APPLIED TRADE POLICY MODELING IN 16 COUNTRIES

Insights and Impacts from
World Bank CGE Based Projects

World Scientific Studies in International Economics

(ISSN: 1793-3641)

Vol. 27 European Economic Integration, WTO Membership, Immigration and Offshoring
by Wilhelm Kohler (University of Tübingen, Germany)

Vol. 28 Services Trade Reform: Making Sense of It
by Philippa Dee (Australian National University, Australia)

Vol. 29 The Social Value of the Financial Sector: Too Big to Fail or Just Too Big?
edited by Viral V Acharya (New York University, USA & Centre for Economic Policy (CEPR), UK), Thorsten Beck (Tilburg University, The Netherlands & Centre for Economic Policy (CEPR), UK), Douglas D Evanoff (Federal Reserve Bank of Chicago, USA), George G Kaufman (Loyola University Chicago, USA), & Richard Portes (London Business School, UK & Centre for Economic Policy (CEPR), UK)

Vol. 30 The Role of Central Banks in Financial Stability: How Has It Changed?
edited by Douglas D Evanoff (Federal Reserve Bank of Chicago, USA), Cornelia Holthausen (European Central Bank, Germany), George G Kaufman (Loyola University Chicago, USA) & Manfred Kremer (European Central Bank, Germany)

Vol. 31 Exchange Rates and Global Financial Policies
by Paul De Grauwe (London School of Economics, UK)

Vol. 32 Asian Free Trade Agreements and WTO Compatibility: Goods, Services, Trade Facilitation and Economic Cooperation
by Shintaro Hamanaka (Asian Development Bank, Philippines)

Vol. 33 Economics and Politics of Trade Policy
by Douglas R Nelson (Tulane University, USA)

Vol. 34 Applied Trade Policy Modeling in 16 Countries: Insights and Impacts from World Bank CGE Based Projects
by David G Tarr (Consultant and Former Lead Economist, The World Bank, USA)

Vol. 35 The Floating World: Issues in International Trade Theory
by Wilfred J Ethier (University of Pennsylvania, USA)

The complete list of the published volumes in the series can be found at
http://www.worldscientific.com/series/wssie

34 World Scientific Studies in International Economics

APPLIED TRADE POLICY MODELING IN 16 COUNTRIES

Insights and Impacts from World Bank CGE Based Projects

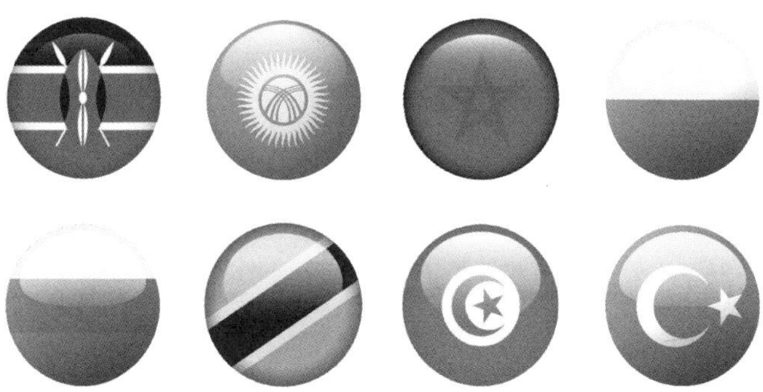

David G. Tarr

Consultant and Former Lead Economist, The World Bank, USA

World Scientific

NEW JERSEY • LONDON • SINGAPORE • BEIJING • SHANGHAI • HONG KONG • TAIPEI • CHENNAI

Published by

World Scientific Publishing Co. Pte. Ltd.
5 Toh Tuck Link, Singapore 596224
USA office: 27 Warren Street, Suite 401-402, Hackensack, NJ 07601
UK office: 57 Shelton Street, Covent Garden, London WC2H 9HE

Library of Congress Cataloging-in-Publication Data
Tarr, David G.
Applied trade policy modeling in 16 countries : insights and impacts from World Bank CGE based projects / authored by David G. Tarr.
pages cm. -- (World Scientific studies in international economics, ISSN 1793-3641 ; vol. 34)
Other title: Applied trade policy modeling in sixteen countries
ISBN 978-9814551427 -- ISBN 9814551422
1. Commercial policy. 2. International trade--Econometric models. 3. Computable general equilibrium models. I. Title. II. Title: Applied trade policy modeling in sixteen countries.
HF1411.T288 2014
382'.3--dc23

2013047862

British Library Cataloguing-in-Publication Data
A catalogue record for this book is available from the British Library.

In-house Editor: Lum Pui Yee

Typeset by Stallion Press
Email: enquiries@stallionpress.com

Printed in Singapore by B & Jo Enterprise Pte Ltd

Contents

Introduction and Overview

David G. Tarr

In the 26 years that I have worked as an international trade economist or consultant to the World Bank, I have worked in more than 25 developing countries. In general, this work has both led to trade policy advice to developing countries and research papers.[1] In many cases, the government requests for assistance to the World Bank specified that the policy discussion should be informed by the construction of a computable general equilibrium (CGE) model of their economy. In this first of two volumes reproducing many of the research papers from this work, I focus on 18 articles from the CGE based projects in 16 countries: Russia, Kazakhstan, Kyrgyzstan, Armenia, Hungary, Poland, Turkey, Iran, Morocco, Tunisia, Chile, Brazil, Kenya, Tanzania, the European Union and the United States. All of these studies were part of World Bank financed projects in response to government requests, with the exception of the article on the United States (which was based on my work in the U.S. government).

The keys to our willingness to undertake these CGE studies,and to the willingness of the World Bank to finance them, were that the model should help inform and improve the policy discussion with the government, and that the model should be intellectually rigorous. My co-authors[2] and I have introduced several innovations in how to model international trade policy and have obtained insights into international trade theory and policy through these models and applications. As a result, the papers in this volume have appeared in many of the economics profession's more prestigious journals, including the *Journal of International Economics, European Economic Review, Journal of Development Economics, Review of Economics and Statistics, Review of International Economics* and the *World Bank Economic Review.*

[1]The issues involved included, but are not limited to, regional trade policy issues, services liberalization, agricultural reform, WTO accession, trade and poverty linkages, second best trade policies with offsetting distortions, trade and tax policy linkages, product standards, trade policy in economies in transition to a market economy, tariff reduction or tariff uniformity, exchange rate issues, trade facilitation and tariffication of non-tariff barriers.

[2]My co-authors of papers in the volume are various subsets of Thomas Rutherford, Glenn Harrison, Jesper Jensen, Edward Balistreri, Jaime de Melo, Morris Morkre, Angelo Gurgel and Elisabet Rutstrom.

We have focused on explaining model results in clear and intuitive terms since, for discussions with country based policy-makers, economic intuition is absolutely essential. Our experience revealed that in country discussions of results subjects the modeler to a level of detailed examination of results not encountered in academic reviews of the work. In this introductory chapter, I provide some of the policy contexts for the requests for the work, key trade policy insights, conclusions and policy impacts.

In some cases, the recommendations based on our modeling framework may not differ in any way from simple theory. Our model work evaluating elimination of non-tariff barriers in Hungary or tariffication of non-tariff barriers in Iran are examples of where simple theory would have made the same recommendation. But the model and analysis provides some additional credibility with the government and the policy community in the country in making policy recommendations; even in these cases, there are usually other policy issues that the model elucidates, such as the very regressive nature of the energy subsidies in Iran. In other cases, such as preferential trade arrangements, the theory is ambiguous, and policy-makers seek insights into preferred strategies that can be informed by results of a CGE model. For example, in the Kyrgyz Republic, I was informed by high level authorities that the work was decisive in affecting the actions of the government. In Chile, the government was very appreciative of the work and used results in testimony before Parliament for future trade policy changes. And the modeling work in Chile persuaded my co-authors and me of the importance of market access in regional arrangements, something that is sometimes overlooked in theoretical work. In the case of Russia, our models and extensive dissemination effort were able to provide a rationale for why it was in Russia's interest to accede to the World Trade Organization (WTO) and change public opinion, where the business community had not been convinced by the arguments of the government prior to the modeling work. But it took the development of an innovative modeling structure to incorporate foreign direct investment in services with endogenous productivity effects to be able to properly tell the story. In the case of Tanzania, the government did not have the resources to undertake a wide range of reforms across all services sectors, and the model was employed to identify the specific services sectors where the most gains could be obtained from reform of barriers to investment in services and to suggest where the government should focus its efforts. The models in the cases of Russia, Kazakhstan, Kenya, and Tanzania showed how important liberalization of barriers against foreign investors in services is relative to conventional tariff liberalization, and in the cases of Kenya and Tanzania, how important are discriminatory versus non-discriminatory barriers to investors in services. Economic theory alone is not capable of these inferences since this is a quantitative rather than qualitative result. In other cases, first best trade policy options from theory can't be applied due to other distortions that limit free trade, such as replacement tax distortions in Chile and export subsidies in Poland. In these cases, the model was able to inform policy-makers on how far to move toward free trade and still obtain gains.

Outline of the Book

In section 1, I report on applications relating to removal of quantitative restrictions in the United States and Hungary, the impact of tariff and export subsidy uniformity in Turkey and foreign exchange surrender requirements in the presence of export and import subsidies in Poland. These papers present some of the most interesting policy contexts and impacts. I amplify on the policy contexts below in this introductory chapter.

In section 2 of the volume, I report on our efforts to incorporate foreign direct investment in services with endogenous productivity effects from the product variety externality. This modeling framework has been applied in Kazakhstan and multiple applications in Russia, Tanzania and Kenya. We have shown that this class of models produces significantly greater estimated welfare gains than models that ignore foreign direct investment in services with endogenous productivity effects.

In section 3, I report on efforts to assess the link between trade reform and poverty using CGE models. I report applications to Turkey, Brazil, Iran and Russia. We show that the poverty results are crucially affected by whether or not the model includes foreign direct investment in services with endogenous productivity effects. We show that trade and poverty work is dramatically more complicated and can easily report perverse results if the data work is not done carefully.

In section 4, I report on studies we have undertaken that focused on preferential trade arrangements in Chile, Morocco, Tunisia, Turkey, the European Union, Kazakhstan, the Kyrgyz Republic, Kenya and Armenia. Despite the fact that all these studies focused on preferential trade arrangements, it may be surprising how diverse the issues were in the different applications. The importance of market access is highlighted in the application to Chile. The relative greater gains from agreements with technologically advanced countries (from both goods and services liberalization) is shown in the applications to Kenya, Tanzania (not in this volume) and Armenia. The importance of trade facilitation is highlighted in the applications to Armenia and Kazakhstan. And the uneven distribution of benefits and costs of trade diversion is the focus of the analysis for the Kyrgyz Republic and Kazakhstan.

Finally, in section 5, I report on several experiences with training exercises in response to requests from governments to train their representatives to independently run the model or better understand it.

1. Trade Policy: Quantitative Restraints, Foreign Exchange Surrender and Uniformity

1.1. Welfare Costs of U.S. Quotas in Textiles, Steel and Autos, *de Melo and Tarr (1990), Review of Economics and Statistics.*

My two partial equilibrium based monographs with Morkre for the U.S. Federal Trade Commission (Morkre and Tarr, 1980; Tarr and Morkre, 1984) documented the high costs of import trade restrictions in the U.S. Nonetheless, import protection typically increased employment in the protected sector and was often justified in terms of gains in employment. Although economists would usually argue that there were employment losses in the unprotected sectors, partial equilibrium analysis can't identify the sectors that lose from protection or estimate the amount of employment lost. Partly to identify sectors that lose from protection, we developed the first computable general equilibrium model of the United States economy devoted to international trade policy issues. The work was originally done for the U.S. Federal Trade Commission (FTC) to assist the FTC with its consumer protection mission, and led to my report to the FTC (Tarr, 1989). This work was further developed (incorporating imperfect factor and product markets) in de Melo and Tarr (1992).

In the 1980s, the U.S. used quantitative restraints (QRs) to restrain imports of textiles and apparel, autos and steel. de Melo and I estimated that the welfare costs of the QRs were equal to more than $20 billion annually (in 1984 dollars). In terms of welfare costs to the economy, we estimated that the QRs more than reversed the cumulative welfare gains of multilateral trade liberalization achieved in the Kennedy and Tokyo Rounds of multilateral trade negotiations. In order to achieve the same welfare costs of these QRs using tariffs, it would be necessary to radially increase all U.S. tariffs more than 7 times (achieving an average tariff of more than 23 percent). Since the average manufactured tariff in the U.S. declined from more than 10 percent pre-Kennedy Round to about 3.5 percent in 1984, in terms of welfare costs, these three QRs took the U.S. back to pre-World War II tariff levels.

A key reason for these high estimates is how the U.S. administered these QRs. Unlike how developing countries typically administer QRs, the U.S. allowed the exporting country to allocate the quota rights, thereby transferring the rents from the quotas to foreigners. About 75 percent of the costs of the QRs derive from the lost quota rents. Thus, "equivalent tariffs" that provide equal protection to the domestic industries would impose only 25 percent of the welfare costs. In the Uruguay Round, the newly formed World Trade Organization made voluntary export restraints (the type of QR that was employed in autos and steel) illegal, and eventually also eliminated the multi-fiber arrangement (MFA) in textiles and apparel. Causality is difficult to establish, but possibly there was a cumulative effect from this study, my two monographs (Morkre and Tarr, 1980 and Tarr and Morkre, 1984) and other studies that quantified the high relative costs of QRs that contributed to the elimination of these QRs.

I am aware, however, of at least one case where there is a clear causal link between my work in this area and the policy decision of the U.S. government. William Niskanen, the Chairman of Ronald Reagan's Council of Economic Advisors, explained that the cabinet was divided in 1984 when it met to get Reagan's decision on whether to extend the QR (more specifically the voluntary export restraint, VER) against Japanese autos. Niskanen argued for termination of the VER. He was supported by the Treasury Secretary and Secretary of State, but was opposed by the Commerce and Labor Secretaries. Niskanen said that the work that Morkre and I did on the auto VER with Japan (in Tarr and Morkre, 1984), along with two other studies done by two other U.S. government agencies that arrived at the same policy recommendation, were instrumental in convincing President Reagan to terminate the voluntary export restraint.

1.2. Reforming Hungarian Agricultural Trade Policy: A Quantitative Evaluation, *Morkre and Tarr (1995), Weltwirtschaftliches Archiv.*

In 1989, Hungary became one of six Eastern European countries to break away from the influence of the former Soviet Union. As part of its effort to make the transition to a market economy, it rapidly removed price controls on most products, reduced state subsidies to industry and agriculture, eliminated the state monopoly on foreign trade and, with the demise of the CMEA (see Tarr, 1992) in January 1990, eliminated state trading in foreign trade. Hungary sought World Bank support for the adjustment costs of the structural reforms. Between November 1989 and November 1991, I did six World Bank missions to Budapest as the trade negotiator for the two Structural Adjustment Loans of the World Bank to the government of Hungary during this period.

By November 1989, the key barrier remaining in the Hungarian trade regime was pervasive import licensing. Hungarian trade economist Kamilia Lanyi of Kopint-Datorg in Budapest presented an excellent analysis of the import licensing regime in Hungary at a World Bank conference in Budapest in November 1989. She explained that, following an application for a license to import, the government would check with the domestic producer. As a rule of thumb, if the domestic producer could supply the product within six months and wanted the sale, the government would not grant the license. The license application required more than 100 signatures. By November 1989, the government has eliminated licenses on tariff lines corresponding to 16 percent of domestic production — mostly on things like spare parts and key intermediate products. Companies I interviewed in the importing and exporting business broadly confirmed the Lanyi analysis by indicating how much easier it was to import the unlicensed products.

Despite the highly protective nature of the import licensing regime, the government of Hungary had a long standing position of arguing that the licenses were not employed in a protective manner, but were "for statistical monitoring purposes only." Haus (1992) documented that when Hungary negotiated its entry into the GATT, it insisted on being admitted as a market economy where the import licenses were not considered protective; otherwise it would refuse membership. Although many European countries wanted to admit Hungary as a state trading country (as it did with Poland and Romania in the 1970s), the United States wanted to encourage Hungary's steps toward independence from the Soviet Union and pressured the European countries into accepting Hungary's position on its admission to the GATT. Thus, Hungary committed to reducing tariffs over time on entering the GATT, but did not commit to change its import licensing regime. Further, my counterparts in the Ministry of International Economic Relations maintained that the International Monetary Fund and my predecessors in the World Bank had accepted that the import licenses were not trade barriers. Thus, when Hungarian international trade economists complained about the problems of the import licenses, they were told that the international organizations accepted that the import licenses were not protective barriers and they should not criticize the system. This message to keep quiet about the import licenses was sometimes conveyed through visits by the Hungarian version of the KGB, as occurred in the case of Janos Gacs.

I insisted on negotiating the elimination of import licenses as the key aspect of trade policy conditionality in the Structural Adjustment Loans. Given the history of the international organizations of accepting the import licenses, this was difficult for the Ministry of International Economic Relations to accept. But the Finance Ministry agreed with our position, and, in the two Structural Adjustment Loans, I negotiated only on the progressive reduction of the import licenses[3]; by 1992, import licenses were eliminated on tariff lines corresponding to 75 percent of industrial output. **By late 1991, Hungarian officials in the Ministry of Finance and elsewhere mentioned to me that the international trade reforms were among the most important achievement of the government in its efforts to move toward a market economy in the prior two years.**

However, all Hungarian agricultural output and a significant share of food production remained protected by import licenses. In an effort to elucidate the costs of the remaining import licenses, Morkre and I undertook this study of the costs of the agricultural restrictions. To obtain the ad valorem equivalents of the import licenses, the study was supported by the best price comparison study I have seen of imported versus domestic prices for five agricultural products; it was done by Agnes Nagy of Kopint-Datorg. We found that import protection imposes significant costs on the Hungarian economy. Piecemeal removal of the import licenses, however, will result in very small gains. The reason is that Hungary maintained an export subsidy program in agriculture as well. Removal of import protection

[3]Given the considerable reduction in protection from import licenses as well as Hungary's commitments at the GATT for tariff reduction, tariffs were ignored in the two Structural Adjustment Loans.

results in firms making greater use of the export subsidies, increasing the government's subsidy burden with offsetting inefficiency costs. This indicates that in order to realize the benefits of import liberalization in the agricultural area, it would be important to concurrently reduce export subsidies along with the removal of import licenses.

1.3. Second-Best Foreign Exchange Policy in the Presence of Domestic Price Controls and Export Subsidies, *Tarr (1990), World Bank Economic Review.*

The original version of this paper was written as part of the World Bank Country Economic Memorandum for Poland in 1989, and was based on a mission to Poland in February 1989. Poland, in the spring of 1989, was the first of the six countries of Eastern Europe to break away from the Soviet Union and start the transition toward a market economy. High level meetings were underway while we were there on a strong reform agenda. Nonetheless, the break from the Soviet Union and the magnitude of the reform surprised us, along with most others.

I was responsible for recommendations for reform in international trade, and this is one of three papers I wrote on Poland's trade regime. Although this model is a one sector model of the foreign exchange regime, technically it is a CGE model, as it is an economy-wide model and the equilibrium is computed.

Poland, like many developing countries, required its exporters to surrender a share of their foreign exchange earnings to the government at an overvalued exchange rate that was only about 25 percent of the market rate in early 1989. During the late 1980s, Poland progressively increased the share which exporters were allowed to retain (the retention ratio), so that by 1989 the retention ratio was about 30 percent. I estimate that the retention of foreign exchange was equivalent to a tax on exports of about 51 percent, and in the absence of other distortions to the trade regime, full retention of foreign exchange would yield benefits to Poland of about 8 percent of GDP. Poland, however, subsidized exports and implicitly subsidized imports (see Tarr, 1990a). The subsidies to exports and implicit subsidies to imports represent offsetting distortions to the foreign exchange restrictions. I estimate that in the presence of the export and import subsidies, increasing the retention ratio for foreign exchange, up to a retention ratio of about 85 percent, would produce welfare gains of about 7 percent of GDP. But retention ratios higher than 85 percent would reduce welfare in the presence of the subsidies to imports and exports.

In January 1990, as part of its "shock therapy" reform program, Poland massively devalued and unified its exchange rate regime, and, for the most part, simultaneously eliminated the export subsidies and the price controls that were the source of the implicit import subsidies. This analysis supported that policy and the first best estimates can be viewed as the gains to Poland from these aspects of their reform program.

1.4. Trade Reform in the Partially Liberalized Economy of Turkey, *Harrison, Rutherford and Tarr (1993), World Bank Economic Review.*

In the 1970s, Turkey employed import-substitution industrialization policies. In the 1980s, it initiated major trade liberalization, made the Turkish lira convertible, but also provided strong direct export subsidies. It turned away from strong export subsidies in the later 1980s and by 1989, we calculated that the anti-export bias of the trade regime had, on average, been virtually eliminated: the weighted average nominal tariff had been reduced to 8.1 percent; and, although export subsidies had been reduced, combining direct and indirect export subsidies, the average export subsidy remained at 7.4 percent. But the distortions in tariffs and export subsidies were very diverse. Export subsidies were 70 percent in fabricated metal products, 30 percent in electrical machinery, 21 percent in iron and steel and 20 percent in rubber products. Sectors with high import tariffs were: alcoholic beverages, 72 percent; tobacco, 57 percent; while fisheries, mineral products, sugar and food products all had tariffs between 30 and 35 percent.

In this paper, we constructed a 40 sector CGE model of the Turkish economy to assess the welfare effects of trade reform in Turkey. **We show that the principal welfare gains that could be obtained from further trade reform could be achieved by uniformity in the distortions of the trade regime. The welfare gains from combined uniformity of tariffs and export subsidies are almost 90 percent of full free trade, where in full free trade, both tariffs and export subsidies are reduced to zero.** This is explained in part by the fact that there was no significant anti-export bias in the 1989 trade regime. Equally important is the fact that the welfare costs of a tariff or export subsidy increase with the square of the distortion; so it is the high tariff or export subsidies that impose the most welfare costs. Although, I generally argue for tariff uniformity (Tarr, 2002), in my experience, this Turkish example proved to be case of the highest welfare gains from trade distortion uniformity as a share of full free trade welfare gains.

2. Evaluating the Impact of Services and FDI with Endogenous Productivity Effects

2.1. *Introduction*

In this section, I summarize several papers where my co-authors and I have incorporated foreign direct investment in services with imperfect competition and endogenous productivity effects into computable general equilibrium (CGE) models. This work was born out of the necessity of creating a class of models that could appropriately assess the impact of Russian accession to the World Trade Organization (WTO), where negotiations on services commitments were crucial. We show in these models that the innovative features we incorporate (foreign direct investment in services with endogenous productivity effects) are dominant in explaining the impacts of Russian WTO accession. These modeling features are necessary to adapt CGE models to the growing body of evidence and economic theory that suggests that the close availability of a diverse set of business services is important for economic growth.[4] The key idea in the literature is that a diverse set (or higher quality set) of business services allows downstream users to purchase a quality adjusted unit of business services at lower cost. We also show that our innovative modeling features produce estimated welfare gains several multiples of the gains of constant returns to scale models, and we argue our estimates are closer to the econometric estimates of the gains from trade and investment liberalization.

Russia began negotiating its accession to the World Trade Organization (WTO) in 1993. While initially the negotiation effort was tepid, when Vladimir Putin first took office at the turn of the century the accession effort of the Russian government gained momentum. As part of this effort, the Russian government requested that the World Bank develop a model to assess the impact of its WTO accession, where the assessment should include the regional and poverty implications.

With my colleagues Constantine Michalopoulos and Harry Broadman in the World Bank, we assessed that the principal problem for Russian WTO accession was commitments to foreign providers of services. While the 11 percent average Russian tariff was not very high (Shepotylo and Tarr, 2008; forthcoming), the Russian trade negotiators had been unable to even table their initial offer in services due to the fact that they were having trouble getting the regulatory agencies to make any commitments in the area of services. Clearly, to effectively address the issues of Russian WTO accession, the models we would build had to include foreign direct investment in services. Given the accumulating evidence on the endogenous productivity impacts of liberalization of barriers against foreign providers of services, this meant developing a new class of CGE models.

As a first step, we developed a small stylized model with the key modeling features (Markusen, Rutherford and Tarr, 2005). By starting with a small stylized model, we were able to understand and explain the implications of incorporating foreign direct investment in services with Dixit-Stiglitz endogenous productivity effects. While the model is small by CGE standards, it is nonetheless complex enough that analytic solutions would be extremely difficult, leading to an effective use of CGE models to obtain theoretical insights. With Thomas Rutherford we extended this class of model to large real datasets of Russia in multiple stages: first,

[4]See Francois and Hoekman (2010) for a survey of the empirical evidence and the theory. Some of the key papers are Arnold, Javorcik and Mattoo (2011) for the Czech Republic, Fernandes and Paunov (2012) for Chile, Shepotylo and Vakhitov (2012) for Ukraine and Arnold, Javorcik, Lipscomb and Mattoo (2012) for India. These papers use firm level panel data and control for FDI endogeneity; they find a significant positive relationship between FDI in services following liberalization (especially allowing foreign entry) and the performance of downstream domestic firms in manufacturing.

with Jesper Jensen, to a single agent model of Russia as a whole (Jensen, Rutherford and Tarr, 2007); then to a model of Russia as a whole, where we accomplished a methodological breakthrough by incorporating all 50,000 households of the Russian household budget survey as agents of the model (Rutherford and Tarr, 2008); next we extended the model to ten regions of Russia, with a single agent in each region (Rutherford and Tarr, 2010); and finally, we developed an application to multiple regions of Russia with ten representative households (distinguished by income) in each region (Rutherford and Tarr, 2012). These first three papers were the basis of my paper in the *Handbook of Computable General Equilibrium Modeling* (see Tarr, 2013). At the request of lead trade negotiators in Ukraine and Kazakhstan, the model of Jensen, Rutherford and Tarr (2007) was applied to both of these countries (Copenhagen Economics et al., 2006; and Jensen and Tarr, 2008). Subsequently, the methodology was applied and extended to assess regional preferences in services and liberalization of domestic barriers in services in Kenya (Balistreri, Rutherford and Tarr, 2009; Balistreri and Tarr, 2011), Tanzania (Jensen, Rutherford and Tarr, 2010; Jensen and Tarr, 2011), Armenia (Jensen and Tarr, 2011) and Malaysia. In this section, I discuss the conceptual contributions of two of the articles on Russia, the article on Kazakhstan and the first paper on Tanzania. The final subsection, discusses the policy impacts of this work in Russia, Ukraine and Kazakhstan.

2.2. The Impact of Liberalizing Barriers to Foreign Direct Investment in Services: the Case of Russian Accession to the World Trade Organization, *Jensen, Rutherford and Tarr (2007), Review of Development Economics.*

In this paper we developed a 35 sector, small open-economy CGE model of the Russian economy to assess the impacts of Russian WTO accession. The model contains perfectly competitive goods and services sectors, imperfectly competitive goods sectors with imports supplied from abroad and imperfectly competitive services sectors where foreign investors invest and produce in Russia. All imperfectly competitive sectors are monopolistically competitive and users have a love of variety, which yields endogenous productivity effects from additional varieties. Russia is modeled as a single region with a single representative agent.

We estimated that Russia will gain about 7.2 percent of consumption from WTO accession; productivity gains from increased varieties of imperfectly produced goods and services lead to increases in real wages and the return to capital. Decomposition of the components of the policy changes revealed that about 70 percent of the total gains derive from Russia's liberalization of its barriers against foreign investors in services. A key result of the sensitivity results is that a constant returns to scale, perfect competition version of our model would yield gains of only 1.2 percent of consumption. These results show that our innovative modeling framework that incorporated foreign direct investment in services, which produced welfare gains 6 times greater, was crucial to the results.

2.3. Regional Impacts of Liberalization of Barriers against Foreign Direct Investment in Services: The Case of Russia's Accession to the WTO, *Rutherford and Tarr (2010), Review of International Economics.*

Given the vast geographic diversity of Russia and the request of the government of Russia for a multi-region model of Russia, in this paper, Rutherford and I extend the single agent, small open economy model of Russia of Jensen, Rutherford and Tarr (2007), to a ten region model of Russia. In our model, there is a single representative agent in each of the ten regions of Russia. The ten regions of Russia are modeled with the features of a multi-region global trade model, while Russia is modeled as a small open economy with respect to the rest of the world. The model retains the foreign direct investment and imperfect competition features of the aggregate model of Russia.

We show that the regions of Russia can be expected to gain substantially from WTO accession. The gains for each region will come primarily from liberalization of barriers against multinational providers of business services, with remaining gains coming from tariff liberalization and improved market access. The results vary considerably across the regions of Russia depending on their ability to attract FDI. This depends primarily on the region's initial share of multinational investment. But regions that are able to improve their policies and institutions to attract foreign direct investment will improve their relative position in gains from WTO accession.

2.4. Impact of Local Content Restrictions and Barriers Against Foreign Direct Investment in Services: The Case of Kazakhstan Accession to the WTO, *Jensen and Tarr (2008), Eastern European Economics.*

In this paper Jensen and I developed a single agent, 56 sector small open-economy model of Kazakhstan with all the features of our model of Russian WTO accession. Kazakhstan is highly dependent on its oil and gas sectors. In its effort to diversify its economy, Kazakhstan has imposed local content restrictions on the multinational investment in oil and gas. Given its crucial role in the policy discussion in Kazakhstan, we extended the model to allow for foreign direct investment by multinational oil and gas companies with local content restrictions. We suggested and evaluated policies that achieve the objective of the local content restrictions (to encourage multinational oil and gas companies to use Kazak inputs), but which, unlike the local content restrictions, do not violate the TRIMS agreement of the WTO. We show that our imperfect competition model features, with foreign direct investment and endogenous productivity effects are crucial to the results as the estimated gains are more than ten times larger than the gains from a constant returns to scale model.

2.5. Modeling Services Liberalization: The case of Tanzania, *Jensen, Rutherford and Tarr (2010), Journal of Economic Integration.*

In this paper and in the companion paper for Kenya (Balistreri, Rutherford and Tarr, 2009) we extended earlier work which was limited to the impact of reducing discriminatory barriers against foreign investors in services. In these papers, we also analyzed the impact of reducing non-discriminatory barriers against investors in services, i.e., those that impact domestic investors as well as foreigners. This paper employs a 52-sector, small open-economy computable general equilibrium model of the Tanzanian economy and, as in our papers on Russia, incorporates foreign direct investment in services and productivity effects in both goods and services markets endogenously through a Dixit-Stiglitz framework.

The extension to non-discriminatory reforms proved crucial, as we found that the largest gains would derive from non-discriminatory services reforms. Given that the government did not have the capacity to implement the reforms across all services sectors, in response to requests from our World Bank colleagues in Tanzania, we decomposed the impacts and found that the largest gains would come from reforms in maritime transportation followed by banking and road transportation. The principal barrier in maritime transportation (a perverse contract to a multinational port operator) was subsequently removed.[5]

We also consider a "constant returns to scale" (CRTS) version of the model. In this version, there are no endogenous productivity effects from additional varieties of imperfectly supplied goods or services. The estimated gains under CRTS are less than 40 percent of the total gains in our central model. While the gains are considerably smaller without the endogenous productivity gains from services varieties, the gains are large by the standards of CRTS trade models. The reason is that we assume that the regulatory barriers impose real resource costs in the initial equilibrium, i.e., there are large "rectangles" of rent losses in the CRTS model. The value of 50 percent of the rents in the benchmark is 1.34 percent of GDP. The economy gains the use of these resources with liberalization in the CRTS scenario and more resources efficiently shift into the services sectors as a result of the reduction of the distortions.

2.6. *Policy Impacts in Russia, Ukraine and Kazakhstan*

The models and results were the core contribution in the effort of the World Bank to assist the government of Russia in its WTO accession effort, especially in its public awareness campaign. It was, however, only part of multifaceted research and

[5]Robin Curruthers, a former staff member and consultant to the World Bank, identified the perverse incentives in the port contract, and together with the World Bank team in Dar es Salaam, worked to remove the perverse incentives that encouraged inefficient port operation.

dissemination effort that was sustained over several years.[6] Although the Russian government was convinced of the benefits of WTO accession, prior to this work there was widespread public skepticism and Russian businessmen were calling for an explanation of the impacts on their sectors. Russian leaders and independent internal World Bank evaluators of the work have concluded that the work was instrumental in shifting public opinion in favor of WTO accession, and in explaining to businessmen and politicians in convincing terms the consequences of WTO at the sector level. Surveys taken after this work was done showed that, regarding the impacts of WTO accession on the sectors of Russia, the views of informed laymen (such as political leaders in the regions of Russia), were coincident with the assessments of the models discussed above. An internal review by a World Bank evaluation team (as part of a broader review of economic work on Russia by World Bank teams) concluded the following:

> The WTO analytical work for Russia consists of a large number of very high quality papers and publications assessing the economic and social effects of Russia's planned accession to WTO. . . .The body of analytical work (about 15 papers) was disseminated through training events (a number of them requested by the authorities) attended by (prospective) civil servants, representatives of labor and industry and the academic community. It has clearly made a contribution to the policy dialogue and is seen as instrumental for establishing a sense that WTO accession would be beneficial for Russia among the government's trade reform team and parts of the research community. Prior to this project, editorials were rampant in the Russian press expressing fears of WTO accession and focusing on the fact that the government has not explained the consequences of WTO accession or the source of the benefits. Now polls of regional politicians reveal that they anticipate exactly the impacts suggested by the analytic studies. Moreover, polls of the public have shown progressively increasing endorsement, and now significant majority supporting WTO accession. Finally, as the analytic studies strongly emphasized the crucial role of liberalization against barriers to foreign direct investment in business services, Russian has agreed to major openings in the business services markets as part of its bilateral market access agreements in the WTO negotiations (see Tarr, 2007).

As noted in the review, the work was very widely disseminated over a period of years.[7] Crucially the dissemination efforts involved writing several short policy

[6]Research papers included the following: Jensen, Rutherford and Tarr (2006, 2007); Rutherford and Tarr (2008; 2010); Rutherford, Tarr and Shepotylo (2005; 2006); Shepotylo and Tarr (2008; forthcoming); Tarr (2006; 2007; 2010; 2010a); Tarr and Thomson (2004); Tarr and Volchkova (2010; 2013).

[7]The evaluation noted that dissemination was good on several fronts. It stated:

> First, the information was presented in a readable way that was easy to follow for non-experts. A selection of the materials were summarized in book form for teaching purposes and translated into Russian. Second, an intensive training course on Trade policies and WTO accession was

papers and op-eds, where the results could be explained in clear terms understandable to a non-technical audience. We regard the extensive and sustained dissemination efforts over several years as a key aspect of the success on the policy front, possibly equally important as the innovative feature of incorporating foreign direct investment in services with endogenous productivity impacts.

In addition to the impact of this work and model in Russia, lead negotiators for WTO accession in both Kazakhstan and Ukraine became aware of the work in Russia and requested similar studies in their countries. The model was adapted and

organized with the World Bank Institute and held twice. In addition to the World Bank Institute training (attended by about 200 participants from civil service and academia), the findings were presented in several conferences in Russia and abroad. A two day workshop for Russian counterparts was organized in London in 2006 to help assist the government in formulating an international trade strategy. Two GDLN events (80 participants each) organized by the World Bank Institute linking up several Russian, one Belarusian university and one Kazak location were held in 2008 and 2009. Third, findings were reflected in the Bank's poverty assessment and highlighted in one of the country office on-line reports to the country. Fourth, a bilingual website was established listing the key outputs of this exercise and other relevant publications. www.worldbank.org/trade/russia-wto. Fifth, in order to transfer the model to Russian experts, seven days of training on the model was provided to economic modelers from Russia and the CIS during which they were provided with the software to run for the models and were given the software. Summaries and PowerPoint presentations were prepared for various audiences including a conference organized with the Ministry of Communications; the CEFIR trade conference; the New Economic School tenth anniversary conference; the CEFIR conference on telecommunications; the conference of labor, business and government officials in Saint Petersburg led by the International Labor Organization; a GDLN presentation to Russian regional officials through the RAGS network; presentations were made to: 800 participants in the conference organized by the Russian Union of Industrialists and Entrepreneurs in Moscow in 2007; to 110 Russian small and medium businessmen in Washington; to a large conference of CIS businessmen in Evian France; to the Russia-US Business Council in Washington; to the government officials representing the CAREC countries at their meetings in Mongolia in 2009, and several smaller gatherings of Russian business interests in both Moscow and visiting in Washington. Short policy papers appeared in the bilingual journal of the American Chamber of Commerce in Russia, the International Labor Organization and a short policy paper was prepared for the Ministry of Economic Development and Trade website. Two op-eds were published in Russia, and other Russian researchers, such as Ksenia Yudaeva, also wrote op eds based on results of the analytic work. In Moscow, there were four large press conferences, several additional interviews with members of the press as well as a television interview on the network "Russia Today."

applied in Ukraine and Kazakhstan, and had a significant impact in those countries in developing a framework for assessing the gains from WTO accession. This helped the lead negotiators with their public awareness obligations.

In requesting the involvement of the team that executed this work in Russia, the Ukrainian lead negotiator said that he had people telling him the impact of WTO accession in agriculture, or in various services sectors or in manufacturing. But he needed to know how it all fit together. This is a perspective that a general equilibrium modeler can appreciate. Jesper Jensen and colleagues working in the Institute for Economic Research in Kiev adapted the model developed for Russia to Ukraine, and helped the lead negotiator with his public awareness need. (See Copenhagen Economics *et al.*, 2006).

In Kazakhstan, Jensen and Tarr (2008) adapted the Russia model to assess the impact of WTO accession in Kazakhstan. The lead negotiator in Kazakhstan wanted to know how WTO accession could be used to increase the productivity and competitiveness of manufacturing in Kazakhstan. As in Russia, the results showed that the largest gains to Kazakhstan would come from its own liberalization in services, due to the productivity gains to industry, agriculture and services in Kazakhstan from additional providers of services. Subsequent to this work, the lead negotiator for WTO accession in Kazakhstan has repeatedly made it her message that the principal benefit to Kazakhstan from WTO accession will be the increase in productivity it will reap from the liberalization of services barriers.

3. Trade and Poverty

3.1. *Introduction*

As international trade as a share of GDP increased in the world, interest in the impact of globalization on poverty in the world also increased. In the mid-1990s, the World Bank adopted the elimination of poverty as its goal, and, many of the aid agencies that donate internationally, such as the Department for International Development (DFID) in the United Kingdom, placed increased focus on poverty elimination. In the decade that followed, the streets in front of the World Bank and the International Monetary Fund were regularly filled with demonstrators during their annual meetings. Many of those demonstrators and other critics of the international financial organizations (IFIs) claimed that the open economy agenda of the IFIs was contributing to poverty.

In response to the increased interest, the economics profession responded with an expanded research agenda on the links between international trade and investment and poverty. This included substantial increased research within the World Bank itself, involving increased data gathering efforts to assess the evolution of household living standards, econometric assessments of the role of trade and investment on poverty and computable general equilibrium modeling to assess the likely distributional and poverty impacts of proposed policy changes. Research in all these areas had been going on, but it intensified in the 1990s.

As part of the effort, I was involved in projects with the governments of Turkey, Iran, Brazil and Russia. All these projects included CGE analysis of proposed trade policy and other changes in which we assessed the distributional and poverty impacts. I first discuss the key points from these papers and then briefly discuss the four journal articles that came out of these projects which are in this volume.

3.2. Trade Policy and Poverty Reduction in Brazil, *Harrison, Rutherford, Tarr and Gurgel (2004), World Bank Economic Review.*

In the early years of the 21st century, the government of Brazil was concerned about avoiding the foreign exchange collapse that had recently fallen on its southern neighbor and customs union partner, Argentina, and it requested a trade study from the World Bank. As part of that trade study, we developed a multi-region, multi-sector constant returns to scale model to evaluate multilateral, regional and unilateral trade policy options of Brazil.

Our estimates supported the apparent strategy of the government of Brazil of simultaneously urging the MERCOSUR Customs Union (of which it is a member) to reach a free trade agreement with the EU plus the Free Trade Agreement of the Americas, while supporting multilateral trade liberalization at the WTO. Brazil saw multilateral trade negotiations under the World Trade Organization as the best hope for improved agricultural market access. We found that Brazil can optimize its choice of trade policies by combining regional arrangements in both the Americas and the EU with multilateral liberalization. If tariff uniformity is added to the regional and multilateral liberalization, further gains would be realized.

We found that the distributional aspects of the trade reforms to be progressive, as the poorest households in Brazil would gain the most. The reasons are the following. International trade theory argues that following trade liberalization, the price of the factor of production used intensively in the protected sector should fall relative to the price of the factor of production in the unprotected sector (the Stolper-Samuelson theorem). In countries where unskilled labor is relatively abundant (as in most developing countries), the country has a comparative advantage in the goods that use unskilled labor intensively, and these countries would be expected to protect the capital intensive sectors which can't compete in open competition on world markets. Trade liberalization would therefore be expected to move resources from the capital intensive sectors to the unskilled labor intensive sectors, which would increase the wage rate of unskilled labor. Since the poor depend on the wage rate of unskilled labor for most of their earned income, trade liberalization in developing countries would be expected to have a progressive impact in these cases. This is precisely what happens in our trade policy scenarios for Brazil. As a legacy of Brazil's import-substitution-industrialization past, sectors such as motor vehicles, other metal products, and other manufacturing were the most protected and they are also among the most capital intensive sectors. These are the sectors that decline in our trade policy liberalization scenarios. On the other hand, it is the key agriculture sectors that, due to export expansion, expand output. And these sectors are the most intensive in unskilled labor in our data. Consequently, in our simulations of the impacts of trade liberalization in Brazil, we assess that they would have a progressive impact.

3.3. Trade Liberalization, Poverty and Efficient Equity, *Harrison, Rutherford and Tarr (2003), Journal of Development Economics.*

In this paper, we extended the single household CGE model we had developed for our World Bank project with the government of Turkey in our work on the customs union with the European Union. We analyze impacts in a model of Turkey with 40 households, 20 urban and 20 rural, distinguished by level of income. We found that a movement to free trade increased aggregate income, but the poorest four urban households and the poorest two rural households lost from the free trade reform. We believe that the distributional results are not accurate (in fact, opposite of the likely impacts) and are due to inaccurate factor intensity data in the Turkish input-output table. Consequently, we did not discuss these results with the government of Turkey. We emphasize three points from this work.

3.3.1. *Factor Intensities in Input Output tables*

Our application to the models we developed for Turkey and Brazil, showed that in CGE analysis of poverty impacts, **it is not possible to rely on input-output tables for factor intensities**. We caution CGE modelers and consumers of policy advice from CGE models to question the reasons for the distributional results and, in particular, to question the source of the factor intensities. The reason is that trade reform, due to real exchange rate depreciation, will tend to benefit the exporting sectors relative to sectors selling on the domestic market; consequently, (from Stolper-Sameuleson) the factor used intensively in the export sector will see its relative return increase. The problem is that national statistical authorities typically calculate the share of capital residually, after payments for intermediates, labor and taxes are subtracted from revenues. Then profitable sectors that export, such as apparel production in Turkey, are reported as capital intensive; and loss making sectors that sell only domestically, such as the state-owned locomotive sector in Turkey, are reported as labor intensive. In fact, the factor intensities of these sectors are the opposite of the data in the input-output table, so our CGE model of Turkey based on the input-output table, reported changes in the relative returns to factors opposite of what would actually occur. Since the poor rely on wage income, a CGE model based on the input-output factor intensities will report distributional impacts opposite of what will likely occur. In our model of Brazil, we employed supplemental data from Brazil for the factor intensities and showed that this significantly impacted the distributional results relative to the factor intensity data in input-output tables of the GTAP dataset.

3.3.2. *Side-payment feasibility*

We demonstrated the feasibility of a side-payment compensation mechanism. That is, we calculate the side payments funded by the existing value-added tax in Turkey (and take the effect of side-payments into account in deriving the general equilibrium) such that the free trade reform will result in no losers. We find that there is only a small loss in overall efficiency compared with an uncompensated free trade reform. This indicates that the existing VAT in Turkey was not very distortionary.

3.3.3. *Decomposition analysis*

We executed a decomposition analysis that identified the removal of the motor vehicle tariff as the tariff change that had the strongest adverse impact on the poor. This is because the VAT on motor vehicles is among the highest in Turkey. The tariff provides second best benefits partly offsetting the VAT distortion by moving resources into the motor vehicle sector and is welfare improving up to a point.

3.4. Poverty Effects of Russia's WTO Accession: Modeling "real" households with endogenous productivity effects, *Rutherford and Tarr (2008), Journal of International Economics.*

3.4.1. *Solving the Problem of Incorporating all Households in the Household Budget Survey as Agents in the Model*

In this paper, we achieved a methodological breakthrough by incorporating all the 55,098 households of the Russian household survey as agents in the model of Russia. The integration of all the households of a household budget survey into a CGE model had been an innovation that poverty analysis specialists had sought for many years. The key was the development of a new algorithm for solving general equilibrium models with a large number of agents that it exploits the economics of the problem. (See the appendix of Rutherford, Tarr and Shepotylo (2005) for an intuitive explanation of the algorithm as well as the GAMS code.)

All other modeling features of the single agent model of Russia discussed above (Jensen, Rutherford and Tarr, 2007) remained unchanged. In particular, the model contained foreign direct investment in services and Dixit-Stiglitz endogenous productivity effects from additional varieties of imperfectly produced goods and services.

3.4.2. *Overcoming Stolper-Samuelson Pessimism*

As we demonstrated in Markusen, Rutherford and Tarr (2005), the model with endogenous productivity effects from the Dixit-Stiglitz externality yields welfare gains much larger than neoclassical constant returns to scale models and overcomes the Stopler-Samuelson pessimism in that it **allows for the possibility that all factor returns will increase relative to an index of the cost of living in response to trade or FDI reform.** We present considerable econometric evidence that indicates that the model with endogenous productivity effects is the better model.

Figure 1.1 encapsulates the key policy results for the distributional effects of Russian WTO accession. It displays two histograms. The histogram on the right is the distribution of benefits across the households in the model based on our central model with foreign direct investment in services and endogenous productivity effects. In our central model, 99.9 percent of the households are estimated to gain between 2 and 25 percent of their income, with a mean gain of 7.3 percent on income. The histogram on the left displays the estimated gains across households based on a constant returns to scale model without foreign direct investment in services. The mean gain for households based on the constant returns to scale model is 1.2 percent, with about 7 percent of the households estimated to lose. The striking feature of the figure is that the two distributions only slightly overlap in the tails. *Figure 1.1 shows that to estimate household impacts, it is important to incorporate household diversity. But incorporating foreign direct investment in business services and Dixit Stiglitz effects in imperfectly competitive sectors is as important*

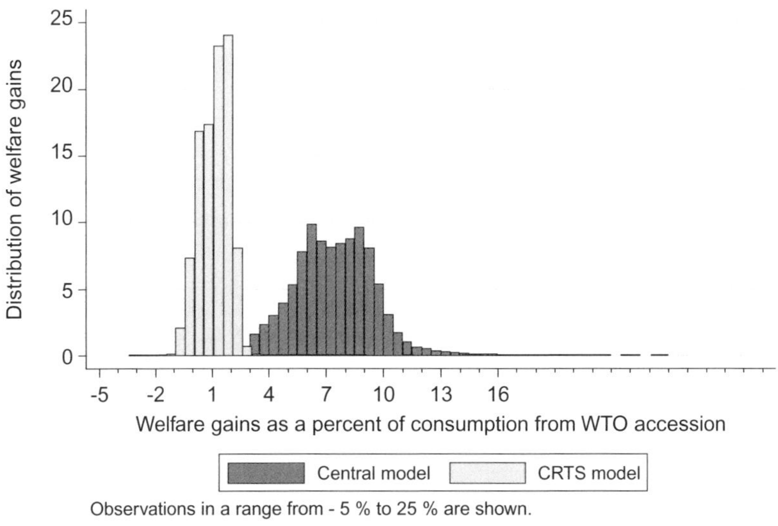

Figure 1.1. Distributions of Estimated Welfare Gains from Russian WTO Accession. Central and CRTS Models Comparison. 55098 Households Sampled.

for our policy simulation. While the figure supports the view that it is important to incorporate household diversity through a real household model, it is evident that incorporating foreign direct investment liberalization and endogenous productivity effects will decisively affect the results relative to a constant returns to scale model.

3.4.3. *Reconciliation of Data Between the Household Survey and the Input-Output table*

Researchers who do poverty analysis of policy changes often use a "top down" or "sequential" approach to micro-simulation analysis, where the results of a single agent CGE model are fed into a household model. This approach is often criticized because the feedback effects on prices from changes in household behavior are ignored. In our application to Russia (Rutherford and Tarr, 2008), we found that the bias from ignoring the quantity feedback effects on prices is very small if the data are reconciled first between the household and representative consumer models. But failure to reconcile the data can lead to opposite results for the overall impacts between the CGE model and the micro-simulation results.[8] Based on our results, we believe that a sequential approach to assess household impacts of trade policy changes is likely to be a good approximation to the results of our more difficult to implement integrated approach, provided three conditions are satisfied: (1) the household data are reconciled with national accounts data; (2) the factor and consumption shares of the representative agent in the sequential approach are equal to factor and consumption shares that are the sum over all households; and (3) the representative agent and the households exhibit the same optimizing behavior (World Bank, 2001). The latter implies that the first order effects are the same.

A policy based version of this paper appeared as a chapter in the World Bank poverty study with the government of Russia (Tarr, 2005). It was part of the longer term project to assess the impacts of Russian WTO accession and influence the public policy debate that eventually led to the accession of Russia to the WTO.

3.5. Trade, Exchange Rate and Energy Pricing Reform in Iran: Potentially Large Efficiency Effects and Gains to the Poor, *Jensen and Tarr (2003), Review of Development Economics.*

This paper was part of the output of a larger World Bank report (World Bank, 2001) that I led for a project with the government of Iran. The government at the time was interested in moving toward a market economy, and asked the World Bank to lead an international trade reform study, as well as examine economic reforms of the foreign exchange regime and energy pricing.

[8]Ianchovichina and Martin (2004) estimated that China will gain from WTO accession based on their representative agent model. But Chen and Ravallion (2004) estimate overall losses for China from WTO accession based on their household model using price changes from Ianchovichina and Martin.

As part of that project, Jesper Jensen and I developed a 43 sector CGE model for the government of Iran with ten rural and ten urban households distinguished by level of income. We analyzed: (i) the removal of non-tariff barriers (with tariffication); (ii) tariff reduction with uniformity or free trade; (iii) unification of the market and official exchange rates (where the market rate was four times the official rate); and (iv) market pricing of petroleum products, where petroleum prices were only 10 percent of world market prices and the energy subsidies were about 18 percent of GDP. There were two key points in this paper.

3.5.1. *Unusually large welfare gains due to massive distortions*

Despite the fact that the model was a constant returns to scale perfect competition model, we estimate that the aggregate welfare gains came to almost 50 percent of aggregate consumer income. This very unusually large welfare gain for a constant returns to scale model derives from the very large distortions present in the Iranian economy. About two-thirds of the gains are from energy pricing reforms, with the balance of the gains coming from tariffication combined with imposition of a 15% uniform tariff and exchange rate unification.

3.5.2. *Commodity subsidies are an inefficient method of helping the poor and may be very regressive*

In Iran, energy and other commodity subsidies were justified on the grounds of helping the poor. We found, however, that these subsidies were not only unusually inefficient and costly, but they are strongly regressive. The wealthy consume more of the commodities and benefit disproportionately from the commodity subsidies, especially the energy subsidies. Even **non-targeted revenue-neutral** direct income support in equal lump sum amounts to all households would dramatically benefit the poor. We estimated that the combined reforms with this non-targeted revenue-neutral distribution scheme would increase the income of the poorest rural household by 292 percent of its initial income and increase the income of the poorest urban household by 140 percent of its initial income.

4. Regionalism

4.1. *Introduction*

It is well known that the impact of preferential trading arrangements on welfare is ambiguous at a theoretical level. Many questions regarding regional trade arrangements only have quantitative answers that are specific to the particular structural features of the economy and the policy considered. Thus, to determine the impact of prospective regional arrangements, governments often rely on a quantitative evaluation. At the request of the governments involved, my co-authors and I have implemented computable general equilibrium (CGE) models of regional trade agreements in Morocco, Tunisia, Chile, Brazil, Turkey, Armenia, Kazakhstan, Kenya and Tanzania. In addition, we evaluated the single market program of the European Union to provide insights for the neighboring developing countries. See Harrison, Rutherford and Tarr (2003a) for a summary of the policy results of these analyses.

4.2. Trade Policy Options for Chile: The Importance of Market Access, *Harrison, Rutherford and Tarr (2002), World Bank Economic Review.*

The analysis of regional trade arrangements is typically conducted in the framework of trade creation versus trade diversion, under which preferential tariff reduction is welfare inferior to non-preferential tariff reduction.Wonnacott and Wonnacott [1981] showed, however, that regional trade arrangements *could* produce more gains due to improved market access to trading partners. The logical extension of this argument is that if a country were to negotiate free trade agreements with all of its trade partners, it would end up with zero effective tariffs on all imports, or free trade, despite the legal existence of positive MFN tariffs. In the process it would achieve preferential access to its partners' markets. Hence, absent transition dynamics, this strategy may produce gains which are considerably larger than unilateral free trade.

Chile has pursued a process of sequentially negotiating bilateral free trade agreements with all significant trading partners, a process we call "additive regionalism." Critics of Chile's additive regionalism strategy argued that agreements with Southern countries are unlikely to be beneficial, and that it is not worth delaying the benefits of unilateral and multilateral tariff liberalization to pursue these agreements. They argue that only agreements with the EU, the US or Japan offer sufficient access to be worth pursuing. Advocates for the government's strategy, however, believe that there are gains to be achieved from the agreements with smaller Southern countries as well. They also argue that additive regionalism will progressively reduce trade diversion costs, lower the effective average tariff in Chile, and provide considerably improved market access. Furthermore, they note that Chile can unilaterally lower its external tariff while simultaneously pursuing additive regionalism to further reduce trade diversion costs. Faced with the controversy, representatives of the Central Bank of Chile requested that we evaluate the additive regionalism strategy.

In this paper, we develop an 11 region multi-sector global computable general equilibrium model with which we examine Chile's additive regionalism strategy. Since Chile started with an 11 percent uniform tariff when we conducted the initial analysis, the trade regime had low distortions. Thus, while Chile reaps gains from further unilateral tariff reduction to 6 percent (as it sequentially implemented between 1998 and 2003), we find that Chile's additive regionalism strategy of combining free trade agreements with four regions, NAFTA, MERCOSUR, the EU and

Rest of South America, produces welfare gains for Chile many multiples of the value of unilateral free trade, provided it attains tariff-free access to all these markets. If the most highly protected sectors in the EU and Rest of South America are excluded from the agreements, however, the gains from additive regionalism are dramatically reduced.

We find that taking Chile's regional arrangements bilaterally, only Chile's agreements with "Northern" partners provide sufficient market access to overcome trade diversion costs for Chile with the 11 percent tariff in place. In particular, the free trade agreement with MERCOSUR was welfare reducing. But we evaluate the agreement with MERCOSUR as welfare increasing after Chile reduced its tariffs to 6 percent since this reduced the trade diversion costs in the MERCOSUR agreement. Furthermore, if an agreement with the US or NAFTA is in place for Chile, adding an agreement with MERCOSUR is welfare increasing, as competition from the US in the Chilean market reduces the trade diversion costs of MERCOSUR. Clearly these results are nuanced and consistent with theory, and in particular, provide some numerical support for the theory of Wonnacott and Wonnacott.

When there is an optimal tariff, as there is in this model, the amount by which a country can reduce its tariff is limited by the distortions of the replacement tax. Consequently, we have produced an updated estimate of the collected VAT rates by sector in Chile. We find that the *benefits of trade liberalization or regional trade arrangements are considerably reduced if tariff revenue must be replaced by the existing distorting alternative taxes.* Similarly, in our optimal tariff calculations, we find that unilateral trade liberalization can proceed to a three percent uniform tariff (rather than a six percent uniform tariff) if efficient replacement taxes are in place.

We find that at least one *partner* country loses from *each* of the regional agreements we consider, and excluded countries as a group always lose. Gains to the world from global free trade are estimated to be vastly larger than any of the regional arrangements (compare Harrison, Rutherford and Tarr, 1997a).

Regarding policy impacts, by quantifying the gains from improved market access, the results provided support for the strategy of additive regionalism, which was controversial in Chile at the time of this study. Chile proceeded to negotiate free trade agreements that led to over 90 percent of its imports coming in tariff free by 2010. Further, when the Chilean Parliament was considering lowering the tariff from 11 percent to 6 percent, the Vice President of the Central Bank of Chile used results of our study (that showed the benefits of such an action) as part of his testimony in favor of lowering the Chilean tariff. By passing this legislation that lowered tariffs, the Chilean government answered its critics who argued that additive regionalism would impede unilateral or multilateral tariff reduction. As a follow-up to this action, the Research Director of the Central Bank of Chile requested a more extensive analysis of the reduction of the tariff from 11 percent to 6 percent (which we did in Harrison, Rutherford and Tarr, 2005).

4.3. Increased Competition and Completion of the Market in the European Union: Static and Steady State Effects, *Harrison, Rutherford and Tarr (1996), Journal of Economic Integration, 1996. This paper won the $10,000 Daeyang Prize as the best article of the year in the Journal of Economic Integration for 1996.*

The single market program of the European Union, also known as "EC92," generated considerable interest among the neighboring developing countries. We developed a global 12 region (9 regions of the European Community, Morocco, Turkey and an aggregate rest of the world), 26 sector CGE model to assess the EC92 program. Our model captures the idea that EC92 will increase competition and rationalization in imperfectly competitive markets.

The impetus for change comes first from the standard, 2.5 percent reduction of border costs and supply side standards costs. In addition, increased competition will come from an increase in the willingness of EU buyers to substitute among the products of producers in different countries. In part, this is because of the single market program on standards; in part, due to rules on government procurement; and, in part, due to an increase in intra-EU trade (from border costs reductions) which is likely to lead to consumers trying new varieties they sometimes like. These effects are best modeled as a change in the elasticity of substitution of consumers in EC countries for the varieties of output of other EC firms. We develop a monopolistic competition model in which each firm's post-1992 markup is endogenously determined as a function of the substitutability of the outputs of different EC firms in the preference structure of national consumers.

We find that there would be a strong increase in intra-EC trade, with EU firms relying less on their domestic markets and more on sales to other EU countries.[9] We find that the EU would trade less with the rest of the world, but since their economies become more trade intensive and expand, the impact on imports from the rest of the world is very small.

Our estimates are that the reduction of border and standards costs associated with the EC92 program will result in welfare gains of about 0.5% of EC welfare. Allowing for the additional effects of standardization on consumer substitution elasticities (our version of integration), however, more than doubles the estimated welfare gains. We estimate that the benefits in the steady state more than quadruple the estimate of the welfare benefits (about 2.4% of EC GDP) compared to the segmented markets comparative statics estimate, explaining some of the anticipatory

[9]While econometric evidence shows that price discrimination will persist,earlier model estimates of others imposed complete elimination of firm level price discrimination across the European Union and led to the perverse result that intra-EU trade declined.

euphoria. For the rest of the world, we estimate welfare changes that are virtually zero in the comparative static model and are positive but extremely small in the steady state model.

4.4. Economic Implications for Turkey of a Customs Union with the European Union, *Harrison, Rutherford and Tarr (1997), European Economic Review.*

We developed a small open economy CGE model to assess the impacts of Turkey joining a customs union with the European Union. We evaluated various aspects of a "deep" agreement and grouped the policy changes into four categories: (1) access–improved market access on exports to the EU in textiles and apparel, steel and to a lesser extent agriculture; (2) standards–improved export prices due to adaptation to EU standards and reduction of non-tariff barriers that the EU applies against Turkey; (3) tariff reduction–tariff reductions in Turkey on manufactured products as Turkey adopts the common external tariff of the EU. This includes Turkey providing improved market access to third countries with whom the EU has negotiated preferential market access; and (4) reciprocal market access–improved market access for Turkish exporters due to reciprocal market access it might obtain with countries that have negotiated free trade agreements with the EU.

We found all four would have positive impacts on Turkish welfare, with reciprocal market access providing the largest benefits. Our results therefore supported the decision of the Turkish government to join the Customs Union. In addition, our results showed that there would be larger revenue losses from joining the Customs Union than anticipated by the government (due to tariff free access to third countries that the EU has free trade agreements); this alerted the government to address revenue replacement issues more seriously.

Over time, however, the government of Turkey was disappointed with what it was able to achieve in reciprocal market access with third countries with whom it was obligated to provide tariff free access under EU negotiated agreements. This indicates that there were likely benefits from the Customs Union from Turkish tariff reduction and improved market access in the EU. However, Turkey had hoped for larger gains from reciprocal market access, and these gains have not materialized.

4.5. Morocco's Free Trade Agreement with the EU: A Quantitative Assessment, *Rutherford, Rutström and Tarr (1997), Economic Modeling.*

In 1992, the Moroccan Minister of Trade, Hassan Abouyoub, proposed to the European Union that Morocco and the EU enter into a reciprocal free trade agreement. Pursuit of a reciprocal free trade agreement by Morocco was seen as surprising to many, including negotiators in the European Union, since Morocco already had tariff free access to EU markets in non-agricultural goods, with minor exceptions such as trousers. However, EU agricultural protection impeded Moroccan exports. Minister Abouyoub preferred to employ an open economy model of development for Morocco, but did not have political support for unilateral free trade. He was, however, able to put together a coalition of agricultural interests, who sought improved market access in the EU, and industrial interests who favored reciprocal free trade with the EU. He saw reciprocal market access with the EU as a means of injecting competition into the Moroccan economy as it required Morocco to lower its moderately high tariffs to its most important trade partner. His initiative led to the EU developing its "Mediterranean Policy," which imposed reciprocal free trade agreements on several countries who had one way preferential market access in the EU.[10]

We developed a small open economy CGE model of Morocco to assess the impacts of a free trade agreement with the EU. Morocco was modeled endogenously, with the European Union and an aggregate rest of the world modeled parametrically. We found that Morocco would gain 1.5% of GDP from the agreement with the EU. About 1.3% of the gains derived from the lowering of tariffs against EU imports, which increased competition in the Moroccan market and reduced the effective dispersion of its effective tariffs; the remainder of the gains were due to some hoped for improved market access for Moroccan exporters in EU markets (primarily in agricultural products). But the gains would increase to 2.5% of GDP if free trade with the rest of the world in goods were added.

Our work provided support for Minister Abouyoub in his efforts to negotiate a reciprocal free trade agreement with the EU. Although Morocco did obtain some additional market access in agriculture, it was quite limited and disappointing to the agricultural interests. Nonetheless, our simulations indicated that the majority of the gains were due to increased competition in Moroccan markets from EU suppliers, so I would continue to assess the agreement as positive for Morocco.

Following the development of the European Union's "Mediterranean Policy," the government of **Tunisia** requested an assessment of the reciprocal free trade agreement it was discussing with the European Union (EU). Unlike the Moroccan case where the government sought reciprocity with the EU, Tunisia grudgingly accepted reciprocity in order to retain its preferential access in the EU market. Tunisian officials hoped that the agreement would facilitate more foreign direct investment from EU investors and, like Morocco, more market access in agriculture. We undertook a project in Tunisia similar to the one in Morocco that produced similar results. See Rutherford, Rutstrom and Tarr (2000).

[10]The Mediterranean policy of the EU covered Morocco, Algeria, Tunisia, Libya, Egypt, Malta, Cyprus, Turkey, Israel, Jordan, Lebanon and Syria.

4.6. Introduction and Key Tables From: Services Liberalization in Preferential Trade Arrangements: The Case of Kenya, *Balistreri and Tarr.*[11]

This chapter summarizes key results from the paper by Balistreri and Tarr (2011) for Kenya and the parallel and similar study on Tanzania (Jensen and Tarr, 2010). These papers were the first to develop a modeling framework to analyze preferential commitments to foreign investors in services in regional arrangements, where the endogenous productivity impacts of services are incorporated. The key contribution of these papers, which is more prominent in the results for Kenya, is that we show that there is an imperfect competition analogy to trade diversion in goods, whereby preferential commitments in services could be immizerising. Further, agreements with technologically advanced regions are very likely to be welfare enhancing. Preferential services agreements with Southern regions incur risks of being immizerising (especially in our Kenya model); but with our parameters and sensitivity analysis, this result depends strongly on initial rent capture from barriers in the home country.

We developed a CGE model of Kenya (Tanzania) to assess preferential commitments by Kenya (Tanzania) to foreign services providers. Who captures the initial rents from barriers to foreign investors in services is crucial to the results, however, as without some initial rent capture by Kenyans (Tanzanians) of their services barriers against foreigners, we find that Kenya (Tanzania) should gain from any of its potential preferential agreements in services, under all plausible elasticity values. (Sensitivity analysis shows that losses are more likely the more technologically advanced the excluded regions are, relative to the partner region, and the greater the rent capture on initial barriers in services.) So an agreement with the European Union is both worth more to Kenya (Tanzania) and is more likely to be welfare increasing than an agreement with its African partners.

Regarding policy implications, the work in Kenya was requested by both the Permanent Secretary and the Chief Economist of the Ministry of East African and Regional Cooperation. In my dissemination meetings with the Chief Economist, he indicated that this study would be useful to him in his negotiations with his regional counterparts. Moreover, he requested the companion study on Tanzania, which he indicated he would use in his discussions with his Tanzanian counterparts on liberalization commitments. Although when we began the study, services were not part of the East African Customs Union (EACU) agenda, when we presented this study, the EACU had committed to preferential services liberalization in some areas, especially professional services.

[11]For this paper, which is in the review process, we provide the introduction, selected key tables and the link to the Working Paper; but we do not reproduce the full paper in this volume.

4.7. Deep Trade Policy Options for Armenia: The Importance of Trade Facilitation, Services and Standards Liberalization, *Jensen and Tarr (2012), Economics — the Open Access, Open Assessment E-Journal.*

At the time this paper was written, Armenia, along with Ukraine, Georgia and Moldova, was negotiating what the European Union calls a "Deep and Comprehensive Free Trade Agreement (DCFTA)." The Armenian Deputy Minister of Economy, Mushegh Tumasyan, met me at a conference in Vienna and requested that I lead a team that would assist the government of Armenia in assessing the impact of the agreement.

At the request of Deputy Minister Tumasyan, we expanded the models of Balistreri and Tarr (2011) on Kenya and Jensen and Tarr (2010) on Tanzania to include trade facilitation and standards issues. As a result, we believe it is the most comprehensive model of modern preferential trading arrangement available.

We developed a 21 sector small open economy, comparative static computable general equilibrium model of Armenia. We find that a DCFTA with the EU will likely result in substantial gains to Armenia, but a shallow free trade agreement with the EU that focuses only on preferential tariff liberalization in goods will likely lead to small losses to Armenia due to traditional trade diversion (tariff losses on displaced imports from the Rest of the World region) and, more importantly, due to a loss of productivity from lost varieties of technologies from the Rest of the World region in manufactured products. We estimate that the gains to Armenia from a DCFTA with the EU derive from further liberalization of barriers in services, harmonization of standards and most importantly, from a trade facilitation and a reduction in border costs. We estimate very small gains from preferential liberalization of barriers against CIS, but find that unilateral liberalization of services and trade barriers on a non-discriminatory basis would yield gains that are about three times the gains from preferential liberalization of goods and services with the EU alone.

Regarding the policy implications, the study supported the government's broad strategy of negotiating a DCFTA with the EU, emphasizing the benefits of the trade facilitation and services components. It also helped the government formulate a nuanced strategy for harmonization of standards with the EU.[12]

[12]While we expect gains from harmonization of standards with the EU, we do not recommend that Armenia adopt all technical regulations and sanitary and phyto-sanitary (SPS) requirements of the European Union. The costs are likely to exceed the benefits for many products, especially regarding the SPS conditions.

4.8. The Eurasian Customs Union among Russia, Belarus and Kazakhstan: Can it succeed where its predecessor failed? *Tarr (2013).*[13]

Failure of the Eurasec Customs Union

There is a network of free trade agreements among the 11 countries in the Commonwealth of Independent States (CIS) and Georgia that provides for tariff free access among these countries on virtually all trade. Nonetheless, in 1995 Russia joined with Belarus and Kazakhstan in forming a customs union. In 1996, the Kyrgyz President, Askar Akaev, agreed to have the Kyrgyz Republic become the fourth member. Later Tajikistan and Uzbekistan joined the Customs Union that came to be known in 2000 as "Eurosec."

Unlike the EU, where the various member states influence the common external tariff, the common external tariff of Eurosec was the Russian tariff. By 1995, Russia had introduced a tariff structure that protected the less competitive manufacturing sectors of Russia, with products like cars getting high protection. Since the common external tariff protected Russian industry, by extending Eurosec, the costs of protecting Russian industry would partly be borne by consumers of new member states.

The political economy in the cases of the less industrialized members, especially the Kyrgyz Republic and eventual member Tajikistan, was just the opposite. If the common external tariff were enforced, these countries would bear the trade diversion costs. Consumers of these countries would have to pay high prices for Russian imports that could only compete under the preferential tariff umbrella. But the products these countries exported were subject to low tariffs in Russia, so the exporters from these countries were not protected in Russian markets.

Work in Kyrgyzstan and Its Policy Implications

At the request of the Kyrgyz authorities, in 1996 I conducted an evaluation of the impact of the participation of the Kyrgyz Republic in the customs union, which I discussed with several Kyrgyz Ministers. This analysis (which was based on theory and partial equilibrium modeling) appeared as part of Michalopoulos and Tarr (1997). This work emphasized the disproportionately high share of the trade diversion costs that the Kyrgyz Republic would bear by implementing the common external tariff. This work helped influence the government to avoid passing into law the common

[13]The CGE analysis in these countries is World Bank (2012). An abbreviated version of the paper that appears in this volume was published in French, English and Russian. The French version is available as Tarr (2013a).

external tariff of the Customs Union and to expedite its accession into the World Trade Organization with tariff commitments that would prevent high trade diversion costs in a customs union.

Recognizing the uneven costs and benefits of the customs union, the member countries of the Eurosec customs union began to apply the common external tariff on an "a la carte" basis. For example, as early as 1996, Kazakhstan suspended application of the common external tariff on cars, since its consumers complained about trade diversion costs away from Korean cars. Estimates are that the common external tariff was applied on only about 50–60 percent of the tariff lines, depending on the country.

The New Eurasian Customs Union of Russia, Kazakhstan and Belarus

In 2010, Russia started the Eurasian Customs Union with Belarus and Kazakhstan, but in 2013 other countries in the region were discussing membership. The most important lesson from the earlier experience of the Eurosec Customs Union is that widening protection of industries through a customs union is really an import substitution policy that has proven to be unsuccessful. The Eurasian Customs Union is too small an economic region to approximate world market prices on most products. But reformers in Russia (who are diminished in number and influence) would like to see the Customs Union focus on trade facilitation and the reduction of non-tariff barriers. This kind of deeper integration could yield benefits, including benefits to excluded countries.

Work in Kazakhstan and its Policy Implications

In response to a request from the government of Kazakhstan, in 2010 and 2011, the World Bank supported a CGE analysis of the impacts on Kazakhstan of joining the Customs Union led by Jesper Jensen and myself (World Bank, 2012). Like the Eurosec Customs Union, the initial tariff of the Customs Union was the tariff of the Russian Federation. In the case of Kazakhstan, imposition of the Customs Union tariff resulted in almost doubling of their average tariffs with an increase in the variance as well, resulting in an estimated loss of real income. Improvements in trade facilitation and a reduction in non-tariff barriers could compensate for these losses and motivate Kazakhstan to effectively implement the Customs Union in the long run. Our analysis and discussions with the government highlighted and strengthened their efforts to reduce non-tariff barriers within the Customs Union and to improve trade facilitation. The paper in this volume summarizes these results and key developments since the time of the World Bank report.

5. Training Exercises

In several cases, we responded to requests from governments to provide a training component to allow training participants designated by the government to independently run the model we developed for their country. Our training exercises in Morocco, Tunisia, Moscow (for Russia, Armenia and the Commonwealth of Independent States), Tanzania (for sub-Saharan Africa) and Malaysia have involved multiple weeks of full time face to face training plus additional training by e-mail.[14] From our experience, we emphasize that governments must be realistic in their expectations about CGE modeling transfer. Depending on the time available and background of the participants, we now offer a menu of training objectives, ranging from the development of independent modeling capacity in GAMS and MPSGE at one extreme, to, at the other extreme when less time is available, the capacity to effectively understand and communicate with modelers. To achieve independent modeling capacity, the trainees should have a good background in economic theory, facility with computers and, most importantly, be allocated substantial time for skill development. In our most successful cases, where our participants or collaborators have become internationally competitive as CGE modelers, the participants had a Master's degree in economics or better, and the modeling work was part of the objectives or work responsibilities of the participant; so the participant devoted substantial time to the endeavor outside of the training provided.[15] In training programs with a more modest objective, we have had success in contributing to an understanding of international trade principles and the consequences of liberalization through the use of CGE models. We find that the application of a CGE model to the country of the participant often provides motivation to understand principles that otherwise appear abstract and less relevant.

References

Arnold, Jens M., Beata S. Javorcik, Mary Lipscomb and Aaditya Matoo (2012). "Services Reform and Manufacturing Performance: Evidence from India," World Bank Policy Research Working Paper 5948, January.

Arnold, Jens M., Beata S. Javorcik and Aaditya Mattoo (2011). "Does Services Liberalization Benefit Manufacturing Firms: Evidence from the Czech Republic," *Journal of International Economics*, **85**(1), 136–146.

Balistreri, Edward J., Thomas F. Rutherford and David G. Tarr (2009). "Modeling Services Liberalization: The Case of Kenya," *Economic Modeling*, **26**(3), 668–679.

[14]My collaborators in the training were various combinations of Thomas Rutherford, Jesper Jensen, Glenn Harrison, Miles Light, James Markusen, Elisabet Rutstrom and Calvin Djofack.

[15]Angelo Gurgel, Natasha Tourdyeva and Oleg Lugovoy are examples where as collaborators or participants in work with us, they became internationally competitive as modelers.

Balistreri, Edward J. and David G. Tarr (2011). "Services Liberalization in Preferential Trade Arrangements: The case of Kenya," World Bank Policy and Research Working Paper No. 5552, January. Available at: http://econ.worldbank.org/external/default/main?pagePK=64165259&theSitePK=469372&piPK=64165421&menuPK=64166093&entityID=000158349_20110131090808.

Chen, Shaohua and Martin Ravallion (2004). "Welfare Impacts of China's Accession to the WTO," *The World Bank Economic Review*, **18**(1), 29–57.

Copenhagen Economics, East Europe Institute of Munich and the Institute for Economic Research and Policy Consulting (2006). "Analysis of Economic Impacts of Ukraine's WTO Accession to the WTO: Overall Impact Assessment." Available from www.ier.kiev.ua.

Fernandes, Ana M. and Caroline Paunov (2012). "Foreign direct investment in services and manufacturing productivity: evidence for Chile," *Journal of Development Economics*, **97**(2), 305–321.

Francois, Joseph and Bernard Hoekman (2010). "Services Trade and Policy," *Journal of Economic Literature*, **48**, 642–692.

Harrison, Glenn W., Thomas F. Rutherford and David G. Tarr (2005). "Chile's Regional Arrangements: The Importance of Market Access and Lowering the Tariff to Six Percent," in Romulo Chumacero and Klaus Schmidt Hebbel (eds.), *General Equilibrium Models for the Chilean Economy*, Santiago, Chile: Central Bank of Chile.

Harrison, Glenn W., Thomas F. Rutherford and David G. Tarr and Angelo Gurgel (2004). "Trade Policy and Poverty Reduction in Brazil," *The World Bank Economic Review*, **18**, 289–317.

Harrison, Glenn W., Thomas F. Rutherford and David G. Tarr (2003). "Trade Liberalization, Poverty and Efficient Equity," *Journal of Development Economics*, **71**(1), 97–128.

Harrison, Glenn W., Thomas F. Rutherford and David G. Tarr (2003a). "Rules of Thumb for Evaluating Preferential Trading Arrangements: Evidence from Computable General Equilibrium Assessments," *Cuadernos de Economía*, **40**(121), 460–468.

Harrison, Glenn W., Thomas F. Rutherford and David G. Tarr (2002). "Trade Policy Options for Chile: The Importance of Market Access," *World Bank Economic Review*, **16**(1), 49–79.

Harrison, Glenn W., Thomas F. Rutherford and David G. Tarr (1997). "Economic Implications for Turkey of a Customs Union with the European Union," *European Economic Review*, **41**(3–5), 861–870.

Harrison, Glenn W., Thomas F. Rutherford and David G. Tarr (1997a). "Quantifying the Uruguay Round," *Economic Journal*, **107**(444), 1405–1430.

Harrison, Glenn W., Thomas F. Rutherford and David G. Tarr (1996). "Increased Competition and Completion of the Market in the European Union: Static and Steady State Effects," *Journal of Economic Integration*, **11**(3), 332–365.

Harrison, Glenn W., Thomas F. Rutherford and David G. Tarr (1993). "Trade Reform in the Partially Liberalized Economy of Turkey," *The World Bank Economic Review*, **7**(2), 191–217.

Haus, L. (1992). *Globalizing the GATT: The Soviet Union's Successor States, Eastern Europe and the International Trading System*, Washington D.C.: The Brookings Institution.

Ianchovichina, Elena and Will Martin (2004). "Impacts of China's Accession to the World Trade Organization," *World Bank Economic Review*, **18**(1), 3–27.

Jesper Jensen, Thomas F. Rutherford and David G. Tarr (2010). "Modeling Services Liberalization: The Case of Tanzania," *Journal of Economic Integration*, **25**(4), 644–675.

Jensen, Jesper, Thomas F. Rutherford and David G. Tarr (2007). "The Impact of Liberalizing Barriers to Foreign Direct Investment in Services: The Case of Russian Accession to the World Trade Organization," *Review of Development Economics*, **11**(3), 482–506.

Jensen, Jesper, Thomas F. Rutherford and David G. Tarr (2006). "Telecommunications Reform within Russia's Accession to the WTO," *Eastern European Economics*, **44**(1), 25–58.

Jensen, Jesper and David G. Tarr (2012). "Deep Trade Policy Options for Armenia: The Importance of Trade Facilitation, Services and Standards Liberalization," *Economics: The Open Access–Open Assessment E-Journal*, 6, 2012-1. http://dx.doi.org/10.5018/economics-ejournal.ja.2012-1.

Jensen, Jesper and David G. Tarr (2010). "Regional Trade Policy Options for Tanzania: the importance of services commitments," World Bank Policy and Research Working Paper No. 5481, November.

Jensen, Jesper and David G. Tarr (2008). "Impact of local content restrictions and barriers against foreign direct investment in services: the case of Kazakhstan accession to the WTO," *Eastern European Economics*, **46**(5), 5–26.

Jensen, Jesper and David G. Tarr (2003). "Trade, Exchange Rate and Energy Pricing Reform in Iran: Potentially Large Efficiency Effects and Gains to the Poor," *Review of Development Economics*, **7**(4), 543–562.

Markusen, James R., Thomas F. Rutherford and David G. Tarr (2005). "Trade and Direct Investment in Producer Services and the Domestic Market for Expertise," *Canadian Journal of Economics*, **38**(3), 758–777.

Melo, Jaime de and David G. Tarr (1992). *A General Equilibrium Analysis of US Foreign Trade Policy*, Cambridge, MA.: MIT Press.

Melo, Jaime de, and David G. Tarr (1990). "Welfare Costs of US Quotas in Textiles, Steel and Autos," *Review of Economics and Statistics*, August, 489–497.

Michalopoulos., Constantine and David G. Tarr (1997). "The Economics of Customs Unions in the Commonwealth of Independent States," *Post-Soviet Geography and Economics*, **38**(3), 125–143.

Morkre, Morris and David G. Tarr (1995). "Reforming Hungarian Agricultural Trade Policy: A Quantitative Evaluation," *Weltwirtschaftliches Archiv* Band 131, Heft 1, 106–131.

Morkre, Morris and David G. Tarr (1980). *The Effects of Restrictions on United States Imports: Five Case Studies and Theory*, Bureau of Economics Report to the Federal Trade Commission, Washington, D.C.: U.S. Government Printing Office, June.

Rutherford, Thomas F., Elisabet E. Rutström and David G. Tarr (2000). "A Free Trade Agreement Between the European Agreement and a Representative Arab Mediterranean Country: A Quantitative Assessment," in Bernard Hoekman and Jamel Zarrouk (eds.), *Catching Up with the Competition: Trade Opportunities and Challenges for Arab Countries*, Ann Arbor: University of Michigan Press.

Rutherford, Thomas F., Elisabet Rutström and David G. Tarr (1997). "Morocco's Free Trade Agreement with the EU: A Quantitative Assessment," *Economic Modelling*, **14**(9), 237–269.

Rutherford, Thomas F. and David G. Tarr (2012). "Services Liberalization in the Regions of Russia under WTO Accession: Regional Household and Poverty Effects," *International Journal of Services Technology and Management*, **17**(2, 3, 4), 181–204.

Rutherford, Thomas F. and David G. Tarr (2010). "Regional Impacts of Liberalization of Barriers against Foreign Direct Investment in Services," the case of Russia's accession to the WTO," *Review of International Economics*, **18**(1), 30–46.

Rutherford, Thomas F. and David G. Tarr (2008). "Poverty Effects of Russia's WTO Accession: modeling 'real households' with endogenous productivity effects," *Journal of International Economics*, **75**(1), 131–150.

Rutherford, Thomas F. and David Tarr (2003). "Regional Trading Arrangements for Chile: Do the Results Differ with a Dynamic Model?" *Integration and Trade*, **7**(18), 117–139.

Rutherford, Thomas F. and David G. Tarr (2002). "Trade Liberalization, Product Variety and Growth in a Small Open Economy: A Quantitative Assessment," *Journal of International Economics*, **56**(2), 247–272.

Rutherford, Thomas F. and David G. Tarr (1998). "Trade Liberalization and Endogenous Growth in a Small Open Economy," World Bank Policy and Research Working Paper Number 1970.

Rutherford, Thomas F., David G. Tarr and Oleksandr Shepotylo (2006). "The Impact on Russia of WTO Accession and The Doha Agenda: the importance of liberalization of barriers against foreign direct investment in services for growth and poverty reduction," in Thomas Hertel and L. Alan Winters (eds.), *Putting Development Back into the Doha Agenda: Poverty Impacts of a WTO Agreement*, New York: Palgrave McMillan and the World Bank. Reprinted in: L. Alan Winters (ed.), *The WTO and Poverty and Inequality*, An Elgar Reference Collection, Cheltenham, UK: Edgar Elgar Publishing, 2007.

Rutherford, Thomas F., David G. Tarr and Oleksandr Shepotylo (2005). "Poverty Effects of Russia's WTO Accession: modeling "real" households and endogenous productivity effects," World Bank Policy and Research Working Paper No. 3473, February.

Shepotylo, Oleksandr and David G. Tarr (forthcoming). "Impact of WTO Accession on the Bound and Applied Tariff Rates of Russia," *Eastern European Economics*.

Shepotylo, Oleksandr and David G. Tarr (2008). "Specific tariffs, tariff simplification and the structure of import tariffs in Russia: 2001–2005," *Eastern European Economics*, **46**, 49–58.

Shepotylo, Oleksandr and Volodymyr Vakhitov (2012). "Impact of services liberalization on productivity of manufacturing firms: evidence from the Ukrainian firm-level data," World Bank Policy and Research Working Paper Number 5944, January.

Tarr, David G. (2013). "Putting Services and Foreign Direct Investment with Endogenous Productivity Effects in Computable General Equilibrium Models," in Dixon, Peter B. Dixon and Dale W. Jorgenson (eds.), *Handbook of Computable General Equilibrium Modeling*, Amsterdam: North Holland, Elsevier B.V., pp. 303–377.

Tarr, David G. (2013a). "L'Union douanaire Russia-Bielorussie-Kazakhstan peut-elle reussir la ou les precedents projets integration ont echoue?" in Arnaud Dubien (ed.), *Russie 2013: regards de l'Observatoire franco-russe*, Available at: http://www.ccifr.ru/uploaded/Actualites/Yearbook-Bondesouscription-BAT2_med.pdf.

Tarr, David G. (2010). "The Economic Impact of Export Restraints on Russian Gas and Raw Timber," in *The Economic Impact of Export Restrictions on Raw Materials*, OECD, Paris: OECD, 131–154.

Tarr, David G. (2010a). "The Crucial Role for Competition in the Russian Gas Market: Implications for Russia and Europe," *IAEE Energy Forum*, Fourth Quarter, 31–35.

Tarr, David G. (2007). "Russian Accession to the WTO: An Assessment," *Eurasian Geography and Economics*, **48**(3), 306–319.

Tarr, David G. editor, (2006). *Trade Policy and WTO Accession for Development in Russia and the CIS: A Handbook*, in Russian, Moscow: Ves Mir.

Tarr, David G. (2005). "The Impact of World Trade Organization Accession on Living Standards and Poverty," in *Reducing Poverty through Growth and Social Policy*

Reform in Russia, Radwan Shaban and others, Directions in Development Series, World Bank: Washington DC., 2006, 114–126. Also appeared as chapter 7 in *Russian Federation: Reducing Poverty through Growth and Social Policy Reform*, Report No. 28923-RU, World Bank: Washington DC., February 2005, 77–85.

Tarr, David G. (2002). "On the Design of Tariff Policy: Arguments for and Against Uniform Tariffs," in B. Hoekman, A. Mattoo and P. English (eds.), *Development, Trade and the WTO*: A Handbook, Washington: World Bank.

Tarr, David G. (1992). "Problems in the Transition from the CMEA: Implications for Eastern Europe," *Communist Economies and Economic Transformation*, **4**(1), 22–43.

Tarr, David G. (1990). "Second-Best Foreign Exchange Policy in the Presence of Domestic Price Controls and Export Subsidies," *The World Bank Economic Review*, **4**(2), 171–193.

Tarr, David G. (1990a). "Quantifying Second Best Effects in Grossly Distorted Markets: The Case of the Butter Market in Poland," *Journal of Comparative Economics*, **14**, 105–119.

Tarr, David G. (1989). *A General Equilibrium Analysis of US Quotas on Autos, Steel and Textiles*, Bureau of Economics Report to the Federal Trade Commission, Washington, D.C.: U.S. Government Printing Office.

Tarr, David G. and Morris Morkre (1984). "*Aggregate Costs to the United States of Tariffs and Quotas on Imports,*" Bureau of Economics Report to the Federal Trade Commission, U.S. Government Printing Office, December.

Tarr, David G. and Peter Thomson (2004). "The Merits of Dual Pricing of Russian Natural Gas," *The World Economy*, **27**(8), 1173–1194.

Tarr, David G. and Natalya Volchkova (2013). "Foreign trade and direct investment, patterns and policy issues," in Michael V. Alexeev and Shlomo Weber (eds.), *Handbook of the Russian Economy*, Oxford: Oxford University Press, pp. 593–616.

Tarr, David G. and Natalya Volchkova (2010). "Foreign Economic Policy at a Crossroads," in Anders Aslund, Sergei Guriev and Andrew Kutchins (eds.), *Russia After the Global Economic Crisis*, Washington DC: Peterson Institute for International Economics and Center for Strategic and International Studies, pp. 200–222.

Wonnacott, Paul and Ronald Wonnacott (1981). "Is Unilateral Tariff Reduction Preferable to a Customs Union? The Curious Case of the Missing Foreign Tariffs", *American Economic Review*, **71**(4), 704–714.

World Bank (2012). "Assessment of Costs and Benefits of the Customs Union for Kazakhstan," Report Number 65977-KZ, Washington DC, January 3, 2012. Available at: http://documents.worldbank.org/curated/en/2012/01/15647043/assessment-costs-benefits-customs-union-kazakhstan.

World Bank (2001). "Trade and Foreign Exchange Policies in Iran: Reform Agenda, Economic Implications and Impact on the Poor," Report No. 22953-IRN, October 31. Available at: http://lnweb90.worldbank.org/CAW/cawDoclib.nsf/vewAsiaPacific/E5BCD8C710B98AD185256C5E0066CCB8/$file/Iran22953.pdf.

Part I

Trade Policy: Quantitative Restraints, Foreign Exchange Surrender and Uniformity

WELFARE COSTS OF U.S. QUOTAS IN TEXTILES, STEEL AND AUTOS

Jaime de Melo and David Tarr*

Abstract—This paper quantifies the welfare effects and resource shifts that would occur if U.S. quantitative restrictions (QRs) in textiles, steel and autos were removed. Estimates are derived from a static ten-sector general equilibrium model of the U.S. economy. The welfare loss from the QRs is estimated at approximately U.S. $20 billion (1984 dollars) Due to the high rent transfer component of QRs (about 75%), the average across-the-board tariff equivalent of QRs (in terms of welfare costs) is estimated at about 20%, a rate which predates the early days of multilateral tariff reduction.

I. Introduction

RECENTLY, several studies have estimated the costs of U.S. special protection arrangements.[1] All these studies, using a partial equilibrium (PE) framework, provide a useful range of estimates of the costs of non-tariff protection. These studies are especially valuable when taken individually because then the assumptions of PE analysis provide an adequate approximation of reality. But, as we quantify below, when the costs of all restrictions are taken together, the underlying assumptions are much less tenable. In particular, the general equilibrium (GE) approach used here accounts for three effects omitted by PE estimates. First, the inclusion of a balance of trade constraint (expressed in world prices) removes an upward bias present in PE analysis. Second, the effects of income transfers to and from the rest of the world are properly accounted for so that, unlike in the PE analysis, capturing quota rents affects resource allocation. Third, economy-wide resource constraints and interindustry linkages provide a more accurate estimate of welfare and sectoral employment effects.

This paper deals with the problems of PE analysis by presenting estimates from a static ten-sector computable general equilibrium (CGE) model of the U.S. economy calibrated to the year 1984 when quantitative restrictions (QRs) in textiles and autos were in effect, and those on steel were in negotiation. To our knowledge, the treatment of QR-associated effects here is more satisfactory than in previous CGE applications. While the U.S.-negotiated voluntary export restraint (VER) on automobiles has expired, demand in the United States for protection through non-tariff barriers (NTBs) remains strong and may be on the rise. A new round of estimates of the costs of protection is therefore all the more welcome.

The remainder of the paper is organized as follows. Section II outlines the model. Section III details the sources of estimates of premia on preexisting QRs in 1984 and the sources for the parameters describing demand and supply elasticities. Estimates of the welfare and employment effects of QR removal are presented by industry and in the aggregate in sections IV and V. Conclusions follow in section VI.

II. Model Outline[2]

The simulation model is a static CGE model with assumptions that correspond closely to those followed by the partial equilibrium estimates cited above, namely, a neoclassical perfect-competition Walrasian model in which a representative consumer maximizes utility subject to a budget constraint, atomistic producers minimize costs, and the government redistributes tax revenues from trade policy in a lump sum. The economy has a fixed endowment of labor and capital and faces

Received for publication January 12, 1989. Revision accepted for publication November 16, 1989.

* The World Bank, University of Geneva, and CEPR; and the World Bank, respectively.

This is a revised and shortened version of de Melo and Tarr (1988) which extends an earlier study by Tarr (1989). We thank Morris Morkre and two referees for comments. The views are those of the authors, not those of the World Bank. We thank Julie Stanton for extremely valuable research assistance, Maria Ameal for logistic support and Soren Nielsen for computer support.

[1] Among the most widely known studies that provide estimates of the welfare costs of non-tariff barriers (NTBs) in the United States are individual sector studies for textiles (Morkre (1984); Tarr and Morkre (1984); Cline (1987); Keesing and Wolf (1980); for automobiles (Winston and Associates (1987); Tarr and Morkre (1984); Feenstra (1984, 1985, 1988); Dinopoulos and Kreinin (1988)); and for steel (Tarr and Morkre (1984)). Perhaps the most comprehensive recent estimates come from the 31 case studies of special protection by Hufbauer, Berliner and Elliott (1986).

[2] A full description of the model is contained in the appendix to de Melo and Tarr (1988) and is available from the authors upon request.

This article originally appeared in the *Review of Economics and Statistics* (1990), August, pp. 489–497. MIT Press retains the copyright for this article.

an exogenous balance of trade constraint expressed in world prices. Because we are interested in the static welfare costs of protection, we abstract from investment, thereby simplifying the welfare analysis. The components of demand, therefore, include only consumer and intermediate demand.

Under these assumptions, it is clear that the welfare changes due to a change in trade policy are the usual production and consumption costs of protection referred to in the literature on the costs of protection. Our measure of the welfare change due to a policy change is given by the equivalent variation (EV) measure associated with the Stone-Geary utility function describing the representative consumer's preferences, i.e.,

$$EV = C[IU(p^1, y^1), p^0] - C[IU(p^0, y^0), p^0]$$

where C is the cost function, IU is indirect utility which depends on prices and income, p is the vector of final goods prices, and superscripts 0 and 1 refer to the equilibrium before and after the counterfactual trade policy experiment. If EV is positive, the consumer is better off as a result of the policy shift.

The structure of the ten-sector model is as follows.[3] Commodities supplied (or purchased) abroad and domestic commodities sold on the domestic market are imperfect substitutes. This assumption of product differentiation is commonly used in applied general equilibrium analysis and is also adopted in most of the PE studies alluded to above. On the export side, the assumption of product differentiation is reflected in the constant elasticity of transformation (CET) function between domestic and foreign sales.[4] A symmetric functional form is specified for intermediate demand by sector (see below). The assumption of product differentiation allows for the cross-hauling observed in trade statistics.

Production possibilities are parametrized by assuming constant elasticity of substitution (CES) functions for value-added and Leontief functions between intermediates (as a whole) and value-added and across intermediates. However, within each sector, intermediate demand is a CES function between the domestically produced intermediate and the competing foreign intermediate. To give an example, no substitution is allowed between purchases of steel and other manufacturing intermediates, but substitution in purchases is allowed between domestically produced and foreign produced steel when their relative prices change as a result of a change in trade policy. Likewise, in consumption demand, the demand system derived from the Stone-Geary utility indicator allows for non-unitary income elasticities of demand and non-zero cross-price elasticities of demand between domestically produced and foreign produced consumer goods.

Finally, we note that in previous single-country partial equilibrium estimates, authors have invariably assumed that the United States is a small supplier and demander in world markets. In our preferred estimates, we retain this assumption except for the supply of auto imports and the demand for agricultural exports. However, because of the controversy about the importance of terms of trade effects reported in multi-country models (e.g., Whalley (1985), Deardorff and Stern (1986)), we report separately results under the assumption that the United States possesses generalized monopoly and monopsony power.

The description of the model is complete except for our treatment of QRs. In the United States, for the sectors considered here, there are no government controls or direct quota allocations with resale prohibition. Hence, unlike the case of many QR allocation schemes in developing countries, the U.S. system of QRs allows for market-clearing prices. Since in 1984 quotas were already in place in autos and textiles, we assume that observed purchases were at the premia-inclusive prices in that year. (The estimation of premia is discussed in section III.)[5]

III. Elasticity and Premia Estimates

Considerable effort was devoted to a "parameter search" for elasticities of demand and supply and to constructing premia estimates for existing

[3] The ten sectors are agriculture (1), food (2), mining (3), textiles and apparel (4), autos (5), steel (6), consumer goods (7), other manufacturing (8), traded services (9), and non-traded services (10). All sectors are traded with the exception of sector 10. See Tarr (1988) for details on aggregation.

[4] The CET was first introduced by Powell and Gruen (1967).

[5] Our calibration procedure assumes that the prices and quantities observed in 1984 correspond to an equilibrium of the U.S. economy with normal capacity utilization and in which the only distortions are the QRs and tariff on imports. This may be viewed as a strong assumption but it is implicit as well in most other estimates of the costs of protection.

TABLE 1.—ELASTICITY SPECIFICATION (CENTRAL CASE)

Sector	Column Notes (1)	(2)	(3)	(4)	(5)	Elasticity of Substitution Intermediates (1)	Elasticity of Substitution Capital/Labor (2)	Elasticity of Transformation Domestic/Export Sales (3)	Price Elasticities of Final Demand: Domestic (4)	Imports (5)	Premia Rates (6)
Agriculture	a	c	e	k	f	1.4	0.6	4.0	0.75	0.8	
Food	a	c	e	f	f	0.3	0.8	3.0	0.90	1.1	
Mining	b	b	e	j	f	0.5	0.8	3.0	0.50	1.0	
Iron and Steel	a	d	e	i	f	3.0	1.0	3.0	1.0	1.4	
Motor Vehicles	a	c	e	h	h	2.0	0.8	3.0	1.2	1.1	31.9%
Textiles and Apparel	a	c	e	l	f	2.6	1.0	3.0	0.4	3.9	40.5%
Other Manufactures	a	c	e	f	f	3.6	0.8	3.0	1.5	1.8	
Other Consumer	a	c	e	f	f	3.2	0.8	3.0	1.9	2.4	
Traded Services	b	c	e	g	g	2.0	0.8	0.7	0.5	0.6	
Non-traded Services		b		g			0.8		0.5		

Note CES and CET functions imply that the corresponding elasticities of substitution (transformation) correspond to compensated import demand (export supply) elasticities

All price elasticities of demand are defined as positive numbers For premia estimates, see text. Column notes correspond to the sources from which estimates are interpolated. For interpolation details see Tarr (1988)

(a) Shiells, Stern and Deardorff (1986); (b) Dixon et al. (1982); (c) Caddy (1976); (d) Hekman (1978), (e) own estimates, (f) Stern, Francis and Schumacher (1976), (g) Houthakker and Taylor (1970); (h) Levinsohn (1988); (i) Crandall (1981), (j) Bohi and Russell (1978), (k) USDA (1984), (l) Hufbauer, Berliner and Elliott (1986)

QRs in textiles and autos. We discuss these briefly below. (Tarr (1989, chaps. 5 and 6) is devoted to a detailed discussion of how these estimates were derived.)

Table 1 presents all elasticities and our constructed estimates of pre-existing premia. These elasticities correspond to the "central" elasticities. (When we report in table 3 the likely range of the welfare effects of removing all trade restrictions, we are reporting results from the "low" and "high" elasticities that are derived from the "central" elasticities in table 1 by subtracting and adding, respectively, a standard deviation.[6]) Because much econometric work has been done to estimate the capital/labor substitution elasticities, we are fairly confident about the accuracy of these elasticities. We are also fairly confident of the import demand elasticities, for which a number of estimates are available. Less confidence can be placed on export supply elasticities. However, because these latter elasticities enter only indirectly into our estimations, we have found that our welfare estimates are quite insensitive to considerable changes in their values.[7]

For the premia rate estimates for apparel (expressed as a percentage of landed U.S. import price inclusive of tariffs), we have relied on Hamilton (1988). Hamilton's data are based on the sale of rights to export apparel products to the United States. His data give an estimate of the quota rents captured by Hong Kong. In order to understand the problem of premia rate estimation, it is crucial to recognize that the existing Multifiber Arrangement (MFA) allows a number of marginally inefficient foreign suppliers to sell in the United States. If the MFA were abolished, many of them would be squeezed out of the U.S. market by competition. The quota premium rate earned by these inefficient suppliers is less than the quota premium rate paid by U.S. consumers as a result of the MFA. Thus, we had to determine the marginal supplier to the United States if the MFA were abolished. Data in Hamilton (1988) allow us to determine that Hong Kong, which had a quota premium rate of 47% for apparel sold to the United States in 1984, or a supplier more

[6] As the sources for table 1 detail, the estimates were obtained from many studies. These studies generally provide standard errors of estimates. For those elasticities taken from Stern, Francis and Schumacher, the high and low estimates are generally the high and low estimates from their survey, which are not based on standard deviations. In a few cases the high and low estimates are obtained by doubling and halving the central estimate. See Tarr (1988, ch. 5) for details.

[7] For example, doubling (halving) the elasticity estimates in column (3) increases (decreases) our estimates of the welfare gains with the central elasticity estimates from US$22.0 billion (with infinite foreign trade elasticities) to $22.1 ($22.9) billion, respectively, or ±0.5%.

efficient than Hong Kong, would be the marginal supplier if quotas were removed.[8]

The United States is much more competitive in textiles than in apparel. Consequently, for textiles we take 5% as the premium rate, which is much more conservative than the 15% proposed by Cline (1987, p. 167). A positive rate is indicated, however, based on data in a study by the U.S. International Trade Commission (1987). For autos we relied on the quality-adjusted premia estimates of Feenstra (1988) for Japanese car imports by the United States. For European car imports, we relied on the quality-adjusted price increase of European cars sold in the United States estimated by Dinopoulos and Kreinin (1988). Our resulting premia estimates, which are weighted averages, are 41% for textiles and apparel and 32% for autos.[9]

IV. Welfare Cost Estimates

The costs of QRs reported in tables 2 and 3 below are based on estimates of the premia that accrue to the exporting countries rather than to the United States. One can therefore distinguish two components of the costs of the QRs: (1) the income or rent transfer to foreigners and (2) the distortionary cost due to the usual consumption and production costs of protection.[10] Table 2 summarizes these costs for each of the three industries: textiles and apparel, autos and steel. Since the restrictions on steel—which resulted in approximately a 15% reduction in imports of steel starting in early 1985—were not implemented until 1985, we obtain the estimates for steel by reducing intermediate and final consumption of imported steel products by 15% from the observed levels in 1984. This restriction results in a 7% premium on imported intermediate steel products. The employment figures in column 2 are only for the industry subject to quota removal; the total economy-wide relocation of workers is reported in column 3. This latter measure is a summary of interindustry effects (see Deardorff and Stern (1986)).

The figures in table 2 reveal that the largest welfare costs are due to the QRs in textiles and apparel. This may seem surprising since that sector is smaller than autos, and imports are three-fourths of auto imports in value (including premia). Also, the proportion of the total welfare costs due to distortionary costs are much higher in textiles and apparel than in autos even in the case of an infinite elasticity of import supply in autos. This is so because the premium rate is higher and because the price elasticity of demand for textiles and apparel is almost four times higher than the corresponding elasticity for autos. Furthermore, the relative homogeneity of domestic and imported steel reduces the production costs of distortion.[11]

Because elasticity estimates are not precise, we report in table 3 a range of welfare gains from removing all QRs simultaneously for the cases of low, central, and high elasticities. Because the marginal benefit to the economy of an income transfer is a decreasing function of demand and supply elasticities, the welfare gains from capturing rents from foreigners is higher in the low elasticity case than in the high elasticity case. Of course, these estimated welfare gains due to the

[8] We note that estimates of quota premia, in both textiles and automobiles, vary from year to year. We obtained estimates of quota premia for 1984, the year for which we benchmarked the model. Thus, our estimates apply to the conditions prevailing in that year. For other years, the premia rates and our cost estimates may differ.

[9] If the marginal supplier is more efficient than Hong Kong, our premium rate estimate is conservative and the associated welfare gain estimate is downward-biased. There is evidence that, during the quota era, U.S. dealers of Japanese autos captured about $550 per vehicle in rents above those rents captured by foreigners. This would correspond to a higher premium rate on autos of 43%, of which foreigners capture 80% of the rents. We shall provide separate estimates for this scenario.

[10] In the cases where there are terms of trade effects, the estimates of the distortionary costs of protection are reduced because the terms of trade effects partially offset the distortionary cost component of the QRs.

[11] The United States imposes QRs in other sectors in addition to textiles, autos and steel. For example, Hufbauer, Berliner and Elliott (1986) reported QRs in book manufacturing, motorcycles, shipbuilding and maritime industries, sugar and food products containing sugar, cheese and other dairy products, peanuts and meat. We have simulated the effects of removing all the QRs in the economy by assuming a high (low) premia rate (tariff equivalent) of the QRs (with rents going to the foreigners) of 5% (2.5%) in agriculture; 3% (1.5%) in other manufactures, other consumer goods and food; and zero in the remaining sectors. Given these premia rates, the welfare gain from removing all QRs, including those in textiles, autos and steel, is $27.6 billion in the high and $24.0 billion in the low premia rate cases. These estimates of the benefits of removing all QRs, however, can only be considered suggestive because, unlike the case of our estimates of the premia rates in textiles, autos and steel, we have not done a careful estimate of the premia rates in the remaining sectors of our model.

TABLE 2.—WELFARE COSTS AND EMPLOYMENT EFFECTS OF QRs: INDIVIDUAL SECTORS

	Welfare[a] Gain	Employment Change in the Industry Losing Its QR[b]	Economy-Wide Employment Relocation[c]
Textiles and Apparel			
Remove QRs	11.92	−157.2	157.2 (0.15)
Capture Rents from Foreigners	6.05	−3.05	28.35 (0.03)
Autos			
Remove QRs	7.50 (9.10)	−1.2	1.3 (0.001)
Capture Rents from Foreigners	7.95[d] (7.92)	+1.3	37.2 (0.035)
Steel			
Remove QRs	0.86	−20.7	22.3 (0.021)
Capture Rents from Foreigners	0.74	−0.1	3.5 (0.003)

Note. Estimates based on central elasticities, with infinite foreign trade elasticities, except for $\epsilon^{s}_{auto} = 5$, and $\epsilon^{d}_{agr} = 4$, where ϵ^{s}_{auto} is the foreign elasticity of import supply of autos and ϵ^{d}_{agr} is the foreign elasticity of demand for exports of agriculture

[a] Welfare is the *EV* measure expressed in billions of 1984 U S dollars Numbers in parentheses are based on infinite foreign trade elasticities in all sectors

[b] Employment is expressed in thousands of work-years

[c] One-half of the sum of the absolute value of the employment changes expressed in thousand work-years The numbers in parentheses are the percentage of employees in the economy who must relocate For example, (0 15) means that fifteen-hundredths of 1% of the economy's employees must relocate

[d] If U S dealers of Japanese autos capture additional rents (explained in footnote 9), the welfare gain from removing QRs is $9 87 billion with infinite foreign trade elasticities

TABLE 3.—WELFARE COSTS OF QRs AND TARIFF PROTECTION

	Preferred Foreign Trade Elasticities			Strong Foreign Trade Elasticities
	Low Elasticity[a]	Central Elasticity[a b]	High Elasticity[a]	Central Elasticity[c]
Remove QRs	20.5	20.3 (22.0)	21.6	15.0
Capture Rents from Foreigners (retain QRs)	16.8	14.9 (14.8)	14.5	15.0
Eliminate Remaining Tariff Protection (after QR removal)	0.33	0.57 (0.94)	0.90	−4.3

Note: Welfare is the *EV* measure expressed in billions of 1984 U S dollars Let ϵ^{d}_{i} = elasticity of demand for exports of sector i and ϵ^{s}_{i} = elasticity of supply of imports in sector i

The central elasticity estimates are not between the high and low elasticity estimates, because we create a new base for comparison by imposing QRs on steel, and then estimate the effects of removing QRs in all 3 sectors

[a] $\epsilon^{d}_{agr} = 4$, $\epsilon^{s}_{auto} = 5$ Small country assumption for all other export demand and import supply elasticities

[b] Results in parentheses are the welfare estimates with infinite foreign trade elasticities

[c] ϵ^{d}_{i} for exports = 3 and ϵ^{s}_{i} of supply of imports = 4 where i ranges over all traded sectors.

capturing of rents from foreigners are overestimates to the extent that rent-seeking activities dissipate them. For this reason, an auction quota mechanism is superior to a direct allocation of quota rights to imports. Thus our estimate of the annual cost of QRs in these three industries for 1985 protection levels is between $20 billion and $22 billion.

Insofar as removing QRs leads to increases in agricultural exports and auto imports, the U.S. terms of trade will decline and hence the welfare gain will be less. For the central elasticity case, the welfare gain is $20.3 billion, of which $5.4 billion is the distortionary cost component of QRs. Obtaining the quota rents is a pure income transfer from the rest of the world to the United

States, and its effect is a real appreciation of the dollar (about 1%) which is accompanied by a small improvement in the terms of trade.

It is conceivable that the United States would have monopoly and monopsony power in all sectors in which it trades. Although this seems unlikely because the U.S. market share is usually small in its main import and export markets, we have experimented with generalized terms of trade effects across all sectors for the central elasticity case. In column 4 of table 3, we assume constant import supply elasticities of 4 and constant export demand elasticities of 3 for all traded sectors. The gains from QR removal are smaller, but still substantial ($15.0 billion). However, in this case the terms of trade effects (from expanded trade volume at higher import prices and lower export prices) exactly offset the distortionary costs in total QR costs. Finally, adding unilateral tariff reduction now results in a welfare loss of $4.3 billion because of the dominating terms of trade effect, a result similar to those found in the global simulations mentioned above.

Evidence of pure profits in autos and of economies of scale in autos and, to a lesser extent, in steel raises the question of the extent to which our estimates would be affected by imperfect competition and economies of scale in autos and steel. We view the empirical effects of imperfect competition and economies of scale as offsetting. Due to the fact that costs will increase, QR removal will result in lower benefits than we have estimated to the extent that there are unrealized economies of scale in autos and steel. Following Krishna (1983), however, QRs should be viewed as a practice facilitating pricing above competitive levels. QR removal, therefore, will induce a reduction in oligopolistic pricing practices and lead to greater benefits (relative to our estimates) from a reduction in the distortion costs of these pricing practices. Thus, we do not know, a priori, the direction of the bias in our estimates due to imperfect competition and economies of scale. The issue, however, is clearly worthy of further investigation.

In the introduction, we said that PE estimates are upwardly biased because they fail to include the balance of trade constraint. An order of magnitude of the difference between PE and GE estimates due to this effect is obtained by solving the model with a fixed real exchange rate and hence an endogenous trade balance. This would correspond to what is typically done in PE estimates, which implicitly assume that the real exchange rate is unchanged as a result of QR removal and that resulting import increases need not be compensated by increased exports (or reduced imports from other sectors). For the central elasticity case, removing all QRs would lead to a trade balance deterioration of $12.1 billion and an EV estimate of $33.9 billion. This estimate is about one and two-thirds times the estimate obtained when the balance of trade constraint is properly taken into account. Economy-wide welfare costs estimates derived by adding up individual industry PE estimates are likely to be significantly upward-biased.

Our welfare cost estimates are significantly higher than previous GE estimates.[12] This is so for several reasons. First we properly account for the $14.9 billion transfer associated with the U.S. system of QRs.[13] Thus, even with generalized terms of trade effects which are stronger than we believe reasonable,[14] the QRs cost the U.S. economy $15 billion. Second, in comparison with most previous PE and GE estimates, we have benefited from the detailed work on premia estimates by Feenstra (1988), Hamilton (1988) and Dinopoulos and Kreinin (1988), which are higher than previous estimates.

V. Employment

Table 4 gives estimates of the employment effects of simultaneous removal of QRs in textiles, autos and steel for the central elasticity case. The simultaneous removal of QRs also points out the conflicting worker interests across the three industries subject to QRs. While the steel and textiles and apparel sectors would lose almost as many jobs when all QRs are removed

[12] For example, Whalley (1985, table 10.2) estimates welfare losses from unilateral U.S. removal of non-tariff barriers and tariffs. Deardorff and Stern (1986, table 4.6) obtain small welfare gains.

[13] Most previous GE studies of the costs of protection (e.g., Deardorff and Stern (1986) and Whalley (1985)) that have dealt with QRs have done so in the context of global models that treat QRs by their tariff equivalents without including the associated rent transfer that occurs with the U.S. QRs.

[14] In addition, Brown (1987) has shown that the structure of many previous GE models has required excessive estimates of terms of trade effects. See also de Melo (1986) and Deardorff and Stern (1986, p. 41).

as when they are removed in their sector alone, the auto sector gains 1,700 jobs when QRs on steel and textiles and apparel are removed concurrently with the VER on autos. This is so because steel, an important input into auto production, becomes cheaper and because the income elasticity of demand for autos is high. Both effects benefit the domestic auto industry which expands even when QR protection is removed.

Given that QR protection is obtained through the political process, one can argue that the U.S. Congress has decided to value a job in the protected sectors more highly than a job in other sectors. In our experiment, 172,000 jobs in textiles and steel were protected by the QRs on the three sectors at a cost of $20.3 billion. Hence, the annual cost per protected job is about $118,000, approximately 8 (3) times the average annual total compensation of workers in the textile (steel) industry.

If QRs are removed, displaced workers will incur search, relocation, and retraining costs (see Mussa (1978)). Net benefits from QR removal are obtained by subtracting these costs. A proxy for these costs is the discounted value of a displaced worker's earnings losses over a lifetime.[15] This measure allows us to estimate how much gainers will have left after compensating displaced workers for their earnings losses. Earnings losses for displaced workers last approximately six years.[16] A conservative estimate of net benefits, *NB*, is obtained as

$$NB = \sum_{t=0}^{5} \frac{[EV - C_t]}{(1+r)^t}$$

where EV is the equivalent variation measure, C_t is estimated earnings losses in year t, and $r = 7\%$ is the discount rate. (This estimate is conservative since earnings losses are zero after six years, while yearly benefits do not decay.) NB is $104 billion, with an associated benefit/cost of 65.

TABLE 4.—EMPLOYMENT EFFECTS OF REMOVING QRs IN AUTOS, STEEL AND TEXTILES (CENTRAL ELASTICITY CASE)[a] (thousand jobs)

Agriculture	6.4
Food	0.8
Mining	4.5
Textiles and Apparel	−156.4
Autos	1.7
Steel	−15.5
Consumer Goods	17.5
Other Manufacturing	87.1
Traded Services	35.4
Non-Traded Services	18.5

[a] Foreign trade elasticities defined in table 3

That is, for every dollar of earnings losses saved, the economy loses $65.

VI. Conclusions

Perhaps the most striking result is the high cost of protection from NTBs relative to that from tariffs. While this is repeatedly mentioned in policy discussions, few relative estimates are available. The figures in table 3 suggest that the welfare cost of tariff protection is between 2% (low elasticity case) and 4% (high elasticity case) of the welfare cost of QRs in textiles, autos and steel. Since there are other QRs in the United States beyond those examined here, this estimate is a lower bound.

An alternative way to evaluate the costs of QRs is to ask what tariff structure would give the same welfare loss as existing QRs in the three sectors. In the central elasticity estimates (with infinite foreign trade elasticities), the total welfare cost is estimated at $22.0 billion (1984 dollars), of which $7.2 billion is the distortionary component. For that set of elasticities, moving from the actual tariff structure to a uniform tariff structure yielding the same (import weighted) average protection would represent a welfare gain of $0.70 billion. (Removing tariffs altogether would give a welfare gain of $0.94 billion.) Starting from the existing tariff dispersion, to get the distortionary cost element of QRs would require multiplying each tariff by 3.6 times its 1984 value, which would amount to an average (import weighted) nominal protection of 12.5%. Adding the loss due to rent transfers would require multiplying tariffs by 7.4 times their 1984 value,

[15] We call our estimate a proxy for these adjustment costs because we have not incorporated into our model an endogenous sector that moves resources, as suggested by the theoretical work by Mussa.

[16] See Jacobson (1978). To be conservative, we measure total compensation losses, which exceed earnings losses by the amount of fringe benefits. Morkre and Tarr (1980, chapter 3) discuss the merits of this measure and the alternative unemployment cost measure.

amounting to an average protection of 19.8%.[17] It is no exaggeration to say that, in terms of protection costs, QRs are taking us back to the early days of multilateral tariff negotiations, especially if one includes the rent transfer element.

REFERENCES

Baldwin, R. E., J. Mutti, and D. Richardson, "Welfare Effects on the United States of a Significant Multilateral Tariff Reduction," *Journal of International Economics* 10 (1980), 405–423.

Bohi, D., and M. Russell, *Limiting Oil Imports: An Economic History and Analysis* (Baltimore: Johns Hopkins University, 1978).

Brown, D. K., "Tariffs, the Terms of Trade and National Product Differentiation," *Journal of Policy Modelling* 9 (1987), 503–526.

Caddy, V., "Empirical Estimation of the Elasticity of Substitution: A Review," Preliminary Working Paper OP-09, IMPACT Project. IAC, Melbourne, Australia (1976).

Cline, W. *The Future of World Trade in Textiles and Apparel* (Washington, D.C.: Institute for International Economics, 1987).

Crandall, R., *The U.S. Steel Industry in Recurrent Crisis* (Washington, D.C.: Brookings Institution, 1981).

Deardorff, A., and R. Stern, *The Michigan Model of World Production and Trade* (Cambridge, MA: MIT Press, 1986).

Dinopoulos, E., and M. Kreinin, "Effects of the U.S. -Japan Auto VER on European Prices and U.S. Welfare," this REVIEW 70 (1988), 484–491.

Dixit, A., "Optimal Trade and Industrial Policies for the U.S. Automobile Industry," in R. Feenstra (ed.), *Empirical Methods for International Trade* (Cambridge, MA: MIT Press, 1988), 141–165.

Dixon, P., B. Parmenter, J. Sutton, and D. Vincent, *ORANI: A Multisectoral Model of the Australian Economy* (Amsterdam: North-Holland, 1982).

Elliott, K., J. Schott, and W. Takacs, *Auction Quotas and U.S. Trade Policy* (Washington, D.C.: Institute for International Economics, 1987).

Feenstra, R., "Voluntary Export Restraints in U.S. Autos, 1980–81: Quality, Employment and Welfare Effects," in R. Baldwin and A. Krueger (eds.), *The Structure and Evolution of Recent U.S. Trade Policy* (Chicago: University of Chicago Press for National Bureau of Economic Research, 1984).

[17] In that experiment we are increasing the variance of nominal protection by 3.6 and 7.4 times the variance prevailing in 1984. Since the distortionary cost of tariff protection is positively related to the average level of protection and to the variance of tariffs (see Johnson (1962)), another hypothetical calculation would consist of computing the average tariff under the assumption of no tariff dispersion across sectors. In that case, starting from a uniform tariff protection (3.5%) equivalent to the existing tariff protection in 1984, the distortionary cost element of QRs would require an average uniform protection of 24%. Adding the rent transfer loss would raise the average uniform protection to 50%. With linear, rather than constant elasticity demand and supply curves, welfare calculations would yield lower estimates as the corresponding elasticities would increase as one moves up the demand and supply curves.

______, "Automobile Prices and Protection: The U.S.-Japan Trade Restraint," *Journal of Policy Modelling* 7 (1985), 49–68.

______, "Quality Change Under Trade Restraints: Theory and Evidence from Japanese Autos," *Quarterly Journal of Economics* 103 (1988), 131–146.

Hamilton, C., "Restrictiveness and International Transmission of the 'New' Protectionism," in R. Baldwin, C. Hamilton, and A. Sapir (eds.), *Issues in US-EC Trade Relations* (Chicago: University of Chicago Press for National Bureau of Economic Research, 1988), 199–224.

Hekman, J., "An Analysis of the Changing Pattern of Iron and Steel Production in the Twentieth Century," *American Economic Review* 68 (1978), 123–133.

Houthakker, H., and L. Taylor, *Consumer Demand in the United States: Analyses and Projections* (Cambridge: Harvard University Press, 1970).

Hufbauer, G., D. Berliner, and K. Elliott, *Trade Protection in the United States: 31 Case Studies* (Washington, D.C.: Institute for International Economics, 1986).

Jacobson, L., "Earnings Losses of Workers Displaced from Manufacturing Industries," in W. Dewald (ed.), *The Impact of International Trade and Investment on Employment* (Washington, D.C.: U.S. Department of Labor, 1978), 87–98.

Johnson, H. G., "The Cost of Protection and the Scientific Tariff," *Journal of Political Economy* 68 (1960), 327–345.

Keesing, D., and M. Wolf, *Textile Quotas Against Developing Countries* (London: Trade Policy Research Centre, 1980).

Krishna, K., *Trade Restrictions as Facilitating Practices* Discussion paper Number 55 Princeton University (1983).

Levinsohn, J., "Empirics of Taxes on Differentiated Products: The Case of Tariffs in the U.S. Automobile Industry," in R. E. Baldwin (ed.), *Trade Policy Issues and Empirical Analysis* (Chicago: University of Chicago Press, 1988), 11–44.

Melo, J. de, "A Comparison of 50% Multilateral Tariff Reductions in Two Global Trade Models," in T. N. Srinivasan and J. Whalley (eds.), *General Equilibrium Trade Policy Modelling* (Cambridge, MA: MIT Press, 1986).

Melo, J. de, and D. Tarr, *Welfare Costs of US Quotas in Textiles, Steel and Autos*, PPR Working Paper No. 83, Washington D.C.: World Bank (1988).

Morkre, M., *Import Quotas on Textiles: The Welfare Effects of United States Restrictions on Hong Kong* (Washington, D.C.: Bureau of Economics Report to the U.S. Federal Trade Commission, 1984).

Morkre, M., and D. Tarr, *The Effects of Restrictions on U.S. Imports: Five Case Studies and Theory* (Washington, D.C.: Bureau of Economics Report to U.S. Federal Trade Commission, 1980).

Mussa, M., "Dynamic Adjustment in the Heckscher-Ohlin-Samuelson Model," *Journal of Political Economy* 86 (5), 775–791.

Powell, A., and F. Gruen, "The Constant Elasticity of Transformation Production Frontier and Linear Supply System," *International Economic Review* 8 (1967), 315–328.

Shiells, C., R. Stern and A. Deardorff, "Estimates of the Elasticities of Substitution between Imports and Home Goods for the United States," *Weltwirtschaftliches Archiv* 122 (3) (1986), 497–519.

Stern, R. M., J. Francis and B. Schumacher, *Price Elasticities in International Trade: An Annotated Bibliographer* (London: Macmillan Press, 1976).

Tarr, D., *A General Equilibrium Analysis of the Welfare and Employment Effects of US Quotas on Textiles, Autos, and Steel* (Washington, D.C.: U.S. Federal Trade Commission, 1989).

Tarr, D., and M. Morkre, *Aggregate Costs to the United States of Tariffs and Quotas on Imports: General Tariff Cuts and Removal of Quotas on Automobiles, Steel, Sugar, and Textiles* (Washington, D.C.: U.S. Federal Trade Commission, 1984).

U.S. Department of Agriculture, *Dairy: Background for the 1984 Farm Legislation* (Washington, D.C., 1984).

U.S. International Trade Commission, *US Global Competitiveness: the US Textile Mill Industry*, Publication No. 2048, Dec. 1987.

Whalley, J., *Trade Liberalization Among Major World Trading Areas* (Cambridge, MA: MIT Press, 1985).

Winston, C., and Associates, *Blind Intersection? Policy and the Automobile Industry* (Washington, D.C.: Brookings Institution, 1987).

Reforming Hungarian Agricultural Trade Policy: A Quantitative Evaluation

By

Morris Morkre and **David Tarr**

Contents: I. Introduction. – II. Recent Policy Changes Affecting Hungarian Agriculture. – III. Basic Data and Overview of the Model. – IV. Costs of Licensing of Imports and Export Subsidies. – V. Costs of a CAP Type System. – VI. Conclusion.

I. Introduction

Hungary has made great strides in recent years in moving toward a market oriented economy, including reforming its external trade regime. Although all imports were subject to an import licensing requirement as of December 1988, by 1992 tariff lines corresponding to over 75 percent of *industrial* output were liberalized, i.e., free of import licensing. However, certain problems remain. Hungarian agricultural production remained fully protected through import licensing, and a significant share of the remaining industrial output protection was in the food sector, justified in part due to high cost agricultural output. Moreover, agricultural export subsidies have become a large share of total government subsidies.

Since Hungary has signed an Association Agreement with the European Union (EU), some are sanguine regarding the future of Hungary's trade policy, taking the view that long-term harmonization of Hungary's trade policies with the EU will correct remaining distortions. But the most significant remaining protected sectors in Hungary are those sectors termed "sensitive" by the EU,[1] in which policies of the EU itself are quite distorted. Thus, it cannot be presumed that EU

Remark: The authors would like to thank Mrs. Agnes Nagy of Kopint Datorg, Budapest Hungary for her extensive assistance in the price comparisons study; Gabor Oblath, Ulrich Thumm, Rory O'Sullivan, Csaba Csaki, Wayne Ringlein and an anonymous referee of this journal for their comments; officials too numerous to mention in the Ministries of International Economic Relations and Agriculture of Hungary for their assistance and informative discussions during several missions; and Jeff Hayden and Nellie Artis for their logistical support. The views expressed are those of the authors and do not necessarily reflect those of the U.S. Federal Trade Commission, the World Bank, the Government of Hungary or its Ministries, or those acknowledged.

[1] In addition to agriculture and a large share of the food sector, a significant share of the textiles and apparel and pharmaceuticals sectors remain subject to import licenses.

This article originally appeared in *Weltwirtschaftliches Archiv* (1995), 131(1), pp. 106–131.

pressure will correct these distortions. Worse still, harmonization of Hungarian policies to those of the EU in the agricultural sector (a policy informally suggested by some policymakers in Hungary) would mean the introduction of a "Common Agriculture Policy" (CAP) type system and the continuation of export subsidies. Given that GDP originating in Hungarian agriculture is about 12 percent of total GDP, compared to 3 percent in the EU, a CAP type system in Hungary would be expected to impose a more significant deadweight loss burden on the rest of the relatively fragile Hungarian economy.

In its international negotiations, the Government of Hungary took a progressive position on these issues. It was a member of the "Cairns" group in the Uruguay Round of GATT negotiations, i.e., it supported reduction of agricultural subsidies and increased transparency of import barriers through tariffication, which included the elimination of licenses on imported products.[2] Hungary justified its interventionist policies in agriculture due to the fear of dumping on the part of the EC, and preferred a multilateral rather than unilateral reduction in these policies (see GATT 1991).[3]

As a result of the recently concluded Uruguay Round negotiations, the measures supported by Hungary promise to be realized. Thus, Hungary will have both an opportunity as well as an obligation to implement the policy recommendations it supported in the GATT. Specifically, under the agricultural provisions of the Uruguay Round, contracting parties are required to reduce export subsidies and convert nontariff barriers (such as nondiscretionary import licensing) to bound tariffs, and to reduce these tariffs (as well as pre-existing tariffs).[4] The reduction in export subsidies and in tariffs are scheduled to begin in 1995. The Uruguay Round will therefore obligate Hungary to partially liberalize its agricultural trade policies.

---

[2] We show in the Appendix to Morkre and Tarr (1993), however, that agricultural import licensing in Hungary is more extensive than in OECD countries outside of the EC.

[3] It should be noted that tariffication of non-tariff barriers retains protection against dumping, and, since about 80 percent of Hungary's agricultural tariff lines are not bound under the GATT, tariffication appears feasible. Tariffication offers a number of advantages including: its transparency will tend to reduce the dispersion in the protection regime as less protected interests become aware of the level of protection received by the highly protected sectors; and since licenses provide rents to those who obtain the licenses, licensing could generate costly rent-seeking which would be significantly reduced by tariffication.

[4] See Office of the U.S. Trade Representative, "Final Act Embodying the Results of the Uruguay Round of Multilateral Trade Negotiations," Agreement on Agriculture, U.S. Government Printing Office, Washington D.C.

In this paper, we quantitatively assess the consequences of three categories of unilateral policy action by the Government of Hungary: (1) the costs to Hungary of its import restraints in agriculture, both in aggregate for all of agriculture and in each of five separate agricultural products: butter, pork, cheese, chicken and milk powder. The tariff equivalent of the import licenses was estimated through detailed empirical work based on price comparisons between the Hungarian and world markets; (2) the costs of the Hungarian export subsidy program; and (3) the costs of a CAP type system in Hungary. The consequences of all policies are estimated through the use of a small open economy computable general equilibrium model for Hungary, calibrated to the year 1990. We provide a thorough intuitive explanation of the results, however, through the use of partial equilibrium graphs of the agricultural sector (which itself is divided into three markets).

We find that import protection, export subsidies and a potential CAP program are all costly to the country in terms of lost welfare, and the CAP system would contribute significantly to the Government's fiscal problems. We also find that the benefits of import liberalization are considerably muted in the presence of an export subsidy program in the same industry, because, in response to the decrease in domestic demand, exporters substitute export sales (increasing the government's subsidy burden). This indicates from a sequencing perspective, it is important to concurrently reduce export subsidies in the process of import liberalization.

Although the magnitude of the costs of protective and interventionist policies in the agriculture sector in East and Central Europe will surely vary across the different economies, similar policies and proposals have been discussed in other countries in East and Central Europe (since most now have Association Agreements with the EU).[5] Thus, the information gained from this exercise should be relevant to the policies of some of these other East and Central European countries as well.

In Section II, we briefly survey the recent reforms in Hungarian agriculture policy as well as the principal remaining policy problems. In Section III, the basic data of the model are presented. Most notably, this includes the details of a price comparisons study to determine the tariff equivalence of the import licensing regime. This price com-

[5] In 1992, a CAP type system was being discussed in Poland and Czechoslovakia, and in Romania in 1993.

parisons study is the first of its kind to our knowledge for Hungary, which is remarkable given the longstanding claim of the pre-1990 Government that the licenses do not represent a restraint to trade.[6] An overview of the model is presented in Section III. The results are presented in Sections IV and V. In Section IV, the results are interpreted through consumers' and producers' surplus using three ordinary supply-demand diagrams of the agriculture sector. Despite the fact that they are partial equilibrium diagrams, since the linkages within the agriculture sector are incorporated, they are helpful for understanding the principal effects of the policy changes in general equilibrium models of this type. The equations of the model, as well as a comparison of the OECD countries import licensing regimes in agriculture are available in Morkre and Tarr (1993).

II. Recent Policy Changes Affecting Hungarian Agriculture

The regulatory environment affecting Hungarian agriculture has changed dramatically in recent years. These changes include: removal of virtually all central controls on prices; reduction in government subsidies; unification of current account transactions and elimination of state trading (following the demise of the CMEA trading system); and an opening of the types and numbers of firms that can engage in external trade, i.e., removal of the state monopoly of foreign trade.

1. Regulatory Reform

Price Decontrol. Before 1989, 85 percent of the prices of Hungarian agricultural products were either set or regulated by the government. By January 1991, only consumer prices of white bread and one type of milk (2.9 percent milkfat) remained regulated.

Subsidies. Overall subsidies to the agriculture sector (such as export, production, input and investment subsidies) fell from 3.7 to 1.6 percent of GDP between 1988 and 1990 (GATT 1991, Vol. I, p. 128). Plans called for a further slash in production subsidies and a complete

[6] See Haus (1992) for a fascinating account of the negotiations in the early 1970s under which Hungary entered the GATT. Hungary maintained that with the introduction of the "New Economic Mechanism," it had departed sufficiently from central planning that the tariff was the principal import regulatory mechanism. The Hungarian representative steadfastly resisted quantitative import commitments characteristic of the accession agreements of Romania and Poland (due to their status as state trading countries), and insisted on (and received) tariff concessions as the "price" of its admission to GATT.

elimination of input subsidies. In fact, the reduction of production and input subsidies combined with the removal of price controls had an offsetting effect which left farm income relatively unchanged.[7] Export subsidies, however, have not declined as significantly. For most products, export subsidies were available in 1990 at between 15 and 35 percent of the value of exports (see Table 1); as a result, by 1990 export subsidies rose to about three-fourths of total subsidies to the agriculture sector.[8]

State Trading. With the demise of the CMEA, the highly distortionary state trading structures involved in the massive intergovernmental barter agreements have been disbanded. All trade is settled on a similar basis, i.e., there is no separate transferable ruble balance of payments accounting for trade with the CMEA countries. While buffeted by an adverse terms-of-trade shock in the switch-over to world prices in its CMEA trade (Oblath and Tarr 1992), Hungary has reoriented its agricultural exports so that by 1990 over two-thirds of its exports were to developed countries (up from 42 percent in 1985), with declines in exports to socialist markets accounting for almost all of the decrease (Varga et al. 1991).

Demonopolization of Foreign Trade. Beginning in 1987, the state monopoly of foreign trade was relaxed for foreign trade settled in convertible currency, which now comprises all trade. The number of enterprises engaged in exporting (importing) of agricultural products exploded from 81 (39) in 1987 to 495 (205) in 1990. These developments have facilitated competition and removed a tool of regulatory control from the hands of the state.[9]

2. Remaining Policy Problems: Import Licenses, Export Subsidies and a Potential CAP

Given this extensive progress, the principal regulatory problems that remain are, as discussed above, the import licenses and the export subsidies. In addition, Hungary introduced a new program in January 1991 that has elements of a CAP type program. This program runs counter to the reforms mentioned above as well as 25 years of gradual

[7] Tarr (1990, pp. 111–114), using 1988 conditions, estimates that similar results would have occurred in Poland for farmers producing butter. Tarr estimates that a policy of simultaneously lifting price controls and removing producer subsidies would have resulted in an improvement in producers' surplus of farmers.

[8] GATT (1991, Vol. II, p. 40) estimated export subsidies at 73 percent of total subsidies.

[9] See GATT (1991) and Bognar et al. (1991) for further details.

Table 1 – *Basic Policy and Industry Data, 1990*

	Butter	Cheese	Chicken	Milk powder	Pork	Agri-culture (aggre-gate)	Rest of economy (nonagri-culture)
				Percent			
Import licensing premium	23.4	12.3	8.8	7.1	19.2	16.6	n.a.
Export subsidy	37.5	37.5	37.5	37.5	18.75	16.7	0
Tariff	66.0	31.0	26.0	26.0	21.0	9.5	8.3
Imports/consumption	0.1	0.7	1.5	1.8	0.8	27.8	32.5
Exports/production	10.3	27.2	57.6	25.3	25.6	46.5	30.1
				Billion Forint			
Imports	0.01	0.04	0.04	0.04	0.40	52.8	610.2
Exports	0.75	2.56	7.97	0.91	17.04	139.3	545.8
Consumption	6.26	5.92	2.91	2.40	46.76	190.2	1,879.8
Production	7.29	9.40	13.82	3.61	66.61	299.9	1,815.4

Note: Consumption is calculated residually and equals production plus imports minus exports.

Source: Import licensing premia: premia for individual products are derived in Table 2. Premium for aggregate agriculture is weighted average of the individual products. – *Export subsidy rates:* rates for individual products are from Kereskedelmi Kozlony (Official Journal of the Ministry of Commerce), Vol. II, No. 1 (Jan 25, 1990); Vol. II, No. 6 (Apr 17, 1990) and Kulgazdasagi Kozlony (Official Journal of the Ministry of International Economic Relations), Vol. 1, No. 1 (Aug 15, 1990). Rate for aggregate agriculture is calculated using total export subsidies to agriculture from GATT (1991) and total exports explained below. – *Tariff rates:* rates for individual products are given in Table 2. Rate for aggregate agriculture calculated from Kopint-Datorg database of customs data. Rate for all exports based on GATT (1991) and total imports explained below. – *Import and Exports:* values for individual products and for aggregate agriculture from Statistical Yearbook of External Trade, 1990, Hungarian Central Statistical Office (CSO); total values from IMF, International Financial Statistics, Dec. 1991. – *Production:* values for individual products are production value at farmgate from unpublished data provided by Division of Agriculture, CSO; value for aggregate agriculture is GDP originating in agriculture and food industry from Division of National Accounts, CSO, total GDP from IMF, International Financial Statistics, Dec. 1991.

deregulation of the agriculture sector in Hungary.[10] In particular, it set minimum prices for grains and some slaughter animals. In July 1991, in the face of large excess supply, the Government intervened in the domestic wheat market to support deteriorating prices. As is known from the experience of the EU, high support prices for grains inflated internal prices of grains for animal feeds. The consequent

[10] Indeed, agriculture was the first sector to benefit from decentralizing reforms that began in the late 1960s. These reforms included abolishing obligatory plan targets, increasing prices paid to producers, and loosening controls over private plots. For a discussion of agricultural reforms by Hungary since 1965 see Marrese (1990).

increased cost of production for EU producers of animal products contributed substantially to high support prices of animal products relative to world prices for these products (see BAE 1985, p. 188). Thus, the prospect of the introduction of a CAP raises concern for the costs of the regulatory environment in Hungary in the future.

III. Basic Data and Overview of the Model

1. Basic Data

Import and Export Shares. In Table 1, we summarize the basic data relevant to our investigation of the trade policy instruments in Hungarian agriculture. It reveals that imports are a very small share of domestic consumption in the individual agricultural products we have investigated; on the other hand, aggregate agricultural imports are a significant one-quarter of consumption. This fact is important in the welfare analysis. On the other hand, exports of all agricultural products in the table are an important part of Hungarian output.

Export Subsidies. Export subsidy rates of row 2 are an average for the year. Export subsidy rates available at any point in time are announced by the Ministry of International Economic Relations and are publicly available in a number of Hungarian sources.[11]

Price Comparisons Estimate of Quota Premia. In row 1 of Table 1, we report the premia rate (or tariff equivalent of the import license) for each of the products for which we conducted an empirical investigation. As elaborated fully in Table 2, these data were obtained by a price comparisons investigation.[12] The percent increase in price induced by the license (after adjusting for transportation and tariff charges) is referred to as the license premium. For the products listed in the table we estimate that the import licenses represent a binding import constraint, and we therefore model the import licenses as quotas in our model. Although Hungarian products are generally viewed as being of lower quality, we have not adjusted for these

[11] See Kereskedelmi Kozlony (Official Journal of the Ministry of Commerce), Vol. II, No. 1, p. 27 (Jan 25, 1990); Vol. II, No. 6, p. 194 (April 17, 1990); and Kulgazdasagi Kozlony (Official Journal of the Ministry of International Economic Relations), Vol. 1, No. 1, p. 7 (August 15, 1990).

[12] We thank Ms. Agnes Nagy of Kopint-Datorg of Budapest, Hungary, for her detailed work in providing these price comparisons.

Table 2 – *Calculation of Licensing Premium for Certain Hungarian Agricultural Products, 1990*

	Butter	Cheese	Chicken	Milk powder	Pork
1. World price ($ per metric ton)[a]	1,363	1,700	1,225	1,458	1,499
2. Transportation and handling charges to the Hungarian border ($ per metric ton)[b]	87	91	34	65	86
3. Border price: 1+2 ($ per metric ton)	1,450	1,791	1,259	1,523	1,585
4. Tariff rates and levies (%)					
MFN tariff	60	25	20	20	15
Other levies[c]	6	6	6	6	6
Total levies in percent	66	31	26	26	21
Total levies in dollars	957	555	327	395	333
5. Delivered price including levies ($)	2,407	2,346	1,586	1,918	1,918
6. Delivered price including levies in Hungarian Forint[d]	151,689	147,845	99,950	120,872	120,872
7. Domestic market farmgate (fob) price (Ft)[e]	187,253	165,946	108,700	129,509	144,050
8. Estimated license premium: [(7/6)−1]×100	23.4	12.3	8.8	7.1	19.2

[a] World prices: Butter, milk (whole) powder, and cheese (hard cheese): The 1990 world price is taken as the average price fob in North-European ports and selected world ports, including New Zealand. Butter is 82 percent butter and requires refrigeration in transportation. Chicken: Average 1990 price for frozen whole carcass chicken broiler, weighing 900–1200 grams (giblet included) delivered to Mideast port in refrigerated container. Pork: Average 1990 price for extra EC exports of fresh or chilled swine carcasses and half carcasses, HTS 0203.11.10 of Eurostat. – [b] Transportation costs: Transportation costs vary depending on the city of origin and method of transportation; in all cases the low cost source was selected. Butter is from Rotterdam by refrigerated truck, which is cheaper than refrigerated rail; milk powder is from Amsterdam by truck; cheese is from the Parisien Basin by refrigerated truck; chicken is from the north Yugoslavian port of Koper by refrigerated rail; pork is from Rotterdam by refrigerated truck. – [c] The six percent levies are decomposed into two percent customs clearance fee, three percent statistical fee, and one percent licensing fee for licensed products. – [d] The exchange rate used was the average exchange rate for 1990: 63.02 Forint = $1. – [e] Domestic prices: The domestic price of cheese, butter and milk powder is the average producers' price for the year.

Source: Calculations are by the authors and Mms. Agnes Nagy of Kopint-Datorg, Budapest, Hungary. – *World prices:* butter, milk powder and cheese: United States Department of Agriculture, Foreign Agricultural Service; chicken: National Broiler Council, Washington, D.C. and Goldkist, Atlanta, Georgia; pork: data of the Statistical Office of the European Community. – *Transportation costs:* estimates were provided by the Hungarian General Forwarding Enterprise (Magyar Altalános Szállítmányozási Vállalat – MASPED). – *Tariff rates:* MFN rates are from Kereskedelmi Vámtarifa, 1988–89 (Commercial Tariff Rates 1988–89 published by the Chamber of Commerce of Hungary). These rates were valid in 1990. – *Exchange rate:* GATT (1991). – *Domestic prices:* butter, milk powder and cheese: sales statistics of the Central Statistical Office; chicken: poultry slaughtering and processing factory in Budapest; pork: meat slaughtering and processing factory in Székesfehérvár.

quality differences; this implies that the license premium is higher than we have estimated to the extent of unadjusted quality differences.[13]

2. Model Overview

The model is a single-country, two-sector CGE model for a small open economy benchmarked to data for 1990. One sector is either the agricultural sector as a whole or a specific agricultural product (e.g., butter) while the second sector is the rest of the economy. The economy has a given endowment of productive resources and chooses from given technologies in the employment of these resources. There exists a given production possibility frontier that describes the trade-off in production between the two sectors. Several CGE models with these supply-side features have been constructed recently to examine trade policy issues for various products, including steel, textiles, and wheat.[14] As is typical of small open economy models, we aggregate all other countries into the "rest of the world" and treat this aggregate parametrically.[15]

The model assumes that market prices are sufficiently flexible to ensure that demands from utility maximizing consumers are consistent with the supplies of cost minimizing producers, resulting in market equilibrium. This assumption would be of doubtful validity in Hungary prior to 1990, due to the widespread use of price controls for many products. In 1990, however, there was significant liberalization of prices as the country moved toward a market system, allowing us to reasonably employ a market clearing model.

The demand side of the model assumes consumption decisions are made by a representative consumer with a Stone–Geary utility function leading to a linear expenditure system (LES). There are two composite consumption goods. The significant product differentiation between similar domestic and imported goods in Hungary (with Hungarian goods being of somewhat lower quality) is incorporated through the use of the Armington assumption, i.e., each composite consumption good is a constant elasticity of substitution (CES) function of domestic and imported goods.

---

[13] There were some agricultural products subject to licensing for which our price comparisons study did not show a positive licensing premium. We attribute this to the lack of adjustment for quality.

[14] For example, see Trela and Whalley (1990) and Trela et al. (1987).

[15] The structure of our model draws extensively on de Melo and Tarr (1992, Chapters 2 and 3). The reader may consult this source for an elaboration of the economics of models of this type.

The supply side of the model assumes that the economy's total endowment of productive resources is fixed and employed in the two sectors. Although productive resources are not modelled explicitly, it is assumed that at least one input (e.g., labor) is mobile between the two sectors. The degree of flexibility between sectors is indicated by the elasticity of the constant elasticity of transformation (CET) production possibility frontier for the two sectors. In addition, each domestically produced product is a composite product that is a CET function of two specific varieties or qualities, one for the domestic market and the other for the export market. This specification captures the important product differentiation feature between exports and domestic products. For example, in the case of meat, exported pork is commonly frozen while pork for the home market is typically fresh or chilled.

Although the Armington assumption has been the standard method of modelling sectors in applied general equilibrium models, one must be careful of its limitations in certain situations. In particular, what may not be apparent is that under the Armington assumption, in response to a change in trade policy (such as tariff or quota reductions) in a given sector, resource movement and the welfare impact will be extremely muted in sectors with a small initial import share. For example, with a point-estimate Armington elasticity (elasticity of substitution) of 2, a 50 percent decline in the relative price of imports will induce a 100 percent increase in the ratio of imports to domestic sales in consumption. But if imports were less than 0.5 percent of consumption, they will remain under 1 percent after their relative price reduction, i.e., the absolute increase in the import share of consumption is less than 0.5 percent. With the same elasticity of substitution, if a sector has a significant initial share, the same relative price reduction will result in a much larger absolute increase in imports as a percent of total consumption in the sector. That is, ceteris paribus, the Armington assumption suggests that there would be dramatically less resource movement (and consequently less welfare impact) in the case of a small initial import share. In some of the agriculture sectors of Hungary, the licenses are regarded as quite important for the protection of the sector, and such a small change in imports (given the small share of imports as shown in Table 1) from a large relative price decline of imports appears unrealistic.

On the other hand, the homogeneous product assumption will tend to result in excessive resource movement, and is equally unrealistic. Our solution to this problem has been to employ the Armington assumption, but to use elasticities that are rather high by the usual standards, since the share of imports is rather small in all individual sectors; this results in a change in quantity demanded for imports that, while still somewhat muted, is more realistic.

Finally, the balance of payments is constrained such that total exports minus total imports (expressed in world prices) is constant, i.e., there is no free lunch either provided to or received from the rest of the world in response to a policy shift. The real exchange rate adjusts to satisfy the constraint. We measure the change in welfare by the Hicksian equivalent variation. The model is written and solved using the GAMS programing language (see Brooke et al. 1988).

IV. Costs of Licensing of Imports and Export Subsidies

In Table 3, we present the results of our examination of trade policy changes in particular agricultural sectors; the scenarios consider the impact of eliminating export subsidies, eliminating import licensing and eliminating both. In the top part of Table 4, we present similar results for the aggregate agriculture sector. In all cases, the two-sector model is employed. The rest of the economy changes size depending on the size of the agriculture sector under consideration.

For each scenario, we consider the impact on four important variables: welfare (the Hicksian equivalent variation), composite output of the sector, net government revenue and the real exchange rate. In all cases, the results are presented in percentage terms. The central elasticity scenario presents the results with our best guess of the elasticities. In order to determine whether the results are robust, all scenarios are rerun with high and low elasticities, where the high and low elasticity cases generally are obtained by doubling and halving the elasticities.

The static welfare benefits are somewhat modest. In the central elasticity case for aggregate agriculture, the benefits are 74 thousandths of one percent for export subsidy removal (this equals 1.52 billion 1990 forint out of a GDP of 2,070 billion forint), 51 thousandths of one percent for import license removal and 11 hundredths of one percent for removal of both. These results, however, should not be surprising to those who are familiar with previous estimates of the welfare effects of policy reform in constant returns to scale models without rent capture or rent seeking. Whether in partial or general equilibrium, measuring "Harberger" triangles or its equivalent in general equilibrium models, has typically produced estimates similar to

Table 3 – *Effects of Removing Export Subsidies and Import Licenses in Agricultural Sectors*[a]

Product & policy[b]	Welfare[c] (% of GDP)			Sector output (% of initial output)			Government revenue (% of initial government revenue)			Real exchange rate[d]		
	H	C	L	H	C	L	H	C	L	H	C	L
Butter, remove:												
Export subsidy	0.003	0.002	0.001	−15.02	−14.39	−12.50	0.026	0.027	0.027	−0.035	−0.040	−0.037
	(13.0)	(11.6)	(13.8)									
Import licenses	0.007	0.001	0.0003	−6.44	−1.82	−0.68	0.011	0.002	0.0005	−0.019	−0.006	−0.003
Both	0.005	0.002	0.001	−16.92	−14.87	−12.81	0.030	0.028	0.027	−0.041	−0.042	−0.038
Cheese, remove:												
Export subsidy	0.012	0.007	0.004	−26.45	−22.18	−19.22	0.087	0.089	0.090	−0.051	−0.059	−0.062
	(4.7)	(3.7)	(3.2)									
Import licenses	0.004	0.001	0.0004	−3.47	−1.37	−0.76	0.007	0.002	0.0008	−0.015	−0.008	−0.005
Both	0.013	0.007	0.004	−27.20	−22.45	−19.38	0.088	0.089	0.090	−0.054	−0.060	−0.063
Chicken, remove:												
Export subsidy	0.028	0.015	0.008	−46.81	−36.87	−30.91	0.272	0.276	0.279	−0.128	−0.135	−0.138
	(0)	(0)	(0)									
Import licenses	0.001	0.0004	0.0001	−0.86	−0.40	−0.25	0.002	0.0008	0.0005	−0.013	−0.009	−0.007
Both	0.028	0.015	0.008	−46.81	−36.87	−30.91	0.272	0.276	0.279	−0.128	−0.135	−0.138
Milk powder, remove:												
Export subsidy	0.005	0.003	0.001	−26.36	−21.56	−18.09	0.031	0.032	0.032	−0.016	−0.019	−0.021
	(2.0)	(1.2)	(0.7)									
Import licenses	0.001	0.0004	0.0002	−3.06	−1.55	−1.00	0.002	0.0007	0.0004	−0.004	−0.003	−0.003
Both	0.005	0.003	0.001	−26.99	−21.77	−18.18	0.031	0.032	0.032	−0.017	−0.019	−0.021
Pork, remove:												
Export subsidy	0.017	0.009	0.005	−14.26	−11.69	−10.23	0.287	0.296	0.301	−0.244	−0.259	−0.266
	(13.0)	(12.7)	(12.5)									
Import licenses	0.046	0.017	0.006	−6.09	−3.43	−1.85	0.061	0.025	0.010	−0.199	−0.143	−0.090
Both	0.045	0.020	0.008	−17.69	−13.54	−11.30	0.333	0.315	0.309	−0.348	−0.332	−0.316

[a] Based on 1990 data, in percent change in variable. The effects are calculated for three different elasticity scenarios: high (H), central (C), and low (L) scenarios. – [b] The benchmark export subsidy and license premium for each product and the rest of the economy is taken from Table 1. – [c] Value in parentheses equals the endogenously determined import license premium (in percent) in the new equilibrium. [d] A negative sign indicates a depreciation of the real exchange rate.

Table 4 – *Effects of Removing Import Licenses and Export Subsidies and Implementing a CAP System in Aggregate Agriculture Sector*[a]

	Welfare (% of GDP)			Sector output (% of initial output)			Government revenue (% of initial government revenue)			Real exchange rate[b]		
	H	C	L	H	C	L	H	C	L	H	C	L
Policy change[c]												
Remove export subsidies	0.144 (7.2)	0.074 (6.9)	0.037 (6.8)	−26.1	−18.7	−14.5	2.07	2.15	2.19	−1.96	−2.06	−2.10
Remove import licenses	0.107	0.051	0.025	−3.7	−2.4	−1.7	−0.04	−0.01	0.004	−0.80	−0.74	−0.71
Remove both	0.225	0.112	0.055	−28.2	−19.9	−15.3	2.19	2.21	2.23	−2.30	−2.35	−2.38
CAP System[d]												
Increase prices by:												
5%	−0.253 (25.0; 21.5)	−0.124 (25.1; 21.5)	−0.061 (25.1; 21.6)	15.5	10.1	7.5	−1.68	−1.39	−1.24	1.05	1.04	1.03
10%	−0.624 (33.4; 26.5)	−0.301 (33.6; 26.5)	−0.148 (33.7; 26.5)	32.2	20.7	15.2	−3.77	−2.96	−2.58	2.11	2.07	2.05
20%	−1.717 (50.3; 36.6)	−0.802 (50.8; 36.6)	−0.387 (51.2; 36.6)	69.2	43.0	31.1	−9.15	−6.63	−5.48	4.31	4.15	4.07

[a] H, C and L are the estimates for high, central and low elasticity scenarios, respectively. – [b] A negative sign indicates a depreciation in the real exchange rate. – [c] Initial export subsidies and license premium in effect in all scenarios are taken from data in Table 1. Value in parentheses equals the endogenously determined import license premium (in percent) in the new equilibrium. – [d] Values in parentheses equal the endogenously determined export subsidy and import license premium (in percent), respectively, in the new equilibrium.

those of Tables 3 and 4.[16] However, models that estimate the dynamic effects of trade liberalization suggest that the dynamic benefits of trade liberalization are many times the benefits suggested from static models (see e.g., Baldwin 1989). These estimates of the dynamic benefits, however, are based on estimates derived from static models such as ours so that our estimates are an important step in the process of estimating the total benefits of trade liberalization.

Comparing the effects of removing export subsidies to removing import licenses reveals that the welfare benefits and sectoral adjustment of output are typically much larger with export subsidy removal. This may appear surprising, especially in the aggregate agriculture case, where the export subsidy and the import license premium are about equal.[17] The reason is that separate or piecemeal removal of the import quotas has important second-best effects which reduce the welfare benefits and output adjustment of the agricultural sector.

We utilize Figures 1, 2 and 3 to explain the results of the three policy type scenarios in Table 3 and the top of Table 4. These figures each have three panels, representing ordinary supply – demand diagrams; panel A refers to the export market, panel B refers to the domestic market and panel C refers to the import market. These figures are partial equilibrium because they only picture the agricultural sector. Nonetheless, since the linkages within the agriculture sector are incorporated, they are helpful for understanding the principal effects of the policy changes in our general equilibrium model. The domestic product and the imported product are pictured separately since consumers regard the two varieties as heterogeneous (the Armington assumption). Thus, in addition to their own prices, the demand curves for imports and the domestic product depend on the price of their substitute. Similarly, for producers, the domestic product and

[16] For example, de Melo and Tarr (1990, 1992, 1993) found that the benefits of removing U.S. quotas were about 0.5 percent of GDP. But their estimates incorporated a rent-transfer component of the quotas (which was about four-fifths of the costs) which is not present in the Hungarian context. Trela and Whalley (1990) found the benefits to the U.S. of global removal of the MFA would be about 0.3 percent of GDP, where again a rent-transfer component was involved. Morkre (1990) found the benefits of agricultural liberalization in sugar and dairy products in the U.S. would be about 0.5 billion U.S. dollars, or about 0.01 percent of 1987 GDP. The above were general equilibrium studies, but Morkre and Tarr (1980) and Tarr and Morkre (1984) estimated the benefits of removing import restriction in numerous industries in partial equilibrium with similar results.

[17] Butter and pork have higher import quota premia relative to their export subsidy rates, so removing the import quota premium is more important in relative terms.

Figure 1 – *Benefits of Piecemeal Removal of an Import Quota Are Reduced by Increased Export Subsidies*

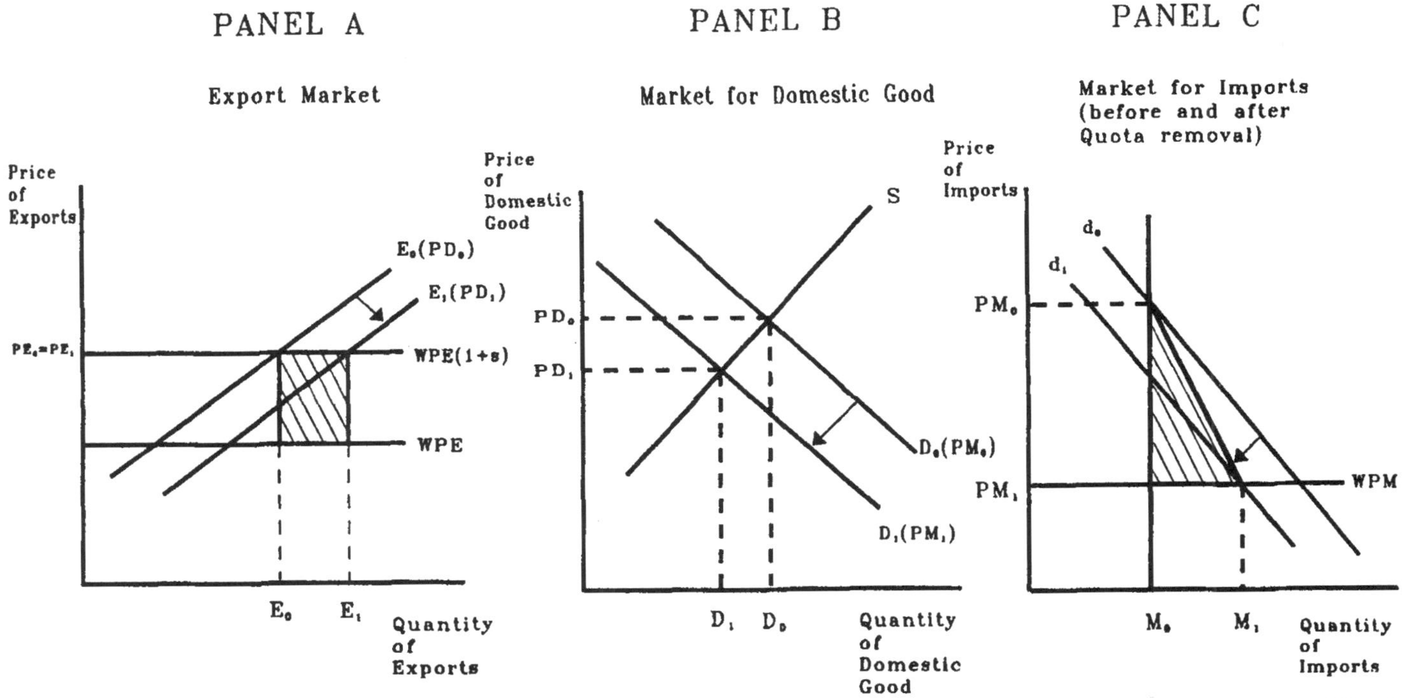

Removal of the import quota lowers the tariff-exclusive price of imports to PM_1, which induces a downward shift in the demand for the domestic variety (to D_1) and lowers its price (to PD_1). Due to the lower price of the domestic variety, producers then shift supply to the export market (E_1). The subsidy provided by the government increases by the size of the rectangle in the export market. ***Net benefits:*** The triangle of benefits in the market for imports minus the rectangle of increased subsidies in the export market.

the export product are heterogeneous, and are pictured separately. Since producers can switch markets subject to their technical possibilities expressed by the CET function, in addition to its own price, the export (domestic) supply curve is a function of the price of the domestic (export) good. Due to the small-country assumption, the supply of imports is perfectly elastic at the world price of imports (WPM), and the demand for exports is perfectly elastic at the world price of exports (WPE). WPM includes transportation costs but excludes tariffs; the "tariff ridden" demand curve for imports is pictured, since the quota premia rate must be determined residually after the tariff is collected. The export subsidy rate, denoted s, allows producers to obtain WPE $(1+s)$ per unit of exports.

Figure 1 illustrates the effects of removing an import quota in the presence of an export subsidy in the same industry. In all three figures, variables in the initial equilibrium are denoted by the subscript 0; in the new equilibrium by 1. The initial impact of quota removal results in a decline in the price of imports to PM_1.[18] Since the demand for the domestic variety depends on the price of imports, the demand for the domestic variety shifts down and its price declines to PD_1. The lower price of the domestic variety induces two feedback effects: (1) consumers will reoptimize by shifting demand away from imports, i.e., the demand for imports shifts in to d_1. Thus, the triangle of benefits measured in the import market is the shaded area shown;[19] (2) producers will reoptimize by shifting production toward the export variety, which continues to sell at the world price times one plus the export subsidy rate (denoted $WPE[1+s]$), i.e., the export supply curve shifts out to the right. The government subsidy burden will increase by the size of the shaded rectangle in the export market. *This rectangle in the export market is a second-best type loss to the economy which must be subtracted from the triangle of benefits in the import market to assess overall benefits to the economy.*[20] It follows that the net benefits of

[18] Since our model is a comparative statics model, the "dynamics" discussed in the context of Figures 1, 2 and 3 is for pedagogical purposes only.

[19] See Burns (1974) for the justification of the measurement of the benefits of quota removal in the import market as the triangle created by connecting the equilibrium points.

[20] The rectangle of losses to the economy in the export market follows from equation 8 (or its special case equation 5‴) in Harberger (1971). Harberger considers the case where there is a change in the tax (broadly interpreted as any price-cost distortion) on good 1 (in our case the removal of the import quota) in the presence of taxes on other goods in the economy, say goods $2, \ldots, n$. In our case, the most notable other tax is the export subsidy on exports in the same sector. Then the change in welfare is the change

quota removal are equal to the shaded triangle in the market for imports minus the shaded rectangle in the market for exports.[21] It is apparent from Figure 1 why the results show very little increase in welfare from a reduction in the import quota alone in the presence of an export subsidy: producers substitute in the export market (and obtain increased government subsidies) for reduced demand in the domestic market.

Figure 2 illustrates the principal effects of removing an export subsidy on a piecemeal basis in the presence of an import quota on the substitute import variety. The height BC equals the difference between the marginal cost of production of the initial output E_0 and the price paid by foreigners. If we were to ignore the interaction effects involved in reaching a new equilibrium, the triangle ABC would equal the benefits to the economy of removing the export subsidy; but the interaction effects between the markets reduces the benefits of export subsidy removal.

Removal of the export subsidy causes the export price of producers to fall to the world price ($PE_1 = WPE$). Since the export price to producers falls, producers shift supply to the domestic market, which induces a fall in the price of the domestic variety. The drop in the price of the domestic variety induces a shift down in the demand for imports, which reduces the price of imports. There are further feedback effects as the lower import price induces a downward shift in the demand for domestic goods, which in turn induces an increase in the supply of exports. Applying the Burns methodology again, the latter effect reduces the benefits of export subsidy reduction to the shaded triangle in the export market.[22] By contrast with Figure 1, there are no welfare consequences other than in the market in which the distor-

in surplus on good 1, plus the change in surplus on goods $2, \ldots, n$, where the latter is equal to the tax on the other goods times the change in quantity of those goods, summed over all such goods.

[21] There are additional second-best effects not shown in Figures 1 and 2 including the change in dead-weight losses due to change in demand in the presence of tariffs in agriculture or the rest of the economy. Most notably, import quota removal results in additional benefits in the agriculture sector equal to the tariff rate times the change in the quantity of imports. Since our approach is general equilibrium, which measures the welfare change by equivalent variation, we consider all second-best effects, even though not depicted in the diagram.

[22] Figure 2 is drawn for the case where the quota remains binding after the removal of the export subsidy. This holds for our results for aggregate agriculture and for most of the individual sectors as well. In the case of pork, however, the cross-elasticity effect is sufficiently strong that the import quota is no longer binding after the export subsidy is removed.

Figure 2 – *Benefits of Piecemeal Removal of an Export Subsidy*

PANEL A PANEL B PANEL C

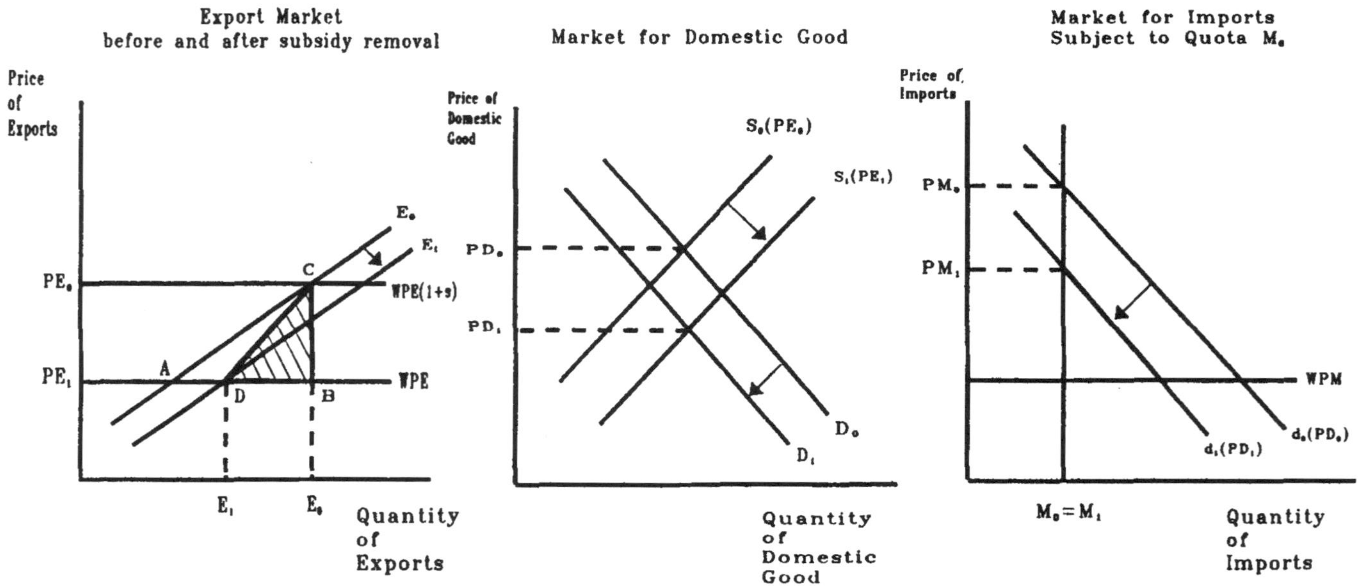

Removal of the export subsidy causes the export price of producers to fall to the world price ($PE_1 = WPE$). The export price reduction induces producers to increase supply to the domestic market. The lower price of domestic goods induces a downward shift in the demand for imports and a lower import price, which induces a downward shift in the demand for domestic goods, a lower domestic price and an increase in the supply of exports. The latter effect reduces the benefits of export subsidy reduction to the shaded triangle in the export market.

tion is changing. This follows from the Harberger principle mentioned in the footnote above: since there is no change in the quantity of imports, there is no welfare change in the import market.[23]

In Figure 3, we depict the benefits of removing both the export subsidy and the import quota. Since distortions are removed in both markets, there are triangles of benefits in both the import market and the export market. What may appear puzzling is that despite the triangle of benefits in the import market in Figure 3, in most of the cases in Table 3 the welfare benefits of removing export subsidies alone are as large as the combined benefits of removing both export subsidies and import quotas. Comparing Figures 2 and 3, one can observe that due to the greater decline in the price of the imported variety in Figure 3, the decline in the price of the domestic good is greater in Figure 3. Then the increase in export supply is greater in Figure 3, which implies that the triangle of benefits in the export market alone is smaller in Figure 3 than in Figure 2, ceteris paribus. These reduced benefits in the export market are typically approximately just offset by the triangle of benefits in the import market.

The third column in Tables 3 and 4 refers to the net change in tariffs minus subsidy expenditures as a percentage of initial government revenue. Export subsidy reduction improves the Government's fiscal position as expected in all cases – an important consideration given the Government's efforts to control inflation.[24] The removal of import licenses provides mixed results on the Government's fiscal position, depending on the elasticities. In Table 4, where smaller elasticities of substitution in demand are employed, for reasons explained above, the Government's fiscal position worsens. As shown in Figure 1, the Government will have to increase its expenditures on export subsidies when it removes import licenses. Another effect on government expenditures which is not pictured in Figure 1, is that the Government increases its tariff collections as a result of the increase in the quantity of imports after the quota is removed. With high import demand elasticities, the increase in imports and the tariff collections are large, and these increased tariff collections exceed the increase in expenditures on export subsidies.

---

[23] That is, without resource movement, there are no gains from improved resource allocation.

[24] Formally in our model, any change in the fiscal position of the government is exactly offset by lump-sum taxes on or transfers to the consumer. To the extent that a reduction of export subsidies allows the government to reduce distortionary taxation, the benefits of export subsidy reduction would exceed the benefits we have estimated.

Figure 3 – *Benefits of Simultaneous Removal of an Export Subsidy and an Import Quota*

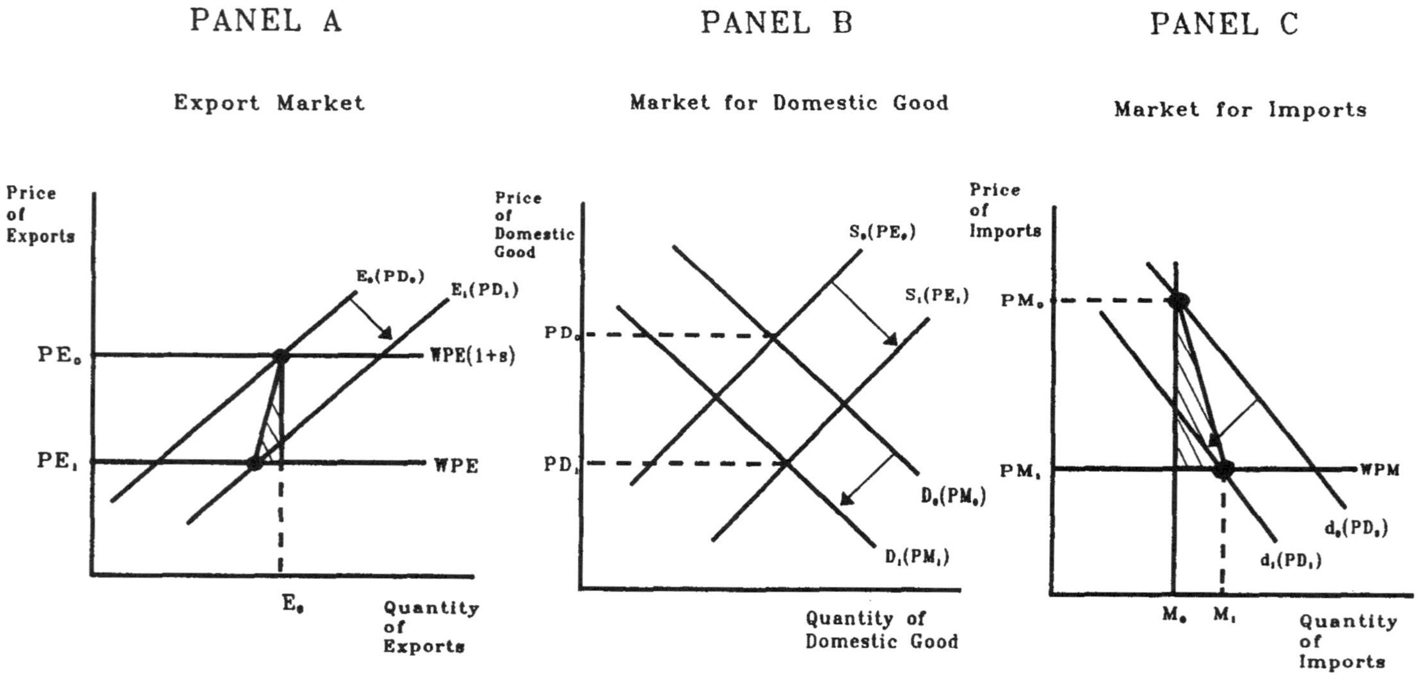

Removal of the export subsidy causes the export price to fall to the world price ($PE_1 = WPE$), and removal of the import quota causes the tariff-exclusive import price to fall to $PM_1 = WPM$. Producers increase their supply to the domestic market and consumers decrease their demand for the domestic product, resulting in a lower domestic price PD_1. This results in an increase in supply to the export market and a decrease in import demand, reducing the triangles of benefits in these markets. *Net benefits:* The sum of the two triangles in the export and import markets.

The fourth column in Tables 3 and 4 shows that the real exchange rate must depreciate when export subsidies or import licenses are removed. The removal of import licenses increases imports; the removal of export subsidies decreases exports. Thus, the price of traded goods must increase relative to non-traded goods in order to restore equilibrium in the balance of trade, i.e., a real depreciation.

V. Costs of a CAP Type System

As mentioned above, the Government initiated a CAP type system in 1991. Since the amount budgeted was rather modest, the consequences of the program were minimal; thus the real concern is whether the system is a harbinger of larger programs in the future. On the one hand, during the Uruguay Round negotiations at the GATT, in which Hungary was member of the "Cairns" group, many Hungarian Government officials came to appreciate that establishing a CAP type system would be a step diametrically opposed to international efforts of the "Cairns" group in the Uruguay Round (as well as the U.S.) to liberalize agricultural trade. On the other hand, other officials anticipate that Hungary will eventually join the EU, and believe that they should harmonize their regulatory environment to the EU CAP system which they believe will continue to exist.

Furthermore, agreement on the Uruguay Round was, in important measure, linked to recent efforts in the EU to make a substantial reform of the CAP.[25] While the key external elements of the CAP continue – specifically, variable levies on imports and subsidies for exports – the EU has adopted changes that include reductions in price guarantees for important commodities (including major cereals, butter, and beef) combined with product-specific subsidies to compensate farmers for consequent losses in income. These subsidies are accompanied by measures to constrain or reduce output, including land set asides for cereals and new or more severe production quotas (on milk and sheep). The consequences of CAP reform are, however, uncertain in part because further reform measures may be introduced, and in part because the effects of supply control measures such as land set asides are likely to be smaller than initially anticipated.[26]

---

[25] For details of the CAP reform, see Folmer et al. (1993).

[26] For example, Herlihy and Madell (1994) suggest that the actual reduction in EU cereals production resulting from the CAP land set asides will be roughly 50 percent of the expected reduction. They attribute this production slippage to base area inflation,

While the objective of the CAP is to support EU farmers, the instruments to accomplish this now include direct subsidy payments in addition to traditional price supports. To examine the effects of policies to support Hungarian farmers, we consider below the less complex case of domestic agricultural price supports. Since domestic price supports also imply export subsidies and import restraints, which remain key to the CAP, we refer to this as a CAP type system. As suggested earlier, due to input-output linkages in the agricultural sector, price supports for feed grains inflate costs for domestic producers (e.g., of animal products) that use grains as inputs and generate pressures for price supports for a wide variety of products. Thus, we shall counterfactually estimate the impact of a price support system in all of agriculture. Moreover, a price support system requires import restraints, since otherwise imports would enter and undermine the price support program. That is, a CAP system would undermine the effort of Hungary to liberalize its trade regime. We simulate a system of price support at three different levels: 5 percent, 10 percent and 20 percent higher than the initial prices.

We assume that the higher prices are achieved by increasing export subsidies and limiting imports to their initial level. That is, we implement the CAP by allowing the export subsidy to endogenously vary to achieve a desired level of domestic prices, holding the import quotas in place, and allowing the quota premium on imports to vary endogenously. Then we may use Figure 2 to analyze the effects of this policy (by inverting the subscripts 0 and 1 and interpreting the subsidy rate s of the figure as the increase in the subsidy rate) since Figure 2 depicts the same type of policy in reverse.[27] The costs of the system therefore are an increase in the inefficiency costs in the export market as the costs of production exceed the value of the goods paid by foreigners.

The results are reported in Table 4. As expected, agricultural output expands due to the price support program. In the case of a 10 percent increase in price supports for example, production increases by

---

intensification of production, intrafarm and interregional differences in land quality, noncompliance, and administration and enforcement difficulties.

[27] Although we may employ Figure 2 to facilitate understanding of the effects of the CAP system, there are important differences between the economics of reducing export subsidies and the CAP system. First, with a CAP system, both the export subsidy rate and the import quota premium are endogenously determined; with the export subsidy, only the import premium is endogenous. In addition, with a CAP (but not with export subsidy removal) there is a rectangle of costs, not shown in Figure 3 but captured by our model; it is the initial subsidy rate times the increase in the quantity of exports.

about 21 percent, but government export subsidies increase by more than 100 percent and the government loses substantial revenue. The export subsidy rate increases from 16.7 percent (Table 1) to 33.6 percent. Without an offsetting revenue increase or expenditure decrease, the government budget would move into deficit by almost 3 percent of its initial revenue. The loss in welfare is about 0.3 percent of GDP. The real exchange rate appreciates with the introduction of a CAP system because the initial effect is to increase exports.

The estimates would be expected to be lower bound estimates of the costs of the price support system for two reasons. *First*, the introduction of a CAP system increases the demand for imported agricultural products as consumers would like to substitute for the higher-priced domestic products. Consumers are prevented from additional importing, however, by the quota restraints. The licensing premium on imports increases from 16.6 percent (Table 1) to 26.5 percent. As a consequence, the rents on imported products under license increase. It would be expected that costly rent-seeking behavior to obtain the more valuable licenses would also increase. The costs to the economy of this likely increase in rent-dissipating activity are an additional cost of the price support system, which are ignored in the estimates of Table 4. *Second*, the government will have to obtain additional revenue (or reduce other expenditures) to compensate for the additional expenditures of the price support system. In practice, additional taxes would impose a dead-weight loss on the economy, but we have employed lump-sum nondistortionary taxes in our model.

VI. Conclusion

We have developed a computable general equilibrium model for the purpose of evaluating the consequences of reform of Hungarian agricultural policy. An important empirical step in the exercise was the price comparisons study, the results of which were presented in Table 2. These results show that the import licenses were a binding constraint on imports for the products mentioned in the table. The results were interpreted through the use of graphs which should facilitate the understanding of models of this type.

The results show that the imposition of a CAP type system would indeed be a costly step backwards for Hungary, especially since the long-run trend in Hungarian agricultural policy has been toward less intervention and greater reliance on the market. Import licenses and export subsidies are also shown to be costly inefficient policies. Perhaps the most important policy conclusion is in the area of the piecemeal sequencing of reforms in the presence of both export subsidies and import licenses. The removal of import licenses in the presence of export subsidies will generate byproduct distortions in the export market; little gain in welfare may ensue. On the other hand, the piecemeal removal of export subsidies will not generate byproduct distortions so that substantial gains can be expected. These greater gains will come, however, at the expense of greater adjustment costs.

References

Balazs, P. (1989). Trade Relations between Hungary and the European Community. In: M. Maresceau (ed.), *The Political and Legal Framework of Trade Relations between the European Community and Eastern Europe*, pp. 55–74. Boston, Mass.: Dordrecht Press.

Baldwin, R. (1989). The Growth Effects of 1992. *Economic Policy*, Vol. 9, pp. 248–281.

Bognar, I., M.F. Feketene, A. Hontvari, and I. Karascony (1991). Size Distribution of Export & Import Enterprises Between the Years 1987 and 1990. Ministry of Agriculture, Centre of Statistics and Economic Analysis, Budapest (mimeo).

Borszeki, E., S. Meszaros, and G. Varga (1985). Agricultural Price and Foreign Trade Study. Research Institute for Agricultural Economics (AKI) Working Paper, Budapest.

Borszeki, E., L. Harza, S. Meszaros, and G. Varga (1988). Prices, Taxes and Subsidies in the Food Producing Sector. Research Institute for Agricultural Economics (AKI) Working Paper, Budapest.

Brooke, A.D., and A. Meeraus (1988). *GAMS, A User's Guide*. Palo Alto, Calif.: Scientific Press.

BAE (Bureau of Agricultural Economics) (1985). Agricultural Policies in the European Community: Their Origins, Nature and Effects on Production and Trade. Policy Monograph No. 2, Canberra: Australian Government Publishing Service.

Burns, M. (1974). A Note on the Concept and Measure of Consumers' Surplus. *American Economic Review*, Vol. 63, pp. 335–344.

Folmer, C., M.A. Keyzer, M.D. Merbis, H.J.J. Stolwijk, and P.J.J. Veenendal (1993). CAP Reform and Its Differential Impact on Member States. Central Planning Bureau Research Memorandum 105, Den Haag.

Gardiner, W., V. Roningen, and K. Liu (1989). Elasticities in the Trade Liberalization Database. U.S. Dept. of Agriculture, Economic Research Service, AGES 89-20. Washington, D.C.

GATT (1991). *Trade Policy Review Mechanism: The Republic of Hungary*. Report by the Secretariat, Vol. A (Text), Vol. B (Tables and Appendices). Geneva.

Harberger, A. (1971). Three Basic Postulates for Applied Welfare Economics: An Interpretative Essay. *Journal of Economic Literature*, Vol. 9, pp. 785–797.

Harrison, G.W., T.F. Rutherford, and D.G. Tarr (1992). Piecemeal Trade Reform in Partially Liberalized Economies: An Evaluation for Turkey. *The World Bank Economic Review,* Vol. 7, pp. 191–217.

Haus, L. (1992). *Globalizing the GATT: The Soviet Union's Successor States, Eastern Europe, and the International Trading System.* Washington, D.C., The Brookings Institution.

Herlihy, M.T., and M.L. Madell (1994). The Effectiveness of the EC's New Set-Aside Program: An Assessment Based on U.S. Experience and Interviews with EC Farmers. In: G. Anania, C.A. Carter, and A.F. McCalla (eds.), *Agricultural Trade Conflicts and the GATT: New Dimensions in North American-European Agricultural Trade Relations.* Boulder, Colorado: Westview Press.

Marrese, M. (1990). Hungarian Agriculture: Lessons for the Soviet Union. *Comparative Economic Studies,* Vol. 32, pp. 155–169.

— (1991). Progress in Transforming Hungarian Agriculture. *Comparative Economic Studies.* Vol. 33, pp. 159–177.

Melo, J. de, and D. Tarr (1990). The Welfare Costs of U.S. Quotas in Textiles, Autos and Steel. *Review of Economics and Statistics,* Vol. 77, pp. 489–497.

— (1992). *A General Equilibrium Analysis of US Foreign Trade.* Cambridge, Mass.: MIT Press.

— (1993). Industrial Policy in the Presence of Wage Distortions: The Case of the U.S. Automobile and Steel Industries. *International Economic Review,* Vol. 34, pp. 833–851.

Morkre, M. (1990). *Effects of U.S. Import Restraints on Agricultural and Other Products: General Equilibrium Results.* Posthearing submission by Staff of Bureau of Economics, Federal Trade Commission to U.S. International Trade Commission on USITC Investigation No. 332-262.

Morkre, M., and D. Tarr (1980). *The Effects of Restriction on United States Imports: Five Case Studies and Theory.* Washington, D.C., U.S. Government Printing Office.

— (1993). Reforming Hungarian Agricultural Trade Policy: A Quantitative Evaluation. The World Bank, Policy Research Working Paper No. 1185, Washington, D.C.

Oblath, G., and D. Tarr (1992). The Terms-of-Trade Effects from the Elimination of State Trading in the Soviet-Hungarian Trade. *Journal of Comparative Economics,* Vol. 16, pp. 75–93.

Rosenblatt, J., et al. (1988). The Common Agricultural Policy of the European Community. International Monetary Fund, Occasional Paper No. 62, Washington, D.C.

Tarr, D. (1990). Quantifying Second Best Effects in Grossly Distorted Markets: The Case of the Butter Market in Poland. *Journal of Comparative Economics,* Vol. 14, pp. 105–119.

Tarr, D., and M. Morkre (1984). *Aggregate Costs to the United States of Tariffs and Quotas on Imports: General Tariff Cuts and Removal of Quotas on Automobiles, Steel, Sugar and Textiles.* Washington, D.C.: U.S. Government Printing Office.

Trela, I., and J. Whalley (1990). Global Effects of Developed Country Trade Restrictions on Textiles and Apparel. *Economic Journal,* Vol. 100, pp. 1190–1205.

Trela, I., J. Whalley, and R. Wigle (1987). International Trade in Grain: Domestic Policies and Trade Conflicts. *Scandinavian Journal of Economics*, Vol. 89, pp. 271–283.

Valdes, A., and J. Zietz (1990). Examination of Proposals for Tariffication and Disciplines on Subsidies and Quantitative Controls Currently Under Negotiation. In: N. Islam and A. Valdes (eds.), *The GATT, Agriculture, and the Developing Countries*. International Food Policy Research Institute, Working Paper, Washington, D.C.

Varga, G., J. Kartali, and M.N. Orban (1991). Initial Steps of Market Orientation in the Hungarian Agricultural and Food Exports. Agricultural Economic Research Institute (AKI), Budapest.

* * *

Abstract: Reforming Hungarian Agricultural Trade Policy: A Quantitative Evaluation. – In this paper, the authors quantitatively assess the consequences for Hungary of: (i) removing its quantitative import restraints in agriculture, (ii) removing the export subsidy program in agriculture, and (iii) adopting an EU-type "CAP" system in Hungary. The consequences are estimated through the use of a small open economy computable general equilibrium model for Hungary, calibrated to the year 1990. The tariff equivalent of the import licenses was estimated through a detailed price comparisons study, the first of its kind for Hungary. Import protection, export subsidies and a potential CAP system would contribute significantly to the Government's fiscal problems. JEL No. F13, P33, Q17

*

Zusammenfassung: Zur Reform der ungarischen Handelspolitik mit Agrarprodukten. Eine quantitative Bewertung. – Die Autoren schätzen die quantitativen Folgen, die in Ungarn eintreten würden, wenn (i) die mengenmäßigen Importbeschränkungen für Agrarprodukte aufgehoben würden, (ii) das Subventionsprogramm für Agrarprodukte abgeschafft würde, (iii) ein System vom Typ der gemeinsamen EG-Agrarpolitik in Ungarn eingeführt würde. Die Folgen werden unter Verwendung eines rechenbaren allgemeinen Gleichgewichtsmodells für eine kleine offene Volkswirtschaft – angepaßt an die ungarischen Verhältnisse des Jahres 1990 – geschätzt. Das Zolläquivalent der Einfuhrlizenzen wurde mit Hilfe detaillierter Preisvergleiche geschätzt, die erstmals für Ungarn angestellt wurden. Importprotektion, Exportsubventionen und ein potentielles System nach dem Vorbild des Gemeinsamen Agrarmarktes würden die Fiskalprobleme des Landes erheblich vergrößern.

THE WORLD BANK ECONOMIC REVIEW, VOL. 4, NO. 2: 175-193

Second-Best Foreign Exchange Policy in the Presence of Domestic Price Controls and Export Subsidies

David Tarr

Poland, like many developing countries, has required its exporters to surrender a share of their foreign exchange earnings to the government at an overvalued exchange rate. During the late 1980s, it progressively increased the share which exporters were allowed to retain (the retention ratio), but other distortions to the trade regime remained. A model developed here estimates the effects of these policies on welfare under different foreign exchange elasticities, export and import subsidies, official exchange rates, and policies on exporter retention of foreign exchange earnings. The retention ratios in effect in early 1989 were equivalent to a 51 percent tax on exports or an import tariff of 130 percent. As economic theory would suggest, maximum social benefit would derive from removal of the full range of distortions. Full retention of foreign exchange by exporters in the absence of other distortions would provide social benefits equivalent to 8 percent of gross domestic product. But the net effect of the other policies together is a bias toward tradables, so that a policy of somewhat less than full retention of foreign exchange is optimal in this second-best world.

Foreign exchange restraints are not uncommon in developing countries, and they are typical in centrally planned economies. Exporting enterprises are required to remit to the government all or part of their foreign exchange earnings, and they receive payment at the official (overvalued) exchange rate. In this article I develop a model to analyze the welfare consequences of partial or full liberalization of foreign exchange restraints, in which enterprises are allowed to retain a greater share or all of their foreign exchange earnings.

In the empirical application of the model, I estimate the welfare costs of foreign exchange restraints in Poland, incorporating all significant distortions to the trade regime. As of early 1989, that involved export subsidies and—a novelty—implicit subsidies to imports because of domestic price controls. In January of 1990, as part of its "shock" stabilization program, Poland massively devalued its exchange rate, unifying its official and parallel market rates (see Lipton and Sachs 1990). Thus the findings here can be viewed as estimates of

The author is an economist in the Technical Department, Europe, Middle East, and North Africa Region, the World Bank. He would like to thank Bohdan Wyznikiewicz for helpful comments.

the benefits Poland will likely receive from the foreign exchange reforms of 1990.

The estimates confirm the conventional wisdom that if there were no other trade distortions, full foreign exchange liberalization would be optimal, or that if other distortions were removed, full foreign exchange liberalization would be the best policy. In Poland, however, foreign exchange restraints are an offsetting distortion to the export subsidies and implicit subsidies to imports, so that full liberalization of foreign exchange is not optimal. Thus the optimal share of foreign exchange to be retained by the firm (the retention ratio), from the government's perspective, is estimated as a function of the level of other distortions.

The model is also used to calculate the anti-export bias of less than full retention of foreign exchange. Moreover, because a tax on exports is equivalent to a tax on imports (in that both will lower the equilibrium level of foreign exchange use), this calculation is also made in terms of the equivalent level of tariff protection.

The Polish trade and exchange rate regime, as it existed in 1989, is first described. The model is then presented and the benefits to Poland from various retention ratios are estimated, and the optimal retention ratio is calculated, given various assumptions regarding the extent of subsidies to imports. I have also estimated the benefits to Poland of foreign exchange liberalization, with subsidies to imports and exports removed. In the concluding section, most of the important simulations in the article are consolidated in the two summary figures.

I. The Trade and Exchange Rate Regime in Poland: 1989

In 1989 Poland embarked on a dramatic trade liberalization effort. Principally this occurred through three institutional changes: the state monopoly on importing was greatly liberalized, foreign exchange was made available at market rates, and foreign exchange obtained through the market was expected to finance the majority of imports.

Previously, importing and exporting were restricted to state foreign trade organizations, which are organized along product lines. Exporters turned over to the government their foreign exchange, and the government allocated it to those imports it desired.

The first liberalization in this area came with the introduction of accounts for exporters that allowed them to retain a share of their foreign exchange earnings (known as ROD accounts). For 1989, in addition, the government intended to auction a substantial share of the foreign exchange, so that only about one-third of it would be obtained through central allocation. The majority of imports thus were to be financed out of ROD accounts or from foreign exchange purchased at market rates. The combination of these two reforms meant that importers could purchase foreign exchange at market rates and import most goods through competitive trade organizations.

Given these reforms, the principal (but not only) distortions which remained in the trade regime involved foreign exchange, for which there were multiple exchange rates. The three most important were the official rate for centrally allocated foreign exchange, the parallel market rate for nonrestricted and illegal transactions, and the rate received by exporters for the dollar value of their exports.

First, those institutions that received centrally allocated foreign exchange paid the official price. This included in 1989 the import demands of the health and education sectors, which had little income. The official exchange rate, which was frequently subject to devaluation, was 239 zloty to one U.S. dollar as of March 1987; 400 in March of 1988; and slightly less than 550 as of March 10, 1989.

Second, there is the parallel or black market exchange rate, which in the three years before July 1988 was between 3.3 and 4.6 times the official exchange rate. The parallel market rate has been very volatile: it began to rise in August 1988 and by December 1988 reached 3,380 zloty to the dollar, or 6.7 times the official rate. By March 1989 it was about 2,900, and it rose by about 1,000 zloty per dollar in April 1989.

In early 1989 there were a variety of auctions at which foreign exchange could be purchased, yielding a variety of parallel exchange rates. Enterprises could sell their unrestricted foreign exchange from ROD accounts at the Export Development Bank auctions. Early in 1989 these rates closely approximated the parallel market rate, and it was expected that $200 million would be auctioned there in 1989. Foreign exchange to import any one of fifty-two important intermediate products was sold at the Bank Handlowy auctions. It was expected that between $1.5 and $2 billion (billion = 1,000 million) would be auctioned through Bank Handlowy. At the first auction, prices varied from 100 zloty above the official rate to 3,100 above it. Generally, lower prices were paid for larger contracts and for contracts further in the future. Lower prices for the future contracts were efficient because the buyer had to pay immediately, forwent interest, and bore the risk of exchange rate changes. Lower prices for the larger contracts were the result of lack of competition. As of April 1, 1989, individuals have been able to purchase foreign exchange at exchange counters established for this purpose. In addition, about $60 million was expected to be auctioned for the import of consumer goods, for which mostly wholesale enterprises were to be the buyers. These auctions were new and a considerable amount of inefficiency in the markets existed, most notably at Bank Handlowy, so that one price for similar transactions did not emerge.

The third important exchange rate is the rate received by exporters for their export earnings. Exporters retain a share of their foreign exchange and must sell the balance to the government at the official exchange rate. The ratio that they are allowed to retain varies by product but is generally between 10 and 50 percent and averages about 30 percent overall. This means that the exchange rate received by the exporter is a weighted average of the official exchange rate and the parallel market exchange rate. Given the average retention ratio of 30 percent, in March 1989 exporters were receiving on average an exchange rate of 1,255 zloty per dollar, compared with the 2,900 parallel market rate.

II. Foreign Currency Markets: The Model

The model estimated here is explained in detail in Harberger (1988) and discussed in other international trade texts, such as Salvatore (1987) and Dornbusch and Helmers (1988). This model has been widely used to estimate the effects on the real exchange rate of policy changes generally, and specifically of foreign exchange restraints (Bhagwati 1978). I focus here on the hard currency market and convert all hard currencies to U.S. dollars, so that we can use the term "dollars" interchangeably with "hard currency foreign exchange." The model formulates a system of supply and demand for foreign exchange.

The supply of dollars comes principally from the sale of exports. Exporters in each industry have a supply function that expresses their willingness to export as a function of their real exchange rate received, E_r. Nominal Polish exchange rates deflated by the ratio of Polish to world prices are real exchange rates. Exchange rates used in the model are real unless otherwise specified.

If units of each commodity are chosen so that one unit yields one dollar at world prices, then the aggregate of the supply functions of all of the exporters of the economy is the total supply function of dollars (Harberger 1988). Exporters are willing to supply more dollars the higher the exchange rate that they receive. Thus the supply of foreign exchange, F_s, is written as a linear function of the real exchange rate received:

$$F_s = a + bE_r(1 + s) \tag{1}$$

In equation 1, E_r is the real exchange rate received (it is derived by deflating the ratio of Polish to world prices), and s is the rate of subsidies on exports. If exporting firms receive subsidies at a positive rate, they will be willing to supply foreign currency (dollars) at a lower exchange rate. Equation 1 is depicted in figure 1; with no subsidy ($s = 0$), foreign exchange supplied is curve SS. Given a positive subsidy rate, the curve shifts down and to the right and is labeled $S(1 + s)$. (Other sources of foreign exchange that are sensitive to the real exchange rate are discussed in the appendix.)

The exchange rate received is a weighted average of the official exchange rate, E_o, and the parallel market exchange rate, E_p:

$$E_r = RE_p + (1 - R)E_o \tag{2}$$

where R is the firm's foreign exchange retention ratio. Note that when $R = 1$, $E_r = E_p$.

Figure 1. *Model of Real Exchange Rate Determination*

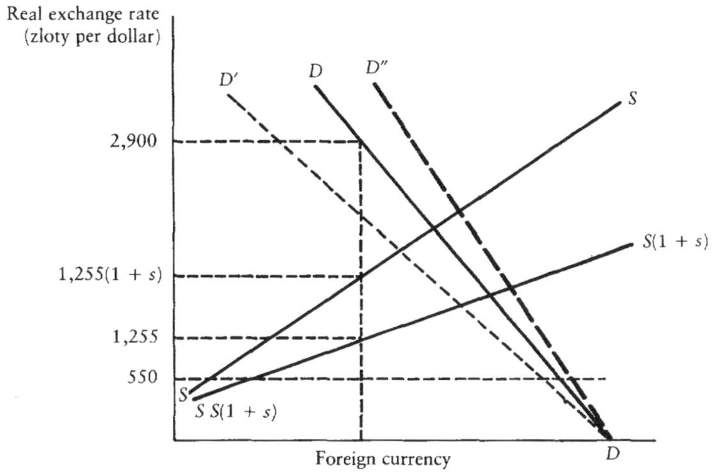

Note: D = foreign exchange demand; $D'D$ = foreign exchange demand given a positive import tariff; $D''D$ = foreign exchange demand given a positive implicit import "subsidy equivalent"; S = foreign exchange supply; s = export subsidy.

The demand for foreign exchange derives from a number of sources, but first from the demand for imports. Real exchange rate depreciation raises the number of zloty required per dollar and reduces the quantity of imports demanded. Demand (and supply) in individual sectors will also be affected by nontariff barriers. The aggregate of these sectoral demand functions represents the import demand for dollars, F_d, which is assumed to be a linear function and is written as

$$F_d = c - dE_p(1 + t) \tag{3}$$

where t, most easily thought of as the tariff rate, is a parameter that measures the policy-induced bias against imports. Payments for external debt would be incorporated in the parameter c. Equation 3 is depicted in figure 1 as the curve DD, and is drawn with $t = 0$. With a positive tariff rate, equation 3 would shift in and to the left, as is depicted in figure 1 as the dotted line $D'D'$.

Finally, we require equilibrium between demand and supply of foreign exchange:

$$F_d = F_s \tag{4}$$

In most economies we think of the parameter t as positive, reflecting a tariff rate that discourages purchase of imports. This does not appear appropriate for Poland, because tariffs average less than 10 percent and price controls and shortages produce implicit import subsidies. This occurs because price controls generate widespread shortages, that is, the quantity supplied is less than the quantity demanded, given Polish incomes. Given that imports could be purchased if dollars were obtained, the excess demand for domestic goods spills over into increased demand for imported consumer goods. Thus, the demand for imports would decrease if the shortages in the economy were reduced through the removal of price controls. That is, the price controls induce a bias toward import purchases that we think of as an implicit "subsidy equivalent," creating a *negative* value for t in equation 3 ($D''D''$ in figure 1).

In related analyses (Tarr 1990a), I have estimated this implicit subsidy equivalent for imports in automobiles and color televisions, two industries which have been subject to severe shortages and price controls. It was found that the elimination of the price controls in autos and color televisions would result in a sizable reduction in imports in the long run. Although obviously the government of Poland did not wish to subsidize the import of autos or color televisions, and there was no financial payment for their import, the impact on import demand of price controls on the domestically produced products was equivalent to a subsidy for the import of autos of 43 percent and imports of color televisions of 22 percent. Similar general results were found in the Polish butter market (see Tarr 1990b).

One cannot, however, generalize these partial equilibrium results of the television and auto industries to all goods simultaneously. If only price controls on autos are removed, producers can attract labor and capital from other sectors of the economy. If price controls are removed in the aggregate, when all sectors attempt to increase supply, the limited factors of production will result in a bidding up of the prices of those factors, and not all sectors will be able to expand. After a period of adjustment, however, one would expect that liberalization of price controls would result in a more efficient allocation of resources across industries, producing some increase in the value of Polish gross domestic product (GDP).

On the basis of these considerations, it is assumed (given best-guess estimates) that the import-increasing effect of the price controls is moderately stronger than the disincentive from the tariff, shifting the demand for imports out and to the right. The parameter t in equation 3 is interpreted as the difference between the tariff rate and the import subsidy equivalent of the price controls. That is, if t' is the tariff rate and p is the rate at which imports are encouraged as a result of price controls, then the net ad valorem effect on import demand is: $t = t' - p$. Given the uncertainty regarding its value, however, I simulate the effects of a number of positive and negative values of t.

These equations constitute the model. In a full general equilibrium model, a firm's export supply function depends on all its output and factor prices, not just the relative price of exports to domestic sales. This model, however, focuses on the relative price of exports, including taxes and subsidies, because this is the most important of the variables that affects export supply. In comparison with literally dozens of variants of general equilibrium models, this simple model has always reliably predicted the qualitative change in the real exchange rate found in the full general equilibrium models (including versions which incorporate labor-leisure choice). (These comparisons are presented in detail in de Melo and Tarr, forthcoming.)

The welfare analysis is based on the concept of net consumers' and producers' surplus, using measurement of Harberger triangles. Welfare estimates based on consumers' surplus have been shown to be good proxies for exact welfare estimates because measures of consumers' surplus are found to lie between the two "exact" measures: the Hicksian equivalent and compensating variations (Willig 1976). Hausman (1981) has taken a critical view of consumers' surplus; he has managed to construct examples in which the Hicksian equivalent and compensating variations differ by a significant amount. But to the extent that consumers' surplus differs from the equivalent variation, it will be closer to the compensating variation, and the latter is as good a welfare measure in most instances. Moreover, in hundreds of simulations using a general equilibrium model we found values based on the Hicksian equivalent and compensating variation measures to be within 1 percent of each other (de Melo and Tarr, forthcoming).

III. Liberalization of Foreign Exchange Policy: The Simulation Results

Impact of Full Retention of Foreign Exchange Earnings

The model described above is used to simulate an increase in the firms' retention ratio to 100 percent and to simulate the effects on the real exchange rate, welfare, and foreign exchange earnings. Six initial simulations are performed assuming: (1) high elasticities; (2) low elasticities; (3) high elasticities but a (high) initial parallel market exchange rate of 4,000 zloty to the dollar; and for (4), (5), and (6), high elasticities and net implicit subsidies to imports of 5, 20, and 50 percent, respectively. Aside from these varying parameter values, the values of the macroeconomic variables are based on best estimates for March 1989.

High elasticities. For this simulation we begin with the official exchange rate at 550, the parallel market exchange rate in the initial equilibrium at 2,900, the initial retention ratio at 0.3, net tariffs at zero, net subsidies at 0.121, initial foreign exchange supplied at $9.644 billion, and the elasticities of foreign exchange supply and demand at 1.16 and –1.0, respectively. The effects of increasing the retention ratio to 1 are presented in figure 2. With full retention, Polish exporters received real exchange rate increases, inducing additional exports and thus a greater supply of foreign exchange. The additional supply of foreign exchange drives down the price of the dollar in the parallel market until

Figure 2. *Simulation of Welfare Effects of Foreign Exchange Liberalization Assuming High Elasticity of Foreign Exchange Supply and Demand*

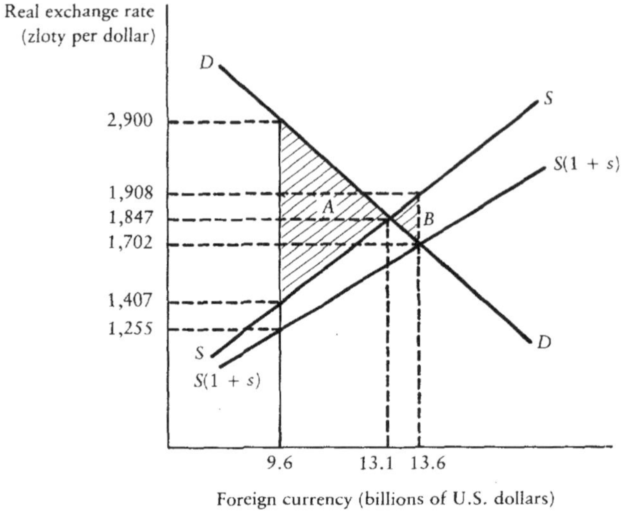

Note: D = foreign exchange demand; S = foreign exchange supplied; s = export subsidy rate.

demand and supply equalize and the market is in equilibrium at a parallel market exchange rate of 1,702 zloty. Note that, excluding subsidies, exporters were receiving a weighted average rate of exchange of 1,255 in the initial equilibrium as a result of partial retention, so that 1,702 is an increase of only 477 zloty; that is, one should *not* consider 1,702 an increase to exporters of 1,152 from the official exchange rate of 550. Including the average 12.1 percent export subsidy, exporters received 1,407 zloty for every dollar of export earnings in the initial equilibrium, 1,255 zloty from foreign exchange earnings, and 152 zloty from a government subsidy. The increased real exchange rate raises foreign exchange earnings by 41 percent—an additional $3.984 billion dollars—for total earnings of $13.628 billion.

What are the welfare costs and benefits of these shifts? The demand curve *DD* represents at any point the marginal value of an additional unit of foreign exchange to the Polish economy. The supply curve *SS* represents the marginal opportunity costs to the Polish economy of providing the goods and services that yield the foreign exchange. As long as *DD* exceeds *SS*, the economy benefits from raising the firms' retention ratios to increase the supply of foreign exchange. But 100 percent retention is not optimal, because of the presence of the export subsidies. The large triangle, *A*, represents the benefits of increasing retention ratios. To the left of $13.145 billion, *DD* exceeds *SS*, so that the

Table 1. *Welfare and Exchange Rate Effects of Full Retention of Foreign Exchange Earnings*

Macroeconomic variable	No import subsidies: High elasticity (1)	No import subsidies: Low elasticity (2)	No import subsidies: High elasticity and parallel exchange rate[a] (3)	High elasticity and import subsidies of: 5 percent (4)	High elasticity and import subsidies of: 20 percent (5)	High elasticity and import subsidies of: 50 percent (6)
Welfare						
In billions of zloty	2,564	733	4,247	2,106	730	−2,019
In percentage of GDP	9.1	2.6	15.0	7.4	3.9	−7.1
Shadow exchange rate (zloty per dollar)	1,847	1,895	2,392	1,819	1,720	1,427
Equilibrium exchange rate (zloty per dollar)	1,702	1,752	2,199	1,702	1,702	1,702
Optimal retention ratio	0.85	0.85	0.85	0.79	0.60	0.35
Increased foreign exchange earnings at optimal retention ratio (billions of dollars)	3.501	1.003	3.876	3.227	2.493	0.156
Increased foreign exchange earnings at 100 percent retention (billions of dollars)	3.984	1.145	4.340	3.984	3.984	3.984

Note: The estimates assume existing export subsidies (at 0.121). Column numbers refer to the respective simulations.

a. 4,000 zloty to the U.S. dollar.

Source: Author's calculations, based on data sources described in the appendix.

value of an additional dollar exceeds the cost of supplying it. The exchange rate is 1,847 at this "optimal" quantity of foreign exchange.

Because subsidies encourage exports, however, the economy will supply more foreign exchange than is optimal once full retention is granted. This will drive down the exchange rate to 1,702, which is slightly appreciated relative to the optimal rate (or shadow price of foreign exchange). The small triangle, *B*, represents the cost to the economy of supplying too much foreign exchange. The net benefits of providing full retention, given the export subsidies, are equal to the value of area *A* less that of *B*—2,564 billion zloty, which is about 9 percent of the estimated GDP for 1988. These results are summarized in column 1 of table 1.

We calculate the optimal retention ratio of foreign exchange to be 85 percent, given the official exchange rate of 550 and the continuation of export subsidies. Once full retention of export earnings is achieved, there is no anti-export bias in the system, and there would be no value in continuing with the export subsidies, which are justified as a means of countering the net anti-export bias. Thus, having a retention ratio of 100 percent and simultaneously removing the export subsidies would yield optimal results; this would increase welfare by a further 49 billion zloty (or 0.1 percent of GDP).

If we consider only the foreign exchange market, this model indicates that a retention ratio of 85 percent and a 12 percent export subsidy yield the same benefits as 100 percent retention ratios without subsidies. But both subsidies and the multiple exchange rate regime create administrative and lobbying costs and incentives to seek rents. When lobbying or administrative failures result in uneven application of subsidies or exchange rates across sectors, this will also distort intersectoral allocation and production. Thus 100 percent retention rates without subsidies is the preferred policy.

Low elasticities. The elasticities of supply and demand are now assumed to be 0.3 and –0.3, respectively; otherwise, parameter selection is identical to the high-elasticity case.

Because of the lower elasticities, the increase from 30 percent to full retention brings forth a much smaller rise in foreign exchange earnings—only 1.145 billion dollars. The equilibrium exchange rate (given the subsidies) falls to 1,752, but the shadow exchange rate is 1,895; these are not dramatically different from the high-elasticity case. Only if the difference in the supply elasticities in the two cases is much larger or smaller than the difference between the demand elasticities will significantly different exchange rates be generated.

There is, however, a considerable decrease in the estimate of the benefits to the economy from full retention. The benefit is equal to 733 billion zloty; this is equal to 2.6 percent of estimated GDP. Because the economy makes a smaller adjustment to the change in retention policy, there is less to be gained from liberalization. Again, there is an overadjustment because of the subsidies, and the optimal retention ratio is 85 percent, given the continuation of subsidies. A policy of 100 percent foreign exchange retention and elimination of the subsidies would also yield the optimal result. These results are summarized in column 2 of table 1.

High initial parallel exchange rate and high elasticities. Inasmuch as the parallel exchange rate is somewhat volatile, and depreciated during April 1989 by more than 1,000 zloty relative to the value that we simulated for March 1989, we have also simulated the results with an initial parallel exchange rate of 4,000 zloty to the U.S. dollar. With a more depreciated parallel exchange rate, the tax on exports from less than full retention of foreign exchange earnings is greater. Thus, as shown in column 3 of table 1, the benefits of full retention reach 15 percent of GDP in this case.

Simulations 4, 5, and 6—high elasticities and subsidies to imports. Empirical evidence suggests and the final set of simulations assumes that the bias to import purchases as a result of price controls is stronger than the import taxes (that is, in equation 3, $t < 0$). Otherwise, parameter values are set as in the high-elasticity case.

Compared with the high-elasticity case without import subsidies, the optimal increase in foreign exchange supplied is smaller and the optimal retention ratio lower for all levels of import subsidy (see table 1). A retention ratio of 100 percent will now lead to greater excess foreign exchange supplied, so that net benefits are reduced. At an import subsidy of 50 percent, the bias to importing is so great that full retention of foreign exchange reduces welfare by 7 percent of GDP. As discussed above, our best assessment of the actual distortions in the Polish economy is that net implicit subsidies to imports in Poland are about 5 percent. Thus, the benefits of full retention are best characterized by the results of simulation 4, shown in column 4 in table 1.

The Anti-Export Bias and the Level of Protection

Calculating the anti-export bias. The system of less than full retention of foreign exchange earnings creates a disincentive to export. The model is now used to estimate how high the tax rate on exports would have to be to produce the initial (lower) level of exports if full retention of foreign exchange were in effect, assuming high elasticities and no import subsidy. In order to offset the 3.984 billion dollar increase in exports which would result from a 100 percent retention ratio, it would be necessary to impose a net export tax of 51.5 percent without the existing 12.1 percent export subsidy, or 63.6 percent if the subsidies remained in effect. That is, it would require an average net export tax of 51.5 percent just to prevent an increase in export earnings if full retention of export earnings were allowed.

Calculating the equivalent level of protection. It is intuitive to think of less than full retention of foreign exchange as a tax on exports. But a basic theorem of international economics (the Lerner symmetry theorem, first established in the 1930s) states that a tax on imports is equivalent to a tax on exports. Applied in this situation it means that the same effects of less than full retention of exchange earnings would result from full retention and imposing a tax on imports. This results because a tax on exports reduces foreign exchange earnings and, because the quantity of foreign exchange demanded and supplied must be equal, demand must be reduced to reestablish equilibrium. This occurs as the excess demand for foreign currency drives up its price, raising import prices and lowering import quantities. Thus giving full retention would increase the amount of imports in the economy, not just increase the amount of exports. By identical reasoning, a subsidy to imports is equivalent to a subsidy to exports. In particular, to the extent that domestic price controls induce additional imports, they depreciate the real exchange rate and encourage additional exports.

An import tax of 131 percent would be necessary to reduce imports to their original level if 100 percent retention rates were granted. Thus the overvalued average exchange rate at which exporters were paid for the surrendered foreign exchange was equivalent to providing import protection of 131 percent. Because the majority of Latin American and Asian countries have had average tariff rates of between 20 and 40 percent, the system of foreign exchange surrender meant that Poland was highly protected in early 1989.

Varying the Retention Ratio and Trade Distortions

No implicit net subsidies to imports; existing subsidies to exports. I first assume that the average 12.1 percent export subsidy remains in place and there are no net subsidies to imports. That is, I assume that the implicit subsidy to imports from price controls is 8.1 percent, which exactly offsets the 8.1 percent import tariff. In table 2, welfare estimates and the exchange rates vary with alternate retention ratios under these assumptions. The greatest welfare increase occurs at a retention ratio of 85 percent; at ratios greater than that, the cost of foreign exchange supplied is greater than the benefits, because of the export subsidy.

The Polish government increased retention rates by about 5 percent between 1985 and 1989. The first column in table 2 shows the costs of a 5 percent *reduction* of retention ratios from the 30 percent base. Thus the absolute value of the welfare changes shown there could be interpreted as the *benefits* Poland has gained from its policy of increasing the retention ratio in the four years before 1989.

Implicit net subsidies to imports of 5 or 20 percent; existing export subsidies retained. As shown in tables 3 and 4, with implicit net import subsidies of 5 and 20 percent, the optimal retention ratios (which yield the maximum gain in welfare) are reduced to 79 and 60 percent, and the benefits to the economy of full retention are reduced to 7.4 and 2.6 percent of GDP, respectively. As suggested above, given macroeconomic resource constraints, it is unlikely that the true net import subsidy is above 5 percent. Thus, the results of tables 2 and 3 are most relevant for the Polish case.

Table 2. *Simulated Effects of Different Foreign Exchange Retention Ratios with No Implicit Import Subsidies*

	Retention ratio				
Macroeconomic variable	*0.25*	*0.5*	*0.75*	*0.85*	*1.0*
Welfare changes					
In billions of zloty	−1,020	1,990	2,584	2,613	2,564
As a percentage of GDP (1988)	−3.6	7.0	9.1	9.2	9.1
Shadow exchange rate	1,847	1,847	1,847	1,847	1,847
Equilibrium parallel exchange rate	3,089	2,361	1,958	1,847	1,702

Note: Assumes 12.1 percent export subsidy and initial retention ratio of 30 percent.
Source: Author's calculations, based on data sources described in the appendix.

Table 3. *Simulated Effects of Different Foreign Exchange Retention Ratios with 5 Percent Implicit Import Subsidies*

	Retention ratio				
Macroeconomic variable	*0.25*	*0.5*	*0.75*	*0.79*	*1.0*
Welfare changes					
In billions of zloty	926	1,754	2,204	2,209	2,106
As a percentage of GDP (1988)	−3.3	6.2	7.8	7.8	7.4
Shadow exchange rate	1,819	1,819	1,819	1,819	1,819
Equilibrium parallel exchange rate	3,089	2,361	1,958	1,910	1,702

Note: Assumes 12.1 percent export subsidy and initial retention ratio of 30 percent.
Source: Author's calculations, based on data sources described in the appendix.

Implicit net subsidies to imports of 50 percent; existing export subsidies retained. Under this simulation (not shown), any retention ratio in excess of 32 percent has a negative impact on welfare. The optimum retention ratio is about a 2 percent increase from the assumed existing retention ratio, to 32 percent. Thus, if existing implicit import subsidies are this high, the import incentives are so great that a liberalization of the foreign exchange regime almost immediately becomes counterproductive.

No net subsidies to imports or subsidies to exports. In this experiment, initially, export subsidies are removed and net subsidies to imports are set at zero; subsequently the effects of different retention ratios are simulated and reported. Because liberalization of the other trade distortions occurs first, increasing the retention ratio is unambiguously beneficial (table 5). The most striking result is that a reduction of 5 percent in the retention ratio (to 25 percent) results in a loss of 9.1 percent of GDP, which is considerably greater than the losses from a reduction in the retention ratio to 25 percent in the previous simulations. This occurs because at the initial equilibrium (given the 30 percent retention ratio) there is already too little foreign exchange supplied. Reduction of the export subsidies in addition to the reduction in the retention ratio further reduces foreign exchange supplied, exacerbating losses.

Table 4. *Simulated Effects of Different Foreign Exchange Retention Ratios with 20 Percent Implicit Import Subsidies*

	Retention ratio				
Macroeconomic variable	*0.25*	*0.5*	*0.6*	*0.7*	*1.0*
Welfare changes					
In billions of zloty	−645	1,048	1,137	1,106	730
As a percentage of GDP (1988)	−2.3	3.7	4.0	3.9	2.6
Shadow exchange rate	1,720	1,720	1,720	1,720	1,720
Equilibrium parallel exchange rate	3,089	2,362	2,175	2,024	1,701

Note: Assumes 12.1 percent export subsidy and initial retention ratio of 30 percent.
Source: Author's calculations, based on data sources described in the appendix.

Table 5. *Simulated Effects of Foreign Exchange Restraints, Export Subsidies, and Implicit Import Subsidies*

	Retention ratio			
Macroeconomic variable	*0.25*	*0.5*	*0.75*	*1.0*
Welfare changes				
In billions of zloty	−2,584	1,060	2,030	2,209
As a percentage of GDP (1988)	−9.1	3.7	7.2	7.8
Shadow exchange rate	1,819	1,819	1,819	1,819
Equilibrium parallel exchange rate	3,198	2,494	2,085	1,819

Note: Initial 12.1 percent export subsidies and 5 percent implicit net import subsidies are reduced to zero, and the initial retention ratio is 30 percent.

Source: Author's calculations, based on data sources described in the appendix.

IV. LIMITATIONS OF THE ANALYSIS

There are two weaknesses in the methodology used here that should be noted. First, the model does not account for the demand or supply of dollars created by asset accumulation. People may wish to hold dollars as an asset, not as a means to purchase imports, especially during periods of domestic inflation. In the short run, these financial reasons may dominate the trade-related factors emphasized above. In the long run, however, people will not continue to acquire dollars as an asset, without those dollars entering the market for goods and services. Moreover, elasticities of trade-driven foreign exchange supply and demand are greater in the long than the short run, and should dominate in a longer time frame. As Caves and Jones (1985, p. 361) have stated: "We can hardly imagine commodity markets running permanently out of equilibrium with unexploited opportunities to arbitrage goods from one country to another. . . . Therefore we expect that financial forces will determine the exchange rate in the short run following any disturbance to equilibrium, but trade flows must dominate the long run result." Thus this model appears to be a reasonable representation of the factors which influence the exchange rate in the long run.

Second, the supply of and demand for dollars here is derived from the supply of exports and demand for imports. These underlying demand and supply schedules are dependent on domestic prices, including factor market prices. To the extent that the underlying prices are distorted, the demand and supply schedules may not represent the marginal social costs or benefits of the goods. In that case, the supply and demand for dollars similarly may not represent society's valuation of the benefits or costs of an additional dollar. This implies that our measure of welfare is subject to error.

In a related paper (Tarr 1989, available upon written request), a model is constructed in which the price of foreign exchange differs from the marginal social benefits and costs. Those differences are characterized by random variables which may be interpreted as reflecting measurement error from all the sources of uncertainty, but most notably from uncertainty about the difference between the price of foreign exchange and marginal social benefits and costs. The paper shows that the variance of the net benefits of a foreign exchange retention policy increases as the retention ratio increases. Consequently, the risk-averse decisionmaker will desire a lower foreign exchange retention ratio than either a decisionmaker who is risk-neutral or a decisionmaker who operates under less uncertainty as a result of less distortion in the underlying supply and demand curves. The qualitative impact of risk aversion under uncertainty is the same as the effect of export subsidies: a further departure from 100 percent retention of foreign exchange is optimal.

V. Conclusions

Using the model outlined above in an application to Poland in 1989, changes in welfare have been related to the share of foreign exchange earnings retained by exporters given various foreign exchange elasticities, degrees of overvaluation, and trade subsidy levels. On the basis of the results of the various simulations (tables 2–4), the change in welfare (as a percentage of GDP) is graphed against the foreign exchange retention ratio in figure 3. All curves have the export subsidy at its level in March 1989, and different levels of implicit import subsidies assumed in the initial equilibrium. The higher curves are associated with an assumed lower initial level of trade distortions. The subsidies to exports and implicit subsidies to imports (t) represent offsetting distortions to the foreign exchange restrictions. Less than 100 percent retention of foreign exchange discourages exports and imports, but the net effect of the other trade distortions is to encourage exports and imports. Thus foreign exchange liberalization produces greater benefits the lower are other trade distortions in the initial equilibrium. Without reduction of the other trade distortions, increasing foreign exchange retention ratios beyond 65–85 percent will reduce welfare. Other trade distortions must be reduced if retention ratios of less than 85 percent are to produce additional benefits. These are "second-best" experiments that simulate the effects of changing the foreign exchange restrictions, given the presence of other distortions to the trade regime.

First-best policies are then simulated, assuming first the best estimate of the March 1989 level of trade distortions, then simulating their elimination and increases in foreign exchange retention ratios (table 5). Figure 4 shows increased benefits up to 100 percent retention of foreign exchange, which yields benefits equivalent to 7.8 percent of GDP. This is the estimated benefit from more efficient allocation of foreign exchange; reducing other distortions, such as domestic price controls, will produce a more efficient allocation of domestic resources and yield additional benefits that are not estimated by this model.

In the application to Poland, less than full retention of foreign exchange is estimated to be equivalent to either a net export tax of 51.5 percent or an import tariff of 131 percent.

Figure 3. *Simulated Welfare Effects of Foreign Exchange Retention Ratios under Differing Trade Policies*

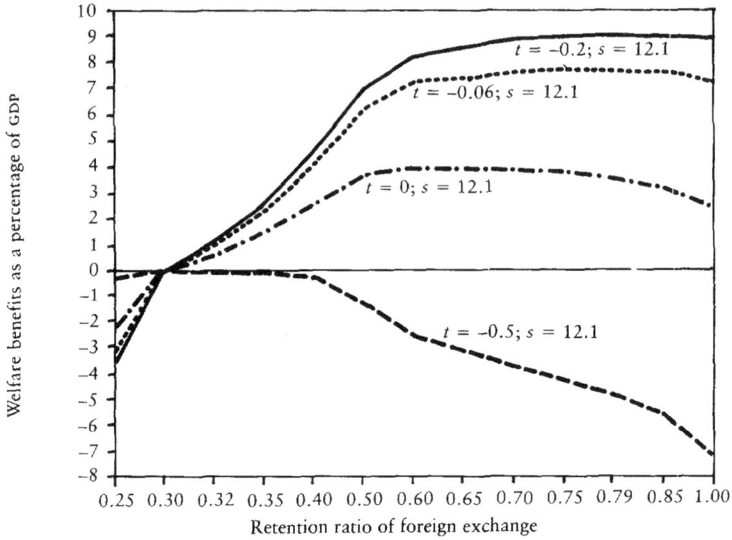

Note: s = rate of subsidy as a percentage of export value; t = net policy (dis)incentive to imports as the difference between tariffs and the implicit subsidy equivalent resulting from price controls on domestic substitutes.

Figure 4. *Simulated Welfare Effects of Foreign Exchange Retention Ratios Given Liberalization of Trade Policy*

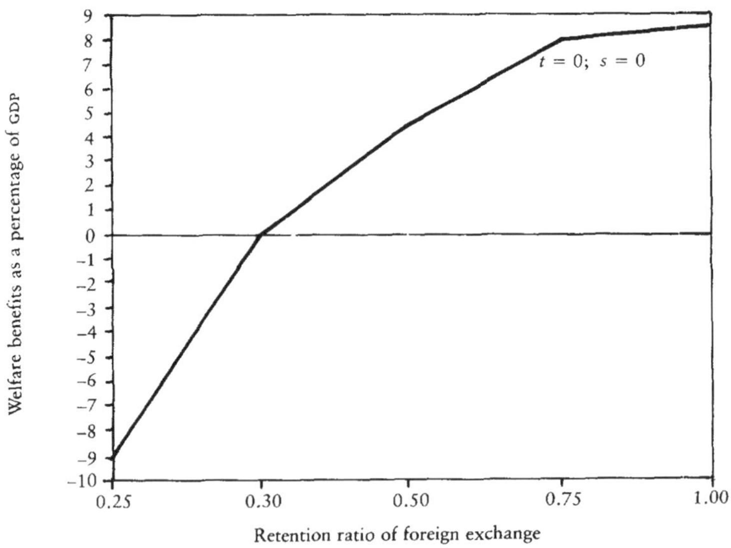

Note: s = rate of subsidy as a percentage of export value; t = net policy (dis)incentive to imports as the difference between tariffs and the implicit subsidy equivalent resulting from price controls on domestic substitutes.

Appendix. The Data, Assumptions, and Parameter Estimates

The official exchange rate was slightly less than 550 during early March 1989, and the parallel rate was 2,900 at that time. The retention rate is taken to be 30 percent. Without loss of generality, indexes were chosen so that relative prices between Poland and the rest of the world are initially unity. Thus, the nominal exchange rates are initially identical to the real rates, but as relative prices change over time, the nominal and real exchange rates will differ.

The subsidy rate to exports has two parts: fiscal incentives and the price equalization payments. Fiscal subsidies in 1988 were 7.1 percent of the value of exports. Data on subsidies and tariffs are taken from UNDP / World Bank (1989). Some enterprises were taxed on exports and some were subsidized, but on balance in 1987 the price equalization payments created an 8.2 percent subsidy to exports to hard currency areas. In an efficiency enhancing reform, payments to exporters under the price equalization fund were reduced over time, so that we take 5 percent as the price equalization subsidy in 1989. This yields a 12.1 percent subsidy from fiscal subsidies and price equalization payments.

Net customs duties were 4.1 percent in 1987. In addition, through the operation of the price equalization account, firms paid varying import taxes, but on balance additional import taxes of 5.9 percent were collected in 1987. As above, the import taxes under the price equalization account are assumed to be lower (4 percent) as a result of the reforms, so that in aggregate we take import duties to be 8.1 percent in 1989. There is an opposite bias on imports deriving from the price controls, however, which appears to be at least as strong as the tariff.

The supply of foreign exchange is derived from data on the balance of payments in convertible currencies in 1988. The sources of foreign exchange in the current account were merchandise exports ($7.248 billion), private remittances ($1.433 billion), and sales of services ($0.963 billion), for a total supply of foreign exchange in the initial equilibrium of $9.644 billion. The demand for foreign exchange is based on merchandise imports ($6.307 billion), nonfactor services ($0.544 billion), and debt payments which are derived as the difference between foreign exchange supply and merchandise and service import demand so that foreign exchange demand and supply is equilibrated. There is also a supply and demand for foreign exchange deriving from capital movements and government import programs, respectively. The effects of moving to greater retention of foreign exchange are completely independent of the *initial* value of foreign exchange supplied or demanded. The additional foreign exchange generated simply shifts the supply and demand curves out to the right, but it does not affect variables otherwise influenced by policy shifts. This is the one parameter in the model that does not affect the results. Thus the supply of foreign exchange deriving from capital movements is ignored.

The final parameters required are the elasticities of supply and demand with respect to the real exchange rate. Two estimates of the supply elasticity are available: an elasticity of 0.2, from annual data for three years ending in 1987, (UNDP / World Bank 1989) and, from monthly export data between December 1985 and December 1987, 1.16 during the first sixteen months and 0.19 during the last nine months (Marczewski 1988). Because the model here is long-run and elasticities are larger in the long run than the short run, and because recent institutional changes allow increased price response of exports, 1.16 is used as the best (high) estimate, but results for a low-elasticity estimate of 0.3 are also calculated.

There is less information available on the elasticity of demand, but the results are estimated for a range of elasticities from 1.0 to 0.3, comparable to the supply elasticities.

I solve for the unknown parameters in equations 1–4 (a, b, c, and d). Given the value of the supply and demand elasticities, I first determine the value of *b* in equation 1 and *d* in equation 3. Given the values of *b* and *d*, I solve equations 1–3 for the unknown parameters *a* and *c*. Given the values of these parameters, other parameters in the model are then changed to simulate policy experiments.

REFERENCES

Bhagwati, Jagdish. 1978. *Anatomy and Consequences of Foreign Exchange Controls*. Cambridge, Mass.: Ballinger.

Caves, Richard, and Ronald Jones. 1985. *World Trade and Payments*. Boston: Little, Brown.

de Melo, Jaime, and David Tarr. Forthcoming. *A General Equilibrium Analysis of U.S. Trade Policy*. Cambridge, Mass.: MIT Press.

Dornbusch, Rudiger, and F. L. Helmers, eds. 1988. *The Open Economy: Tools for Policymakers*. New York: Oxford University Press.

Harberger, Arnold. 1988. "Trade Policy and the Real Exchange Rate." World Bank Economic Development Institute. Processed.

Hausman, Jerry. 1981. "Exact Consumer's Surplus and Deadweight Loss." *American Economic Review* 11: 662–76.

Lipton, David, and Jeffrey Sachs. 1990. "Creating a Market Economy in Eastern Europe: The Case of Poland." *Brookings Papers on Economic Activity*, no. 1.

Marczewski, K. 1988. "The Real Exchange Rate in Poland and Hungary in the 1980s." *Handel Zagraniczny* 33: 11–15.

Salvatore, Dominick. 1987. *International Trade*. New York: Macmillan.

Tarr, David. 1989. "The Implications of Distortion–Induced Uncertainty on Optimal Foreign Exchange Policy." Technical Department, EMENA Region, World Bank. Washington, D.C. Processed.

———. 1990a. "A Disequilibrium Model of the Welfare Effects of Foreign Exchange Restraints and Price Controls: The Case of Automobiles and Color Televisions in

Poland." World Bank Europe, Middle East, and North Africa Region Working Paper IDP0058. Processed.

———. 1990b. "Quantifying Second Best Effects in Grossly Distorted Markets: The Case of Butter in Poland." *Journal of Comparative Economics* 14: 105–09.

UNDP (United Nations Development Programme) / World Bank. 1989. "Poland: Policies for Trade Promotion." Trade Expansion Program, Country Report 1. New York. Processed.

Willig, Robert. 1976. "Consumer Surplus without Apology." *American Economic Review* 66: 589–97.

THE WORLD BANK ECONOMIC REVIEW, VOL. 7, NO. 2: 191-217

Trade Reform in the Partially Liberalized Economy of Turkey

Glenn W. Harrison, Thomas F. Rutherford, and David G. Tarr

Recent reforms in trade policy in Turkey have produced a foreign trade regime that exhibits very little antiexport bias on average. A quantitative, multisectoral general equilibrium model of the Turkish economy shows that piecemeal trade policy reform, based on first-best rationales that are appropriate for highly distorted economies, would not now be appropriate. Further tariff reductions must be coordinated with export subsidy reductions to attain significant welfare benefits. The dispersion of distortions, especially export subsidies, is more important than their level. A policy of harmonizing tariffs to the common external tariff of the European Community has virtually no effect on welfare.

Turkey undertook a major liberalization of trade policies in the 1980s. Import quotas have become virtually nonexistent, the Turkish lira has been made convertible, and tariffs have generally been lowered so that the average nominal tariff rate is less than 10 percent. Given these changes and remaining export subsidies, Turkey has, on average, removed the antiexport bias from its external incentive regime.

The impact on Turkey of its import-substitution trade policies in the 1970s and of its trade liberalization in the early 1980s has been the subject of several earlier studies, notably Baysan (1984); Baysan and Blitzer (1988, 1991); Rodrik (1988b); and Grais, de Melo, and Urata (1986). Although few analysts object to the reduction in import barriers and the real exchange rate depreciation as an aid to exporters, the effectiveness of more direct export incentives has been questioned by Milanovic (1986), Rodrik (1988a), and Arslan and van Wijnbergen (1990). The welfare effects of either the direct or indirect incentives, however, have not been estimated.

Starting with the relatively liberal trade regime of Turkey in the late 1980s, we use a 40-sector computable general equilibrium model to consider several fur-

Glenn W. Harrison is in the Department of Economics, College of Business Administration, at the University of South Carolina; Thomas F. Rutherford is in the Department of Economics at the University of Colorado at Boulder; and David G. Tarr is in the Policy and Research Department in the World Bank. This study is part of the World Bank's research on "The Impact of EC 1992 and Trade Integration in Selected Mediterranean Countries," supported under grant RPO 67564. The authors would like to thank Deborah Bateman, Marylou Uy, Omer Karasapan, and Michael Klein for data and helpful comments and two referees for their suggestions.

ther trade liberalization options that are now open to the Turkish government. The first option is across-the-board liberalization. Under this option, Turkey would completely reduce or remove its trade distortions, that is, its import tariffs and export subsidies. The second option is to consider sectoral liberalizations of tariffs or export subsidies. In this connection, we evaluate the reduction of tariffs and export subsidies that Turkey implemented during the late 1980s. The final option is the principal trade policy change Turkey is planning to implement: harmonization of its tariff structure to the common external tariff of the European Community (EC). This option is part of Turkey's effort to continue to press its case for membership in the EC.

The evaluation of removing trade barriers yields what is perhaps our most important finding: first-best rules of thumb that may be appropriate for highly distorted economies are not necessarily appropriate for economies that have liberalized as much as Turkey. (Other developing countries that achieved a relatively liberal trade regime in the 1980s include Chile, Indonesia, Mexico, and Poland.) In particular, piecemeal across-the-board tariff reductions in Turkey are not always beneficial from a welfare perspective and generally must be coordinated with export subsidy reductions to ensure welfare gains. The counterfactual assumption that the tariff level of Turkey is at the level of 1985 (about twice the 1989 level of our benchmark model) reintroduces an antiexport bias in the external incentive regime. In this case piecemeal tariff reduction to the 1989 tariff level is beneficial.

We show that, because there is no antiexport bias, the principal distortions remaining in the trade regime derive from the dispersion of external incentives. The primary source of this dispersion is the export subsidy structure. Neutrality of external incentives is therefore able to achieve a high proportion of the benefits of full external liberalization.

As Turkey turned away from import substitution in the early 1980s, it adopted strong export promotion measures. We estimate that Turkey's policy in the late 1980s of reducing direct export incentives yielded very substantial welfare benefits. We also show that the policy of applying export subsidies in individual sectors with high tariffs, as a way to encourage exports in a sector that may otherwise rely only on the highly protected domestic market, is particularly counterproductive. The reason is that at the multisector level the distortion that the export subsidy adds by encouraging too many resources into the protected sector dominates the reduction in the overall antiexport bias.

If Turkey harmonizes its tariff to the common external tariff of the EC, there will be only small welfare changes. Whether these changes result in gains or losses will depend on how "harmonization" is done, because the EC and Turkey have different interpretations of what such a harmonization would mean. The welfare changes will be losses if the interpretation of the EC is followed, or gains if the interpretation of Turkey is followed. Harmonization to EC tariffs will require Turkish tariffs to be lowered from already low levels in the presence of export subsidies almost as large as the existing average effective tariff rate.

Beyond small reductions in the tariffs, the export subsidies become the dominant distortion to the trade regime, and the economy becomes too export oriented. Harmonization to the EC tariff structure can be a welfare-enhancing policy, however, if accompanied by a policy of removing or reducing export subsidies.

We exploit the ability of a "simulation laboratory" to control for revenue effects by adopting an explicit "replacement tax," that is, a tax that enables government revenue to remain constant. We allow the value added tax (VAT) or a lump-sum tax to serve as replacement taxes for any changes in revenue. Given the structure of our model for Turkey (the model has no untaxed goods) and the range of replacement taxes, we find that the VAT produces results extremely close to a lump-sum replacement tax. In other words, the VAT has a relatively small marginal excess burden in this model.

Section I outlines the model, including the procedures used to empirically estimate the model to the Turkish economy using 1985 input-output data and 1989 protection data. Section II reports the results of the policy simulations. Finally, section III draws conclusions for policy. Appendix A presents the equations of the model, and appendix B subjects the conclusions to systematic sensitivity analysis.

I. A Model for a Small Open Economy

Our small open economy (SOE) model is designed for trade policy analysis with a large number of sectors. The model is a generic, static general equilibrium model of a single economy along the lines of de Melo and Tarr (1992: ch. 3). The equations of the model are in appendix A. A description of the data set, the elasticities used, and more general features of the model may be found in Harrison, Rutherford, and Tarr (1992).

The General Structure of the Model

Goods are produced using labor, capital, and intermediate inputs. In export sectors a composite output is produced that distinguishes between goods destined for domestic and for export markets. This tradeoff is characterized by a constant elasticity of transformation frontier. Production is characterized by constant returns to scale. Producers behave competitively, selecting output levels such that marginal cost equals the given market price. Although the model allows increasing or decreasing returns to scale and imperfect competition, these features are not utilized here.

Final demand by private households arises from nested constant elasticity of substitution utility functions. At the top level, different types of goods enter in a constant elasticity aggregate. All income elasticities are unity. At the next lower level, composite imported goods trade off with corresponding domestic products, and there are possibly different elasticities of substitution by commodity. Imports from different sources substitute for one another at a lower nest in utility to form a composite import good for each sector. To capture the effects of geographically discriminatory protection policies, we allow imports and exports to bear different tariffs or subsidies, depending on their source or destination. This feature allows us to study policies such as harmonization or accession to a free trade area, albeit without any terms of trade effects.

Given the level of aggregation in the model, the data contradict the homogeneous product model assumption because they reveal that there are imports, exports, and domestic production in most sectors. Although at a more disaggregated level we would like fewer sectors with both imports and exports in the same sector, our assumption of product differentiation between imports and domestic production (the "Armington" assumption) as well as between exports and domestic production will explain these data.

Government expenditures and investment demand are exogenous. Government expenditures are funded by net tax revenues. There are three components of government income in addition to import tariffs and export subsidies: VATS on factor inputs to production, ad valorem production subsidies or excise taxes on production output, and lump-sum taxes on domestic consumers. In a counterfactual scenario one or more of the tax instruments adjusts endogenously to balance government (net) tax revenues with expenditures. This equal-yield constraint is accommodated through an endogenous proportional adjustment of VAT rates or lump-sum transfers. Thus the welfare effects of changes in trade policy explicitly incorporate the appropriate marginal excess burden of raising government revenue from other sources. Walras's law is satisfied because private consumption equals the income from primary factors plus transfers to consumers by the government (from taxes and import and export quota rents), and public consumption is balanced with the value of public endowments and tax revenue net of transfers.

World market import and export prices are given, that is, import supplies and export demand are infinitely elastic. This implies that the model affects a simple closure with respect to foreign trade so that the economy experiences no endogenous changes in the terms of trade. The current account balances the value of exports and imports, taking into account exogenously specified capital inflows.

There is only one private household in the model. Dixit and Norman (1980: 78–80; 1986) have shown, however, that providing there are aggregate (real) income gains from trade liberalization and accepting some weak conditions (that hold in our model), it is possible to effect Pareto-efficient reforms for multiple households by taxing commodities.[1] The SOE model is generated with the GAMS software developed by Brooke, Kendrick, and Meeraus (1988); it is solved with the MPS/GE software developed by Rutherford (1989).

1. Dixit and Norman (1986) show that if the government imposes commodity and factor taxes that restore autarchy prices for all consumer goods and factors of production (and therefore leave all consumers no worse off), but does so in a situation where firms face the undistorted prices, then the government will have positive revenues (more precisely, positive accumulation of commodities) in a free-trade equilibrium.

The Turkish SOE *Model*

We employed the 1985 Turkish input-output table distinguishing 64 production sectors. We aggregated the 64 sectors to 40 sectors by individually adding or aggregating each of the smallest 24 sectors into the sectors closest to them. The 24 sectors account for only 5.1 percent of the value added to the economy in 1985. Table 1 displays the names of the 40 sectors. Given that one of the trade policy options that we sought to evaluate was the neutrality of external incentives, we were anxious not to bias results by aggregating the model excessively. Aggregating further (at least according to the criteria of value added) would have biased the model toward showing smaller welfare costs from disperse incentives because benchmark export subsidies would be less disperse in the benchmark equilibrium solely as an artifact of the process of aggregation. An alternative to employing a disaggregated model, which would reduce aggregation bias, is to use an explicit decision-theoretic metric to select sectors to be aggregated, an approach advocated by Harrison and Manning (1987). This approach aggregates sectors having similar levels of protection and export subsidies. Given that the current state of modeling technology does not constrain us to aggregate significantly, we elected not to do so.

The column headings in table 1 are the policy instruments in the Turkish model. Domestic distortions consist of the VAT and production subsidies. The VAT rates listed in table 1 vary a great deal across sectors. One reason is that there is some slight statutory difference in the rates. More important, however, is that the rates are derived from observed collections in 1985, the year the VAT was barely introduced. There were a great many administrative difficulties in collection procedures, yielding different observed collection rates. Foreign trade distortions consist of import tariffs and export subsidies. The revenue instruments are tariffs and the VAT. There are no import quotas or voluntary export restraints (VERs) in the Turkey model, reflecting their virtual absence from the economy in 1989, the benchmark year for the tax and trade policies.

Turkish export subsidies consist of indirect measures (such as duty drawback and the waiver of corporate income tax and VAT obligations) and direct budgetary transfers for exports of eligible products. Using benchmark import and export shares as weights, the average import tariff in the model is 8.1 percent and the average export subsidy is 7.4 percent. There is considerable dispersion in these rates across sectors, and this dispersion turns out to be important for our welfare evaluation of the distortionary effects of tariffs and subsidies.

The structure of the export subsidy rates across sectors is adapted from Milanovic (1986, table VII.4). As explained in Harrison, Rutherford, and Tarr (1992), we regard the rates in table 1 as appropriate because they are somewhat low if one accounts for indirect export subsidies available through the tax code without sectoral discrimination and high only if direct budgetary subsidies are considered. We also performed simulations with larger export subsidy rates that reflect the earlier years. Regarding tariff dispersion, nine sectors account for 79

Table 1. *Sectors and Policies in the Turkish Model*

Production sector	*Tariff* 1985	*Tariff* 1989	*Export subsidy*	VAT	*Production subsidy*
Agriculture	4.1	6.0	0.0	0.9	4.2
Air transport	n.a.	n.a.	n.a.	2.3	0.0
Alcoholic beverages	22.0	72.3	8.2	4.7	0.0
Animal husbandry	15.6	6.0	0.0	0.9	0.0
Building construction	n.a.	n.a.	n.a.	16.5	0.0
Cement	3.9	2.6	18.0	7.5	0.0
Coal mining	0.7	0.7	0.0	7.8	3.4
Communication	2.5	6.3	2.8	2.0	0.0
Electrical machinery	35.3	11.0	29.7	9.4	0.0
Electricity	n.a.	n.a.	n.a.	3.6	2.0
Fabricated metal products	46.4	10.0	69.7	12.8	0.0
Fertilizers	1.3	2.5	15.7	2.5	0.9
Financial institutions and insurance	n.a.	n.a.	n.a.	9.7	0.0
Fisheries	23.5	34.9	0.0	0.3	0.0
Forestry	20.5	3.9	0.0	1.1	0.0
Gas manufacture and waterworks	n.a.	n.a.	n.a.	3.4	0.0
Glass and glass products	63.0	31.8	16.9	5.2	0.0
Iron and steel	16.3	4.6	21.4	20.1	0.0
Machinery (except electrical)	20.2	10.5	9.6	6.0	0.6
Manufacture of other food products	38.7	30.1	8.2	15.0	0.0
Meat processing	13.7	4.2	8.2	1.8	0.0
Motor vehicles and equipment	24.6	20.1	15.1	25.8	0.0
Other chemical products	19.8	15.7	15.7	11.4	2.4
Other construction	n.a.	n.a.	n.a.	4.5	0.0
Other land transport	n.a.	n.a.	n.a.	3.6	0.8
Other nonmetallic mineral production	27.1	32.5	0.0	9.5	0.0
Ownership of dwellings	n.a.	n.a.	n.a.	2.0	0.0
Personal and professional services	0.6	0.0	0.0	18.9	0.0
Petroleum refineries	150.7	16.2	0.0	15.7	0.0
Public services	n.a.	n.a.	n.a.	0.0	0.0
Restaurants and hotels	n.a.	n.a.	n.a.	9.2	0.0
Rubber products	49.8	25.3	20.0	7.7	0.0
Sugar	16.9	32.3	8.2	8.4	9.0
Textiles	26.2	19.4	13.5	14.1	0.0
Tobacco	52.1	57.3	0.0	2.4	0.0
Vegetable and animal oils and fats	2.9	3.9	8.2	12.1	0.6
Water transport	n.a.	n.a.	n.a.	2.3	2.8
Wearing apparel	8.3	22.8	13.5	12.8	0.0
Wholesale and retail trade	n.a.	n.a.	n.a.	10.5	0.0
Wood and cork products	23.0	13.7	1.6	13.6	0.0

n.a. Not applicable because the product was not traded.

Note: Tariffs are the percentage of the value of imports, export subsidies are the percentage of the value of exports, and production subsidies are the percentage of the value of production.

percent of the total tariff revenue: electrical machinery, 7.3 percent; iron and steel, 4.2 percent; machinery (except electrical), 13.4 percent; motor vehicles and equipment, 14.1 percent; other chemical products, 20.7 percent; other nonmetallic mineral production, 5.2 percent; petroleum refineries, 6.1 percent; textiles, 4.5 percent; and tobacco, 3.5 percent.

Estimates of elasticities had to be assembled for primary factor substitution, import demand, import source, domestic demand, and the transformation of domestic supply into domestic and exported products. Virtually all of the elasticity values were selected from a literature search, as described in Harrison, Rutherford, and Tarr (1992). Elasticity estimates are subject to a margin of error. Our "remedy" for this problem, which is endemic to any large-scale model of this kind, was to undertake systematic sensitivity analyses of the major results with respect to plausible bounds on these elasticities. (Harrison and others 1993 and Harrison and Vinod 1992 review the major issues in undertaking such analyses.) Even if we were unable to specify a point estimate with any precision, our priors over the likely bounds that these elasticities could take were quite strong. To the extent that our major conclusions are robust to perturbations over these bounds, we do not see our uncertainty over the specific values of these elasticities as a weakness of the model.[2] We report the results of these sensitivity analyses, which involve 1,000 simulations for each counterfactual policy, in appendix B. They allow us to conclude that our main results are robust, at least with respect to plausible uncertainty over elasticities.

II. Policy Analysis

We present our results by examining the principal trade policy options currently facing Turkey: across-the-board liberalization, sectoral liberalization, and harmonization with the external tariff of the EC.

Across-the-Board Liberalization

Quantitative restraints have been virtually eliminated in Turkey, and tariffs have been lowered, but some export subsidies remain. Does it enhance welfare to continue to reduce tariffs across the board while leaving export subsidies in place? Conversely, as a second-best measure to reducing the tariff, would it be beneficial to increase export subsidies to offset the antiexport bias of the tariff? We first consider the theory and conventional policy advice on this question in the context of the arguments for export subsidies.

The classic argument for export subsidies rests on the theoretical foundation of the Lerner (1936) symmetry theorem, which states that a tax on imports is equivalent to a tax on exports. It follows that if a two-sector economy has an unremovable import tax in the import-competing sector, it can offset the result-

2. Any effort that could generate better bounds on these point estimates would help to generate policy conclusions that carry greater credibility, even if those conclusions will still be probabilistic in nature.

ing antiexport bias with an export subsidy to the exporting sector.[3] Based largely on this argument, Balassa (1989) argues that for most developing countries an antiexport bias will likely prevail, even after tariff reduction and devaluation, which call for export promotion measures. Krueger (1984: 528) has noted that many "export promotion" measures employed by policymakers in developing countries are nothing more than partial offsets to the overall bias in the regime toward import substitution. Large export subsidies, however, generally create problems and are thus typically not recommended. These problems may include budgetary problems for the government and various types of rent-seeking behavior, such as falsifying export documents, lobbying to seek higher subsidy rates, and exporting a product and then reimporting it to obtain the subsidy.

Nogues (1990), for example, has shown that in Argentina export subsidies lead to fraud, corruption, and rent seeking. He concludes that in Latin America the level of import protection has been so dominant that the provision of fully offsetting subsidies would introduce budgetary problems and rent-seeking behavior that would be counterproductive and clearly inferior to the first-best policy of reducing the import protection. Based on evidence such as this, Thomas, Nash, and associates (1991) have concluded that large export subsidies should not be recommended.

Export subsidies per se in the manufacturing sector are proscribed by the General Agreement on Tariffs and Trade (the GATT); those who argue for export subsidies suggest the use of export subsidies that are legal under the GATT. Thus Balassa (1989) has recommended that developing countries rebate, both to direct and to indirect exporters, the import duties and indirect taxes on exports and that they provide, as well, preferential export credit and export insurance in the absence of private insurance. These "duty drawback" schemes have the effect of automatically linking tariff and tax reform with export subsidy reform.

Welfare effects of across-the-board reductions in tariffs and export subsidies. Figure 1 displays the welfare effects of reducing tariffs and export subsidies across the board. Reductions of tariffs alone cause some welfare gains initially, but these deteriorate into a welfare loss for reductions greater than 40 percent. This welfare loss is attributable to the Lerner symmetry effect. The average tariff is only slightly above the average export subsidy, so there is only a slight antiexport bias in external incentives. When tariffs are progressively reduced in a piecemeal manner, external incentives eventually become biased toward exports.

The benefits of export subsidy reductions continue up to a 70 percent reduction and are much more substantial at about 1 percent of gross domestic product

3. Alternative theoretical justifications for export subsidies are in Itoh and Kiyono (1987) on nontraditional exports, Brander and Spencer (1985) and Eaton and Grossman (1986) on strategic policy considerations and oligopolistic industries, Krugman (1988) on positive externalities, and Romer (1989) on imports of new technologies. Because our model is a static, perfectly competitive model with no terms of trade effects, we abstract from all these arguments.

Figure 1. *Welfare Effects of Simulated Across-the-Board Trade Liberalization in Turkey*

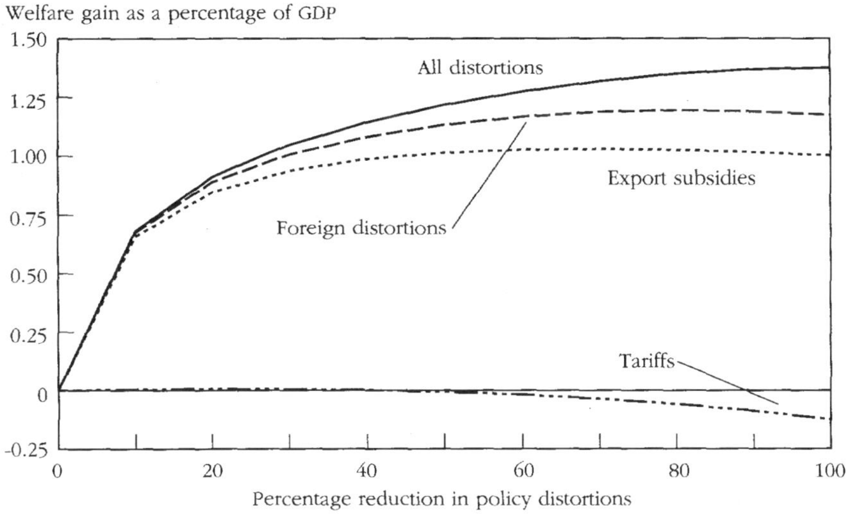

(GDP) because there is significantly greater dispersion in benchmark export subsidies. In this model the Turkish economy would gain about 1 percent of GDP from providing neutral incentives to all export sectors but less than 0.2 percent from tariff uniformity.[4] The process of taking an across-the-board reduction in export subsidies has the simultaneous effect of also reducing the dispersion in export subsidies, and it is the reduction in dispersion that is driving the result of figure 1 for export subsidy reduction.

Because of the offsetting effects of tariffs and export subsidies, reducing export subsidies and tariffs jointly leads to even greater welfare gains than just reducing export subsidies does. Similarly, because of the presence of domestic distortions, reductions in foreign distortions fail to generate welfare gains at the margin when they reach the 80 percent level. Only when all distortions are removed is the optimal policy to reduce export subsidies and tariffs jointly by 100 percent. This is the first-best policy. Removing all domestic as well as foreign distortions results in further, small enhancements of welfare.

4. Our model is ill-suited for analyzing the question of optimal commodity taxation. Because there is no labor-leisure choice in our model, and all goods are taxable, the optimal nondiscriminatory commodity tax is uniform (see Atkinson and Stiglitz 1980). Because import taxes do not tax the domestic variety of the good, however, there are 40 untaxed goods in our model when import taxes are employed; hence, there are optimal departures from uniform import taxation. Our results show that the existing pattern of import taxes in Turkey is inferior to a uniform pattern of import taxation.

Dispersion in the export subsidy regime. We performed further simulations, depicted in figure 2, to bolster our interpretation that the dispersion in the export subsidy regime is the principal cause of the gains from reducing export subsidies. We eliminated the dispersion in export subsidies and import tariffs before reducing the level of the policy. In this case the results are much more consistent with the practical rule of thumb derived from the Lerner symmetry theorem. The average benchmark tariff of 8.1 percent is slightly higher than the average export subsidy of 7.4 percent, indicating a slight import bias in this new benchmark with uniform tariffs and export subsidies. Reductions in export subsidies result in welfare losses even at the margin because the regime becomes biased further toward imports. There is a very slight welfare gain from reducing tariffs by as much as 30 percent, with the maximal gain occurring at around the 10 percent level, when import tariffs just offset export subsidies exactly. When tariffs are reduced by more than 30 percent, the welfare losses are much larger, paralleling the losses obtained from reducing export subsidies alone. The welfare effects of reducing the level of foreign distortions, given that tariffs and subsidies are both initially neutral, are small compared with a welfare gain of 1.2 percent from providing a neutral external incentive regime.

The reason that neutral external incentives yield welfare benefits almost as large as full liberalization is that Turkey starts from a trade regime that is not significantly biased toward import substitution or export promotion. Other

Figure 2. *Welfare Effects of Simulated Trade Liberalization from Neutral Initial Distortions in Turkey*

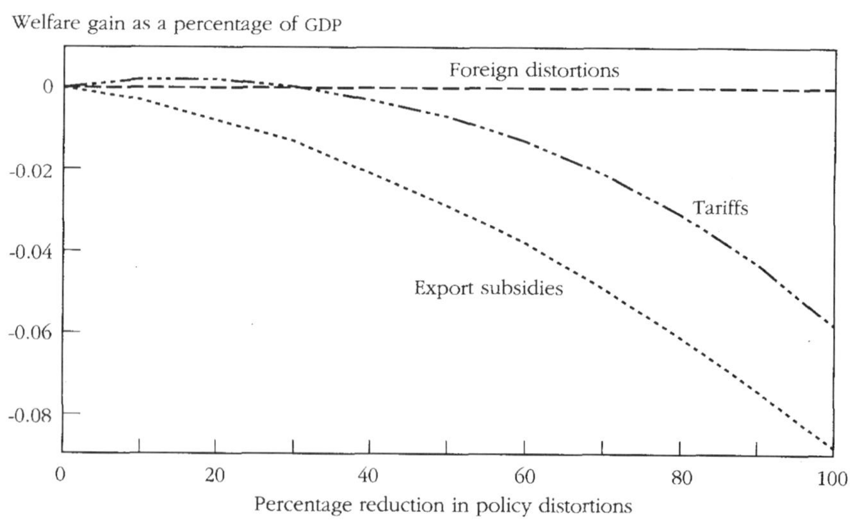

things being equal, the more the economy is protected and the greater the antiexport bias, the smaller the proportion of the welfare benefits of liberalization that neutral external incentives will achieve.

We performed some additional experiments to verify this interpretation. We benchmarked our model to the tariff rates prevailing in 1985, which were reported in table 1. Averaging 17.6 percent, these rates were about double those applying in 1989, weighted by 1985 shares of imports. Although the average 1985 tariff rate is somewhat small compared with rates of nominal protection in many developing countries, it does introduce an antiexport bias into the Turkish external regime. A piecemeal reduction in the 1985 tariff rates to the level of 1989 results in an increase in Turkish welfare of 0.07 percent of GDP, and the benefits of uniformity (of all distortions) are reduced from 99.9 to 94.1 percent of the benefits of fully removing all external and domestic distortions. These results also show that the tariff reductions that Turkey undertook in the late 1980s enhanced welfare.

If the external incentive regime were biased toward import substitution (that is, if the economywide average level of import protection exceeded the average level of export promotion), as is common in developing economies, then piecemeal lowering of import protection would improve welfare. The important lesson is that when a country has liberalized imports as much as Turkey, while at the same time maintaining significant export subsidies, further import liberalization must be balanced with further reductions in export subsidies.[5] Similarly, these results support the view that some small export subsidies are efficient if a country starts from an import regime that is significantly protected.

To the extent that export or production subsidies in Turkey are effected by a "duty drawback" on customs duties on imports or VAT, interaction effects such as we have examined will be built into any liberalization of those subsidy schemes. In other words, anything that lowers tariffs would endogenously lower export subsidies, generating these beneficial interaction effects. This may well be an unplanned advantage of using such drawback schemes.

Counterfactual simulation from higher export subsidies. The strong export promotion measures adopted by Turkey in the early 1980s have been questioned as excessive. We counterfactually scaled up all export subsidies to levels estimated to prevail in earlier years in Turkey and simulated the effects of the Turkish policy of lowering export subsidies toward the level of 1989. Doing so tilts the external incentives toward export promotion but greatly increases the dispersion in the export subsidies. We estimated that the Turkish export subsidy reduction policy of the late 1980s yielded very substantial welfare benefits.

We performed simulations with three new export subsidy rates of 2.0, 2.62, and 3.4 times the export subsidies of our original benchmark equilibrium. These new rates corresponded to export subsidies of 14.8, 19.4, and 25.2 percent, which were reported as the export subsidy rates prevailing in Turkey in 1988,

5. Similar results for the Polish economy are discussed by Tarr (1990).

1985, and 1986, respectively. As a percentage of GDP, the welfare benefits of reducing the export subsidies to the level of our original benchmark equilibrium are 3.6, 6.5, and 12.1 percent, respectively, the higher welfare benefits corresponding to reduction of the higher export subsidies. The welfare benefits of reducing export subsidies increase more than proportionately to the scalar multiple of the export subsidy because the quantity of resources distorted increases with the price distortion of the subsidy and acts multiplicatively on the price distortion in calculating the welfare costs. These estimates are rather large compared with most estimates of the welfare benefits of trade liberalization in models with constant returns to scale. This finding runs contrary to the conventional wisdom that only models with increasing returns to scale will achieve large welfare benefits from trade liberalization and is due to the fact that without specific factors in our model the elasticity of supply in the sectors receiving export subsidies is very large. Thus, the export subsidy induces a large amount of resource movement. Interestingly, the welfare effects of subsidy reduction are only slightly affected by rebenchmarking with 1985 tariff rates, reflecting the fact that the dispersion of the export subsidy is of primary importance in these results.

Distributional effects across sectors. Finally, we assessed distributional effects of across-the-board liberalization by noting which sectors are the biggest winners and losers when all foreign and domestic distortions are removed. The six sectors with the largest increase in total value added (with the absolute increase in their percentage of total value added) are air transport, 1.4; other land transport, 0.23; ownership of dwellings, 0.11; personal and professional services, 0.25; restaurants and hotels, 0.23; and wholesale and retail trade, 1.25. From table 1, none of these sectors received either export subsidies or import tariffs. Moreover, the six sectors are primarily nontraded goods, and the incentives to the nontraded goods sectors will improve after the tariffs and export subsidies are removed.

The six sectors with the largest decrease in total value added (with their absolute decrease in their percentage of total value added) are agriculture, −0.83; fabricated metal products, −0.36; iron and steel, −0.45; other chemical products, −0.18; textiles, −0.40; and wearing apparel, −0.32. Except for agriculture, these sectors lose their substantial export subsidies, which explains the decline in their shares. In agriculture, the loss of the production subsidy induces the loss of the share in value added. Because nominal export subsidies are concentrated in manufacturing industries, there has been some debate over the claim that export subsidies in Turkey have an "antiagriculture" bias. We tested this claim by examining value added in agriculture before and after the export subsidies were removed. We defined "agriculture" broadly as consisting of nine sectors in our model: agriculture, animal husbandry, fisheries, forestry, manufacture of other food products, meat processing, sugar, tobacco, and vegetable and animal oils and fats. Defining agriculture as solely the sector "agriculture" in table 1 would not change the following conclusions. Value added in the broadly defined agricultural sector increases by 1.2 percent after all export subsidies were completely removed. Alternatively, if both export subsidies and import tariffs are completely removed, value added in agriculture declines by 0.7 percent.

Sectoral Liberalization

Krueger (1984, p. 528) has noted that in some developing countries firms have been required or induced to export in return for privileges accorded in the domestic market. Presumably the argument is that the sector is not motivated to export without the export subsidy or requirement because the sector receives a relatively high price on the domestic market as a result of the import protection.

On the contrary, however, an export subsidy will not offset the effect of a high tariff. Rather it will exacerbate the problem of misallocating too many resources to the protected sector. We investigated the impact on the Turkish economy of removing or reducing tariffs or export subsidies, or both, from individual sectors. Given piecemeal policy change in a particular sector, the interaction with the VAT in the sector will become important. In particular, if a sector enjoys a high tariff and high export subsidy, excessive resource allocation to the sector will be reduced by a high VAT.

Table 2 summarizes the welfare effects of piecemeal reform in individual sectors. The results show the consequences of removing existing export subsidies and import tariffs one sector at a time, leaving protection in all other sectors at benchmark levels. The column titled "tariff and export subsidy" simultaneously removes both tariffs and export subsidies in the sector. The first three columns represent total removal of the policy, whereas the last two columns, labeled "marginal reform," report results for scenarios in which sectoral tariffs and export subsidies are reduced by 10 percent. To provide a consistent basis for comparison, we multiplied the welfare effect of these marginal 10 percent reductions by 10 to indicate the welfare consequences of complete reform that would be "predicted" by a marginal analysis. We do not report the "tariff and export subsidy" column for the marginal changes because the results are roughly additive in the two components that are displayed.

The first result on which we focus is the welfare effects of export subsidy and tariff reduction in those sectors for which both the export subsidies are greater than 15 percent and tariffs are above average. From table 1, there are six sectors in this group: electrical machinery, fabricated metal products, glass and glass products, motor vehicles and equipment, other chemical products, and rubber products. For a marginal reduction in export subsidies, there is a welfare gain in all sectors except motor vehicles. Similarly, for a marginal reduction in tariffs, there is a welfare gain in all sectors except electrical machinery. Motor vehicles experienced the highest VAT rate in the economy at 25.8 percent, which means that export subsidies offset the impact of too little resources in motor vehicles as

Table 2. *Welfare Effects of Simulated Piecemeal Sectoral Reform in Turkey*

	Complete removal of subsidy or tariff			*Marginal reform*[a]	
Production sector	*Export subsidy*	*Tariff*	*Tariff and export subsidy*	*Export subsidy*	*Tariff*
Agriculture	0.000000	−0.000840	−0.000840	0.000000	0.000835
Alcoholic beverages	−0.001730	0.010399	0.008353	−0.000230	0.015240
Animal husbandry	0.000000	−0.001000	−0.001000	0.000000	−0.000310
Cement	0.000930	−0.000010	0.000907	0.005899	0.000237
Coal mining	0.000000	−0.002840	−0.002840	0.000000	−0.002840
Communication	−0.001410	−0.000960	−0.002410	−0.001310	−0.000410
Electrical machinery	0.024585	−0.011380	0.013431	0.101528	−0.003870
Fabricated metal products	0.769165	0.008477	0.767100	5.693816	0.010337
Fertilizers	0.002663	−0.001050	0.001471	0.013099	−0.000910
Fisheries	0.000000	0.000166	0.000166	0.000014	0.000992
Forestry	0.000000	−0.000590	−0.000590	0.000000	−0.000340
Glass and glass products	0.000280	0.000427	0.000579	0.010503	0.001970
Iron and steel	0.191486	−0.096300	0.131224	0.617817	−0.089550
Machinery (except electrical)	−0.010280	−0.006420	−0.015410	0.005135	0.001286
Manufacture of other food products	−0.018640	0.002069	−0.016130	−0.009620	0.005472
Meat processing	−0.001960	−0.000340	−0.002300	0.000560	−0.000220
Motor vehicles and equipment	−0.012730	−0.017150	−0.030660	−0.007540	0.015335
Other chemical products	0.003322	−0.028500	−0.026600	0.028970	0.013773
Other nonmetallic mineral production	0.000000	−0.000720	−0.000720	0.000000	0.003740
Petroleum refineries	0.000000	0.000403	0.000403	0.000000	0.003821
Rubber products	0.000104	0.000380	0.000209	0.006920	0.002601
Sugar	0.001557	0.000057	0.001614	0.003080	0.000157
Textiles	−0.070480	−0.008660	−0.079150	0.006692	0.009843
Tobacco	0.000000	0.029122	0.029122	0.000000	0.052881
Vegetable and animal oils and fats	−0.007360	−0.002240	−0.009760	0.002079	−0.001440
Wearing apparel	−0.078830	−0.004260	−0.087360	−0.013090	0.010655
Wood and cork products	−0.002380	−0.005380	−0.007760	−0.002310	−0.000610

Note: The values in the table are the changes in welfare (using the equivalent variation measure) as a percentage of GDP.

a. Tariffs and export subsidies are initially reduced by 10 percent; the results are multiplied by 10 to indicate the welfare consequences of a complete reform that would be predicted by using a marginal analysis.

Source: Authors' estimations.

a result of the VAT. In electrical machinery, there is also an above-average VAT rate; moreover, the tariff rate, which is close to the average rate in the benchmark, is also offsetting the VAT at the margin. Because welfare increases from export subsidy reduction, these results support the view that using high export subsidies in sectors with above-average tariffs is counterproductive.

Theory suggests that the distortion costs of a tariff or subsidy increase more than proportionally with the size of the tariff or subsidy because the quantity of resources misallocated also increases and acts multiplicatively on the tariff or subsidy in calculating the value of the distortion costs. Thus the greater the export subsidy, the greater the benefits of export subsidy reduction at the margin. The concentration of high export subsidies in a few sectors in Turkey is likely to be a problem for this reason. Examining the three cases of export subsidies above 20 percent—electrical machinery, fabricated metal products, and iron and steel—there are indeed substantial benefits from reducing the export subsidy at the margin, even though for iron and steel the tariff rate is below average. The same general policy conclusion also holds for the seven sectors with tariffs greater than 30 percent.

In many sectors there are welfare losses from reductions in tariffs or export subsidies, or both, either in terms of marginal or complete liberalization. In addition, in several sectors marginal liberalization can be beneficial in welfare terms and yet complete liberalization can be harmful.[6] These results are explained by the fact that after some point further reduction of tariffs or export subsidies results in a bias in incentives against the sector, given that tariffs and export subsidies remain in place in the rest of the economy.

Harmonization with the EC

Turkey has long aspired to becoming a member of the EC. As part of the negotiations with the EC on this matter, Turkey has adopted a policy of harmonizing its tariff structure with the Common External Tariff (CET) of the EC. There has been some dispute, however, as to exactly what harmonization would mean.

Turkey's "effective (nominal) tariff" consists of a statutory customs duty and a series of import surcharges, such as stamp taxes and wharf charges. The customs duty varies across sectors, but the surcharges are generally uniform. We refer to the sum of the customs duty and the surcharges as the "total duty" to be applied to dutiable imports.

Turkey exempts a significant portion of imports from duties, however, through a number of mechanisms including duty drawbacks and the investment code. The result of these exemptions is that the share of imports that is dutiable varies greatly across sectors. Hence the effective (nominal) tariff is the product of the total duty and the share of imports that is dutiable in each sector. This effective duty is the best measure of the nominal protection in each sector.

These distinctions become crucial in attempting to implement a political commitment to "harmonize the tariff structure." Turkey initially interpreted harmonization to mean that it would levy a zero customs duty and reduced import

6. With respect to export subsidies, examples (in table 2) include machinery (except electrical), meat processing, textiles, and vegetable and animal oils and fats. With respect to tariffs, examples include machinery (except electrical), motor vehicles and equipment, other nonmetallic mineral production, textiles, and motor vehicles and equipment.

surcharges on imports from the EC. According to this interpretation of harmonization, the customs duty on non-EC imports would be set equal to the CET of the EC, and all import surcharges on non-EC imports would remain unchanged. The net effect of this interpretation, as far as the EC was concerned, was that the EC would face positive tariffs on exports to Turkey. Instead, the EC may have expected "harmonization" to mean that goods from the EC would be imported duty-free into Turkey.

After negotiation with the EC, Turkey has considered revising the harmonization policy to accord better with the initial expectations of the EC. According to this view all surcharges would be incorporated into the customs duty, and only this single total tariff would apply to imports. The total tariff on EC imports would be zero and would be equal to the CET on non-EC imports.

Assuming the continued use in Turkey of exemptions from import duties, the effective (nominal) tariff on non-EC imports would be lower than the CET that the EC itself applies on those imports. That is, after harmonization Turkey would be applying lower average tariffs than the EC does.

Given the political importance of harmonization with the EC, we considered the effects of each interpretation. With either interpretation of the CET and with VAT as the replacement tax, the change in welfare from CET harmonization is small. Under Turkey's interpretation of the CET, Turkey's welfare would increase by 0.007 percent of GDP. Under the EC's interpretation of the CET, Turkey's welfare would be reduced by 0.024 percent of GDP.

CET harmonization reduces Turkey's average tariff. For small reductions in the tariff, such as those implied by the Turkish version of harmonization, there is a slight gain in welfare. As explained above, further uncoordinated reductions in the tariff level from the already low level eventually result in welfare losses. Thus, although the difference is slight, the EC version of harmonization results in a loss simply because the tariff reduction is larger.

Alternatively, by combining CET harmonization with removal of export subsidies Turkey can expect to obtain significant welfare gains from EC tariff harmonization. This result follows from our analysis of the joint effects of removing tariffs and export subsidies in figure 2, along with our interpretation of CET harmonization as a de facto across-the-board reduction in tariffs. Irrespective of the final policy package, the main policy lesson here is that the welfare effects of quibbling over the proper interpretation of CET harmonization are in the second order of smalls.

III. Conclusions

The principal trade liberalization exercise currently being considered by Turkey is harmonization to the common external tariff of the EC. We find that harmonization would have little beneficial effect on welfare compared with several other options. It is important to accompany a harmonization policy with export subsidy reduction to achieve significant benefits.

The most important policy conclusion from our analysis concerns the fragility of first-best rules of thumb as to the welfare benefits of piecemeal trade policy reforms for countries that have reduced trade barriers as much as Turkey has but that have retained export subsidies. The results of trade policy reforms then depend crucially on both the level and the dispersion of import tariffs and especially of export subsidies. In other words, it is not the case that any partial movement toward the first-best trade policy for Turkey will result in some fraction of the welfare gains from that first-best package. Of course this is a restatement of well-known second-best results. What is new, however, is an attempt to assess the quantitative significance of these effects for Turkey. In doing so we are able to gain some insights into which particular distortions have more or less severe second-best effects.

APPENDIX A. AN ALGEBRAIC FORMULATION OF THE MODEL

The model is formulated as a system of nonlinear equations corresponding to the three classes of equilibrium conditions associated with an Arrow-Debreu general equilibrium: price-cost relations for producers, supply-demand balance for commodity and factor markets (including balance of payments), and income-expenditure balance for domestic consumers and government. The model is generated using the GAMS programming language. It is solved using the software of Rutherford (1989), which employs the modified Newton (SLCP) algorithm created by Mathiesen (1985). A central set of variables (prices, activity levels, and income levels) characterizes the economic equilibrium. All important notation is summarized in table A-1.

Technology, Preferences, and Market Clearance Conditions

Domestic production is an aggregate of domestic and exported varieties of goods with a constant elasticity of transformation:

$$\text{(A-1)} \qquad Y_i = \phi_i(D_i, X_i) = (\delta_{Di}\, D_i^{\,(\epsilon_i - 1)/\epsilon_i} + \delta_{Xi}\, X_i^{\,(\epsilon_i - 1)/\epsilon_i})^{\,\epsilon_i/(\epsilon_i - 1)}.$$

This relation can be interpreted as implying differences in the technical processes associated with production for domestic and export markets. The elasticity of transformation defined by ϵ_i will be lower for goods that are highly differentiated and higher for goods that are relatively homogeneous. The specification of this elasticity may be influenced by the intended time frame of the analysis. In the short run it is more difficult to transform plants between domestic and export-oriented products.

Imports from different trading partners trade off with domestic varieties in intermediate demand, investment demand, and final demand. For simplicity (and because of data limitations) we assume that the import composition and import-domestic substitution possibilities in investment, intermediate, and final demand are identical. Under these conditions we can represent inputs as though they were composed of a single import-domestic aggregate for each commodity.

Table A-1. *Notation Used in the SOE Model*

Variable or parameter	*Definition*
	MA Variables
C_i	Private consumer demand for good i
D_i	Domestic sales of good i
f_{ki}	Variable input of primary k in sector i
ff_{ki}	Fixed input of primary k in sector i
K_i	Capital inputs to sector i
L_i	Labor inputs to sector i
M_i	Composite import of good i
m_{ir}	Import of good i from region r
p_i	Price of domestic produced good i
p_i^X	Export price of good i (exogenous)
p_{ir}^M	Import price of good i from region r(exogenous)
S_i	Armington aggregate of domestic supply and imports
V_i	Value added function for variable factors
W	Welfare index for the representative domestic consumer
w_k	Factor prices k
X_i	Export of good i
x_{ki}	Intermediate inputs of good k in sector i
Y_i	Domestic production of good i
π_i	Price of domestic import good i composite
τ_T	Replacement tax multiplier on lump-sum transfers
τ_v	Replacement tax multiplier for factor taxes
τ_t	Replacement tax multipliers for tariffs
Parameters	
a_{ij}	Intermediate input requirements, good i in sector j
B	Current account balance (net capital inflows)
E_k	Endowment of factor k
F_k	Primary factor supplies
G_i	Government demand for good i from region
I_i	Final demand for output of sector i for investment purposes
s_i	Elasticity of substitution in consumption in sector i between imports from different regions
s_i^P	Rate of production subsidy for good i
s_i^X	Export subsidy rate for good i
T	Lump-sum tax on consumers
t_{ir}	Import tariff rate on commodity i from region r
ν_i	Tax rate on factor inputs to sector i
ϵ_i	Elasticity of transformation between domestic production and exports in sector i
σ_i	Elasticity of substitution between domestic consumption and aggregate imports in sector i

The aggregation of domestic and imported varieties is characterized by a nested constant-elasticity function of domestic and imported goods:

$$\text{(A-2)} \qquad S_i \equiv \psi_i(D_i, M_i) = (\alpha_{Di}^{1/\sigma_i} D_i^{(\sigma_i-1)/\sigma_i} + \alpha_{Mi}^{1/\sigma_i} M_i^{(\sigma_i-1)/\sigma_i})^{\sigma_i/(\sigma_i-1)}$$

where M_i represents a composite import from two or more regions, r:

$$M_i \equiv \left(\sum_r \beta_{ir} m_{ir}^{(s_i-1)/s_i}\right)^{s_i/(s_i-1)}.$$

The market clearance condition for domestic supply balances output from the Armington aggregation function with intermediate, investment, and final demand. This condition is

(A-3)
$$S_i = \sum_j a_{ij} Y_j + G_i + I_i + C_i$$

in which Y_j is the activity level of sector j; a_{ij} is the input requirements of good i in sector j; and G_i, I_i, and C_i are components of final demand associated with government, investment, and final consumption.

Variable inputs to production include primary factors as well as intermediate inputs of commodities. These are combined in a linearly homogeneous nested Leontief-CES form:

(A-4)
$$Y_i = \min\left[\frac{x_{1i}}{a_{1i}}, \frac{x_{2i}}{a_{2i}}, \ldots, \frac{x_{ni}}{a_{ni}}, \frac{V_i(f_i) + \sum_k f_{ki}^F}{a_{VA}}\right]$$

where

$$V_i(f_i) = \left(\sum_k \delta_{ki} f_{ki}^{(\sigma_i - 1)/\sigma}\right)^{\sigma/\sigma - 1}.$$

In this equation x_{ki} represents intermediate inputs of good k in sector i, f_{ki} is the variable input of primary factor k in sector i, $V_i(\ )$ represents the value-added function for variable factors, f_i represents primary factor inputs to variable cost in sector i, and f_{ki}^F represents the input of factor k to the formation of fixed costs in sector i (taken as zero in the present model).

Domestic welfare is defined by consumption levels of market goods:

(A-5)
$$W = U(C_1, \ldots, C_n).$$

The current account (B) is balanced at international prices (p_i^X and p_i^M), taking into account exogenous capital flows:

(A-6)
$$\sum_i p_i^X X_i + B = \sum_{ir} p_{ir}^M m_{ir}.$$

The prices that appear in this equation are exogenous parameters, the international prices of imports and exports. This constraint has an associated variable, which is the "real exchange rate." The model, however, contains no monetary instruments and determines only relative prices.

Factor markets always clear with flexible prices:

(A-7)
$$\sum_i f_{ki} + f_{ki}^F = F_k.$$

Income-Expenditure Balance

Consumer income includes primary factor earnings plus foreign capital inflows less transfers. Final demand is modeled by budget-constrained utility maximization by a representative agent. The budget constraint is:

$$\sum_i \pi_i C_i = \sum_k w_k E_k + B - \tau_T T. \tag{A-8}$$

In this equation w_k represents the market price of primary factor k, B represents the foreign exchange balance, and $\tau_T T$ represents the level of lump-sum transfer.

Unlike private households, government demands are held constant in all simulations. The government budget constraint is accommodated through endogenous scaling of one of the three government tax instruments so that revenue balances with expenditure. Government income consists of five components: (1) lump-sum transfers from households, T; plus (2) import tariffs, t_{ij}; plus (3) VATS on factor inputs to production, v_i; less (4) production subsidies, s_i^P; less (5) export subsidies, s_i^X. The government budget is

$$\begin{aligned} \sum_i \pi_i G_i = {} & \tau_t T + \tau_t \sum_{ir} p_{ir}^M t_{ir} m_{ir} \\ & + \tau_v \sum_{ik} v_i w_k f_{ki} \\ & - \sum_i s_i^P (p_i D_i + p_i^X X_i) \\ & - \sum_i s_i^X p_i^X X_i. \end{aligned} \tag{A-9}$$

In the government budget equation, parameters that endogenously adjust to balance income and expenditure are τ_T for lump-sum transfers, τ_t for tariffs, and τ_v for VATS. In any given equilibrium only one of these parameters departs from the default value of unity.

Price-Cost Balance

Producers price at marginal cost. In production the marginal cost of supply for sector i (c_i) is defined by

$$c_i Y_i = \sum_j \pi_j x_{ji} + (1 + \tau_v v_i) \sum_k w_k f_{ki}. \tag{A-10}$$

With constant-returns-to-scale technology and no barriers to entry, excess profits go to zero. Producers then equate marginal cost with market price gross of subsidy, providing the following zero-profit condition:

$$(1 + s_i^P)(p_i D_i + p_i^X X_i) + p_i^X X_i s_i^X = c_i Y_i. \tag{A-11}$$

In this equation the first term represents the value of output gross of production subsidy, and the second term captures the effect of the export subsidy.

The import aggregation always equates price with marginal cost. This means that the value of domestic supply equals the cost of domestic inputs plus imports gross of tariffs and rents:

(A-12) $$\pi_i S_i = p_i D_i + \sum_r (1 + \tau_t t_{ir}) p_{ij}^M m_{ir}.$$

Appendix B. Sensitivity Analysis

How robust are the major policy conclusions to the many assumptions of our numerical model? This question is answered partially by considering a systematic sensitivity analysis of the main results with respect to the elasticities in the model. We appreciate that there are many other assumptions that remain fixed as we just vary elasticities, but we regard those extensions as beyond the scope of this study. For example, an important question is how our results might change as we examine alternative market structure assumptions or move from a static framework to a growth setting. We plan to examine these extensions using the SOE model, but we do not believe that they can be treated briefly enough to be included here.

The sensitivity analysis uses the procedures developed by Harrison and Vinod (1992). Essentially these procedures amount to a Monte Carlo simulation exercise, in which a wide range of elasticities are independently and simultaneously perturbed from their benchmark values. These perturbations follow prescribed distributions, such as a *t*-distribution with a specified standard deviation and degrees of freedom, or a uniform distribution over a specified range. The exact distributional assumptions used are documented in Harrison, Rutherford, and Tarr (1992). The MPSS software used to implement the Monte Carlo simulations is documented in Harrison (1990).

For each Monte Carlo run, we solve the counterfactual policy with the selected set of elasticities. This process is repeated until we arrive at the desired sample size, in our case 1,000. The results are then tabulated as a distribution, with equal weight being given (by construction) to each Monte Carlo run. The upshot is a probability distribution defined over the endogenous variables of interest. In our case we focus solely on the welfare effects of each policy.

The policies that we examine and the results of the sensitivity analysis are reported in table B-1. The "sample size" column refers to the number of Monte Carlo runs that were actually completed. In each case we have at least 1,000 runs, which should be enough to obtain a reliable picture of the distribution of results. The "point estimate" column shows the welfare effect of the policy when all elasticities are set equal to their benchmark, or point estimate (PE), values. These are the results reported and discussed in the results section of the text. The point estimate is the change in welfare caused by the policy as a percentage of GDP.

Table B-1. *Descriptions of the Policy Simulations and Results of the Sensitivity Analysis for Turkey*

Simulation	Sample size	Change in welfare (percentage of GDP)[a]: Point estimate	Mean	Median	Standard deviation
1. Set tariffs equal to a uniform value of 8.1 percent for all sectors.	1,000	0.161	0.210	0.210	0.030
2. Set export subsidies equal to a uniform value of 7.4 percent for all sectors.	1,000	1.073	0.841	0.866	0.114
3. Set all foreign trade distortions (tariffs and export subsidies) equal to their average benchmark values.	2,662	1.173	1.005	1.034	0.118
4. Set all domestic and foreign distortions equal to their average benchmark value.	1,041	1.373	1.301	1.307	0.139
5. Liberalize tariffs by setting them to zero across the board.	1,000	−0.125	−0.218	−0.211	0.108
6. Liberalize export subsidies by setting them to zero across the board.	1,000	1.004	0.844	0.875	0.117
7. Liberalize export subsidies by 20 percent across the board.	1,000	0.848	0.751	0.782	0.129
8. Liberalize foreign trade distortions by setting them to zero across the board.	1,000	1.174	1.003	1.030	0.122
9. Liberalize all distortions by setting them to zero: the "first-best" policy.	1,000	1.374	1.299	1.308	0.144
10. Set tariffs and export subsidies to their uniform values and then liberalize tariffs.	1,000	−0.058	−0.167	−0.172	0.033
11. Set tariffs and export subsidies to their uniform values and then liberalize export subsidies.	2,000	−0.088	−0.050	−0.050	0.020
12. Liberalize the VAT by setting it to zero across the board.	1,000	−0.342	−0.097	−0.090	0.085

Note: All simulations (the last six columns of the table) use a lump-sum tax replacement.
a. Using the equivalent variation measure.
b. Probability that the welfare increased under the counterfactual policy.
c. Probability that the welfare effect under the counterfactual policy, using perturbed elasticities, is greater than or equal to the welfare effect obtained under the counterfactual policy point estimate.

The remaining columns report the results of the sensitivity analysis proper. The mean, median, and standard deviation are given to provide simple indicators of the location and dispersion of the distribution of welfare results. The skewness and kurtosis statistics that are necessary to gain a more complete impression of the distribution are not reported in the table. In all cases we find that there is indeed significant skewness in the distribution, but insignificant kurtosis. The skewness in these distributions manifests itself in a systematic

		Symmetric confidence interval around the median			
		50 percent		75 percent	
Prob. ≥ 0[b]	Prob. ≥ PE[c]	Lower bound	Upper bound	Lower bound	Upper bound
1.000	0.97	0.190	0.230	0.180	0.250
1.000	0.00	0.710	0.930	0.650	0.960
1.000	0.03	0.870	1.090	0.800	1.120
1.000	0.33	1.200	1.400	1.110	1.460
0.010	0.22	−0.310	−0.140	−0.360	−0.100
1.000	0.03	0.700	0.930	0.650	0.960
1.000	0.38	0.570	0.850	0.520	0.870
1.000	0.04	0.860	1.090	0.800	1.120
1.000	0.34	1.180	1.400	1.100	1.460
0.000	0.00	−0.190	−0.130	−0.200	−0.120
0.001	0.98	−0.066	−0.034	−0.074	−0.025
0.135	1.00	−0.170	−0.020	−0.210	0.000

difference between the mean and median reported. Thus comparison of these two statistics indicates the direction of the skewness.

Why do we get such significant skewness in the distributions? There are two general reasons why this might occur: induced skewness as a result of our explicit distributional assumptions, and intrinsic skewness in the (implicit) function linking the set of elasticities and welfare. Each can be evaluated.

The explicit assumptions made in our sensitivity analysis result in a large number of skewed distributions for production activities that have benchmark Leontief technologies. The activities that fall into this category combine intermediate inputs and value added. In this case we allow perturbations of 0.25, 0.5, 0.75, and 1.0, as well as the benchmark value of zero. To see if this is the source of the skewness, we can remove these perturbations for these activities and rerun the sensitivity analysis to see if the skewness disappears. We have done this for the uniformity policy simulation (making all export subsidies uniform) and find that it does not account for the skewness.

The other possible reason for skewed results is more subtle than the presence of skewed distributional assumptions but could well be more important. It has to do with the "asymmetry" of the implicit function that takes a given set of elasticities and generates the welfare effect. It is perfectly possible that equi-sized perturbations of a given elasticity can have different absolute effects on welfare.[7] We can evaluate this source of skewness with respect to blocks of elasticities of the same type by setting those elasticities equal to their PE value. We do this for the simulation of uniformity of policy and with respect to each elasticity block. No single block can account for the skewness. We conclude that there is no single block of elasticities that is causing this skewness.

The "probability" columns indicate the qualitative policy results. The "welfare increased" column shows the probability from the empirical distribution that welfare increased in the counterfactual policy. This gives a measure of the confidence that we have the sign right when we look at the point estimate welfare effect, the mean, or the median. Similarly, the next column shows the probability that a welfare effect greater than or equal to the PE welfare effect was obtained. If the PE result perfectly represents the location of the distribution of results, this value should be around one-half; this would be the case if the PE result exactly equaled the reported median result. A value lower (higher) than one-half indicates that the distribution generally lies below (above) the PE result.

Finally, to gain a better sense of the confidence to be attached to the PE or mean result, we report lower and upper bounds from 50 and 75 percent symmetric confidence intervals around the median result. These confidence intervals show the smallest and largest values that lie within 50 or 75 percent of the distribution centered on the median. Thus a 50 percent confidence interval between 1.1 and 2.3 can be interpreted to mean that 50 percent of the Monte Carlo runs produced welfare results between these values.

Six observations can be made from these sensitivity analyses regarding our policy conclusions.

7. For example, our sensitivity analysis allows equal increases and decreases in the elasticity of substitution between domestically produced and imported goods in our Armington aggregate. However, it is plausible that increasing this elasticity from 2 to 3 has very little impact on welfare, whereas reducing it from 2 to 1 has a large impact. The source of our priors on this is no more than visual and casual inspection of isoquants with the relevant elasticities of substitution: once the elasticity gets above 2 it stays pretty flat, but dropping it down to 1 adds significant curvature.

First, the welfare gains from the first-best liberalization policy are robust to uncertainty over elasticities. The median and PE estimates are of the same order of magnitude—around 1.3 percent.

Second, the welfare gains from reform of export subsidies are not as large as they were with the PE elasticities. This applies to the policy of uniformity as well as to the policy of liberalization. In each case the welfare gains drop to around 0.87 percent, rather than to the initial results of 1.0 percent or so when PE elasticities are used. It is noteworthy, however, that just reducing export subsidies by 20 percent continues to generate a relatively large fraction of the welfare gains from the complete liberalization of export subsidies. Given the decline in welfare gains as a result of the uniformity and liberalization policies, this fraction is even larger than before. The higher fraction confirms the policy conclusion that it is important to have the highest export subsidies reduced, at the very least.

Third, there continues to be a welfare loss from unilateral liberalization of tariffs. This loss increases from 0.1 percent of GDP to around 0.2 percent when we allow for uncertainty over elasticities.

Fourth, the welfare gains from moving toward uniformity of foreign distortions or of all distortions appear to be very robust.

Fifth, the welfare losses obtained when tariffs or export subsidies are liberalized from a benchmark in which all foreign distortions are uniform are qualitatively robust. The welfare loss for tariff liberalization is somewhat larger than before, strengthening our earlier policy conclusion in this respect.

Finally, the welfare effects of removing the VAT with a lump-sum replacement are even "more neutral" then before. Rather than a welfare loss of 0.342 percent, we now find a median welfare loss of only 0.09 percent, with a standard deviation of approximately the same value. This confirms the earlier finding that the existing VAT serves well as a practical alternative to the lump-sum tax as a distortion-free replacement tax.

References

The word "processed" describes informally reproduced works that may not be commonly available through library systems.

Arslan, Ismail, and Sweder van Wijnbergen. 1990. "Turkey: Export Miracle or Accounting Trick?" WPS 370. World Bank, Latin America and the Caribbean Regional Office, Washington, D.C. Processed.

Atkinson, Anthony, and Joseph Stiglitz. 1980. *Public Economics*. New York: McGraw-Hill.

Balassa, Bela. 1989. "Subsidies and Countervailing Measures: Economic Considerations." In Bela Balassa, ed., *Subsidies and Countervailing Measures: Critical Issues in the Uruguay Round*. Discussion Paper 55. Washington D.C.: World Bank.

Baysan, Tercan. 1984. "Some Economic Aspects of Turkey's Accession to the EC: Resource Shifts, Comparative Advantage, and Static Gains." *Journal of Common Market Studies* 23: 15–34.

Baysan, Tercan, and Charles Blitzer. 1988. "Turkey's Trade Liberalization in the 1980s and Prospects for Its Sustainability." Paper presented at the Conference on Turkey's Economic Development in the 1980s. Harvard University, Cambridge, Mass. Processed.

———. 1991. "The Timing and Sequencing of a Trade Liberalization: The Case of Turkey." In D. Papageorgieu, M. Michaely, and A. Chokski, eds., *Liberalizing Foreign Trade,* vol. 6. Cambridge, Mass.: Blackwell.

Brander, James, and Barbara Spencer. 1985. "Export Subsidies and International Market Share and Rivalry." *Journal of International Economics* 18: 83–100.

Brooke, Anthony, David Kendrick, and Alexander Meeraus. 1988. *GAMS: A User's Guide.* Redwood City, Calif.: Scientific Press.

de Melo, Jaime, and David Tarr. 1992. *General Equilibrium Analysis of U.S. Foreign Trade Policy.* Cambridge, Mass.: MIT Press.

Dixit, Avinash K., and Victor Norman. 1980. *Theory of International Trade.* Welwyn, U.K.: Nisbet.

———. 1986. "Gains from Trade without Lump-Sum Compensation." *Journal of International Economics* 21: 111–22.

Eaton, Jonathan, and Gene Grossman. 1986. "Optimal Trade and Industrial Policy under Oligopoly." *Quarterly Journal of Economics* 101: 383–406.

Grais, Wafik, Jaime de Melo, and Shujiro Urata. 1986. "A General Equilibrium Estimation of the Effects of Reductions in Tariffs and Quantitative Restrictions in Turkey in 1978." In T. N. Srinivasan and John Whalley, eds., *General Equilibrium Trade Policy Modeling.* Cambridge, Mass.: MIT Press.

Harrison, Glenn W. 1990. "The Sensitivity Analysis of Applied General Equilibrium Models with MPSS: User's Guide." University of South Carolina, Department of Economics, Columbia. Processed.

Harrison, Glenn W., Richard Jones, Larry Kimbell, and Randall Wigle. 1993. "How Robust Is Applied General Equilibrium Modelling?" *Journal of Policy Modelling* 15 (1):99–115.

Harrison, Glenn W., and Richard J. Manning. 1987. "Best Approximate Aggregation of Input-Output Systems." *Journal of the American Statistical Association* 82 (December): 1027–31.

Harrison, Glenn W., Thomas Rutherford, and David Tarr. 1992. "Piecemeal Trade Reform in Partially Liberalized Economies: An Evaluation for Turkey." WPS 951. World Bank, Country Economics Department, Washington, D.C. Processed.

Harrison, Glenn W., and H. D. Vinod. 1992. "The Sensitivity Analysis of Applied General Equilibrium Models: Completely Randomized Factorial Sampling Designs." *The Review of Economics and Statistics* 79 (May): 357–62.

Itoh, Motoshige, and Kazuharu Kiyono. 1987. "Welfare-Enhancing Export Subsidies." *Journal of Political Economy* 95: 115–37.

Krueger, Anne O. 1984. "Trade Policies in Developing Countries." In Ronald Jones and Peter B. Kenen, eds. *Handbook of International Economics.* Amsterdam: North Holland.

Krugman, Paul. 1988. "Endogenous Innovations, International Trade, and Growth." Paper presented at the SUNY-Buffalo Conference on Development. Massachusetts Institute of Technology, Department of Economics, Cambridge, Mass. Processed.

Lerner, Abba. 1936. "The Symmetry between Import and Export Taxes." *Economica* 3: 306–13.

Mathiesen, Lars. 1985. "Computation of Economic Equilibria by a Sequence of Linear Complementarity Problems." *Mathematical Programming Study 23*. Amsterdam: North Holland.

Milanovic, Branko. 1986. *Export Incentives and Turkish Manufactured Exports, 1980–84*. World Bank Working Paper 768. Washington, D.C.

Nogues, Julio. 1990. "The Experience of Latin America with Export Subsidies." *Weltwirtschaftliches Archiv* 126: 97–114.

Rodrik, Dani. 1988a. "Some Policy Dilemmas in Turkish Macroeconomic Management." In T. Aricanly and D. Rodrik, eds., *Turkey's Economic Development in the 1980s: Changing Strategies for the Next Decade*. New York: Macmillan.

———. 1988b. "Imperfect Competition, Scale Economies, and Trade Policy in Developing Countries." In R. Baldwin, ed., *Trade Policy Issues and Empirical Analysis*. University of Chicago Press.

Romer, Paul. 1989. "What Determines the Rate of Growth of Technological Change?" WPS 279. World Bank, Country Economics Department, Washington, D.C. Processed.

Rutherford, Thomas F. 1989. "General Equilibrium Modelling with MPS/GE." University of Western Ontario, London, Ontario. Processed.

Tarr, David. 1990. "Second-Best Foreign Exchange Policy in the Presence of Domestic Price Controls and Export Subsidies." *The World Bank Economic Review*. 4:175–93.

Thomas, Vinod, John Nash, and associates. 1991. *Best Practices in Trade Policy Reform*. New York: Oxford University Press.

Part II

Evaluating the Impact of Services and FDI with Endogenous Productivity Effects

Review of Development Economics, *11(3)*, *482–506*, *2007*
DOI:10.1111/j.1467-9361.2007.00362.x

The Impact of Liberalizing Barriers to Foreign Direct Investment in Services: The Case of Russian Accession to the World Trade Organization

*Jesper Jensen, Thomas Rutherford, and David Tarr**

Abstract

In this paper a computable general equilibrium model of the Russian economy is used to assess the impact of accession to the World Trade Organization (WTO), which encompasses improved market access, Russian tariff reduction, and reduction of barriers against multinational service providers. It is assumed that foreign direct investment in business services is necessary for multinationals to compete well with Russian business services providers, but cross-border service provision is also present. The model incorporates productivity effects in both goods and services markets endogenously, through a Dixit–Stiglitz framework. It is estimated that Russia will gain about 7.2% of the value of Russian consumption in the medium term from WTO accession and up to 24% in the long run. It is also estimated that the largest gains to Russia will derive from liberalization of barriers against multinational service providers. Piecemeal and systematic sensitivity analysis shows that the results are robust.

1. Introduction

Russia applied for membership in the General Agreement on Tariffs and Trade (GATT) in June 1993 and the GATT Working Party was transformed into the World Trade Organization (WTO) Working Party in 1995. After many years of negotiations, momentum for accession built when President Vladimir Putin made accession to the WTO a priority of his administration.

Within Russia, numerous industrialists, policy analysts and even the former Prime Minister have called for an assessment of the gains and losses from WTO accession and for an assessment of the impact on different sectors of the economy. Russian goods providers are concerned that a fall in tariffs will imply increased competition from foreign goods providers and a decline in their market share. Russian service providers are concerned that liberalized rules on new foreign direct investment (FDI) will lead to increased competition from multinational service providers in Russia. The government has appropriately replied that when the economy as a whole is considered, the reduction in the tariff in any one sector does not mean that sector will decline, i.e. in general equilibrium the effects may be favorable for many sectors whose protection is cut. Moreover, the government argues that Russian exporters will obtain improved access to the markets of WTO member countries. But some commentators remain

---

*Jensen: Teca Training ApS, Mosevej 55, 2970 Hørsholm, Denmark. Tel: 45 4570-1130; Fax: 45 4570-1131; E-mail: jensen@tecatraining.dk/. Rutherford: University of Colorado, 4829 Northgate Drive, Ann Arbor, MI 48103, USA. Telefax: (734) 424-3563; E-mail: tom@mpsge.org. Tarr: The World Bank, MSN 3-303, The World Bank, 1818 H. St. NW, Washington, DC 20433, USA. Tel: (202) 473-7677; Fax: (202) 522-1159; E-mail: dtarr@worldbank.org. The authors would like to thank Ekaterina Krivonos, Sergei Ovechin, Oleksandr Sheoptylo and Maria Kasilag for their help and also seminar participants at the CEFIR and NES conferences in Moscow and the ASSA meetings in Washington for helpful comments. Financial support from the United Kingdom's DFID is gratefully acknowledged. The views expressed are those of the authors and do not necessarily reflect those of the World Bank or its Executive Directors.

skeptical, in part because there is a lack of quantitative estimates of the impacts, and in part because the sources of the gains have not been well articulated.

In this paper we develop a 35-sector small open economy comparative static computable general equilibrium model of Russia that we believe is appropriate to evaluate the impact of Russian accession to the WTO. We document that, although the Russian tariff structure has some problem areas and can be liberalized, it is not a highly distorted tariff structure. On the other hand, barriers to foreign direct investors in several key business services sectors are quite substantial and are the focus of intense negotiations between Russia and the WTO Working Party. Consequently, a serious evaluation of Russian WTO accession requires developing a model that is capable of assessing the impact of liberalization of barriers against FDI in an applied context.

Our key modeling assumptions are: we assume that a substantial portion of business services require a domestic presence; multinational service providers import some specialized capital or labor as part of their decision to establish a domestic presence; and business services supplied with a domestic presence are supplied by imperfectly competitive firms who produce a unique variety of the service. We adopt the Dixit–Stiglitz–Ethier structure for business services (and for increasing returns to scale goods) that implies endogenous productivity gains from the net introduction of new varieties.[1]

We argue that the gains to Russia from WTO accession derive from four principal effects:

1. Improved access to the markets of non-CIS countries in selected products. Russia has already negotiated most-favored nation (MFN) status on a bilateral basis with most of its important trading partners, so Russia's exporters will not see an immediate reduction in the tariffs they face and this effect is not expected to be large. But Russia will have improved rights under antidumping and countervailing duty investigations in its export markets, which is the source of the improved access we model.[2]
2. Tariff reduction on goods will induce improved domestic resource allocation and increase the number of varieties of imports in imperfectly competitive sectors. The latter will increase total factor productivity in downstream sectors due to a Dixit–Stiglitz–Ethier externality.
3. Reduction in barriers against multinational service providers will increase the number of service varieties available in Russia. The variety increase will increase total factor productivity (or lower the quality adjusted costs) in sectors that use business services.
4. Positive effects on the investment climate from increases in the rate of return to capital. We model this impact in a comparative steady state model, which produces an upper bound estimate of the gains from an increase in capital stock due to trade liberalization.

There have been a number of theoretical papers modeling foreign direct investment liberalization in services (Markusen, 1989, 1990; Markusen and Venables, 1998). Regarding numerical efforts, Markusen et al. (2005) developed a stylized model where foreign direct investment is required for entry of new multinational competitors in services, but they did not apply this model to the data of an actual economy and there was no foreign direct investment in the initial equilibrium of the model. Brown and Stern (2001) and Dee et al. (2003) employ multi-country numerical models with many of the same features of Markusen et al. Their models contain three sectors: agriculture, manufacturing, and services, and are thus also rather stylized. Results in the Brown and Stern paper depend crucially on capital flows between nations, with capital importing nations typically gaining and capital exporting nations typically losing. In Dee et al. (2003), multinationals are assumed to capture the quota rents initially. So results of liberalization depend crucially on the fact that liberalization transfers rents to capital importing countries. This paper is innovative in a couple of respects relative to the above papers. First, it numerically assesses liberalization of barriers against foreign direct investors in business services in a model with considerable sector detail (35 sectors in our model). This allows the crucial estimates of the barriers to foreign direct investment to be estimated at the level of a particular business service. Unlike Brown and Stern and Dee et al., the Dixit–Stiglitz endogenous productivity effects are important in interpreting the results from the impact of service sector liberalization.[3]

We estimate that the gains to Russia (measured as Hicksian equivalent variation) from WTO accession are 7.2% of Russian consumption (or 3.3% of GDP) in the medium term, and could be as high as 23.6% of Russian consumption (11.0% of GDP) in the long run (using our comparative steady state model). To understand the sources of these gains, we execute several scenarios that allow us to decompose the impacts. Tariff reform is responsible for only 1.3 percentage points of the gain in consumption. Improved market access accounts for 0.6 percentage points of the welfare gain. We estimate the gains from FDI liberalization in services to be 5.2% of the value of Russian consumption, which amounts to over 70% of the total gains from Russian WTO accession. Thus, while improving its offer to foreign services providers within the context of the General Agreement on Trade in Services (GATS) has been one of the most difficult aspects of Russia's negotiation for WTO accession, our estimates suggest that the most important component of WTO accession for Russia in terms of the welfare gains is liberalization of its barriers against FDI in services sectors.

The crucial importance in the Russian context of liberalization of barriers to FDI reflects the starting point of the analysis; that is, we assess that Russia has done more to lower it tariffs on goods than it has to liberalize its barriers to FDI in services sectors. The *ad valorem* equivalence of the barriers to foreign direct investors in business services has been estimated specifically for this study, as explained below. These estimates were based on surveys we commissioned of specialized service sector institutes in Russia to obtain data on the regulatory environment in the key business services sectors.

We examine the robustness of the results through extensive sensitivity analysis both with respect to modeling assumptions and with respect to parameter choice. This includes "systematic sensitivity analysis" where we execute the model 30,000 times with random selection of parameter values within their specified probability distributions. We produce sample distributions and 50 and 95% confidence intervals of all key variables.

The paper is organized as follows. In section 2 we describe the model and the most important data. In section 3 we describe and interpret the central policy scenarios. In section 4 we examine the impact of different modeling assumptions (or model closures) on the results and present the results of our piecemeal and systematic sensitivity analysis.

2. Overview of the Model and Key Data

Overview of the Model Formulation

An algebraic formulation of the model is available in Jensen et al. (2004) at www.worldbank.org/trade/Russia-wto. Here we provide a general description. We depict the

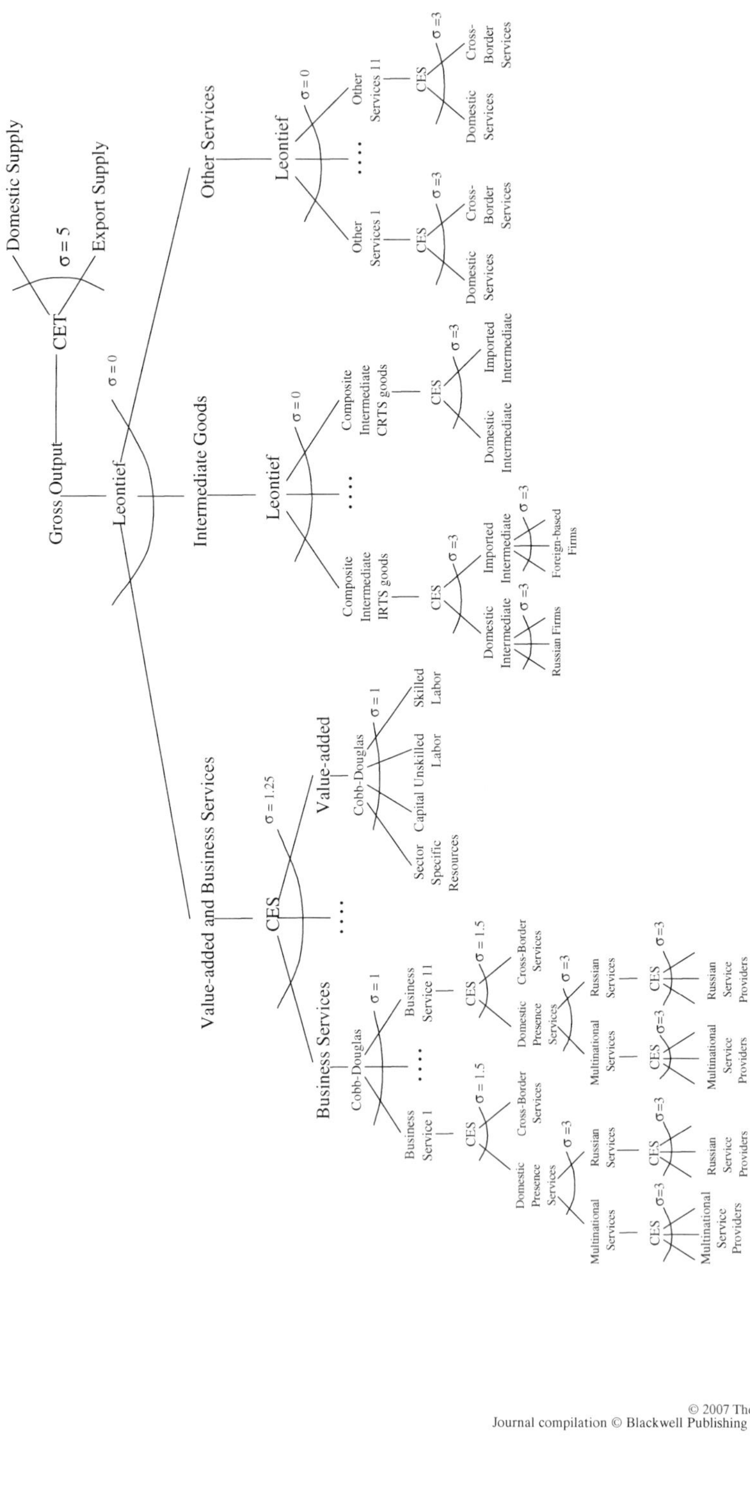

Figure 1. Production and Allocation of Output

structure of production in Figure 1. Primary factors include skilled and unskilled labor; mobile capital; sector-specific capital in the energy sectors reflecting the exhaustible resource; sector-specific capital in imperfectly competitive sectors; and primary inputs imported by multinational service providers, reflecting specialized management expertise or technology of the firm. The existence of sector-specific capital in several sectors implies that there are decreasing returns to scale in the use of the mobile factors, and supply curves in these sectors slope upwards.

There are 35 sectors shown in Table 1. Regardless of sector, all firms minimize the cost of production. One category of sectors is *competitive goods and services sectors*

Table 1. List of Sectors

1. Sectors where foreign direct investment from new multinational services providers is possible	
RLW	Railway transportation
TRK	Truck transportation
PIP	Pipelines transportation
MAR	Maritime transportation
AIR	Air transportation
TRO	Other transportation
TMS	Telecommunications
SCS	Science & science servicing
SSM	Public health & sports & social security
ECM	Education & culture & art
FIN	Financial services
2. Sectors where new foreign firms may provide new goods from abroad	
FME	Ferrous metallurgy
NFM	Non-ferrous metallurgy
CHM	Chemical & oil-chemical industry
MWO	Mechanical engineering & metal-working
TPP	Timber & woodworking & pulp & paper industry
CNM	Construction materials industry
CLO	Light industry
FOO	Food industry
OTH	Other industries
3. Competitive sectors subject to constant returns to scale	
ADM	Administration & public associations
AGF	Agriculture & forestry
COA	Coal mining
PSM	Communal & consumer services
CON	Construction
ELE	Electric industry
GAS	Gas
GEO	Geology & hydrometeorology
OLE	Oil extraction
OLP	Oil processing
OFU	Other fuel industries
OIN	Other goods-producing sectors
PST	Post
CAT	Public catering
TRD	Trade

produced under constant returns to scale and where price equals marginal costs with zero profits. This includes agriculture, forestry, and construction. It also includes certain public services, like education and post office facilities, and key mineral industries.[4] In these sectors, products are differentiated by country of origin, i.e. we employ the Armington assumption. All Russian goods-producing firms (including imperfectly competitive firms) can sell on the domestic market or export. Russian firms optimize their output decision between exports and domestic sales based on relative prices and their constant elasticity of transformation production function.

Goods produced subject to increasing returns to scale are differentiated at the firm level. We assume that manufactured goods may be produced domestically or imported. Firms in these industries set prices such that marginal cost (which is constant) equals marginal revenue; and there is free entry, which drives profits to zero. For domestic firms, costs are defined by observed primary factor and intermediate inputs to that sector in the base year data. Foreigners produce the goods abroad at constant marginal cost but incur a fixed cost of operating in Russia. The c.i.f. import price of foreign goods is defined simply by the import price, and, by the zero profits assumption, in equilibrium the import price must cover fixed and marginal costs of foreign firms. We employ the standard Chamberlinian large group monopolistic competition assumption within a Dixit–Stiglitz framework, which results in constant markups over marginal cost.

For simplicity we assume that the composition of fixed and marginal cost is identical in all firms producing under increasing returns to scale (in both goods and services). This assumption in a Dixit–Stiglitz based Chamberlinian large-group model assures that output per firm for all firm types remains constant, i.e., the model does not produce rationalization gains or losses.

The number of varieties affects the productivity of the use of imperfectly competitive goods based on the standard Dixit–Stiglitz formulation. The effective cost function for users of goods produced subject to increasing returns to scale declines in the total number of firms in the industry.

The third category of sectors is *services sectors that are produced in Russia under increasing returns to scale and imperfect competition,* such as telecommunications, financial services, most business services, and transportation services. In services sectors, we observe that some services are provided by foreign service providers on a cross-border basis analogous to goods providers from abroad. But a large share of business services are provided by service providers with a domestic presence, both multinational and Russian.[5] Our model allows for both types of foreign service provision in these sectors. There are cross-border services allowed in this sector and they are provided from abroad at constant costs—this is analogous to competitive provision of goods from abroad. Cross-border services, however, are not good substitutes for service providers who have a presence in Russia.[6]

There are also multinational service firm providers that choose to establish a presence in Russia in order to compete with Russian firms directly in the Russian market. When multinational service providers decide to establish a domestic presence in Russia, they will import some of their technology or management expertise. That is, FDI generally entails importing specialized foreign inputs. Thus, the cost structure of multinationals differs from Russian service providers. Multinationals incur costs related to both imported primary inputs and Russian primary factors, in addition to intermediate factor inputs. Foreign provision of services differs from foreign provision of goods, since the service providers use Russian primary inputs. Domestic service providers do not import the specialized primary factors available to the multinationals. Hence, domestic service firms incur primary factor costs related to Russian labor and capital only. These services are characterized by firm-level product differentiation. For multinational firms, the barriers to foreign direct investment affect their profitability and entry. Reduction in the constraints on FDI will induce foreign entry that will typically lead to productivity gains because, when more varieties of service providers are available, buyers can obtain varieties that more closely fit their demands and needs (the Dixit–Stiglitz variety effect).

Comparative steady state formulation In this version of our model, we allow the capital stock to adjust to its steady state equilibrium along with all of the model features we employ in our WTO reference case, i.e. we allow for tariff and FDI liberalization with endogenous productivity effects as above. We call this our comparative steady state model. In the comparative static model, we assume that the capital stock is fixed and the rental rate on capital is endogenously determined. In the comparative steady state model, the logic is reversed. We assume that the capital stock is in its initial steady state equilibrium in the benchmark dataset, but that the capital stock will adjust to a new steady state equilibrium based on a fixed rate of return demanded by investors. That is, if the trade policy shock happens to induce an increase in the rate of return on capital so that it exceeds the initial rate of return, investors will invest and expand the capital stock. Expansion of the capital stock drives down the marginal product of capital, i.e. it drives down the rental rate on capital, until the rate of return on capital falls back to the initial level.[7] To analyze trade policy, this comparative steady state approach has been employed by many authors, including Harrison et al. (1996, 1997), Baldwin et al. (1999), and Francois et al. (1996). The approach, however, dates back to the 1970s, when both Hansen and Koopmans (1972) and Dantzig and Manne (1974) used it. The approach ignores the foregone consumption necessary to achieve the higher level of investment and thus is an upper bound estimate of the long-run gains within the framework of the model assumptions.

Key Data

Ad valorem equivalence of barriers to foreign direct investment in services sectors Among the key restrictions against multinational service providers in Russia are: Rostelecom maintains a monopoly on long distance fixed-line telephone services, affiliate branches of foreign banks are prohibited, and there is a quota on the multinational share of the insurance market.[8] Estimates of the *ad valorem* equivalence of these and other barriers to FDI in services are key to the results. Consequently, we commissioned 20-page surveys from Russian research institutes that specialize in these sectors and econometric estimates of these barriers based on these surveys.

These questionnaires provided us with data, descriptions, and assessments of the regulatory environment in these sectors.[9] Using this information and interviews with specialist staff in Russia, as well as supplementary information, Kimura et al. (2004a, 2004b, 2004c) then estimated the *ad valorem* equivalence of barriers to FDI in several Russian sectors, namely in telecommunications; banking, insurance and securities; and maritime and air transportation services. The process involved converting the answers and data of the questionnaires into an index of restrictiveness in each industry. Kimura et al. then applied methodology explained in the volume by Findlay and Warren (2000), notably papers by Warren (2000), McGuire and Schuele (2000) and Kang (2000). For each of these service sectors, authors in the Findlay and Warren volume evaluated the

Table 2. Tariff Rates, Export Tax Rates, Estimated Ad Valorem Equivalence of Barriers to FDI in Services Sectors and Estimated Improved Market Access (ad-valorem in %—by sector)

	Tariff rates	Export tax rates	Estimated change in world market price	Barriers to FDI	
				Base Year	Post-WTO Accession
Electric industry	4.5	0.0	0.0		
Oil extraction	0.0	7.9	0.0		
Oil processing	3.8	4.6	0.0		
Gas	0.5	18.8	0.0		
Coal mining	0.0	0.0	0.0		
Other fuel industries	2.6	2.6	0.0		
Ferrous metallurgy	2.9	0.4	1.5		
Non-ferrous metallurgy	7.4	5.3	1.5		
Chemical & oil-chemical industry	7.1	1.6	1.5		
Mechanical engineering & metal-working	7.2	0.0	0.0		
Timber & woodworking & pulp & paper industry	9.9	6.9	0.0		
Construction materials industry	10.6	1.6	0.0		
Light industry	11.8	4.1	0.5		
Food industry	11.3	3.1	0.5		
Other industries	6.4	0.0	0.5		
Agriculture & forestry	8.2	0.6	0.0		
Other goods-producing sectors	0.0	0.0	0.5		
Telecommunications				33.0	0.0
Science & science servicing (market)				33.0	0.0
Financial services				36.0	0.0
Railway transportation				33.0	0.0
Truck transportation				33.0	0.0
Pipelines transportation				33.0	0.0
Maritime transportation				95.0	80.0
Air transportation				90.0	75.0
Other transportation				33.0	0.0

Source: Authors' estimates.

regulatory environment across many countries. The price of services is then regressed against the regulatory barriers to determine the impact of any of the regulatory barriers on the price of services. Kimura et al. then assumed that the international regression applies to Russia. Applying that regression and their assessments of the regulatory environment in Russia from the questionnaires and other information sources, they estimated the *ad valorem* impact of a reduction in barriers to FDI in these services sectors.[10] The results of the estimates are listed in Table 2.[11] In the case of maritime and air transportation services, we assume that the barrier will be cut by only 15 percentage points, since pressure from the Working Party in these sectors is not strong.

Share of expatriate labor employed by multinational service providers The impact of liberalization of barriers to FDI in business services sectors on the demand for labor in these sectors will depend importantly on the share of expatriate labor used by multinational firms. We explain in the results section that despite the fact that multinationals use Russian labor less intensively than their Russian competitors, if multinationals use mostly Russian labor, their expansion is likely to increase the demand for Russian labor in these sectors.[12] We obtained estimates of the share of expatriate labor or specialized technology not available to Russian firms that is used by multinational service providers in Russia from Russian research institutes that specialize in these sectors. In general, we found that multinational service providers use mostly Russian primary factor inputs and only small amounts of expatriate labor or specialized technology. In particular, the estimated share of foreign inputs used by multinationals in Russia is: telecommunications, 10%, plus or minus 2%; financial services, 3%, plus or minus 2%; maritime transportation, 3%, plus or minus 2%; and air transportation, 12.5%, plus or minus 2.5%.

Tariff and export tax data We estimate the tariff and export tax rates by sector in our model based on the following data and methodology. For the purpose of calculating the tariff and export tax rates, we obtained data on the trade flows from the 2001 Customs Statistics on the External Trade of the Russian Federation ("Таможенная Статистика Внешней Торговли Российской Федераций"), a yearly publication from the Russian Customs Committee.[13] Import tariff rates and export taxes at the tariff line level were obtained from official government decrees available online; the data are current as of August 2002.[14]

Based on a Goskomstat mapping from the tariff line data of the Customs Committee to the sectors in our input–output table, we calculated a weighted average tariff rate for the sectors of our model. We calculated these rates two ways: based on all imports (where the collected tariff rate as a percentage of all imports is 8.1%) and on non-CIS imports (where the collected tariffs as a percentage of non-CIS imports is 11.1%). The rates we employ in the model are the rates based on all imports. The rates based on all imports are lower since the base on the calculation includes CIS imports on which no tariffs are imposed. We believe collected tariff rates more closely approximate the protection a sector receives and the incentives it faces. Similar procedures are applied for export taxes. The results at the sector level are in Table 2.

Applying these tariff rates across all sectors implies that tariff revenue in our model is about 1.6% of GDP in the initial equilibrium. Collected tariffs in Russia are closer to 1.1% of GDP.[15] There are several reasons that the collected tariffs in Russia are less than the legal rates on most favored nation (MFN) imports. Most notably, exemptions to the Russian tariff are available for regional agreements (most notably the CIS), personal imports, and shuttle trade. Since we have data for the CIS trade, we adjust for this and apply the MFN rates on all imports from the non-CIS trade. This slightly, but not significantly, biases upward the rates we employ relative to collected rates.

Export tax data Analogous to the import trade data, the Russian State Customs Committee publishes data on export volumes and values. These data were also entered manually at the tariff line level. Unlike the tariff data that are listed by the Customs Committee, it was necessary to consult numerous regulations of the government of Russia to obtain the export taxes. Similar to the tariff data, the export taxes are sometimes *ad valorem* or sometimes the maximum of the *ad valorem* or specific tax rate. The results are reported in Table 2.[16]

Input–output table The core input–output model is the 1995 table produced by Goskomstat. The official table contained only 22 sectors, and importantly has little service sector disaggregation. Consequently, Russian input–output expert S. P. Baranov disaggregated this table into a 35-sector input–output table (Baranov, 2000). Baranov used unpublished data available to Goskomstat based on the surveys that were used to construct the 1995 table. The principal elements of this disaggregation were: a split of the oil and gas sector into oil, gas, and oil processing; a split of the transport sector into railroad, maritime, air, pipeline, truck, and other transportation services; the breakup of communication into post services and telecommunications; and disaggregation of the data in several business services sectors regarding market and non-market activities. The documentation by Baranov is available on the website listed above.

3. Results

In our general WTO scenario, we assume that barriers against foreign direct investment are reduced as indicated in Table 2; seven sectors subject to antidumping actions in export markets receive slightly improved market access. This is implemented as an exogenous increase in their export price as shown in Table 2; and the tariff rates of all sectors are reduced by 50%.[17] We first discuss (and present in Table 3) our estimates of the impact of Russian WTO accession on aggregate variables such as welfare and the real exchange rate, aggregate exports, the return to capital, skilled labor and unskilled labor, and the percentage change in tariff revenue. In order to obtain an assessment of the adjustment costs, we estimate the percentage of labor and mobile capital that must change industries. The gains come from a combination of effects, so we also estimate the comparative static impacts of the various components of WTO accession in order to assess their relative importance.

First we discuss the comparative static results. We shall also consider the results of assuming the time frame is long enough for capital to adjust to its new long-run steady state equilibrium in a scenario we call comparative steady state. In addition, we evaluate a "short-run" scenario, in which all labor is "sector specific".

Aggregate Welfare Effects of WTO Accession

We estimate that the welfare gains to Russia are equal to 7.2% of Russian consumption (or 3.3% of GDP) in the medium term. These gains derive from three key effects: (1) improved access to the markets of non-CIS countries in selected products; (2) Russian tariff reduction; and (3) liberalization of barriers to FDI in services sectors. We execute three scenarios that allow us to understand the relative impact of these various elements and the mechanisms through which they operate.

Impact of tariff reduction The results for this scenario are presented in column (2) of Table 3. We lower tariffs by 50%, but there is no liberalization of the barriers to FDI or improved market access. The estimated welfare gains to the economy are 1.3% of consumption or 0.6% of GDP.

The gains to the economy from tariff reduction alone come about for two reasons. Tariff reduction in Russia will lead to improved domestic resource allocation since tariff reduction will induce Russia to shift production to sectors where production is valued more highly based on world market prices. This is the fundamental effect of trade liberalization in constant returns to scale models (CRTS). In addition, tariff

Table 3. Impact of WTO Accession on Economy-Wide Variables in Russia: Policy Results and Decomposition of Effects (results are percentage change from initial equilibrium)

	Benchmark	*WTO accession (1)*	*Tariff reform only (2)*	*Improved market access only (3)*	*Reform of FDI barriers only (4)*	*WTO accession in steady state model (5)*	*WTO accession with partial reform of FDI barriers (6)*	*WTO accession with domestic rent dissipation (7)*	*WTO accession in short run model (8)*
Aggregate welfare									
Welfare (EV as % of consumption)		7.2	1.3	0.6	5.2	23.6	4.1	7.7	5.9
Welfare (EV as % of GDP)		3.3	0.6	0.3	2.4	11.0	1.9	3.6	2.8
Government budget									
Tariff revenue (% of GDP)	1.4	0.9	0.8	1.4	1.4	1.0	0.8	0.9	0.8
Tariff revenue (% change)		–33.4	–38.4	8.4	10.6	–23.3	–35.4	–33.2	–35.8
Aggregate trade									
Real exchange rate (% change)		2.6	2.0	–0.5	1.1	4.8	1.8	2.7	3.0
Aggregate exports (% change)		13.2	7.9	1.5	3.5	24.3	10.8	13.5	9.5
Returns to mobile factors									
Unskilled labor (% change)		2.5	0.4	0.1	1.9	13.2	1.0	2.7	1.9
Skilled labor (% change)		4.7	1.5	0.6	2.5	17.6	2.6	4.9	3.4
Capital (% change)		4.9	2.0	0.7	3.1	19.5	3.6	4.9	4.3
Factor adjustments									
Unskilled labor (% of workers who change jobs)		2.6	1.1	0.5	1.6	4.4	1.7	2.6	0.0
Skilled labor (% of workers who change jobs)		2.1	0.4	0.4	1.5	2.5	1.0	2.2	0.0
Capital		0.6	0.4	0.4	0.2	0.1	0.6	0.6	0.4

Source: Authors' estimates.

reduction on imports in imperfectly competitive sectors raises the tariff ridden demand curve for imports. This increases profitability for foreigners selling in the Russian market thereby inducing new entry by foreign suppliers until zero profits are restored. Although there is a loss of domestic varieties due to increased foreign competition, there is a net increase in varieties. The additional varieties in the imperfectly competitive sectors of Russia result in a productivity improvement for users of these goods through the Dixit–Stiglitz–Ethier effect (Dixit and Stiglitz, 1977; Ethier, 1982). This result is analogous to the result found by Rutherford and Tarr (2002) in a fully dynamic model.

Impact of improved market access In column (3) of Table 3, we present the results of a scenario in which we allow for improved market access (according to the terms of trade improvements of Table 2), but we do not lower tariffs or barriers to FDI in services sectors. We estimate the impact of improved market access at 0.6% of consumption (0.3% of GDP). Gains derive from improved prices for exports. But also a higher value for exports allows Russia to buy more imports and more varieties of imports increase productivity. Thus, the impact of improved market access is greater in a model with Dixit–Stiglitz variety effects than in a constant return to scale model.

Impact of FDI liberalization in business services In this scenario, labeled reform of FDI barriers in column (4) of Table 3, we eliminate or reduce the discriminatory tax on multinationals in the services sectors (as shown in Table 2), but there is no reduction in tariffs or improved market access. The reduction in the discriminatory tax on multinationals increases profitability for provision of services in Russia by multinationals, thereby inducing new entry by multinational service providers until zero profits are restored. Although there is a loss of domestic service varieties due to increased multinational foreign competition, there is a net increase in varieties. Russian businesses will then have improved access to the services of multinational service providers in areas like telecommunication, banking, insurance, transportation, and other business services. The additional service varieties in the business services sectors should lower the cost of doing business and result in a productivity improvement for users of these goods through the Dixit–Stiglitz–Ethier effect. We estimate that the gains to Russia from liberalization of barriers to FDI in services are about 5.2% of the value of Russian consumption or about 72% of the total gains to Russia of WTO accession.

Sector Results

Expanding manufacturing sectors Sectors we estimate will expand are those that either: export a relatively large share of their output; obtain an exogenous increase in export prices as a result of WTO accession; are relatively unprotected initially compared to other sectors of the economy; or experience a significant reduction in the cost of their intermediate inputs, typically because they have a large share of intermediate inputs that come from sectors that experience productivity advances due to trade or FDI liberalization.

The manufacturing sectors that we estimate are likely to expand their output the most are non-ferrous metals, ferrous metals, and chemicals. (See Jensen et al. (2004) for detailed sector results.) These three sectors are among the sectors that we assume will gain an exogenous increase in the price of their exports upon WTO accession. They are also among those that export the highest share of their output—they all export over 30% of the value of their output. Export intensity is important because a reduction in tariffs generally depreciates the real exchange rate. As the real exchange rate depreciates, sectors that export intensively will gain more domestic goods for a unit of their exports.[18]

Declining manufacturing sectors The sectors that contract the most are the sectors that are the most protected prior to tariff reduction and which have a relatively small share of exports. Most notably this includes machinery and equipment, food and light industry, and construction materials. All of these sectors do little exporting and light industry and food are the sectors with the highest tariff rates.

Business services sectors Russian business and labor interests in these sectors are not the same, and we discuss the impact on labor in these sectors first. We find that skilled and unskilled employment will expand in most, but not all, of the business services sectors. This is an application to a full economy model of the result found by Markusen et al. (2005). They have shown in a more stylized model that even when FDI is a partial equilibrium substitute for domestic skilled labor, it may be a general equilibrium complement. The reason is as follows. As a result of a reduction in the barriers to FDI in these sectors, we estimate that there will be an expansion in the number of multinational firms who locate in Russia to provide business services from within Russia, and a contraction in the number of purely Russian firms. Although multinationals also demand Russian labor, they use Russian labor slightly less intensively than Russian firms. In other words, since multinationals import primary inputs, FDI is a partial equilibrium substitute for Russian labor. But as more service firms enter the market, the quality adjusted price of services falls, and industries that use services expand their demand for business services. On balance, the increase in labor demand from the increase in the demand for business services typically exceeds the decline in labor demand from the substitution of multinational supply for Russian supply in the Russian market. That is, FDI is a partial equilibrium substitute but a general equilibrium complement to Russian labor. Thus, we estimate that labor in the business services sectors will typically gain from an expansion in FDI and multinational provision of services in Russia.

Regarding capital, as a result of the removal of restrictions, we estimate there would be significant increase in foreign direct investment and an increase in multinational firms operating in Russia. We estimate that specific capital owners in imperfectly competitive sectors will lose from this increase in competition. We expect, however, the increase in FDI to have diverse impacts on Russian firms. We define a firm as a multinational even if a foreign firm and a Russian firm have formed a joint venture. Multinationals will often look for Russian joint venture partners when they want to invest in Russia. Russian companies that become part of the joint ventures in the expanding multinational share of the business services market will likely preserve or increase the value of their investments. Russian capital owners in business services who remain wholly independent of multinational firms, either because they avoid joint ventures or are not desired as joint venture partners, will likely see the value of their investments decline, and the least efficient will exit the industry.[19]

This suggests that domestic lobbying interests within a service sector could be diverse regarding FDI liberalization. We estimate that labor should find it in their interest to support FDI liberalization even if capital owners in the sector oppose it. But capital owners themselves may have diverse interests depending on their prospects for acquisition by multinationals.

4. Sensitivity Analysis

The results depend on the choice of parameters in the model as well as certain assumptions or "closures." In this section, we evaluate the impact on the results of changing the values of the key parameters or modeling assumptions in the model. We begin with key model assumptions. We then discuss the results of "piecemeal sensitivity" analysis on the parameters. Finally, we discuss the results of our "systematic sensitivity" analysis.

Model Assumptions

Sensitivity of results to a 50% cut in the barriers to FDI In this scenario, we simulate a cut in the barriers by one-half as much as in our central scenario (shown in column 6 of Table 3). But we allow for improved market access and a 50% cut in tariff barriers. We find that the gains to the economy are reduced to about 4.1% of consumption. From Table 3, we can see this is slightly less than the sum of three components: (i) half of the gains from FDI liberalization; (ii) tariff reduction; and (iii) improved market access.

Rent capture or dissipation Resource loss from rent seeking of licenses is a significant problem in Russia. In our central scenario we have ignored these costs. It may be appropriate, however, to assume that those that obtain the licenses used Russian capital and labor in wasteful license seeking activities and the like. Then the *ad valorem* equivalence of the barriers to multinational investment are a real resource cost. As a result the estimated gains from WTO accession increase from 7.2% to 7.7% of consumption (as shown in column 7 of Table 3) because the resources that were used to capture the rents become available for productive activities.

Similarly, if foreigners capture the rents initially, liberalization of the barriers will allow competition among foreigners that will result in a transfer of the rents from foreigners to Russia. Then we estimate the gains to Russia from WTO accession will increase from our central estimate of 7.2% to 7.5% of consumption.

Sector-specific labor Although we have some sector-specific capital (varying by sector), in our central scenario all labor is mobile. To evaluate short-run effects, where a significant portion of labor will be unable to switch jobs between sectors, we assume that labor cannot move between sectors, that is labor is "sector-specific." With sector-specific labor, wages of skilled and unskilled labor will vary across sectors in response to shifts in demand coming from WTO accession.

The aggregate results are presented in column 8 of Table 3. The welfare gains fall to 5.9% of consumption. This decline in the gains is expected when labor is sector-specific since when labor is immobile, it cannot move to the sectors where it is valued most highly. What is striking about this scenario is that the gains remain very substantial. This shows how important productivity effects are since without productivity effects a model with no labor market resource reallocation would produce very small gains.

While the welfare gains are smaller, no labor changes jobs in this scenario (see the rows on factor adjustments in Table 3). So the "social" adjustment costs of labor are zero. Despite no dislocation of labor, the wages of workers in each sector will have their wages go up or down relative to the average wage in the economy for skilled or unskilled labor; thus, there are private adjustment costs of WTO accession, even if there are no social costs of adjustment in this short-run model.[20]

CRTS model—no productivity effects We also executed a CRTS version of our model where we reduced tariffs by 50%, allowed improved access and lowered FDI barriers. Without the Dixit–Stiglitz structure that provides the possibility of productivity gains, the welfare gains are reduced to 1.2% of consumption.[21]

Long-run comparative steady state results of WTO accession In a long-run analysis, we should allow for the fact that WTO accession could improve the investment climate in Russia. In this scenario, we employ our comparative steady state model. As explained in section 2, the principal feature is that we allow for the fact that accession to the WTO could increase the rate of return on investment.[22] This would induce an increase in the capital stock until the marginal productivity of capital declines sufficiently that the rate of return on investment is no higher than the initial steady state equilibrium rate of return on investment. With our comparative steady state model, we estimate that the gains to Russia from WTO accession are 23.7% of consumption (11% of GDP). This is more than three times the estimated comparative static welfare gains. The reason the gains are larger is that we estimate that WTO accession will induce an increase in the rental rate on capital in Russia in the comparative static model by 4.9%. In the comparative steady state model, this induces an expansion of the capital stock in the new equilibrium. We estimate that the capital stock will increase by about 14.4% of its initial level in the long-run steady state equilibrium. With a higher capital stock, the economy is able to produce more output and there is more consumption. We typically argue that this type of model produces an upper bound estimate of the welfare gains because the foregone consumption necessary to achieve the higher capital stock is not taken into account.[23] However, Rutherford and Tarr (2002) have shown that a fully dynamic model which incorporates productivity effects like those in our present model, and which takes into account foregone consumption from investment decisions, could produce estimated welfare gains that are as large or larger than these comparative steady state results.

Piecemeal Sensitivity Analysis

In Table 4, we present the impact on welfare of varying the value of key parameters. In these scenarios, we retain the central value of all parameters except the parameter in question. In general, the gains to the economy (welfare gains) increase with an increase in elasticities, since higher elasticities imply that the economy is able to shift more easily to sectors or products that are cheaper after trade and FDI liberalization.[24] There are two parameters in the table that have a strong impact on the results: the elasticity of substitution between value-added and business services (esubs) and the elasticity of multinational firm supply (etaf). A liberalization of the barriers to FDI will result in a reduction in the cost of business services, both from the direct effect of lowering the costs of doing business for multinational service providers and from the indirect effect that additional varieties of business services allow users to purchase a quality adjusted unit of services at lower cost. When the elasticity of substitution between value-added and business services is high, users have the greater potential to substitute the cheaper business services and this increases productivity. The elasticity of multinational and Russian firm supply (etaf, etad) is primarily dependent on the sector-specific factor for each firm type (foreign or domestic). When etaf is high, a reduction in the barriers to FDI results in a larger expansion in the number of multinational firms

Table 4. Piecemeal Sensitivity Analysis–Welfare Effects

	Parameter value			*Hicksian equivalent variation[b] with corresponding parameter*		
Parameter[a]	*Lower*	*Intermediate*	*Upper*	*Lower*	*Intermediate*	*Upper*
esubs	0.5	1.25	2.0	5.6	7.2	9.7
esub	2.0	3.0	4.0	7.3	7.2	6.8
sigmadm	2.0	3.0	4.0	7.1	7.2	7.3
esubprimary	0.70	1.00	1.30	7.1	7.2	7.2
esubintermed	0.0	0.0	0.25	7.2	7.2	7.4
esubconsumer	0.5	1.0	1.5	6.8	7.2	7.5
etadx	3.0	5.0	7.0	7.1	7.2	7.2
etad	5.0	7.5	10.0	6.9	7.2	7.4
etaf	10.0	15.0	20.0	5.1	7.2	8.7
theta_m(i)	see table below			7.1	7.2	7.2
theta_fdi(i)	see table below			5.2	7.2	8.4

[a]The piecemeal sensitivity analysis employs central values for all parameters (see below) other than the tested parameter and lump sum tax replacement.
[b]Hicksian equivalent variation as a percent of the value of consumption in the benchmark equilibrium.

Key:

Parameter	*Central value*	*Definitions of the parameter*
esubs	1.25	Elasticity of substitution between value-added and business services
esub	3.0	Elasticity of substitution between firm varieties in imperfectly competitive sectors
sigmadm	3.0	"Armington" elasticity of substitution between imports and domestic goods in CRTS sectors
esubprimary	0.0	Elasticity of substitution between primary factors of production in value added
esubintermed	0.0	Elasticity of substitution in intermediate production between composite Armington aggregate goods
esubconsumer	1.0	Elasticity of substitution in consumer demand
etadx	5.0	Elasticity of transformation (domestic output versus exports)
etad	7.5	Elasticity of Russian service firm supply with respect to price of output
etaf	15.0	Elasticity of multinational service firm supply with respect to price of output
theta_m(i)	varies	Share of specialized imports V as a share of value added in multinational firms in sector I in the benchmark equilibrium
theta_fdi(i)	varies	Share of output of service sector I captured by multinational firms in the benchmark equilibrium

Table 4. Continued

	theta_fdi(i)			theta_m(i)		
Parameter values for:	*low*	*central*	*high*	*low*	*central*	*high*
railway transportation	0.01	0.03	0.05	0.02	0.04	0.06
truck transportation	0.03	0.05	0.07	0.01	0.03	0.05
pipelines transportation	0.01	0.03	0.05	0.05	0.1	0.15
maritime transportation	0.25	0.35	0.4	0.01	0.03	0.05
air transportation	0.15	0.25	0.35	0.1	0.125	0.15
other transportation	0.02	0.04	0.06	0.03	0.05	0.07
telecommunications	0.05	0.15	0.25	0.08	0.1	0.12
science and science servicing (market)	0.05	0.1	0.15	0.1	0.15	0.2
financial services	0.05	0.1	0.15	0.01	0.03	0.05

supplying the Russian market, and hence more gains from additional varieties of business services. In addition, the share of the services market captured by multinationals has a strong effect, since a liberalization results in a larger number of new varieties introduced.

Share of expatriate labor employed by multinational service providers The impact of liberalization of barriers to FDI in business services on the demand for labor in the business services sectors will depend on the share of expatriate labor used by multinational firms. If multinationals use mostly Russian labor, their expansion is likely to increase the demand for Russian labor in these sectors. We employed the estimates of the share of expatriate labor or specialized technology not available to Russian firms that is used by multinational service providers in Russia provided by the various Russian research institutes mentioned above. Here we estimate the impact of employing the upper or lower bound estimates of this share in all business services sectors.

We find that the impact on the welfare estimates of lower or higher share of imported inputs in the business services sectors is only one-tenth of a percentage point of consumption. But the impact on labor demand in the business services sector is more significant. For example, skilled labor demand in telecommunications increases by 6.0% with our central estimates of labor demand change, but would increase by 7.5% with the lower shares of imported inputs by multinationals and by 4.5% with higher shares of labor demand by multinationals. There is a similar range of results for labor demand in most of the business services sectors. With sufficiently high share of expatriate labor use by the multinationals, the demand for labor in the business services sectors would decline, but based on the expert estimates of the use of expatriate labor, we expect to see an increase in the demand for labor in telecommunications, financial services, and truck transportation, but a decline in air transportation services and science servicing. In all these cases, the shift in employment is less than 15% of initial employment.

Systematic Sensitivity Analysis

Piecemeal sensitivity analysis shows how the results change when we vary the value of key parameters one by one, with central values of all parameters except the one under consideration. In the systematic sensitivity analysis, we allow all parameters to change simultaneously. A probability distribution for each parameter is chosen. We typically choose uniform probability distribution, with the lower and upper bounds for the values of the parameters taken from the lower and upper values of the key parameters presented in Table 4. We furthermore assume that all distributions are stochastically independent.

We then run the model 30,000 times. Each time the program chooses a random configuration of parameters and executes the model with this configuration. For each variable in our model, we then harvest the sample distribution based on the 30,000 solutions. Consequently the sample distribution is not dependent on any particular set of parameter values, but represents results representative of the full distribution of parameter values.

We present the distribution of the results below for three key variables: welfare change as a percent of consumption, output change, and skilled employment changes. A full compendium of results with the sample distributions and confidence intervals can be found in Jensen et al. (2004). For each report variable, we calculate the percentage of solutions associated with a given result for the variable. The top panel of Figure 2 shows that the welfare gains as a percentage of consumption are, in most cases, between 6 and 8%. The minimum value is 4.5% and the maximum value is 11.4%. The bottom panel of Figure 2 shows the corresponding cumulative distribution of the welfare gains. The statistics shows that only 6.4% of the solutions are below a welfare gain of 6% and that 13.0% are above a gain of 8%. More than 80% of the solutions yield a gain between 6% and 8%. This shows that the welfare results are very robust within the 6 to 8% of consumption range.

In Figure 3, we focus on the employment impacts in the six sectors where the impacts are the greatest: the three sectors with the largest increase in employment and the three sectors with the largest decline in employment. We only show the results for skilled labor, as the results for unskilled labor are very close to the results for skilled labor. We assume total employment is unchanged, so employment must expand in some sectors and contract in others. The sectors where employment expands the most are: ferrous metallurgy, non-ferrous metallurgy, and chemical industry. The manufacturing sectors where employment declines the most are: mechanical engineering, light industry, and food industry. The results for all six sectors show that our central results are robust to most parameter configurations, and in particular that the expanding (declining) sectors are expanding (declining) for virtually all configurations. The figure also shows that the magnitude of the results for the expanding sectors is more uncertain than the results for the declining sectors. This is explained by the relatively greater use of business services and goods from imperfectly competitive sectors.[25]

In Figure 4, we display the frequency distributions of the output changes in the same six sectors. The pattern of which sectors expand or contract is the same as for employment, but the results are more positive. Whereas economy-wide employment is fixed by assumption, output increases overall. Output expands due to greater efficiency in the use of resources, and, more importantly, due to greater productivity of factors of production from the increase in varieties of business services and differentiated goods.

Finally, in order to display systematic sensitivity results for all industries in one figure, in the upper panel of Figure 5 we display bars that represent 50% confidence intervals for aggregate output (export plus domestic sales) for all industries (the point on the bar is our point estimate). In the lower panel of Figure 5, we show 50%

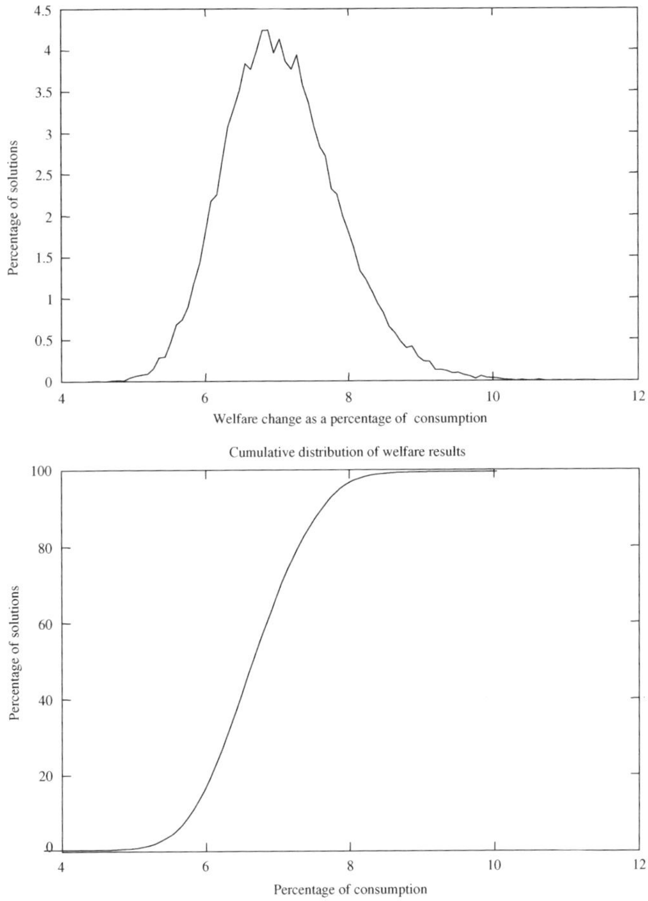

Figure 2. Frequency and Cumulative Distribution of Welfare Results

confidence intervals for domestic output by industry. Similar figures for other variables are in Appendix B of Jensen et al. (2004).

5. Conclusions

In this paper we have developed an innovative small open economy computable general equilibrium model of the Russian economy that is capable of assessing the impact of the liberalization of barriers against foreign direct investment. Surveys and estimates of the *ad valorem* equivalence of the barriers against FDI were prepared for this model. We find that the source of the largest gains to Russia from WTO accession is that additional multinational service providers will reduce the quality

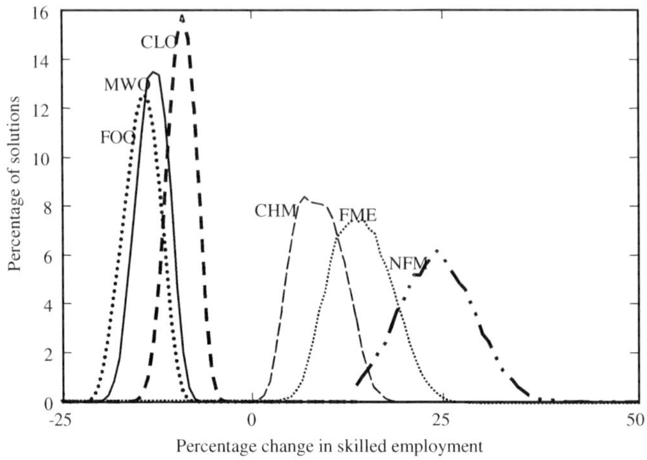

Figure 3. Frequency Distributions of Skilled Employment Impacts

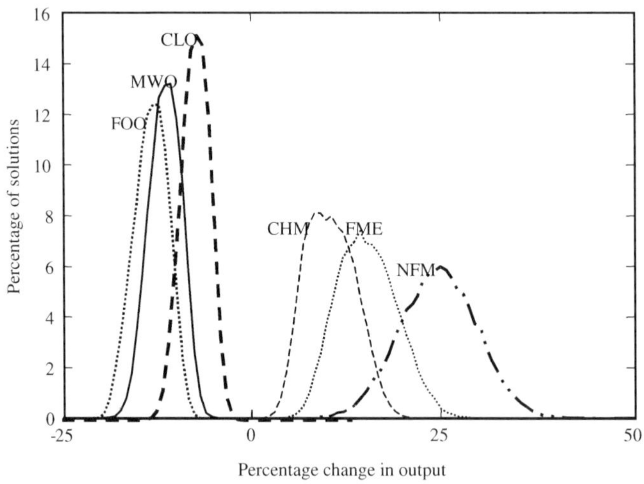

Figure 4. Frequency Distributions of Output Impacts

adjusted cost of purchasing business services in Russia and that these gains are rather substantial when compared with the typical gains from constant returns to scale models of tariff liberalization. We believe that these results are consistent with the economic geography literature and the earlier urban economics literature that suggest that access to a diverse set of service providers with a domestic presence is crucial for growth.

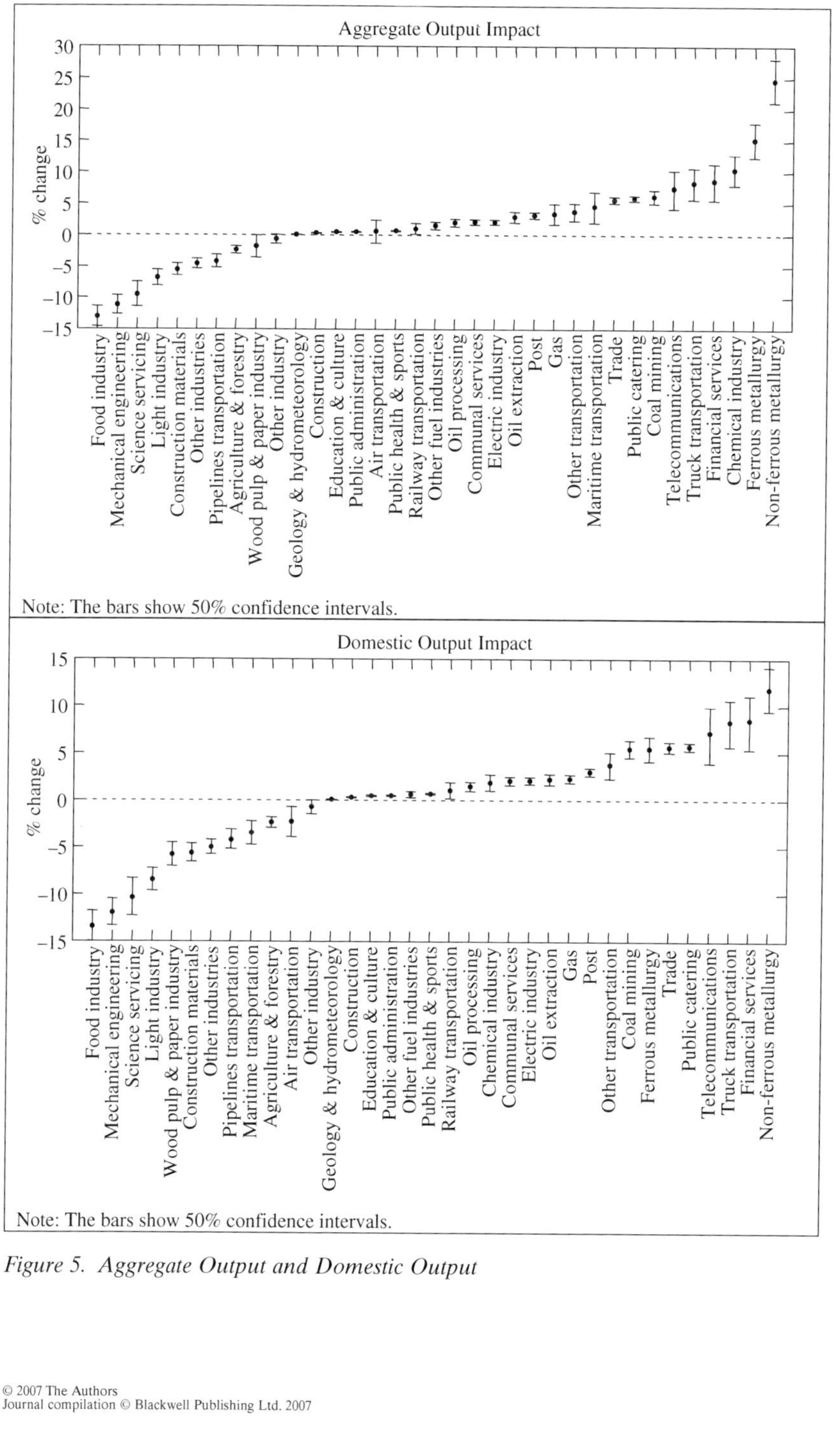

Note: The bars show 50% confidence intervals.

Note: The bars show 50% confidence intervals.

Figure 5. Aggregate Output and Domestic Output

References

Baldwin, Richard E., Rikard Forslid, and Jan Haaland, "Investment Creation and Investment Diversion: Simulation Analysis of the Single Market Programme," in R. Baldwin and J. Francois (eds), *Dynamic Issues in Applied Commercial Policy Analysis*, Cambridge: Cambridge University Press (1999).

Baranov, S.P., "Compiling the disaggregated version of 'input-output' tables of the Russian Federation for 1995 year for consequent use as a basic data for building the general equilibrium model for the Russian Federation," mimeo (2000).

Broda, Christian and David Weinstein, "Globalization and the Gains from Variety," NBER Working paper number 10314. www.nber.org/papers/10314 (2004).

Brown, Drusilla and Robert Stern, "Measurement and Modeling of the Economic Effects of Trade and Investment Barriers in Services," *Review of International Economics* 9(2) (2001): 262–86.

Brown, Drusilla, Alan Deardorf, Alan Fox, and Robert Stern, "Liberalization of Services Trade," in Will Martin and L. Alan Winters (eds), *The Uruguay Round and the Developing Countries*, Cambridge: Cambridge University Press (1996).

Chinitz, B., "Contrast in Agglomeration: New York and Pittsburgh," *American Economic Review, Papers and Proceedings* 51 (1961):279–89.

Daniels, P.W., *Service Industries: A Geographical Appraisal*, New York: Methuen & Co. (1985).

Dantzig, George and Alan Manne, "A Complementary Algorithm for an Optimal Capital Path with Invariant Proportions," *Journal of Economic Theory* 9 (1974):312–23.

Dee, Philippa, Kevin Hanslow, and Tien Phamduc, "Measuring the Costs of Barriers to Trade in Services," in Takatoshi Ito and Anne Krueger (eds), *Trade in Services in the Asia-Pacific Region*, Chicago: University of Chicago Press (2003).

Dixit, A. and J. Stiglitz, "Monopolistic Competition and Optimum Product Diversity," *American Economic Review* 76(1) (1977):297–308.

Ethier, W.J., "National and International Returns to Scale in the Modern Theory of International Trade," *American Economic Review* 72(2) (1982):389–405.

Findlay, Christopher and Tony Warren (eds), *Impediments to Trade in Services: Measurement and Policy Implications*, London: Routledge (2000).

Francois, Joseph, Bradley McDonald, and Hakan Nordstom, "Assessing the Uruguay Round," in Will Martin and L. Alan Winters (eds), *The Uruguay Round and the Developing Countries*, Cambridge: Cambridge University Press (1996).

Fujita, Masahisa, Paul Krugman, and Anthony J. Venables, *The Spatial Economy: Cities, Regions, and International Trade*, Cambridge: MIT Press (1999).

Hansen, Terje and Tjalling Koopmans, "On the Definition and the Computation of a Capital Stock Invariant Under Optimization," *Journal of Economic Theory* 5 (1972):487–523.

Harrison, Glenn W., Thomas F. Rutherford, and David G. Tarr, "Increased Competition and Completion of the Market in the European Union: Static and Steady State Effects," *Journal of Economic Integration* 11(3) (1996):332–65.

———, "Quantifying the Uruguay Round," *Economic Journal* 107 (September 1997):1405–30.

Holmes, T., "Localization of Industry and Vertical Disintegration," Federal Reserve Bank of Minneapolis (1995).

Hummels, D., "Global Income Clustering and Trade in Intermediate Goods," Graduate School of Business, University of Chicago (1995).

Jensen, Jesper, Thomas Rutherford and David Tarr, "The Impact of Liberalizing to Foreign Direct Investment in Services: The Case of Russian Accession to the WTO," (2004), available at www.worldbank.org/trade/russia-wto.

Kang, Joog-Soon, "Price Impact of Restrictiveness on Maritime Transportation Services," in Christopher Findlay and Tony Warren (eds), *Impediments to Trade in Services: Measurement and Policy Implications*, London: Routledge (2000).

Kimura, Fukunari, Mitsuyo Ando, and Takamune Fujii, "Estimating the Ad Valorem Equivalent

of Barriers to Foreign Direct Investment in the Telecommunications Services Sectors in Russia." Available at http://www.worldbank.org/trade/russia-wto (2004a).
———, "Estimating the Ad Valorem Equivalent of Barriers to Foreign Direct Investment in the Maritime and Air Transportation Service Sectors in Russia." Available at http://www.worldbank.org/trade/russia-wto (2004b).
———, "Estimating the Ad Valorem Equivalent of Barriers to Foreign Direct Investment in Financial Services Sectors in Russia." Available at http://www.worldbank.org/trade/russia-wto (2004c).
Markusen, James R., "Trade in Producer Services and in Other Specialized Intermediate Inputs," *American Economic Review* 79 (1989):85–95.
———, "Derationalizing Tariffs with Specialized Intermediate Inputs and Differentiated Final Goods," *Journal of International Economics* 28 (1990):375–84.
Markusen, James R. and Anthony Venables, "Multinational Firms and the New Trade Theory", *Journal of International Economics* 46 (1998):183–204.
Markusen, James R., Thomas Rutherford, and David Tarr, "Trade and Direct Investment in Producer Services and the Domestic Market for Expertise," *Canadian Journal of Economics* 38(3) (2005):758–77.
Marshall, J.N., *Services and Uneven Development*, London: Oxford University Press (1988).
Matusz, Steven J. and David G. Tarr, "Adjusting to Trade Policy Reform," in A. Krueger (ed.), *Economic Policy Reform*, Chicago: University of Chicago Press (2000).
McGuire, Greg and Michael Schuele, "Restrictiveness of International Trade in Banking Services," in Christopher Findlay and Tony Warren (eds), *Impediments to Trade in Services: Measurement and Policy Implications*, London: Routledge (2000).
McKee, D.L., *Growth, Development, and the Service Economy in the Third World*, New York: Praeger Publishers (1988).
Rutherford, Thomas F., "Applied General Equilibrium Modeling with MPSGE as a GAMS Subsystem: An Overview of the Modeling Framework and Syntax", *Computational Economics* 14(1–2) (1999):1–46.
Rutherford, Thomas F. and David G. Tarr, "Trade Liberalization and Endogenous Growth in a Small Open Economy," *Journal of International Economics* 56 (2002):247–72.
———, "Regional Trading Arrangements for Chile: Do the Results Differ with a Dynamic Model?" *Integration and Trade* 7(18) (2003):117–39.
United Nations Conference on Trade and Development and World Bank, *Liberalizing Trade in Services: A Handbook*, New York and Geneva: United Nations (1994).
United Nations Conference on Trade and Development, Division on Transnational Corporations and Investment (1995 and 1996), *World Investment Report 1995 and 1996*, New York and Geneva: United Nations.
Vernon, R., *Metropolis 1985*, Cambridge: Harvard University Press (1960).
Warren, Tony, "The Impact on Output of Impediments to Trade and Investment in Telecommunications Services," in Christopher Findlay and Tony Warren (eds), *Impediments to Trade in Services: Measurement and Policy Implications*, London: Routledge (2000).

Notes

1. Elasticities of substitution for product categories in the Dixit–Stiglitz framework (1977) have been estimated by Broda and Weinstein (2004). They estimate that, although there are variances within the groups, for agriculture, services, and goods, the Dixit–Stiglitz elasticitiy of substitution is close to three. We choose three as our central Dixit–Stiglitz elasticity of substitution.
2. WTO accession will grant an "injury determination" to Russia in antidumping cases in WTO member countries. Combined with the decision by the US to treat Russia as a market economy, this will imply Russian exporters may have considerably improved rights in these cases in the US. But market economy status may be denied in particular cases, so it will be necessary to see how this is implemented in practice.

3. There have also been numerical estimates of the benefits of services liberalization where services trade is treated analogously to goods trade, i.e. trade in services is assumed to be entirely cross-border and subject to tariffs. For example, see Brown et al. (1996).
4. Although electricity and gas are monopolistically controlled, prices are controlled by the government. Thus, market determined pricing to exploit market power is excluded by the government, and we maintain the assumption of price equal to marginal costs.
5. One estimate puts the world-wide cross-border share of trade in services at 41% and the share of trade in services provided by multinational affiliates at 38%. Travel expenditures 20% and compensation to employees working abroad 1% make up the difference. See Brown and Stern (2001, table 1).
6. Daniels (1985) found that service providers charge higher prices when the service is provided at a distance.
7. The rate of return on investment in our model is the rental rate on capital divided by the cost of a unit of the capital good.
8. The protocol on Russian accession signed between the European Union and Russia on May 21, 2004 calls for the termination of the Rostelekom monopoly by 2007 and allows for an increase in the upper limit on the multinational share of the Russian insurance market. See UNCTAD (1996) or Brown and Stern (2001, table 2) for a complete list of barriers to FDI worldwide.
9. This information was provided by the following Russian companies or research institutes: ZNIIS in the case of telecommunications, ExpertRA for banking, insurance and securities; Central Marine Research and Design Institute (CNIIMF) for maritime transportation services, and InfoMost for air transportation services. We thank Vladimir Klimushin of ZNIIS; Dmitri Grishankov and Irina Shuvalova of ExpertRA; Boris Rybak and Dmitry Manakov of InfoMost; and Tamara Novikova, Juri Ivanov and Vladimir Vasiliev of CNIIMF. The questionnaires are available at www.worldbank.org/trade/russia-wto. The same sources provided the data on share of expatriate labor discussed below.
10. Warren estimated quantity impacts and then, using elasticity estimates, was able to obtain price impacts. The estimates by Kimura et al. that we employ are for "discriminatory" barriers against FDI. Kimura et al. also estimate the impact of barriers on investment in services that are the sum of discriminatory and non-discriminatory barriers.
11. Kimura et al. estimated that the price of telecommunications services in Russia are elevated by 10% due to barriers to multinational service providers. We believe that in telecommunications it is crucial to employ a differentiated product model to characterize competition between multinational and Russian telecommunications providers. This means that we interpret the estimates of Kimura et al. to indicate that the discriminatory tax on multinational service providers results in a 10% increase in the ***composite price*** of domestic and multinational service provision. Then the *ad valorem* tax on multinationals, say at rate x, must be above 10% since there is no discriminatory tax on domestic service providers and the composite price is a weighted average of domestic prices (which are untaxed) and multinational prices which are taxed at a rate x. More precisely, if x is the *ad valorem* equivalent of the barriers to multinational investment in telecommunications in Russia, s is the share of the market in Russia of multinationals, 10% is the amount by which telecommunications prices are elevated due to the barriers, and if we assume Russian domestic service providers' prices are unaffected, then we may solve for x from: $sx + (1 - s) * 0 = 0.10$. That is, $x = 0.10/s$. Our data indicate that $s = 0.15$, and therefore $x = 0.67$ or 67%.

Barriers to FDI, however, have an indirect effect on the price of Russian telecommunications services. Consequently, $sx + (1 - s) * y = 0.10$ may be more appropriate, where y is the amount by which the price of Russian telecommunications services are increased in the benchmark as a result of barriers on multinational telecommunications service providers. The value of y would have to be less than the value of the increase in composite services (0.1). It is likely that the indirect effect of barriers to FDI on the price of domestic Russian telecommunications services is less than 0.05, since the composite price increased by only 0.1 and lower values of y yield higher estimates of x. But if we take $y = 0.05$, then x equals 0.38, which is approximately the value estimated for financial services, of 0.33. We take a conservative estimate here of 0.33 for telecommunications.

12. See Markusen et al. (2005) for a detailed explanation on why FDI may be a partial equilibrium substitute for domestic labor but a general equilibrium complement.
13. The data in this paper, which were entered manually, are based on a level of aggregation reported by the Customs Committee that yields about 2000 tariff lines. We thank Ekaterina Krivonos and Eshref Trushin for their work on these data.
14. The regulations can be found on the web page of the Customs Computer Service: www.tks.ru in the document database (Базы данных → Документы).
15. International Monetary Fund, "Russian Federation: Selected Issues and Statistical Appendix," 2002.
16. We thank Jan Strelka for painstaking work on the export data, which he compiled into a spreadsheet. He has also documented this work, including his sources for the export tax data.
17. Actual tariff reductions remain a part of the accession negotiations and are not known with certainty.
18. The real exchange depreciates because the increased demand for imports accompanying the decline in tariffs induces an increase in the price of foreign exchange. In addition, the reduction in barriers to multinational investment in the services sector depreciates the real exchange rate. This is because multinationals use more foreign skilled labor, and they must pay in foreign exchange for the foreign skilled labor from domestic sales. The depreciation of the real exchange rate encourages exports and mutes the import expansion.
19. We assume that firms in the business services sectors must use a specific factor in order to produce output. This specific factor results in an upward-sloping supply curve in each business services sector.
20. See Matusz and Tarr (2000) for an elaboration of the distinction between private and social costs of adjustment.
21. Without increasing returns to scale, removing barriers to FDI has no effect.
22. Rutherford and Tarr (2003) explain why we typically, but not always, find in models with product differentiation that the rate of return on investment (the rental rate on capital divided by the cost of a unit of capital) increases. This despite the fact that we have no *a priori* expectation that the rental rate on capital will rise relative to the wage rate.
23. On the other hand, Russia has had a substantial trade surplus in the past several years; the trade surplus was $46 billion in 2002, approximately the value of aggregate imports, which reflected decisions by Russian investors to invest abroad. If WTO accession can improve the investment climate in Russia, the large annual capital outflow of Russia could be turned around and invested in Russia. Then, it may be possible to achieve a larger capital stock without the foregone consumption that is typically required.
24. An increase in the elasticity of substitution between varieties reduces the welfare gain. This is because when varieties are good substitutes, additional varieties are worth less to firms and consumers.
25. Thus, variation in the values of etaf, esubs and theta_fdi have a greater impact on these sectors.

Review of International Economics, 18(1), 30–46, 2010
DOI:10.1111/j.1467-9396.2009.00879.x

Regional Impacts of Liberalization of Barriers against Foreign Direct Investment in Services: The Case of Russia's Accession to the WTO

*Thomas F. Rutherford and David G. Tarr**

Abstract

In this paper, the authors develop a 10-region comparative static computable general-equilibrium model of Russia to assess the impact of accession to the World Trade Organization on the regions of Russia. The model allows for foreign direct investment in business services and endogenous productivity effects from additional varieties of business services and goods produced under imperfect competition. The authors then show that these features are crucial to the results, as the welfare gains are about 20 times greater than in a constant-returns-to-scale model. The results for the estimated gains vary considerably across the regions; this is principally explained by the ability of the different regions to benefit from a reduction in barriers against foreign direct investment.

1. Introduction

Russia is the largest economy in the world that is not a member of the World Trade Organization (WTO), and, as of 2008, it was among 30 countries in the long process of negotiating its accession to the WTO. Russia applied for membership in the General Agreement on Tariffs and Trade (GATT) in June 1993, and the GATT Working Party was transformed into what became the largest ever WTO Working Party on accession. By late 2008, Russia had reached bilateral agreements with all nations on its WTO Working Party and had reduced the multilateral issues to just the aggregate measure of support in agriculture and a couple of others. But significant differences with Georgia remained on the highly contentious border posts issue.

In response to numerous calls for a quantitative assessment of the impact of WTO accession in Russia, Jensen et al. (2007) have estimated the economy-wide and sector impacts of Russian WTO accession, while Rutherford and Tarr (2008) have examined the household and poverty effects. Russia, however, is geographically very large and diverse. There are parts of European Russia close to the markets of Western Europe and parts of Far Eastern Russia that are close to the markets of China and Japan, while large portions of Siberia are relatively isolated. We can expect the impacts across the regions to be very diverse, even for the same industry. Consequently, it would be useful to determine how the impacts can be expected to differ among the regions of Russia.

* Rutherford: ETH, Department of Management, Technology and Economics, Zürichbergstrasse 18, Zürich 8032, Switzerland. Tel: (41) 44 632 63 59; Fax: (41) 44 632 16 22; E-mail: TRutherford@ethz.ch. Tarr: The World Bank, MSN MC 3-303,1818 H St, NW, Washington, DC 20433, USA. Tel: (202) 473-7677; Fax: (202) 522-1159; E-mail: dtarr@worldbank.org. We gratefully acknowledge financial support from the United Kingdom's Department for International Development and the Bank-Netherlands Partnership Program. We thank Oleksandr Shepotylo for help with the data and estimates of parameters in this paper and Maria Kasilag for help with the logistics. The views expressed are those of the authors and do not necessarily reflect those of the World Bank, its Executive Directors, or those cited.

In this paper we develop a 10-region, comparative static, computable general-equilibrium model of Russia for the purpose of assessing the impacts across these 10 regions. Jensen et al. (2007) have shown that, regarding Russian WTO accession, a model which allows foreign direct investment (FDI) in business services and endogenous productivity effects from liberalization of goods and services via the Dixit–Stiglitz–Ethier productivity effect from greater varieties produces estimated welfare gains many times larger than a constant-returns-to-scale (CRTS) model. A CRTS model will capture only the resource allocation efficiency gains from trade in goods, as well as any terms-of-trade gains. Given that insight, we regard it as essential to go beyond a multi-regional model of Russia based on constant returns to scale. Our model is innovative in that it is the first to allow FDI in the business services sectors in a multi-region model of a small open economy, and the first multi-region model of any kind in which Dixit–Stiglitz endogenous productivity effects from liberalization of FDI in services plays a role in the interpretation of results.[1] More specifically, the structure of the model for each region of Russia is the same productive structure as in the national model of Russia of Jensen et al. (2007); but we have constructed the regional models based on the data for the regions, including adding regional markets, and we have incorporated data on FDI in business services in the regions of Russia.

The key messages from this paper are that it is the liberalization of barriers against multinational providers of business services that we expect to provide the greatest gains to from WTO accession, and that there is a lot more at stake in WTO accession for Russia (and we believe in trade and FDI liberalization more generally) than the Harberger triangle gains from resource reallocation effects due to tariff reduction or from the terms-of-trade gains due to improved market access. Liberalization of barriers against multinational providers of business services results in additional varieties of business services. Through the Dixit–Stiglitz–Ethier endogenous productivity mechanism, this leads to welfare gains that dominate the results. To demonstrate this we simulate Russian WTO accession in a CRTS model and find that the estimated gains in our central model with imperfect competition and FDI liberalization in services are about 20 times greater than in the CRTS model.

At the regional level, regions vary significantly in their gains based on their capacity to attract additional multinational providers of business services. Thus, while improving its offer to foreign service providers within the context of the General Agreement of Trade in Services (GATS) has been one of the most difficult aspects of Russia's negotiation for WTO accession, our estimates suggest that the most important component of WTO accession for Russia and its regions in terms of the welfare gains is liberalization of its barriers against FDI in service sectors.

2. Overview of the Model and Key Data

Production and Geographic Structure

There are 30 sectors in the model; they are listed in Table 1 along with the distortions by sector. There are three types of sectors: perfectly competitive goods and services, imperfectly competitive goods sectors, and imperfectly competitive business service sectors where FDI is present (along with cross-border trade in services).

The model contains 10 regions within Russia that we call regions or regional markets (RMs). The dataset is built on the data for the 88 Russian "*oblasts*," which are analogous to states in the US. Each RM is modeled fully endogenously. Goods and FDI can flow across regions, but primary factors of production are not able to move between

Table 1. Sectors, Tariff Rates, Export Tax Rates, Barriers to FDI in Service Sectors, and Estimated Improved Market Access (ad valorem in % by sector)

Sector and type of sector	Tariff rates	Export tax rates	Change in world market price	Equivalent % barriers to FDI: Base year	Equivalent % barriers to FDI: Post-WTO accession
Perfectly competitive goods					
Electric industry	2.6	0.0	0.0		
Oil extraction	0.0	7.9	0.0		
Oil processing	4.5	4.6	0.0		
Gas	5.0	18.8	0.0		
Coalmining	2.2	0.0	0.0		
Other fuel industries	5.0	2.6	0.0		
Textiles and apparel	16.8	4.1	0.5		
Agriculture and forestry	8.4	0.6	0.0		
Other goods-producing sectors	14.6	0.0	0.5		
Imperfectly competitive goods					
Ferrous metallurgy	5.9	0.4	1.5		
Nonferrous metallurgy	8.5	5.3	1.5		
Chemical and oil-chemical industry	7.5	1.6	1.5		
Mechanical engineering and metalworking	10.7	0.0	0.0		
Timber, woodworking, pulp and paper	13.5	6.9	0.0		
Construction materials industry	12.0	1.6	0.0		
Food industry	14.1	3.1	0.5		
Other industries	12.4	0.0	0.5		
Business services with FDI					
Telecommunications				33.0	0.0
Science and science servicing (market)				33.0	0.0
Financial services				36.0	0.0
Railway transportation				33.0	0.0
Truck transportation				33.0	0.0
Pipelines transportation				33.0	0.0
Maritime transportation				95.0	80.0
Air transportation				90.0	75.0
Other transportation				33.0	0.0

Note: There are four perfectly competitive sectors with no distortions that are not listed in the table: Post; Trade; Public Services; and Arts.
Source: Shepotylo and Tarr (forthcoming) for tariff rates; Kimura et al. (2004a,b,c) for barriers to FDI; Rosstat for export tax rates; authors' estimates for change in world market prices.

regions. Each region also has a balance-of-trade constraint so that any change in the value of imports (either from the rest of the world or another regional market within Russia) is matched by an increase in the value of exports. Wage rates and the rental rates on capital adjust in each regional market so that there is no change in aggregate employment or use for any primary factor of production. Consequently, within Russia, the model shares many features common to multi-region trade models. Descriptive data on value-added, exports, and imports by sector for our 10 regions of Russia, and how we group several contiguous *oblasts* into the 10 regions of our model, are presented in Rutherford and Tarr (2006, R&T hereafter).

Russia as a whole, represented as an aggregate of the regional markets, must satisfy a typical economy-wide balance-of-trade constraint. The real exchange rate adjusts to ensure that any change in the aggregate value of regional imports from the rest of the world is matched by an equal change in the value of aggregate exports to the rest of the world.

Export and import prices from the rest of the world are exogenous. In that sense, the model shares many features of small open-economy models.

Price Determination for Competitive Goods and Service Sectors

In each competitive sector, homogeneous competitive firms in each regional market (RM) produce three varieties of their product distinguished by region of destination: one variety for sales in their own RM; one variety to sell to other parts of Russia; and a third to export to the rest of the world. Firms maximize revenue for any given composite output level based on a constant elasticity of transformation function between the three varieties. For each sector in each RM, it follows that there will be only three prices: the price of the good in the home RM; the price of the good in other parts of Russia; and the price of the good in the rest of the world.

The structure of demand for goods or services from competitive sectors follows an Armington nested structure that is depicted in Figure 2 of R&T.

Goods Produced Subject to Increasing Returns to Scale

Broda and Weinstein (2004) find that increased product variety contributes to a fall of 1.2% per year in the "true" import price index. Schott (2004) and Hummels and Klenow (2005) have shown that product variety and quality are important in explaining trade between nations. Based on these and other studies, a key feature of our model is that we assume that an increase in the number of varieties increases the productivity of the use of imperfectly competitive goods or services based on the Dixit–Stiglitz–Ethier formulation. Dual to the Dixit–Stiglitz quantity aggregator is the Dixit–Stiglitz cost function, which shows the productivity-adjusted cost of purchasing inputs declines in the total number of firms in the industry. Consumer and firm demand for goods produced under increasing returns to scale is governed by firm-level product differentiation within a CES (Dixit–Stiglitz) framework.

We assume that imperfectly competitive manufactured goods may be produced in each region or imported. Both Russian and foreign firms in these industries set prices such that marginal cost (which is constant) equals marginal revenue in each regional market. There is a fixed cost of operating in each region and there is free entry, which drives profits to zero for each firm on its sales in each regional market in which it sells. Quasi-rents just cover fixed costs in each region in the zero-profit equilibrium. We assume that all firms that produce from the same regional market have the same cost structure—the standard symmetry assumption.

Foreigners produce the goods abroad at constant marginal cost but incur a fixed cost of operating in each RM in Russia. The c.i.f. import price of foreign goods is simply defined by the import price. By the zero-profits assumption, in equilibrium the import price (less tariffs) must cover the average costs that foreign firms incur in each regional market.

Similar to foreign firms, Russian firms also produce their goods in their home regions; they incur a fixed cost of operation if each RM in which they operate. By the zero-profit constraint, if they operate in a RM, the price of their product must just cover the average costs of operation in that RM.

Regional firms use intermediate inputs (which can be foreign inputs, inputs from other regions of Russia, or from its own region) and primary factors of production to produce output. The detailed structure is depicted in Figure 4 of R&T). We emphasize that business services are not part of the "other services" nest; rather, business services substitute for primary factors of production in a CES nest.[2]

We assume that Russian firms do not have any market power on world markets and thus act as price-takers on their exports to world markets. On the exports to the rest of the world then, price equals marginal costs. On sales to Russia, firms must use a specific factor in addition to the other factors of production. The existence of the specific factor implies that additional output or firms can only come at increasing marginal costs. Imperfectly competitive Russian goods producers sell in all of Russia; but services firms do not sell in other Russian regional markets.

We employ the standard Chamberlinian large group monopolistic competition assumption within a Dixit–Stiglitz framework, which results in constant markups over marginal cost. For simplicity we assume that the composition of fixed and marginal cost is identical in all firms of the same type in a sector (in both goods and services). This assumption in a Dixit–Stiglitz-based Chamberlinian large-group model assures that output per firm for all firm types remains constant, i.e. the model does not produce rationalization gains or losses.

Hummels and Klenow (2005) have shown, however, that contrary to the standard Dixit–Stiglitz model, varieties expand less than proportionately to market size. As noted by Ardelean (2006), models based on the standard Dixit–Stiglitz love of variety framework will then overstate the gains from trade liberalization. Hummels and Lugovsky (2005) adopt an interesting approach that can explain this phenomenon: they modify the demand structure so that goods become more substitutable as more varieties enter the market; then the marginal benefit of new varieties falls with market size. Another interesting approach is by Ardelean (2006). She develops a general CES framework that nests the Armington structure and the Dixit–Stiglitz structure that allows consumers to choose between more varieties and greater quantities of existing varieties. Her approach yields an estimated increase in varieties consistent with the data. In our model, varieties also expand less than proportionately with market size, but it is due to the costs of production. We assume that in each imperfectly competitive goods or services industry, there are two specific factors: one used by domestic firms and one used by foreign firms. Both fixed and variable costs require the use of a specific factor.[3] The expansion of the industry bids up the price of the specific factor, so additional varieties are acquired at increasing costs, and therefore the number of varieties expands less than proportionately to market size. We show in the sensitivity analysis that the welfare results are quite sensitive to the parameter in our model ($\varepsilon(f_i)$) that is determined by the share of costs due to the specific factor.

We have assumed that imperfectly competitive firms within a regional market have symmetric cost structures and face symmetric demand for their outputs. It follows from these assumptions that all imperfectly competitive firms from a regional market will obtain the same price in any regional market of Russia in which they operate, although the price will differ across regional markets since the fixed costs associated with entering any regional market vary across the regional markets.

Service Sectors that are Produced in Russia under Increasing Returns to Scale and Imperfect Competition

These sectors include telecommunications, financial services, most business services, and transportation services. What is crucial for our model is that barriers against foreign firms will be reduced, thereby allowing additional foreign firms and varieties to enter the Russian market. But we begin by discussing the public–private composition of the domestic business services market in Russia. In the telecommunications sector, the leading fixed-line company Rostelekom is 51% owned by the public holding company Svyazinvest, but the leading mobile companies MTS, Vimpelcom, Megafon, Golden Telecom, and PeterStar are private. In banking, Sberbank had 37% of the lending market in 2006 and is 60% owned by the Russian central bank. Although trucking and maritime transportation is predominantly private in Russia, railroad, airline, and pipeline transportation services are predominantly supplied by government-controlled companies. Personal professional services like lawyers and accountants are provided privately.

Overview of Russian Barriers against FDI in Business Services As Russia began seriously negotiating its barriers in services as part of its WTO accession, key barriers to FDI were the following. Rostelecom had a monopoly on long-distance fixed-line telephone services. In banking and insurance, foreign banks and foreign insurance companies were restrained to a maximum of about 15% of the market. Foreign insurance companies were prohibited from selling insurance in the mandatory insurance markets, and branches of foreign banks are prohibited. In transportation services, China made liberalization of Russian barriers against its providers of truck transportation services a significant issue in its bilateral talks on Russian WTO accession. While several large multinational oil companies would like to construct a gas pipeline, only Gazprom may construct or operate a gas pipeline. Consequently, at least 20 billion cubic meters of gas that is associated with the production of oil must be flared each year.

Russian Commitments to Reduce Barriers against Foreign Investors in Business Services The business service sectors have been the subject of some of the most intense negotiations associated with Russian accession. Russia has made numerous commitments in this area. Some of the key concessions are the following. Russia has agreed to increase the quota on the maximum share that foreign banks and insurance companies can attain from 15% to 50%, and Russia will phase out the prohibition on foreign participation in mandatory insurance lines. Russia reportedly agreed to terminate the Rostelecom monopoly on long-distance fixed-line telephone services as part of the Russia–EU bilateral agreement. (There are multinational telephone operators already operating in the Russian mobile telephone market.) Russia will ensure national treatment and market access for a wide variety of professions, including lawyers, accountants, architects, engineers, marketing specialists, and healthcare professionals. Foreign-owned companies will be permitted to engage in wholesale and retail trade, franchise sectors, and express courier services.[4] The European Union has negotiated intensely for the rights of companies other than Gazprom to construct a gas pipeline, but no success in this area has been reported.

Modeling Business Service Sectors In service sectors, we observe that some services are provided by foreign service providers on a cross-border basis analogous to goods providers from abroad. But a large share of business services are provided by service providers with a domestic presence, both multinational and Russian.[5] Our model allows for both types of foreign service provision in these sectors. There are cross-border services allowed in this sector and they are provided from the firms outside of Russia at constant costs—this is, analogous to the competitive provision of goods from abroad. Cross-border services from the rest of the world, however, are not good substitutes for service providers who have a presence within the regional market of Russia where consumers of these services reside.[6]

Russian firms providing imperfectly competitive business services operate at the regional level and organize production in a manner fully analogous to imperfectly competitive Russian firms producing goods. Other assumptions we made for imperfectly competitive goods producers—such as entry conditions, pricing, and symmetry—also apply to imperfectly competitive service providers. The only difference is that we assume that regional service providers sell only in their own regional market. It follows from these assumptions that there is a unique price for all Russian providers of imperfectly competitive business services in a regional market.

There are also multinational service firm providers that choose to establish a presence in a RM of Russia in order to compete with regional Russian firms. The decision to locate in a regional market by a multinational must take into account the existence of a fixed cost of operating in a regional market. Foreign service providers also must use a specific factor to produce the output, and this implies that additional output can only be obtained at increasing marginal costs. Since the structure of costs for all multinational firms that provide a service in a given region is identical and demand is symmetric, there is a unique price for all multinational providers of a service in a regional market. As with imperfectly competitive goods producers, price must cover the average costs of producing in a regional market, and we have a zero-profit equilibrium.

For multinational firms, the barriers to FDI affect their profitability and entry. Reduction in the constraints on FDI in a region will induce foreign entry that will typically lead to productivity gains because when more varieties of service providers are available, buyers can obtain varieties that more closely fit their demands and needs (the Dixit–Stiglitz variety effect).

Factors of Production

Primary factors include skilled and unskilled labor and three types of capital: (i) mobile capital (within regions); (ii) sector-specific capital in the energy sectors reflecting the exhaustible resource; and (iii) sector-specific capital in imperfectly competitive sectors. We also have primary inputs imported by multinational service providers, reflecting specialized management expertise or technology of the firm. The existence of sector-specific capital in several sectors implies that there are decreasing returns to scale in the use of the mobile factors, and supply curves in these sectors slope up.

The above list of primary factors exists in all regions. In the case of skilled and unskilled labor it is natural to assume that the representative agent in the region obtains the returns from these factors of production. Consistent with standard trade models, in our central model we assume that capital and labor are immobile between regions.[7] However, this model is a regional disaggregation of a national model of Russia; consequently, it does not seem reasonable to assume that all capital in a region is *owned* by the agents in that region. Thus, we make the assumption that a fraction of the capital in any region is held by agents outside of the region; but all the capital is held by residents of Russia. We take the fraction of the capital held by agents in the region to be 50%, but this percentage is not crucial to the solution of the model.

Regarding the capital of each region that is held outside of the region, it is convenient to think of a national mutual fund that holds the remaining capital in each region. For all three capital types, 50% of the capital used in the region is owned by this mutual fund and the balance is owned by the representative agent in the region. The national mutual fund invests in all regions and obtains an overall return. The representative agent in the region also holds shares in the national mutual fund.

Key Data[8]

Estimates of the *ad valorem* equivalents of the barriers to FDI in services are key to the results. Consequently, for each of the key sectors, we commissioned 20-page surveys from Russian research institutes that specialize in these sectors and used these surveys and supplementary information as a basis for the econometric estimates of these barriers. Details are in R&T.

Tariff rates, reported by sector in Table 1, are taken from the paper by Shepotylo and Tarr (2008). Export tax rates are calculated from the 2001 input–output table of Rosstat and are reported in Table 1. Since we do not change export taxes in the counterfactual simulations, these parameters are considerably less important to the results than the tariff rates.

Improved Market Access

Although many in the Russian government have argued that improved market access from accession to the WTO is a major reason for WTO accession, Russia has already negotiated most-favored-nation (MFN) status on a bilateral basis with most of its important trading partners, so Russia's exporters will not see an immediate reduction in the tariffs they face and this effect may not be expected to be large. But Russia will have improved rights under antidumping and countervailing duty investigations in its export markets. Consequently, we assume that Russian exporters in seven sectors which have been subject to antidumping actions in Russia's export market, will receive an improvement in their terms of trade by either 1.5% or 0.5% (see Table 1 for details.).[9]

Input–Output Tables

The core input–output model is the 2001 table produced by Rosstat. The official table contained only 22 sectors, and importantly has little service sector disaggregation. In order to disaggregate the table, we used costs and use shares from our 35-sector Russian input–output table for 1995 prepared by expert S. P. Baranov. (For details see www.worldbank.org/trade/russia-wto.) When we broke up a sector such as oil and gas into oil, gas and oil processing, we assumed that the cost shares and use shares of the sector were the same in 2001 as they were in the 1995 table. For example, steel is an input to the oil and gas sector. Suppose in 1995, that oil purchased 55% of the steel used in oil and gas. Then we assume that in 2001, oil purchased 55% of the steel used in oil and gas.

Regional IO Tables

We constructed input–output (IO) tables of the 88 *oblasts* that are based on data from the *oblasts* (described below) and the national IO table. The IO tables for our 10 regional markets are aggregates of the IO tables of the *oblasts* in their respective regional markets.

We assume that the technology of production is common across *oblasts*, so that the IO coefficients from the national IO table apply across all *oblasts*. As a first step, for each industrial sector, we took the national output from the national IO table for 2001, and we used the data in Regions of Russia (Rosstat, 2002, 2003) to allocate the shares of that output across the 88 *oblasts*. That is, from the Regions of Russia 2001, we have, by *oblast*, the value of total industrial output and industry shares of *oblast* industrial output for the year 2000 (Table 13.3); thousands of tons of oil recovery, including gas condensate, for the year 2000 (Table 13.13); extraction of natural gas (in millions of cubic meters for the year 2000, Table 13.14); and thousands of tons of mined coal for the year 2000 (Table 13.15). This allows us to calculate the value of industry output by sector and *oblast*. For each industrial sector, we then proportionally scaled the value of *oblast*-level output so that the sum of industrial output across all *oblasts* was equal to the value of national output of the sector from the national IO table.

We infer *oblast* demand (and supply) of services, assuming that intermediate and final demand for services share a common intensity of demand in all *oblasts* as in the national model. For example, if telecommunications costs are 10% of the costs of nonferrous metals production in the national model, we assume that telecommunications costs are 10% of nonferrous metals costs in each of the *oblasts*. Demand for telecommunications from nonferrous metals will differ across *oblasts*, however, since the share of total output attributable to nonferrous metals differs across regions.

We have total external exports and imports by *oblast*, as well as the commodity structure of external exports and imports by *oblast* for the year 2001 (Tables 23.1 and 23.2). We also have unpublished data supplied to us by Rosstat on inter-*oblast* exports and imports by sector. That is, for each of over 250 key commodities, we have an 88 × 88 matrix of bilateral trade flows among the *oblasts*.

Supply-and-demand balance by *oblast* and by commodity requires adjustment of *oblast* import and export intensities. These adjustments assure that *oblast* exports and imports in aggregate are consistent with national import and export values. We did this by using a methodology that minimized the sum of squares of the difference between the original data on exports and imports and the adjusted exports and imports data, subject to the constraints of supply–demand balance and consistency with the national model data. Since we had greater confidence in the validity of the *oblast* output data than the inter-*oblast* trade flow matrix, in this optimization process, we fixed the output levels of the *oblasts* at the levels we had calculated above. We do not need to make any other adjustments, as the production technologies are assumed consistent across the regions.

Since in every step of the process, we calculated *oblast* shares of the national IO table, the process yields a set of 88 regional IO tables which portray a regional disaggregation of the national IO table. That is, summing over all the 88 IO tables will yield the national IO table, including wholesale and retail distribution margins, investment demand, and government expenditure. Crucially, we may aggregate the 88 *oblasts* into a set of nonoverlapping subsets and any such aggregation will yield a set of IO tables that is fully consistent with the national IO table. In particular, our 10-region model is consistent with the national IO table.

FDI Shares[10]

We first employed the NOBUS[11] survey to obtain the shares of employees working in multinational service sectors in each business service sector in each *oblast*. We used this as a proxy for the share of output in each service sector in each *oblast*. We also obtained information from (1) our estimates from Russian service sector institutes of the share by sector of multinational ownership in the key services sectors;[12] (2) regions of Russia (2003) by Rosstat; and (3) the Business Environment and Enterprise Performance Survey (BEEPS). Only the NOBUS survey provides data that allow us to estimate shares of multinational ownership by both region and sector. We thus start with our calculations based on the NOBUS information.

We found, however, that when we aggregate the NOBUS shares across *oblasts* or sectors, the other three sources of information show considerably higher foreign ownership shares than the NOBUS survey. We believe that the NOBUS survey estimates are too small, and adjust them. We adjusted our estimates from the NOBUS to be consistent with the estimates of the service sector institutes. The estimates of the service sector institutes are lower than those from the BEEPS or regions of Russia, and thus involve less adjustment of the NOBUS data. We employed least-squares adjustment of the NOBUS data so that the weighted average over all of Russia in each sector is consistent with the national estimates we received from the specialist service sector research institutes in Russia. This process will give us a *structure* of ownership based on the NOBUS survey, with the economy-wide average by sector determined by the national data. Results are presented in Table 4 of R&T.

3. Estimated Impacts of WTO Accession

In our central scenario, we assume that tariffs on goods are cut by 50%, that barriers to FDI are eliminated or reduced (depending on the sector) and that seven industrial sectors receive an improvement in their market access between 0.5% and 1.5% (see Table 1 for details by sector). Owing to space constraints, full tables of results for the decomposition scenarios, sensitivity analysis and the results for output, employment, and exports and imports by sector are available only in R&T.

In Table 2, we show that the estimated weighted average of the welfare gains across all regions is 4.3% of GDP, or 7.8% of consumption. By region, the welfare gains as a percent of GDP range from 3.1% in Tumen to 6.2% in the Northwest region. Except for Tumen, the gains as a percent of consumption range from 6.2% in the Urals regional market to 11.2% in the Northwest regional market.[13] In Figure 1 of this paper, we depict the results by region.

Explaining Differences across Regions

The principal explanation for the differences across regions is the ability of the different regions to benefit from a reduction in barriers against FDI. Some regions may attract FDI much more easily than others. A key parameter in our model is the initial share of multinational investment in each sector in each region. Multinational firms have widely different shares of the business service sectors in the different regions. A 10% expansion of multinational firms will be a much larger absolute amount in a region that has substantial FDI initially. Thus, larger initial shares of FDI in a region will lead to larger absolute increases in FDI in the region when the barriers against FDI are reduced.

The three regions with the largest welfare gains as a percent of GDP, Northwest, St. Petersburg, and Far East, are clearly the regions with the estimated largest shares of multinational investment (along with a fourth region, the North region, which also gains substantially). All have estimated multinational shares of the service sector that

Table 2. Impact of WTO Accession on Regional Markets (% change from base year)

	Overall average	Moscow	St. Peters.	Tumen	North-west	North	Central	South	Urals	Siberia	Far East
Aggregate welfare											
Welfare (EV as % of consumption)	7.8	7.0	10.6	13.8	11.2	9.8	7.6	8.3	6.2	7.6	9.7
Welfare (EV as % of GDP)	4.3	4.7	5.7	3.1	6.2	4.7	4.2	4.7	3.3	4.2	5.2
Aggregate trade											
Regional terms of trade (% change)	3.3	4.9	6.4	4.4	6.1	5.2	4.8	4.4	3.7	3.6	5.4
Regional exports (% change)	1.9	2.6	2.1	1.8	2.1	2.2	2.2	1.7	1.6	1.6	2.4
Real exchange rate (% change)	2.5	2.6	3.4	2.7	2.9	2.7	2.8	2.8	1.9	1.9	3.0
International exports (% change)	9.4	13.3	19.1	2.8	17.3	7.7	23.0	10.9	10.8	8.0	11.1
Return to primary factors (% change)											
Unskilled labor	4.1	4.7	6.6	4.2	6.1	5.5	3.8	4.9	2.5	4.1	6.2
Skilled labor	4.2	3.5	7.4	3.8	7.2	5.7	5.3	5.1	2.9	4.4	6.9
National capital	4.0	4.2	4.9	4.2	4.4	4.2	4.4	4.3	3.4	3.4	4.6
Regional mobile capital	6.5	6.6	10.2	5.4	10.2	7.6	6.9	6.5	5.5	6.1	8.0
Crude-oil resources	4.9			5.6	4.1	5.3		5.4	2.9	2.8	5.9
Natural-gas resources	1.8			2.9	–17.2	–9.1		–5.0	–9.9	–12.3	–9.1
Coal resources	10.8					14.1	13.7	13.6	10.6	9.8	14.2
Specific capital in domestic firms	–24.7	–32.3	–26.4	–47.5	–23.7	–27.4	–19.7	–26.3	–18.6	–21.0	–30.4
Specific capital in multinational firms	101.4	60.4	45.6	228.1	79.2	148.3	116.6	130.6	144.1	165.2	118.0
Factor adjustments											
Unskilled labor (% changing sectors)	2.3	2.1	3.2	1.5	4.2	2.1	2.6	1.7	2.3	2.1	2.8
Skilled labor (% changing sectors)	2.5	2.6	3.9	1.9	4.1	2.5	2.9	2.0	2.4	2.4	3.2

Source: Authors' calculations.

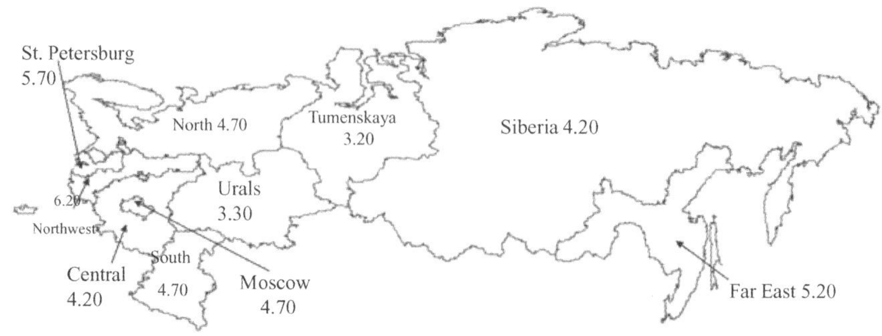

Figure 1. Welfare Effects of WTO Accession by Region of Russia as a Percentage of Regional GDP

are twice the national average in maritime services, rail services, truck services, air transportation services, telecommunications, science, and financial services. On the other hand, we estimate that the Urals will gain only 3.3% of GDP, considerably less than the national average. But the Urals has relatively little FDI in the service sectors, as the Urals share of FDI ranges from about 50% to 70% of the national average depending on the sector (see R&T, Table 4).

Given the aggregate balance-of-trade constraint, the real exchange rate depreciates until the value of the increase in exports equals the value of increased imports. The percentage change in the overall value of increased international exports is presented in Table 2 and equals 9.4% in our central scenario.[14] The expansion of exports varies across regions ranging from a low of 2.8% from Tumen to a high of 23% from the Central region.[15]

Decomposition of Welfare Impacts from Exogenous Changes

In order to assess what is causing these results we have undertaken several additional simulations in which we allow only one of the components of our WTO scenario to change, while holding others constant. First we assess the **impact of FDI liberalization in business services**. We reduce barriers against FDI in the service sectors according to the cuts in Table 1, but there is no reduction in tariffs or improved market access. Russian commitments to reduce barriers against multinational service providers will allow multinationals to obtain greater after-tax returns on their investments in Russia. This will encourage them to increase FDI to supply the Russian market. Although we expect some decline in the number of purely Russian-owned businesses serving the service markets, on balance there will be additional service providers. Russian users of business services will then have improved access to the providers of services in areas like telecommunication, banking, insurance, transportation, and other business services. We estimate that the gains to Russia from liberalization of barriers to FDI in services are about 6.7% of the value of Russian consumption or 3.7% of the value of GDP (R&T, Table 13b). Thus, we estimate that about 85% of the total gains from Russian WTO accession come from the liberalization of barriers against FDI in the business service sectors.

Next we assessed the results of a scenario in which we allow for **improved market access** (according to the terms-of-trade improvements of Table 1), but we do not lower tariffs or barriers to FDI in service sectors. We estimate that the impact of improved market access at 0.3% of consumption (0.2% of GDP; R&T, Table 13d). The gains come from two effects: (i) improved prices for exports and (ii) a higher value for exports allows Russia to buy more imports, and more varieties of imports increase productivity. The gains are quite small compared with the gains from liberalization of barriers against FDI in services. In part this is because the *ad valorem* equivalent of the barriers against FDI are much higher than the percentage improvement in export prices in the sectors that obtain improved terms of trade.

Improved market access has a small but positive effect on all regions except Tumen. The reason the impact is negative for Tumen is that it exports mainly oil and gas, products that do not gain from the improved market access. The improved market access results in greater exports for the economy, which has the effect of appreciating the real exchange rate, and thereby reducing the value of the principal exports of Tumen. This is analogous to the Dutch disease problem, except it is non-oil and gas exports that are hurting the oil and gas exports in this scenario.

Finally, we execute a scenario where we **lower tariffs by 50%**, but there is no liberalization of the barriers to FDI or improved market access. The estimated welfare gains to the economy are 0.7% of consumption or 0.4% of GDP (R&T, Table 13e).

The gains to the economy from tariff reduction alone come about for two reasons: (i) tariff reduction in Russia will lead to improved domestic resource allocation since tariff reduction will induce Russia to shift production to sectors where production is valued more highly based on world market prices. This impact, known as the "gains from trade," is the fundamental effect from trade liberalization and is often stressed by international trade economists; (ii) tariff reduction will increase the profitability of exporting to Russia by imperfectly competitive foreign producers. More foreign firms will enter the Russian market until zero profits are restored. The additional varieties of foreign goods as inputs will increase Russian productivity in sectors that use these goods as inputs.

Decomposition of Welfare Results into Factor Price and Transfer Effects

In R&T, Table 14, we present the details of our decomposition of the welfare effects for each region into their factor price effects, terms of trade, and transfer effects. For each region we report returns to capital as returns to the three types of regional capital held by the region's representative agent. The largest gains derive from increases in the real wages, which increase from a low of 3.8% for unskilled labor in the central region to 7.4% for skilled labor in the St. Petersburg region.

Key to the results is to recognize that the Dixit–Stiglitz–Ethier endogenous productivity effect means that we escape the pessimism of Stolper–Samuelson trade liberalization—that is, the price of all factors of production may increase in real terms. With one exception, the price of all factors of production increases in real terms. Owing to liberalization of barriers to FDI, the rental rate on specific capital for domestic firms declines, negatively impacting welfare across the regions. But the rental rate on specific capital for use in multinational firms increases, positively impacting welfare across regions. In addition, the contribution of capital flows to welfare is negative. Russia has a very large capital outflow in relation to its trade, as exports are approximately twice the value of imports. Given the real depreciation that accompanies trade and FDI liberalization, it will become necessary for Russia to consume a smaller amount of domestic goods to maintain the same value of capital outflow in real terms.

4. Sensitivity Analysis

Sensitivity to Investment Potential of the Regions

In our central scenario, results differ across regions due, to a significant extent, to the inherited FDI of the regions—the greater the initial FDI, the more the regions are capable of attracting new FDI for the same elasticities. In this scenario, we augment the assessment of how regions may adapt and attract FDI based on the ranking of their investment potential. For investment potential ranking we use the rankings of Expert RA, which we explain in Appendix B of R&T. We use the investment potential rankings to adjust a parameter in our model ($\varepsilon(f_i)$) that reflects the responsiveness (elasticity) of foreign investment supply to an increase in the price of their product in the region. We assign higher values of $\varepsilon(f_i)$ to regions with above-average investment potential rankings and conversely for low investment potential rankings.

The principal result (details are in R&T, Table 19) is that the estimated gains for Moscow, St. Petersburg, and Tumen increase, and the estimated gains for Siberia, Northwest, North, Central, and Far East decline. Despite smaller estimated gains in this scenario, Far East and Northwest are still estimated to receive above-average gains. The results suggest that the gains for a region could vary considerably depending on whether it succeeds in creating an atmosphere conducive to investment.

Sensitivity to Results to a 50% Cut in the Barriers to FDI

In this scenario, we cut in the *ad valorem* tax equivalence of the barriers to FDI in the service sectors by 50% of the cut we executed in our central scenario, but we still allow for improved market access and a 50% cut in tariff barriers. We find (R&T, Table 13c) that the gains to the economy are reduced to about 4.2% of consumption or 2.4% of GDP. St. Petersburg and the Northwest regions still are those that gain the most, but the ranking of gains among other regions changes slightly—reflecting different relative gains from FDI, versus tariff reduction or improved market access.

Constant Returns to Scale

In this scenario we evaluate the impact of WTO accession in a traditional-type CGE model with constant returns to scale and no FDI in services. As in our general WTO scenario, we reduce tariffs by 50% and improve the export prices of seven key sectors. FDI in our model is based on a finite number of firms that only makes sense with imperfect competition. Thus, we know from our results above that the most important impact (liberalization of barriers against FDI in services) will be ignored in this scenario. Moreover, the productivity impact from additional varieties of goods in imperfectly competitive goods sectors will also be ignored.

We find that the overall welfare gains to the economy drop to only 0.3% of consumption, from 7.8% of consumption with our full model. This demonstrates that a traditional model that focuses on the Harberger triangle-type resource allocation gains from trade liberalization, and terms-of-trade effects would miss the most important aspects of the impact of WTO accession on Russia.

Piecemeal Sensitivity Analysis

We perform piecemeal sensitivity analysis on all the parameters of the model, where in each case we retain the central value of all parameters except the one in question. In general (R&T, Table 19), the gains to the economy (welfare gains) increase with an increase in elasticities, since higher elasticities imply that the economy is able to more easily shift to sectors or products that are cheaper after trade and FDI liberalization.[16] There are two parameters in the model that have a strong impact on the results: the elasticity of substitution between value-added and business services and the elasticity of multinational firm supply ($\varepsilon(f_i)$). A liberalization of the barriers to FDI will result in a reduction in the cost of business services, both from the direct effect of lowering the costs of doing business for multinational service providers and from the indirect effect that additional varieties of business services allow users to purchase a quality-adjusted unit of services at less cost. When the elasticity of substitution between value-added and business services is high (*esubs* = 2 as opposed to a central value of 1.25), users have the greater potential to substitute the cheaper business services and this increases productivity. The elasticity of multinational and Russian firm supply ($\varepsilon(f_i)$, $\varepsilon(d_i)$) is related to the share of capital that is sector-specific for each firm type (foreign or domestic), but we also allow this parameter to vary with the ability of the regional market to attract capital. When $\varepsilon(f_i)$ is high, a reduction in the barriers to FDI results in a larger expansion in the number of multinational firms supplying the Russian market, and hence more gains from additional varieties of business services. In addition, the share of the services market captured by multinationals has a strong effect, since liberalization results in a larger number of new varieties introduced.

5. Conclusions

In this paper we have shown that the regions of Russia can be expected to gain substantially from WTO accession, and that the gains will come primarily from liberalization of barriers against multinational providers of business services. Although we estimate that all regions of Russia will gain significantly, the results vary considerably across the regions of Russia depending on their ability to attract FDI. Their ability to attract FDI is partly related to geographic proximity to Western Europe or the Far East, as well as their policies and institutions that affect their investment climate.

These results depend crucially on our model, which incorporates endogenous productivity effects from additional varieties. Then the liberalization of barriers against FDI in business services, and to a lesser extent from tariff reduction in imperfectly competitive goods sectors, induces productivity growth in sectors that use these goods and services. We have shown that a traditional constant-returns-to-scale model, by focusing on resource allocation and terms-of-trade effects, would miss the most important features of the trade and FDI liberalization that accompanies Russian WTO accession.

References

Ardelean, Ardina (2006), "How Strong is the Love of Variety?" Available at http://www.mgmt.purdue.edu/centers/ciber/publications/pdf/2006/Ardelean%202006-006.pdf, November (2006).

Broda, Christian and David Weinstein, "Variety, Growth and World Welfare," *American Economic Review* 94 (2004):139–44.

Brown, Drusilla and Robert Stern, "Measurement and Modeling of the Economic Effects of Trade and Investment Barriers in Services," *Review of International Economics* 9 (2001):262–86.

Daniels, P. W. *Service Industries: A Geographical Appraisal*, New York: Methuen (1985).

Dee, Philippa, Kevin Hanslow, and Tien Phamduc, "Measuring the Costs of Barriers to Trade in Services," in Takatoshi Ito and Anne Krueger (eds), *Trade in Services in the Asia-Pacific Region*, Chicago: University of Chicago Press (2003).

Hummels, David and Peter Klenow, "The Variety and Quality of a Nation's Trade," *American Economic Review* 95 (2005):704–23.

Hummels, David and Volodymyr Lugovsky, "Trade in Ideal Varieties: Theory and Evidence." Available at http://www.nber.org/papers/w11828, December (2005).

Ivanova, Nadezhda, "Estimates of Own and Cross-Price Elasticities of Disaggregated Imported and Domestic Goods in Russia." Available at www.worldbank.org/trade/russia-wto, September (2005).

Jensen, Jesper, Thomas F. Rutherford, and David G. Tarr, "The Impact of Liberalizing Barriers to Foreign Direct Investment in Services: The Case of Russian Accession to the World Trade Organization," *Review of Development Economics* 11 (2007):482–506.

Kimura, Fukunari, Mitsuyo Ando, and Takamune Fujii, "Estimating the Ad Valorem Equivalent of Barriers to Foreign Direct Investment in the Telecommunications Services Sectors in Russia." Available at http://www.worldbank.org/trade/russia-wto (2004a).

———, "Estimating the Ad Valorem Equivalent of Barriers to Foreign Direct Investment in the Maritime and Air Transportation Service Sectors in Russia." Available at http://www.worldbank.org/trade/russia-wto (2004b).

———, "Estimating the Ad Valorem Equivalent of Barriers to Foreign Direct Investment in Financial Services Sectors in Russia." Available at http://www.worldback.org/trade/russia-wto (2004c).

Markusen, James R., Thomas Rutherford, and David Tarr, "Trade and Direct Investment in Producer Services and the Domestic Market for Expertise," *Canadian Journal of Economics* 38 (2005):758–77.

Rosstat, *Regions of Russia: Social and Economic Indicators*, Moscow: Federal Service of State Statistics (2002, 2003).

Rutherford, Thomas F. and David G. Tarr, "Regional Impacts of Russia's WTO Accession," World Bank Policy and Research Working Paper 4015. Available at www.worldbank.or/trade/russia-wto, June (2006).

———, "Poverty Effects of Russia's WTO Accession: Modeling 'Real Households' and Endogenous Productivity Effects," *Journal of International Economics* 75 (2008):131–50.

Schott, Peter, "Across-Product versus Within-Product Specialization in International Trade," *Quarterly Journal of Economics* 119 (2004):647–78.

Shepotylo, Oleksandr and David G. Tarr, "Specific Tariffs, Tariff Simplification and the Structure of Import Tariffs in Russia: 2001–2005," *Eastern European Economics* 46 (2008):49–58.

Tarr, David G., "Russian Accession to the WTO: An Assessment," *Eurasian Geography and Economics* 48 (2007):306–19.

Notes

1. Markusen et al. (2005) developed a stylized model where FDI is required for entry of new multinational competitors in services, and this is the core model in the Jensen et al. (2007) and Rutherford and Tarr (2008) models mentioned above. Brown and Stern (2001) and Dee et al. (2003) employ three-sector multi-country numerical models with many of the same features of Markusen et al. (2005). Brown and Stern (2001), however, depend crucially on capital flows between nations, with capital-importing nations typically gaining and capital-exporting nations typically losing. In Dee et al. (2003), multinationals are assumed to capture the quota rents initially. So the results of liberalization depend crucially on the fact that liberalization transfers rents to capital-importing countries.
2. For example, firms can employ an accountant or a lawyer, or contract for accounting or legal services. They can employ a driver and buy a truck, or contract for delivery services. These examples make it evident that it is more appropriate to allow substitution between business services and primary factors of production than to assume a Leontief structure.

3. Since the longer the time period, the less factors of production can be assumed to be specific, our model is more appropriate in the short to medium term.
4. See Tarr (2007) for details.
5. One estimate puts the worldwide cross-border share of trade in services at 41% and the share of trade in services provided by multinational affiliates at 38%. Travel expenditures (20%) and compensation to employees working abroad (1%) make up the difference. See Brown and Stern (2001, Table 1).
6. Daniels (1985) found that service providers charge higher prices when the service is provided at a distance.
7. In the long run, factors of production would be mobile between regions, at least to some extent. Thus, analogous to the implication of our use of specific factors, the model is more appropriate for short- to medium-term analysis.
8. Several Armington elasticities have been estimated for Russia by Ivanova (2005). We took these values where they were available, as explained in Figures 2 and 3 of R&T. Otherwise, elasticities were taken from Jensen et al. (2007).
9. WTO accession will grant an "injury determination" to Russia in antidumping cases in WTO member countries.
10. We explain the methodology further in Appendix A of Rutherford and Tarr (2006).
11. NOBUS is a cross-section survey of Russian households available online through the World Bank.
12. The institutes are the Central Science Institute of Telecommunications Research (ZNIIS), Expert RA for banking, insurance, and securities; Central Marine Research and Design Institute (CNIIMF) for maritime transportation services, and Infomost for air transportation services.
13. The gains to Tumen as a percent of consumption are much higher because a larger share of the GDP of Tumen is invested, so consumption is a smaller share of GDP.
14. The change in the value of international exports must equal the change in the value of international imports. Since international exports exceed international imports in the benchmark equilibrium, the percentage change in exports is smaller than the percentage change in imports.
15. Since the initial value of exports exceeds the initial value of imports in our dataset, a smaller percentage increase in exports is equal in absolute dollar value to a larger percentage increase in imports.
16. An increase in the elasticity of substitution between varieties reduces the welfare gain. This is because when varieties are good substitutes, additional varieties are worth less to firms and consumers.

Eastern European Economics, vol. 46, no. 5,
September–October 2008, pp. 5–26.

ISSN 0012–8775/2008 $9.50 + 0.00.
DOI 10.2753/EEE0012-8775460501

Jesper Jensen and David Tarr

Impact of Local Content Restrictions and Barriers Against Foreign Direct Investment in Services

The Case of Kazakhstan's Accession to the World Trade Organization

ABSTRACT: *We employ a computable general equilibrium model of the Kazakh economy to assess the effect of accession to the World Trade Organization (WTO). Our model incorporates foreign direct investment by multinational business service providers and by multinational oil and gas companies; it contains endogenous productivity effects in both goods and services markets through a Dixit–Stiglitz (1977) framework. Our model is innovative in that we assess the effect of local content provisions for multinational oil and gas companies, provisions that are highly contentious in WTO accession negotiations. We show that our model features are crucial to the results, as the estimated gains are more than ten times larger than the gains from a constant return-to-scale model.*

The working party on the accession of Kazakhstan to the World Trade Organization (WTO) was established on February 6, 1996. Bilateral market access negotiations

Jesper Jensen is a director at TECA Training, Hørsholm, Denmark. David Tarr is a consultant and former lead economist at the World Bank. The authors thank Pedro Rodriguez, Mark Davis, Laura Lucas, and Ilyas Sarsenov of the World Bank for many helpful discussions. They thank numerous officials of the government of Kazakhstan for insights into the issues important to Kazakhstan in the accession negotiations, especially Zhanar Aitzhanova, vice minister of industry and trade and lead negotiator for Kazakh accession to the WTO; K. Abdiyev of the Kazakhstan Agency of Statistics; K. Sagadiev, chairman of the parliament's Finance and Budget Committee; and Lilia Musina, vice minister of agriculture. The authors also received helpful comments from numerous members of the business and academic communities of Kazakhstan, including participants of seminars in Almaty and Astana. They thank Gulmira Akshatyrova, Ainoura Alzhanova, and Maria Kasilag for logistical support. The views expressed are those of the authors and do not necessarily reflect those of the government of Kazakhstan, the World Bank, or its executive directors.

began in October 1997 and are continuing on the basis of revised offers in goods and services. Since 2004, the accession negotiations have acquired increased momentum. A draft report of the working party was prepared by the WTO secretariat in May 2005. Based on this report, the chairman of the working party on the accession of Kazakhstan indicated that Kazakh accession "has taken an important step forward."[1] He stated further that progress would not have been possible without key domestic reforms and the enthusiasm of the Kazakh negotiating team. By 2007, some Kazakh officials were (over-) optimistically forecasting accession by the end of the year.

We document that the Kazakh tariff structure is not highly distorted. On the other hand, barriers to foreign direct investors remain significant in several key business service sectors and are the focus of negotiations between Kazakhstan and the WTO working party. Despite the important role that the rights of multinational investors in business services play in WTO accession negotiations—and in the Kazakh negotiations in particular—until recently, modelers have been unable to assess the effect of the liberalization of barriers to foreign direct investment (FDI) in business services. This paper follows the recent innovative structure of the models for Russia of Jensen et al. (2006; 2007). That is, we numerically assess the liberalization of barriers to foreign direct investors in business services in a multisector applied general equilibrium model, for which Dixit–Stiglitz (1977) variety-productivity effects are crucial to the results.

Local content policies in crude oil and gas are an important aspect of the accession negotiations. At issue is whether multinational oil producers that invest in Kazakhstan are encouraged to purchase Kazakh inputs in a manner that is inconsistent with the Trade-Related Investment Measures (TRIMS) agreement of the WTO. Modeling local content policies requires a modeling framework that distinguishes domestic from foreign firms and gives foreign firms a domestic presence through FDI. Based on the theoretical model of Grossman (1981), this paper is innovative in that we extend the Jensen et al. (2006; 2007) analysis to examine the effect of local content policies in an applied general equilibrium model. We also use that framework to examine a policy option being considered in Kazakhstan: the waiver of the value-added tax (VAT) on domestic inputs into oil and gas. The intent is to place domestic inputs on an equal VAT footing with imported inputs in the crude oil and gas sectors, as multinationals in those sectors are reported to have negotiated a waiver of the VAT on imported inputs.

We develop a fifty-six-sector, small, open economy comparative static computable general equilibrium model of Kazakhstan, which we believe is appropriate to evaluate the effect of Kazakhstan's accession to the WTO. Our key modeling assumptions are as follows. We assume that additional varieties of business services—and those goods that are produced under increasing returns to scale—result in a reduction of the quality-adjusted cost of their use, according to the Dixit–Stiglitz framework. We also assume that a substantial portion of business services require a domestic presence, that is—FDI; multinational service providers import specialized capital or labor as part of their decision to establish a domestic presence; and business services supplied with a domestic presence are supplied by imperfectly competitive firms that produce a unique variety of the service.

We estimate that the gains to Kazakhstan from WTO accession, measured as Hicksian equivalent variation, are 6.7 percent of Kazakh consumption, or 3.7 percent of the gross domestic product (GDP) in the medium run; the gains could be as high as 17.5 percent of Kazakh consumption, or 9.7 percent of GDP, in the long run, using our comparative steady-state model. We show that the gains from FDI liberalization in services are 4.9 percent of the value of Kazakh consumption, which amounts to over 70 percent of the total gains from Kazakh WTO accession. We show that these gains are more than ten times the gains from a constant returns-to-scale model.

Overview of the Model and Key Data

Overview of the Model Formulation

Our small, open economy (SOE) computable general equilibrium model is based on the model of Jensen et al. (2007). An algebraic formulation of the model may be found in Jensen et al. (2004), which is based on Markusen et al. (2005). Consequently, we describe the model structure only briefly here. Because it is new in this paper, we discuss in more detail how we model local content policies and specialized VAT treatment for the multinationals in the oil and gas sectors. Primary factors include labor, mobile capital, sector-specific capital in the energy sectors reflecting the exhaustible resource, sector-specific capital in imperfectly competitive sectors, and primary inputs imported by multinational service providers, reflecting specialized management expertise or technology of the firm. The existence of sector-specific capital in several sectors implies decreasing returns to scale in the use of the mobile factors. Supply curves in these sectors slope upward.

There are fifty-six sectors in the model. Excepting crude oil and natural gas, the sectors fall into one of three categories (see Table 1). The categories are competitive goods and services sectors; imperfectly competitive goods produced subject to increasing returns to scale; and business services that are produced in Kazakhstan under increasing returns to scale and imperfect competition. In the imperfectly competitive sectors we allow for Dixit–Stiglitz, Ethier (1982) variety effects, whereby an additional variety results in endogenous productivity gains for downstream sectors that use the new variety as an input.

In business services, we allow for both cross-border trade and FDI by multinational service providers that choose to establish a presence in Kazakhstan to compete with Kazakh firms directly in the Kazakh market. These services are characterized by firm-level product differentiation. For multinational firms, the barriers to

8

Table 1

Tariff Rates, Barriers to FDI, and World Prices

			Tariff rates (percent)		Tariff-equivalent barriers (percent)		World prices (change in percent)
		Type of sector*	Base year	WTO	Base year	WTO	WTO
Agriculture and hunting	AGR	Competitive	6	3			
Forestry	FRS	Competitive	3	2			
Fishery	FIS	Competitive	6	3			
Coal & lignite	COA	Competitive	3	2			
Crude oil & gas	CRG	Imperfectly competitive	3	2			
Metal extraction	MTE	Competitive	3	2			
Other mineral resources	OMI	Competitive	3	2			
Food products	FOP	Imperfectly competitive	8	4			
Tobacco	TOB	Imperfectly competitive	3	2			
Textiles	TEX	Imperfectly competitive	7	4			
Clothing and furs	CLO	Competitive	5	3			
Leather products	LEA	Competitive	7	4			
Wood products	WOO	Imperfectly competitive	9	4			
Paper and pulp	PAP	Imperfectly competitive	2	1			
Publishing	PUB	Imperfectly competitive	8	4			
Oil products	OIL	Competitive	3	2			
Chemicals	CHM	Competitive	3	2			
Rubber and plastic	RUB	Imperfectly competitive	4	2			

Other nonmetallic products	ONM	Imperfectly competitive	9	4			
Basic metals	BME	Imperfectly competitive	3	2			1.50
Metal products	MET	Imperfectly competitive	5	3			1.00
Machinery	MAC	Imperfectly competitive					
Office equipment	OFE	Imperfectly competitive					
Electrical equipment	EEQ	Imperfectly competitive					
Communication equipment	CEQ	Imperfectly competitive					
Medical equipment	MEQ	Imperfectly competitive	10	5			
Vehicles and trailers	VEH	Imperfectly competitive	4	2			
Other transport equipment	OTE	Competitive	5	2			
Furniture and other industry	FOI	Competitive	4	2			
Processing of raw materials	PRA	Competitive					
Heat and power and gas	HPG	Competitive					
Water	WAT	Competitive					
Construction	CST	Competitive					
Repair of vehicles	REP	Competitive					
Wholesale trade	WTD	Competitive					
Retail trade	RTD	Competitive					
Hotels	HOT	Competitive					
Restaurants	RES	Competitive					
Food delivery	FOD	Competitive					
Land and pipeline transport	LTR	Business service			33	17	
Water transport	WTR	Business service			92	69	
Air transport	ATR	Business service			98	74	
Communication	COM	Business service			25	13	
Financial intermediation	FIN	Business service			11		

(continues)

9

10

Table 1 (Continued)

			Tariff rates (percent)		Tariff-equivalent barriers (percent)		World prices (change in percent)
		Type of sector*	Base year	WTO	Base year	WTO	WTO
Insurance	INS	Business service			53	27	
Real estate services	REE	Competitive					
IT services	ITS	Business service			25	13	
Research and development	RDE	Competitive					
Public administration	PAD	Competitive					
Education	EDU	Competitive					
Health and social services	HEA	Competitive					
Waste services	WAS	Competitive					
Public associations	PUA	Competitive					
Recreation	REC	Competitive					
Other services	OTS	Competitive					

Source: Authors' estimates.

* Sectors are competitive, imperfectly competitive goods, or imperfectly competitive business services.

FDI affect their profitability and entry. Reducing the constraints on FDI induces foreign entry that typically leads to productivity gains, because when more varieties of service providers are available, buyers can obtain varieties that more closely fit their demands and needs (the Dixit–Stiglitz variety effect).

Crude Oil and Gas Sector

We view oil and gas as goods produced under increasing returns to scale and imperfect competition. Unlike other goods in this model, we assume, for obvious reasons in the case of Kazakhstan, that there is FDI in the sector. The modeling of this sector is similar to the modeling of the increasing returns to scale services sectors except that several new features have been added to incorporate a treatment of local content policies and specialized VAT treatment for the multinationals in the sector. In addition, we assume that a specific factor in this sector reflects the need for crude oil and gas reserves.

Local content policies encourage multinational oil firms to purchase some share of their inputs locally. The policies are reportedly negotiated on an individual basis as part of the contracts between the oil and gas firms and the government. Also, we understand that the policies could be characterized as voluntary agreements, whereby the oil and gas firms commit to making an effort to purchase inputs locally and regularly report on the local content in the contracts that they enter. We are not aware of specific local content requirements, such as a required percentage-cost share of specified domestic inputs with an associated direct penalty for non-compliance. VAT policies are reportedly also negotiated on an individual basis. Multinational oil firms are reported to be exempt from VAT on imported inputs, but with some exemptions, pay a nonrefundable VAT of around 15 percent on the purchase of domestic inputs.

Policies in the sector have offsetting effects on multinational firms' use of Kazakh inputs. The discriminatory VAT encourages the use of imported inputs, whereas local content favors Kazakh inputs. Local content requirements imply a distortion that increases the use of domestic inputs beyond the point where the (true) value of its marginal product equals its cost. In our model, the nonrefundable VAT is incorporated as an ad valorem tax rate applying to all domestic inputs that multinational firms purchase. Following the theoretical model of Grossman (1981), we represent the Kazakh local content policies as a 20 percent price preference (subsidy) by multinationals for domestic inputs, which is financed out of the gross revenues of multinational oil firms. These modeling assumptions imply that both policies distort multinationals' input choice, but only the VAT policies involve a transfer of funds to the government.

The modeling of the oil and gas sectors differs from other services sectors in two more respects. First, we assume that all firms, domestic and multinational, use sector-specific capital, which is perfectly mobile across all oil and gas firms. This factor reflects that oil and gas are exhaustible resources. Second, we assume national product differentiation (in addition to firm-level product differentiation) to add convexity to the model.

Key Data

Key Barriers

We first highlight the key barriers in the business services sectors. See the appendices of Jensen and Tarr (2007) for an elaboration of the barriers and the key policy objectives.

In telecommunications, there is strong restriction on entry in some areas of services; incumbent operators have excessively long exclusivity rights in areas such as long-distance and international telephone services and with respect to interconnection for mobile operators; foreign ownership of a company cannot exceed 49 percent; and cross ownership among the incumbents limits competition. The costs of long-distance telephone services and broadband Internet access are three to six times the costs in countries such as Russia, selected EU countries, and Australia.

In banking, up to the end of 2005, branches of foreign banks were prohibited and banks with foreign participation were limited to a maximum of 50 percent of the aggregate authorized capital of the sector. In addition, banks with foreign participation could be subjected to additional requirements, such as the type of business in which they could engage, reporting procedures, and the makeup of their boards of directors. In transportation services, railroad tariffs differentiate between imports, exports, and domestic freight destinations. In addition, a major reform of the sector is planned, introducing competition into freight and passenger services. Network or infrastructure services are to be subjected to monopoly regulation. Existing railroad service, however, is quite slow, contributing to very long delivery times for external trade. In air transportation services, domestic route licensing is rather restrictive.

Ad Valorem Equivalence of Barriers to Foreign Direct Investment in Services Sectors

Estimates of the ad valorem equivalence of the barriers to FDI in services are crucial to the results. Consequently, we commissioned twenty-page surveys from Kazakh research institutes that specialize in these sectors. Our econometric estimates of these barriers are based on these surveys.

These questionnaires provided us with data and descriptions and assessments of the regulatory environment in these sectors.[2] Using this information and interviews with specialists in Kazakhstan, we estimated the ad valorem equivalence of barriers to FDI in several Kazakh sectors—namely, telecommunications, financial services, insurance and securities, and maritime and air transportation services. The process involved converting the answers and data of the questionnaires into an index of restrictiveness in each industry. We applied the methodology explained in Findlay and Warren (2000). For details, including the data, see Jensen and Tarr (2007, appendix B).

Share of the Output of the Sector Produced by Multinational Service Providers

The effect of liberalization of barriers to FDI in business services sectors on the demand for labor in these sectors depends on the share of the output of the sector sold by multinationals. For crude oil and gas, land transport, water transport, financial intermediation, insurance, and information technology services, we employ an average of two proxies. One proxy is the share of employees in large and medium enterprises with foreign ownership (Labor Statistics Department, Statistical Agency of Kazakhstan 2003; www.stat.kz). The other source is the share of total value added captured by firms with foreign ownership (National Accounts Department, Statistical Agency of Kazakhstan 2003). Because these data sources produce unequal estimates, we average the two for our central estimate, using the actual values as the bounds for the sensitivity analysis.

For communication, we have detailed data on revenue by type of telecommunication services (Interfax Kazakhstan 2005; www.aic.gov.kz). We aggregate the data to three types of services: fixed line, mobile, and Internet. Fixed-line and Internet services are dominated by Kazakh firms, whereas mobile services are almost exclusively provided by firms with significant foreign ownership. We use the revenue share for mobile firms to estimate the market share of foreign firms in the telecommunications sector. For air transport, our estimate is based on interviews with Kazakh experts.

Share of Expatriate Labor

Due to lack of data in Kazakhstan on the share of expatriate labor that multinational firms use, our estimates for this parameter are from our Russia model. However, we do perform sensitivity analysis with respect to this parameter.

Tariff and Export Tax Data

We begin with tariff rate data at the four-digit harmonized system (HS) level based on government decree 1389 of the Republic of Kazakhstan, with updates and amendments as of May 5, 2005.[3] We then aggregate the four-digit data to two-digit categories using a simple average method of tariff rate aggregation. Subsequently, we map the two-digit tariff lines to the sectors of our model, again using a simple average of the tariff rates to obtain the tariff rates at the level of aggregation of our model. The export tax rate data were taken from the rates implied by the input–output table.

Input–Output Table

The core input–output model is the 2003 table produced by the Statistical Agency of the Republic of Kazakhstan. We use this table along with the data on tariff rates, estimates of the ad valorem equivalents of barriers to FDI, data on local content and VAT policies in the oil and gas sectors, and data discussed above on services sectors to calibrate the model following the calibration procedure in Jensen et al. (2004). In all sectors except oil and gas, we calibrate an identical cost function for intermediate inputs for both national and multinational firms (in the absence of firm-specific data). In the oil and gas sectors, we calibrate separate cost functions for national and multinational firms as the VAT and local content policies affect their cost functions differently. We first calibrate identical cost shares for intermediate inputs, as in other sectors. Incorporating a 20 percent price preference then reduces the cost shares of domestic inputs that multinational firms purchase. The price preference (an ad valorem subsidy) is then financed by an ad valorem tax on output. The revenue of this tax equals the value of the subsidy to domestic inputs, leaving the output of the multinational firms unchanged. Incorporating the discriminatory VAT finally increases the same cost shares by 15 percent.[4]

Results

In our general WTO scenario, we assume that barriers to FDI are reduced by 50 percent, except as indicated in Table 1; basic metals and metal products, which are subject to antidumping actions in export markets, receive an exogenous increase in their export prices (1.5 percent and 1 percent, respectively); and the tariff rates of all sectors are reduced by 50 percent.[5] We first discuss (and present in Table 2) our estimates of the effect of Kazakh WTO accession on aggregate variables. The gains come from a combination of effects, so we also estimate the comparative static effects of the various components of WTO accession to assess their relative importance. We discuss sector effects and then, given the innovative nature of the work on local content policies, we discuss the local content results in some detail. We also consider the results of assuming that the time frame is long enough for capital to adjust to its new long-run steady-state equilibrium in a scenario we call comparative steady state.

Aggregate Welfare Effects of WTO Accession

We estimate that the welfare gains to Kazakhstan are equal to 6.7 percent of Kazakh consumption (or 3.7 percent of GDP) in the medium term. These gains derive from four key effects: improved access to the markets of non–Commonwealth of Independent States (CIS) countries in selected products; Kazakh tariff reduction; liberalization of barriers to FDI in services sectors; and the elimination of local content policies for multinational oil companies, combined with VAT exemption on

Table 2

Impact of WTO Accession on Economy-Wide Variable: Policy Results and Decomposition of Effects (results are percentage change from initial equilibrium)

	Benchmark	WTO accession	VAT and local content only	Tariff reform only	Improved market access only	Reform of FDI barriers only	WTO accession in CRTS model	WTO accession in steady-state model
FDI liberalization?	No	Yes	No	No	No	Yes	—	Yes
Improved market access?	No	Yes	No	No	Yes	No	Yes	Yes
Reduction in tariffs?	No	Yes	No	Yes	No	No	Yes	Yes
Oil VAT reform?	No	Yes	Yes	No	No	No	—	Yes
Removal of local content policies?	No	Yes	Yes	No	No	No	—	Yes
	(1)	(2)	(3)	(4)	(5)	(6)	(7)	(8)
Aggregate welfare								
Welfare (EV as percent of consumption)	0.0	6.7	0.9	0.4	0.5	4.9	0.5	17.5
Welfare (EV as percent of GDP)	0.0	3.7	0.5	0.2	0.3	2.7	0.3	9.7
Government budget								
Tariff revenue (percent of GDP)	0.8	0.5	0.8	0.4	0.8	0.8	0.5	0.5
Tariff revenue (percent change)	0.0	–41.5	2.5	–45.3	0.3	4.2	–48.0	–38.5
Aggregate trade								
Real exchange rate (percent change)	0.0	1.9	0.1	0.4	0.0	1.4	0.1	3.2
Aggregate exports (percent change)	0.0	7.3	1.7	2.3	0.0	2.9	1.1	13.5

(continues)

16

Table 2 (Continued)

	(1)	(2)	(3)	(4)	(5)	(6)	(7)	(8)
Return to factors								
Wage (percent change)	0.0	5.2	0.9	0.9	0.2	3.1	0.7	14.7
Capital (percent change)	0.0	6.6	1.8	0.5	0.2	4.0	0.5	16.2
Factor adjustments								
Labor adjustment (percent of workers who change jobs)	0.0	2.3	1.3	0.3	1.1	0.8	0.9	0.8
Capital adjustment (percent of mobile capital released to other sectors)	0.0	1.1	0.6	0.4	0.7	0.4	0.7	0.0
Capital stock, percent change	0.0	0.0	0.0	0.0	0.0	0.0	0.0	12.9

Source: Authors' estimates.

their input purchases from domestic sources (parallel treatment to the VAT treatment on imported inputs). We execute four scenarios to understand the relative effects of these various elements and the mechanisms through which they operate.

Effect of Tariff Reduction

The results for the effect of tariff reduction are presented in Table 2, column 4. We lower tariffs by 50 percent, but do not liberalize the barriers to FDI, improve market access, or reform local content. The estimated welfare gains to the economy are 0.4 percent of consumption or 0.2 percent of GDP. From Table 1, we can see that tariffs rates are not high in Kazakhstan: The maximum rate when aggregated to the sectors of our model is 10 percent. Thus, additional welfare gains from tariff reform alone are limited.

The gains to the economy from tariff reduction alone come about for two reasons. Tariff reduction in Kazakhstan leads to improved domestic resource allocation, as tariff reduction induces Kazakhstan to shift production to sectors in which production is valued more highly at world market prices. This is the fundamental effect from trade liberalization in models of constant returns to scale (CRTS). In addition, tariff reduction on imports in imperfectly competitive sectors raises the tariff-ridden demand curve for imports. This increases the profitability for foreigners of selling in the Kazakh market, thereby inducing new entry by foreign suppliers until zero profits are restored. Although there is a loss of domestic varieties due to increased foreign competition, there is a net increase in varieties. The additional varieties in the imperfectly competitive sectors of Kazakhstan result in productivity improvement for users of these goods through the Dixit–Stiglitz–Ethier effect. The result is analogous to the result found by Rutherford and Tarr (2002) in a fully dynamic model.

Impact of Improved Market Access

Table 2, column 5, presents the results of a scenario that allows for improved market access in basic metals by 1.5 percent and metals by 1 percent, but does not lower tariffs or barriers to FDI in services sectors or change local content or VAT policy in oil and gas. We estimate the effect of improved market access at 0.5 percent of consumption (0.3 percent of GDP). Gains derive from improved prices for exports. But a higher value for exports also allows Kazakhstan to buy more imports, and in turn, more varieties of imports increase productivity. Thus, the effect of improved market access is greater in a model with Dixit–Stiglitz variety effects than in a CRTS model.

Effect of FDI Liberalization in Business Services

In the next scenario, labeled reform of FDI barriers in Table 2, column 6, we cut the discriminatory tax on multinationals in the services sectors by 50 percent, but do not reduce tariffs or improve market access. The reduction in the discriminatory tax on multinationals increases profitability for multinationals providing services in Kazakhstan, thereby inducing new entry by multinational service providers until zero profits are restored. Although there is a loss of domestic service varieties due to increased multinational competition, there is a net increase in varieties. Kazakh businesses then have improved access to multinational service providers in areas such as telecommunications, banking, insurance, transportation, and other business services. The additional service varieties in the business services sectors should lower the cost of doing business and result in improved productivity for users of these goods through the Dixit–Stiglitz–Ethier effect. We estimate that the gains to Kazakhstan from liberalizing barriers to FDI in services are about 4.9 percent of the value of Kazakh consumption or over 70 percent of the total gains to Kazakhstan of WTO accession.

Effect of Removal of Local Content Provisions in Oil and Gas and Provision of Parallel Exemptions on the VAT

In the last scenario, the requirement for multinationals to purchase some share of inputs locally is removed. We model this requirement as a 20 percent price preference by multinationals for domestic inputs, financed out of multinational oil company revenues from their output. Multinational oil companies are reportedly exempt from the VAT on imported inputs, but pay the 15 percent VAT on the purchase of domestic inputs. This scenario also imposes parallel treatment of the VAT by exempting multinationals from the VAT on the purchase of domestic inputs. Table 2, column 3, presents the results. Implementing the combined policies in the oil and gas sectors results in a gain of 0.9 percent of consumption or 0.5 percent of GDP. More detailed analysis of these policies is presented below.

Sector Results

We estimate that sectors will expand if they export a relatively large share of their output, obtain an exogenous increase in export prices as a result of WTO accession, are relatively unprotected initially compared to other sectors of the economy, or experience a significant reduction in the cost of their intermediate inputs, typically because they have a large share of intermediate inputs that come from sectors that experience productivity advances due to trade or FDI liberalization. The sectors expanding the most are electrical equipment, chemicals, and crude oil and gas; basic metals; and communication equipment.

The sectors that contract the most are those that are the most protected before tariff reduction and have a relatively small share of exports. These include the sectors for wood products, medical equipment, vehicles and trailers, other non-metallic products, and publishing. See Jensen and Tarr (2007, p. 25, table 6) for estimated changes, for all sectors in our model, of output, exports, imports, and employment.

In the business services sectors, we find that output expands in several sectors—communications, financial intermediation, and land transport—but falls in water and air transport services. Domestic lobbying interests within a service sector should be diverse regarding FDI liberalization. We estimate that labor should find it in their interest to support FDI liberalization even if capital owners in the sector oppose it. Capital owners may have diverse interests, depending on their prospects for joint venture partnerships with multinationals.

Oil- and Gas- Sector Policies: Local Content Requirements and Value-Added Exemptions for Multinationals

In the oil and gas sectors, local content requirements and the value-added exemption for multinationals work in opposite directions regarding the incentive for multinationals to use Kazakh inputs. On one hand, local content requirements for multinationals encourage multinationals to use Kazakh inputs. On the other hand, the exemption of the 15 percent value-added tax on multinational use of imported intermediates discourages multinationals from using Kazakh inputs. We find (Table 3, column 4) that simultaneously exempting multinationals from the VAT on the purchase of domestic inputs and eliminating local content requirements results in a gain of 0.9 percent of consumption or 0.5 percent of GDP. If we provide independently for an exemption of multinational oil companies from the VAT on their purchases of Kazakh inputs (parallel VAT treatment of Kazakh and imported inputs), we find (Table 3, column 6) that the Kazakh economy gains 1.1 percent of consumption (0.6 percent of GDP). However, we also estimate that eliminating local content policies, in the presence of discriminatory VAT treatment, results in a loss of welfare to the Kazakh economy of 0.3 percent of consumption (Table 3, column 5). The explanation for the local content estimate is a "second-best" story. Discriminatory VAT treatment has a powerful effect in discouraging multinational oil companies from using Kazakh inputs. Local content policies offset that distortion, so their removal diminishes welfare.

To verify our second-best explanation, column (7) displays results from a scenario starting from no discriminatory VAT treatment and then eliminating local content policies. As expected, the result of unilateral elimination of local content policies results in a gain in welfare equal to 0.2 percent of consumption (Table 3, column 7). Further, if local content were equal to a 30 percent subsidy on Kazakh purchases rather than a 20 percent subsidy (as assumed in our central scenario), then unilaterally eliminating local content policies with no discriminatory VAT treatment results in a gain to the Kazakh economy of 0.9 percent of consumption (Table 3, column 8).[6] The scenarios verify that the local content policies are harmful to the economy absent the offsetting VAT distortion and that the adverse

20

Table 3

Impact of Removal of VAT Discrimination and Local Content Policies: Policy Results and Decomposition of Effects (results are percentage change from initial equilibrium)

	Benchmark	WTO accession	WTO accession without VAT and local content reform	VAT and content reform only	Local content reform only	VAT reform only	Local content reform only (no VAT on oil firms)	Local content reform only (30 percent and no VAT on oil firms)
FDI liberalization?	No	Yes	Yes	No	No	No	No	No
Improved market access?	No	Yes	Yes	No	No	No	No	No
Reduction in tariffs?	No	Yes	Yes	No	No	No	No	No
Oil VAT reform?	No	Yes	No	Yes	No	Yes	No	No
Removal of local content policies?	No	Yes	No	Yes	Yes	No	Yes	Yes
	(1)	(2)	(3)	(4)	(5)	(6)	(7)	(8)
Aggregate welfare								
Welfare (EV as percent of consumption)	0.0	6.7	5.8	0.9	–0.3	1.1	0.2	0.9
Welfare (EV as percent of GDP)	0.0	3.7	3.2	0.5	–0.1	0.6	0.1	0.5

21

Government budget								
Tariff revenue (percent of GDP)	0.8	0.5	0.5	0.8	0.8	0.8	0.8	0.8
Tariff revenue (percent change)	0.0	–41.5	–42.9	2.5	1.9	0.3	2.4	4.6
Aggregate trade								
Real exchange rate (percent change)	0.0	1.9	1.8	0.1	0.0	0.0	0.0	0.0
Aggregate exports (percent change)	0.0	7.3	5.3	1.7	1.2	0.4	1.5	3.0
Return to factors								
Wage (percent change)	0.0	5.2	4.2	0.9	0.0	1.0	0.1	0.3
Capital (percent change)	0.0	6.6	4.7	1.8	0.0	1.9	0.1	0.6
Factor adjustments								
Labor adjustment (percent of workers who change jobs)	0.0	2.3	1.2	1.3	0.7	2.0	0.8	1.3
Capital adjustment (percent of mobile capital released to other sectors)	0.0	1.1	0.8	0.6	0.7	1.2	0.8	1.3
Capital stock (percent change)	0.0	0.0	0.0	0.0	0.0	0.0	0.0	0.0

Source: Authors' estimates.

consequences of local content policies increase more than proportionately with the level of the distortion.

Sensitivity Analysis

The results depend on the choice of parameters in the model as well as certain assumptions, or closures. In this section, we evaluate the effect on the results of changing the values of the key parameters or modeling assumptions in the model.

Model Assumptions

CRTS Model: No Productivity Effects

We executed a CRTS version of our model in which we reduced tariffs by 50 percent and allowed improved access.[7] Without the Dixit–Stiglitz structure that provides the possibility of FDI and productivity gains, the welfare gains are dramatically reduced, to 0.5 percent of consumption, or 0.3 percent of GDP (Table 2, column 7)—that is, we return to typically small gains under CRTS.

Long-Run Comparative Steady-State Results of WTO Accession

This scenario employs our comparative steady-state model (see Jensen and Tarr 2007). We allow the capital stock to adjust and hold the rate of return on capital investments constant. With our comparative steady-state model, we estimate that the gains to Kazakhstan from WTO accession are 17.5 percent of consumption (9.7 percent of GDP), more than twice the estimated comparative static welfare gains. We estimate that the capital stock increases by about 12.9 percent of its initial level in long-run steady-state equilibrium. We typically argue that this type of model produces an upper-bound estimate of welfare gains because the foregone consumption necessary to achieve higher capital stock is not taken into account. However, Rutherford and Tarr (2002) have shown that a fully dynamic model that incorporates productivity effects, such as those in our present model, and that account for foregone consumption from investment decisions could produce estimated welfare gains that are as large as or larger than these comparative steady-state results.

Piecemeal Sensitivity Analysis

Table 4 presents the effect on welfare of varying the values of key parameters. These scenarios retain the central value of all parameters except the parameter in question. In general, the gains to the economy (welfare gains) increase with an increase in elasticities, as higher elasticities imply that the economy can more easily shift to sectors or products that are cheaper after trade and FDI liberalization. The parameters that significantly affect the results are the elasticity of substitution

Table 4

Piecemeal Sensitivity Analysis–Welfare Effects

	Parameter value			Hicksian equivalent variation[a] with corresponding parameter		
Parameter[b]	Lower	Intermediate	Upper	Lower	Intermediate	Upper
esubs	0.5	1.25	2.0	4.5	6.7	10.7
esub	2.0	3.0	4.0	11.5	6.7	5.7
sigmadm	2.0	3.0	4.0	6.5	6.7	6.9
esubva	0.70	1.00	1.30	6.6	6.7	6.8
esubt	0.0	0.0	0.25	6.7	6.7	7.0
esubc	0.5	1.0	1.5	6.2	6.7	7.3
etadx	3.0	5.0	7.0	6.5	6.7	6.9
etad	5.0	7.5	10.0	6.8	6.7	6.8
etaf	10.0	15.0	20.0	5.3	6.7	7.7
theta_m(i)		see below		6.7	6.7	6.8
theta_fdi(i)		see below		4.2	6.7	8.2

(continues)

Table 4 (Continued)

Parameter	Value	Definitions of the parameter
esubs	1.25	Elasticity of substitution between value-added and business services
esub	3.0	Elasticity of substitution between firm varieties in imperfectly competitive sectors
sigmadm	3.0	"Armington" elasticity of substitution between imports and domestic goods in CRTS sectors
esubva	0.0	Elasticity of substitution between primary factors of production in value added
esubt	0.0	Elasticity of substitution in intermediate production between composite Armington aggregate goods
esubc	1.0	Elasticity of substitution in consumer demand
etadx	5.0	Elasticity of transformation (domestic output versus exports)
etad	7.5	Elasticity of national service firm supply with respect to price of output
etaf	15.0	Elasticity of multinational service firm supply with respect to price of output
theta_m(i)	varies	Share of specialized imports V as a share of value added in multinational firms in sector *i* in the benchmark equilibrium
theta_fdi(i)	varies	Share of output of service sector *i* captured by multinational firms in the benchmark equilibrium

Parameter values for		theta_fdi(i)			theta_m(i)	
	low	central	high	low	central	high
Crude oil and gas	0.40	0.60	0.80	0.07	0.10	0.13
Communication	0.35	0.55	0.75	0.07	0.10	0.13
Financial intermediation	0.10	0.20	0.30	0.01	0.03	0.05
Insurance	0.03	0.06	0.09	0.01	0.03	0.05
IT services	0.01	0.05	0.10	0.07	0.10	0.13
Land and pipeline transport	0.05	0.15	0.25	0.03	0.05	0.07
Water transport	0.10	0.15	0.20	0.01	0.03	0.05
Air transport	0.10	0.25	0.50	0.10	0.125	0.15

Notes: [a] Hicksian equivalent variation as a percent of the value of consumption in the benchmark equilibrium. [b] The piecemeal sensitivity analysis employs central values for all parameters (see below) other than the tested parameter and lump sum tax replacement.

between value-added and business services (esubs); the elasticity of substitution between varieties of firms (esub);[8] the elasticity of multinational firm supply (etaf); and the share of foreign ownership (theta_fdi).

Conclusions

This paper developed a small, open economy computable general equilibrium model of the Kazakhstan economy that can assess the effect of liberalizing barriers to FDI in business services. Given the contentious nature of the WTO accession negotiations, we innovatively developed the model to assess the effect of eliminating local content policies applying to multinational oil and gas companies. We found that the source of the largest gains to Kazakhstan from WTO accession is that additional multinational service providers reduce the quality-adjusted cost of purchasing business services in Kazakhstan. Due to these innovative modeling features, we estimate that the gains are more than ten times the gains that we would obtain from a CRTS model.

Notes

1. See the WTO press release on Kazakh accession of June 7, 2005, at www.wto.org.

2. This information was provided by Kazakh research institutes. We thank Il Kalimulin, head of infrastructure and transport department at the Economic Research Institute under the Ministry of Economy for preparation of the questionnaires on air transport, maritime transport, and telecommunications; Gulbakhyt Kalieva for preparation of the banking questionnaire; Dinara Aldabergenov for preparation of the insurance questionnaire; and Altyn Jumanbaeva for preparation of the securities questionnaire.

3. The data were extracted from Jurist, a source of data on the laws of Kazakhstan, as of September 29, 2005. Jurist is an online data source, available at http://base.zakon.kz. Tariff rates for Kazakhstan may be found at http://zakon.kz, an electronic reference database of the legislation of Kazakhstan.

4. We understand that multinational oil firms prefer to deal with the same global suppliers for a number of reasons, including cost savings from using the same suppliers in all of the countries in which they operate and a major concern for quality and safety standards that national firms may not be able to deliver. Our calibration procedure implies cost shares of domestic inputs purchased by multinationals close to the average of both national and multinational firms. We may therefore overestimate the true cost shares for multinationals and underestimate the same shares for national firms. We have not been able to identify data that allow us to verify this or to improve our calibration procedure.

5. Actual tariff reductions remain part of the accession negotiations and are not known with certainty.

6. The welfare costs of distortions tend to increase geometrically with the level of the distortion.

7. Without increasing returns to scale, removing barriers to FDI has no effect.

8. An increase in the elasticity of substitution between varieties reduces the welfare gain because, when varieties are good substitutes, additional varieties are worth less to firms and consumers.

References

Dixit, A., and J. Stiglitz. 1977. "Monopolistic Competition and Optimum Product Diversity." *American Economic Review* 76, no. 1: 297–308.

Ethier, W.J. 1982. "National and International Returns to Scale in the Modern Theory of International Trade." *American Economic Review* 72, no. 2: 389–405.

Findlay, C., and T. Warren, ed. 2000. *Impediments to Trade in Services: Measurement and Policy Implications.* London: Routledge.

Grossman, G.M. 1981. "The Theory of Domestic Content Protection and Content Preference." *Quarterly Journal of Economics* 96, no. 4 (November): 583–603.

Jensen, J.; T. Rutherford; and D. Tarr. 2004. "The Impact of Liberalizing Barriers Against Foreign Direct Investment: The Case of Russian Accession to the WTO." Policy and Research Working Paper no. 3391, World Bank, Washington, DC (available at www.worldbank.org/russia-wto).

———. 2006. "The Importance of Telecommunications Reform in Russia's Accession to the WTO." *Eastern European Economics* 44, no. 1 (January–February): 25–58.

———. 2007. "The Impact of Liberalizing Barriers Against Foreign Direct Investment: The Case of Russian Accession to the WTO." *Review of Development Economics* 11, no. 3 (August): 482–506.

Jensen, J., and D. Tarr. 2007. "The Impact of Kazakhstan Accession to the World Trade Organization: A Quantitative Assessment." Policy and Research Working Paper no. 4142, World Bank, Washington, DC (available at http://econ.worldbank.org/external/default/main?pagePK=64165259&theSitePK=469372&piPK=64165421&menuPK=64166093&entityID=000016406_20070223161209).

Markusen, J.R.; T. Rutherford; and D. Tarr. 2005. "Foreign Direct Investment in Services and the Domestic Market for Expertise." *Canadian Journal of Economics* 38, no. 3: 758–777.

Rutherford, T.F., and D. Tarr. 2002. "Trade Liberalization and Endogenous Growth in a Small Open Economy." *Journal of International Economics* 56, no. 2: 247–272.

Journal of Economic Integration
25(4), December 2010; 644-675

Modeling Services Liberalization: The Case of Tanzania

Jesper Jensen
Teca Training

Thomas F. Rutherford
The Swiss Federal Institute of Technology

David G. Tarr
The World Bank

Abstract

Despite economic theory and empirical literature that have shown that wide availability of business services contributes significantly to productivity gains and growth, economic modelers have been slow to meaningfully incorporate services into their models. This paper employs a 52-sector, small, open-economy computable general equilibrium model of the Tanzanian economy to assess the impact of the liberalization of regulatory barriers against foreign and domestic business service providers in Tanzania. The model incorporates foreign direct investment in services, and productivity effects in both goods and services markets endogenously through a Dixit-Stiglitz framework. The paper summarizes and builds on the surveys and policy notes of the regulatory regimes in business services in Tanzania, and estimates the ad valorem equivalent of barriers to foreign direct investment. The paper estimates significant gains to Tanzania from services reforms, especially in banking, maritime and road transportation.

*Corresponding address: Jesper Jensen, Director of Teca Training, Denmark, Agern Allé 3, Hørsholm 2970 / Thomas F. Rutherford, ETH Zürich, Centre for Energy Policy and Economy, Department of Management, Technology and Economics, Zürichbergstrasse 18, Zürich, Switzerland / Professor of Economics at the Swiss Federal Institute of Technology (ETH-Zürich) / David G. Tarr, The World Bank, MSN MC 3-303 1818 H St., N.W., Washington D.C. 20433, Tel (202) 473-7677, Fax (202) 522-1159, E-mail: dtarr@worldbank.org.

Decomposition exercises reveal that the largest gains will derive from liberalization of non-discriminatory regulatory barriers.

• **JEL Classification:** C68; D58; F12; F13; F14

• **Keywords:** Services Liberalization; General Equilibrium; Endogenous Productivity; Tanzania; Foreign Direct Investment; Imperfect Competition.

I. Introduction

Both economic theory and empirical literature have shown that wide availability of business services results in productivity gains to the manufacturing sector and contributes to its international competitiveness.[1] Despite this, economic modelers have been slow to incorporate services into their models in a way that would allow a meaningful assessment of the impact of services reforms.

In many of the service sectors in Tanzania, the regulatory regime imposes significant burdens on the cost of providing services, both by Tanzanian service providers and by multinationals. Consequently, the number of service providers and their quality is lower than it could be. Reform of the regulatory regimes in Tanzanian services sectors could therefore result in an increase in the number of providers and the quality of business service provision in Tanzania.

Moreover, Tanzania is involved in negotiations of commitments in services in various regional arrangements, such as the European Partnership Agreements, SADC[2] and the East African Customs Union.[3] And in the context of its international negotiations under the Doha Development Agenda, Tanzania may be called upon to make further commitments in the business services area. We shall argue that while there are barriers against foreign investment in business services, in practice, the more significant regulatory barriers in Tanzania are those that raise the costs of providing business services in a non-discriminatory manner. Moreover, Tanzanian commitments at the WTO or in its regional arrangements are

[1]We provide a brief review of the literature below. See Jensen *et al.* (2007) for a more extensive review of the literature.

[2]The South African Development Community (SADC) is a preferential trade area among Botswana, Lesotho, Madagascar, Malawi, Mauritius, Mozambique, Namibia, South Africa, Swaziland, Tanzania, Zambia and Zimbabwe.

[3]The East African Customs Union is a customs union among Tanzania, Uganda, Kenya, Rwanda and Burundi.

considerably less open than its practice. Binding commitments made at the WTO or in regional agreements provide a signal to investors in the services sectors that they are welcome and that the regulatory regime will not be turned against them arbitrarily.

In this paper we develop a 52-sector small open economy comparative static computable general equilibrium model of Tanzania that we believe is appropriate to evaluate the impact of Tanzanian liberalization of services barriers. We adopt the Dixit-Stiglitz-Ethier structure for business services (and for increasing returns to scale goods). The key feature of this framework is "love of variety" which implies endogenous productivity gains from the net introduction of new varieties of service providers or from additional varieties of imperfectly competitive goods.[4] Key to our model is that we allow foreign direct investment in business services. We estimate that a reduction in the regulatory barriers in services would yield substantial welfare gains in Tanzania, and that the innovations in our model are crucial to the estimates.

We have commissioned surveys and policy notes on the key business services sectors in Tanzania. Based on these surveys and policy notes, we estimate the ad valorem equivalents of the regulatory barriers in business services in Tanzania, both discriminatory against foreign investors as well as non-discriminatory barriers that apply to domestic and multinational service providers. We find that the regulatory costs are higher for foreign firms, but they are very high for domestic firms as well.

This paper is innovative since it numerically assesses liberalization of barriers against both domestic and multinational service providers in a multi-sector applied general equilibrium model where the Dixit-Stiglitz endogenous productivity effects are important to the results. Earlier related work includes the following. Markusen, Rutherford and Tarr (2005) developed a stylized model where foreign direct investment is required for entry of new multinational competitors in services, but they did not apply this model to the data of an actual economy. Brown and Stern (2001) and Dee *et al.* (2003) employ multi-country numerical models with many of the same features of Markusen, Rutherford and Tarr. Their models contain three sectors, agriculture, manufacturing and services, and are thus also rather stylized.

[4]Elasticities of substitution for product categories in the Dixit-Stiglitz framework have been estimated by Broda and Weinstein (2004). They estimate that, although there are variances within the groups, for agriculture, services and goods the Dixit-Stiglitz elasticitiy of substitution is close to three. We choose three as our central Dixit-Stiglitz elasticity of substitution.

The Dixit-Stiglitz endogenous productivity effect from the impact of service sector liberalization on product variety is not mentioned in the results of Brown and Stern and are interpreted as of little relevance in Dee *et al.*[5] Konan and Maskus (2006) execute a careful evaluation of the liberalization of barriers against foreign service providers in Tunisia. All sectors in their model are constant returns to scale and perfect competition; barriers in services sectors raise the costs of producing services and allow monopoly rents. They note that their results are likely to be an underestimate of the gains since they do not allow entry of foreign service providers nor endogenous productivity gains from additional varieties of service providers-issues we address in this paper. The papers by Jensen, Rutherford and Tarr (2007) and Rutherford and Tarr (2008) on Russian WTO accession are full economy applications with similar modeling features, but the impact of liberalization of domestic regulatory barriers is not considered in those papers. The paper by Balistreri, Rutherford and Tarr (2009) in Kenya is closest to this model, but tourism is a crucial sector in Tanzania and there are several key issues in the treatment of tourism revenues that are crucial to the results in Tanzania that did not arise in the Kenya model.

The paper is organized as follows. In section II, we summarize the key regulatory issues in the business services sectors, and summarize our procedure for the estimation of the ad valorem equivalents of the regulatory barriers. In section III, we describe the model and the most important data. We describe and interpret the results of our central policy scenarios in section IV. In section V, we examine the impact of different modeling and parameter assumptions on the results. This includes "systematic sensitivity analysis" of the results to the parameters of the model by executing the model 30,000 times.

II. Overview of the Tanzanian Service Sectors and Estimation of the Ad Valorem Equivalence of the Regulatory Barriers

In this section, we summarize the key institutional and policy issues in telecommunications, financial services and transportation and explain how we estimated the ad valorem equivalents of regulatory barriers in services. Below we focus on the regulatory problems in ports, insurance and telecommunications. For a

[5]There have also been numerical estimates of the benefits of services liberalization where services trade is treated analogously to goods trade, i.e. trade in services is assumed to be entirely cross-border and subject to tariffs. For example, see Brown, Deardorff, Fox and Stern (1996).

discussion of regulatory problems in roads, rail, air transport and banking, see Jensen, Rutherford and Tarr (2008).

A. Transportation

Tanzania's port, rail and road facilities are serious impediments to trade, as highlighted by the ranking of Tanzania as 137th out of 150 countries on the 2007 Logistics Performance Index.[6] Although some of the problems are related to infrastructure and require investment, there are serious regulatory barriers and governance problems in regulation that significantly aggravate the problems.

As of early 2008, there were widespread complaints about the container terminal at the port of Dar es Salaam. Tanzanian businessmen complain that congestion in the container terminal of the port is the greatest transport impediment to an increase in exports. The multinational company Tanzania International Container Terminal Services (TICTS) received a concession to operate the container terminal in 2000, when the throughput was less than 100,000 tons of equivalent units (TEU). As the throughput passed the nominal capacity of 250,000 TEU (it was about 350,000 TEU in 2008), the number of containers loaded or offloaded per hour fell to less than half of what was achieved in 2004 and 2005, at the peak of the port's efficiency. The waiting time for ships to access a berth was 12 days in December 2007, and the average total time for an import container to remain in the terminal ("dwell time") more than doubled from 2004 to 2008 from about 13 days to close to 30 days in 2008. As a consequence, some shipping lines were reducing the frequency of calls to the port, while at least one major shipping line has suspended all services to Dar es Salaam until the crisis is resolved. This congestion is raising costs for both importers and exporters and undermining firms that rely on speed and reliability to market.

Long-term solutions to this problem require investment. There are, however, several regulatory problems that have significantly aggravated the problems. Most importantly, the structure of tariffs for the container terminal operator provides an incentive to keep containers in the port. Container terminal operators typically expect to make most of their revenue from the throughput of containers, and this is what happened in the early years of the concession. However, between 2005 and 2008, more than half of the revenue (and in 2008 more than three quarters) came

[6]See http://go.worldbank.org/88X6PU5GV0.
http://web.worldbank.org/WBSITE/EXTERNAL/TOPICS/EXTTRANSPORT/EXTTLF/0,,contentMDK:21514122~menuPK:3875957~page PK:210058~piPK:2100 62~the Site PK:515434,00.html

from storage charges, and this is possible because of the long dwell times.

In addition to the above primarily non-discriminatory cost increasing regulatory barriers, there are discriminatory barriers against foreign firms. A commercial presence in Tanzania is required in order to offer shipping services and foreigners are prohibited from operating in Tanzania, but must operate through a Tanzanian agent. Moreover, formally, although not in practice, the maximum ownership share allowed in a local shipping firm is one percent.

B. Insurance

Although the structure of the non-life insurance market is competitive (but not the life insurance market), the insurance sector is not well developed. Current regulations impede the growth of the sector. These rules include restricting foreign ownership to two-thirds of capital, requiring insurers to be locally incorporated entities, not allowing foreign branches or wholly owned subsidiaries of foreign insurers, not allowing cooperative and mutual insurance companies and limits that make it less attractive for banks to participate in the distribution of insurance.

There are no foreign reinsurance companies operating in Tanzania. This is partly due to the fact that reinsurance arrangements have, at their core, compulsory reinsurance requirements to TanRe, a company indirectly owned by the government. Moreover, reinsurance companies are prohibited to operate as either branches or as wholly owned subsidiaries of foreign domiciled reinsurers. Reinsuring externally, and insuring for that matter, also requires approval.

C. Telecommunications

The government has implemented significant reforms in the sector since the reform program began in 1993. At that time, fixed line telephone services were all that was available and less than 1% of the population were subscribers. As of September 2008, fixed line subscription had not increased as there were only 123 thousand fixed lines available in Tanzania for a population of almost 38 million. However, the mobile telephone service network has been rapidly expanding, from 127 thousand in 2000, to over 13 million as of end 2008.[7] These subscribers were receiving service at very competitive prices.

The Tanzanian telecommunications regulatory environment is based on the modern "converged" licensing framework, and is not restrictive regarding entry

[7]See http://www.tcra.go.tz/publications/telecom.html.

requirements. The non-restrictive regulatory environment has introduced competition in the telecommunications sector, and should be credited with much of the success of the mobile telephone build-out. Nonetheless significant problems remain in the telecommunications sector. Notably: (i) there is a need to develop the Information and Communication Technology (ICT) network efficiently; (ii) internet and data transmission services are very costly. But apart from efficient procurement, this is largely an investment issue beyond regulatory control; and (iii) electronic commerce is seriously constrained by the need to develop credit reference bureaus, the lack of a national payments system, and a legislative framework appropriate for e-business.

D. Estimation of the Tariff Equivalence of the Regulatory Barriers

Estimates of the ad valorem equivalents of the regulatory barriers in services are key to the results. In order to make these estimates, we first need to assess the regulatory environment in the services sectors in our model. We commissioned a 54 page survey of the regulatory regimes in key Tanzanian business services sectors, namely, insurance, banking, fixed line and mobile telecommunications services and maritime transportation services.[8] We supplemented this information based on the policy notes discussed above. These questionnaires and papers provided us with data, descriptions and assessments of the regulatory environment in these sectors.

This methodology involves building on the estimates and methodology of Warren (2000), McGuire and Schulele (2000) and Kang (2000). In different services sectors, these authors evaluated the regulatory environment across many countries. The price of services was then regressed against the regulatory barriers to determine the impact of any of the regulatory barriers on the price of services.

Mircheva (2008) then estimated the ad valorem equivalents of barriers to foreign direct investment in fixed line and mobile telecommunications, banking, insurance and maritime transportation services in Tanzania by assuming that the international regression applies to Tanzania. Mircheva's methodology involves classification of the possible restrictions into separate categories with unique weights summing to one, where the weights are determined based on the international regressions mentioned in the paragraph above.[9] Mircheva assigned a score to each potential

[8]We thank Mr. Cyril Pesha and his law firm associates in Dar es Salaam for leading this research effort.
[9]Mircheva followed the methodology of Kimura, Ando and Fujii (2004) to generate these estimates.

restriction, where the score reflects the level of restriction imposed by the economy. Mircheva estimated two indices: an index of "regulatory barriers" (RB index) where the regulatory barriers impose costs on both domestic and multinational firms in a non-discriminatory manner; and an index of discriminatory barriers against multinational service providers, which we call the foreign discriminatory index (FDR index).[10]

Applying the international regressions and her assessments of the regulatory environment in Tanzania from the questionnaires and other information sources, Mircheva estimated the ad valorem impact of a reduction in barriers[11] both for

Table 1. Sector Definitions and Initial Ad Valorem Distortions

			Regulatory barriers	
	Tariff	Sales Tax	All firms	Foreign firms
IRTS Goods and Services	**6.3**	**5.4**		
CRTS Goods and Services	**4.3**	**1.1**		
Business Services				
Telecommunication			3.0	8.0
Insurance			18.0	36.0
Banking			37.0	25.0
Professional business services			10.0	15.0
Air transport			20.0	2.0
Road transport			30.0	5.0
Railway transport			40.0	
Water transport			86.0	39.0
Dixit-Stiglitz Goods	**7.4**	**6.8**		
Processed food	11.1	7.1		
Beverages & tobacco products	28.4	11.4		
Textile & leather products	29.7	14.1		
Wood paper printing	11.6	3.0		
Manufacture of basic & industrial chemicals	3.6	14.2		
Manufacture of fertilizers & pesticides		0.1		
Petroleum refineries	3.2	1.5		
Rubber plastic & other manufacturing	6.0	7.1		
Glass & cement	7.1	18.5		
Iron steel & metal products	5.5	2.8		
Manufacture of equipment	6.3	0.0		

[10] In order to obtain the estimated score for each restriction, the assigned score is multiplied by the corresponding weight. Finally, the estimated scores for all categories are summed to obtain the restrictiveness indices.

[11] Warren estimated quantity impacts and then using elasticity estimates was able to obtain price impacts. The estimates by Mircheva that we employ are for "discriminatory" barriers against foreign direct investment.

Table 1. Sector Definitions and Initial Ad Valorem Distortions (Continued)

Agriculture	**15.1**	**1.9**
Maize	0.2	0.1
Paddy	20.5	
Sorghum or millets	4.6	0.0
Wheat	8.7	0.9
Beans	25.1	0.8
Cassava	25.0	5.3
Other cereals	8.8	2.0
Oil seeds	1.1	0.2
Other roots & tubes	0.5	5.0
Cotton	1.2	2.0
Coffee	11.8	27.8
Tobacco	11.1	2.6
Tea	18.9	28.0
Cashew nuts	22.2	6.2
Sisal fiber		
Sugar	22.3	1.8
Fruits & vegetables	6.7	0.1
Other crops	4.3	12.4
Poultry & livestock	4.4	2.8
Other CRTS	**3.9**	**0.9**
Fish	22.7	2.5
Hunting & forestry		3.6
Mining & quarrying	3.2	4.2
Meat & dairy products	27.2	13.0
Grain milling	8.6	0.4
Utilities		
Construction		
Wholesale & retail trade		
Hotels & restaurants		
Postal communication		
Real estate		
Other services		
Public administration health & education		
Tourism		

discriminatory and non-discriminatory barriers. Mircheva then weighted her fixed line and mobile telecommunications estimates by their market shares to obtain her estimate for communications. The results of the estimates are listed in Table 1.

III. Overview of the Model and Key Data

A. Overview of the Model Formulation

This paper follows the algebraic structure of the model of Jensen, Rutherford and Tarr (2007) and Rutherford and Tarr (2008).[12] Here we provide a general description. There are 52 sectors in the model shown in Table 1. These include eight imperfectly competitive business services sectors, eleven imperfectly competitive manufacturing sectors, nineteen competitive agricultural sectors and fourteen competitive manufacturing or services sectors. Primary factors include 8 types of labor grouped both according to gender and to one of four levels of education; child labor; agricultural land; mobile capital; sector-specific capital in imperfectly competitive sectors; and primary inputs imported by multinational service providers, reflecting specialized management expertise or technology of the firm. In each imperfectly competitive sector there is sector specific capital which implies that there are decreasing returns to scale in the use of the mobile factors and supply curves in these sectors slope up. In our central model, we assume that 50% of the capital in each of the imperfectly competitive sectors is sector specific. We conduct sensitivity analysis with respect to this share by allowing 25% and 75% of the capital in each sector to be sector specific.

The are three types of sectors in our model. Regardless of sector, all firms minimize the cost of production.

1. Competitive goods and services sectors

In these sectors, production is subject to constant returns to scale and price equals marginal costs with zero profits. This includes all 19 of the agriculture sectors, some food processing sectors such as meat and dairy products and grain milling, and services such as construction, hotels and restaurants, postal communication, real estate, public administration, health and education. In these sectors, products are differentiated by country of origin (what is known as the Armington assumption). All goods producing firms (including imperfectly competitive firms) can sell on the domestic market or export. Firms optimize their output decision between exports and domestic sales based on relative prices and

[12] A full algebraic description of the model may be found at: http://siteresources.worldbank.org/INTRANETTRADE/Resources/Topics/Accession/Jensen-Rutherford-Tarr_servicesliberalization-mathappen.pdf.

their constant elasticity of transformation production function.

Tourism is one of the sectors in this category, and given its importance in the Tanzanian economy, it deserves its own discussion. All sales to tourists are considered exports, i.e., the sector does not produce for the domestic market. Based on a Bank of Tanzania (2007a) survey, we have that the inputs of the sector are domestic transportation services, hotel and restaurant services, clothing, gold items, and certain food products, as well as foreign inputs such as international travel expenditures. Given that we have data only on tourist expenditure by sector and on tourism imports and exports, we assume that the output of this sector is produced without value added. But the tourism sector demands domestically produced services and goods that lead to value-added in the Tanzanian economy. Moreover, the sector is intensive in services and this way we capture the impacts on services liberalization on services exports. We discuss the special data issues related to this sector in the data section below.

2. Goods produced subject to increasing returns to scale[13]

These goods are differentiated at the firm level. We assume that manufactured goods may be produced domestically or imported. Firms in these industries set prices such that marginal cost (which does not vary with output) equals marginal revenue; and there is free entry, which drives profits to zero. For domestic firms, costs are defined by observed primary factor and intermediate inputs to that sector in the base year data. Foreigners produce the goods abroad at constant marginal cost but incur a fixed cost of operating in Tanzania. The cif import price of foreign goods is simply defined by the import price, and, by the zero profits assumption, in equilibrium the import price must cover fixed and marginal costs of foreign firms. We employ the standard Chamberlinian large group monopolistic competition assumption within a Dixit-Stiglitz framework, which results in constant markups over marginal cost.

For simplicity we assume that the composition of fixed and marginal cost is identical in all firms producing under increasing returns to scale (in both goods and services). This assumption in our Dixit-Stiglitz based Chamberlinian large-group model assures that output per firm for all firm types remains constant, i.e., the model does not produce rationalization gains or losses.

The number of varieties affects the productivity of the use of imperfectly

[13] The classification is based on estimates of minimum efficient scale.

competitive goods based on the standard Dixit-Stiglitz formulation. The effective cost function for users of goods produced subject to increasing returns to scale declines in the total number of firms in the industry.

3. Service sectors characterized by increasing returns to scale and imperfect competition

These sectors in our model are telecommunications, financial services, transportation services and professional business services. In these services sectors, we observe that some services are provided by foreign service providers on a cross border basis analogous to goods providers from abroad. But a large share of business services are provided by service providers with a domestic presence, both multinational and Tanzanian.[14] Our model allows for both types of foreign service provision in these sectors. There are cross border services allowed in this sector and they are provided from abroad at constant costs-this is analogous to competitive provision of goods from abroad. Cross border services, however, are not good substitutes for service providers who have a domestic presence.[15]

There are also multinational service firm providers that choose to establish a presence in Tanzania in order to compete with Tanzanian firms directly. When multinationals service providers decide to establish a domestic presence in Tanzania, they will import some of their technology or management expertise. That is, foreign direct investment generally entails importing specialized foreign inputs.[16] Thus, the cost structure of multinationals differs from national only service providers. Multinationals incur costs related to both imported primary inputs and Tanzanian primary factors, in addition to intermediate factor inputs. Foreign provision of services differs from foreign provision of goods, since the service providers use Tanzanian primary inputs. Domestic service providers do not import the specialized primary factors available to the multinationals. Hence, domestic service firms incur primary factor costs related to Tanzanian labor and capital only. These services are characterized by firm-level product differentiation. For multinational firms, the barriers to foreign direct investment affect their profitability and entry. Reduction in the constraints on foreign direct investment

[14]One estimate puts the world-wide cross-border share of trade in services at 41% and the share of trade in services provided by multinational affiliates at 38%. Travel expenditures 20% and compensation to employees working abroad 1% make up the difference. See Brown and Stern (2001, Table 1).

[15]Daniels (1985) found that service providers charge higher prices when the service is provided at a distance.

[16]See Markusen, Rutherford and Tarr *et al.* (2005) for theoretical development of this type of model.

will induce foreign entry that will typically lead to productivity gains because when more varieties of service providers are available, buyers can obtain varieties that more closely fit their demands and needs (the Dixit-Stiglitz variety effect).

4. Comparative Steady State Formulation

In this version of our model, we allow the capital stock to adjust to its steady state equilibrium along with all of the model features we employ in our central scenario, i.e., we allow for tariff and FDI liberalization with endogenous productivity effects as above. The increased availability of services results in an endogenous increase in productivity and an increase in the marginal productivity of capital in particular. An increase in the marginal productivity of capital should increase the accumulation of capital and, in the long run steady state, increase the capital stock. In this scenario the impact on the accumulation of capital from an improvement in the productivity of capital is taken into account. We call this our comparative steady state model.

In the comparative static model, we assume that the capital stock is fixed and the rental rate on capital is endogenously determined. In the comparative steady state model, the logic is reversed. We assume that the capital stock is in its initial steady state equilibrium in the benchmark dataset, but that the capital stock will adjust to a new steady state equilibrium based on a fixed rate of return demanded by investors. That is, if the trade policy shock happens to induce an increase in the rate of return on capital so that it exceeds the initial rate of return, investors will invest and expand the capital stock. Expansion of the capital stock drives down the marginal product of capital, i.e., it drives down the rental rate on capital, until the rate of return on capital falls back to the initial level.[17] To analyze trade policy, this comparative steady state approach has been employed by many authors, including Harrison, Rutherford and Tarr (1996, 1997) and Baldwin *et al.* (1999) and Francois *et al.* (1996). The approach ignores the foregone consumption necessary to achieve the higher level of investment and thus, is an upper bound estimate on the long run gains within the framework of the model assumptions.

B. Empirical Basis for Our Modeling Assumptions

Our model assumes: (1) that discriminatory and non-discriminatory barriers against providers of business services exist in Tanzania; (2) that the removal or

[17]The rate of return on investment in our model is the rental rate on capital divided by the cost of a unit of the capital good.

reduction of the barriers will stimulate an increase in FDI and domestic entry in business services; and (3) that additional varieties of business services (and goods in imperfectly competitive sectors) will produce endogenous productivity gains through the Dixit-Stiglitz mechanism. We have discussed the regulatory barriers in business services, and how, in response to a reduction of the barriers, entry has occurred (as in telecommunications and banking) or would be expected to occur (as in maritime services). More systematically, Alessina *et al.* (2005) find, for a sample of a large number of OECD countries, that regulatory reform, especially liberalization of the barriers against entry, plays a strong role in increasing investment in the sector.

Regarding the productivity impacts in our model, it is the greater availability of varieties that is the engine of productivity growth. Broda and Weinstein (2004) find that increased product variety was responsible for a fall of 1.2% per year in the "true" U.S. import price index. Hummels and Klenow (2005) and Schott (2004) have shown that product variety and quality are important in explaining trade between nations. Arnold, Mattoo and Javorcik (2007) show that in the Czech Republic, services sector liberalization led to increased productivity of downstream industries, and the key channel through which reform led to increased productivity was allowing foreign entry. Fernandes and Paunov (2008) found a positive and significant effect of foreign direct investment in services on productivity growth in Chile. Fernandes (2007) finds a positive and significant effect of services liberalization in both finance and infrastructure on the productivity of downstream manufacturing in fifteen Eastern European countries.

C. Data

The core of the model data is the Social Accounting Matrix (SAM) for 2001 developed by Thurlow and Wobst (2003). The SAM contains 43 sectors, most of which are agricultural and food-producing sectors and only a few are service sectors.

Two sectors in the SAM, "Transport and communication" and "Business and other service activities", account for most business services in Tanzania. Given our focus on services, we disaggregated these sectors into 10 sectors using unpublished national accounts data for the year 2006 from the National Bureau of Statistics of Tanzania.

Data for gross domestic product for the sectors "Transport," "Communications," "Financial intermediation," and "Real estate and business services" is officially published (National Bureau of Statistics (2007)). In response to our request, we received a breakdown of these data for the main types of services within each sector. Specifically, the data allows us to disaggregate "Transport and communication" into road transport, railway transport, water transport, air transport, postal services and telecommunication. We disaggregated "business and other service activities" into insurance, banking, business services and other services.

Within each of the two aggregate sectors, the share of gross domestic product by disaggregate sector is used to decompose the corresponding aggregate sector. It is furthermore assumed that the input output structure for all the disaggregate sectors is identical to the input output structure of the corresponding aggregate sector. Along with the addition of the tourism sector, the resulting table has 52 sectors as shown in Table 1.

The SAM contains nine types of labor: Adults are grouped both according to gender and to one of four levels of education. All child labor (age 10 to 14) is the 9th and final category. Capital and agricultural land and a factor called a subsistence factor are the three remaining primary factors of production.

The subsistence factor is a composite of land, labor and capital used in the production for home (own) consumption by households.[18] The subsistence factor is used in the agricultural and food-producing sectors. In each sector the SAM shows the value of output allocated for home consumption and of output allocated to the market, both of which are coming from the same activity.

1. Tariff Data

We were fortunate to receive unusually detailed unpublished collected tariff data at the tariff line level from the Tanzania Revenue Authority. That is, we received data on collected import duties (tariffs) and import values at the eight digit tariff line level. The collected tariff rates for the sectors in our model are obtained by first aggregating the eight digit tariff line level tariff collections and import values to the sectors of our model. The ratio of tariff collections to import values for each sector of our model is then calculated to give estimates of the collected tariff rates, which in turn are incorporated into our SAM. The tariff rates are shown in Table 1. Applying these tariff rates across all sectors implies that tariff revenue in the revised database is about 1.3% of GDP, which is consistent with collected revenues

[18]Data do not allow a breakdown of the subsistence factor into its shares of the other primary factors.

in Tanzania.[19] The SAM has some detail on taxes, which include direct taxes on households and enterprises, import tariffs, producer taxes, indirect (sales) taxes and factor taxes. The data for import tariffs are replaced with collected tariff rate data for the year 2006.

2. Tourism Sector

The Thurlow and Wobst SAM does not contain the important tourism sector. It allocates international travel expenditure (mainly international tourism) to the "Transport and communication" sector. According to a survey conducted by the Bank of Tanzania (2007a), this is grossly contradicted by the facts. Given our focus on services and the importance of tourism to the Tanzanian economy, we had to correct this problem with the data and add a tourism sector along the lines discussed above. For further details, see Jensen, Rutherford and Tarr (2008).

3. Share of Market Captured by Multinational Service Providers

We estimated the market share captured by foreign banks based on asset data for all major banks operating in Tanzania as provided in Appendix II in Bank of Tanzania (2007b). Foreign banks are identified as banks with a foreign ownership share of more than 20%, and the market share is estimated as the share of assets held by foreign banks. Our central values are presented in the table on sensitivity analysis.

4. Share of Expatriate Labor Employed by Multinational Service Providers

We obtained estimates of the share of expatriate labor or specialized technology not available to Tanzanian firms that is used by multinational service providers in Tanzania from the survey mentioned above. We found that multinational service providers use mostly local primary factor inputs and only small amounts of expatriate labor or specialized technology. Our estimated share of foreign inputs used by multinationals in Tanzania is presented in the table on sensitivity analysis.[20]

[19]For the year 2006, aggregate data from Tanzania show that tariff collections are 1.47% of GDP.

[20]See Markusen, Rutherford and Tarr (2005) for a detailed explanation on why FDI may be a partial equilibrium substitute for domestic labor but a general equilibrium complement.

IV. Results

In our "full reform" scenario, we assume that regulatory barriers in business services sectors against both foreign direct investment and domestic investors are cut in half. Given the high dispersion in the tariff (see Table 1), we set tariffs at a uniform tariff level that leaves tariff revenue unchanged. We assume that there is a representative consumer in the economy, and we measure the Hicksian equivalent variation of the consumer.[21] Except for the "comparative steady state" scenario, all results are based on a comparative static model. The gains come from a combination of effects, so we conduct several scenarios to assess their relative importance.

A. Aggregate Effects

We estimate that the welfare gains to Tanzania of full reform are equal to 5.3% of Tanzanian consumption (or 4.8% of GDP) in the medium term. In the long run, we estimate that the gains could be as high as 16% of consumption. These medium terms gains derive from three key effects: (1) removal of non-discriminatory inefficient regulatory barriers against service providers; (2) removal of discriminatory regulatory barriers against multinational service providers in Tanzania; and (3) gains from moving to a uniform tariff. We execute several scenarios that allow us to understand the relative impact of these various elements and the mechanisms through which they operate. We discuss three of these below.

The improvement of aggregate welfare is accompanied by a significant increase in factor earnings including the wages of the various types of labor in our model (with the exception of females without a primary school education).[22] Given the relatively strong expansion of business services (which intensively employs the two more relatively educated males), wages of the two more educated types of male labor increase relatively strongly. Our data indicates that the business services sectors are the most capital intensive sectors in the economy, which explains why the return on capital increases by 5.7%. Land is used only in agriculture and agriculture experiences a slight contraction. Nonetheless, with Dixit-Stiglitz productivity gains, we escape the pessimism of Stolper-Samuelson and we observe

[21]See de Melo and Tarr (1992, chapter 3) for an explanation of how to calculate equivalent variation in computable general equilibrium models.

[22]Females without a prime school education are employed more intensively in agriculture, which contracts relative to other sectors.

Table 2. Summary of Macro Estimates
(%-change from initial equilibrium, unless otherwise indicated)

Scenario definition	Bench-mark	Full Re form	All services barriers	Only non-discrimi-natory services barriers	Only barriers against FDI in services	Only uniform tariffs	CRTS	Steady State
Liberalization of regulatory barriers for all services firms	No	Yes	Yes	Yes	No	No	Yes	Yes
Liberalization of discriminatory barri-ers on foreign services firms	No	Yes	Yes	No	Yes	No	Yes	Yes
Uniform import tariffs?	No	Yes	No	No	No	Yes	Yes	Yes
Steady-state capital stock	No	No	No	No	No	No	No	Yes
Dixit-Stiglitz variety-induced produc-tivity gains	Yes	Yes	Yes	Yes	Yes	Yes	No	Yes
Aggregate welfare								
Welfare (EV as % of consumption)		5.3	5.0	3.7	0.8	0.2	19	15.9
Welfare (EV as % of GDP)		4.8	4.5	3.3	0.7	0.2	1.7	14.4
Government budget								
Tariff revenue (% of GDP)	1.3	1.2	1.3	1.3	1.3	1.3	1.2	1.0
Tariff revenue		0.0	11.3	9.6	1.0	0.0	0.0	0.0
Aggregate trade								
Real exchange rate		-1.6	-2.4	-2.3	0.1	0.6	-0.7	-4.9
Aggregate exports		31.4	17.3	16.3	-0.3	9.5	13.0	71.4
Factor Earnings								
Subsistence Factor		6.5	5.8	4.4	0.9	0.4	2.3	21.7
Child labor (age 10 to 14)		4.7	4.1	3.1	0.5	0.3	1.6	19.2
Female labor (no formal education)		5.6	4.3	3.3	0.4	1.0	1.9	20.0
Female labor (not finished primary school)		-2.2	2.5	1.6	0.7	-4.4	-3.7	6.3
Female labor (not finished secondary school)		5.0	4.6	3.4	0.7	0.1	1.7	18.3
Female labor (secondary or higher education)		3.2	3.1	1.9	1.1	-0.1	1.4	12.7
Male labor (no formal education)		4.8	3.1	2.3	0.2	1.4	1.6	19.7
Male labor (not finished primary school)		2.4	2.6	1.7	0.4	-0.4	-0.1	16.8
Male labor (not finished secondary school)		4.4	4.0	2.7	0.9	0.3	1.7	20.6
Male labor (secondary or higher education)		4.3	3.9	2.6	1.2	0.2	1.9	16.2
Capital		5.7	4.3	3.2	0.7	1.0	2.2	-6.9
Agricultural land		3.6	2.9	2.2	0.2	0.4	0.5	17.2

Table 2. Summary of Macro Estimates
(%-change from initial equilibrium, unless otherwise indicated) (Continued)

Factor adjustments							
Subsistence Factor	0.5	0.4	0.3	0.1	0.2	0.3	1.0
Child labor (age 10 to 14)	1.4	1.1	0.8	0.3	0.9	0.5	1.2
Female labor (no formal education)	1.3	1.4	1.1	0.4	0.9	0.7	1.7
Female labor (not finished primary school)	5.2	2.1	1.8	0.3	3.0	3.6	7.5
Female labor (not finished secondary school)	1.9	1.4	1.1	0.3	0.9	0.9	2.5
Female labor (secondary or higher education)	2.4	2.1	1.5	0.5	0.7	1.1	3.6
Male labor (no formal education)	1.3	1.6	1.2	0.6	1.0	0.6	1.7
Male labor (not finished primary school)	2.8	2.0	1.5	0.5	1.7	1.7	4.0
Male labor (not finished secondary school)	2.4	2.0	1.5	0.5	1.0	1.0	4.0
Male labor (secondary or higher education)	2.7	2.4	1.8	0.6	0.5	1.2	4.8
Capital	2.7	2.4	1.9	0.5	1.0	1.3	0.1
Agricultural land	2.0	1.7	1.4	0.5	1.2	1.3	2.4
Capital stock and investment							27.1

Source: Authors' estimates.

an increase in agricultural rents, albeit at a more modest rate than other factors.

The impact on the movement of workers is not strong as for most categories. Except for females without formal education, less than 3% must change jobs.

1. Impact of Removing Non-discriminatory Regulatory Barriers against Tanzanian and Multinational Service Providers

In this scenario, labeled "only non-discriminatory services barriers," we reduce by 50% the ad valorem equivalent of the non-discriminatory barriers on domestic and multinational service providers in Tanzania, but there is no reduction in the discriminatory tax on multinationals in the services sectors; nor is there any movement toward tariff uniformity. At 3.7% of the value of Tanzanian consumption, the largest share of the gains derives from the liberalization of non-discriminatory regulatory barriers. The results are explained by the fact that the estimated non-discriminatory barriers are rather high in the services sectors, especially in the banking (37%), water (86%), rail (40%) and road (30%) transportation sectors. In addition, we assume that there are real resource costs of the barriers which are freed through the liberalization.

The reduction in the regulatory barriers on the provision of services in Tanzania reduces the cost of providing services in Tanzania for both Tanzanian and multinational service providers. This increases profitability for the provision of services in Tanzania, thereby inducing new entry by both domestic and multinational service providers until zero profits are restored. Consequently, there is an increase in new varieties of services. Tanzanian businesses will then have improved access to services in areas like telecommunication, banking, insurance, transportation and other business services. The additional service varieties in the business services sectors should lower the cost of doing business and result in a productivity improvement for users of these goods through the Dixit-Stiglitz-Ethier effect.

2. Impact of Foreign Direct Investment Liberalization in Business Services

In this scenario, labeled "only barriers against FDI in services," we reduce by 50% the ad valorem equivalent of the discriminatory barriers against multinational service providers who may wish to serve the Tanzanian market, but there is no reduction in the non-discriminatory tax equivalent of the regulatory burden on business service; nor is there any movement toward tariff uniformity. Reducing discriminatory barriers against multinational service providers yields a gain of 0.8% of Tanzanian consumption. The reduction in the discriminatory tax equivalent on multinational service providers increases profitability for multinational provision of services in Tanzania, thereby inducing new entry by multinational service providers until zero profits are restored. Although there is a loss of domestic service varieties due to increased competition from multinational service providers, there is a net increase in varieties. Tanzanian businesses will then have improved access to services.

3. Impact of Tariff Uniformity

In this scenario, labeled only tariffs, we impose tariff uniformity, but we do not change the ad valorem tax equivalent of regulatory barriers on domestic or multinational service providers. In moving to tariff uniformity, the average level of the Tanzanian tariff is unchanged. The level of the tariff is imposed that results in the same average collected tariff rate in Tanzania-the difference in the highs and lows are eliminated and replaced with a unique tariff for all sectors. Moving to uniform tariffs yields and estimated welfare gain of 0.2% of consumption. Our result of gains from tariff uniformity is consistent with the results of Martinez de Pereira (2000) in 13 countries and Harrison, Rutherford and Tarr (1993) for Turkey. These authors have found that moving to tariff uniformity leads to welfare benefits. These results show that, in practice, tariffs do not differ from uniformity due to inverse elasticity-Ramsey optimal tax considerations. The reason for the welfare gains is that the distortion costs of a tariff increase with the square on the tariff. Then moving to uniformity can be expected to benefit the country since it is the very high tariffs that cause the most of distortion costs.

4. Most Important Sectors

We have simulated removal of 50% of the ad valorem equivalents of the non-discriminatory barriers in individual sectors. The results are that three of the four sectors with the high estimated ad valorem equivalents of the regulatory barriers dominate the comparative static gains. In terms of EV as a percent of consumption, the results are 1.8% for maritime transportation, 1.3% for road transport and 1.0% for banking.[23]

5. Comparative Steady State Formulation

The increased availability of services results in an increase in the productivity of capital, which (as discussed above) should increase the accumulation of capital and, in the long-run steady state, increase the capital stock. In this scenario, we allow the capital stock to adjust to its long-run equilibrium.

Then the gains to the Tanzanian economy increase to 15.9% of consumption or 14.4% of GDP per year. In this formulation, the incentive to accumulate more capital due to an increase in the marginal productivity of capital is taken into account, but the costs of foregone consumption to achieve the higher capitals stock are not taken into account. So in the context of this model, the estimates should be considered upper bound estimates. On the other hand, Rutherford and Tarr (2002) have shown that in a fully dynamic model with endogenous productivity effects, the gains can be even larger than those estimated here.

[23]The fourth sectors, rail transportation, is a much smaller sector and therefore reduction of the regulatory barriers has a lesser welfare impact.

Table 3. Impact on sector activity (% change from initial equilibrium)

	Full Reform	All services barriers	Only non-discriminatory services barriers	Only barriers against FDI in services	Only uniform tariffs	CRTS	Steady State
IRTS Goods and Services	**11.4**	**12.8**	**8.3**	**3.1**	**-1.1**	**5.8**	**30.1**
CRTS Goods and Services	**7.0**	**5.0**	**4.5**	**0.2**	**1.2**	**2.8**	**20.8**
Business Services	**37.5**	**36.2**	**24.4**	**8.4**	**0.8**	**16.1**	**67.4**
Telecommunication	21.7	22.2	13.4	5.7	-0.6	7.7	43.6
Insurance	51.2	52.6	27.7	17.8	-1.0	20.1	79.9
Banking	59.2	60.6	38.8	15.8	-1.0	27.4	88.4
Professional business services	39.9	41.4	22.1	11.8	-1.0	13.5	67.6
Air transport	31.6	25.8	20.9	2.7	4.2	13.8	69.7
Road transport	35.1	29.0	24.2	2.8	4.2	16.3	73.8
Railway transport	35.0	29.0	24.5	2.5	4.2	17.1	72.6
Water transport	24.5	25.0	21.7	9.7	-0.6	13.9	44.9
Dixit-Stiglitz Goods	**-0.9**	**1.9**	**0.8**	**0.6**	**-2.0**	**0.9**	**12.6**
Processed food	4.8	2.7	1.9	0.5	2.1	3.8	15.5
Beverages & tobacco products	0.1	5.0	3.4	0.9	-4.4	0.8	11.6
Textile & leather products	-8.9	1.6	0.7	0.5	-9.3	-2.3	-2.2
Wood paper printing	-4.2	1.1	-0.7	1.2	-4.1	0.0	4.6
Manufacture of basic & industrial chemicals	5.8	4.9	3.1	1.1	1.6	1.7	11.8
Manufacture of fertilizers & pesticides	0.5	-10.0	-8.6	-1.6	9.9	2.8	13.1
Petroleum refineries	6.5	0.4	-1.5	1.1	7.9	4.4	30.2
Rubber plastic & other manufacturing	2.9	2.6	0.8	1.1	1.2	1.7	28.1
Glass & cement	0.9	1.3	0.6	0.4	-0.3	0.8	20.6
Iron steel & metal products	1.3	-0.2	-1.1	0.5	2.5	1.4	22.6
Manufacture of equipment	-2.0	-2.0	-2.9	0.6	1.2	0.2	38.3
Agriculture	**-1.0**	**-0.8**	**-0.7**	**-0.4**	**-0.1**	**-1.0**	**6.3**
Maize	1.6	1.1	0.8	0.2	0.5	1.0	4.5
Paddy	-2.4	1.3	0.9	0.3	-2.9	-2.5	0.7
Sorghum or millets	2.8	2.6	2.0	0.4	0.1	1.2	8.6
Wheat	-5.7	-3.3	-3.2	0.0	-1.4	-2.9	-8.7
Beans	2.2	2.1	1.6	0.3	0.1	0.9	9.0
Cassava	0.3	0.4	0.3	0.0	0.0	0.1	1.2
Other cereals	2.3	2.7	1.9	0.4	-0.3	1.1	9.9
Oil seeds	2.0	1.5	1.1	0.3	0.5	1.1	9.2

Table 3. Impact on sector activity (% change from initial equilibrium) (Continued)

Other roots & tubes	1.6	1.5	1.2	0.2	0.1	0.7	6.1
Cotton	-4.1	1.6	1.0	0.4	-6.3	-0.4	11.1
Coffee	-13.1	-23.8	-19.5	-7.0	8.3	-9.3	9.6
Tobacco	12.5	10.0	6.8	1.9	0.4	7.13	8.7
Tea	-2.4	-4.1	-3.9	-0.1	-0.6	-1.6	20.9
Cashew nuts	-4.5	-20.0	-13.7	-9.2	17.4	-3.2	19.0
Sisal fiber	-8.9	1.6	0.7	0.5	-9.3	-2.3	-2.2
Sugar	-14.9	-3.1	-3.0	0.1	-10.4	-11.3	-15.5
Fruits & vegetables	0.8	0.6	0.5	0.1	0.2	0.4	5.3
Other crops	3.0	2.2	1.9	0.2	0.5	1.3	10.5
Poultry & livestock	1.6	1.4	1.1	0.1	0.2	0.5	8.4
Other CRTS	**4.0**	**3.6**	**2.6**	**0.6**	**0.3**	**1.7**	**14.7**
Fish	0.8	-0.4	-0.1	-0.2	0.9	0.3	8.9
Hunting & forestry	1.1	1.5	1.0	0.3	-0.3	0.5	4.9
Mining & quarrying	0.8	-2.2	-2.3	0.0	3.1	1.7	31.1
Meat & dairy products	-0.1	1.2	0.9	0.2	-1.1	-0.6	3.8
Grain milling	3.1	2.8	2.1	0.4	0.2	1.4	10.3
Utilities	3.1	5.0	3.3	1.1	-1.6	1.6	20.3
Construction	1.9	2.0	1.4	0.4	-0.1	0.8	23.5
Wholesale & retail trade	2.6	2.6	1.7	0.5	-0.1	1.2	18.4
Hotels & restaurants	18.2	13.7	12.0	1.1	2.8	7.6	44.5
Postal communication	8.6	9.2	5.2	2.4	-0.5	3.4	28.9
Real estate	6.7	6.7	4.7	1.3	-0.1	2.5	16.7
Other services	6.5	7.6	1.9	3.7	-0.8	2.4	29.2
Tourism	81.5	49.7	52.0	-1.6	19.9	34.6	164.6
Public administration health & education	0.9	0.7	0.2	0.2	0.2	0.3	0.1

Source: Authors' estimates.

B. Sector Results

In Table 3, we present point estimates for the output effects by sector based on the scenario with our central parameter values. In the next section we display confidence intervals for the sector output changes, where we have run the model 30,000 times with different parameter values. See Jensen, Rutherford and Tarr (2008) for results for imports, exports, employment and price changes by sector.

Various scenarios are presented in the table, but we focus the discussion on the comparative static full reform scenario.

In the full reform scenario, reduction in the cost of business services (both from removal of regulatory barriers and from the Dixit-Stiglitz variety externality) leads to an increase in the demand for business services and their expansion. The expansion is greatest in the banking and insurance sectors, at 59 and 51%, respectively (this includes multinational output in these sectors). This is primarily explained by the fact that these sectors are among the sectors with the highest level of barriers (both non-discriminatory and discriminatory).

The tourism and hotel and restaurant sectors are the sectors that we estimate will expand the greatest (tourism almost doubles in size). The tourism sector is an intensive user of business services, such as transportation and banking services. Regulatory reforms will decrease the price and allow for quality improvements in these business services, which permits the tourism sector to operate more cheaply and offer better quality services.

Given that we assume that total employment and the capital stock is fixed in the medium term, if labor expands in some sectors, it must contract in other sectors. Given the large expansion in several sectors, especially services, we must have declines in others in the medium term. We estimate declines in output in several sectors, especially those that use business services less intensively. Moreover, since we assume uniform tariffs in our full reform scenario, sugarcane, which is the one of the more highly protected sectors, is estimated to decline.

Since the tourism sector is a major exporter, exports increase and the real exchange rate is estimated to appreciate as a result. Other sectors that rely heavily on exports for their earnings, but do not use business services significantly, are estimated to decline. This includes small declines in the cashew and coffee sectors (5 and 13%, respectively).

V. Sensitivity Results

We have discussed the impact of steady state versus comparative static modeling assumptions above. We focus now on the impact of constant returns to scale, barriers that generate rents to dometic agents rather than dissipate real resources, and parameter assumptions for our comparative static results.

A. Constant Returns to Scale Formulation

In order to assess the importance of the modeling assumption of endogenous productivity effects from additional varieties, we also consider a "constant returns to scale" (CRTS) version of the model. In this version, there are no endogenous productivity effects from additional varieties of imperfectly supplied goods or services. We estimate that the gains fall to 1.9% of consumption or 1.7% of GDP. Thus, the estimated gains are less than 40% of the total gains when we include endogenous productivity effects of additional services varieties. While the gains are considerably smaller without the gains from services varieties, the gains are large by the standards of CRTS trade models. The reason is that we are considering reforms of regulatory barriers against both foreign and domestic service providers and we assume that the regulatory barriers impose real resource costs in the initial equilibrium, i.e., there are large "rectangles" of rent losses in the CRTS model. The value of 50% of the rents in the benchmark is 1.34% of GDP.

B. No Rent Dissipation in the Initial Equilibrium

In this simulation, we estimate the welfare impacts under an assumption that the barriers generate rents captured by Tanzanian agents. In our central scenario, we assume the costs of firms in terms of their capital, labor and intermediates costs are higher due to the requirements of these barriers. This means that there are "rectangles" of real resource costs that the economy loses due to the barriers. Since the value of rents in the benchmark are equal to 2.68% of GDP, when we simulate our 50% liberalization of the barriers, the liberalization frees up resources for productive use by the economy, in an amount equal to 1.34% of GDP. Then welfare increases, in part due to the additional resources available for productive use.

When the initial rents are captured by domestic agents, they are not losses to the economy. Consequently, no additional resources are freed up as a result of reduction of the barriers, and liberalization should yield lower gains compared with our central scenario. In the comparative static case, the overall welfare gains in this scenario are reduced to 3.5% of GDP as compared to 4.8% when the barriers are real resource costs. Thus, the overall benefits of reform are smaller by an amount very close to the value of the rectangle of real resource costs (rents).

C. Impact of Parameter Assumptions: Piecemeal Sensitivity Analysis

Three parameters stand out in Table 4 as having a strong impact on the results.

Table 4. Piecemeal sensitivity analysis – welfare effects

	Parameter value			Hicksian equivalent variation[b] with corresponding parameter		
Parameter[a]	Lower	Central	Upper	Lower	Central	Upper
$\sigma(va, bs)$	0.5	1.25	2	4.0	5.3	8.5
$\sigma(q_i, q_j)$	2	3	4	14.5	5.3	3.8
$\sigma(D, M)$	2	4	6	4.6	5.3	5.9
$\sigma(L, K)$	0.7	1	1.3	5.3	5.3	5.3
$\sigma(A_1, \ldots A_n)$	0	0	0.25	5.3	5.3	5.4
$\sigma(D, E)$	2	4	6	5.1	5.3	5.6
$\varepsilon(d_i)$	2	4	6	4.9	5.3	5.6
$\varepsilon(f_i)$	2	4	6	3.6	5.3	6.7
$\theta m(i)$		see table below		5.3	5.3	5.3
$\theta fdi(i)$		see table below		5.1	5.3	5.6

[a] The piecemeal sensitivity analysis employs central values for all parameters other than the tested parameter and lump sum tax replacement.
[b] Hicksian equivalent variation as a percent of the value of consumption in the benchmark equilibrium.

Key:

Parameter	**Definition of the parameter**
$\sigma(va, bs)$	Elasticity of substitution between value-added and business services
$\sigma(q_i, q_j)$	Elasticity of substitution between firm varieties in imperfectly competitive sectors
$\sigma(D, M)$	"Armington" elasticity of substitution between imports and domestic goods in CRTS sectors
$\sigma(L, K)$	Elasticity of substitution between primary factors of production in value added
$\sigma(A_1, \ldots A_n)$	Elasticity of substitution in intermediate production between composite Armington aggregate goods
$\sigma(D, E)$	Elasticity of transformation (domestic output versus exports)
$\varepsilon(d_i)$	Elasticity of national service firm supply with respect to price of output
$\varepsilon(f_i)$	Elasticity of multinational service firm supply with respect to price of output
$\theta m(i)$	Share of value added in multinational firms in sector I due to specialized primary factor imports in the benchmark equilibrium
$\theta fdi(i)$	Share of output of service sector I captured by multinationals firms in the benchmark equilibrium

Parameter values for:	$\theta fdi(i)$			$\theta m(i)$		
	Lower	Central	Upper	Lower	Central	Upper
Telecommunication	0.85	0.9	0.95	0.025	0.05	0.1
Insurance	0.2	0.3	0.4	0.025	0.05	0.1
Banking	0.3	0.4	0.5	0.025	0.05	0.1
Professional business services	0.2	0.3	0.4	0.025	0.05	0.1
Road transport	0.1	0.2	0.3	0.025	0.05	0.1
Railway transport	0.5	0.6	0.7	0.025	0.05	0.1
Water transport	0.7	0.8	0.9	0.025	0.05	0.1
Air transport	0.3	0.4	0.5	0.025	0.05	0.1

The strongest impact comes from $\sigma(q_i, q_j)$, the elasticity of substitution between firm varieties in imperfectly competitive sectors. Unlike other elasticities, a lower value of $\sigma(q_i, q_j)$ increases the welfare gains. This is because lower values of this elasticity imply that varieties are less close to each other, so additional varieties are worth more. The next strongest impact comes from σ(va, bs), the elasticity of substitution between value-added and business services. The better firms are able to substitute business services for labor and capital, the more the economy will gain from the reforms that reduce the quality adjusted price of business services. Finally, larger values of $\varepsilon(f_i)$, the elasticity of multinational service firm supply with respect to the price of output, also significantly increase the gains, since it means that reforms that open opportunities for multinational service firms, will not be so quickly choked by the increased cost of the specific factor required for multinational firm expansion.

D. Systematic Sensitivity Analysis

In the systematic sensitivity analysis, we allow all parameters to change simultaneously. A probability distribution for each parameter is chosen. We typically choose uniform probability distributions, with the lower and upper bounds for the values of the parameters taken from the lower and upper values of

Figure 1. Frequency distribution of sample distribution of welfare gains (based on 30,000 simulations)

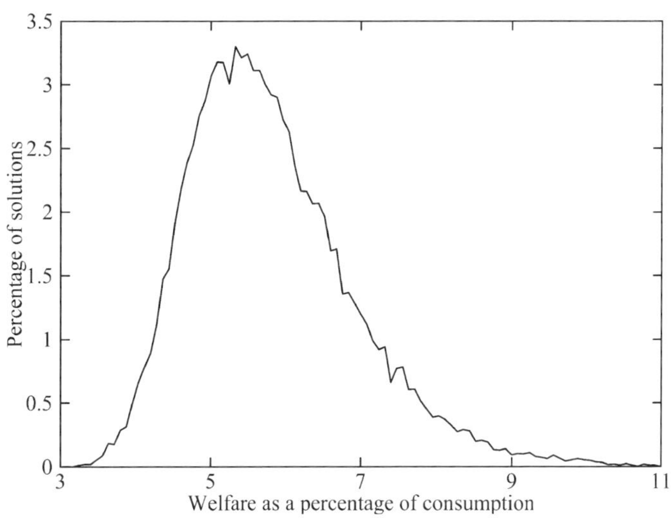

the key parameters presented in Table 4. We furthermore assume that all distributions are stochastically independent. We then run the model 30,000 times. Each time the program chooses a random configuration of parameters and executes the model with this configuration. For each variable in our model, we then harvest

Figure 2. 50% confidence intervals of percent changes in sector output from the sample distribution (based on 30,000 simulations)

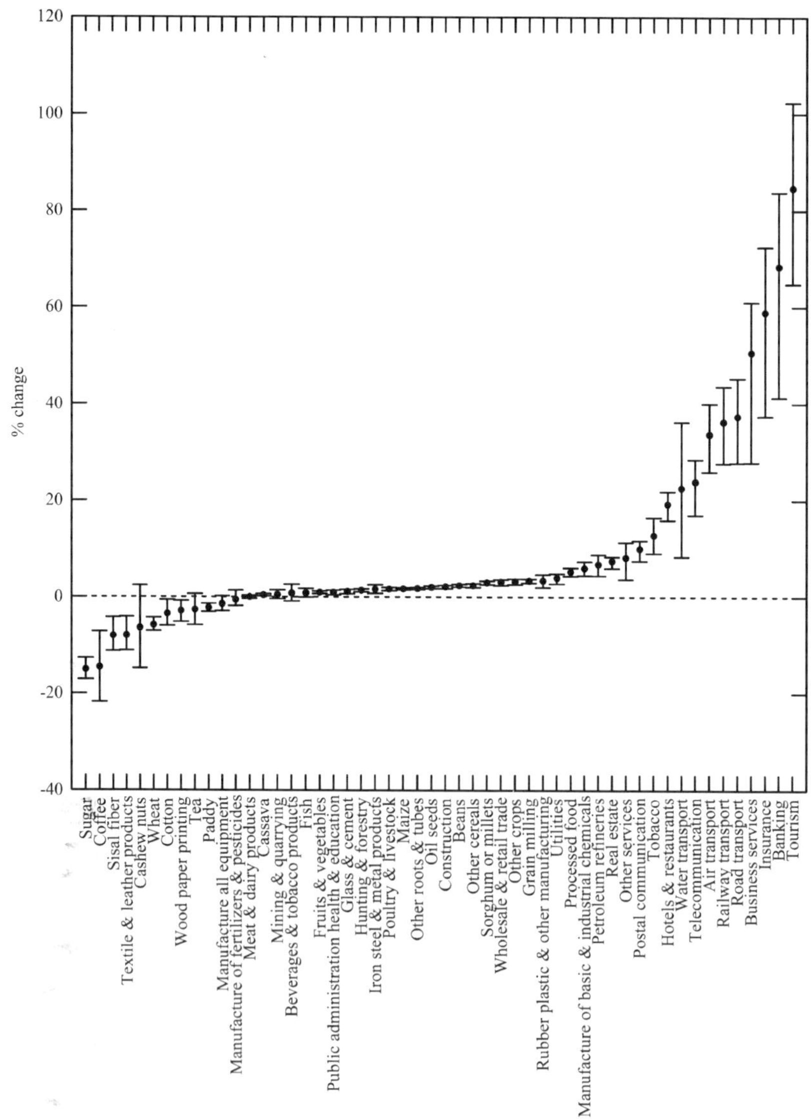

the sample distribution based on the 30,000 solutions. Consequently the sample distribution is not dependent on any particular set of parameter values, but represents results representative of the full distribution of parameter values.

1. Welfare Results

Figure 1 shows the frequency distribution of the sample results of the welfare gains as a percent of consumption. The distribution is not symmetric around our central value, since (as Table 4 shows) low values of the Dixit-Stiglitz elasticity generate very large welfare gains. In our 30,000 simulations, the minimum welfare gain was 3.11%, and 99% of the estimates fall in the range of 3.11 to 9.47%. This shows that the result for substantial welfare gains is robust to parameter specification.

2. Output Change

In Figure 2, we display bars that represent fifty percent confidence intervals for aggregate output changes (the point on the bar is our central point estimate). The results suggest robustness for most sectors that we estimate to significantly expand (or contract) with our central elasticities. In particular, we estimate that these sectors will expand (or contract) for virtually all parameter configurations. The figure also shows that the variance in the estimates for the sectors that significantly expand is larger than for other sectors. This is partly explained by the relatively greater use of business services and goods from imperfectly competitive sectors.

VI. Conclusions

In this paper we have developed an innovative small open economy computable general equilibrium model of the Tanzanian economy that is capable of assessing the impact of the liberalization of regulatory barriers against both domestic and multinational service providers. We find that reduction of the barriers against potential service providers, both foreign and domestic, can yield substantial gains to the Tanzanian economy, and that the innovations in our model are crucial to capturing these impacts.

Received 28 October 2009, Revised 6 October 2010, Accepted 11 October 2010

References

Arnold, Jens, Aaditya Matoo and Beata Javorcik (2007), Does Services Liberalization Benefit Manufacturing Firms: Evidence from the Czech Republic, *World Bank Policy and Research Working Paper 4109.*

Baldwin, Richard and R. Forslid (1999), Putting Growth Effects in CGE Models, R. Baldwin and J.Francois (eds.), *Dynamic Issues in Applied Commercial Analysis,* The World Bank, Cambridge: Cambridge University Press.

Balistreri, Edward J., Thomas F. Rutherford and David G. Tarr (2009), Modeling Services Liberalization: the case of Kenya, *Economic Modelling*, **26**, pp. 668-679.

Bank of Tanzania (2007a), *Tanzania Tourism Sector Survey: The 2005 International Visitors' Exit Survey Report*, October.

Bank of Tanzania (2007b), *Directorate of Banking Supervision Annual Report for 2006.*

Broda, Christian and David Weinstein (2004), Variety, Growth and World Welfare, *American Economic Review*, **94(2)**, pp. 139-144.

Brown, Drusilla, Alan Deardorf, Alan Fox and Robert Stern (1996), Liberalization of Services Trade, W. Martin and L. A. Winters, eds., *The Uruguay Round and the Developing Countries*, Cambridge: Cambridge University Press.

Brown, Drusilla and Robert Stern (2001), Measurement and Modeling of the Economic Effects of Trade and Investment Barriers in Services, *Review of International Economics*, **9(2)**, pp. 262-286.

Daniels, P.W. (1985), *Service Industries: A Geographical Appraisal*, New York: Methuen & Co.

Dee, Philippa, Kevin Hanslow and Tien Phamduc (2003), Measuring the Costs of Barriers to Trade in Services, Takatoshi Ito and Anne Krueger (eds.), Trade in Services in the Asia-Pacific Region, Chicago: University of Chicago Press.

Dixit, A. and J. Stiglitz (1977), Monopolistic Competition and Optimum Product Diversity, *American Economic Review*, **76(1)**, pp. 297-308.

Fernandes, Ana M. and Caroline Paunov (2008), Foreign direct investment in services and manufacturing productivity growth: evidence for Chile, *Policy and Research Working Paper 4730*, The World Bank.

Fernandes, Ana M. (2007), Structure and performance of the services sector in transition economies, *Policy and Research Working Paper 4357*, The World Bank.

Francois, Joseph, Bradley McDonald and Hakan Nordstom (1996), Assessing the Uruguay Round, Will Martin and L. Alan Winters (eds.), *The Uruguay Round and the Developing Countries*, Cambridge: Cambridge University Press.

Hansen, Terje and Tjalling Koopmans (1972), On the Definition and the Computation of a Capital Stock Invariant Under Optimization, *Journal of Economic Theory*, **5**, pp. 487-523.

Harrison, Glenn, Thomas Rutherford and David Tarr (1997), Quantifying the Uruguay Round, *Economic Journal*, **107(444)**, pp. 1405-1430, September.

Harrison, Glenn, Thomas Rutherford and David Tarr (1996), Increased Competition and Completion of the Market in the European Union: Static and Steady State Effects, *Journal of Economic Integration*, **11(3)**, pp. 332-365.

Harrison, Glenn, Thomas Rutherford and David Tarr (1993), Trade Reform in the Partially Liberalized Economy of Turkey, *The World Bank Economic Review*, May.

Hummels, David and Peter Klenow (2005), The Variety and Quality of a Nation's Trade, *American Economic Review*, **95(3)**, pp. 704-723.

Jensen, Jesper, Thomas Rutherford and David Tarr (2007), The Impact of Liberalizing Barriers to Foreign Direct Investment in Services: The Case of Russian Accession to the World Trade Organization, *Review of Development Economics*, **11(3)**, pp. 482-506.

Jensen, Jesper, Thomas Rutherford and David Tarr (2008), Modeling Services Liberalization: The Case of Tanzania, *World Bank Policy and Research Working Paper*, No. 4801, December. Available at: http://econ.worldbank.org/external/default/main?pagePK=64165259&theSitePK=469372&piPK=64165421&menuPK=64166093&entityID=000158349_20081228230212.

Kang, Joog-Soon (2000), Price Impact of Restrictiveness on Maritime Transportation Services", in Findlay, Christopher and Tony Warren (eds), *Impediments to Trade in Services: Measurement and Policy Implications*, London: Routledge.

Kimura, Fukunari, Mitsuyo Ando and Takamune Fujii (2004), Estimating the Ad Valorem Equivalent of Barriers to Foreign Direct Investment in the Telecommunications Services Sectors in Russia, Available at http://www.worldbank.org/trade/russia-wto.

Konan, Denise Eby and Keith E. Maskus (2006), Quantifying the impact of services liberalization in a developing country, *Journal of Development Economics*, **81**, pp. 142-162.

Markusen, James R, Thomas Rutherford and David Tarr (2005), Trade and Direct Investment in Producer Services and the Domestic Market for Expertise, *Canadian Journal of Economics*, **38(3)**, pp. 758-777.

Martinez de Prera, Josefina (2000), Revenue-Neutral Tariff Reform: Welfare Effects of Uniform Tariffs in 13 Developing Countries, Chapter 3 of Ph.D Dissertation, University of Colorado. Available at http://ussub.colorado.edu/~martindp/.

Melo, Jaime de and David G. Tarr (1992), *A General Equilibrium Analysis of US Foreign Trade Policy*, Cambridge, MA.: MIT Press.

McGuire, Greg and Michael Schuele (2000), Restrictiveness of International Trade in Banking Services, in Findlay, Christopher and Tony Warren (eds), *Impediments to Trade in Services: Measurement and Policy Implications*, London: Routledge.

Mircheva, Bladislava (2008), Ad valorem equivalence to FDI restrictiveness, Tanzania, Available at: http://sites.google.com/site/davidgtarr/Home/estimates-of-services-barriers.

National Bureau of Statistics of Tanzania, Gross Domestic Product at Current Prices by Selected Economic Activities for the Years 2001-2006, unpublished data.

National Bureau of Statistics of Tanzania (2007), Revised National Accounts Estimates For Tanzania Mainland - Base Year, 2001, *Dar es Salaam*, July.

Rutherford, Thomas F. and David Tarr (2008), Poverty Effects of Russian WTO accession: modeling "real" households with endogenous productivity effects, *Journal of International Economics,* **75(1)**, pp. 131-150.

Rutherford, Thomas F. and David Tarr (2003), Regional Trading Arrangements for Chile: Do the Results Differ with a Dynamic Model?, *Integration and Trade*, **7(18)**, pp. 117-139.

Rutherford, Thomas F. and David Tarr (2002), Trade Liberalization and Endogenous Growth in a Small Open Economy, *Journal of International Economics*, **56(2)**, March, pp. 247-272

Rutherford, Thomas F. (1999), Applied General Equilibrium Modeling with MPSGE as a GAMS Subsystem: An Overview of the Modeling Framework and Syntax, *Computational Economics*.

Schott, Peter (2004), Across-Product Versus Within-Product Specialization in International Trade, *Quarterly Journal of Economics*, **119(2)**, pp. 647-678.

Tarr, David (2002), On the Design of Tariff Policy: Arguments for and Against Uniform Tariffs, B. Hoekman, A. Mattoo and P. English (eds.), Development, *Trade and the WTO: A Handbook*, Washington: The World Bank.

Thurlow, James and Peter Wobst (2003), Poverty-Focused Social Accounting Matrices For Tanzania, TMD Discussion Paper No. 112, International Food Policy Research Institute, Washington D.C. USA.

Warren, Tony (2000), The Impact on Output of Impediments to Trade and Investment in Telecommunications Services, Findlay, Christopher and Tony Warren (eds), *Impediments to Trade in Services: Measurement and Policy Implications*, London: Routledge.

Part III
Trade and Poverty

Trade Policy and Poverty Reduction in Brazil

Glenn W. Harrison, Thomas F. Rutherford, David G. Tarr, and Angelo Gurgel

A multiregion computable general equilibrium model is used to evaluate the regional, multilateral, and unilateral trade policy options of Mercosur from the perspective of the welfare of all potential partners in several proposed agreements. The focus for Brazil is on poverty impacts. The results show that the poorest households in Brazil experience gains of 1.5–5.5 percent of their consumption, which are about three to four times the average gains for Brazil. Protection in Brazil favors capital-intensive manufacturing relative to unskilled labor-intensive agriculture and manufacturing. So trade liberalization raises the return to unskilled labor relative to capital and disproportionately helps the poor.

Brazil has several trade policy options. This study evaluates those options from the perspective of the welfare of all potential partners in several proposed trade agreements, looking particularly at the impacts on poor people to determine which trade policy contributes most to poverty reduction in Brazil. The objective is to determine whether there is a tradeoff between aggregate welfare gains to Brazil from trade liberalization and the welfare gains to the poor. The article concludes that there is no tradeoff and explains why.

As part of the Mercosur customs union with Argentina, Paraguay, and Uruguay, Brazil is engaged in negotiations to implement the Free Trade Agreement of the Americas (FTAA). Mercosur is also negotiating a potential free trade

Glenn W. Harrison is professor of economics at the University of Central Florida; his e-mail address is glenn.harrison@bus.ucf.edu. Thomas F. Rutherford is professor of economics at the University of Colorado; his e-mail address is rutherford@colorado.edu. David G. Tarr is lead economist at the World Bank; his e-mail address is dtarr@worldbank.org. Angelo Gurgel is professor of economics at the Universidade de São Paulo in Brazil; his e-mail address is angelo_gurgel@yahoo.com.br. The authors thank seminar participants at the Institute for Applied Economic Research in Brasilia, the Brazilian Development Bank in Rio de Janeiro, and the GTAP conference in Taiwan, China; agencies of the government of Brazil and Brazilian research institutes; and Brazilian scholars including Francisco Ferreira, Renato Flores, Claudio Fritschak, Marcelo Neri, Armando Castelar Pinheiro, Lia Valls Pereira, Octavio Tourinho, and William Tyler. They also thank Mary Burfisher, Mauricio Carrizosa, Carsten Fink, Paul Gibson, Bernard Hoekman, Maria Kasilag, Peter Lanjouw, Daniel Lederman, Aaditya Mattoo, Johan Mistian, Sherman Robinson, Maurice Schiff, Claudia Paz Sepulveda, Mark Thomas, Vinod Thomas, Alberto Valdes, Dominique van der Mensbrugge, and Joachim von Amsberg for help and comments. The authors gratefully acknowledge research support under the Bank-Netherlands Partnership Program to examine the impact of trade policy on poverty.

THE WORLD BANK ECONOMIC REVIEW, VOL. 18, NO. 3,

doi:10.1093/wber/lhh043 18:289–317

agreement with the European Union, along with less notable regional arrangements. In addition, Brazil has supported further multilateral negotiations within the World Trade Organization (WTO 2000).

Brazil is concerned that these regional integration initiatives will provide much less market access than agreements that do not constrain the exports of partner countries. Notably, significantly improved access to EU agricultural markets will be very difficult to achieve for the usual EU internal political reasons. As a major agricultural exporter, Brazil believes that the WTO is the best negotiating forum for obtaining freer access to agricultural markets. Moreover, antidumping and stringent rules of origin may limit access to the markets of the main industrial country partners in these regional agreements, especially the Free Trade Agreement of the Americas (FTAA).

Extending the analysis of Harrison and others (2002) on Chile, this study evaluates the value of trade policy options to Brazil if the key industrial country partner in these regional agreements denies access to specific products. For the EU, that means exclusion of preferred access to Mercosur exporters in the most highly protected agricultural products. For the FTAA, that means denial to Brazil of access to the most highly protected products in the United States because of antidumping measures or restrictive rules of origin.

A major policy concern is the link between trade policy changes and poverty in Brazil. Although interest in the topic has increased dramatically in recent years, using general equilibrium modeling with multiple households to examine equity issues dates to pioneering studies by Adelman and Robinson (1978) and Piggot and Whalley (1985). This has typically been done by aggregating households from a household survey into 5–40 households.[1] Recently modelers have focused attention on the impact of trade policy on poverty, and Harrison and others (2003a) have showed that a concern with equity is not equivalent to a concern with poverty.[2]

A second approach is to take price changes from a representative consumer general equilibrium model and feed these into a micro-simulation model of household behavior, such as in Chen and Ravallion (2003) and Bussolo and Lay (2003). This approach allows examination of the diversity of impacts across households: Even if the aggregated poor households gain, many individual poor households could lose. But the approach ignores feedback effects of the quantity changes on the equilibrium outcome in the general equilibrium model and does not reconcile inconsistent information on household income from the national accounts and the household surveys.[3]

The analysis here is in the tradition of the first approach. The model incorporates 20 types of Brazilian households: 10 rural and 10 urban, with

1. For recent applications see the papers for the conference on Poverty and the International Economy (available online at www.worldbank.org/trade).

2. The trade policy change they evaluated resulted in an increase in aggregate real income and greater equity as measured by the Gini coefficient, but the poorest households were worse off.

3. See Cockburn (2001) for an attempt to combine the two approaches.

households further classified by income level. The results show clear and crucial links among trade policy changes, factor intensities at the industry level, economy-wide factor returns, and poverty—the links suggested by the Heckscher-Ohlin and Stolper-Samuelson models. But only because of the attention to detail in the empirical estimation of factor shares are results obtained that can be sensibly used to analyze the poverty dimension of trade policy changes. The results also show the importance of agricultural liberalization for the poor.

The aggregate policy results show that both the FTAA and the EU–Mercosur arrangements are net trade creating for member countries, but excluded countries almost always lose. But multilateral trade liberalization (a 50 percent cut in tariffs and export subsidies) results in estimated gains to the world that are more than four times greater than the returns for either the FTAA or the EU–Mercosur agreement, demonstrating the continuing importance of multilateral negotiations.

A fully implemented agreement with the European Union is about 1.5 times more valuable to Brazil than the FTAA because of access to highly protected EU agricultural markets. But if agriculture is excluded from the agreement, it becomes of very little value to Brazil. Application of antidumping and restrictive rules of origin by the United States against Brazil on the most protected products in the U.S. market similarly reduces the value of the FTAA to Brazil. Nonetheless, the FTAA still has significant value to Brazil because other markets in the Americas and the less protected sectors in the United States are assumed to remain open to Brazilian exporters.

Most of the evaluated trade policy options result in a progressive distribution of the gains, so that the poorest households experience the greatest percentage increase in their incomes. Although Brazil undertook substantial trade liberalization in the 1990s, vestiges of its import-substitution industrialization strategy of the 1960s remain. Trade policy reforms in Brazil tend to shift resources from capital-intensive manufacturing to unskilled labor-intensive agriculture and less capital-intensive manufacturing, increasing the wages of unskilled labor relative to returns to capital and skilled labor. The percentage increase in the incomes of the eight poorest types of households is several times greater than the average percentage increase for the economy as a whole.[4]

Previous work has shown that multilateral agricultural trade liberalization will lead to aggregate gains for agricultural exporting nations. The results here suggest that agricultural trade liberalization, whether multilateral or in a regional arrangement with the European Union, is particularly important for the realization of poverty reduction benefits for agricultural exporters, such as Brazil.

4. These results are consistent with two other analyses of the impact of trade liberalization on the poor in Brazil: Barros and others (2000) and World Bank (2001).

I. A Multiregional Trade Model

A comparative static, constant returns to scale, multiregional, and multisectoral quantitative model is developed to evaluate the impact of trade policy on poverty in Brazil. The model is relatively detailed in the Americas, with 13 countries or regions from that area (table 1). Also included are the European Union 15, Japan, and a residual rest of the world. Of the Mercosur members, Brazil, Argentina, and Uruguay are represented explicitly in the model, whereas Paraguay is represented as part of the rest of South America. The general specification of this model follows the earlier multiregional model of the effects of the Uruguay Round in Harrison and others (1997c) and even more closely their model of trade policy options for Chile (Harrison and others 2002).[5]

Because most of the documentation of the data and model and additional simulations are available in Harrison and others (2003b), only the main features

Table 1. List of Commodities, Regions, and Factors of Production Used in the Model

Commodities		Regions		Factors
PDR	Paddy rice	BRA	Brazil	Capital
GRO	Cereal grains	ARG	Argentina	Unskilled labor
OSD	Oilseeds	URY	Uruguay	Land
AGR	Other agriculture	CHL	Chile	Natural resources
OCR	Other crops	COL	Colombia	Skilled labor
CMT	Bovine meat products	PER	Peru	
OMT	Other meat products	VEN	Venezuela	
MIL	Dairy products	XAP	Rest of Andean pact	
PCR	Processed rice	MEX	Mexico	
SGR	Sugar	XCM	Central America and Caribbean	
OFD	Other food products	XSM	Rest of South America	
ENR	Energy and mining	CAN	Canada	
TEX	Textiles	USA	United States	
WAP	Wearing apparel	E_U	European Union 15	
LEA	Leather products	JPN	Japan	
LUM	Wood products	ROW	Rest of world	
MAN	Other manufacturing			
I_S	Iron and steel			
FMP	Other metal products			
MVH	Motor vehicles and parts			
SER	Services			
CGD	Savings good			
DWE	Dwellings			

5. Harrison and others (1997c, 2002). The model is formulated using the GAMS-MPSGE software developed by Rutherford (1999) and solved using the PATH algorithm of Ferris and Munson (2000). See de Melo and Tarr (1992) for an exposition of the general form of the within-country equations of the model.

are summarized here.[6] Production uses intermediate inputs and primary factors (labor, capital, and land) that are mobile across sectors within a region but immobile internationally. The amount of capital and labor available to any economy is fixed. Output is differentiated between domestic output and exports, but exports are not differentiated by destination country. Except for Brazil, each region has a single representative consumer who maximizes utility, as well as a single government agent. Demand is characterized by a nested Armington structure for each of the 22 sectors (see table 1). The Armington aggregate good is a constant elasticity of substitution (CES) composite of domestic production and aggregate imports, and aggregate imports are a CES aggregate of imports from different regions of origin. This structure allows multistage budgeting. So government revenue remains unchanged in any counterfactual scenario, a tax is imposed to compensate for lost tariff revenue. Each country has a balance of trade constraint, so any change in the value of imports is matched by an equal value change in exports. The model is "real," in the sense that it contains no financial assets. Thus there is only a "real" exchange rate, defined as the price of a country's tradable goods relative to the price of its nontradable goods.

The model does not incorporate increasing returns to scale or endogenous productivity effects of trade policy, despite a number of studies by Brazilian researchers identifying a correlation between the opening of Brazil to external trade in the early 1990s and an increase in productivity in Brazilian manufacturing (Muendler 2001 found a causal relationship). A model that incorporates both of these, such as that developed in Rutherford and Tarr (2002), would be expected to produce much larger gains than this constant returns to scale model, with a resulting further reduction in Brazilian poverty. But because the productivity advances are not likely to be concentrated in the labor-intensive sectors, the relative share of the gains at the household level for the poor may be less progressive than that found here.[7]

Brazilian Households

The most important new feature in this model is the extension to multiple households in Brazil: 10 rural households and 10 urban households, distinguished by income levels (as defined in table 2). The structure of demand for each household is a nested Armington structure, based on CES demand functions, similar to representative households in other regions.

6. These appendixes present details of the model specification, tables with low elasticity results and detailed sectoral results for Brazil, procedures for updating the input-output tables and estimating factor intensities, calculation of the tariff rates in Mercosur, systematic sensitivity analysis, steps for incorporating the household survey information, and some additional references.

7. Most of the trade policy options were also evaluated in separate simulations in a comparative steady-state model. Because the rental rate on capital falls in most of the scenarios, the new equilibrium capital stock does not rise, and the estimated welfare gains to the economy also do not rise.

TABLE 2. Household Types and Characteristics

Rural Households	Mean per Capita Income[a]	Mean Household Income[a]	% of Sample	Representative no. Individuals[b] (millions)	No. Individuals in Survey	Urban Households	Mean per Capital Income	Mean Household Income[a]	% of Sample	Representative no. Individuals[b] (millions)	No. Individuals in Survey	No. Individuals in Survey in Household i[c]	Monthly Household Income (1996 reals)
1	48	129	5.89	6.10	1,090	1	63	135	4.38	4.54	707	1,797	0–206
2	103	259	3.92	4.06	868	2	131	264	5.54	5.74	955	1,823	207–313
3	116	364	2.64	2.73	661	3	155	375	6.14	6.36	1,152	1,813	314–431
4	140	489	2.31	2.39	556	4	196	497	6.78	7.03	1,260	1,816	432–564
5	165	647	1.87	1.94	470	5	239	649	7.34	7.61	1,347	1,817	565–741
6	228	838	1.41	1.46	328	6	286	846	8.74	9.05	1,486	1,814	742–964
7	286	1,074	0.7	0.73	194	7	390	1,123	9.27	9.60	1,624	1,818	965–1,290
8	385	1,528	0.96	0.99	235	8	479	1,561	8.06	8.35	1,582	1,817	1,291–1,889
9	615	2,282	0.32	0.33	103	9	752	2,449	8.99	9.31	1,716	1,819	1,890–3,196
10	2,363	7,864	1.52	1.58	408	10	2,187	6,728	13.22	13.70	2,648	3,056	3,197–66,809
Total			21.54	22.31	4,913	Total			78.46	81.27	14,477	19,390	

[a]Income figures are in 1996 reals.

[b]The number of individuals the stratified sample is estimated to represent.

[c]Rural household 1 plus urban household 1.

Because the CES function is homothetic, changes in the income level of individual consumers will not change the proportions in which they consume commodities. Despite the fact that each individual consumer has homothetic utility functions, relative prices will vary with income levels in the model. This is because the CES demand function parameters calibrated for each household necessarily differ across households, because the initial shares of income spent on different commodities vary by household. This implies that the elasticities of demand with respect to prices and income differ across Brazilian households. Hence if income shifts from household A to household B, aggregate demand will shift toward the commodities consumed more intensely by household B.[8]

General Data and Elasticities

The Global Trade Assistance and Protection 5 (GTAP5) database, described in Dimaranan and McDougall (2002), is used for countries other than Brazil. It includes key protection data (table 3). The 57 sectors in the full GTAP database have been aggregated to 22 sectors, resulting in a model with approximately 2,500 equations. This retains the sectors that are most important to Brazilian trade policy, sectors with high protection in U.S., EU, or Mercosur markets. Aggregating sectors with similar protection levels should not significantly affect the results.[9]

In the scenarios using central elasticities, the lower level elasticity of substitution between imports from different regions, σ_{MM}, is assumed to be 30 and the higher level elasticity between aggregate imports and domestic production, σ_{DM}, to be 15. Although these elasticities are high by the standards of some econometric studies, such as Reinert and Roland-Holst (1992) and Shiells and Reinert (1993), they are supported by the estimates of Reidel (1988) and Athukorala and Reidel (1994). Moreover, elasticities would be expected to increase over time, and this model presumes an adjustment of about 10 years, a long period in the context of these econometric estimates. The higher elasticities are needed in the model to produce results for terms of trade changes that are closer to the results of Chang and Winters (2002).[10]

8. The model was also executed with the linear expenditure system (LES) demand functions at the top level in place of CES for all Brazilian households. Given that the change in real income is not large in the simulations, the welfare results and returns to factors change only negligibly.

9. That is, sectors were aggregated that are not important in trade or that have low rates of protection. Although aggregation may significantly change the results in applied trade policy analysis, this type of aggregation creates quite small aggregation bias. It is acknowledged, however, that services are not treated seriously in this model. Readers interested in the role of services in regional agreements of Brazil may consult Mattoo and others (2002).

10. Larger elasticities in the model result in larger terms of trade effects. The Chang and Winters (2002) results provide support for the higher choice of elasticities, because even the highest elasticities chosen fall short of the terms of trade effects they find for the United States and Japan. The welfare calculations here, however, are broadly consistent with those of Chang and Winters (2002).

TABLE 3. Structure of Protection for All Countries in the Sample (import share trade-weighted average import tariff defined over the set of countries subject to positive tariffs)

	BRA	USA	CAN	MEX	ARG	CHL	COL	PER	VEN	URY	XCM	XAP	XSM	EUR	JPN	ROW
PDR	12	5	[a]	15	12	11	13	22	13	12	25	12	15	65	409	7
GRO	7	1	9	38	7	11	12	12	12	7	9	11	5	44	20	77
OSD	6	18	[a]	3	6	11	11	12	11	6	5	8	4	3	76	52
AGR	10	3	12	17	10	11	17	12	17	10	12	17	7	13	18	24
OCR	8	14	2	12	9	11	12	16	12	9	9	9	7	10	46	20
ENR	4	0	1	7	5	11	9	12	6	5	6	6	4	1	−1	5
CMT	12	5	16	35	12	11	19	15	19	12	15	18	11	95	36	34
OMT	14	4	72	68	14	11	18	20	18	14	20	19	13	61	58	33
MIL	19	42	215	38	19	11	19	19	17	19	24	18	16	90	287	43
PCR	15	5	1	15	15	11	20	20	20	15	36	20	18	86	409	19
SGR	19	53	5	4	19	11	18	12	18	19	20	17	24	76	116	17
OFD	18	8	29	22	18	11	18	15	19	18	16	18	17	28	34	32
TEX	16	11	16	15	16	11	17	16	17	16	16	11	16	10	8	16
WAP	20	13	21	33	20	11	20	20	20	20	24	15	23	12	13	17
LEA	26	13	15	25	26	11	16	18	18	23	15	15	19	8	15	13
LUM	15	2	7	13	13	11	17	12	16	14	15	15	20	3	3	11
MAN	13	2	3	10	13	11	9	12	10	13	9	9	11	4	1	7
I_S	13	3	5	8	12	11	10	12	12	12	6	9	11	3	3	8
FMP	16	4	6	14	16	11	14	12	15	16	10	12	16	4	1	12
MVH	26	2	5	14	26	10	21	12	25	29	13	20	14	5		13

Note: See table 1 for definitions of countries and products.

[a]Imports are from the United States only and are not subject to duties.

Source: Authors' calculations based on GTAP database (Dimaranan and McDougall 2002), updated 1996 input-output table for Brazil, and the 1996 LSMS survey conducted by the Brazilian Institute of Geography and Statistics.

The policy simulations are also performed with lower elasticity values of $\sigma_{MM} = 8$ and $\sigma_{DM} = 4$.[11] Lower elasticities typically lower the welfare gains for the countries that gain from the regional arrangements and reduce the losses for countries excluded from the regional arrangements, but they rarely change the qualitative results in the scenarios examined.[12] Similarly, results at the household level in Brazil are muted with lower elasticities, but the relative gains to the poor in Brazil remain several multiples of the overall gain.

The elasticity of transformation between exports and domestic production is assumed to be 5 for each sector. Elasticities of substitution between primary factors of production is unity. Fixed coefficients are assumed between all intermediates and value added.

Protection Data

All distortions are represented as ad valorem price wedges. Border protection estimates combine tariff protection and the tariff equivalents of nontariff barriers into a single measure of protection referred to as the tariff rate.

Trade in goods within Mercosur was tariff-free by 2000. Members were allowed a list of exceptions to the common external tariff, but the common tariff is being phased in for the exceptions and all members are obligated to fully converge to it by 2006 (WTO 2000, p. 20). Because changes in protection data are crucial to the results and protection rate data are usually available for a more recent period than input-output tables, the protection data used are typically more recent than the data in the input-output tables.[13] Similarly, tariffs on imports of goods between Argentina, Brazil, and Uruguay are assumed to be zero. Because the common external tariff was largely in place in 2003 and is scheduled to be fully implemented by 2006, Argentina, Brazil, and Uruguay are all assumed to apply it.[14]

The North American Free Trade Association (NAFTA), too, is assumed to operate as an effective free trade area, with zero tariffs between Canada, Mexico, and the United States, but with each country maintaining its own external tariff. The model does not incorporate the preferential tariff rates

11. The results for low elasticites reported in Harrison and others (2003a) were erroneously reported as being based on $\sigma_{MM} = 8$ and $\sigma_{DM} = 4$; in fact, they are based on $\sigma_{MM} = 16$ and $\sigma_{DM} = 8$.

12. The impact of unilateral trade liberalization on Argentina is one exception, for reasons explained later.

13. Several sources of protection data were examined, and the data in the GTAP database were assessed as the best. The trade flow data are also from the GTAP database, which is for 1997. Because the input-output table and estimated factor payments in Brazil were updated, a balanced social accounting matrix (SAM) had to be created. An optimization procedure was employed in creating the new SAM that minimizes the sum of the squares of the difference between all the values in the new SAM and the original GTAP database, subject to the constraints of a SAM.

14. The common external tariff is imposed at the tariff-line level but is applied at the level of aggregation of the model. This involves no loss of generality, because if the common external tariff holds at the tariff-line level, then it must hold for more aggregate levels.

found in the many other regional trading arrangements in the Americas that are implemented at various levels of effectiveness.

Table 3 shows the (trade-weighted) average protection rates by product category across all countries. The common external tariff of Mercosur is implemented by imposing the external tariff of Brazil as the external tariff of Argentina and Uruguay. Nonetheless, the trade-weighted average tariff is not precisely equal in all cases for the three countries because of product mix differences across sources of imports.

Brazilian Data for Poverty Analysis

Most of the data for Brazil, which are crucial to effective trade and poverty analysis, were independently constructed for this study. In addition to the protection data, the most important steps were to estimate factor shares in Brazilian industries, update the 1996 input-output table of the Brazilian economy from the 1985 base table in the GTAP database and use the household expenditure survey for Brazil to construct information on household expenditure patterns and sources of income.

The share of value added attributed to capital in input-output tables is notoriously overestimated in agriculture and services and is poorly represented in many manufacturing sectors. The convention of input-output authorities is to take capital's share as the residual from revenue after payments for intermediates, labor, and taxes. Agriculture's lack of official reported wage payments means that input-output authorities often report these sectors as the most capital-intensive sectors in the economy.[15] Similar but less severe problems prevail in services. In manufactures, unprofitable sectors (which often do not export) have a low share of capital in the input-output tables, whereas profitable sectors (which more often export) have a high share of capital. In developing economies the result is that labor-intensive sectors, which may be the most profitable and export-oriented, are likely to be reported as capital-intensive sectors. Harrison and others (2003a) show how this problem can lead to perverse results.

Factor shares in Brazilian industries were thus independently estimated for this study. The reestimation raised labor's share significantly in agriculture and, to a lesser extent, in services. For manufactures there were no significant differences between these estimates and the input-output table. This adjustment is fundamental to the results on the relative impact on the poor.

Household expenditure and income patterns were extracted from the Living Standards Measurement Study (LSMS) survey for Brazil. The survey was designed and conducted by the Brazilian Institute for Geography and

15. Researchers at the International Food Research Institute and the Economic Research Service of the U.S. Department of Agriculture have noted this problem and adjusted for it (see Arndt and others 1998; Thomas and Bautista 1999; Hausner 1999; Burfisher and others 1992).

Statistics. The LSMS survey is a stratified sample, with each household representing a share of the total population in the area sampled. The LSMS focused on the eastern part of Brazil, but it is estimated to represent 103.6 million people in the region (about 63 percent of the total population), 22.3 million of them in rural areas and 81.3 million in urban areas. Although much of the country is not sampled in the survey, experts who have worked with the poverty data in Brazil believe that the poor are proportionally represented or at least are not underrepresented.[16] The Gini coefficient for the entire survey sample is estimated at 0.585.

To aggregate the approximately 5,000 Brazilian households in the survey into 20 households, all households in the sample were first ranked from poorest to richest based on per capita income. Per capita rather than household income was chosen to enable comparisons with the standard per capita poverty measures of the World Bank (World Bank 1990, 2000) and of Ferreira and others (1999) for Brazil. The sample was then divided into deciles, with an equal number of households in each decile (except for the richest decile, which has more households, because they were to receive less emphasis in the analysis). Each decile was then partitioned into two representative households: one rural and one urban. This partition means that the *i*th representative rural household and the *i*th representative urban household have about the same per capita income. Although the *i*th representative rural and the *i*th representative urban household do not have an equal number of households or individuals, the sum of the households they represent is equal, and the sum of individuals they represent is approximately equal. As a result, there are roughly 1,800 individuals in each household group, apart from the richest household group, which has just over 3,000 individuals (see table 2).

The shares of income each household spent on each commodity group and the shares of income each household obtained from capital, rent on land, unskilled wages, and skilled wages were extracted from the LSMS survey. Data on factor incomes were also available from national accounts, so the data from the two sources had to be reconciled before implementing the model.[17] For reasons to be explained, the total payments to factors were taken from the national accounts, and the factor shares of each representative household in the model were adjusted accordingly.[18] This reconciliation minimized aggregate deviations between household factor shares and expenditure shares from the

16. The authors thank Francisco Ferreira, Peter Lanjouw, and Marcelo Neri for helpful conversations on several aspects of assessing poverty in Brazil.

17. A two-stage process in which price changes from a general equilibrium model are fed into a second-stage micro-simulation model can ignore this reconciliation. Of course, inconsistencies then arise if one then wants to allow for feedback from the second stage to the first stage after some policy shock.

18. This rebalancing also required adjusting expenditure shares of households for broad categories of goods, to ensure consistency with the broad patterns of consumer expenditure in the national accounts.

values obtained from the LSMS survey prior to rebalancing, and the shares were weighted by the value of household income and expenditure. The results are reported in table 4 and explained in Harrison and others (2003b, appendix D).

This reconciliation of the two databases significantly increased the share of capital owned by wealthy households, particularly wealthy urban households. Income estimates from LSMS surveys are known to be lower than income estimates from national accounts (see Ravallion 2003; Deaton 2003). Although there are biases in collection of both databases, so that neither source is clearly correct, Deaton (2003) believes that the most likely explanation for the difference is that households fail to respond to the survey, with the probability of nonresponse increasing monotonically with income. It also appears to be the case that the LSMS surveys report a lower share of income for capital than the national accounts do. Vanos (2003) mapped income from the LSMS surveys in 14 countries into factor shares and compared these with the GTAP database. Capital's share from the LSMS surveys was 21 percent of household income, but it was 52 percent of household income based on national account information in the GTAP database. The presumed pattern of nonresponse to the household survey

TABLE 4. Household Income Shares from Factors of Production and Transfers (percent)

Household Type	Skilled Labor	Unskilled labor	Rent from Capital	Rent from Land	Transfers
Rural					
1	6	68	3	1	22
2	8	80	0	0	11
3	11	87	0	2	1
4	8	64	3	2	22
5	11	57	32	0	0
6	22	47	31	0	0
7	9	49	42	0	0
8	15	62	20	3	0
9	18	45	35	1	0
10	7	75	15	3	0
Urban					
1	1	70	0	0	28
2	18	67	1	0	14
3	10	74	3	0	14
4	13	68	8	0	10
5	27	57	16	0	1
6	28	52	19	0	0
7	27	30	42	0	0
8	33	28	39	0	0
9	30	21	49	0	0
10	17	15	69	0	0

Source: Authors' calculations based on the 1996 LSMS survey conducted by the Brazilian Institute of Geography and Statistics.

would also help explain this difference in capital's share, because the rich are likely to have more capital than the poor.[19]

What percentage of the households are poor based on the LSMS data? Poverty lines are defined in several ways. Two well-known measures are $1 a day per person or $2 a day per person at a purchasing power parity exchange rate. From the LSMS data 7.3 percent of the population lives on $1 a day or less and 17.8 percent lives on $2 a day or less. To calculate poverty in Brazil, Ferreira and others (1999) developed a measure of poverty based on a "minimum food basket" in the reference region, metropolitan São Paulo, that would generate the Food and Agriculture Organization–defined minimum intake of 2,288 calories a day. They also developed indices that allow them to define "equivalent" income levels across individual households in different regions of the LSMS. Using purchasing power parity adjustments for 1996, this measure amounts to a poverty line of $1.50 per person per day.[20] Taking the poverty headcounts for each region in Brazil as reported in Ferreira and others (1999, table 3) and sample weights for the individuals in each of the regions of the LSMS in Brazil, their measure implies a national poverty index of 13.03 percent for Brazil using the LSMS.[21]

Based on the Ferreira and others (1999) measure of poverty incidence and the full LSMS database, 82 percent of the households in the poorest two households, urban household 1 and rural household 1, fall below this poverty line. The poorer households are more populous, however, so that this amounts to 13 percent of the individuals in Brazil who are below the poverty line.[22]

II. Results at the Country Level

The model estimates the aggregate change in welfare, measured by Hicksian equivalent variation, in Brazil and the other countries in the model as a result of the trade policy choices hypothetically made by Brazil (tables 5–7). The aggregate estimate of the change in welfare is the weighted sum of the welfare changes for the 20 individual households in the model, reported as a percentage

19. In Brazil, capital's share of factor income from the input-output tables is between 52 percent and 54 percent between 1995 and 1997. Capital's share of factor income is 54 percent in the Brazilian Survey of Industry for 1998 and 76 percent in the Brazilian Census of Agriculture for 1996. Factor shares in production were reestimated to correct for biases in agriculture and services, so that capital's share of income is 50 percent based on the national accounts. But Vanos (2003) estimates capital's share at 22 percent based on the LSMS survey. From our mapping of LSMS data, capital's share is about 10 percent.

20. Specifically, they report a poverty level of 65.07 reals per month. This is divided by 30.417, the average number of days in a month, and then further divided by 1.44 to get the purchasing power parity equivalent in U.S. dollars. This is $1.48656, rounded to $1.50 for ease of recollection.

21. They also report comparable numbers from an alternative survey, known as the PPD, which imply a national poverty index of 24.7 percent using comparable income measures.

22. The average number of people is 5.8 in rural household 1 and 5.0 in urban household 1. This compares with an average of 3.9 for the entire survey.

TABLE 5. Impact of Mercosur Trade Policy Options on Selected Countries As a Share of Consumption, Central Elasticities (welfare change, percent)

Country or region	FTAA (1)	FTAA with Excluded Products (2)	EU–Mercosur (3)	EU–Mercosur with Excluded Products (4)	FTAA and EU–Mercosur (5)	Unilateral 50% Tariff Cut (6)	Multilateral Tariff Liberalization by 50% (7)	FTAA with no Mercosur Liberalization (8)
Brazil	0.6	0.4	0.9	0.1	1.8	0.4	0.9	0.4
Argentina	−0.2	−0.2	2.3	0.2	2.2	0.2	0.8	0.2
Uruguay	1.7	1.6	43.9	1.2	43.4	1.4	7.8	0.4
Chile	1.1	1.1	−0.2	0.0	0.9	0.1	1.3	0.8
Colombia	1.7	2.0	−0.1	−0.1	1.7	0.0	1.0	1.7
Peru	1.0	1.0	−0.1	0.0	0.9	0.0	1.3	1.0
Venezuela	1.1	1.1	0.0	−0.1	1.1	0.0	0.9	1.1
Rest of Andean pact	1.9	2.0	0.0	0.0	1.9	0.1	2.5	1.8
Mexico	0.3	0.4	0.0	0.0	0.3	0.0	0.5	0.0
Central America and Caribbean	4.3	4.8	0.0	0.0	4.4	0.0	2.1	4.6
Rest of South America	0.8	0.8	−1.2	0.1	0.0	0.3	4.1	0.1
Canada	0.0	0.1	0.0	0.0	0.0	0.0	0.2	0.1
United States	0.0	0.0	0.0	0.0	0.0	0.0	0.1	0.0
European Union 15	−0.1	0.0	0.5	0.1	0.4	0.0	0.8	−0.1
Japan	0.0	0.0	0.0	0.0	0.0	0.0	1.8	0.0
Rest of the world	−0.1	−0.1	0.0	0.0	−0.1	0.0	2.3	−0.2

Note: FTAA with excluded products: FTAA with U.S. antidumping policy denying improved access to its four protected sectors. EU-Mercosur with excluded products: a free trade agreement between Mercosur and the European Union with the seven most protected food and agricultural products in the European Union excluded from the agreement. FTAA and EU-Mercosur: the FTAA combined with a free trade agreement between Mercosur and the European Union. Unilateral 50% tariff cut: a Mercosur-only tariff cut of 50 percent. Multilateral tariff liberalization: all regions reduce tariffs and export subsidies by 50 percent. FTAA with no Mercosur liberalization: the FTAA but Mercosur does not change its external tariff to the rest of the Americas.

Source: Authors' computations based on GTAP database (Dimaranan and McDougall 2002), updated 1996 input-output table for Brazil, and the 1996 LSMS conducted by the Brazilian Institute of Geography and Statistics.

TABLE 6. Impact of Mercosur Trade Policy Options on Selected Countries, Central Elasticities (welfare gain in billions of 1996 U.S. dollars)

Country	FTAA	FTAA with Excluded Products	EU–Mercosur	EU–Mercosur with excluded products	FTAA and EU–Mercosur	Unilateral 50% Tariff Cut	Multilateral Tariff Liberalization by 50%	FTAA with no Mercosur Liberalization
	(1)	(2)	(3)	(4)	(5)	(6)	(7)	(8)
Brazil	3.1	2.3	5.0	0.5	9.5	1.9	4.6	2.3
Argentina	−0.5	−0.5	5.9	0.5	5.7	0.5	2.0	0.5
Uruguay	0.2	0.2	6.5	0.2	6.4	0.2	1.2	0.1
Chile	0.5	0.6	−0.1	0.0	0.5	0.1	0.7	0.4
Colombia	1.1	1.3	−0.1	−0.1	1.1	0.0	0.6	1.1
Peru	0.4	0.4	0.0	0.0	0.4	0.0	0.6	0.4
Venezuela	0.7	0.7	0.0	0.0	0.7	0.0	0.5	0.6
Rest of Andean pact	0.4	0.4	0.0	0.0	0.4	0.0	0.5	0.3
Mexico	0.9	1.0	0.0	0.0	0.7	0.0	1.2	0.0
Central America and Caribbean	3.4	3.8	0.0	0.0	3.5	0.0	1.7	3.6
Rest of South America	0.1	0.1	−0.1	0.0	0.0	0.0	0.3	0.0
Canada	0.1	0.3	0.0	0.0	−0.1	0.0	0.8	0.2
United States	2.3	2.0	−0.4	−0.4	1.7	0.3	3.0	−0.5
European Union 15	−2.6	−2.2	25.0	5.6	21.2	1.6	39.3	−3.2
Japan	−1.0	−0.9	0.7	0.4	−0.5	0.3	45.7	−1.2
Rest of the world	−4.8	−4.2	−0.2	−0.2	−5.0	1.3	83.6	−5.6
Sum for included countries	12.7	12.4	42.3	6.9	51.6	NA	NA	9.1
Sum for excluded countries	−8.4	−7.2	−0.2	−0.4	−5.5	NA	NA	−9.9
Sum for all countries	4.3	5.2	42.2	6.4	46.1	NA	186.0	−0.9

Note: FTAA with excluded products: FTAA with U.S. antidumping policy denying improved access to its four protected sectors. EU-Mercosur with excluded products: a free trade agreement between Mercosur and the European Union with the seven most protected food and agricultural products in the European Union excluded from the agreement. FTAA and EU-Mercosur: the FTAA combined with a free trade agreement between Mercosur and the European Union. Unilateral 50 percent tariff cut: a Mercosur-only tariff cut of 50 percent. Multilateral tariff liberalization: all regions reduce tariffs and export subsidies by 50 percent. FTAA with no Mercosur liberalization: the FTAA but Mercosur does not change its external tariff to the rest of the Americas.

Source: Authors' computations based on GTAP database (Dimaranan and McDougall 2002), updated 1996 input-output table for Brazil, and the 1996 LSMS conducted by the Brazilian Institute of Geography and Statistics.

TABLE 7. Impact of Trade Policy Options on Macro Variables, Central and Low Elasticities (percentage change)

Macrovariable	Elasticity	FTAA (1)	FTAA with Excluded Products (2)	EU–Mercosur (3)	EU–Mercosur with Excluded Products (4)	FTAA and EU–Mercosur (5)	Unilateral 50% Tariff Cut (6)	Multilateral Tariff Liberalization by 50% (7)	FTAA with no Mercosur Liberalization (8)
Real exchange rate	Central	2.61	2.73	2.25	2.70	3.00	1.97	1.43	−0.2
	Low	1.86	2.01	1.08	1.89	1.98	1.82	1.20	1.9
Change in tariff revenue	Central	0.60	0.56	0.56	0.55	0.69	0.10	0.12	0.0
(% of GDP)	Low	0.52	0.50	0.50	0.48	0.72	0.20	0.24	0.5
Unskilled labor wage rate	Central	2.91	1.87	4.24	2.42	5.81	0.94	3.02	0.0
	Low	1.61	1.05	2.51	1.38	3.64	0.73	2.04	0.7
Skilled labor wage rate	Central	0.97	1.01	1.12	0.60	1.77	0.54	0.31	1.1
	Low	0.66	0.65	0.85	0.44	1.37	0.46	0.48	1.6
Rental rate on capital	Central	−0.13	0.18	−0.47	−0.39	−0.31	−0.08	−0.59	−0.1
	Low	0.17	0.32	0.00	−0.04	0.22	0.10	−0.09	0.2
Rental rate on land	Central	14.21	9.19	25.12	14.84	31.00	5.79	30.00	4.4
	Low	6.31	3.94	13.19	7.38	16.76	3.56	16.27	6.3

Note: FTAA with excluded products: FTAA with U.S. antidumping policy denying improved access to its four protected sectors. EU-Mercosur with excluded products: a free trade agreement between Mercosur and the European Union with the seven most protected food and agricultural products in the European Union excluded from the agreement. FTAA and EU-Mercosur: the FTAA combined with a free trade agreement between Mercosur and the European Union. Unilateral 50 percent tariff cut: a Mercosur-only tariff cut of 50 percent. Multilateral tariff liberalization: all regions reduce tariffs and export subsidies by 50 percent. FTAA with no Mercosur liberalization: the FTAA but Mercosur does not change its external tariff to the rest of the Americas.

Source: Authors' computations based on GTAP database (Dimaranan and McDougall 2002), updated 1996 input-output table for Brazil, and the 1996 LSMS conducted by the Brazilian Institute of Geography and Statistics.

of consumption and in 1996 U.S. dollars. The central elasticity results are presented explicitly, and important differences with low elasticities are also mentioned. Key macrovariables that are important for the interpretation of the household results are presented in table 7.

Regional Arrangements

As part of Mercosur, Brazil is negotiating participation in the FTAA as well as an EU–Mercosur free trade agreement. Brazil will gain an estimated 0.6 percent of personal consumption from the FTAA (about $3 billion; see tables 5 and 6, column 1). The gains to Brazil from a Mercosur–EU agreement are about 1.5 times greater.

Both the FTAA and the EU–Mercosur agreement create very large economic areas, each with one large industrial country partner. These partners have export supply capacities that are large relative to the demand from smaller partners. For a given absolute change in demand resulting from a regional agreement, the larger capacity of these partner countries allows them to supply their smaller partners with relatively elastic supply curves. This prevents the supply price for imports from large partner countries from rising significantly. Finally, large countries offer improved market access, as emphasized in Harrison and others (1997a, 2002). Although in several cases preferential arrangements among small countries have been found to be welfare reducing,[23] for the reasons just mentioned the estimates show that Brazil and most countries in the Americas would gain from an FTAA and that Mercosur countries would gain from a free trade agreement with the European Union.

The one exception to this pattern in the Americas is Argentina, which is estimated to lose slightly from the FTAA. Without FTAA it enjoys preferential access to the markets of the other Mercosur countries. The FTAA provides equivalent access to the other countries in the Americas to the Mercosur market, eroding Argentina's preferential access. The effects of this loss of preferential access plus the trade diversion effects are larger than the trade creation effects.[24]

The combined gains to Argentina, Brazil, and Uruguay are more than 50 percent larger from an EU–Mercosur agreement than from the FTAA (see tables 5 and 6, column 3). The European Union has several agricultural and food products with very high tariffs (see table 2). If Argentina, Brazil, and Uruguay obtain tariff-free access to these markets while the European Union continues to apply these tariffs on other countries, the three countries would receive large terms of trade gains in EU markets. The gains for Uruguay, a relatively small economy, would

23. See Harrison and others (2002) and Bakoup and Tarr (2000). Uruguay also loses from participation in Mercosur.

24. Pereira (1999) and Teixera and others (2002) find the same result for Argentina in the FTAA. Although the gains to Brazil from the FTAA are also eroded because of erosion of preferential access in Argentina, Argentina is a smaller market than the Brazilian market. Thus the erosion of preferential access in the partner's market is more important for Argentina.

be between 6 percent (with low elasticities) and 44 percent (with the central elasticities).[25]

Countries excluded from the agreements typically lose. The European Union, Japan, and the rest of the world all lose from the FTAA, for a combined loss of $8.4 billion (see table 6, column 1). The excluded countries suffer a decline in demand for their exports to the Americas as importers in the Americas shift demand toward suppliers from the Americas. Hence there is both a terms of trade loss on sales that continue and an efficiency loss from having to shift to alternate markets or products. The European Union is estimated to lose $2.6 billion, slightly more than the $2.3 billion the United States is estimated to gain. One exception is Japan under the EU–Mercosur agreement. Japan obtains a small terms of trade improvement in the markets of the rest of the world as countries included in that agreement shift their trade toward each other's markets. The gains to Japan, however, are very small and round to zero at the nearest 0.1 percent of Japan's consumption.

The benefits to Brazil from these two agreements exceed the sum of the benefits for each agreement separately. This is because the combined economic area of the Americas plus the European Union is vast, so Brazil is the less likely to face adverse terms of trade effects as a result of consuming a large share of any exporter's supply. Lost tariff revenues from diverting trade to partner countries that are part of either agreement taken separately are reduced by combining the two agreements. Thus negotiating an agreement with the European Union in addition to the FTAA appears likely to increase the welfare gains to Brazil.[26]

Limitations on Market Access: The Impact of Antidumping, Rules of Origin, and EU Agriculture Exclusions

Although preferential trade arrangements with large industrial countries offer developing economies the promise of increased access to large markets, in practice limitations on improved access significantly reduce the benefits. The European Union has steadfastly refused to grant tariff-free access in its highly protected agricultural products in its association agreements with Central and Eastern European countries, its customs union agreement with Turkey, and its free trade area agreements with various Mediterranean countries (Morocco, Tunisia). Hence it is a priori unlikely to offer such concessions to Mercosur

25. The gains to Uruguay come primarily from the meat sector. Attracted by the tariff umbrella of 95 percent tariffs in the large EU market, Uruguay will dramatically expand meat output and exports to the European Union in the long run. Meat exports are a much more significant share of gross domestic product in Uruguay than they are in Argentina or Brazil. Thus the welfare gain from an improvement in the export price in the European Union in this sector can be expected to result in a larger welfare gain than in Brazil or Argentina. It is likely, however, that such a large expansion of the meat sector would be constrained by "specific factors" in Uruguay that were not modeled.

26. These results are similar to those Harrison and others (2002) found for the "additive regionalism" strategy of Chile, which yielded significantly larger benefits than the agreements taken separately.

when it has refused to offer them to countries for which it might be viewed as having more to gain geopolitically.

As for the FTAA, the United States has strongly resisted efforts to limit the use of antidumping actions as part of the FTAA despite a proposal by Chile to include such a limitation. As the use of tariffs and nontariff barriers has declined, the use of antidumping as a protectionist device has risen significantly in the United States (Finger 1993) (and more recently in the European Union as well; see Messerlin and Reed 1995). Antidumping actions have focused on four sensitive sectors: chemicals, metals, nonelectrical machinery, and electrical equipment. Thus Brazilian authorities have expressed the fear that the benefits of nominally improved access to U.S. markets will be denied by antidumping actions.

Finally, free trade agreements involve rules of origin, requiring that exporters source a share of inputs from within the preferential area. Evidence is accumulating that these rules of origin significantly limit the improved market access of preferential tariff concessions. The Africa Growth and Opportunity Act provides preferential access for African exports to the U.S. markets. Mattoo and others (2002) found that African nonoil exports to the United States would increase by about 50 percent without the stringent rules of origin but by only 10 percent with them. Estevadeordal (2000) found that restrictive rules of origin limited Mexico's improved access to the U.S. market under NAFTA. Brenton and Manchin (2003) argue that EU preferential trade agreements have been ineffective in delivering improved market access, most likely because of the restrictive rules of origin and the costs of proving compliance.

Two simulations illustrate how these limitations of market access by the European Union and the United States can affect the potential gains.

Excluded Agricultural Products in the EU–Mercosur Agreement. This scenario assumes that the European Union fails to provide improved market access to its most highly protected agricultural products in an EU–Mercosur agreement. The EU tariff rates in the database are 65 percent for paddy rice, 44 percent for cereal grains, 86 percent for processed rice, 28 percent for other food products, 95 percent for bovine meat products, 90 percent for dairy products, 61 percent for other meat products, and 76 percent for sugar. These are products in which the Mercosur countries have a comparative advantage, so if the free trade agreement between the European Union and Mercosur excludes these products, the expected benefits would be significantly reduced.

Under the central elasticity results the denial of full market access to these key agricultural products reduces the value of the EU–Mercosur agreement to Brazil from 0.9 percent of consumption to 0.1 percent (see tables 5 and 6, column 4). The estimated gains for Uruguay are also dramatically reduced. The gains to the European Union are also reduced, from 0.5 percent of its consumption to 0.1 percent, reflecting the importance of agriculture liberalization if EU consumers are to reap gains from the agreement.

Antidumping and Rules of Origin in the FTAA. Limitations on access to the U.S. market are more likely to come from restrictive rules of origin and the use of antidumping actions than from explicit exclusion of certain products. Indeed, Brazilian authorities have expressed the fear that the benefits of improved access to U.S. markets will be denied by antidumping actions, as in the steel sector. This scenario estimates the costs to Brazil of continued U.S. protection of its most protected markets even with the FTAA. Protection is 53 percent on sugar, 42 percent on dairy products, 18 percent on oil seeds, and 14 percent on other crops.[27] For these sectors the United States is assumed to employ antidumping duties or stringent rules of origin to neutralize the impact of the FTAA on Brazil's exports (in other words, the U.S. tariff on exports of these products from Brazil does not change).[28]

The impact is to reduce the benefits to Brazil to about two-thirds of the gains it would receive with full market access in the FTAA (see tables 5 and 6, column 2). The reduction is not as severe as with the excluded products in the EU agreement. The large impacts tend to be driven by the tariff peaks, which are not as high in the U.S. market as in the European Union. If the United States fails to provide preferential access to its highly protected products, Brazil can sell these products in other markets in the Americas that also open up to Brazil on a preferential basis as part of the FTAA. With the EU–Mercosur agreement there are no alternate markets in which Brazil has preferential access.

FTAA *with No Change in Mercosur's External Tariffs.* To identify the source of gains, especially at the household level, the impact of the FTAA with no improved access to Mercosur markets is also evaluated. This scenario shows how much of the gains to Brazil come from improved access to the markets of the Americas and how much from lowering Mercosur tariffs, thereby achieving improved resource allocation in Brazil. In this scenario the countries in the Americas outside of Mercosur are assumed to lower their tariffs preferentially to all countries in the Americas (so Brazil obtains improved market access), but the Mercosur countries do not lower their common external tariffs against partner countries in the Americas (so Brazil does not offer any improved market access).

Under this scenario the gains to Brazil are reduced to 0.4 percent of consumption. This shows that improved market access is responsible for about two-thirds of the gain to Brazil from the FTAA and that the remaining one-third of the gain comes from the preferential lowering of the Mercosur tariff (see tables 5 and 6, column 8).

27. The category "other crops" is an aggregate of the following sectors from the full GTAP data set: wheat, vegetables and fruits, fiber-based plants, wool, forestry, fishing, and other crops. Simulations were also performed with wheat as part of grains rather than other crops. Argentina gains more from the EU–Mercosur agreement, but otherwise most of the results change by very small amounts.

28. This is not a full treatment of the potential use of antidumping or rules of origin within the FTAA or of the impact on Brazil. Such treatment would have to account for antidumping duties and stringent rules of origin by the United States against other products and partners in the Americas as well and for the use of antidumping and stringent rules of origin by countries other than the United States.

Tariff Cuts and Uniformity in Mercosur or Multilateral Liberalization—or Both

Simulations were also run for unilateral tariff cuts by Mercosur and for cuts through multilateral trade liberalization under the WTO.

Unilateral Trade Liberalization by 50 Percent and Tariff Uniformity. A 50 percent cut in Mercosur tariffs will result in a welfare increase of about 0.4 percent of Brazilian consumption or about $1.9 billion a year (see tables 5 and 6, column 6). Thus the gains from the FTAA with excluded access to the U.S. market on selected products results in about the same gains as a unilateral tariff cut by Mercosur of 50 percent. With low elasticities, however, the gains are only about 0.2 percent of consumption for Brazil, or $0.4 billion, and the impact on Argentina is negative.[29] The larger terms of trade effects with the lower elasticities account for the lower gains from tariff reduction.

Tariff uniformity (with the same collected tariff revenue) in Mercosur will result in slightly larger welfare gains than a 50 percent cut in tariffs. These results are consistent with earlier results on the benefits of tariff uniformity for Turkey and Chile (Harrison and others 1993, 2002). Similarly, Martinez de Prera (2000) found welfare gains from tariff uniformity in all 13 countries evaluated. Although theory indicates that taxes are more efficient if they are higher on products with relatively low elasticities of demand, evidently tariffs do not typically differ from uniformity in these economies for tax efficiency reasons.[30] On the contrary, the large gains from trade liberalization typically come from reducing tariff peaks, which is effectively accomplished through tariff uniformity. Reducing low tariffs results in proportionately smaller gains and may even result in losses if the importing country possesses monopsony power.

Multilateral Trade Liberalization. Brazilian authorities have also encouraged multilateral trade negotiations and supported the Doha Development Agenda—in part because of a belief that it is the most likely way to achieve agricultural liberalization. In this scenario all countries in the world reduce their tariffs and export subsidies and their taxes by 50 percent.

Brazil gains about 0.9 percent of personal consumption from multilateral trade liberalization in the static model, or about $4.6 billion a year (see tables 5 and 6, column 7). These are larger than the gains from the FTAA and those from an agreement with the European Union that excludes the highly protected

29. Harrison and others (1997c, appendix C) show that the optimal tariff t in any sector of the model is bounded below by $t^* = \{[\sigma_{MM}/(\sigma_{MM} - 1)] - 1\}$. Thus even in the central elasticity case with $\sigma_{MM} = 30$ the optimal tariff is more than 3 percent. But in the low elasticity scenarios, with $\sigma_{MM} = 8$, the optimal tariff is more than 14 percent. With an average Mercosur tariff of 12 percent, the optimum uniform tariff is lower than the existing average tariff in the central elasticity scenarios. The small gains that remain are due to lowering the tariff peaks.

30. The set of elasticities that were chosen, however, makes uniformity beneficial in general. That is, the Ramsey optimal taxation rule suggests that higher taxes should be placed on goods with the lower elasticity of demand. With the virtually homogeneous choice of elasticities here, the Ramsey optimal tariffs are close to uniform.

agricultural and food products. Because these products are likely to be excluded from a Mercosur agreement with the European Union, the results support the strategy of the Brazilian authorities to pursue multilateral liberalization along with the regional options.

The gains to the world from the 50 percent cut in tariffs and export subsidies are estimated at $186 billion with central elasticities (see table 6, column 7) and $87 billion with low elasticities. As Harrison and others (1997b) argue in assessing the Uruguay Round, elasticities play an important role in explaining differences in aggregate gains from multilateral trade liberalization.

Impact on Households and the Poor

The household results follow a similar pattern across all of the policy scenarios (table 8). The poorest household will typically gain several times the aggregate gains for the economy expressed as a percentage of household consumption.[31] Although the impact on household incomes is not strictly progressive, the four poorest urban households and four poorest rural households are among the biggest gainers from the reforms as a percentage of their own household consumption.

What accounts for this robust and encouraging result? Trade protection in Brazil favors capital-intensive manufactures, so liberalization shifts resources toward more unskilled labor-intensive agriculture. Thus the wage rate of unskilled labor increases significantly more that the rent on capital (see table 7).[32] The poorest households earn most of their income from unskilled labor (see table 4), so they gain proportionally more than other households.

Although the impact on sectors depends on the specific agreement, there is a general pattern. Oilseeds, other agriculture (excluding grains and wheat), other crops (which includes fruits and vegetables and wheat), processed food, and leather sectors expand production and exports. These sectors, especially the agricultural sectors,[33] are the most intensive users of unskilled labor in the model. Several manufacturing sectors decline, including motor vehicles, other metal products, and other manufacturing. These declining sectors are among the most capital-intensive in Brazil.

These outcomes reflect relative protection in Brazil, which favors manufacturing at the expense of agriculture and processed food products. Despite substantial trade liberalization, vestiges of Brazil's import-substitution indus-

31. The percentage gains for the poor relative to the aggregate percentage gains are similar for low trade elasticities.

32. The poor typically have not accumulated large stores of real assets or financial assets, so they do not earn significant capital income or income from the rent of land. Nor have the poor typically accumulated much human capital, so they earn a much smaller share of their income from skilled labor than do the middle classes.

33. The EU–Mercosur agreement (without exceptions) induces a much larger increase in agricultural output in Brazil than do the other agreements because of the large increase in preferential access for Mercosur countries in the European Union.

TABLE 8. Impact of Mercosur Trade Policy Options on Brazilian Households as a Share of Consumption, Central Elasticities (welfare change, %)

Household type	FTAA (1)	FTAA with Excluded Products (2)	EU–Mercosur (3)	EU–Mercosur with Excluded Products (4)	FTAA and EU–Mercosur (5)	Unilateral 50% Tariff Cut (6)	Multilateral Tariff Liberalization by 50% (7)	FTAA with no Mercosur Liberalization (8)
Rural								
1	2.5	1.7	4.0	2.1	5.5	1.5	2.9	0.8
2	2.3	1.5	3.9	1.8	5.4	1.2	2.8	1.0
3	2.5	1.5	4.5	1.9	6.2	1.1	3.5	1.3
4	2.5	1.8	3.9	2.2	5.4	1.5	3.1	0.8
5	1.3	0.8	2.3	0.7	3.5	0.6	1.8	0.8
6	1.5	1.0	2.3	0.8	3.6	0.7	1.7	0.8
7	1.3	0.9	2.0	0.7	3.2	0.6	1.6	0.7
8	3.1	2.0	4.8	2.4	6.9	1.2	4.1	1.4
9	0.9	0.4	1.7	0.6	2.6	0.4	1.8	0.7
10	3.7	2.3	6.0	2.8	8.3	1.4	4.9	1.6
Urban								
1	2.5	1.8	3.8	2.1	5.2	1.5	2.7	0.7
2	2.3	1.6	3.8	1.8	5.2	1.3	2.6	0.8
3	2.2	1.4	3.6	1.7	5.0	1.2	2.6	0.9
4	2.0	1.3	3.1	1.5	4.5	1.0	2.4	0.8
5	1.3	0.7	2.4	0.8	3.5	0.7	1.8	0.8
6	1.6	1.0	2.6	1.0	3.9	0.7	1.9	0.8
7	0.4	0.3	0.9	0.0	1.6	0.3	0.7	0.4
8	0.3	0.2	0.7	−0.1	1.4	0.3	0.7	0.4
9	−0.5	−0.4	−0.3	−0.7	−0.1	0.0	0.1	0.2
10	0.0	0.2	−0.2	−0.5	0.5	0.1	0.0	0.2

Note: FTAA with excluded products: FTAA with U.S. antidumping policy denying improved access to its four protected sectors. EU-Mercosur with excluded products: a free trade agreement between Mercosur and the European Union with the seven most protected food and agricultural products in the European Union excluded from the agreement. FTAA and EU-Mercosur: the FTAA combined with a free trade agreement between Mercosur and the European Union. Unilateral 50 percent tariff cut: a Mercosur-only tariff cut of 50 percent. Multilateral tariff liberalization: all regions reduce tariffs and export subsidies by 50 percent. FTAA with no Mercosur liberalization: the FTAA but Mercosur does not change its external tariff to the rest of the Americas.

Source: Authors' computations based on GTAP database (Dimaranan and McDougall 2002), updated 1996 input-output table for Brazil, and the 1996 LSMS conducted by the Brazilian Institute of Geography and Statistics.

trialization protection structure remain. When protection in the economy is reduced, resources shift toward the agriculture and food sectors that had been disadvantaged relative to manufacturing. The expanding sectors tend to be less capital-intensive than the contracting sectors. International trade theory argues that the price of the factor of production used intensively in protected sectors should fall relative to the price of the factor of production in the unprotected sectors following trade liberalization.[34] Thus the wage rate of unskilled labor rises relative to the rent on capital, benefiting the poor. Because the value of land rises even more than the wage rate of unskilled labor, two of the richest rural households are the biggest gainers from the reforms.

To document this interpretation of why the poor can be expected to gain proportionally more than wealthier households, the impact of the FTAA on households was decomposed in table 9. Column 1 reproduces the base results from table 8 for the FTAA. Column 2 presents the results of assuming that all households consume the commodities in the same proportions. Although the gains to the poorest households decline slightly, they remain three to four times greater than the percentage gains for all households together. Thus, disparate consumption shares do not explain why poor households gain more from the trade policy changes.

Column 3 presents the results of the FTAA scenario in which all households are assumed to earn the same shares of income from the wages of unskilled labor and skilled labor and rent on capital and land. Most of the poorest households would obtain only a slightly greater increase in income than the average for all households of 0.6 percent. This confirms that it is the more than proportionate rise in the price of the factors of production important to the income of poor households that explains why poor households gain more from these trade policy options. The factor most important to the poor is the wage rate of unskilled labor (see table 4), which rises fastest among the important household income factors (see table 7).

An additional simulation offers further support for this explanation. For reasons explained earlier, the capital intensity in agriculture sectors is estimated to be significantly less than reported in the Brazilian input-output table. There is a dramatic difference in the results for the estimated welfare gains from the FTAA to Brazilian households when the biased factor shares in the GTAP data are used instead of the corrected data. The poorest rural household is estimated to gain 0.5 percent of its consumption and the poorest urban household 0.4 percent, equal or slightly less than the aggregate average percentage gain (see table 9, column 4). This shows that the corrections to the factor share data are crucial to the results at the household level and supports the interpretation that the shift of

34. This is known as the Stolper-Samuelson theorem. In this model, however, product differentiation mutes strict application of the Stolper-Samuelson results.

TABLE 9. Decomposition of the Impact of the FTAA on Brazilian Households as a Share of Consumption, Central Elasticities (change in welfare, %)

	FTAA	FTAA with Uniform Consumption Shares	FTAA with Uniform Income Shares	FTAA with Factor Shares from Input-Output Table
	(1)	(2)	(3)	(4)
All households	0.6	0.6	0.6	0.5
Rural				
1	2.5	2.0	1.0	0.5
2	2.3	1.8	0.7	0.3
3	2.5	2.0	0.5	0.1
4	2.5	2.1	0.9	1.0
5	1.3	0.8	0.5	0.4
6	1.5	0.7	0.9	0.7
7	1.3	0.6	0.7	0.5
8	3.1	2.8	1.0	2.2
9	0.9	1.2	0.0	0.8
10	3.7	3.2	1.1	2.0
Urban				
1	2.5	2.0	1.0	0.4
2	2.3	1.8	0.9	0.2
3	2.2	1.8	0.7	0.0
4	2.0	1.6	0.7	0.9
5	1.3	1.0	0.3	0.1
6	1.6	1.4	0.6	0.4
7	0.4	0.2	0.3	0.1
8	0.3	0.3	0.2	0.0
9	−0.5	0.0	−0.3	−0.3
10	0.0	0.1	0.9	0.9

Source: Authors' computations based on GTAP database (Dimaranan and McDougall 2002), updated 1996 input-output table for Brazil, and the 1996 LSMS conducted by the Brazilian Institute of Geography and Statistics.

resources toward agriculture is important in increasing the incomes of the poor and reducing poverty.

The results also show that the Mercosur tariff changes are more important to the poor than improved market access (see tables 5 and 8, column 8). In this scenario Mercosur does not change its own tariffs but obtains improved access to the markets of the Americas. The average gains to the economy fall by about one-third compared with the FTAA gains, but the gains to the poorest households fall by two-thirds. This is because Mercosur's tariff changes induce output expansion in the sectors that intensively use unskilled labor, thus increasing unskilled wages relative to other factor prices. Improved market access does not increase the price of unskilled labor relative to capital. With only improved market access, the poor gain, but not progressively as they do with internal liberalization in Mercosur.

Although the trade reforms are significantly propoor, the model implicitly assumes a time horizon long enough to reestablish equilibrium after some policy shock. Thus it is possible that during the transition to a new equilibrium some poor households will be hurt. This is especially likely among households that move out of the declining sectors, such as the more highly protected manufacturing sectors. This emphasizes the need for an effective safety net to assist the poor.

To test the robustness of the results with respect to parameter specification, 500 simulations were conducted of the impact of the FTAA. Key parameter values were drawn randomly from specified probability distributions (see Harrison and others 2003b, appendix F on systematic sensitivity analysis). As a result of the FTAA, the following results will hold with virtual certainty: Brazil will gain at least 0.3 percent of its consumption, FTAA members will gain at least $12 billion a year, excluded countries will lose at least $6.7 billion a year, and the poorest urban and rural households will gain at least 1 percent of their income. The sensitivity results confirm the conclusions drawn from the point estimates of the gainers and losers at the household level and the aggregate country level.

Conclusions

Both the FTAA and an EU–Mercosur agreement would benefit Brazil, but exceptions to the agreements (rules of origin, antidumping, and agricultural exclusions) would significantly diminish the gains. The estimates presented here indicate that Brazil can optimize its choice of trade policies by combining regional arrangements in both the Americas and Europe with multilateral liberalization. If tariff uniformity is added to the regional and multilateral liberalization, further gains could be realized.

Both the FTAA and the EU–Mercosur arrangements are net trade creating for the countries involved, but excluded countries almost always lose. Multilateral trade liberalization results in gains to the world more than four times greater than either of these relatively beneficial regional arrangements, showing the importance of multilateral negotiations.

Most of the trade policy options evaluated result in a progressive distribution of the gains to Brazilian households, with the poorest households experiencing the greatest percentage increase in their incomes. Trade policy changes tend to shift resources from capital-intensive manufacturing toward unskilled labor-intensive agriculture and less capital-intensive manufacturing, inducing an increase in unskilled labor wages relative to the prices of other factors of production. The percentage increase in the incomes of the poorest households is three to four times greater than the average percentage increase in income for the economy as a whole.

A micro-simulation model would likely find that some poor households could lose, especially in the short run. This emphasizes the need for having effective safety net policies in place. But because the sectors that are important to the poor tend to be disfavored by the structure of protection, the medium- to long-run effects of these trade reforms should be positive for the vast majority of the poorest households.

References

Adelman, Irma, and Sherman Robinson. 1978. *Income Distribution Policies in Developing Countries.* Stanford, Calif.: Stanford University Press.

Athukorala, Premachandra, and James Reidel. 1994. "Demand and Supply Factors in the Determination of NIE Exports: A Simultaneous Error-Correction Model for Hong Kong: A Comment." *Economic Journal* 104(427):1411–14.

Arndt, C., A. Cruz, H. T. Jensen, S. Robinson, and F. Tarp. 1998. "Social Accounting Matrices for Mozambique 1994 and 1995." TMD Discussion Paper 28. International Food Policy Research Institute, Trade and Macroeconomics Division, Washington D.C.

Bakoup, Ferdinand, and David Tarr. 2000. "The Economic Effects of Integration in the Central African Economic and Monetary Community: Some General Equilibrium Estimates for Cameroon." *African Development Review* 12(3):161–90.

Barros, R. P., C. H. Corseuil, and S. Cury. 2000. "Trade Opening and Liberalization of Capital Flows in Brazil: Impacts on Poverty and Inequality." In R. Henriques, ed., *Desigualdade e pobreza no Brasil.* Rio de Janeiro: Instituto de Pesquisa Econômica Aplicada.

Brenton, Paul, and Meriam Manchin. 2003. "Making EU Trade Agreements Work: The Role of Rules of Origin." *World Economy* 26(5):755–69.

Burfisher, M., K. Thierfelder, and K. Hanson. 1992. "Data Base for a Computable General Equilbrium Model of the Agricultural Sectors of the United States and Mexico and Their Interaction." Staff Report AGES9225. U.S. Department of Agriculture, Economic Research Service, Washington, D.C.

Bussolo, Maurizio, and Jann Lay. 2003. "Globalization and Poverty Changes in Columbia." Paper presented at the Annual World Bank Conference on Development Economics, Europe, May 15–16, Paris.

Chang, Won, and L. Alan Winters. 2002. "How Regional Blocs Affect Excluded Countries: The Price Effects of Mercosur." *American Economic Review* 92(4):889–904.

Chen, Shaohua, and Martin Ravallion. 2003. "Household Welfare Impacts of China's Accession to the WTO." World Bank, Washington, D.C.

Cockburn, John. 2001. "Trade Liberalization and Poverty in Nepal: A Computable General Equilibrium Micro Simulation Analysis." CREFA Working Paper 01-18. University of Laval, Center for Applied Economic and Financial Research, Quebec. Available online at www.crefa.ecn.ulaval.ca/cahier/0119.pdf.

Deaton, Angus. 2003. "Measuring Poverty in a Growing World (or Measuring Growth in a Poor World)." Working Paper, Princeton University, Department of Economics. Available online at www.wws.princeton.edu/~deaton/working.htm.

de Melo, Jaime, and David Tarr. 1992. *General Equilibrium Analysis of U.S. Foreign Trade Policy.* Cambridge, Mass.: MIT Press.

Dimaranan, Betina V., and Robert A. McDougall. 2002. *Global Trade, Assistance, and Production: The GTAP 5 Data Base.* Purdue University, Center for Global Trade Analysis. Available online at www.gtap.agecon.purdue.edu/databases/v5/v5_doco.asp.

Estevadeordal, Antoni. 2000. "Negotiating Market Access." *Journal of World Trade* 34(1):141–66.

Ferreira, Francisco H. G., Peter Lanjouw, and Marcelo Neri. 1999. "The Urban Poor in Brazil in 1996: A New Poverty Profile Using PPV, PNAD and Census Data." Unpublished manuscript. World Bank, Washington, D.C.

Ferris, M. C., and T. S. Munson. 2000. "Complementarity Problems in GAMS and the PATH Solver." *Journal of Economic Dynamics and Control* 24(2):165–88.

Finger, J. Michael, ed. 1993. *Antidumping: How It Works and Who Gets Hurt.* Ann Arbor: University of Michigan Press.

Harrison, Glenn W., Thomas F. Rutherford, and David Tarr. 1993. "Piecemeal Trade Reform in the Partially Liberalized Economy of Turkey." *World Bank Economic Review* 7(2):191–217.

———. 1997a. "Economic Implications for Turkey of a Customs Union with the European Union." *European Economic Review* 41(3–5):861–70.

———. 1997b. "Quantifying the Uruguay Round." *Economic Journal* 107(444):1405–30.

———. 1997c. "Trade Policy Options for Chile: A Quantitative Evaluation." Policy Research Working Paper 1783. World Bank, Washington, D.C. Available online at www.worldbank.org/research/trade/archive.html.

———. 2002. "Trade Policy Options for Chile: The Importance of Market Access." *World Bank Economic Review* 16(1):49–79.

———. 2003a. "Trade Liberalization, Poverty and Efficient Equity." *Journal of Development Economics* 71(1):97–128.

Harrison, Glenn W., Thomas F. Rutherford, David G. Tarr, and Angelo Gurgel. 2003b. "Regional, Multilateral and Unilateral Trade Policies of Mercosur for Growth and Poverty Reduction in Brazil." Policy Research Working Paper 3051. World Bank, Washington, D.C. Available online at www.worldbank.org/research/trade.

Hausner, U. 1999. "A 1995 Social Accounting Matrix for Zambia." TMD Discussion Paper Series 49. International Food Policy Research Institute, Trade and Macroeconomics Division, Washington, D.C.

Martinez de Prera, Josefina. 2000. "Revenue-Neutral Tariff Reform: Welfare Effects of Uniform Tariffs in 13 Developing Countries." PhD dissertation. University of Colorado, Department of Economics. Available online at http://ussub.colorado.edu/~martindp.

Mattoo, Aaditya, Devesh Roy, and Arvind Subramaniam. 2002. "The Africa Growth and Opportunity Act and Its Rules of Origin: Generosity Undermined?" Policy Research Working Paper 2908. World Bank, Washington, D.C. Available online at www.worldbank.org/research/trade/archive.html.

Mattoo, Aaditya, Carsten Fink, Mario Marconini, and Lia Valls Pereira. 2002. "Brazil's Services Trade and International Trade Negotiations." Working Paper. World Bank, Washington, D.C.

Messerlin, Patrick, and Geoffrey Reed. 1995. "Antidumping Policies in the United States and the European Community." *Economic Journal* 105(433):1565–75.

Muendler, Mark-Andreas. 2001. "Trade, Technology, and Productivity: A Study of Brazilian Manufacturers: 1986–98." Working Paper. University of California, Department of Economics, Berkeley.

Pereira, Lia Valls. 1999. "Estudo sobre linhas estrutuais da posicao brasileira, nos principais setores produtivos, de interesse do Brasil, no ambito do exercicio de conformacao da ALCA no ambito das negociacoes do Mercosul com a uniao Europeia." Fundação Getulio Vargas, o Ministério de Desenvolvimento, Indústria e Comércio do Brasil.

Piggott, John, and John Whalley. 1985. *UK Tax Policy and Applied General Equilibrium Analysis.* New York: Cambridge University Press.

Ravallion, Martin. 2003. "Measuring Aggregate Welfare Effects in Developing Countries: How Well Do National Accounts and Surveys Agree?" *Review of Economics and Statistics* 85(3):645–52.

Reidel, James. 1988. "The Demand for LDC Exports of Manufactures: Estimates from Hong Kong." *Economic Journal* 98(389):138–48.

Reinert, Kenneth A., and David W. Roland-Holst. 1992. "Armington Elasticities for United States Manufacturing Sectors." *Journal of Policy Modelling* 14(5):631–39.

Roland-Holst, David, and Dominique van der Mensbrugghe. 1992. "Trade Liberalization in the Americas: Are Regionalism and Globalization Compatible?" Paper presented at the conference on the Impact of Trade Liberalization Agreements on Latin America and the Caribbean, November 5–6, Inter-American Development Bank and Centre d'Etudes Prospectives et d'Information Internationales, Washington, D.C.

Rutherford, Thomas F. 1999. "Applied General Equilibrium Modeling with MPSGE as a GAMS Subsystem: An Overview of the Modeling Framework and Syntax." *Computational Economics* 14(1/2):1–46.

Rutherford, Thomas F., and David G. Tarr. 2002. "Trade Liberalization, Product Variety and Growth in a Small Open Economy: A Quantitative Assessment." *Journal of International Economics* 56(2): 247–72.

Shiells, C. R., and K. A. Reinert. 1993. "Armington Models and Terms-of-Trade Effects: Some Econometric Evidence for North America." *Canadian Journal of Economics* 26(2):299–316.

Teixera, Erly, Luiz Cypriano, and Wildson Pinto. 2002. "Impacts of AFTA and MERCOEURO on Agribusiness in the MERCOSUL Countries." Paper presented at the Fifth Annual Conference on Global Economic Analysis, June 5–7, Taipei, Taiwan, China. Available online at www.gtap.agecon.purdue.edu/resources/res_display.asp?recordid= 1017.

Thomas, M., and M. Bautista. 1999. "A 1991 Social Accounting Matrix (SAM) for Zimbabwe." TMD Discussion Paper 36. International Food Policy Research Institute, Trade and Macroeconomics Division, Washington, D.C.

Vanos, Maros. 2003. "Reconciliation of the GTAP and Household Survey Data." Working Paper. Purdue University, Department of Agricultural Economics. Available online at www.gtap.agecon.purdue.edu/events/board_meetings/2003/docs/maros_survey.pdf.

World Bank. 1990. *World Development Report 1990: Poverty*. New York: Oxford University Press.

———. 2000. *World Development Report 2000/2001: Attacking Poverty*. New York: Oxford University Press.

———. 2001. *Rural Poverty Alleviation in Brazil: Towards an Integrated Strategy*. Washington, D.C.: World Bank.

WTO (World Trade Organization). *Trade Policy Review, Brazil 2000*. Geneva.

ELSEVIER Journal of Development Economics 71 (2003) 97–128

JOURNAL OF Development ECONOMICS

www.elsevier.com/locate/econbase

Trade liberalization, poverty and efficient equity

Glenn W. Harrison[a], Thomas F. Rutherford[b], David G. Tarr[c,*]

[a] *The Moore School of Business, University of South Carolina, Columbia, SC, USA*
[b] *Department of Economics, University of Colorado, Denver, CO, USA*
[c] *Development Research Group, The World Bank, MSN 3-303 1818 H. St., N.W. Washington, DC 20433, USA*

Received 1 July 2001; accepted 1 April 2002

Abstract

Even if trade liberalization results in aggregate welfare gains over all households, it is possible that the poorest households could lose. We illustrate two approaches to designing trade liberalization in Turkey which ensure that the poor will not lose. The first approach uses direct compensation to losers. The second approach uses limited policy reform, where exceptions to the across-the-board reform are chosen to meet the equity goal. In each case, we map out some of the efficiency costs of attaining these equity goals so as to inform policy makers about the least costly way of attaining them.

JEL classification: F13; D63; D58
Keywords: Trade liberalization; Poverty; Efficient equity

1. The issue

Trade policy reforms typically result in some households winning and some households losing. Given the diversity of households in an actual economy, even the most attractive reforms will typically result in some households losing, at least in the short run. One approach is just to accept these losses if they are "acceptable" as the price of achieving some greater good. Another approach is to argue against any reform that hurts even one household, especially if that household is poor. These stylized positions sound extreme, but we have encountered them repeatedly.

* Corresponding author. Tel.: +1-202-473-7677; fax: +1-202-522-1159.
E-mail addresses: HARRISON@MOORE.SC.EDU (G.W. Harrison), RUTHERFORD@COLORADO.EDU (T.F. Rutherford), DTARR@WORLDBANK.ORG (D.G. Tarr).

0304-3878/02/$ - see front matter
doi:10.1016/S0304-3878(02)00135-9

We believe that these are false alternatives. We develop a computable general equilibrium (CGE) model with 40 households, distinguished by income level and urban or rural location, and show how it is possible to *combine policies* such that no poor household is harmed from trade policy reform. One general theme of our policy analyses is that we seek to mitigate the negative welfare effects on the poor at least cost. Equity goals can be achieved efficiently, but it is often the case that they are achieved inefficiently (e.g. Coller et al., 1996). Our goal is to identify the equity–efficiency tradeoffs available in Turkey, and to indicate the most attractive and least attractive alternatives given certain equity objectives.

The approach we propose involves three steps in the design of trade policy reform.

The steps we propose are the following. First, within the range of feasible policy options, find a combination of policy options that generate the *greatest aggregate welfare gains*. This step recognizes that the "top level" of analysis cannot be bogged down in extreme detail, lest the analysis becomes sidetracked. In our experience, the first step typically involves complementary policies to trade policy reform such as domestic tax uniformity (e.g. see Harrison et al., 1993, 1997a). Labor market reforms may also offer opportunities for complementary policies.[1]

Second, if a representative poor household losses in welfare terms, consider the explicit use of *sidepayments to compensate* them. These sidepayments would be extracted from the "winners" and would be designed so as to ensure that there are no "losers" from the reform among the poor households. Indeed, one could attempt to build in a stricter criterion that all households gain by some specified amount or more. The general idea is to make explicit the notion of hypothetical sidepayments that underlie the Compensation Principle in welfare economics, and take into account the effects of the sidepayments on relative prices (and hence welfare).

Third, exploit the laboratory simulation afforded by a CGE model to undertake a policy "instrument decomposition" in order to identify *which specific components of the policy affect the poor most*. That decomposition information can then be used to design complementary reforms or limited reforms that avoid reform in those sectors which have the most impact on the poor.

In both the second and third steps, we must take account of the possible efficiency loss from the application of the compensation or limited reform. There is likely to be a price to pay for attaining the equity goal of avoiding welfare losses for the poor, and our job is to simply characterize that price tag. We expect that there will always be less costly ways of attaining the equity goal, and that our characterization will make that apparent.

We view these steps as a feasible and constructive response to the controversy that otherwise seems to beset trade reforms. They are not a panacea. Without complementary

[1] In many developing countries, the poor are concentrated in "informal" labor markets. Frequently, there are practices or laws that limit labor mobility between the formal and informal sectors. The impact of trade reform can have a multiplicative effect on reducing poverty when combined with policies that improve labor market flexibility, allowing the poor to move into the formal sector. Reforms in Panama in the later half of the 1990s are a case in point. In Panama, labor market reforms undertaken prior to trade reform had little effect, but after trade reform was also implemented, the combined effect was significant in reducing poverty (see World Bank, 1999). It would be useful to develop a model in which the formal and informal labor markets are distinguished. This will allow an assessment of trade reform on the poor with and without the complementary labor market reforms.

reforms, due to second best effects, it might be that no trade reform package exists which improves welfare, even in the classic utilitarian sense of the simple sum of real income gains. If lost tariff revenue is replaced with increases in sufficiently distortionary domestic taxes, the welfare gains that might be expected from the tariff reform could be more than offset. One such example we have encountered was a proposal to replace lost tariff income in Turkey with increases in the "luxury tax". Or it could be the case that the welfare gains to winners are much smaller than the welfare losses to losers, again measured in terms of equivalent real income, so that there is simply not enough to effect sidepayments. Or it could be that there do not exist tax or subsidy mechanisms for effecting sidepayments that allow those to be made without engendering distortions that reduce aggregate welfare. Or it could be that the available survey data do not provide enough detail to identify those that actually lose.

We emphasize, however, that there is a grave danger to providing a rationale for sector-specific exemptions from trade reform since it provides an invitation to political lobbying. Lobbyists are likely to maintain that protection of their sector will help the poor, and governments are likely to find it difficult to verify the validity of these claims. Models can help make the distinction, but we must use this rationale for limiting trade reform judiciously, with a focus on the use of models to find complementary reforms and the least distortionary instrument.

The issues examined here are also more general than a concern with poverty. Economists are often chided for ignoring equity considerations and only focusing on the effects of policies on overall efficiency. Unfortunately, the complaint is generally true. In most cases, this is a logical habit born of analyses that assume the existence of lump-sum transfers such that winners can compensate losers without any effects on the real economy. Such frictionless transfer mechanisms simply do not exist. If they do exist in some proximate form, they are sufficiently unpopular politically as to be infeasible instruments of policy grounded in reality. Absent such frictionless transfer mechanisms, there is a need for the type of quantitative detail, and attention to simultaneity, which only a CGE framework can provide.

Although there have been many CGE models that include multiple households in an attempt to capture the equity effects of policy, equity effects have not been studied very much.[2] In recent years, there have been several policy developments that have driven a renewed interest in examining equity effects. First, domestic concerns with inter-generational burden sharing in the design of pension schemes and health benefit schemes necessitate some proper accounting for equity effects (e.g. Fougère and Mérette, 2000). Second, international concerns with contemporaneous geographic burden sharing in the design of policies to combat global warming require some proper accounting for equity effects (e.g. Harrison and Rutherford, 1999). Third, given the fact that many trade and

[2] Piggot and Whalley (1985) incorporated 100 households in their CGE model of the United Kingdom, utilizing every available representative household of the Family Expenditure Survey available to them. Households were differentiated by income, family structure and occupation. Ballard et al. (1985) included 12 households in their CGE model of the United States, differentiated by gross income. In his global four-region model, Whalley (1985, p. 71) even carried along 10 household types in the United States region, 1 representative household for the European Communities, and 16 household types in the Japanese region. However, it is fair to say that none of these major early studies made much of the distributional effects incorporated in their models.

global tax policies will burden current generations and benefit future generations, quite apart from the geographic dimension, explicit attention to equity effects is required (e.g. Keuschnigg and Kohler, 2000; Rutherford, 2000).

We examine some of the methodological issues that arise when one extends a small, open economy CGE model to consider multiple households and the equity effects of trade policy. The goal is not to jump to the fanciest model possible, but to illustrate how one can introduce and examine equity effects in such a model.

In Section 2, we examine the effects of free trade on Turkey using a CGE model developed by Harrison et al. (1997a). We extend our earlier results, which aggregated all private households into one, by examining the detailed effects on 40 household types differentiated by income and urban status. We demonstrate that unilateral free trade does provide aggregate welfare gains for Turkey if we take a utilitarian view of aggregate welfare. That is, the sum of welfare gains over all households is positive. However, some of the poorest households lose from the reform. We use the power of the CGE model as a simulation laboratory to identify the sources of the losses to the poorest households, and they are on the income side and derive from factor price changes.

The key policy question we consider here is whether one can design a trade reform package that includes revenue replacement, which mitigates the negative effects of trade reform on the poorest households. In Sections 3 and 4, we take up this question.

In Section 3, we consider if it is possible to effect sidepayments from "winners" to "losers" so as to effect an actual Pareto improvement for the poorest households. In effect, we are making explicit the compensation principle of welfare economics, whereby a policy is deemed to be a *potential* Pareto improvement if winners could hypothetically compensate losers such that nobody loses. One of the virtues of a CGE model in this context is that one can evaluate the effects of the sidepayments on the real economy, and hence consider the effects of non-hypothetical sidepayments.

In Section 4, we use the CGE simulation laboratory to try to identify which components of the policy reform appear to be driving the welfare losses for the poor. This is implemented by means of a decomposition instrument showing the marginal effect on welfare for each household of incremental changes in each policy instrument. This matrix of welfare effects then allows us to identify certain sectors that appear to have the biggest impact on the poor. We then consider limiting the reform to exclude those sectors.

2. Effects of liberalizing trade with multiple households

2.1. Policy background

In our earlier work,[3] we examined the impact of Turkey joining a customs union with the European Union (EU). We estimated that the gains to Turkey of the customs union with the EU are between 1% and 1.5% of its GDP per year depending on the complementary policies adopted by Turkey. These gains are recurring in the sense that they can be expected each year, and they take into account the costs of imposing higher

[3] Harrison et al. (1996, 1997a).

taxes to compensate for the revenue loss of the tariff. Of course, the results are dependent on the model structure. In particular, productivity gains that Turkey may derive from trade liberalization were not estimated in our model, so the gains from the customs union are likely to be larger than we have estimated.

One aspect of our previous work that is important for the present exercise is the revenue replacement issue. We estimated that Turkey will lose tariff revenue equal to 1.4% of GDP. If the existing Value Added Tax (VAT) was used as the replacement tax, we estimated that VAT rates will have to increase by 16.2% in each sector to compensate for the revenue loss from implementing the full customs union (e.g. from 10% to 11.6%). This represents a challenge for Turkey since some tax experts in the government of Turkey believe that the most obvious choice for a revenue replacement tax, the VAT, will generate little revenue due to tax evasion problems. There is a concern that an increase in VAT rates will increase the relative share of the informal sector in the economy. In our model, use of the VAT imposes distortion costs since the rate of collection varies considerably across sectors. Clearly, subsidy reductions would serve the dual purpose of not only increasing efficiency directly by reducing distortions, but would also reduce the revenue needs of the state and reduce the indirect distortions imposed by subsidies through the requirement of additional taxes.

We depart from our previous work in two respects. First, the policy experiment we consider is the movement to global free trade in Turkey, starting from the level of tariffs and export subsidies that prevailed in the economy in 1993, prior to the implementation of the customs union with the European Union. The customs union with the European Union was presented to Turkey, more or less, in its entirety. It was not possible for Turkey to select certain sectors to exclude from the customs union, or to negotiate deviations from the common external tariff of the European Union. We compare here the impact of general trade reform to a reform that is limited in selected sectors, where those limitations in reform are designed to mitigate the impacts on the poor at least cost. In our view, this type of limited reform is more reasonable if one considers the global free trade option available to Turkey in 1993.

In our previous work, we had a single aggregate household in the model. The second important departure is that we disaggregate the household into 40 households: 20 urban and 20 rural, where rural and urban households are distinguished by income level.[4] This allows us to analyze the impact of reform on poor households as well as general distributional aspects. Our analyses include a comparison of compensation mechanisms and limited trade reform to achieve results that are more favorable to the poor.

2.2. The model

Our Small Open Economy (SOE) model is designed for trade policy analysis with a large number of sectors. With the exception of the disaggregation of households, the model is a "generic" general equilibrium model of a single economy along the lines of De Melo and Tarr (1992), Harrison et al. (1993) and Rutherford et al. (1997). We describe here the general features of the base model, adding details about the version for Turkey later.

[4] De Santis (2000) develops a CGE model of Turkey that uses the same data and distinguishes 39 separate households.

Goods are produced using primary factors and intermediate inputs. Primary factors include eight types of labor and five types of capital. All labor is perfectly mobile within its own type, although some labor types are not used in all sectors.[5] Labor of one type is incapable of transforming itself into another type of labor. This yields a unique wage rate for each type of labor. Capital in agriculture is specific to the agriculture sectors, but the other general type of capital is perfectly mobile among sectors.

Production exhibits constant returns to scale and individual firms behave competitively, selecting output levels such that marginal cost at those output levels equals the given market price. Output is differentiated between goods destined for the domestic and export markets. Exports are further distinguished according to whether they are destined for the EU or the Rest of the World (ROW). This relationship is characterized by a two-level constant elasticity of transformation frontier. Composite output is an aggregate of domestic output and composite exports; composite exports are aggregates of exports for the EU and ROW markets.

Final demand by each private household arises from nested constant elasticity of substitution (CES) utility functions. This allows consumer decision-making to occur in the form of multi-stage budgeting. At the top level, goods from different sectors compete subject to the budget constraint of the consumer, and all income elasticities are unity. The shares of each consumer's expenditure on different commodities may differ. In the second stage, the consumer decides how much to spend on domestic or imported goods in each sector, subject to income allocated to spending in that sector in the first stage. Finally, having decided how much to spend on imports as a whole, the consumer allocates this expenditure on EU and ROW imports. Each allocation decision is modeled as a CES function.

The model allows tariff rates to differ depending on whether the imports are from the EU or the ROW. Exports can be sold at different prices depending on whether they are destined for EU or ROW markets. The same is possible on the import side.

Government expenditures and investment demand are exogenous, with the exception of expenditures on subsidies that we model. Reductions in export subsidies reduce government expenditures and endogenously reduce taxes. Tax and tariff revenues provide funding of government expenditures. In addition to tariffs, the government also derives income from indirect taxes (net of subsidies). These are modeled as VAT. Since the expectation is that tariff revenues will decline, all other things being equal, we would expect the increase in the VAT to be positive to ensure revenue neutrality. Our model solves explicitly for the level of the VAT required for this to be so, taking into account changes in "all other things".

Since private consumption equals the income from primary factors plus net transfers to the consumer by the government (from domestic and foreign trade taxes), Walras law is satisfied. Public consumption is balanced with revenue.

[5] Labor type L_AGRC is only used in agricultural sectors AGR and FRS, and is the dominant labor type used in sector AGR. Labor type L_RETL is only used in sectors FIS, TRD, RES and FIN. Labor types L_PROF, L_ADMN and L_OTHR are not used in agricultural sectors. These restrictions on the sectoral mobility of certain labor types derive from the absence of their use in the benchmark equilibrium in those sectors, and not from some constraint that we otherwise impose on the model.

World market import and export prices are fixed, so there are no endogenous changes in the terms of trade. In other words, import supplies and export demands are infinitely elastic at given world prices. The current account balances the value of exports and imports taking into account exogenously fixed capital inflows. Our model allows for changes in these fixed world prices, such as might be expected to occur after the Uruguay Round reforms have been implemented (see Harrison et al., 1997b).

2.3. Empirical implementation for Turkey

We employ a 1990 Social Accounting Matrix (SAM) for Turkey, due to De Santis and Ozhan (1994), which distinguishes 54 production sectors, 8 types of labor, 2 types of capital and 40 households. This SAM provides a consistent set of relationships showing intermediate, final demand, value added and foreign transactions. The sectors and factors of the model are described in Tables 1 and 2 along with their label.[6]

Table 3 lists the names of the household types and their acronyms. Since many of the social policies of the Turkish government are directed at improving the welfare of rural households and the urban poor, this taxonomy of household types is particularly useful. As we shall see, the distribution of factors by household is one of the most important determinants of the distribution of welfare, since it directly determines the distribution of nominal income once we know the relative prices of factors. In Table 4, we list the percentage distribution for each household of the different occupational categories of labor and capital.

Poor households obtain the largest portion of their income from "production" labor, which we view as the least skilled of the labor types in our model. We can see in Table 4 that households at the four lowest income categories earn between 40% and 68% of their income from production labor.

For urban households, the richer households earn a much larger share of their labor income from professional and administrative employment rather than clerical, service sector and manufacturing sector employment. For rural households, the same patterns tend to apply with some variations. The three richest households earn most of their labor income from working in agricultural occupations. The two richest rural households have extremely high shares of their factor income deriving from K_RENT rather than K_AGRC, suggesting that they represent the class of households that own and operate most of the land, plant, equipment and buildings in rural villages. This is also consistent with the high share of rural income for the richest six households that is derived from retail employment.

The Turkish Input–Output (IO) table classifies 91% of value added in agriculture to capital. The reason is that the returns to individuals who operate their own farms are classified in the Turkish IO table as a return to the owner as a capitalist rather than to the owner as a worker. We chose not to alter the IO data. One consequence is that poor rural households will have a larger share of their income attributed to K_AGRC, compared to L_AGRC, than appropriate in an economic sense. If the relative prices of these factors changed significantly, we would have to be particularly careful in interpreting the results.

[6] In the original SAM, there are three additional types of capital that are used only in the six service and trade sectors. We have aggregated this capital into general capital that is fungible across sectors.

Table 1
Sectors in the model

AGR	Agriculture and animal husbandry
FRS	Forestry
FIS	Fisheries
COL	Coal mining
CRU	Crude petroleum and natural gas production
MIN	Iron ore mining
STO	Non-ferrous ore and non-metallic mineral mining and stone quarrying
MEA	Slaughtering preparation and preparing and preserving meat
CAN	Canning and preserving of fruits and vegetables
VEG	Manufacture of vegetable and animal oils and fats
GRN	Grain mill products
SUG	Sugar
OFP	Manufacture of other food products
ALC	Alcoholic beverages
BEV	Soft drinks and carbonated water industries
TOB	Tobacco manufactures
TXT	Textiles (including ginning)
WAP	Wearing apparel
LEA	Leather and fur products
SHO	Footwear
WOO	Wood and wood products
FRN	Furniture and fixtures
PAP	Paper and paper products
PRN	Printing and publishing and paper products
FRT	Fertilizers
DRG	Drugs and medicine
OCP	Other chemical products
REF	Petroleum refineries
PET	Petroleum and coal products
RBR	Rubber products
PLA	Plastic products
GLA	Glass and glass products
CEM	Cement
NMM	Non-metallic mineral products
IRO	Iron and steel
NFM	Non-ferrous metal
FAB	Fabricated metal products
MAC	Machinery except electrical
AGM	Agricultural machinery and equipment
ELM	Electrical machinery
SHP	Shipbuilding and repairing
RRE	Railroad equipment
VEH	Land transport vehicles and equipment
OTE	Other transport equipment
OMN	Other manufacturing industries
ELE	Electricity
GAS	Gas manufacture and waterworks
CON	Building construction and other construction
TRD	Wholesale and retail trade
RES	Restaurants and hotels
TRN	Railway transport and other land and water and air transport
COM	Communications
FIN	Financial institutions and insurance
SRV	Private and public services and ownership of dwelling

As we shall see below, however, in our principal scenario, the price of both of these factors increases slightly relative to the numeraire, so the consequence for distribution is not likely to be significant.

A more significant problem with the classification of value added derives from the existence of large State-Owned Enterprises (SOEs) in several sectors. The SOEs are generally loss making and represent a drain on the government budget. Turkey has had enormous political difficulty privatizing or closing the loss-making SOEs. This has been a principal cause of its budget deficits and inflation. In the IO table, however, when a SOE is a loss maker, it is presumed to have no return to capital, and so all of its value added is attributed to labor. The sugar sector is an extreme case in point. Table 5a shows that the Turkish IO table reports 100% of value added as a return to labor. Clearly, capital is required to produce sugar, but due to the losses of some of the firms, the accounting procedures indicate this to be the most labor-intensive sector of the economy. On the other hand, wearing apparel is a sector that we know is relatively labor intensive, but since the firms in the industry are profitable, it is reported to have only 22% of its value added as labor. This is a relatively low labor intensity across all sectors of the economy, and inconsistent with our a priori economic judgement as to which sectors use labor intensively.

The decomposition of value added by labor among labor types was performed with the aid of a "RAS" procedure by De Santis and Ozhan (1997, p. 283). In Table 5b, we show that they assigned 75% of labor to production labor in most manufacturing sectors. That is, there is little variation among manufacturing sectors in terms of the intensity with which they use production labor relative to more skilled labor.

Households are distinguished carefully in the SAM regarding the source of their income, and production labor is particularly important for the poor. However, it does not

Table 2
Factors in the model

Labor types	
L_PROF	Scientific, technical, professional and related workers
L_ADMN	Administrative, executive and managerial workers
L_CLER	Clerical and related workers
L_RETL	Sales workers
L_SRVC	Service workers
L_AGRC	Agricultural, animal husbandry and forestry workers, fisherman and hunters
L_PROD	Non-agricultural production workers, transport equipment operators and laborers
L_OTHR	Workers not classifiable by occupation
Capital types	
K_RENT	Rent (sector-specific in COL, CRU, MIN, STO, ELE, GAS and TRN)
K_AGRC	Operating surplus in agriculture

Table 3
Households in the model

Monthly disposable income (1000 TL in 1990)	Urban households	Rural households
0–133	URB_133	RUR_133
134–267	URB_267	RUR_267
268–400	URB_400	RUR_400
401–533	URB_533	RUR_533
534–667	URB_667	RUR_667
668–800	URB_800	RUR_800
801–933	URB_933	RUR_933
934–1067	URB_1067	RUR_1067
1068–1200	URB_1200	RUR_1200
1201–1333	URB_1333	RUR_1333
1334–1600	URB_1600	RUR_1600
1601–1867	URB_1867	RUR_1867
1868–2133	URB_2133	RUR_2133
2134–2400	URB_2400	RUR_2400
2401–2667	URB_2667	RUR_2667
2668–4000	URB_4000	RUR_4000
4001–5333	URB_5333	RUR_5333
5334–13,333	URB_13,333	RUR_13,333
13,334–26,667	URB_26,667	RUR_26,667
26,668–66,667	URB_66,667	RUR_66,667

appear that production labor is mapped into the sectors that use it using defensible economic criteria. Consequently, neither the labor-to-capital intensity data nor the unskilled-labor-to-value-added intensity data in the SAM table reflect our priori judgement as to what constitutes factor intensity. It follows that we may not see simulation results that are expected from trade liberalization for an economy that is relatively heavily endowed with unskilled labor (based on Heckscher–Ohlin considerations).

We also employ some ancillary data on production subsidies from the 1990 IO table provided by the State Institute of Statistics.[7] Import tariffs and export subsidies are calibrated to collected rates in 1993, the most recent year for which we have consistent data. We also use estimates of collected VAT rates for 1990. Table 5a lists the data on taxes, tariffs, export and production subsidies.

Detailed documentation of the model, data and elasticity choices may be found in Harrison et al. (1996). The model is formulated and solved using the MPSGE system developed by Rutherford (1995, 1999).

2.4. *Effects of trade liberalization*

Table 6 reports the results of the elimination of tariffs on all imports. We report results for welfare in terms of billions of 1990 Turkish lira and as a percent of GDP. In

[7] The SAM only reports net indirect taxes, whereas the IO table breaks out production subsidies and indirect taxes by sector.

all experiments, we impose a constraint that the fiscal deficit of the government of Turkey cannot increase. We implement this constraint by allowing the VAT rate to adjust in all sectors. The variable "VAT rate" in Table 6 shows the amount by which the VAT must change. A value of 124.5 means that the collected VAT must rise to 124.5% of its value in the initial equilibrium to compensate for the lost tariff revenue. For example, if the collected VAT rate is 10% in the initial equilibrium, the collected rate will have to rise to 12.45% in the new equilibrium (Table 7). The real exchange rate will depreciate by 8.4%.

In aggregate, there are welfare gains of about three-tenths of a percent of GDP. Welfare is measured in Hicksian equivalent variation as a percent of benchmark GDP. Unfortunately, there are adverse distributional consequences of this particular trade reform: it hurts the two poorest rural households and the four poorest urban households. Interestingly, it also hurts the richest urban and rural households. It is the middle class, especially in the rural households that gain the most from the reform.

The presumption of trade theory is that Turkey, as a country relatively heavily endowed with unskilled labor, would be expected to protect its capital intensive or skilled labor-intensive sectors. This theory suggests that trade reform should help unskilled labor and households that are relatively heavily endowed with unskilled labor who are the poor households in our model. Since we show results that are quantitatively inconsistent with this simple theoretical presumption, we need to identify the source of the disparity.

An important step in that process is to determine if it is changes in factor prices or goods prices that is the source of the adverse impact on the poor. We use the data in Table 8 for that purpose. If all households were identical in their income and expenditure patterns, then Hicksian equivalent variation as a percentage of benchmark income would be identical for all households. The model would then essentially be equivalent to a single household model. We counterfactually impose identical consumption shares for all household and identical factor endowment shares and present the results of that simulation in the three columns on the far right in Table 8. The result is that all households realize a welfare gain of 0.28% of benchmark income.

In the columns labeled "uniform consumption shares", we counterfactually impose a uniform consumption pattern but preserve the diverse factor shares in the data. In the columns labeled "uniform income shares", we counterfactually impose a uniform factor income pattern but preserve the diverse consumption shares in the data. Uniform consumption shares make the two poorest urban and two poorest rural households worse off than diverse consumption shares, so this is not the source of the adverse impact of the trade reform compared to an average household. On the other hand, uniform factor shares make the two poorest urban and two poorest rural households better off than the average household. Clearly, for the poor, it is the source of income not the pattern of expenditure that is driving the adverse impact relative to the average household.

These decompositions of the source of changes in welfare across households represent a general equilibrium analogue, and extension, of the type of factor decompositions of the source of inequality proposed by Shorrocks (1982). His decompositions allowed an exact identification of the contribution from each of the

Table 4
Distribution of factor endowments by household percentages for each household[a]

Household	Income	L_PROF	L_ADMN	L_CLER	L_RETL	L_SRVC	L_AGRC	L_PROD	L_OTHR	K_RENT	K_AGRC
Urban	133	3		7	2	18	1	68	1	1	
Urban	267	6		24	1	17		48	1	1	1
Urban	400	17		20	1	17		40	1	1	2
Urban	533	16	1	17	2	15		42	1	3	3
Urban	667	19	2	16	3	11		41	1	4	4
Urban	800	21	2	15	3	8		38	2	5	5
Urban	933	19	3	17	4	8		35	2	6	6
Urban	1067	22	4	14	4	8	1	32	2	8	6
Urban	1200	22	4	14	6	6		29	1	9	7
Urban	1333	29	5	11	6	6		28	2	9	3
Urban	1600	28	10	11	6	7	1	21	1	10	5
Urban	1867	29	8	8	6	9	1	19		10	10
Urban	2133	32	11	6	6	10	1	14		11	9
Urban	2400	38	11	1	6	4	1	19		15	5
Urban	2667	41	7	6	6	11		12	1	11	4
Urban	4000	32	14	5	6	4	1	15		16	9
Urban	5333	29	17		7	3		12		22	9
Urban	13,000	33	23		7	7		8		16	6
Urban	27,000		54		4		1	12		20	8
Urban	67,000		73		21					7	

Rural	133	5		3	1	15	6	46		1	23
Rural	267	6		9	1	16	5	31		2	31
Rural	400	8	1	8	1	12	4	28		2	36
Rural	533	7	1	10	1	9	4	20		2	47
Rural	667	6	1	6	2	10	4	14		2	55
Rural	800	3	1	7	1	7	4	16		2	60
Rural	933	3	1	2	1	3	4	18		1	67
Rural	1067	2	1	3	1	2	6	10		1	74
Rural	1200	1	1	1	2	1	6	11		1	76
Rural	1333	1		4	1	1	3	7		2	80
Rural	1600	1	1		1	3	5	7		1	81
Rural	1867	1	1		2	5	6	4	1	3	77
Rural	2133	3	1		5	4	5	5		3	74
Rural	2400	7	5		5		2	9		1	71
Rural	2667	6	3		6		4	10			71
Rural	4000	11	2		5	1	4	5		4	69
Rural	5333		5		2		6				86
Rural	13,000		2		2		8			37	52
Rural	27,000						15			72	13

Calculated from De Santis and Ozhan (1994).

[a] Sum for individual households may not equal 100 due to rounding.

Table 5a
Labor intensity by sector and percentage tax and subsidy rate (all tax and subsidy rates shown on a net basis)

Industry	Labor intensity		Tax and subsidy incidence			
	Labor share of value added	Labor share of production	1990 VAT + consumption tax	1993 Import tariffs	1993 Export subsidy	1990 Production subsidy
AGR	9	7	1	21	3	2
FRS	23	19	2		− 1	
FIS	12	9	1	38	5	
COL	72	50	8		7	3
CRU	5	4	15		17	
MIN	68	38	4	1		
STO	19	18	5	3	9	
MEA	25	6	1	25	13	
CAN	25	31	3	44	8	
VEG	24	7	2	4	9	
GRN	32	4	11	39	5	
SUG	100	16	9	18		17
OFP	32	9	2	52	2	
ALC	31	20	32	62	6	
BEV	49	20	37	107	5	
TOB	44	20	35	80	11	
TXT	23	9	7	10	8	
WAP	22	12	4	28	11	
LEA	6	3	4	2	14	
SHO	28	8	4	30	9	
WOO	12	4	2	19	10	
FRN	24	7	7	22	5	
PAP	32	11	4	18	25	
PRN	39	11	28	13	5	
FRT	45	13	8	1	24	
DRG	23	10	3	1	9	
OCP	27	11	2	10	15	
REF	5	1	162	9	16	
PET	25	7	1	4	29	3
RBR	39	12	1	18	10	
PLA	26	8	9	24	5	
GLA	32	21	4	23	10	
CEM	23	12	3	2	8	
NMM	34	17	6	18	9	
IRO	52	12	9	1	21	
NFM	27	10	2	4	19	
FAB	25	10	4	14	8	
MAC	26	11	2	6	8	
AGM	25	9	3	17	9	
ELM	34	13	16	11	13	
SHP	59	37	2	3	8	
RRE	88	50	1	5		
VEH	51	16	43	27	7	
OTE	50	32	16		14	
OMN	36	9	51	10	4	
ELE	41	26	18			1
GAS	29	19	1			

Table 5a (*continued*)

Industry	Labor intensity		Tax and subsidy incidence			
	Labor share of value added	Labor share of production	1990 VAT + consumption tax	1993 Import tariffs	1993 Export subsidy	1990 Production subsidy
CON	55	22	4			
TRD	23	19	6			5
RES	34	18	6			
TRN	9	7	2			1
COM	53	31	24			
FIN	65	46	16			
SRV	59	48	6			

1993 Import Tariffs are based on collected revenues, estimated by the State Planning Organization (SPO); 1993 Export Subsidies are World Bank estimates; 1990 VAT rates plus consumption tax rates are based on collected indirect tax revenues, estimated by SPO; 1990 Production Subsidy rates are based on collections reported in the IO table (De Santis and Ozhan, 1994).

factor components of *factor* income, assuming that those factor components added up to factor income for each of the units of analysis. Our approach considers the (aggregate) factor–income contribution to welfare changes as well as the expenditure–pattern contribution.

Having identified factor price changes as the primary source of disparate effects across households, we can examine the percent change in factor prices in Table 6. All prices in the model, including factor prices, are relative prices, relative to the numeraire. The numeraire in the model is the unit value of representative basket of consumption goods based on aggregate household demand in the benchmark period.

The factor which is most important for poor households is production labor. However, the price of production labor declines by 2.9%, which is the greatest percentage decline of any of the factors. Thus, it appears that the principal reason that the poor lose is that the wage of production labor declines. In Tables 5a and 5b, we show factor intensity among the different types of labor. Production labor is used most intensively in manufacturing industries: it represents about 75% of labor usage in most manufacturing industries (Table 5b). Table 5a shows aggregate labor intensity as a percent of value added or production. We also see in Table 5a that it is the manufacturing sector that is protected relatively heavily, which explains why the relative price of production labor declines in a trade reform.

2.5. Data concerns

The results are obviously dependent on the underlying data. One important problem we identified earlier is the data on factor intensity. Based on Heckscher–Ohlin considerations, we would expect that Turkey, as an economy relatively heavily endowed with unskilled labor, would have that abundant factor aided by trade liberalization. Our results show the contrary: it is the unskilled labor that loses the most. To investigate, we correlated labor's share of value added in a sector with the export percentage and the import percentage. We calculate these correlations to be − 0.16% and 0.081%, respectively. Hence, exports in our

Table 5b
Labor intensity by sector as a percentage of total labor usage

Industry	Labor type							
	L_PROF	L_ADMN	L_CLER	L_RETL	L_SRVC	L_AGRC	L_PROD	L_OTHR
AGR		4	9		4	80	2	
FRS			22		35	3	40	
FIS				7	92	1		
COL	12	2	8		5		73	
CRU	13	1	8		4		73	
MIN	12	1	9		4		73	
STO	12	2	9		4		73	
MEA	5	8	6		3		75	2
CAN	6	8	6		3		75	1
VEG	6	8	6		3		75	2
GRN	6	8	6		3		75	2
SUG	6	8	6		3		75	2
OFP	6	8	6		3		75	2
ALC	6	8	6		3		75	2
BEV	6	8	6		3		75	1
TOB	6	8	6		3		75	2
TXT	6	8	6		3		75	2
WAP	6	8	6		3		75	2
LEA	6	8	6		4		75	2
SHO	6	8	6		3		76	2
WOO	6	8	6		3		75	2
FRN	5	8	5		3		76	1
PAP	6	8	6		3		75	2
PRN	6	8	6		3		75	2
FRT	5	8	6		3		75	2
DRG	6	8	6		3		75	2
OCP	6	8	6		3		75	2
REF	6	8	6		3		75	1
PET	6	9	6		3		75	1
RBR	6	8	6		3		75	2
PLA	6	8	6		3		75	1
GLA	6	8	6		3		75	2
CEM	6	8	6		3		75	2
NMM	6	8	6		3		75	2
IRO	6	8	6		3		75	2
NFM	6	8	6		3		75	2
FAB	6	8	6		3		75	2
MAC	6	8	6		3		75	2
AGM	6	8	5		3		75	2
ELM	6	8	6		3		75	2
SHP	6	8	6		3		76	2
RRE	6	8	6		3		75	2
VEH	6	8	6		3		75	2
OTE	6	9	6		3		72	3
OMN	6	8	6		3		75	2
ELE	21	3	32		8		36	1
GAS	21	3	32		8		36	1
CON	6	10	3		2		79	

Table 5b (*continued*)

Industry	Labor type							
	L_PROF	L_ADMN	L_CLER	L_RETL	L_SRVC	L_AGRC	L_PROD	L_OTHR
TRD	7	1	13	28	40		10	
RES	7	1	13	28	40		10	
TRN	6	5	19		3		67	1
COM	6	5	19		3		67	1
FIN	34	13	44	1	5		3	
SRV	48	5	16		15		15	1

Calculated from De Santis and Ozhan (1994).

data set are less labor intensive in Turkey than imports. We also calculated the correlation coefficient between the labor share and the import share across all countries in the GTAP data set; we found that the value is negative for most developing countries, as expected, but in contrast to Turkey.

Our explanation is that this is due to the widespread existence of loss making State-Owned Enterprises (SOEs) in Turkey, resulting in the IO table showing that it is the export sectors which are relatively capital intensive. That is, capital's share is calculated as the residual after payments for intermediates, labor and taxes are subtracted from revenues. Loss-making SOEs, which are widespread in Turkey, are reported in the IO table as being very labor intensive because they earn no profits. So profitable sectors that export, such as wearing apparel, are reported as being less labor intensive than sectors dominated by loss-making SOEs.

Moreover, the allocation of labor in the SAM among labor types was very similar across all manufacturing sectors. To provide some idea of the consequence of this classification, we undertook a free trade simulation in which we assumed that all labor types are perfect substitutes.[8] Thus, the "arbitrary" allocations of labor across types in some sectors would have no effect on the results. We find that the same qualitative results hold in the sense that free trade results in the poorest four urban households losing in welfare terms and the second poorest urban household loses. However, the poorest rural household now enjoys a small welfare gain.

2.6. Poverty and measures of inequality

A concern for the poor is not the same thing as a concern for equity in general. It is possible that alleviating standard measures of inequality can improve while the poor are worse off. Our results provide one sharp reminder of this point, which is well known in the literature on inequality measures. If one uses the standard Gini coefficient to measure the effect of the free trade reform on the distribution of welfare (or real income), the conclusion would be that the trade reform *improves* the distribution of income. Specif-

[8] This alternative formulation does not address the issue of the excessive labor intensity in SOE-dominated sectors. To address that problem would require a more fundamental reconstruction of the data underlying the SAM as well as the proper analysis of the behavior of SOEs.

Table 6
Effects of free trade on Turkey

(I) Welfare (percentage change in Hicksian Equivalent Variation in income)

Household income	Urban	Rural	Total
133	− 0.84	− 0.07	− 0.36
267	− 0.47	− 0.12	− 0.32
400	− 0.26	0.10	− 0.10
533	− 0.23	0.28	0.00
667	0.19	0.61	0.39
800	0.18	0.71	0.41
933	0.22	0.44	0.30
1067	0.30	0.89	0.53
1200	0.09	0.62	0.29
1333	0.10	0.75	0.30
1600	0.42	0.90	0.58
1867	0.38	1.10	0.58
2133	0.14	0.78	0.31
2400	− 0.24	1.94	0.36
2667	0.46	0.37	0.44
4000	− 0.01	3.09	0.54
5333	0.54	0.97	0.65
13,000	0.48	4.28	0.91
27,000	− 1.74	− 3.90	− 1.93
67,000	− 2.49		− 2.49
TOTAL	0.06	0.67	0.28

(II) VAT rate (% increase required to replace lost revenue)	24.5
(III) Real exchange rate depreciation (%)	8.5

(IV) Factor price change (%)

L_PROF	− 1.0
L_ADMN	− 2.5
L_CLER	− 0.5
L_RETL	2.1
L_SRVC	0.4
L_AGRC	0.3
L_PROD	− 2.9
L_OTHR	− 2.7
K_RENT	− 1.5
K_AGRC	0.2

Authors' estimates.

ically, the Gini coefficient changes from 0.3438 in the benchmark to 0.3430 with free trade.[9] This occurs because some of the richest households lose, thereby offsetting the losses of the poorest households. Thus, if concern is with the poorest households who

[9] The Gini coefficient takes on values between 0 and 1, with 0 being consistent with an egalitarian distribution.

clearly lose under this free trade reform, one must be cautious relying on simple inequality measures.[10]

An alternative approach is to design inequality measures that place greater weight on the poorest households. Several of these measures have been proposed, and the most popular are due to Atkinson (1970) and Donaldson and Weymark (1980). They offer a class of inequality measures parameterized so as to allow more weight to be given to the poorest households. At one extreme is the Gini coefficient, and as the parameter is increased, one ends up with the Rawlsian measure that judges inequality solely with reference to the poorest household. In the case of free trade reform in Turkey, only extremely high values of these parameters result in the conclusion that the distribution of welfare has become less equal.

Of course, one does not have to try to disguise a concern for the poor as a concern for equity in general. Our point is simply to caution against casual identification of the two as identical.

3. Compensation principle and practice

3.1. General issues

In general, major policy reforms result in winners and losers. It would be nice if one could always devise reforms that were "win–win" propositions. Unfortunately, life does not often present reforms that meet the Pareto criterion of economists that nobody can be worse off after the reform than they were before it. What is even more troubling, as our particular reform in Turkey illustrates, is that it may be the poor households who are among the losers, despite aggregate gains.

Following Harrison et al. (1995, 2001), we illustrate how one can use our CGE model of Turkey to determine if trade reform can be accomplished without harm to any of the four poorest households if compensation was allowed. More generally, we ask if the trade reform could be a Pareto improvement if one allowed compensation.

We answer this question in our quantitative model, despite the fact that it is not practical to do so using only theory. The reason is that one must take into account the effects of sidepayments on relative prices and hence on the basis for welfare evaluation made prior to sidepayments. This loop raises interminable difficulties if one does not have information on expenditure patterns of different households, as well as the rest of the structure of the economy. At a theoretical level, any minimally realistic model becomes excessively complex to adequately address the issue. Thus, there is a need for a numerical model to provide insight into the problem.

[10] De Santis (2000, Table 9, p. 230) uses a generalized entropy measure of inequality and concludes from simulations of a CU with the European Union that "... trade is not an important contributor of income inequality." (p. 228). His generalized measure does have parameter values (the top panel of his Table 9) which place greater weight on the poorest households, and they show that there is a worsening of overall income inequality in the standard "flexible wages" specification. However, the casual use of summary measures like these can mask apparent impacts on the poorest households when there are also impacts on richer households.

Table 7
Impact of free trade on the output by sector (percentage change from initial equilibrium)

	Output	Imports	Exports	Tariff	Export subsidy
AGR	0	28	14	21	3
FRS	1	−12	29	0	−1
FIS	0	64	7	38	5
COL	−2	−6	6	0	7
CRU	−2	−4	389	0	17
MIN	−9	−15	0	1	0
STO	0	−12	0	3	9
MEA	−1	7	−11	25	13
CAN	1	36	2	44	8
VEG	2	−5	0	4	9
GRN	3	72	11	39	5
SUG	−1	19	24	18	0
OFP	8	23	31	52	2
ALC	−4	95	−5	62	6
BEV	−2	268	2	107	5
TOB	−10	165	−23	80	11
TXT	−3	−1	−1	10	8
WAP	−13	75	−19	28	11
LEA	−8	−15	−19	2	14
SHO	−2	66	−4	30	9
WOO	0	19	−4	19	10
FRN	0	25	9	22	5
PAP	−3	8	−35	18	25
PRN	−1	10	7	13	5
FRT	−1	−5	−34	1	24
DRG	1	−11	−1	1	9
OCP	−5	2	−20	10	15
REF	−4	−1	−35	9	16
PET	−1	−1	−43	4	29
RBR	−1	11	−4	18	10
PLA	−1	18	9	24	5
GLA	−2	19	−6	23	10
CEM	0	−5	1	2	8
NMM	−3	16	−5	18	9
IRO	−12	−6	−41	1	21
NFM	−8	−5	−34	4	19
FAB	−3	8	−6	14	8
MAC	−1	−2	−2	6	8
AGM	−1	3	−3	17	9
ELM	−5	2	−20	11	13
SHP	2	−1	3	3	8
RRE	0	−2	0	5	0
VEH	−11	28	−12	27	7
OTE	2	0	−17	0	14
OMN	−5	2	−6	10	4
ELE	−2	−16	22	0	0
GAS	1	−14	27	0	0
TRD	2	0	27	0	0

Table 7 (*continued*)

	Output	Imports	Exports	Tariff	Export subsidy
RES	9	− 15	37	0	0
TRN	1	− 13	17	0	0
COM	− 1	− 12	18	0	0
FIN	0	− 12	19	0	0
SRV	1	− 15	27	0	0

Authors' estimates.

The use of sidepayments raises two important issues for the welfare comparison. First, the way in which the funds for compensation are raised by the government can have efficiency effects. There is a marginal excess burden from any attempt to raise extra government revenue, whether or not that revenue is being used to finance government expenditures or compensate private households. If there are aggregate gains, and a distortion-free Lump Sum transfer mechanism, then it is immediate that compensation should be possible. In real world cases, the government will not have the hypothetical distortion-free Lump Sum tax available. Due to different marginal excess burdens

Table 8
Decomposing the welfare effects of free trade in Turkey
The effect of income shares and consumption shares.

Household income	Heterogeneous consumption and income shares			Uniform consumption shares			Uniform income shares			Uniform income and consumption shares		
	Urban	Rural	Total	Urban	Rural	Total	Urban	Rural	Total	Urban	Rural	Total
133	− 0.84	− 0.07	− 0.36	− 1.13	− 0.37	− 0.66	0.57	0.58	0.57	0.28	0.28	0.28
267	− 0.47	− 0.12	− 0.32	− 0.64	− 0.25	− 0.47	0.43	0.42	0.43	0.28	0.28	0.28
400	− 0.26	0.10	− 0.10	− 0.41	− 0.09	− 0.27	0.41	0.48	0.44	0.28	0.28	0.28
533	− 0.23	0.28	0.00	− 0.24	0.12	− 0.08	0.27	0.45	0.35	0.28	0.28	0.28
667	0.19	0.61	0.39	0.13	0.49	0.30	0.32	0.42	0.37	0.28	0.28	0.28
800	0.18	0.71	0.41	0.24	0.51	0.36	0.21	0.51	0.34	0.28	0.28	0.28
933	0.22	0.44	0.30	0.35	0.37	0.36	0.14	0.38	0.23	0.28	0.28	0.28
1067	0.30	0.89	0.53	0.46	0.72	0.56	0.11	0.49	0.26	0.28	0.28	0.28
1200	0.09	0.62	0.29	0.34	0.49	0.40	0.02	0.46	0.18	0.28	0.28	0.28
1333	0.10	0.75	0.30	0.32	0.67	0.43	0.05	0.42	0.16	0.28	0.28	0.28
1600	0.42	0.90	0.58	0.67	0.82	0.72	0.01	0.42	0.15	0.28	0.28	0.28
1867	0.38	1.10	0.58	0.72	0.98	0.80	− 0.08	0.45	0.07	0.28	0.28	0.28
2133	0.14	0.78	0.31	0.54	0.52	0.53	− 0.13	0.56	0.05	0.28	0.28	0.28
2400	− 0.24	1.94	0.36	0.17	1.49	0.53	− 0.14	0.75	0.10	0.28	0.28	0.28
2667	0.46	0.37	0.44	0.66	0.24	0.56	0.07	0.44	0.16	0.28	0.28	0.28
4000	− 0.01	3.09	0.54	0.37	2.89	0.81	− 0.10	0.49	0.00	0.28	0.28	0.28
5333	0.54	0.97	0.65	0.79	0.55	0.73	0.02	0.76	0.21	0.28	0.28	0.28
13,000	0.48	4.28	0.91	0.25	3.38	0.60	0.50	1.19	0.58	0.28	0.28	0.28
27,000	− 1.74	− 3.90	− 1.93	− 1.49	− 4.10	− 1.72	0.03	0.53	0.07	0.28	0.28	0.28
67,000	− 2.49		− 2.49	− 3.03		− 3.03	0.86	0.00	0.86	0.28	0.28	0.28
Total	0.06	0.67	0.28	0.17	0.49	0.28	0.16	0.48	0.28	0.28	0.28	0.28

Welfare effects are Hicksian Equivalent Variation as a percent of benchmark household income.
Welfare impact for homogeneous income and consumption shares = 0.28% for all households.
Author's estimates.

associated with different tax instruments, the tax that the government uses to raise revenue will affect the outcome. Typically, VAT will impose the least marginal excess burden of the tax instruments available to a developing country government. However, the marginal excess burden will still be positive. Given that VAT will be collected at different rates in different sectors, there is a distortion associated with collecting tax revenue from VAT to effect sidepayments (see Ballard, 1988). These distortion costs will typically reduce the welfare gain from the trade reform. This problem is analogous to the problem of replacing tariff revenue from a trade reform. We have shown, for example, that the scope for efficient tariff reduction in Chile is limited by the need to replace tariff revenue (see Harrison et al., 2002). On the other hand, it is possible that second-best considerations mean that one must evaluate specific proposals to see if the marginal excess burden is positive or negative.[11]

Second, the way in which compensation is undertaken can also have efficiency effects. If distortionary subsidies are used to compensate losers, then there may be an efficiency cost from the very act of compensation that must also be taken into account. For example, many countries provide subsidized prices of basic food items as a means of targeting assistance to the poor. Households will optimize their consumption choices based on the subsidy-ridden commodity prices that will impose distortion costs. Thus, the "overall pie" may be diminished by the way in which it is "sliced up". Of course, it is also possible that second best interactions with pre-existing distortions result in an efficiency gain from the use of a distortionary compensation scheme.

Our focus is on the poor. A simple modification of the general Pareto compensation scheme allows us to target sidepayments solely to reduce poverty. We initially consider the impact on the welfare of only the poorest households in the rural and urban households: those whose income is less than or equal to 133,000 Turkish lira/household in 1990. Based on a purchasing power parity (PPP) estimate, US$1 was equal to 1505 Turkish lira in 1990, while US$1 was equal to 2609 Turkish lira based on a nominal exchange rate conversion.[12] This means that 549,000 (952,000) Turkish lira were required to provide US$1/day of income to a Turkish household in 1990 based on a PPP (nominal exchange rate) estimate. By either measure, the poorest households are extremely poor. Since the four poorest urban households lose, we shall also consider sidepayment schemes such that none of the households at the four lowest income levels lose: thus, no household with an income less that 533,000 Turkish lira in 1990 loses in this scenario. This corresponds approximately to all households with incomes less than US$1/day in PPP terms. In this case, we investigate if there is a scheme that compensates these households such that their welfare does not drop from the trade reform. There may be other richer households that lose from the reform, in which case, this would not meet the Pareto criterion.

[11] For example, if a sector receives relatively high border protection, there are too many resources in the sector if that is the only distortion in the economy. In such a case, a relatively high VAT on a sector *may* offset some of the distortion from the high border protection.

[12] Nominal exchange rate information comes from *International Financial Statistics* of the International Monetary Fund. Purchasing power parity conversion factors are from the *World Development Indicators* of the World Bank.

Compensation schemes are well known in theory but are often neglected in practical efforts to evaluate policy reforms. We take all of the potential costs and second-best interactions from the revenue-raising side of compensation schemes into account in our calculations.

3.2. Results for Turkey

Table 9 shows the detailed welfare results of the trade reform simulation when we allow for no sidepayments (Panel A), the full Pareto sidepayment scheme in which all households are ensured to suffer no welfare loss (Panel B), and two scenarios with poverty-oriented sidepayment schemes.[13] In these latter two scenarios, only the two poorest households (Panel C) or eight poorest households (Panel D) are ensured to suffer no welfare loss. In these scenarios, we have employed VAT as the means of generating government revenue to provide the sidepayments (if necessary). The revenue has then been distributed lump sum to the household.

The first result that stands out is that there is no substantial efficiency loss from *any* of the compensation schemes. The aggregate welfare gain is either 0.27–0.28% of GDP in all four scenarios; aggregate welfare does drop by 3.3 billion Turkish liras as we move from no compensation to the full-blown Pareto compensation, but this is a minor impact.[14] This suggests that VAT in Turkey does not impose a significant efficiency costs. Thus, if we ignore potential efficiency losses deriving from recipients altering decisions as a result of distribution mechanisms, it is possible to implement the trade reform such that the poor households that lose are compensated in full for their losses without significant efficiency cost. These results provide support for the policy prescription of a social safety net in which general tax revenues would be used to address the needs of the poor following a trade reform. This result generalizes to include the richer households that lose from free trade as well.

A second result is that there are some middle-class households that remain losers when only the poor are compensated. Worse, in the scenario where the eight poorest households are compensated for their losses (Panel D), two urban households become losers when they were previously unharmed.[15] Thus, we cannot even say that the compensation of poor households always constitutes a Pareto *improvement*. This result suggest that we may observe resistance to compensation schemes in disparate groups in society, even if the distribution scheme imposes relatively little efficiency costs in aggregate. Of course, this concern can be mitigated by focusing on compensation schemes that provide relief to all losers of trade reform, whether or not they are poor.

These calculations have focused on the scope for compensating adversely impacted households through an income subsidy financed by public funds. On the basis of economic theory, we would expect such direct subsidies to be the least costly means of achieving a

[13] Our compensation scheme maintains welfare at the benchmark level. One could design a compensation scheme to maintain income, but then expenditure effects would be ignored.

[14] The aggregate welfare loss for the poverty-reducing compensation schemes is smaller than for the full Pareto scheme.

[15] Specifically households URB_1200 and URB_1333.

Table 9
Effects of sidepayment schemes on welfare

Household income groups	Urban (%)	Rural (%)	Total (%)	Urban	Rural	Total
(A) No compensation						
133	− 0.84	− 0.07	− 0.36	− 14.60	− 1.87	− 16.48
267	− 0.47	− 0.12	− 0.32	− 43.13	− 8.45	− 51.58
400	− 0.26	0.10	− 0.10	− 35.85	10.98	− 24.87
533	− 0.23	0.28	0.00	− 31.15	30.61	− 0.54
667	0.19	0.61	0.39	22.07	64.22	86.29
800	0.18	0.71	0.41	18.93	56.29	75.21
933	0.22	0.44	0.30	23.19	27.93	51.12
1067	0.30	0.89	0.53	26.22	48.88	75.10
1200	0.09	0.62	0.29	6.82	26.96	33.78
1333	0.10	0.75	0.30	6.23	20.85	27.08
1600	0.42	0.90	0.58	52.11	57.95	110.06
1867	0.38	1.10	0.58	38.25	44.27	82.52
2133	0.14	0.78	0.31	10.55	20.20	30.75
2400	− 0.24	1.94	0.36	− 15.38	46.86	31.48
2667	0.46	0.37	0.44	19.69	4.89	24.58
4000	− 0.01	3.09	0.54	− 0.71	87.61	86.90
5333	0.54	0.97	0.65	29.84	19.38	49.22
13,000	0.48	4.28	0.91	65.27	74.37	139.64
27,000	− 1.74	− 3.90	− 1.93	− 44.83	− 9.67	− 54.50
67,000	− 2.49	0.00	− 2.49	− 32.03	0.00	− 32.03
Total	0.06	0.67	0.28	101.50	622.25	723.75
(B) Pareto compensation of all households						
133	0.00	0.00	0.00	0.00	0.00	0.00
267	0.00	0.00	0.00	0.00	0.00	0.00
400	0.00	0.00	0.00	0.00	0.40	0.40
533	0.00	0.18	0.08	0.00	19.63	19.63
667	0.06	0.52	0.27	6.72	54.26	60.98
800	0.05	0.61	0.29	5.17	48.30	53.47
933	0.08	0.33	0.18	8.65	21.44	30.09
1067	0.16	0.79	0.40	13.80	43.47	57.27
1200	0.00	0.52	0.19	0.00	22.37	22.37
1333	0.00	0.66	0.21	0.00	18.39	18.39
1600	0.27	0.81	0.45	33.74	51.83	85.56
1867	0.23	1.00	0.45	23.39	40.23	63.62
2133	0.00	0.66	0.17	0.00	17.01	17.01
2400	0.00	1.77	0.49	0.00	42.67	42.67
2667	0.30	0.22	0.28	12.82	2.86	15.68
4000	0.00	2.93	0.52	0.00	83.16	83.16
5333	0.36	0.82	0.48	20.07	16.41	36.48
13,000	0.31	4.10	0.74	42.45	71.26	113.71
27,000	0.00	0.00	0.00	0.00	0.00	0.00
67,000	0.00	0.00	0.00	0.00	0.00	0.00
Total	0.10	0.60	0.27	166.80	553.68	720.47
(C) Compensation of two poorest households						
133	0.00	0.00	0.00	0.00	0.00	0.00
267	− 0.48	− 0.12	− 0.32	− 43.72	− 8.78	− 52.50

Table 9 (*continued*)

Household income groups	Urban (%)	Rural (%)	Total (%)	Urban	Rural	Total
(C) Compensation of two poorest households						
400	−0.27	0.10	−0.11	−36.73	10.46	−26.28
533	−0.24	0.27	−0.01	−32.06	30.12	−1.94
667	0.18	0.61	0.38	21.25	63.79	85.04
800	0.17	0.71	0.40	18.20	55.97	74.17
933	0.21	0.43	0.30	22.43	27.70	50.12
1067	0.29	0.89	0.52	25.57	48.69	74.26
1200	0.08	0.62	0.28	6.24	26.81	33.05
1333	0.09	0.75	0.30	5.76	20.79	26.55
1600	0.41	0.90	0.57	51.16	57.79	108.95
1867	0.37	1.10	0.58	37.49	44.15	81.63
2133	0.14	0.77	0.30	9.93	20.07	30.00
2400	−0.25	1.94	0.35	−15.87	46.68	30.81
2667	0.45	0.36	0.43	19.33	4.81	24.14
4000	−0.01	3.08	0.53	−1.81	87.42	85.60
5333	0.53	0.96	0.64	29.35	19.29	48.63
13,000	0.47	4.27	0.91	64.12	74.25	138.37
27,000	−1.76	−3.92	−1.95	−45.17	−9.71	−54.88
67,000	−2.50	0.00	−2.50	−32.22	0.00	−32.22
Total	0.06	0.67	0.28	103.23	620.30	723.52
(D) Potential compensation of eight poorest households						
133	0.00	0.00	0.00	0.00	0.00	0.00
267	0.00	0.00	0.00	0.00	0.00	0.00
400	0.00	0.06	0.02	0.00	5.95	5.95
533	0.00	0.23	0.10	0.00	25.63	25.63
667	0.12	0.57	0.33	14.40	59.82	74.22
800	0.12	0.67	0.35	12.09	52.93	65.01
933	0.15	0.40	0.24	16.00	25.34	41.34
1067	0.23	0.85	0.47	20.11	46.75	66.86
1200	0.02	0.58	0.22	1.31	25.23	26.54
1333	0.03	0.72	0.24	1.76	20.03	21.79
1600	0.34	0.87	0.52	43.11	55.81	98.92
1867	0.31	1.06	0.52	31.00	42.76	73.77
2133	0.06	0.73	0.24	4.68	18.83	23.51
2400	−0.32	1.87	0.29	−20.03	45.02	24.99
2667	0.38	0.30	0.36	16.34	4.01	20.34
4000	−0.09	3.02	0.46	−11.25	85.64	74.40
5333	0.45	0.91	0.57	25.12	18.27	43.38
13,000	0.40	4.20	0.83	54.27	73.05	127.32
27,000	−1.87	−4.06	−2.06	−48.10	−10.07	−58.16
67,000	−2.63	0.00	−2.63	−33.87	0.00	−33.87
Total	0.07	0.64	0.28	126.93	595.01	721.95

Pareto improvement. Implementation of practical compensation schemes, however, may be difficult in practice, and their efficacy depends on how resources are transferred. Compensation schemes might, for example, lead to rent-seeking or other inefficiencies. We have ignored these potential losses in these simulations.

4. Limited policy reform

We now consider an alternative approach to the problem of mitigating poverty in the context of a trade liberalization by evaluating the prospects for compensation via the structural details of the tariff reform itself. We employ our numerical model to assess the extent to which sectoral exemptions from tariff reductions could provide a means of assisting the poorest households, which face adverse welfare impacts as a result of tariff elimination.

In order to develop an understanding about the impact of individual tariff and export subsidy rates on the welfare of different households, we first apply a decomposition procedure proposed by Harrison et al. (2000). This calculation decomposes the economic implications for each of the 40 households in our model. The total economic impact for each household is split into contributions from each of the sectoral tariffs and export subsidies. We then use the results of that decomposition to design a limited trade reform for Turkey that mitigates impacts on the poor.

4.1. Instrument decomposition

The main virtue of complex CGE models, the comprehensive and consistent quantification of direct and indirect policy impacts, also constitutes the major challenge for their use. Various partial effects contribute to the overall effect of a policy instrument, but those partial effects can work in opposite directions. As a result, it can become difficult to explain in depth an aggregate policy outcome. Numerical applications inherit some ambiguity in the interpretation of the results to the extent that it is difficult to make transparent the sign and the magnitude of individual effects. Therefore, procedures, which allow the decomposition of general equilibrium effects in a meaningful way, can be helpful for the understanding and interpretation of policy simulations.[16]

The results of this decomposition for the welfare impacts on the eight poorest household groups are presented in Table 10. The top row of this table indicates the aggregate welfare impact on each of the households associated with the reform as a percent of their benchmark income. We separately examine the impact of tariff elimination and export subsidy elimination. The cells corresponding to sectors in the table represent the percentage impact on the income of each household listed as a result of the elimination of the tariff or export subsidy of the product listed in the respective row. We round the effects to the nearest one-tenth of a percent of household income, and do not list products that round to 0%.

The poorest urban and rural households lose as a result of export subsidy elimination, but the rural households gain from tariff liberalization. Elimination of tariff in four or five sectors results in a negative impact on the poorest household, but it is a small effect apart from motor vehicles. Elimination of tariff on vehicles, however, is significant: the poorest urban (rural) household loses 0.6% (0.5%) of its income due to the elimination of vehicle

[16] Details of the decomposition methods we implemented can be found in Appendix A of http://dmsweb.badm.sc.edu/glenn/HRTpoverty.pdf.

Table 10
Decomposition of tariff and export subsidy reductions for poorest households

Household income	Urban households				Rural households			
	133.00	267.00	400.00	533.00	133.00	267.00	400.00	533.00
Aggregate welfare effect (EV) as a percentage of income	− 0.84	− 0.47	− 0.26	− 0.23	− 0.07	− 0.12	0.10	0.28
Aggregate tariff impact	− 0.21	− 0.15	− 0.07	− 0.09	0.14	0.07	0.28	0.35
Tariff impact of:								
Agriculture and animal husbandry	0.30	0.20	0.20	0.20	0.30	0.20	0.20	0.10
Grain mill products	0.10	0.00	0.00	0.00	0.00	0.00	0.00	0.00
Sugar	0.10	0.00	0.00	0.00	0.10	0.00	0.00	0.00
Manufacture of other food products	0.10	0.00	0.00	0.00	0.10	0.10	0.10	0.10
Soft drinks and carbonated water industries	0.00	0.10	0.00	0.00	0.00	0.00	0.00	0.00
Tobacco manufactures	0.40	0.30	0.30	0.30	0.50	0.30	0.40	0.30
Other chemical products	0.10	0.00	0.10	0.00	0.10	0.10	0.00	0.00
Non-metallic mineral products	− 0.10	0.00	0.00	0.00	− 0.10	0.00	0.00	0.00
Machinery except electrical	− 0.20	− 0.20	− 0.10	− 0.10	− 0.20	− 0.10	− 0.10	0.00
Electrical machinery	− 0.20	− 0.10	− 0.10	− 0.10	− 0.10	− 0.10	− 0.10	0.00
Land transport vehicles and equipment	− 0.60	− 0.60	− 0.40	− 0.40	− 0.50	− 0.30	− 0.30	− 0.20
Other manufacturing industries	− 0.10	0.00	0.00	0.00	0.00	0.00	0.00	0.00
Aggregate export subsidy impact	− 0.59	− 0.34	− 0.21	− 0.14	− 0.20	− 0.19	− 0.18	− 0.06
Export subsidy impact of:								
Agriculture and animal husbandry	0.10	0.10	0.10	0.10	0.10	0.00	0.00	− 0.10
Canning and preserving of fruits and vegetables	0.20	0.10	0.20	0.20	0.10	0.00	0.00	− 0.10
Textiles (including ginning)	− 0.20	− 0.20	− 0.20	− 0.10	− 0.10	− 0.10	− 0.10	0.00
Wearing apparel	− 0.30	− 0.10	− 0.10	− 0.10	− 0.10	0.00	0.00	0.10
Other chemical products	− 0.10	− 0.10	0.00	0.00	− 0.10	0.00	0.00	0.00
Iron and steel	− 0.20	− 0.10	− 0.10	0.00	0.00	0.00	0.00	0.10

Due to rounding, the sum of the listed components does not necessarily equal the total.

tariff. Elimination of the export subsidy on textiles, apparel and iron and steel has a small, negative impact on the poorest urban households.

4.2. Designing a (very simple) limited tariff reform

Based on the results of applying our decomposition procedure, we know that tariff or export subsidy removal of some tariff lines has an adverse impact on poor households. This suggests that differentiation of the tariff reform could potentially improve the distributional impacts. We therefore consider alternative reforms in which one-by-one individual sectoral import tariffs are exempt from the policy exercise.

In Table 11, we present the results of the simulation of moving to global free trade while retaining tariff protection in the sector that has the strongest adverse impact on the poor: *Motor Vehicles*. For comparison purposes, we reproduce the results for global free trade in the first two columns on the left. When motor vehicle tariff is retained, the welfare

Table 11
The vehicle tariff and indirect compensation for poor households

	Tariff revenue replacement with existing VAT				Tariff revenue replacement with uniform VAT			
	Global free trade		Retain vehicle tariff		Global free trade		Retain vehicle tariff	
	Urban (1)	Rural (2)	Urban (3)	Rural (4)	Urban (5)	Rural (6)	Urban (7)	Rural (8)
133	−0.84	−0.07	−0.17	0.55	−0.27	0.22	0.21	0.70
267	−0.47	−0.12	0.11	0.26	0.16	0.00	0.54	0.31
400	−0.26	0.10	0.21	0.38	0.23	0.20	0.55	0.42
533	−0.23	0.28	0.20	0.44	0.29	0.21	0.56	0.36
667	0.19	0.61	0.51	0.63	0.68	0.43	0.86	0.47
800	0.18	0.71	0.47	0.66	0.70	0.39	0.84	0.40
933	0.22	0.44	0.49	0.31	0.78	−0.07	0.90	−0.09
1067	0.30	0.89	0.54	0.68	0.89	0.33	0.97	0.23
1200	0.09	0.62	0.32	0.29	0.70	−0.18	0.78	−0.35
1333	0.10	0.75	0.31	0.37	0.75	−0.25	0.78	−0.42
1600	0.42	0.90	0.54	0.46	1.10	0.00	1.05	−0.25
1867	0.38	1.10	0.54	0.75	1.05	0.31	1.04	0.13
2133	0.14	0.78	0.32	0.47	0.95	0.47	0.94	0.21
2400	−0.24	1.94	−0.02	1.25	0.47	1.77	0.51	1.13
2667	0.46	0.37	0.48	0.07	1.23	0.03	1.07	−0.19
4000	−0.01	3.09	0.02	2.10	0.71	3.03	0.55	2.06
5333	0.54	0.97	0.47	−0.19	1.19	−0.26	0.95	−1.24
13,000	0.48	4.28	−0.43	2.68	1.23	3.86	0.02	2.32
27,000	−1.74	−3.90	−1.87	−4.36	−1.39	−4.24	−1.64	−4.65
67,000	−2.49	0.00	−3.52	0.00	−2.45	0.00	−3.46	0.00
Total	0.06	0.67	0.21	0.56	0.67	0.35	0.64	0.29

of all of the poor households improves and, except for the poorest urban household, all gain from the trade reform.

There appears to be two explanations for this effect.

First, *Motor Vehicles* represent imports that are purchased primarily by high-income households. Hence, the poor do not bear the cost of this import tariff. Tariff revenues in this sector are substantial, and when this tariff is cut, a large increase in VAT is required to replace the tariff revenue. The burden of these VAT payments falls in part on the poor household. In essence, tax on vehicle imports is a luxury tax in the sense that it largely falls on individuals who are not poor, and reduces the tax revenue that must be raised through the value-added tax system.

Second, given the actual distortions present in Turkey, tariff on vehicles provides welfare benefits due to second best interaction effects with the distortionary VAT. In Table 5a, we can see that the "VAT plus consumption tax" on motor vehicles is 43%. This is among the highest rates of domestic taxation for any sector. Petroleum refineries are taxed at a higher rate, but only 9% of the value added of refineries is production labor, as opposed to 50% for motor vehicles. Given that there is a relatively high rate of domestic taxation in motor vehicles, other things equal, there are too few resources devoted to the production of *Motor Vehicles*. Tariff and export subsidies on vehicles serve to induce additional resources into vehicle production, which up to a point is efficient and welfare increasing from a second-best perspective.

In order to confirm this analysis, we undertake one further calculation in which tariff reform is preceded by a reform of the VAT. In this reform, VAT is levied on a uniform basis across all production sectors. In order to provide a fair comparison, we omit the welfare gains associated with VAT reform per se when assessing the subsequent welfare impact of tariff elimination. In this case, as can be seen in columns 5 and 6 of Table 11, global free trade provides much more substantial improvements in welfare for all households, rich and poor, compared with the similar reform presented in columns 1 and 2. These results are due to the fact that there are no distortion costs associated with raising government revenue to replace the tariff revenue.

When we implement a limited reform, presented in columns 7 and 8, the *aggregate* welfare results (shown at "Total" in the bottom row) are now less than with global free trade (columns 5 and 6). Since we have eliminated the second best effect, the aggregate welfare gains decline with limited reform. Moreover, the poor households all gain, except for the poorest urban household. On the other hand, although the effect is much less pronounced with a uniform VAT, the poor households still prefer the limited reform to global free trade. As explained above, this is due to the luxury tax element of tariff on vehicles.

The explanation for the importance of motor vehicles for the poor depends on a combination of second best interactions with domestic taxes, the luxury tax aspect of taxes on motor vehicles and the intensity of the use of unskilled labor. Even if we can explain the result after the fact, it is doubtful that this sector could have been identified as this important to the poor without the machinery of our CGE model. It is quite possible, however, that these kinds of insights can be generated as one gains more experience with the practical use of the tool.[17] Moreover, this tool can suggest what complementary reforms to trade reform are indicated to address the needs of the poor. In this case, complementary reform of VAT is clearly indicated. In addition, it would be possible to investigate the optimal mix of a luxury tax on motor vehicles and distortion offsetting tariff.

While the results presented here suggest that tariff exemptions could, in principle, be used to redress adverse distributional impacts of tariff reform, we believe that these preliminary results do not justify such a policy. The obvious danger of sector-specific exemptions from trade reform is that, like the income transfers considered in Section 3, they would clearly induce rent-seeking and political lobbying. Limiting the scope of a trade reform to potentially benefit the poor is one of many possible arguments for a non-uniform tariff structure (Tarr, 2001). Martinez (2000) has demonstrated that as a rule of thumb, tariff uniformity has substantial appeal across CGE models constructed for a wide variety of less developed countries. Panagariya and Rodrik (1993) have shown that the great advantage of the uniform tariff is that it greatly diminishes the incentive to lobby for protection. In fact, experience in Chile has shown that industrialists may lobby for a reduction in the tariff when they are convinced that tariff is uniform. Lobbyists are likely to maintain that protection of their sector will help the poor, and governments are likely to find it difficult to verify the validity of the claims. Models can help make the distinction, but this tool must be used judiciously with due attention paid to finding complementary reforms or the least distortionary instrument.

[17] Böhringer and Rutherford (2000) provide an example of a decomposition which is not so transparent.

5. Conclusions

A great deal can be done to inform policymakers about the efficiency costs of specified equity goals. Direct compensation mechanisms appear to work well in the case of trade reform in Turkey, even when account is taken of the efficiency costs of raising the revenue needed to effect the compensation.

Some important qualifications must be entered, even if our intent is solely to evaluate alternative methodologies for alleviating losses to the poor.[18]

The results presented here are conditional on the data and model used in the simulations. We have discussed variants on both, and we would expect that specific quantitative results would change, and there are likely to be some changes in the qualitative results as well for some households. There are many features of the data and model that we would like to examine in more detail in order to assess the impact on the poor.

The results are also conditional on the way we have specified the policies considered. In practice, there are many risks that compensation, for example, could be effected in an extremely costly manner. Our experience in Turkey during the early 1990s is that many State-Owned Enterprises were geographically located and economically supported in order to attain some political goals. Those political goals may have just been one concrete manifestation of broad equity goals shared by most Turks, as well as more narrow and familiar sectional interests. However, it is apparent that they were not achieving those equity goals in a least-cost manner. So one should not casually assume that *any* intervention program will fit the bill of effecting compensation at low efficiency cost.

Our results also provide one potential danger in policy making: an invitation to strategic lobbying so as to effect preferential treatment for some sector or household. One of the benefits of treating sectors similarly in an across-the-board manner is that it mitigates the tendency to treat some sector in a special way. The limited policy reform approach runs this risk, and hence carries with it an expected cost in terms of a diminished political ability to effect broad reforms. Our point is that these broader risks should be taken into account in addition to the efficiency costs we have calculated.

Acknowledgements

We are grateful for comments from participants at a conference on *Poverty and the International Economy*, organized by The World Bank and The Parliamentary Commission on Swedish Policy for Global Development, held in Stockholm, October 2000.

The views expressed are those of the authors and do not necessarily reflect those of the World Bank or its Executive Directors.

[18] More extensive discussion of some of these issues is contained in Appendix A of http://dmsweb.badm.sc.edu/glenn/HRTpoverty.pdf.

References

Atkinson, A.B., 1970. On the measurement of inequality. Journal of Economic Theory 2, 244–263.

Ballard, C.L., 1988. The marginal efficiency cost of redistribution. American Economic Review 78 (5), 1019–1033 (December).

Ballard, C.L., Fullerton, D., Shoven, J.B., Whalley, J., 1985. A General Equilibrium Model for Tax Policy Evaluation. University of Chicago Press, Chicago.

Böhringer, C., Rutherford, T.F., 2000. "Decomposing the Cost of Kyoto: A Global CGE Analysis of Multilateral Policy Impacts," ZEW Discussion Paper 00-11, Centre for European Economic Research, Mannheim. Available at http://dmsweb.badm.sc.edu/glenn/Decomp.pdf.

Coller, M., Harrison, G.W., Rutherford, T.F., 1996. Efficient equity: removing salary discrimination by meeting statistical legal constraints at least cost. Economics Letters 52, 81–88.

De Melo, J., Tarr, D., 1992. A General Equilibrium Analysis of US Foreign Trade Policy. MIT Press, Cambridge, MA.

De Santis, R.A., 2000. The impact of a customs union with the EU on Turkey's welfare, employment and income distribution: an AGE model with alternative labour market structures. Journal of Economic Integration 15 (2), 195–238 (June).

De Santis, R., Ozhan, H.G., 1994. A Social Accounting Matrix for Turkey 1990. Working Paper, Department of Economics, University of Warwick.

De Santis, R., Ozhan, H.G., 1997. Social accounting matrix for Turkey 1990. Economic Systems Research 9, 281–285.

Donaldson, D., Weymark, J., 1980. A single-parameter generalisation of the Gini indices of inequality. Journal of Economic Theory 22, 67–86.

Fougère, M., Mérette, M., 2000. Population aging, intergenerational equity, and growth: analysis with an endogenous growth overlapping-generations model. In: Harrison, G., Jensen, S.E.H., Pedersen, L.P., Rutherford, T.F. (Eds.), Using Dynamic General Equilibrium Models for Policy Analysis. North-Holland, Amsterdam, pp. 325–361.

Harrison, G.W., Rutherford, T.F., 1999. Burden sharing, joint implementation, and carbon coalitions. In: Carraro, C. (Ed.), International Environmental Agreements on Climate Change. Kluwer Academic Publishing, Amsterdam, pp. 77–108.

Harrison, G.W., Rutherford, T.F., Tarr, D.G., 1993. Piecemeal trade reform in partially liberalized economies. World Bank Economic Review 7 (2), 191–217 (May).

Harrison, G.W., Rutherford, T.F., Wooton, I., 1995. Liberalizing agriculture in the European community. Journal of Policy Modeling 17, 223–255.

Harrison, G.W., Rutherford, T.F., Tarr, D.G., 1996. Economic implications for Turkey of a CU with the European Union. Policy and Research Working Paper No. 1599. The World Bank, Washington, DC.

Harrison, G.W., Rutherford, T.F., Tarr, D.G., 1997a. Economic implications for Turkey of a customs union with the European union. European Economic Review 41, 861–870.

Harrison, G.W., Rutherford, T.F., Tarr, D.G., 1997b. Quantifying the Uruguay round. Economic Journal 107, 1405–1430 (September).

Harrison, J., Horridge, J.M., Pearson, K.R., 2000. Decomposing simulation results with respect to exogenous shocks. Computational Economics 15 (3), 227–249.

Harrison, G.W., Jensen, J., Lau, M.I., Rutherford, T.F., 2001. Policy reform without tears. In: Fossati, A., Weigard, W. (Eds.), Policy Evaluation with Computable General Equilibrium Models. Routledge, New York, pp. 20–38.

Harrison, G.W., Rutherford, T.F., Tarr, D.G., 2002. Trade policy options for Chile: the importance of market access. World Bank Economic Review 16, 49–79.

Keuschnigg, C., Kohler, W., 2000. Eastern enlargement of the EU: a dynamic general equilibrium perspective. In: Harrison, G., Jensen, S.E.H., Pedersen, L.P., Rutherford, T.F. (Eds.), Using Dynamic General Equilibrium Models for Policy Analysis. North-Holland, Amsterdam, pp. 119–170.

Martinez, J., 2000. "Revenue–Neutral Tariff Reform: Welfare Effects of Uniform Tariffs in 13 Developing Countries," Unpublished Manuscript, Department of Economics, University of Colorado; available at http://dmsweb.badm.sc.edu/glenn/Martinez_ch3.pdf.

Panagariya, A., Rodrik, D., 1993. Political-economy arguments for a uniform tariff. International Economic Review, 685–703 (August).

Piggott, J., Whalley, J., 1985. UK Tax Policy and Applied General Equilibrium Analysis. Cambridge Univ. Press, New York.

Rutherford, T.F., 1995. Extensions of GAMS for complementarity and variational problems arising in applied economics. Journal of Economic Dynamics and Control 19 (8), 1299–1324 (November).

Rutherford, T.F., 1999. Applied general equilibrium modeling with MPSGE as a GAMS subsystem: an overview of the modeling framework and syntax. Computational Economic 14 (1/2), 1–46 (October).

Rutherford, T.F., 2000. Carbon abatement, technical change and intergenerational burden sharing. In: Harrison, G., Jensen, S.E.H., Pedersen, L.P., Rutherford, T.F. (Eds.), Using Dynamic General Equilibrium Models for Policy Analysis. North-Holland, Amsterdam, pp. 79–117.

Rutherford, T.F., Rutström, E., Tarr, D., 1997. Morocco's free trade agreement with the EU: a quantitative assessment. Economic Modelling 14 (9), 237–269 (April).

Shorrocks, A.F., 1982. Inequality decomposition by factor components. Econometrica 50, 193–212.

Tarr, D.G., 2002. Arguments for and against uniform tariffs. In: Hoekman, B., Maltoo, A., English, P. (Eds.), Development, Trade and the WTO: A handbook. The World Bank, Washington, DC, pp. 526–534.

Whalley, J., 1985. Trade Liberalization among Major Trading Areas. MIT Press, Cambridge, MA.

World Bank, J., 1999. Panama, Poverty Assessment: Priorities and Strategies for Poverty Reduction The World Bank, Washington, DC, USA.

Journal of
INTERNATIONAL
ECONOMICS

ELSEVIER

Journal of International Economics 75 (2008) 131–150

www.elsevier.com/locate/econbase

Poverty effects of Russia's WTO accession: Modeling "real" households with endogenous productivity effects

Thomas F. Rutherford [a], David G. Tarr [b,*]

[a] *ETH, Zurich, Switzerland*
[b] *The World Bank, USA*

Received 30 July 2007; accepted 7 September 2007

Abstract

We employ a computable general equilibrium model of the Russian economy to assess the impact of accession to the World Trade Organization (WTO) on income distribution and the poor. We incorporate all 55,098 households from the Russian Household Budget Survey as agents in the model. The model includes FDI in services and Dixit–Stiglitz endogenous productivity effects in imperfectly competitive goods and services sectors, features which are crucial to the results. We show that incorporating the diversity of households though a real household model is important for assessing household impacts, but getting the key model features right is equally important.

Keywords: Poverty impacts; Endogenous productivity; Foreign direct investment; Real household model; Dixit–Stiglitz; Computable general equilibrium; Increasing returns to scale; Business services

JEL classification: F12; I32; C68

1. Introduction[1]

In mid-2007, Russia was the largest country among 29 countries that were engaged in the long process of negotiating their accession to the World Trade Organization (WTO). WTO disciplines reach well beyond tariffs on goods and include

* Corresponding author. MSN MC3-303, The World Bank, 1818 H. St., NW, Washington DC 20433, USA.
E-mail address: dtarr@worldbank.org (D.G. Tarr).

[1] This work originated from a request by the Government of Russia to the World Bank for development of a methodology to assess the impact of WTO accession on poverty and social issues in Russia. We thank Jesper Jensen and Oleksandr Shepotylo for extensive help with this paper and the Centre of Policy Studies at Monash University for their hospitality during the time this paper was written. For helpful comments, we thank two anonymous referees of this journal, Aleksander Ananjev, Edward Balestreri, Mikhail Dmitriev, Glenn Harrison, Nanak Kakwani, Michael Lokshin, Marcelo Olarreaga, John Piggott, Guido Porto, Radwan Shaban, and Maria Kasilag for help with the logistics. We gratefully acknowledge financial support from the United Kingdom's Department for International Development (DFID), the Bank-Netherlands Partnership Program (BNPP) and the Research Committee of the World Bank under RF-P077820. The views expressed are those of the authors and do not necessarily reflect those of the Government of Russia, DFID, BNPP, the World Bank or its Executive Directors.

0022-1996/$ - see front matter
doi:10.1016/j.jinteco.2007.09.004

regulations on product standards, technical barriers to trade, intellectual property and the rights of foreign investors in services. WTO membership also forces institutional development and regulatory change in these and related areas. Consequently, accession to the WTO is among the most important policy changes that a country may undertake. In Russia, as in many countries, policy-makers are concerned with not only the aggregate effects and impacts on productive sectors of the economy, but they are also concerned with impacts on the poor and other distributional effects.

In this paper, we evaluate the impact of Russian accession to the WTO on the poor and the income and distributional effects more generally throughout the Russian population. We do so through the use of an innovative comparative static computable general equilibrium model of the Russian economy in which we integrate all the households of the Russian Household Budget Survey (HBS) as agents. Thus, our model is a "real household" model.

Due to the fact that the rights of foreign investors in the business services sectors (but not goods) are crucial aspects of WTO negotiations in general, and in Russia in particular, the model incorporates foreign direct investment in imperfectly competitive business service sectors.[2] We adopt the Dixit–Stiglitz framework in both business services and imperfectly competitive goods sectors, which implies that we have endogenous productivity effects from additional varieties in these sectors. We show that these features are crucial to both the distributional and aggregate results.

Interest in the impact of trade policy on poverty has dramatically increased in recent years. Some modellers (e.g., Harrison et al., 2003, 2004; Jensen and Tarr, 2003), have assessed impacts with a computable general equilibrium multiple representative agent approach; but this approach can mask large differences among the households within each representative household. In order to incorporate information on all available households, but given the difficulty in incorporating large household datasets as multiple agents of a computable general equilibrium (CGE) model, several authors (e.g., Bourguignon et al., 1991; Chen and Ravallion, 2004) have adopted a sequential (also called "open loop" or "top down") micro-simulation approach. In the first step a single representative agent computable general equilibrium model is employed to obtain the estimated price changes from a trade policy change. These price changes are then fed into a micro-simulation household model for predicted household effects. But the sequential approach ignores feedback effects of the quantity changes in the micro-simulation household model on the equilibrium prices in the representative agent general equilibrium model. Moreover, although efforts are sometimes made at data reconciliation, the sequential approach does not require reconciliation of inconsistent information on household income from the National Accounts (which report factor payments) and the household surveys (which report factor income).[3] Consequently, in summarizing the state of the literature, Bourguignon and Pereira da Silva (2003, p.343) have argued that one of the major challenges for the analysis of the impact of economic policies on poverty and income distribution is to integrate a computable general equilibrium model with "real" households from the household survey rather than representative households, but they note that this is empirically difficult.[4]

In our central model, we estimate that the mean welfare gains to Russia, averaged over all households, from WTO accession are a rather substantial 7.3% of Russian consumption (with a standard deviation of 2.2% of consumption) in the medium run. Decomposition analysis reveals that over 70% of the gains are due to the liberalization of barriers against foreign investors in services. We estimate that 99.9% of the households will gain from 2% to 25% of their household income. We find that poor households gain slightly more than rich households on average, since the return on capital does not increase as much as the wages of skilled and unskilled labor. We conduct both piecemeal sensitivity analysis and systematic sensitivity analysis (the latter by executing the model 30,000 times with random parameter selection), and find that our results are robust with respect to parameter specification. But without foreign direct investment, services liberalization and Dixit–Stiglitz externalities, the welfare gains are only one-sixth of the gains in our model and 7% of the households are estimated to lose. Our results show that, while incorporating the diversity of households though a real household model is important, incorporating foreign direct investment in business services with Dixit Stiglitz effects is as important for assessing household impacts.

[2] Based on the rule of thumb that goods producers can compete from abroad, but services providers need a domestic presence, the WTO disciplines only cover the rights of foreign investors in the services sphere. The attempt to introduce an investment code for goods producers into the WTO was one of the issues that caused the Cancun WTO Ministerial meetings to collapse in failure. Since rights of foreign investors in goods are not negotiated in the WTO, we did not include this in our assessment of Russian WTO accession.

[3] Without data reconciliation the household model and the representative agent model can produce very different results. Ianchovichina and Martin (2004) estimated that China will gain from WTO accession based on their representative agent model. But Chen and Ravallion (2004) estimate overall losses for China from WTO accession based on their household model using price changes from Ianchovichina and Martin.

[4] In a recent working paper, Annabi et al. (2005) have incorporated 3278 households into constant returns to scale computable general equilibrium model.

We describe the model, algorithm and data in Sections 2 and 3. Results are presented in Section 4. We show the results of piecemeal and systematic sensitivity analysis in Section 5. Also in Section 5, we assess the estimation error in the sequential approach and suggest conditions under which the sequential approach may be a good approximation for our integrated approach.

2. The model

We employ a small open economy computable general equilibrium model of the Russian economy with multiple households. In this paper we extend our earlier representative agent model of the Russian economy to a model with 55,098 households integrated into a single model. Since we have described the structure of that single representative agent model in Jensen et al. (2007), we only briefly describe the structure of the representative model here. Rather we focus on the features of the model that are necessary to generalize the model to 55,098 households.

The key modeling features that distinguish this paper from previous applied general equilibrium modeling exercises linking trade and poverty is that we permit foreign direct investment in business services and additional varieties of business services to endogenously increase the productivity of sectors using that service through the Dixit–Stiglitz–Ethier variety effect (as in the approach of Markusen et al., 2005). We also allow for Dixit–Stiglitz productivity effects in goods, both for final consumers and for intermediate use, as explained in Ethier (1982). We shall show that these features have a fundamental effect on the results for the estimated impact of WTO accession on poverty in Russia.

The model assumes: (1) that discriminatory barriers against FDI in business services exist in Russia; (2) that WTO accession will result in the reduction or removal of these barriers and that will stimulate an increase in FDI; and (3) that additional varieties of business services (and goods in imperfectly competitive sectors) will produce productivity gains in Russia. After we describe the model, we discuss the empirical basis for these assumptions.

2.1. Overview of the model formulation[5]

There are 35 sectors in the model listed in Table 1. These sectors fall into three categories: competitive sectors producing goods or services; imperfectly competitive goods sectors; and imperfectly competitive services sectors. The structure of production is depicted in Fig. 1.

2.1.1. Competitive sectors

In competitive sectors price equals marginal costs and imports and domestic goods are differentiated (the Armington assumption). See de Melo and Tarr (1992) for a description of the details of how these sectors are modeled or Harrison et al., 1997a,b) for applications.

2.1.2. Imperfectly competitive sectors

In imperfectly competitive goods sectors, goods are produced with a fixed cost and constant marginal costs. Foreign firms supply the Russian market with production facilities abroad. We assume symmetry among domestic firms as well as among foreign firms, but costs differ between domestic and foreign firms. We have firm-level competition with pricing decisions based on large group monopolistic competition. The ratio of marginal costs to average costs is assumed fixed, which together with our large group monopolistic competition pricing assumption, implies that output per firm is fixed, i.e., there are no rationalization gains. Both final and intermediate users of the output of imperfectly competitive sectors obtain a quality adjusted unit more cheaply when there are additional varieties via the Dixit–Stiglitz variety effect. Entry and exit is determined by a zero profit condition.

2.1.3. Business services sectors

Business services are supplied both by competitive firms on a cross-border basis and, since many services are more effectively supplied with a domestic presence, by imperfectly competitive firms (both multinational and Russian) that

[5] The model is solved using MPSGE software as explained in Rutherford (1999). For a mathematical treatment of the model and the algorithm we have developed see the appendices to Rutherford et al. (2005). We intuitively explain our new algorithm there, and why it allows us to integrate all households from any Household Budget Survey into a general equilibrium model, i.e., it has essentially eliminated the constraint on the number of households that can be integrated into a general equilibrium model.

134 T.F. Rutherford, D.G. Tarr / Journal of International Economics 75 (2008) 131–150

Table 1
Structure of value added in Russia: factor shares from the input–output table and after reconciliation with the Household Budget Survey (HBS)

	Sectors	Total	Value added (billions of rubles)	Value added (%)	Input–output table			Reconciled with HBS		
					Unskilled labor %	Skilled labor %	Capital %	Unskilled labor %	Skilled labor %	Capital %
			1354	100.0	28	12	61	21	63	16
IRTS sectors										
Business services	Railway transportation		45	3.3	30	24	45	11	85	5
	Truck transportation		20	1.5	31	33	36	8	88	4
	Pipelines transportation		49	3.6	5	3	92	11	58	31
	Maritime transportation		4	0.3	32	19	48	14	81	5
	Air transportation		8	0.6	48	29	24	14	84	2
	Other transportation		14	1.1	21	20	59	9	85	6
	Telecommunications		16	1.2	31	16	53	16	79	5
	Financial services		21	1.5	33	27	40	10	86	4
	Science and science servicing		11	0.8	56	10	34	35	61	4
		Subtotal	188	13.9						
Differentiated goods	Ferrous metallurgy		26	1.9	18	17	65	9	85	7
	Non-ferrous metallurgy		31	2.3	18	13	69	12	81	7
	Chemical and oil-chemical industry		24	1.8	28	10	61	20	74	7
	Mechanical engineering and metal-working		71	5.2	48	11	41	30	66	4
	Timber and woodworking and pulp and paper industry		19	1.4	37	17	45	17	79	5
	Construction materials industry		21	1.6	33	13	54	19	75	5
	Light industry		9	0.7	66	3	30	63	32	5
	Food industry		45	3.3	25	11	64	17	76	7
	Other industries		9	0.6	54	19	28	22	76	3
		Subtotal	255	18.8						
CRTS sectors										
Extractive industries	Oil extraction		39	2.9	4	9	87	1	12	87
	Gas		12	0.9	4	7	89	1	10	89
	Coalmining		15	1.1	13	41	47	2	52	47
		Subtotal	67	4.9						
Other CRTS industries	Electric industry		48	3.6	19	17	64	9	84	6
	Oil processing		10	0.8	7	17	77	3	89	8
	Other fuel industries		0	0.0	30	2	68	49	33	18
	Construction		116	8.6	30	26	44	10	86	4
	Agriculture and forestry		103	7.6	25	2	73	47	31	22
	Post		4	0.3	23	11	66	15	78	7
	Trade		309	22.9	10	3	87	20	53	27
	Public catering		2	0.1	67	28	5	19	81	1
	Other goods-producing sectors		11	0.8	72	23	5	23	76	1
	Communal and consumer services		76	5.6	24	9	67	19	72	9
	Public health and sports and social security		42	3.1	59	7	34	44	52	4
	Education and culture and art		54	4.0	68	5	28	56	40	4
	Geology and hydrometeorology		3	0.2	63	7	30	45	52	3
	Administration and public associations		65	4.8	66	22	12	22	76	1
		Subtotal	844	62.3						

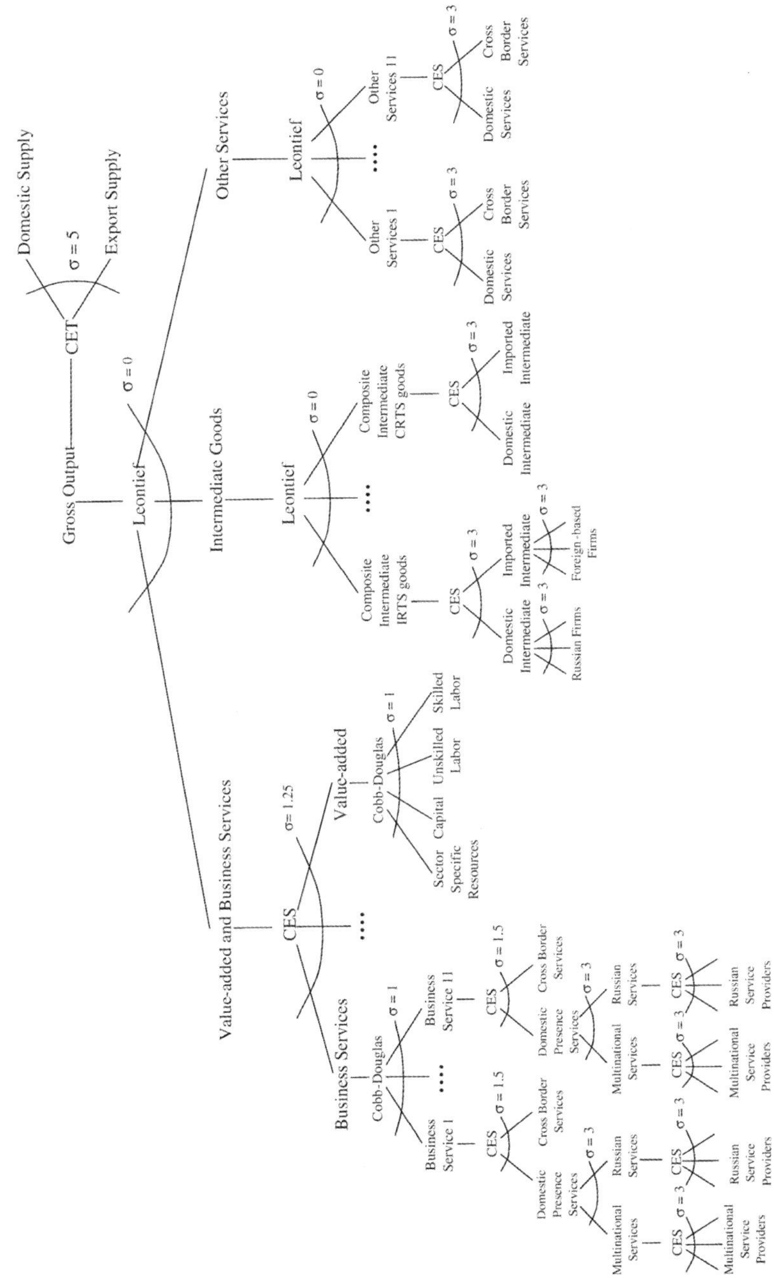

Fig. 1. Production and allocation of output.

have a domestic presence in Russia. For imperfectly competitive firms the cost and pricing structure is similar to imperfectly competitive goods producers except that production of services by multinational service providers is done in Russia. Multinational service providers will import some of their technology or management expertise when they decide to establish a domestic presence in Russia. Thus, their cost structure differs from Russian service providers. They incur costs related to both imported inputs and Russian primary factors, in addition to intermediate factor inputs. These services are characterized by firm-level product differentiation. Restrictions on foreign direct investment, right of establishment, the movement of business personnel, and lack of intellectual property protection and contract enforcement have major, direct impacts on multinational firms providing services to the market.

The number of multinational and Russian firms that are present in the Russian market depends on profitability in the Russian market. For multinational firms, the barriers to foreign direct investment affect the profitability. Reduction in the constraints on foreign direct investment will typically lead to productivity gains from the Dixit–Stiglitz variety effect because when more varieties of services are available, buyers can obtain varieties that more closely fit their demands and needs.

2.1.4. *Primary factors*

Primary factors of production are capital, skilled and unskilled labor. (In the sensitivity analysis we allow for land in agriculture.) There are five types of capital in the model: (1) mobile capital that can be used in any sector without adjustment costs (46% of total capital); (2) sector-specific capital in the energy sectors, namely ownership of the mineral resources in oil extraction, gas and coalmining (representing 15% of total capital); (3) sector-specific capital required for expansion of output in imperfectly competitive domestic firms producing either goods or services (representing 32% of the capital in the benchmark); (4) sector-specific capital required for expansion of output in imperfectly competitive foreign firms producing either goods or services (representing 5% of the capital in the benchmark); and (5) ownership of licenses for monopoly rents in services sectors (representing 2% of capital in the benchmark). We do not have data that would allow us to associate specific capital holdings in given sectors with particular households. Thus, we assume that all households that hold capital, hold the different types of capital in the same proportions.

2.2. *Household consumer demand*

Based on the data work described below, we aggregate individuals within each of the 55,098 households to obtain household factor income shares, expenditure shares on the commodities in our model and transfers between the household and the government and savings. We assume each household maximizes a Cobb Douglas utility function of the aggregate 35 goods in our model subject to its budget constraint (which is factor income net of transfers). Each of the 35 aggregate commodities is a CES ("Armington") aggregate of imported goods or services and goods or services produced in Russia. In imperfectly competitive goods sectors, imported and Russian produced goods are Dixit Stiglitz aggregates of the outputs of foreign or Russian firms. (Since consumer demand is analogous to firm-level demand, the structure is depicted in Fig. 1 under "composite intermediate IRTS goods.") The structure of consumer demand in imperfectly competitive services sectors (equivalent to business services in our model) is depicted on the left side of Fig. 1 under "Business Services." Competitively supplied cross-border services and imperfectly competitive services produced in Russia are a CES (Armington) aggregate. Services produced in Russia are a Dixit–Stiglitz aggregate of services provided by multinational service providers and Russian service providers. Given our elasticity assumptions, we have pure firm-level product differentiation (no preferences for varieties according to country of origin) for all Dixit Stiglitz goods and services.

Consumer demand, as well as firm-level demand, exhibits love of variety in imperfectly competitive goods. Given that we have weak separability and homothetic functions at all levels of consumer demand, the conditions for two-stage (or multi-stage) budgeting are satisfied. Given the initial data on each of the households, and our assumptions on the structure of demand, we solve for the parameter values in each of the 55,098 household utility functions that are consistent with optimization by the households. Thus, the demand functions of all households are dependent on their initial choices and, in general, differ from one another.

2.3. *Empirical basis for our modeling assumptions in imperfectly competitive sectors*

The model assumes: (1) that discriminatory barriers against FDI in business services exist in Russia; (2) that WTO accession will result in the reduction or removal of these barriers; (3) that the removal or reduction of the barriers will stimulate an increase in FDI in business services; and (4) that additional varieties of business services (and goods in imperfectly competitive sectors) will produce productivity gains in Russia. We now address each of these issues in turn.

2.3.1. Barriers to foreign direct investment in Russian services sectors

As Russia began seriously negotiating its barriers in services as part of its WTO accession, key barriers to foreign direct investment were the following. Rostelecom had a monopoly on long distance fixed-line telephone services. In banking and insurance, foreign banks and foreign insurance companies were restrained to a maximum of about 15% of the market. Foreign insurance companies were prohibited from selling insurance in the mandatory insurance markets, and branches of foreign banks are prohibited. In transportation services, China made liberalization of Russian barriers against its providers of truck transportation services a significant issue in its bilateral talks on Russian WTO accession. While several large multinational oil companies would like to construct a gas pipeline, only Gazprom may construct or operate a gas pipeline. Consequently, at least 20 billion cubic meters of gas that is associated with the production of oil must be flared each year.

2.3.2. Will WTO accession reduce the barriers to FDI in business services?

The business services sectors have been the subject of some of the most intense negotiations associated with Russian accession. Russia has made numerous commitments in this area. Some of the key concessions are the following. Russia has agreed to increase the quota on the maximum share that foreign banks and insurance companies can attain from 15% to 50%, and Russia will phase out the prohibition on foreign participation in mandatory insurance lines. Russia reportedly agreed to terminate the Rostelecom monopoly on long distance fixed-line telephone services as part of the Russia–EU bilateral agreement. (There are multinational telephone operators already operating in the Russian mobile telephone market.) Russia will ensure national treatment and market access for a wide variety of professions, including lawyers, accountants, architects, engineers, marketing specialists, and health care professionals. Foreign owned companies will be permitted to engage in wholesale and retail trade, franchise sectors and express courier services.[6] The European Union has negotiated intensely for the rights of companies other than Gazprom to construct a gas pipeline; but no success in this area has been reported.

2.3.3. Will reduction of the barriers against FDI increase FDI?

The value of net FDI inflows into Russia is only about 1% of its GDP annually. This is low compared with countries like China, Brazil, Mexico, Hungary and Poland that typically attract net FDI inflows between 2 and 6% of their GDP. Reasons for low FDI in Russia include lack of good governance, administrative barriers to investment and customs delays that inhibit Russia participating in international production chains. But explicit barriers to FDI are also part of the explanation. Despite these problems faced by foreign investors, there are foreign providers of business services operating in Russia in virtually all of the business services sectors (estimates by our specialist service sector institutes of the shares of the market captured by multinationals are in the sensitivity analysis table), which shows interest in the Russian market by foreign service providers. And the intensity with which the negotiations have been conducted in the business services sectors is due in most cases to lobbying interests by foreign service providers. This suggests that multinational service providers have a desire to expand operations in Russia. Consequently, it is natural to assume then that a reduction of barriers against multinational providers of services will, at the margin, result in an increase in FDI in those sectors, at least with some time.[7]

2.3.4. The impact of additional varieties on productivity

As Romer (1994) has argued, product variety is a crucial and often overlooked source of gains to the economy from trade liberalization. In our model, it is the greater availability of varieties that is the engine of productivity growth, but we believe there are other mechanisms as well through which trade may increase productivity.[8] Consequently, we take variety as a metaphor for the various ways increased trade can increase productivity. Winters et al. (2004) summarize

[6] See Tarr (2007) for details.

[7] More systematically, Alessina et al. (2005) find, for a sample of a large number of OECD countries, that regulatory reform, especially liberalization of the barriers against entry, plays a strong role in increasing investment in the sector.

[8] Trade or services liberalization may increase growth indirectly through its positive impact on the development of institutions (see Rodrik et al., 2004). It may also induce firms to move down their average cost curves, or import higher quality products or shift production to more efficient firms within an industry. Tybout and Westbrook (1995) find evidence of this latter type of rationalization for Mexican manufacturing firms.

the empirical literature by concluding that "the recent empirical evidence seems to suggest that openness and trade liberalization have a strong influence on productivity and its rate of change." Some of the key articles regarding product variety are the following. Broda and Weinstein (2004) find that increased product variety contributes to a fall of 1.2% per year in the "true" import price index. Hummels and Klenow (2005) and Schott (2004) have shown that product variety and quality are important in explaining trade between nations. Feenstra et al. (1999) show that increased variety of *exports* in a sector increases total factor productivity in most manufacturing sectors in Taiwan (China) and Korea, and they have some evidence that increased input variety also increases total factor productivity. Finally, Feenstra and Kee (2004) show that export variety and productivity of a country are positively correlated.

In business services, because of the high cost of using distant suppliers, the close availability of a diverse set of business services may be even more important for growth than in goods. As early as the 1960s, the urban and regional economics literature argued that non-tradable intermediate goods (primarily producer services produced under conditions of increasing returns to scale) are an important source of agglomeration externalities which account for the formation of cities and industrial complexes, and account for differences in economic performance across regions. The more recent economic geography literature has also focused on the fact that related economic activity is economically concentrated due to agglomeration externalities. Evidence comes from a variety of sources. Arnold et al. (2007) show that in the Czech Republic, services sector liberalization led to increased productivity of downstream industries, and the key channel through which reform led to increased productivity was allowing foreign entry. Ciccone and Hall (1996) show that firms operating in economically dense areas are more productive than firms operating in relative isolation. Hummels (1995) shows that most of the richest countries in the world are clustered in relatively small regions of Europe, North America and East Asia, while the poor countries are spread around the rest of the world. He argues this is partly explained by transportation costs for inputs since it is more expensive to buy specialized inputs in countries that are far away. The high cost of using far away inputs is especially true of business services that are not provided locally, as Marshall (1988) shows that in three regions in the United Kingdom (Birmingham, Leeds and Manchester) almost 80% of the services purchased by manufacturers were bought from suppliers within the same region. He cites studies which show that firm performance is enhanced by the local availability of producer services. In developing countries, McKee (1988) argues that the local availability of producer services is very important for the development of leading industrial sectors.

On the other hand, Hummels and Klenow (2005) have shown that, contrary to the standard Dixit–Stiglitz model, varieties expand less than proportionately to market size. Hummels and Lugovsky (2005) adopt an interesting approach that can explain this phenomenon: they modify the demand structure so that goods become more substitutable as more varieties enter the market; then the marginal benefit of new varieties falls with market size. In our model, varieties also expand less than proportionately with market size, but it is due to the costs of production. We assume that in each imperfectly competitive industry there are two specific factors, one used by domestic firms and one used by foreign firms. Both fixed and variable costs require the use of a specific factor. The expansion of the industry bids up the price of the specific factor, so additional varieties are acquired at increasing costs. We show in the sensitivity analysis that the welfare results are quite sensitive to the parameter in our model ($\varepsilon(f_i)$) that is determined by the share of costs due to the specific factor.

2.4. How we quantify the barriers to foreign direct investment in business services

We model barriers against foreign direct investment in business services in Russia as a discriminatory ad valorem tax on foreign owned production in the business services sectors in Russia. In order to estimate this tax, we first commissioned surveys in telecommunications, banking, insurance and securities, and maritime and air transportation services. These surveys were completed by Russian research institutes that specialize in these sectors. Using these surveys, as well as supplementary data, Kimura, Ando and Fujii[9] employed methodology and estimates explained in the volume by C. Findlay and T. Warren (2000) to estimate the barriers to FDI.

For each of these service sectors, authors in the Findlay and Warren volume evaluated the regulatory environment across many countries; the same regulatory criteria were assessed for all countries in a particular service sector. The price of services is then regressed against the regulatory barriers to determine the impact of any of the regulatory barriers on the price of services. Assuming that the international regression applies to Russia and assessing the

[9] The three papers by Kimura, Ando and Fujii as well as the underlying responses to the surveys are available at www.worldbank.org/trade/russia-wto.

Table 2
Tariff rates, export tax rates, estimated ad valorem equivalence of barriers to FDI in services sectors and estimated improved market access[a]

Sectors		Tariff rates	Export tax rates	Estimated change in export prices in world markets	Equivalent % barriers to FDI	
					Base year	Post-WTO accession
ELE	Electric industry	4.5	0	0		
OLE	Oil extraction	0	7.9	0		
OLP	Oil processing	3.8	4.6	0		
GAS	Gas	0.5	18.8	0		
COA	Coalmining	0	0	0		
OFU	Other fuel industries	2.6	2.6	0		
FME	Ferrous metallurgy	2.9	0.4	1.5		
NFM	Non-ferrous metallurgy	7.4	5.3	1.5		
CHM	Chemical and oil-chemical industry	7.1	1.6	1.5		
MWO	Mechanical engineering and metal-working	7.2	0	0		
TPP	Timber and woodworking and pulp and paper industry	9.9	6.9	0		
CNM	Construction materials industry	10.6	1.6	0		
CLO	Light industry	11.8	4.1	0.5		
FOO	Food industry	11.3	3.1	0.5		
OTH	Other industries	6.4	0	0.5		
AGF	Agriculture and forestry	8.2	0.6	0		
OIN	Other goods-producing sectors	0	0	0.5		
TMS	Telecommunications				33	0
SCS	Science and science servicing				33	0
FIN	Financial services				36	0
RLW	Railway transportation				33	0
TRK	Truck transportation				33	0
PIP	Pipelines transportation				33	0
MAR	Maritime transportation				95	80
AIR	Air transportation				90	75
TRO	Other transportation				33	0

(ad valorem in %) — by sector.
[a] Source: Authors' estimates.

regulatory environment based on the surveys, Kimura, Ando and Fujii estimated the ad valorem impact of the discriminatory barriers to foreign direct investment in these services sectors. The results are in Table 2. Kimura et al. also estimated the ad valorem equivalent of the sum of discriminatory and non-discriminatory regulatory barriers, but we do not report those here.

3. Data

In Jensen et al. (2007) we explain how we disaggregated the official Russian input–output table, how we calculated Russian tariff and export tax rates.[10] Here we focus on the features of the model relevant to development of the multi-household model.

3.1. Households

Households are modeled endogenously based on the 55,098 households of the Russian Household Budget Survey (HBS). The HBS, which is representative at the regional level, has very detailed information on household consumption expenditures, and information about age, gender, education, and occupation of each member of the household. It also has information about expenditures and savings and by implication household income.

[10] The export taxes are domestically imposed and are not subject to reduction commitments as part of WTO accession. Therefore, we do not model any change in the export taxes as part of our WTO scenario.

The major shortcoming of the HBS for our purposes is that it does not contain information on the sources of income of the households. For sources of household income, we must turn to the Russian Longitudinal Monitoring Survey (RLMS). The RMLS has less than 5000 observations and is not representative of the population on the regional level. But is has extensive information on individual and household sources of income: wages and profits from first, second, third jobs; pensions and unemployment benefits; profits and dividends from accumulated assets.

We have employed both small area estimation (SAE) and Matching techniques (see Elbers et al., 2003; Rao, 1999; Moriarity and Scheuren, 2003) to generate sources of income data for all 55,098 plus households in the HBS. We describe our procedures in Appendix B of Rutherford et al. (2005) (hereafter RTS). Results from both techniques yield similar results.

The key point is that we chose characteristics of the two datasets that are common to both datasets and which we expect influence factor shares of income. These characteristics, which can be found in both the HBS and the RLMS, are personal, household and geographic characteristics. Personal characteristics include age, gender, skilled or unskilled worker, head of the household, primary, secondary, and other occupation, and income. Household characteristics are family size, members of the household who work and gender of the head of household. Geographic characteristics are the region of Russia and urban or rural.

Using the RLMS data, we then estimate regression equations where the independent variables are those listed above and factor shares are the dependent variables. In the SAE procedure, we assume that the estimated equations based on the RLMS data apply to all the households in the HBS. Using the data on the household characteristics in the HBS, we thereby generate factor shares for the larger HBS. Factor shares and consumption shares aggregated to deciles are presented in RTS (2005).

3.2. Reconciliation of the National Account and Household Budget Survey Data

We have two sources of data for aggregate factor incomes: data from National Accounts and data from the HBS. In our Russian data, capital's share of factor income is much larger in the National Account data than in the HBS (see Table 1). This is typical. Ivanic (2004) mapped income from the Living Standards Measurement Surveys (LSMS) in 14 countries into factor shares and compared factor shares with the input–output tables in these countries. Capital's share from the LSMS surveys was 21% of household income, but it was 52% of household income based on National Account information (based on the "GTAP" dataset).[11]

We must produce a balanced Social Accounting Matrix in order to implement our integrated model, which means we must reconcile those differences. There are biases in both the collection of National Account and Household Survey data so that neither source is clearly correct. A key problem with the factor share data from the National Accounts is that capital's share is calculated residually in the input–output tables. Then in sectors where labor payments are underreported, as in agriculture (where sole proprietors do not report their labor income and temporary workers are often informal workers) and services, the share of capital is biased up. Unprofitable sectors that receive state subsidies will be reported as labor intensive, despite the fact that in developing countries these are typically the capital intensive sectors. Harrison et al. (2003) have shown that this bias can lead to perverse reporting of which sectors are labor intensive in developing countries. On the other hand, income estimates from LSMS surveys are known to be less than income estimates from National Accounts. Deaton (2003) explains that one of the most likely explanations of the difference is that households fail to respond to the survey, and that the probability of non-response plausibly increases monotonically with income. This presumed pattern of non-response to the household survey would also help explain this difference in capital's share, since the rich are likely to have more capital than the poor.

For our central model, we took total value added by sector from the National Accounts, but given our desire to preserve "real households" and our focus on poverty, we did not want to alter the HBS factor shares. Thus, we did not alter the HBS data or value-added data by industry from the National Accounts. Rather we adjusted factor shares at the

[11] Household income (net of taxes and transfers) in Russia exceeds household consumption for almost all households. Part of the reason is savings for investment. But in the case of Russia, an important part of the reason is that Russia has a large current account surplus. Consistency between the macro balances and the household data in construction of the Social Accounting Matrix implies that household factor income must be larger than household consumption for most households to allow for the transfer of capital to foreigners. It follows that the change in factor income as a percent of consumption will be larger than the change in factor income as a percent of household income.

industry level to be consistent with the factor payments implied by the HBS. This reconciliation of the two sets of data significantly decreased the share of capital reported by the input–output table, especially in some of the more capital intensive sectors like ferrous and non-ferrous metals (see Table 1).[12]

We acknowledge that alternate methods of reconciliation are valid. For the purposes of sensitivity analysis, therefore, we have also run the model with the opposite reconciliation. That is, we adjusted factor shares at the household level to be consistent with the factor payments of the National Accounts. We report these results in the sensitivity results.

4. Estimated impacts of Russian WTO accession

4.1. What is the counterfactual?

In our general WTO scenario, we assume: (1) that barriers against foreign direct investment are reduced as indicated in Table 2; (2) seven sectors subject to antidumping actions in export markets receive slightly improved market access. This is implemented as an exogenous increase in their export price as shown in Table 2[13]; and (3) the tariff rates of all sectors are reduced by 50%. Unless otherwise stated, we assume that the government employs lump sum distributions or taxes households in equal percentages of household income so that government revenue remains unchanged. In one scenario (column two of Table 3), we assume that government distributions are in equal absolute amounts. In Section 4.2 we discuss aggregate results and decompose the impacts to show that it is foreign direct investment and services liberalization that is the most important policy change. In Section 4.3 we discuss household and distributional impacts. We show that getting the model right is crucial to the distributional results.

4.2. Aggregate results in the full 55,098 household model

Aggregate results are summarized in Table 3. Aggregate welfare results in Table 3 are obtained by aggregating the equivalent variation gains (as a percent of consumption) of the 55 thousand consumers, using population weights. We report both the mean and the standard deviation of the welfare results across the 55,098 households.[14] For our central WTO scenario (column 1), we obtain rather substantial aggregate gains for a comparative state trade model equal to 7.3% of aggregate consumption. To determine what is driving these results, we decompose the WTO scenario into its three components. The results are shown in columns three, four and five. The key result is that liberalization of barriers to foreign direct investment is responsible for an estimated welfare gain of 5.3% of consumption, or over 70% of the total welfare gain. Reduction of barriers against multinational service providers or foreign goods producers increases the (tariff ridden) demand curve for multinational services or foreign goods. In imperfectly competitive sectors, this induces entry of new multinational service providers or new varieties of foreign goods until zero profit is restored.

[12] Of course as capital's share decreases, labor's share must increase, but reconciliation of data with the household data, also resulted in an increase in the relative share of skilled labor to unskilled labor. This is because, lacking more specific data at the household level, we defined all labor income as skilled labor income if the worker had any post-secondary education. Russia has a highly educated labor force, so this reconciliation resulted in an increase in the share of labor income going to skilled labor.

[13] Although one could also question whether some trade partners would revoke bilateral MFN status if Russia were to fail to accede to the WTO, Russia has already negotiated most-favored nation (MFN) status or better on a bilateral basis with virtually all of its important trading partners. Thus, Russia's exporters will not see a reduction in the MFN tariffs they face as a result of WTO accession. But Russian exporters will be guaranteed an injury determination in antidumping and countervailing duty investigations in its export markets, which is the source of the improved access we model. But given the evidence on discriminatory application of antidumping actions, we do not assess this effect to be large.

[14] For each of our 55,098 households h, we estimate its equivalent variation (ev_h) and we have the value of the household's initial consumption (C_h). Define $100\ ev_h = 100\ [ev_h/C_h]$, which is the increase in the equivalent variation of household h as a percentage of its initial consumption. To calculate the mean and standard deviation of the 55,098 values of $100\ ev_h$ we need to take into account that the households in the sample are statistically representative of the Russian population, and each household in the Household Budget Survey has a weight w_h that reflects the number of people it represents in the overall Russian population. If we multiply the weight of the household times the number of members in the household and sum over households, we obtain the entire Russian population. We normalize the household weights by defining $\alpha_h = w_h / \sum_h w_h$ The weights α_h for $h=1,\ldots,55{,}098$ are each household's share of the total Russian population. Thus, our estimated weighted average increase in equivalent variation as a percent of initial household consumption is $100 \sum_h \alpha_h\ ev_h = \mu$. Calculation of the weighted average variance of the increase in equivalent variation as a percent of initial consumption follows similar principles; it is defined as: $\sum_h [\alpha_h\ 100^2\ \{ev_h - \mu\}^2]$. We report the positive square root of this value in Table 3, i.e., the standard deviation.

Table 3
Impact of WTO accession in 55,098 household model on economy-wide variables in Russia — policy results and decomposition of effects (results are percentage change from initial equilibrium)

	Benchmark	WTO accession (1)	WTO accession (equal ruble transfers) (2)	Improved market access only (3)	Tariff reform only (4)	Reform of FDI barriers only (5)	CRTS model (6)	WTO accession with partial reform of FDI barriers (7)
Aggregate welfare								
Mean welfare (EV as % of consumption)		7.3	7.2	0.7	1.3	5.3	1.2	4.1
Standard deviation of EV as % of consumption [a]		(2.2)	(2.2)	(0.5)	(0.8)	(1.5)	(0.7)	(1.3)
Welfare (EV as % of GDP)		3.4	3.4	0.3	0.6	2.4	0.6	1.9
Government budget								
Tariff revenue (% of GDP)	1.4	0.9	0.9	1.4	0.8	1.4	0.9	0.8
Tariff revenue (% change)		−33.2	−33.2	8.7	−38.3	10.9	−43.5	−35.2
Aggregate trade								
Real exchange rate (% change)		2.6	2.6	−0.5	2.0	1.1	0.3	1.8
Aggregate exports (% change)		14.4	14.4	2.3	8.1	3.7	5.9	11.9
Returns to mobile factors								
Unskilled labor (% change)		3.7	3.7	0.1	0.6	2.9	1.0	1.7
Skilled labor (% change)		5.3	5.3	0.7	1.7	2.8	1.9	3.2
Capital (% change)		1.8	1.8	−0.6	1.0	1.4	0.9	2.2
Percent of factors that must adjust								
Unskilled labor		1.2	1.2	0.3	1.2	0.4	0.8	1.3
Skilled labor		1.4	1.4	0.5	0.6	0.7	0.6	1.0
Capital		0.5	0.5	0.1	0.3	0.1	0.3	0.4

Source: Authors' estimates.
[a] Numbers: The means and standard deviations are the population weighted means and standard deviations of the 55,098 estimates for the households.

Although there is a reduction in domestic varieties, there is a net increase in varieties. The increase in varieties lowers the quality adjusted cost of purchasing the services or goods in downstream industries, and this acts like an externality that increases the total factor productivity in the downstream using sectors.

Given that our estimates are that barriers against FDI in services are much higher than tariff barriers and that there will be only small gains in market access, the relative importance of liberalization of barriers to FDI is not surprising. In column 7 we also show the results of our estimates of the impact of only a 50% reduction in the barriers to FDI, along with the same improved market access and tariff reduction that we implement in our WTO scenario. The gains are reduced to 4.1% of consumption; the gains remain substantial, but significantly reduced due to a less significant reduction in FDI barriers.

To put these numbers in perspective, Rutherford and Tarr (2002) have analytically derived the relationship between a permanent increase in the steady state growth rate and equivalent variation. A welfare gain of 10% of consumption corresponds to a permanent increase in the growth rate of about 0.4%. Although cross-country assessments of the impact of trade liberalization of growth have been criticized, several authors have estimated that trade liberalization could increase the growth rate by between 1 and 2.5%.[15]

[15] These cross-country regression results are controversial, since trade liberalization is often accompanied by macro stabilization and other market reforms, and the open economy variable in the regressions can be picking up these other effects as well. Moreover, institutional reforms may also be rather important. But trade reform may compel complementary reforms, such as the elimination of state subsidies which are often unsustainable in an open economy. And WTO accession involves a number of institutional reforms. For example, liberalization of foreign direct investment in services will put great pressure on the regulatory authorities to improve the institutional environment.

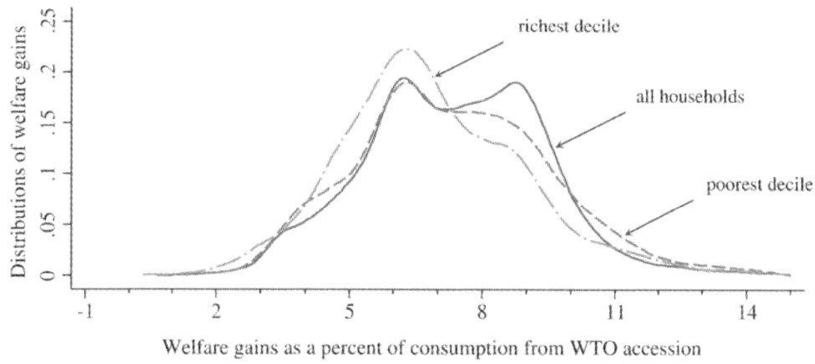

Fig. 2. Distributions of estimated welfare gains from Russian WTO accession for the entire sample, the poorest decile, and the richest decile. Of the 55,098 households, there are 59 with gains less than 2% and 7 households with gains above 25%. Thus, 99.9% of all households have gains that fall in the range of 2 to 25%. 14 households, or two-hundredths of 1% of the households, are estimated to loose. Observations in the range 0% to 15% are shown. Deciles are constructed to be representative of 10% of the Russian population based on the weights of the Household Budget Survey.

If we assume constant returns to scale in all sectors of the economy, the estimated gains (column 6) are reduced to 1.2% of consumption. These results show that incorporating liberalization of barriers to foreign direct investment in the analysis as well as the Dixit–Stiglitz–Ethier formulation for endogenous productivity effects are both crucial in explaining the rather substantial estimated gains from Russian WTO accession.

In the WTO scenario, the wage rate of skilled labor increases by 5.3%, the wage rate of unskilled labor increases by 3.7% and the return on capital increases by 1.8%. Although the return to capital rises relative to a basket of consumption goods, it does not rise as much as wages. The return to capital increases less than wages because owners of "specific capital" in imperfectly competitive sectors that are subject to increased competition from imports or from foreign direct investment and will see a reduction in the value of their returns. Returns to mobile capital increase by over 6%, even faster than returns to skilled labor because the economy shifts resources into the more capital intensive sectors and away from more unskilled labor intensive sectors such as light industry and mechanical engineering and metal-working (see RTS, Table 1). But, the return on sector-specific capital in all imperfectly competitive sectors falls, so that the total return on capital rises less than wages. The ratio of skilled to unskilled labor in the expanding sectors is greater than in the contracting sectors. As a result, the wage of skilled labor rises faster than the wage rate of unskilled labor.

4.3. *Results for individual households*

4.3.1. *Distribution of the results*

The distribution of gains from Russian WTO accession across all 55,098 households is summarized in Fig. 2. We also display in Fig. 2, the distribution of gains for the poorest and richest decile of the population. Fig. 2 shows there is a distribution of income changes across the 55,098 households that is centered around a mean gain of income of 7.3%.[16] Except for fourteen households, we estimate that all households will gain in the new equilibrium relative to the status quo.[17] We find that gains are rather evenly distributed across income groups, but we find that the poor gain slightly more than the wealthy because the wage rate of unskilled labor increases more than the rate of return on capital. The Gini coefficient is only marginally affected: it declines from 0.401 to 0.399.[18] We also find that rural households gain less than urban households because the wage rate of skilled labor increases more than the other factors of production and rural households are less endowed with skilled labor than urban households. These results highlight in a real model what Markusen et al. (2005) showed in their stylized model: with Dixit–Stiglitz productivity impacts, we escape the

[16] Of the 55,098 households, there are 59 with gains less than 2% and 7 households with gains above 25%. Thus, 99.9% of all households have gains that fall in the range of 2 to 25%. Fourteen households, or two-hundredths of 1% of the households, are estimated to lose.

[17] Households that depend disproportionately on specific capital that falls in return would be expected to lose from WTO accession, but the data do not allow this distinction.

[18] Our estimate of the Gini coefficient is virtually identical to Rostat (the statistical agency of Russia). Rostat estimates the Gini coefficient at 0.400 in 2003.

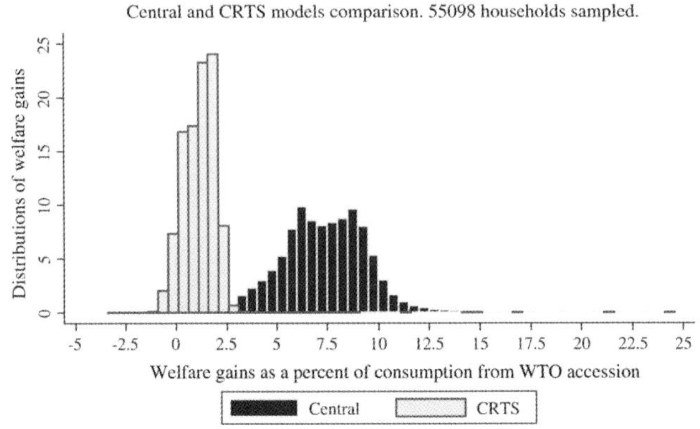

Fig. 3. Distribution of estimated welfare gains from Russian WTO accession. Central and CRTS models comparison. 55098 households sampled. In our central model, two-hundredths of 1% of households are estimated to lose as opposed to 7% of the households with the CRTS model.

pessimism of Stolper–Samuelson. The fact that the model has FDI in business services yields Dixit–Stiglitz productivity effects from services liberalization and further contributes to increase in real returns to all mobile factors. The principal caveat to the widespread gains is the potential loss of income to owners of specific capital in sectors subject to increased competition from FDI.[19]

In Fig. 3 we compare the results across 55,098 households based on two models. On the right side of the diagram, is the histogram of results for all households from our central model. Despite diversity among households, virtually none are estimated to lose. On the left side of the diagram, we present the histogram of results for all households based on a constant returns to scale model. The CRTS distribution is centered around 1.2% of gains in consumption and about 7% of the households are estimated to lose from accession to the WTO.[20]

The striking aspect of Fig. 3 is that the distribution of gains from our central model is centered sufficiently far to the right of the CRTS distribution that there is only a slight overlap of the two distributions in the tails. Fig. 3 *encapsulates the central point of this paper: to estimate household impacts, it is important to incorporate household diversity through a real household model. But incorporating foreign direct investment in business services and Dixit Stiglitz effects in imperfectly competitive sectors is as important for our policy simulation.* It is evident that incorporating foreign direct investment liberalization and endogenous productivity effects will decisively affect the results.

4.4. What is left out of the analysis

4.4.1. Transition costs

We have not modeled the transition costs of achieving a new equilibrium. During a transition period it is likely that many households will lose, so the gains will be less that we estimate to that extent.

[19] While households that are heavily endowed with specific capital in declining sectors will lose on average from WTO accession, those who can form joint ventures with foreign investors will likely see the value of their specific capital holdings increase.

[20] The fact that only 7% of households lose with liberalization under CRTS may be surprising in view of the Stolper–Samuelson theorem. But one should not apply intuition from Stolper–Samuelson in our model. First, we have specific factors in our CRTS model. Second, Ethier (1984) has shown that "the Stolper–Samuelson result in its strong form is inherently a 2 × 2 property and offers no hope for generalization." More importantly, we maintain the assumption of product differentiation by country of origin in CRTS sectors (the "Armington" assumption). To see why this is crucial, consider a two sector CRTS model with products differentiated by country of origin. Suppose factor intensities are identical in the two sectors. Trade will exist due to the product differentiation assumption. Suppose there is one distortion: a tariff on one of the goods, and it is removed. Welfare and real incomes increase on average due to the tariff removal. But since factor intensities are identical, relative factor returns can not change and the returns to both factors increase, i.e., Stolper–Samuelson does not hold as a general principle. Stolper–Samuelson results are more likely to hold, the better the products substitute for each other and the larger the factor intensity differences across sectors.

4.4.2. Intellectual property

The most important part of WTO accession that we have not modeled is the strengthening of the intellectual property regime in Russia, especially enforcement. Contrary to the transition cost issue, it is difficult to assess the direction of the impact on Russia from better intellectual property enforcement. On the one hand, Russia will have to pay more for goods like imported DVDs, software and drugs. On the other hand, Russia is a high human capital country and has the potential to significantly expand its marketable research. President Vladimir Putin reportedly considers the balance of these issues to favor Russia and now encourages more vigorous enforcement of intellectual property laws in Russia.

5. Sensitivity analysis

The results depend on the choice of parameters in the model, alternate ways of reconciling data and method of solution of the model. In this section, we begin, with an assessment of the bias from the sequential approach to micro-simulation analysis. We then assess the impact on the results if we adjust the household data to be consistent with the input output data. We then we turn to "piecemeal sensitivity" analysis on the parameters. Finally, we discuss the results of our "systematic sensitivity analysis."

5.1. Decomposition of the gains and biases from the sequential approach to micro-simulation analysis

We have aggregated the households in our model into deciles, from poorest to richest. Then we have decomposed the equivalent variation gains (as a percent of consumption) of the ten aggregated households into changes in factor prices, goods prices and taxes and transfers. The results are in Table 4 labeled "integrated model." For all the deciles of aggregated households the impact of goods prices is relatively unimportant compared with the impact of factor prices. In part because households cannot easily change their factor endowments between unskilled labor, skilled labor and capital, but they can substitute among commodities consumed, impacts on factor incomes through changes in factor prices tend to dominate the household welfare impacts in these kinds of models.[21]

We have also executed a single representative consumer model based on input output data that is not reconciled with the household data. We feed the factor and good price changes into a household model for the determination of household equivalent variation of the 55,098 households. Aggregation of the household welfare results for households within each decile provides the results at the decile level labeled "unreconciled sequential approach" in Table 4. We find that the richer households are estimated to gain significantly more in the unreconciled sequential approach, since the return to capital increases more in the unreconciled approach (this is not a general result). On the other hand, we find that the bias from ignoring the quantity feedback effects on prices is very small if the data are reconciled first between the household and representative consumer models. See Rutherford, Tarr and Shepotylo for further details.[22]

Based on these results, we believe that a sequential approach to assess household impacts of trade policy changes is likely to be a good approximation to the results of a more difficult to implement integrated approach, provided three conditions are satisfied: (1) the household data are reconciled with National Accounts data; (2) the factor and consumption shares of the representative agent in the sequential approach are equal to factor and consumption shares that are the sum over all households; and (3) the representative agent and the households exhibit the same optimizing behavior. The latter implies that the first order effects are the same.

5.2. Alternate Reconciliation of the National Account and Household Budget Survey Data

As opposed to our central model, in this "national accounts" based model we allow the household factor shares to adjust while keeping the factor shares from the national accounts fixed. Taking a weighted average of the 55,098 household welfare gains, we get an estimated 7.2% of consumption; this is only trivially different than the 7.3% gain in our central model. At the household level, we again estimate that virtually all households should gain from WTO accession.

[21] See, for example, Harrison et al. (2003).

[22] We have also shown that if we are only interested in results at the decile level (as opposed to household results), running a model with thousands of households and then aggregating results to deciles (as we have done in Table 4) does not appear to make much difference compared with aggregating the households to ten households first and then running the model with ten households. See Rutherford et al. (2005) for details regarding this section.

Table 4
Data reconciliation and the welfare impacts of WTO accession — with a decomposition of the impacts

		Percentage change in EV due to changes in factor prices, goods prices or transfers, by aggregated deciles[a]					
		Skilled wages	Unskilled wages	Return to capital	Taxes and transfers	Goods prices	Aggregate EV
Decile 1 (0–10%) — overall	Unreconciled sequential approach	5.3	2.2	0.2	−0.5	0.0	7.2
	Integrated model	5.4	2.8	0.1	−0.3	0.3	7.6
Decile 2 (11–20%) — overall	Unreconciled sequential approach	5.3	2.0	0.3	−0.4	0.0	7.3
	Integrated model	5.5	2.5	0.1	−0.3	0.3	7.6
Decile 3 (21–30%) — overall	Unreconciled sequential approach	5.8	1.7	0.5	−0.5	−0.1	7.6
	Integrated model	5.9	2.2	0.2	−0.3	0.2	7.7
Decile 4 (31–40%) — overall	Unreconciled sequential approach	5.8	1.6	0.6	−0.4	−0.1	7.6
	Integrated model	5.9	2.0	0.2	−0.3	0.2	7.7
Decile 5 (41–50%) — overall	Unreconciled sequential approach	5.7	1.5	0.9	−0.4	−0.1	7.8
	Integrated model	5.9	1.8	0.3	−0.3	0.1	7.7
Decile 6 (51–60%) — overall	Unreconciled sequential approach	5.6	1.4	1.2	−0.5	−0.1	7.9
	Integrated model	5.8	1.7	0.5	−0.3	0.1	7.5
Decile 7 (61–70%) — overall	Unreconciled sequential approach	5.7	1.1	1.6	−0.5	−0.1	8.1
	Integrated model	5.8	1.4	0.6	−0.3	0.0	7.5
Decile 8 (71–80%) — overall	Unreconciled sequential approach	5.9	0.9	1.9	−0.5	−0.1	8.4
	Integrated model	6.0	1.2	0.7	−0.4	0.1	7.5
Decile 9 (81–90%) — overall	Unreconciled sequential approach	5.1	0.9	2.6	−0.5	−0.2	8.3
	Integrated model	5.3	1.1	1.0	−0.3	−0.1	7.2
Decile 10 (91–100%) — overall	Unreconciled sequential approach	4.4	0.6	3.8	−0.5	0.0	8.3
	Integrated model	4.5	0.8	1.4	−0.3	−0.3	6.8

Source: Authors' estimates.
[a] In the integrated (sequential) approach, the percentage change in skilled wages, unskilled wages and return on capital is 5.3% (5.1%), 3.7% (3.0%) and 1.8% (4.9%), respectively. All households face the same factor prices, but depending on the factor endowments of the different households, this will impact the EV of the households differently. Similarly, for goods price changes. We have estimated the decomposed impacts as shown in the table. Aggregate EV for each decile is approximately the horizontal sum of the elements in the same row.

There are, however, differences in the distribution of gains among households, the standard deviation of the estimated gains is somewhat larger and the Gini coefficient slightly increases, rather than slightly decreases. As a result of the national accounts based reconciliation of the factor shares, several sectors are considerably more capital intensive, and among them are three key expanding export intensive sectors — ferrous metals, non-ferrous metals and chemicals. Consequently the return to capital expands considerably more than in our central model. The percentage change in skilled wages, unskilled wages and return on capital in the national accounts based (central model) is 4.7% (5.3%), 2.5% (3.7%) and 4.4% (1.8%), respectively. Then, since rich households depend more on capital income, we estimate slightly regressive results with the national accounts based model, as opposed to very slightly progressive results with our central model based on the household survey based data reconciliation.[23]

We conclude that the aggregate results and the shape of the distribution of gains across all households are not significantly affected by the principal choice of data reconciliation. Although virtually all households gain due to the Dixit–Stiglitz variety effect, which households gain more or less, however, is affected by the choice of how we reconcile the data.

5.3. Piecemeal sensitivity analysis

In Table 5 we present the impact on welfare of varying the value of key parameters. In these scenarios, we retain the central value of all parameters except the parameter in question. In general, the gains to the economy (welfare gains) increase with an increase in elasticities, since higher elasticities imply that the economy is able to more easily shift to

[23] Results, based on the national accounts model, for EV as a percent of consumption by decile are: decile 1, 5.7; decile 2, 5.7; decile 3, 6.1; decile 4, 6.2; decile 5, 6.5; decile 6, 6.6; decile 7, 7.0; decile 8, 7.3; decile 9, 7.5; decile 10, 8.0. With the data reconciled based on the National Accounts data, the Gini coefficient is .403 in this benchmark equilibrium, and it increases to .405 after our WTO accession scenario.

Table 5
Piecemeal sensitivity analysis-welfare effects

Parameter[a]	Parameter value			Hicksian equivalent variation[b] with corresponding parameter		
	Lower	Intermediate	Upper	Lower	Intermediate	Upper
σ(va, bs)	0.5	1.25	2	5.6	7.3	9.9
σ (q_i, q_j)	2	3	4	7.4	7.3	6.9
σ (D, M)	2	3	4	7.2	7.3	7.4
σ (Ls, Lu, K)	0.7	1	1.3	7.2	7.3	7.3
σ (A_1,... A_n)	0	0	0.25	7.3	7.3	7.6
σ (D, E)	3	5	7	7.2	7.3	7.3
$\varepsilon(d_i)$	5	7.5	10	6.9	7.3	7.6
$\varepsilon(f_i)$	10	15	20	5.2	7.3	8.8
$\theta m(i)$	See table below			7.2	7.3	7.4
$\theta fdi(i)$	See table below			5.3	7.3	8.5

Key

Parameter	Central value	Definitions of the parameter
σ (va, bs)	1.25	Elasticity of substitution between value-added and business services
σ (q_i, q_j)	3	Elasticity of substitution between firm varieties in imperfectly competitive sectors
σ (D, M)	3	"Armington" elasticity of substitution between imports and domestic goods in CRTS sectors
σ (Ls, Lu, K)	1	Elasticity of substitution between primary factors of production in value added
σ (A_1,... A_n)	0	Elasticity of substitution in intermediate production between composite Armington aggregate goods
σ (D, E)	5	Elasticity of transformation (domestic output versus exports)
$\varepsilon(d_i)$	7.5	Elasticity of Russian service firm supply with respect to price of output
$\varepsilon(f_i)$	15	Elasticity of multinational service firm supply with respect to price of output
$\theta m(i)$	Varies	Share of value added in multinational firms in sector I due to specialized primary factor imports, in the benchmark equilibrium
$\theta fdi(i)$	Varies	Share of output of service sector I captured by multinationals firms in the benchmark equilibrium

Parameter values for	$\theta fdi(i)$			$\theta m(i)$		
	Low	Central	High	Low	Central	High
Railway transportation	0.01	0.03	0.05	0.02	0.04	0.06
Truck transportation	0.03	0.05	0.07	0.01	0.03	0.05
Pipelines transportation	0.01	0.03	0.05	0.05	0.1	0.15
Maritime transportation	0.25	0.35	0.4	0.01	0.03	0.05
Air transportation	0.15	0.25	0.35	0.1	0.125	0.15
Other transportation	0.02	0.04	0.06	0.03	0.05	0.07
Telecommunications	0.05	0.15	0.25	0.08	0.1	0.12
Science and science servicing (market)	0.05	0.1	0.15	0.1	0.15	0.2
Financial services	0.05	0.1	0.15	0.01	0.03	0.05

[a] The piecemeal sensitivity analysis employs central values for all parameters (see below) other than the tested parameter and lump sum tax replacement.
[b] Mean value of Hicksian equivalent variation as a percent of the value of consumption in the benchmark equilibrium.

sectors or products that are cheaper after trade and FDI liberalization.[24] There are three parameters in the table that have a strong impact on the results: the elasticity of substitution between value-added and business services, σ(va, BS); the elasticity of multinational firm supply, $\varepsilon(f_i)$; and $\theta fdi(i)$, the share of output of service sector i captured by multinational firms in the benchmark equilibrium. A liberalization of the barriers to FDI will result in a reduction in the cost of business services, both from the direct effect of lowering the costs of doing business for multinational service providers and from the indirect effect that additional varieties of business services allow users to purchase a quality adjusted unit of services at less cost. When the elasticity of substitution between value-added and business services is

[24] An increase in the elasticity of substitution between varieties reduces the welfare gain. This is because when varieties are good substitutes, additional varieties are worth less to firms and consumers.

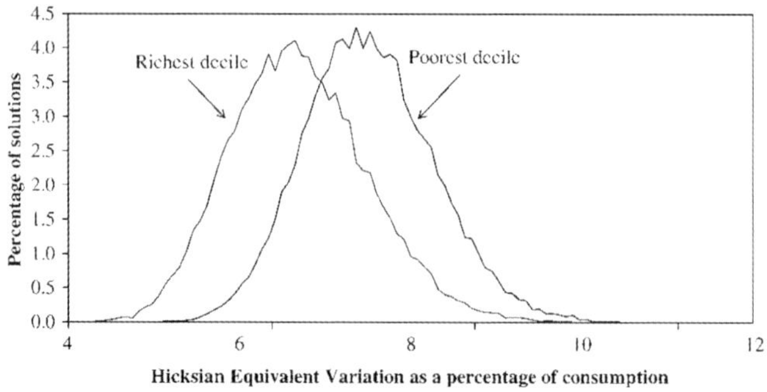

Fig. 4. Systematic Sensitivity Analysis — sample frequency distributions from 30,000 simulations for the richest and poorest deciles. 95% confidence intervals (assuming a normal distribution): Poor (6.1, 9.0); Rich (5.1, 8.3). 99% confidence intervals (assuming a normal distribution): Poor (5.6, 9.5); Rich (4.6, 8.8). In our systematic sensitivity analysis, for each simulation we take a random draw from the probability distributions of all the parameters in our model. In each of our 30,000 simulations, we obtain results for all 55,098 households and calculate the weighted average of the Hicksian equivalent variation as a percent of consumption for the poorest and richest deciles of the population. Fig. 4 shows the sample frequency distributions for these two deciles.

high, users have the greater potential to substitute the cheaper business services and this increases productivity. And when the initial multinational share, $\theta fdi(i)$, is larger, the same percentage increase in multinational varieties results in a larger number of varieties. The elasticity of multinational and Russian firm supply ($\varepsilon(f_i)$, $\varepsilon(D_i)$) is primarily dependent on the sector-specific factor for each firm type (foreign or domestic). When $\varepsilon(f_i)$ is high, a reduction in the barriers to foreign direct investment results in a larger expansion in the number of multinational firms supplying the Russian market, and hence more gains from additional varieties of business services. In addition, the share of the services market captured by multinationals has a strong effect, since a liberalization of results in a larger number of new varieties introduced.

Finally, we have executed a variant of the model with land as a specific factor in agriculture; this reduced the variable capital in agriculture by 50% relative to our central model. The mean of the estimated gains are slightly reduced, from 7.3% to 7.1%, which is explained by the Le Chatelier principle.

5.4. Systematic sensitivity analysis

Piecemeal sensitivity analysis shows how the results change when we vary the value of key parameters one-by-one, with central values of all parameters except the one under consideration. In the systematic sensitivity analysis, we allow all parameters to change simultaneously. A probability distribution for each parameter is chosen. We typically choose uniform probability distributions, with the lower and upper bounds for the values of the parameters taken from the lower and upper values of the key parameters presented in Table 5. We furthermore assume that all distributions are stochastically independent.

We have executed the model with all 55,098 households 30,000 times.[25] Each time the program chooses a random configuration of parameters and executes the model with this configuration. For each variable in our model, we then harvest the sample distribution based on the 30,000 solutions. Consequently the sample distribution is not dependent on any particular set of parameter values, but represents results representative of the full distribution of parameter values.

We present the distribution of the weighted average welfare results in Fig. 4 for the poorest and richest deciles of the population. Results for each decile are the aggregated equivalent variations, as a percent of consumption, for the households in the decile. Fig. 4 shows that there is virtually no chance that the weighted average welfare gains as a percent of consumption for the poorest decile of the population is less than 5% or more than 11%; a 99% confidence

[25] The systematic sensitivity analysis took about four months to complete. We produced about 2300 solutions of the model per week on a 2.8 GHz computer dedicated fully to this task.

interval is 5.6% to 9.5%. For the richest decile, the gains are slightly smaller; a 99% confidence interval for the richest decile of the population is 4.6% to 8.8%. These results are consistent with the central parameter value estimates, where we had the poorest decile gaining 7.6% and the richest 6.8%.[26]

6. Conclusions

We estimate that in the medium term, virtually all households will gain from Russian WTO accession. We have shown that our estimates of the distribution of gains across the 55,098 households are decisively affected the inclusion of liberalization of barriers against foreign direct investment in business services sectors and endogenous productivity effects in business services and goods.

Fig. 3 encapsulates the key point of this article. To estimate income distribution effects, a micro-simulation model is important, given that there is great diversity of impacts for trade liberalization across households. But incorporating foreign direct investment in business services with Dixit Stiglitz effects in imperfectly competitive sectors is as important since these modeling features displace the distribution of results across households to the right from a CRTS model based distribution.

References

Alessina, A., Ardagna, S., Nicoletti, G., Schiantarelli, F., 2005. Regulation and Investment. Journal of the European Economic Association 3, 791–825.

Annabi, N., Cisse, F., Cockburn, J., Decaluwe, B., 2005. Trade liberalisation, growth and poverty in Senegal: a dynamic microsimulation CGE model analysis. CEPII Research Paper.

Arnold, J., Matoo, A., Javorcik, B., 2007. Does services liberalization benefit manufacturing firms: evidence from the Czech Republic. World Bank Policy and Research Working Paper Number 4109.

Bourguignon, F., de Melo, J., Morrison, C., 1991. Poverty and income distribution during adjustment: issues and evidence from the OECD project. World Development 19, 1485–1508.

Bourguignon, F., Pereira da Silva, L., 2003. Conclusion: where do we go from here? In: Bourguignon, F., Pereira da Silva, L. (Eds.), The Impact of Economic Policies on Poverty and Income Distribution: Evaluation Techniques and Tools. World Bank and Oxford University Press, New York, pp. 1–26.

Broda, C., Weinstein, D., 2004. Variety, growth and world welfare. American Economic Review 94, 139–144.

Chen, S., Ravallion, M., 2004. Welfare impacts of China's accession to the WTO. World Bank Economic Review 18, 29–57.

Ciccone, A., Hall, R., 1996. Productivity and the density of economic activity. American Economic Review 86, 54–70.

de Melo, J., Tarr, D., 1992. A General Equilibrium Analysis of US Foreign Trade Policy. MIT Press, Cambridge, MA.

Deaton, A., 2003. Measuring Poverty in a Growing World (or Measuring Growth in a Poor World). National Bureau of Economic Research Working Paper no. 9822.

Elbers, C., Lanjouw, J.O., Lanjouw, P., 2003. Micro-level estimation of poverty and inequality. Econometrica 71, 355–364.

Ethier, W., 1982. National and international returns to scale in the modern theory of international trade. American Economic Review 72, 389–405.

Ethier, W., 1984. Higher dimensional issues in trade theory. In: Jones, R., Kenen, P. (Eds.), Handbook of International Economics, vol. 1. International Trade, North-Holland, Amsterdam.

Feenstra, R., Kee, H., 2004. On the measurement of product variety in trade. American Economic Review 94, 145–149.

Feenstra, R., Madani, D., Yang, T.H., Liang, C.Y., 1999. Testing endogenous growth in South Korea and Taiwan. Journal of Development Economics 60, 317–341.

Findlay, C., Warren, T., 2000. Impediments to Trade in Services: Measurement and Policy Implications. Routledge, London.

Harrison, G., Rutherford, T., Tarr, D., 1997a. Economic implications for Turkey of a customs union with the European Union. European Economic Review 41, 861–870.

Harrison, G., Rutherford, T., Tarr, D., 1997b. Quantifying the Uruguay round. Economic Journal 107, 1405–1430.

Harrison, G., Rutherford, T., Tarr, D., 2003. trade liberalization, poverty and efficient equity. Journal of Development Economics 71, 97–128.

Harrison, G., Rutherford, T., Tarr, D., Gurgel, A., 2004. Trade policy and poverty reduction in Brazil. World Bank Economic Review 18, 289–317.

Hummels, D., 1995. Global Income Clustering and Trade in Intermediate Goods. University of Chicago, Graduate School of Business.

Hummels, D., Klenow, P., 2005. The variety and quality of a nation's trade. American Economic Review 95, 704–723.

Hummels, D., Lugovsky, V., 2005. Trade in ideal varieties: theory and evidence. National Bureau of Economic Research Working Paper No. 11828.

Ianchovichina, E., Martin, W., 2004. Impacts of China's accession to the World Trade Organization. World Bank Economic Review 18, 3–27.

Ivanic, M., 2004. Reconciliation of the GTAP and household survey data. GTAP Resource Memorandum No. 1408. Available at: http://www.gtap.agecon.purdue.edu/resources/res_display.asp?RecordID= 1408.

[26] Note that these systematic sensitivity distributions are the sample probability distributions for the weighted average welfare gains of the households in the decile being considered, based on random parameter selection; whereas the distributions of Figs. 2 and 3 are distributions of welfare gains across all the different households based on our specified central parameter values.

Jensen, J., Tarr, D., 2003. Trade, exchange rate and energy pricing reform in Iran: potentially large efficiency effects and gains to the poor. Review of Development Economics 7, 543–662.

Jensen, J., Rutherford, T., Tarr, D., 2007. The impact of liberalizing barriers to foreign direct investment in services: the case of Russian accession to the World Trade Organization. Review of Development Economics 11, 482–506.

Markusen, J., Rutherford, T., Tarr, D., 2005. Foreign direct investment in services and the domestic market for expertise. Canadian Journal of Economics 38, 758–777.

Marshall, J.N., 1988. Services and Uneven Development. Oxford University Press, London.

McKee, D.L., 1988. Growth, Development, and the Service Economy in the Third World. Praeger Publishers, New York.

Moriarity, C., Scheuren, F., 2003. A note on Rubin's statistical matching using file concatenation with adjusted weights and multiple imputations. Journal of Business and Economic Statistics 21, 65–73.

Rao, J.N.K., 1999. Some recent advances in model-based small area estimation. Survey Methodology 25, 175–186.

Rodrik, D., Subramanian, A., Trebbi, F., 2004. Institutions rule: the primacy of institutions over geography and integration in economic development. Journal of Economic Growth 9, 131–165.

Romer, P., 1994. New Goods, Old Theory and the Welfare Costs of Trade Restrictions. Journal of Development Economics 43, 5–38.

Rutherford, Thomas F., 1999. Applied general equilibrium modeling with MPSGE as a GAMS subsystem: an overview of the modeling framework and syntax. Computational Economics 14 (1/2), 1–46 October.

Rutherford, T., Tarr, D., 2002. Trade liberalization, product variety and growth in a small open economy: a quantitative assessment. Journal of International Economics 56, 247–272.

Rutherford, T., Tarr, D., Shepotylo, O., 2005. Poverty effects of modeling Russia's WTO accession: modeling "real" households and endogenous productivity effects. Policy and Research Working Paper Series No. 3473. The World Bank. Available at www.worldbank.org/trade/russia-wto.

Schott, P., 2004. Across-product versus within-product specialization in international trade. Quarterly Journal of Economics 119, 647–678.

Tarr, D., 2007. Russian accession to the WTO: an assessment. Eurasian Geography and Economics 48, 306–319.

Tybout, J., Westbrook, D., 1995. Trade liberalization and the dimensions of efficiency change in mexican manufacturing industries. Journal of International Economics 39, 53–78.

Winters, L., McCulloch, N., McKay, A., 2004. Trade liberalization and poverty: the evidence so far. Journal of Economic Literature 42, 72–115.

Review of Development Economics, 7(4), 543–562, 2003

Trade, Exchange Rate, and Energy Pricing Reform in Iran: Potentially Large Efficiency Effects and Gains to the Poor

*Jesper Jensen and David Tarr**

Abstract

Iran is committed to substantial trade and market reform in its Third Five Year Development Plan. It started, however, with nontariff barriers on all products, a dual exchange rate regime with the market rate more than four times the official rate, and domestic energy product subsidies of about 90%. The authors develop a multisector computable general-equilibrium model with ten rural and ten urban households to analyze the various reforms, separately and together. Reflecting the large initial distortions, they find that the combined reforms could generate large welfare gains equal to about 50% of aggregate consumer income. Moreover, the results show that well-intentioned policies of commodity subsidies for the poor can have perverse effects. Even nontargeted direct income payments to all households (not just the poor) would enormously and progressively increase the incomes of the poor compared to the status quo.

1. Introduction

Iran has applied for membership in the World Trade Organization (WTO), and with the passage of the law for the Third Five Year Development Plan on 5 April 2000, the government of Iran has committed itself to the use of the market mechanism as a means of regulating foreign trade. Iran began this reform process, however, from a highly distorted trade and exchange rate regime. The principal distortions are: nontariff barriers, the dual exchange rate system, and highly subsidized petroleum product prices.[1] While applied tariffs were low, nontariff barriers (in the form of import licenses) restrained imports of all goods. A dual exchange rate system prevailed in which the market rate was more than four times the official rate. Finally, petroleum product prices in Iran were only about 10% of world market prices. Reforms are proposed or contemplated in all these areas, but the impact on the poor is a major issue in assessing whether the reforms can be implemented.

In this paper, we present quantitative estimates of the impacts of reform of all of the principal distortions mentioned above. We develop a multisector computable general-equilibrium model of the Iranian economy to provide the estimates. The model contains 20 households, ten rural and ten urban grouped according to income, so that in addition to results at the sector and macro levels, the model produces estimates of

*Tarr: MSN 3-303, The World Bank, 1818 H. St, NW, Washington, DC 20433, USA. Tel: (202) 473-7677; Fax: (202) 522-1159; E-mail: dtarr@worldbank.org. Jensen: Copenhagen Economics ApS, Vandflyverhangaren, Refshalevej 100, DK-1452 Copenhagen K, Denmark. Tel: (+45) 7027-0740; Fax: (+45) 7027-0741; E-mail: jj@copenhageneconomics.com. We wish to thank numerous agencies in Iran that provided useful comments and assistance, including the Ministry of Finance, Ministry of Commerce, Ministry of Industry and Mining, Central Bank, Export Guarantee Fund, Customs Department, the Export Development Bank of Iran, and especially the Institute for Trade Studies and Research. The authors would also like to thank Habib Fetini, George Fane, Bernard Hoekman, Dorsati Madani, Radwan Shaban, seminar participants at the World Bank, and two anonymous referees of this journal for helpful comments, and Maria Kasilag for logistical support. The views expressed are those of the authors and do not necessarily reflect those of the World Bank, the government of Iran, or those acknowledged.

the impact on the poor and on the distribution of income. The results for the poor households are crucial, given the importance Iranian policymakers place on the impact of policy change on the poor.

We estimate the impact of changing the policies that were in effect in 2000/01. More specifically, the policy changes we consider and the motivation for examining these are as follows.

Trade Policies

In Article 115 of the law for the Third Five Year Development Plan, the government indicates it plans to eliminate nontariff barriers to foreign trade and substitute tariff barriers at their equivalent level.[2] Estimates of the tariff equivalence on nontariff barriers are notoriously difficult to obtain. We, however, have been fortunate to obtain these estimates from the Iranian Ministry of Industry for virtually all major products in the economy. As a result, our estimates of the value to the economy of tariffication of nontariff barriers is, to our knowledge, the first data-based CGE estimate for an economy that is replete with such barriers. We next consider the marginal impact of lowering tariffs to either a maximum 25% or to a uniform 15%.[3]

Unification of the exchange rate for import purchases (with and without consumption subsidies). It is the intention of the government to unify the exchange rate for imports during the period of the development plan. Certain imports qualify for foreign exchange at the official rate of 1,750 rials per US dollar, whereas the Tehran Stock Exchange (TSE) rate was about 8,150 rials per US dollar in November 2000. In effect, imports of these commodities are subsidized by the government through allocation of foreign exchange at the official exchange rate. These subsidies were equal to almost 7% of GDP in 2000.[4]

Energy Pricing Reform

Petroleum prices in Iran are only about 10% of world prices. We estimate the impact of the elimination of the petroleum product subsidies that are equal to 18% of GDP.

Key Results

Assuming rent dissipation of the nontariff barriers (we also provide estimates without rent dissipation), tariffication will lead to an increase in Iranian aggregate welfare of 3.4% of the value of consumption in the benchmark equilibrium.[5] Lowering tariffs, as discussed above, will result in a further increase in welfare relative to tariffication alone of between 0.7% and 2.1% of consumption.[6] We estimate that the elimination of the subsidies to foreign exchange alone will increase aggregate welfare by 6.9% of consumption. Eliminating the subsidies to domestic energy products alone would result in an enormous estimated gain of 32% of consumption for the economy as a whole. If all these reforms were implemented (tariffication, tariff reduction, exchange rate unification and energy pricing reform), we estimate that the Iranian economy would experience an enormous gain of more than 50% of the value of consumption.

All of the reforms generate revenue for the government. We assume that the additional revenue received by the government is distributed back to households in equal absolute amounts. As a result, the poor gain enormously from these policy reforms. In the case of the combination of all reforms, the poorest rural (urban) household gains about 290 (140)% of their income. The reason is that the poor have such little income that the distributions from the government have a significant effect on their income.

Our results show that well-intentioned policies for the poor can have perverse effects, at least when compared to direct income payments. Even though the direct income payments we consider (equal absolute payments to all households) are not targeted at the poor in our scenarios, they do a better job of improving the welfare of the poor than do commodity subsidies, even though the commodity subsidies are perceived to be aimed at the poor. The commodity subsidies create inefficiencies between sectors. More importantly, the commodity subsidies are not well targeted for the poor since the rich buy more of all commodities, including the subsidized commodities. In summary, we find that direct income payments, even if not well-targeted initially, are much superior to commodity subsidies in assisting the poor. More targeted direct income payments would be even more efficient for the poor.

Regarding the relative importance of the reforms, the largest gains come from the energy pricing reform, as this reform alone results in an estimated gain of 32% of consumption. Exchange rate reform is estimated to yield gains of about 7% of consumption. Tariffication combined with lowering of tariffs to uniform 15% tariffs yields 5.5% of consumption.

The estimated gains in welfare that we find are extremely large by the standards of this type of model (constant returns to scale). Constant-returns-to-scale numerical modeling estimates of the impact of trade liberalization have often found that trade liberalization increases the welfare of a country by only about 0.5% of GDP.[7] The very large estimated welfare gains reflect the unusually high level of distortions present at the starting point of the reform in Iran. The combined fiscal impact of all the reforms (with a 15% uniform tariff) is estimated to be an increase in the fiscal surplus by 18.5% of GDP.

In section 2, we describe the key data on the tariffs, nontariff barriers, and subsidies that are fundamental to the results of the model. In section 3, we briefly describe the model and other aspects of the data. In section 4, we present and interpret the results of the policy scenarios; this includes individual policy reforms and combinations of policy reforms. We provide conclusions in section 5.

2. Data on Tariffs, Nontariff Barriers, and Subsidies[8]

Data on Tariff Rates in the Initial Year

Imports into Iran are subject to both an import duty and the commercial benefit tax (CBT).[9] What would normally be referred to as the tariff on imports is the sum of these two items. Actual collected tariffs, however, in Iran are quite low by international standards. Based on customs department data for collected tariffs in fiscal year 1998/99, aggregate collected tariffs were 0.3% of GDP. Collected tariff rates are rather low for two reasons. First, for the purposes of customs valuation, all imports are valued at the official exchange rate; this amounts to 78% reduction in assessed import duties relative to the market exchange rate as of November 2000. Second, the principal means of import protection has been nontariff barriers exercised through licensing requirements.[10]

For the sectors in our model, we present the average collected duty and CBT in Table 1. These data were calculated as follows. Since up-to-date applied tariff data are important, we obtained the collected tariff data at the tariff-line level for fiscal year 1999/2000. Iran employs the International Harmonized System at the six-digit level, which contains 5,313 tariff lines.[11] These tariff lines were aggregated with simple

Table 1. Production Sectors in the Model and the Policy Instruments (percentage rates of the distortions)

	Sector	Import duty	Commercial benefit tax (pre-reform)	Nontariff barrier (tariff equivalent)	Commercial benefit tax (post tariffication)	Energy subsidy to consumption	Foreign exchange subsidy for imports
1	Farming	0.1	0.7	9.2	10.0		63.0
2	Livestock	0.1	0.7	19.1	20.0		
3	Other agriculture	0.1	0.7	14.2	15.0		
4	Mining	0.5	1.1	13.7	15.0		
5	Crude oil						
6	Sugar						79.0
7	Other food	0.1	0.4	29.5	30.0		31.0
8	Paper & print	0.7	2.4	6.4	9.0		
9	Cement	1.1	1.0	19.6	21.0		
10	Brick	1.1	8.2	11.7	21.0		
11	Gypsum & other minerals	0.7	2.3	18.2	21.0		
12	Glass	1.3	6.5	21.8	30.0		
13	Other nonmetal products	1.1	5.3	14.8	21.0		
14	Textiles	0.4	2.3	69.8	74.0		
15	Clothing	3.1	11.1	69.1	90.0		
16	Weaving & leather products	0.6	3.6	67.6	74.0		
17	Rubber & plastic products	0.4	1.3	23.3	25.0		
18	Pharmaceutical products						79.0
19	Kerosene		0.1		0.1	92.0	
20	Fuel oil		0.1		0.1	94.0	
21	Gasoline		0.1		0.1	74.0	
22	Gas oil		0.1		0.1	91.0	
23	Liquid gas		0.1		0.1		
24	Other materials & chemical products	0.3	1.7	7.2	9.0		
25	Basic metal & steel products	0.4	3.1	16.3	20.0		
26	Copper & aluminum & other basic products	0.4	3.1	16.3	20.0		
27	Metal products	1.0	4.9	4.8	10.0		
28	Industrial machinery	0.6	2.1	7.7	10.0		59.0
29	Radio & TV equipment	1.2	2.8	16.5	20.0		
30	Motor vehicles	1.4	2.1	32.8	36.0		
31	Other industrial products	0.5	2.9	16.5	20.0		
32	Electricity						
33	Water						
34	Natural gas						
35	Construction						
36	Trade						
37	Restaurants						
38	Hotel & motels						
39	Load transport						
40	Passenger transport						
41	Post & telecommunications						
42	Other transport & storage						
43	Other services						

Source: Iranian Ministry of Industry, Iranian Ministry of Oil, and authors' estimates as explained in the text.

averages to obtain the average collected tariff at the level of the sectors in our model. Since it is what the importer pays that affects the decision to purchase, collected tariff rates should be superior to legal tariff rates. Thus, we updated the data in the input–output table for our model with collected tariff rates for 1999/2000.

Tariff Equivalence of the Nontariff Barriers (NTBs)

Tariffication plans and progress With the passage of the Third Five Year Development Plan, Iran has committed itself to tariffication of the NTBs. Prior to 1999, an import license was required for goods that could be legally imported. That is, there was a "Positive List" of goods that were not banned. If the good were on the Positive List it could be legally imported, but it still required a license from the responsible industry, typically the Ministry of Industry, Ministry of Agriculture, or Ministry of Mines.

The commitment to tariffy the NTBs has manifested itself in several ways. First, the Positive List is rapidly expanding. In fiscal year 1998/99 the Positive List consisted of 29 broad categories of products. This was expanded to 41 broad product categories in early 2000 and 77 broad product categories by November 2000. It is expected that the Positive List will include all products except for those banned for religious or health and safety reasons.

Second, the requirement to obtain a license from the relevant line Ministry is being eliminated. Only the registration requirement at the Ministry of Commerce (which is accomplished routinely within a few days) will remain for virtually all goods when the tariffication process is complete.[12] As of November 2000, Ministry licensing had been eliminated for 1,900 tariff lines out of the 5,313 tariff lines in the Iranian system. In addition, the decision was taken by the government to eliminate Ministry licensing for an additional 895 tariff lines categories. Finally, during the transition, if the item is on the Positive List it is reported that even for those products which still require Ministry licensing, the line Ministries are providing the license more rapidly than in the past.

Estimated tariff equivalence of the NTBs The intergovernmental committee chaired by the Ministry of Commerce, which includes the Ministry of Industry, is responsible for recommending the tariff equivalent of the NTBs. International versus domestic price comparisons are being done based on a database of 70 million observations from Iranian customs declarations. The Ministry of Industry has been responsible for providing the licenses for approximately 3,000 of the tariff lines in the manufacturing sectors, and it has estimated the tariff equivalence of the NTBs for the 3,000 tariff lines for which it is responsible. We have obtained estimates from the Ministry of Industry of Iran of the new commercial benefit tax necessary to provide tariff equivalence of the NTBs and have supplemented that information with the following consideration. For imports that are subsidized in the initial period, we take the tariff equivalence to be zero.[13] For imports that are not on the Positive List, the tariff equivalence of the NTB should be very high, since it can't legally be imported. For products on the Positive List, we assume the tariff equivalence is lower than for those products that are not on the Positive List.

Define NTB as the tariff equivalent of the nontariff barrier of a product in *ad valorem* terms. It can be shown (Jensen and Tarr, 2001) that

$$NTB = [1 + TD + CBT(1)]/[1 + TD + CBT(0)] - 1,$$

where $CBT(0)$ is the commercial benefit tax prior to tariffication, $CBT(1)$ is the commercial benefit tax after tariffication, and TD is the unchanged customs duty.

We have data on all of the right-hand-side variables. *CBT*(0) and *TD* are straightforward data, and, as discussed, we have estimates of *CBT*(1) from the Ministry of Industry and other considerations. We calculate of estimated NTBs from this equation and present the results in Table 1. The NTB rate for a sector typically represents the average tariff equivalent in a product category, since each category represents many tariff lines. Textiles and apparel are the sectors with the highest NTBs by far; the tariff equivalents are 74% and 90%, respectively. The next highest is motor vehicles at 36%. There are only three other sectors with tariff equivalents above 20%.

These estimates are based on the Tehran Stock Exchange (TSE) exchange rate; i.e., they are about 20% of the tariff equivalents that would prevail if imports were valued at the official exchange rate. It is the intention of Iran to convert to customs valuation at the TSE rate, but more importantly, we need rates that reflect real costs that induce resource movement, so we must use the TSE rate for the tariff equivalents of the NTBs.

Distribution of the rents from the NTBs What happens to the quota rents when the NTBs are in place? We model this in two ways: (1) all *the rents are dissipated* through rent-seeking; and (2) *no rent dissipation*. One view of the rents is they are dissipated along the lines of the model of Barzel (1974). Given that the license to import has value, competition among license seekers will result in real resources being used in lobbying costs, queuing costs, and inefficiencies in the cost of the delivery that dissipate the rents. Elimination of the NTB through tariffication would eliminate the rent from obtaining the license to import and eliminate the wasteful expenditure of resources on rent-seeking behavior. Thus, this view of license allocation implies there are real resource gains for conversion to the tariff equivalents of NTBs and welfare should increase significantly for all households. In addition, the poor are likely to gain, since we shall assume that the tariff revenue of the government will be distributed to all households in equal amounts. No rent dissipation could occur if recipients of the licenses to import are unable to influence the decision on who gets the licenses. That is, the size of the firm or any payments or lobbying of officials is irrelevant regarding the receipt of the license. When a firm receives the license to import, it receives a windfall profit equal to the difference between the domestic price of the imported product and the tariff-inclusive import price; i.e., it receives the tariff equivalent of the quota. We assume this value accrues to the owners of the factors of production in the firm. This value ultimately is part of household income, since the owners of the factors of production are the households. When we impose tariffs and eliminate the NTBs counterfactually, under this assumption of no rent dissipation, the tariff revenue of the government increases, and the government distributes the tariff revenue back to the households in an equal lump-sum manner. Although there will be little or no efficiency or aggregate welfare effect from this process, there will be significant distribution of income effects. In particular, the poor will be better off and the rich worse off under our distribution mechanism. This is because the rents from the quotas accrue to the owners of the factors of production in the economy (of which the poor hold a small share), whereas the tariff revenue is distributed to the households in equal shares. We believe the appropriate result is between these two extremes, with the true state closer to rent dissipation. We take rent dissipation as our central assumption unless otherwise indicated.

Data on Centrally Allocated Foreign Exchange

In fiscal year 1999/2000, the official rate for a US dollar was 1,750 rials and the market rate was approximately 8,150 rials per US dollar. In general, exporters receive the market exchange rate for their exports, and importers who do not receive centrally allocated foreign exchange pay the market exchange rate. Consequently, the principal impact of the dual exchange rate is to provide a subsidy to those who receive centrally allocated foreign exchange for imports. Since centrally allocated dollars at the official exchange rate cost only about 21% of dollars from the market, those who received centrally allocated dollars received a subsidy of about 79% of the market value of the dollars. Imported goods qualifying for foreign exchange at the official exchange rate fall into one of the following categories: essential food commodities, pharmaceuticals and petroleum products, investment demand for state-owned enterprises, and national defense.[14] At the same time producers in these sectors are disprotected (or are facing an effective negative tariff) by 79%.

Essential food commodities comprise wheat, rice, sugar, cooking oil, and milk powder. The Government Trading Corporation imports these products. They fall into three sectors in our model: farming, sugar, and other food products. Imports of these commodities collectively represent 10% of the value of imports at the official exchange rate. The Ministry of Health imports pharmaceuticals, which is about 1% of the value of imports. The Iranian National Oil Company imports petroleum products, comprising an additional 8% of the value of imports.

Our measure of the subsidy to the sector is adjusted proportionately based on the share of the sector's imports that is subsidized. In the case of sugar and pharmaceuticals, all imports receive the subsidy, so the subsidy is listed at 79%. Farming and other food products have the subsidy reduced in proportion to the share of imports in the sector that receives the subsidy.[15]

Regarding the investment projects of the state-owned enterprises, one of the largest categories of imports in our IO table is "industrial machinery." We assume that 75% of these imports are destined for the investment demand of the state-owned enterprises at the official exchange rate. The subsidy rate is thus estimated at 59% (75% of 79%).

Based on data from the Central Bank of Iran, 50% of imported goods in fiscal year 1999/2000 were imported at the official exchange rate. The sum of the above categories represents 32% of the value of imports based on the data in the input–output table. In addition to the above imports, which are for the purpose of private consumption or intermediate use in industry, the central government allocates foreign exchange for national defense. We take national defense as the residual 18% of centrally allocated foreign exchange at the official exchange rate. We assume that national defense is the central government's own final consumption. That is, the central government holds foreign exchange that is uses to purchase imported goods for its own consumption in the form of national defense expenditures. Given a decision by the government to spend some of its foreign exchange on imports for national defense, the rate at which the foreign exchange is accounted for national defense purposes is irrelevant for economic decision-making, and we ignore national defense expenditures in the analysis that follows.[16]

Energy Subsidies

Direct energy subsidies apply on four of the seven energy products in our model: gasoline (74%), kerosene (92%), gas oil (91%), and fuel oil (94%).[17] That is, for fuel oil for example, domestic prices are 6% of world market prices at the TSE exchange rate. Since the subsidies are on consumption of the products, they apply on imports as well as domestic consumption. (Iran imports small amounts of these products.)

3. The Model

Our small open economy (SOE) model is designed for trade policy analysis with a large number of sectors. The model is a generic constant-returns-to-scale general-equilibrium model of a single small open economy. Explanation of the equations for this type of model may be found in de Melo and Tarr (1992, ch. 3). Four figures that characterize our model are depicted in Jensen and Tarr (2002). We describe here the general features of the model, but refer the reader to de Melo and Tarr (1992) for a mathematical treatment. The principal departure from the earlier model is the treatment of multiple households.

Table 1 lists the 43 production sectors in the model. Goods are produced using primary factors and intermediate inputs. Primary factors include labor and capital. In addition, land is a factor of production that is specific to the production of agriculture. Labor and capital are perfectly mobile, which yields a unique real wage rate and rental rate on capital for the entire economy. Goods used as intermediates are an "Armington" composite of domestic and imported goods. The world prices of imported and exported goods are fixed (the small open economy assumption), which implies the absence of any terms-of-trade effects. Production exhibits constant returns to scale and individual firms behave competitively, selecting output levels such that marginal cost at those output levels equals the given market price. From Euler's theorem, payments to primary factors exhaust value-added. Output in all sectors except for crude oil is differentiated between goods destined for the domestic and export markets. This relationship is characterized by a constant elasticity of transformation (CET) frontier. Composite output is an aggregate of domestic output and exports.

Regarding the crude oil sector, we continue to employ the assumption of constant returns to scale, Armington aggregates for intermediates, cost minimization, and marginal cost pricing. The sector differs from other sectors in that we assume domestic output and exports are homogeneous, following Bernstein et al. (1999), and production of oil requires the use of a sector-specific primary factor; i.e., natural resources (oil). We assume that the government owns this primary factor and consequently the government receives the returns from this primary factor. Capital and labor are mobile factors among all sectors and receive the unique wage rate and return on capital. Given that natural resources are a specific factor of production owned by the government, and constant returns to scale prevail, the royalties or rents to the government vary residually such that zero profits prevail. This structure results in the government, in effect, being the residual claimant to the revenues from the sale of produced oil after the payment of intermediate goods, wages, and rent on capital to produce oil. This appears appropriate in view of the fact that the revenues from the Iranian National Oil Company are reported as part of the government's budget, unlike the treatment of other state-owned enterprises. We report any changes in oil rents as part of changes in government revenue from policy changes.

We have seven sectors in the model that produce refined energy products: gasoline, kerosene, fuel oil, gas oil, liquid gas, natural gas, and electricity. The first four of these are the sectors where consumption is heavily subsidized directly (the estimates were listed above). We assume zero substitution both between energy inputs and, most importantly, between energy inputs and other inputs. This reflects that there is a roughly fixed physical relationship between, for example, the amounts of crude oil required to produce a given amount of gasoline. We continue to apply the CET assumption for sectors where there are exports initially.[18] The principal distinctions for these sectors are the modeling of energy inputs and, crucially, energy subsidies.

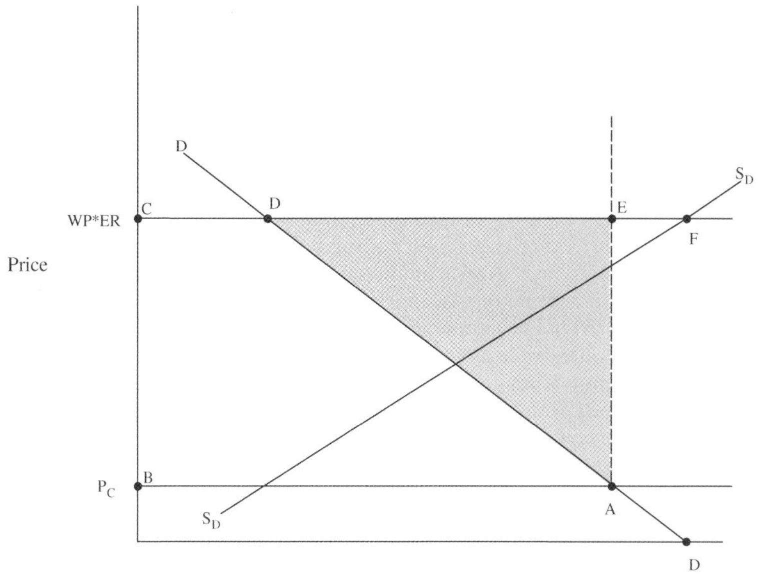

Figure 1. Market for Energy Projects, with Endogenous Consumption Subsidy

Regarding the energy subsidies, we assume that consumers pay an artificially low and controlled price for energy products and that the government pays the difference (i.e., a subsidy), such that demand is met at the controlled price. Sellers of energy receive the payment by consumers plus the subsidy, and domestic producers optimize their output decisions between domestic sales and exports according to a CET. Since the price paid by domestic consumers remains fixed, if the domestic market for energy does not clear, the government will alter the subsidy rate. Thus, the subsidy rate is endogenous to policy changes, and we report in the results the amount by which petroleum product subsidies change in each scenario.

We illustrate this government intervention in Figure 1, where for simplicity, and contrary to our model, we assume that exports and domestic products are homogeneous. Energy product prices are initially subsidized by the government such that the price to domestic consumers is fixed at P_C. WP is the fixed world price and ER is the real exchange rate, so $WP^*\ ER$ is the price domestic firms receive for exports. With S_D as the domestic supply curve, domestic firms produce the quantity CF. Domestic consumers consume CE and domestic firms export EF. *Deadweight loss is the shaded area ADE, and the government subsidy is the area ABCE.* The height of the government subsidy, AE, is endogenous, and depends among other things on the world price and the real exchange rate. As reported later in Table 2, the rectangle of government subsidies in the figure is about 18% of GDP.

There are 20 household types in the model, ten urban and ten rural. Based on the 1999/2000 Iranian Household Expenditure Survey, the urban households are grouped among themselves from the poorest to the richest with an equal number of households represented by each household; i.e., urban household 1 represents the poorest 6.8% of urban households, while urban household 10 represents the richest 6.8% of urban households. Similarly, rural households are grouped within themselves from the poorest rural to the richest rural, where each rural household represents 3.2% of all Iranian households.[19] Our estimates are that the income of urban household 2 is just above the one dollar a day poverty line, while rural household 2 is just below the one dollar a day poverty line. Households higher than the second poorest are not poor by the standards of one dollar a day.

The shares of each consumer's expenditure on different commodities differ. Among the major expenditure categories—food, energy, transportation, and other—the urban households spend more on "other" than the rural. Poor rural households spend almost three-fourths of their income on transportation and food, even more than the urban poor. Details are provided in Jensen and Tarr (2002, Table 2).

Owing to lack of data, we assume that all households obtain their income from the different factors of production in identical proportions.[20] That is, the share of the household's income derived from labor and capital is the same across different households, even though they may work in different industries.

Government demand for goods and services and investment demand are exogenous. Government revenue derives from rents on crude oil, import tariff revenues, and exogenous lump-sum taxes. Government expenditures finance the exogenous government demand for goods and services, plus subsidies to foreign exchange for imports, subsidies to petroleum products, and (in one counterfactual) food subsidies.

We impose an "equal yield constraint" on government revenue; i.e., any loss (gain) of government revenue must be offset by a lump-sum tax (subsidy). In all of our scenarios, the government is reducing subsidies, which reduce government expenditures. In all scenarios we hold the government demand for goods unchanged (otherwise welfare analysis would be meaningless, since only consumers obtain utility and only from private goods). Consequently, when government revenues are increased, they are endogenously distributed back to households so that the government demands are unchanged. Thus, government demand is balanced with revenue (which is consistent with the loose requirement in Iran to balance the budget). We, however, calculate and present the impact of all policy changes on the revenues of the government, and policymakers in practice may consider alternate expenditures for these revenues such as institution building to assist the development of the private sector.

The decision rule we typically adopt is that lump-sum distributions of the government are given to households in equal shares. That is, suppose the government is distributing 10,000 rials. Since rural households in aggregate constitute 32% of all households, it will provide 320 rials to each of the ten rural household types. It will provide 680 rials to each of the ten urban household types, which collectively represent 68% of all households. This implies that all individual households, rural and urban, receive the same rial amount.

We suggest this decision rule for distributions for several reasons. First, although less efficient as a safety net for the poor than lump-sum distributions targeted at the poor, more targeted distributions have the difficulty that it may be administratively difficult to identify who are the poor. Some of the poor, who can ill afford a period of lowered income, may be excluded inadvertently. Second, on political economy grounds, if all households receive distributions, there is likely to be less opposition to the reforms.[21] Third, if all households receive distributions, then there is no disincentive to work as a result of the distribution scheme; that is, no income level at which additional earnings result in ineligibility for distributions and a net reduction in after distribution income.

Criticism of our distribution scheme has taken two forms. First, some argue that distributions to the rich are politically unacceptable. We note, however, that all Iranians are recipients of government commodity subsidies and the wealthy receive larger subsidies than the poor since subsidies are in proportion to consumption. For example, the per capita benefits of fuel subsidies to members of the richest urban quintile were 6.7 times the per capita benefits to those in the poorest urban quintile. For the rural quintiles the corresponding ratio was 5.5 (World Bank, 1999). Thus, compared to commodity subsidies, our distribution rule will be a progressive distribution scheme since the poorest households receive less than an equal share of most commodity subsidies (even the subsidies targeted for the poor) because they consume less of virtually all goods.

Second, some have suggested that the distribution scheme is not feasible—that it is not possible to set up a system to monitor who has received a distribution and that the system will be plagued by fraud. Iran, however, already has a photo identification system for the distribution of ration coupons for edible oils, sugar, and cheese that has been in place since the time of the Iran–Iraq war. Bearers present their ID to a bank and receive the coupons. This system could be expanded to cover cash distributions. The likelihood of fraud would increase if substantial amounts of cash were involved, but fraud would require complicity of the bank teller. Additional study to assess how fraud could be reduced is appropriate, but fraud is prevalent in any safety-net distribution system.

Since private consumption equals the income from primary factors plus net transfers by the households to the government (from domestic and foreign trade taxes), Walras' law is satisfied.

World market import and export prices are fixed, so there are no endogenous changes in the terms of trade. In other words, import supplies and export demands are infinitely elastic at given world prices. The real exchange rate in the model adjusts such that the current account balances the value of exports and imports taking into account exogenously fixed capital inflows. Our model allows for changes in these fixed world prices, such as a change in the price of crude oil on world markets.[22]

4. Policy Results

Results of the main policy simulations are presented in Table 2. In the first column, we present summary data regarding the fiscal situation in the initial equilibrium of the model. Import taxes and foreign exchange subsidies have been discussed above. Petroleum subsidies are due to the energy policy of providing petroleum products at a given domestic price. These subsidies vary with the cost of foreign exchange since some of these products are imported. Oil rent is the revenue that accrues to the government from the sale of oil after payments to labor and capital to produce the oil. Revenues or subsidies from each of these sources can change in any scenario due to a direct change in the policy related to the tax or subsidy or to an indirect effect when another variable is changed. The latter can have "second-best" effects as we will discuss below. The fiscal effects are reported as a percentage change from the benchmark equilibrium (where we consider that the rents from import licensing are dissipated).

Tariffication of Nontariff Barriers

Dissipation of the rents from the NTBs In column (1) of Table 2 we present results of the scenario we call tariffication, where rents from the NTBs are dissipated in the

Table 2. Impact of Trade and Exchange Rate Reforms

	Initial situation (level values)	*Tariffication* (1)	*Tariffication without rent dissipation* (2)	*Tariffication & maximum 25% tariff* (3)	*Tariffication & uniform 15% tariff* (4)	*Exchange rate unification* (5)	*Exchange rate unification & food subsidies* (6)
Aggregate welfare change (% of income)		3.4	–0.4	4.1	5.5	6.9	6.7
Fiscal effects (change as % of GDP)							
Food subsidies							–2.1
Foreign exchange subsidies	–6.4	–0.3	–0.1	–0.8	–0.2	6.4	6.4
Petroleum subsidies	–18.1	–0.8	–0.1	–1.7	–1.9	2.7	2.3
Import taxes	0.3	2.0	2.0	1.7	1.6	0.0	0.0
Oil rent	15.7	0.5	0.1	1.4	1.5	–3.8	–3.7
Net effect		1.4	1.9	0.7	1.0	5.3	2.9
Average effective tariff rate (%)	2.5	19.4	19.5	15.3	13.9	2.8	2.8
Trade effects (% change)							
Real exchange rate		1.1	0.2	3.6	3.8	–13.0	–12.2
Aggregate exports		1.0	0.1	5.6	4.9	–21.9	–22.4
Factor incomes (% change)							
Wage rate		–0.1	0.1	0.2	0.4	3.0	6.8
Return to capital		–0.4	–0.2	1.1	1.4	–4.7	–1.7
Price of essential goods (% change)							
Primary food items		1.2	0.3	1.6	2.5	10.5	
Food products		0.6	0.2	0.8	0.4	6.0	
Sugar		0.0	0.0	0.6	7.4	37.6	
Pharmaceuticals		–0.3	–0.1	0.8	2.3	1.0	
Change in household welfare (% of income)							
Rural 1		23.3	27.9	15.6	20.2	72.0	46.3
Rural 2		15.2	16.6	10.9	14.2	44.6	30.5
Rural 3		10.8	10.4	8.3	10.9	30.4	21.8
Rural 4		9.8	8.9	7.9	10.4	26.6	19.7
Rural 5		8.0	6.3	6.9	9.0	20.9	16.1
Rural 6		6.3	3.9	6.0	7.9	15.6	12.7
Rural 7		5.6	2.9	5.6	7.4	13.0	11.3
Rural 8		5.2	2.4	5.7	7.5	11.7	10.7
Rural 9		3.6	0.1	4.7	6.2	6.7	7.3
Rural 10		1.1	–3.8	2.6	3.6	–0.4	1.9
Urban 1		11.1	10.6	8.3	10.9	32.0	21.9
Urban 2		7.5	5.6	6.3	8.3	19.9	14.9
Urban 3		5.9	3.2	5.4	7.1	14.8	11.6

Table 2. Continued

	Initial situation (level values)	*Tariffication* (1)	*Tariffication without rent dissipation* (2)	*Tariffication & maximum 25% tariff* (3)	*Tariffication & uniform 15% tariff* (4)	*Exchange rate unification* (5)	*Exchange rate unification & food subsidies* (6)
Urban 4		5.0	2.0	5.0	6.7	11.9	9.9
Urban 5		4.4	1.1	4.7	6.2	9.9	8.6
Urban 6		3.9	0.5	4.4	5.9	8.4	7.8
Urban 7		3.3	−0.4	4.1	5.5	6.5	6.5
Urban 8		2.6	−1.6	3.7	4.9	4.0	4.9
Urban 9		1.8	−2.7	3.1	4.2	1.9	3.4
Urban 10		0.9	−4.1	2.4	3.5	−0.7	1.5

Source: Authors' estimates.

benchmark equilibrium. Tariffication then has the effect of increasing aggregate welfare by 3.4% of initial household income. Although all households gain from this scenario, the positive impact on the welfare of the poor households is much stronger: the poorest rural household gains 23% and the poorest urban household gains 11%. The reason for this favorable distribution effect on the poor is that, as a result of converting NTBs to tariffs, the collected tariffs of the government increase by 2% (to 2.3% of GDP). On the other hand, government revenues are endogenously affected by the depreciation of the real exchange rate. The output and income expansion induces an increase in the demand for imports. The real exchange rate must depreciate to restore equilibrium in the balance of trade. The depreciated exchange rate implies that the cost of the government subsides to foreign exchange and to imported petroleum products increases, worsening the government's fiscal position. On the positive side, the revenues the government receives (after factor payments) from the sale of oil on world markets increases with exchange rate depreciation by 0.5% of GDP. On balance, the fiscal impact of the government is positive at 1.4%. Unless otherwise indicated, we assume that the government distributes the additional revenue from the reforms back to households in equal absolute amounts per household. Since the poor have such low incomes, the distribution of these revenues represents a significant share of their income.

An interesting and *unique* aspect of this scenario is that the output of all Iranian industries expands. This is because the rent-seeking behavior consumes real resources, labor and capital. Tariffication frees these resources from wasteful activity to produce output. At the same time, the increase in the supply of labor and capital for production results in a fall in the real wage of 0.1% and a fall in the rental rate on capital of 0.4%. The impact on incomes is more than offset by the additional output available from productive use of the newly available capital and labor and the income transfers from the government.

Tariffication of NTBs without rent dissipation The results of this scenario are presented in column 2 of Table 2. The principal impact of the tariffication of NTBs without rent dissipation is the increase in government revenues. Again the government revenues increase by 2.0% of GDP, and again the increase in government revenue is distributed back to households in equal Iranian rial amounts. As a result the poor households gain substantially, even though the rich households lose in this scenario. The distributional impacts are strictly progressive because we had assumed in this scenario that the rents from the quotas were not dissipated. Rather they accrued to the households in proportion to their income. Thus, tariffication without rent dissipation implies that the households lose the rents from the quotas in proportion to their income.

The aggregate welfare impact of this scenario is slightly negative for two reasons. First, tariffication without rent dissipation results in the same set of international prices and no improved resource allocation regarding the international trade regime. But, tariffication results in a negative second-best effect owing to the increased consumption of food and energy products. Given the change in the distribution of income, expenditure in the economy shifts toward the budget items consumed more intensely by the poorer households. The poor intensively consume food, energy, and transportation (and transportation is an intense direct user of energy subsidies). The increased demand for food and energy results in a slight reduction in economy-wide efficiency and welfare because these products are excessively consumed in the initial equilibrium owing to the subsidies.

On the other hand, the poorest household actually gains more in this scenario. The reason is that while the rents from the licenses are distributed to households in proportion to their income, the poor receive a disproportionately large share of the transfers relative to their incomes. The government budget expands by a larger amount without rent dissipation because the lower output expansion induces a much smaller real exchange rate depreciation. This in turn implies a smaller increase in the cost of petroleum product subsidies (even though the quantity of petroleum products consumed domestically increases). See the tables in Jensen and Tarr (2002) for the impact on domestic output, prices, and exports at the sector level in all scenarios mentioned in this paper.

Unification of the Exchange Rate

We evaluate the impact of unifying the exchange rate for the purpose of imports and exports. More specifically, we simulate the removal of subsidies through centrally allocated foreign exchange at the official exchange rate for essential commodities (wheat, rice, sugar, cooking oil, milk powder, and pharmaceuticals), and for the investment demands of state-owned enterprises. Petroleum product consumption subsidies are considered part of energy policy, so we retain them except in the energy policy scenarios. The results are presented in Table 2, column 5. But so that no needy household is excluded, some would argue that such a broad payment approach is initially required.

The aggregate welfare gain from this policy is a very large 6.9% increase as a percentage of income. This shows how very inefficient a dual exchange rate regime can be when the exchange rate subsidies are as large as four or five to one.

The prices of the essential commodities increase significantly: 11% for farm products, 6% for food, and 38% for sugar. Despite these price increases, what is really striking is the very large increase in the welfare of the poorest households. The poorest two rural households (both earn less than one dollar per day) experience an increase in their welfare of 72% and 45%. The poorest urban households gain 32% and 20%. These households are so poor that the lump-sum distribution payments represent a substantial portion of their income. Note that all individual households gain from this policy but that this distribution scheme is monotonically progressive: the poorer the household, the larger the percentage gain. Thus, even though the distribution scheme is not perfectly targeted at the poor, it is a highly pro-poor distribution scheme.

There is a significant positive output response of the farming sector of 13% as a result of an increase in the price of domestic farm products by 7%. The import subsidies represent an implicit tax on the farming sectors, which have to compete with heavily subsidized imports. Removing subsidies to imports results in an increase in the price of farm products and removes the implicit tax on Iranian farmers. Their output expands as a result. Similarly, the other domestic producing sectors that competed with subsidized imports (sugar, food product producers of oils, pharmaceuticals, and industrial machinery) see demand for their products increase and they respond with increased production in the new equilibrium. These sectors expand considerably and draw resources away from the other sectors. The elimination of subsidies to imports reduces the demand for foreign exchange, so there is a strong appreciation of the real exchange rate by an estimated 13%. Output effects by sector are also partly explained by the appreciation. See Jensen and Tarr (2002) for an interpretation of the results of column 6, in which subsidies to consumption are retained when subsidized imports of the same commodities are removed.

Lowering Tariffs and Introducing Competition

The simulations we perform combine the effects of tariffication of NTBs and lowering tariffs. We use the term "tariff" to refer to the combined import duty plus commercial benefit tax.

Maximum 25% tariffs First consider the simulation in which all sectors with tariffs above 25% have their tariffs lowered to 25% along with tariffication of NTBs in other sectors. The results are presented in Table 2, column 3. Aggregate welfare increases relative to the initial equilibrium by 4.1% of real consumer income. The average effective or collected tariff is initially 2.5% and increases to 19.4%. When the maximum tariff is 25% the average effective tariff is reduced to 15.3%.

Given tariffication of NTBs, we observe that the marginal impact of lowering the high tariffs to 25% maximum is 0.6% of real consumer income. This is a significant gain in welfare from tariff reduction alone, which illustrates that biggest gains in a trade policy reform are derived from lowering protection to moderate levels in the sectors with the very high protection.

Uniform 15% tariffs The impact of tariffication and moving all tariffs to 15% is presented in Table 2, column 4.[23] Combining elimination of NTBs with tariff uniformity at 15% results in an increase in aggregate welfare relative to the initial equilibrium by 5.5% of real consumer income, where the impact of removing the NTBs with rent dissipation is included. The marginal impact of imposing uniform tariffs is 2.0%.

Impact on the poor The combined effect of tariffication and lowering tariff protection has a strong positive impact on the income of the poorest households. Fifteen percent uniform tariffs and elimination of the NTBs results in a 20% increase in the income of the poorest rural household and an 11% increase in the income of the poorest urban household. All households gain, but the percentage increase in income declines monotonically with income, since the equal lump-sum transfers by govern-

Table 3. Impact of Combining Trade, Exchange Rate, and Energy Pricing Reforms

						Energy pricing reform + tariffication + exchange rate unification + tariff reform	
	Initial situation (level values)	Tariffication + exchange rate unification + uniform 15% tariffs (1)	Tariffication + exchange rate unification + zero tariffs (2)	Energy pricing reform (3)	Energy pricing reform + exchange rate unification (4)	(5) (15% uniform tariffs)	(6) (Zero tariffs)
Aggregate welfare change (% of income)		14.0	12.7	32.9	38.8	50.1	50.7
Fiscal effects (change as % of GDP)							
Food subsidies							
Foreign exchange subsidies	–6.4	6.4	6.4	2.1	6.4	6.4	6.4
Petroleum subsidies	–18.1	0.8	–0.3	18.1	18.1	18.1	18.1
Import taxes	0.3	1.6	–0.3	0.1	0.1	2.1	–0.3
Oil rent	15.7	–2.2	–0.6	–7.0	–9.2	–8.1	–6.6
Net effect		6.6	5.1	13.3	15.3	18.5	17.6
Average effective tariff rate (%)	2.5	14.0		2.7	2.9	14.7	
Trade effects (% change)							
Real exchange rate		–8.5	–3.5	–26.1	–35.5	–31.9	–26.1
Aggregate Exports		–17.2	–8.9	30.4	16.6	25.8	35.3
Factor incomes (% change)							
Wage rate		3.1	3.2	2.4	7.7	8.4	7.8
Return to capital		–3.7	–1.3	–6.1	–7.1	–5.8	–3.7
Price of essential goods (% change)							
Primary food items		13.5	13.1	8.2	19.4	24.9	23.9
Food products		7.4	6.9	4.3	8.1	10.3	9.5
Sugar		40.9	41.9	–0.3	36.4	41.6	42.1
Pharmaceuticals		2.1	3.1	–4.0	–1.2	0.4	1.4
Change in household welfare (% of income)							
Rural 1		95.6	77.7	209.8	239.1	292.2	282.9
Rural 2		60.8	50.5	139.0	157.2	193.3	188.7
Rural 3		42.5	36.1	98.5	112.8	140.2	137.4
Rural 4		38.1	32.9	90.0	102.4	128.1	126.2
Rural 5		30.7	27.1	73.1	84.0	105.9	104.7
Rural 6		24.0	21.9	58.7	67.8	86.3	85.8
Rural 7		20.8	19.5	51.6	60.0	77.1	77.2
Rural 8		19.6	18.7	49.5	56.8	73.6	74.2
Rural 9		12.9	13.4	34.6	40.6	53.9	55.0
Rural 10		2.8	5.2	11.9	15.6	21.6	23.2

Table 3. Continued

	Initial situation (level values)	*Tariffication + exchange rate unification + uniform 15% tariffs* (1)	*Tariffication + exchange rate unification + zero tariffs* (2)	*Energy pricing reform* (3)	*Energy pricing reform + exchange rate unification* (4)	*Energy pricing reform + tariffication + exchange rate unification + tariff reform* (5) *(15% uniform tariffs)*	(6) *(Zero tariffs)*
Urban 1		44.3	37.3	102.6	116.3	143.1	139.5
Urban 2		28.9	25.4	70.3	79.8	99.4	97.9
Urban 3		22.4	20.3	55.1	63.5	80.0	79.2
Urban 4		18.9	17.7	47.5	54.9	69.8	69.6
Urban 5		16.3	15.8	41.8	48.4	62.0	62.2
Urban 6		14.4	14.3	37.8	43.9	56.5	56.9
Urban 7		12.0	12.5	32.1	37.7	49.2	49.9
Urban 8		8.8	10.0	25.1	29.9	39.6	40.7
Urban 9		5.7	7.5	18.4	22.6	30.3	31.5
Urban 10		2.3	5.0	10.5	13.9	19.4	21.1

Source: Authors' estimates.

ment of the fiscal surplus represents a higher percentage of income for the poorer households.

The *marginal impact* of lowering tariff protection given tariffication has a negative revenue impact on government revenue. The adverse fiscal impact is greater with the 25% maximum tariff scenario (0.7 decline in revenue) than with the 15% uniform tariff (0.4% decline in revenue). This is because with tariff uniformity the low tariffs are raised to 15%, which increases revenue, partly offsetting the revenue loss for the lowering of the tariffs above 15%. Since the impact on the poor is primarily a function of the lump-sum transfers, the marginal impact on the poor of lowering tariff protection given prior tariffication is negative.

Energy

In this scenario we remove the enormous subsidies to energy products. The results are presented in column 3 of Table 3. Eliminating the subsidy to domestic consumption of petroleum products results in an enormous increase in welfare of 33% of consumption. The large gains are partly the result of starting with such a large distortion: petroleum subsidies are initially 18% of GDP. The poorest rural (urban) household gains over 200 (100)% of income.

The elimination of the energy product subsidies results in a large decline in the domestic demand for crude oil production. Given that exports and domestic sales of crude oil products are homogeneous, crude oil exports expand dramatically by 76%. This results in a significant appreciation of the real exchange rate by 26%. Consequently, there is a Dutch disease problem regarding exports of the rest of the economy that sees its exports decline.[24] Moreover, several energy-intensive sectors suffer large output declines.

Combinations of Trade, Energy, and Exchange Rate Reform

In Table 3, we present various combinations of combining trade (tariffication of NTBs), exchange rate, and energy pricing reform. We consider two tariff policies: a uniform tariff at 15% and zero tariffs. If all reform policies are implemented, the estimates are that the Iranian economy would experience an enormous gain of more than 50% of the value of consumption following the combined reforms. With a uniform 15% tariff, the aggregate welfare gains are 50.1% of consumption. With zero tariffs, the gains are slightly larger at 50.7% of consumption, reflecting further gains from trade liberalization. The poor gain slightly more from the uniform tariff at 15%, since we assume the fiscal surplus is distributed to the poor and there is a greater fiscal surplus to distribute with the 15% uniform tariff. The impact on production is dominated by the sectors that benefit from the elimination of the foreign exchange subsidies.

5. Conclusion

The estimated gains in welfare that we find are extremely large by the standards of constant-returns-to-scale comparative static models. The very large estimated welfare gains reflect the unusually high level of distortions present at the starting point of the reform.

Iran has implemented many of its policies through subsidies and nontariff barriers. We estimate the fiscal impact of all these reforms to be an increase of 18.5% of GDP. We find that despite the fact that many of the policy interventions are rationalized as support for the poor, direct income payments, even if not targeted to the poor, have the potential to enormously increase the income of the poor compared with the market interventions that prevail. In fact, a direct income payment distribution scheme would have to be significantly anti-poor for the poor not be better off.[25] Our results show that well-intentioned policies of commodity subsidies for the poor can have perverse effects.

References

Barzel, Yoram, "A Theory of Rationing by Waiting," *Journal of Law and Economics* 17 (1974):73–95.

Bernstein, Paul M., W. David Montgomery, Thomas F. Rutherford, and Gui-Fang Yang, "Effects of Restrictions on International Permit Trading: the MS–MRT Model," in John Weyant (ed.), *The Costs of the Kyoto Protocol: a Multi-Model Evaluation*, special issue of *The Energy Journal* (1999).

Harrison, Glenn W., Thomas F. Rutherford, and David G. Tarr, "Trade Liberalization, Poverty and Efficient Equity," *Journal of Development Economics* 71 (1), (2003):97–128.

———, "Economic Implications for Turkey of a Customs Union With the European Union," *European Economic Review* 41 (1997b):861–70.

———, "Trade Liberalization, Poverty and Efficient Equity," *Journal of Development Economics* (forthcoming).

Jensen, Jesper and David Tarr, "Trade, Exchange Rate and Energy Pricing Reform in Iran: Potentially Large Efficiency Effects and Gains to the Poor," World Bank policy research working paper 2768 (2002); available at www.worldbank.org/research/trade/majoract.htm.

Melo, Jaime de and David Tarr, "Welfare Costs of US Quotas in Textiles, Steel and Autos," *Review of Economics and Statistics* 72 (1990):489–97.

———, *A General Equilibrium Analysis of US Foreign Trade Policy*, Cambridge, MA: MIT Press (1992).

———, "Industrial Policy in the Presence of Wage Distortions: the Case of the US Auto and Steel Industries," *International Economic Review* 34 (1993):833–51.

Rutherford, Thomas and David Tarr, "Trade Liberalization, Product Variety and Growth in a Small Open Economy: a Quantitative Assessment," *Journal of International Economics* 56 (2002):247–72.

World Bank, *Economic Aspects of Increasing Energy Prices to Border Levels in the Islamic Republic of Iran*, report 1980IRN, Washington, DC (1999).

World Bank, *Trade and foreign exchange policies in Iran: reform agenda, economic implications and impact on the poor*, report No. 22953, Washington, DC (2001). Available at http://imagebank3.worldbank.org

Notes

1. For more details on the institutional background to the trade, exchange rate, and energy sectors, see World Bank (1999, 2002).
2. There is an intergovernmental committee led by the Ministry of Commerce that is responsible for tariffication of nontariff barriers. It decides on the timing of products to be converted to tariff barriers and recommends the equivalent tariff level. Of the 5313 tariff lines in the Iranian code, almost 1900 tariff lines had had the nontariff barriers removed by end 2000.
3. This will also be an important step in the process of entering the WTO, since as a practical matter acceding countries in recent years have been required to have low to moderate tariff barriers in order to gain admission to the WTO.
4. In the spring of 2002, the government of Iran officially unified the exchange rate. The change, however, was one of transparency, rather than a change in incentives that will affect resource allocation. For example, the Wheat Organization will continue to receive its foreign exchange at the rate of 1750 to the dollar from the central bank, but the government was to provide an on-budget payment to the central bank in 2002/03 to compensate for the subsidy. It is expected that the central bank will also receive an on-budget payment for the other categories of imports that have received officially allocated foreign exchange (e.g., national defense, pharmaceuticals, and the investment projects of the state-owned enterprises).
5. Welfare estimates are Hicksian equivalent variation reported as a percentage of Iranian consumption (for aggregate welfare) or as a percentage of household consumption in the case of individual households. Iranian consumption is about 37% of Iranian GDP in our dataset. Thus, the welfare gains as a percentage of GDP are about 37 hundredths of the numbers reported for welfare as a percentage of consumption.
6. Two percent of consumption is about 0.8% of GDP. Thus, changes in the tariff rates alone produce results broadly consistent with estimates of the impact of trade liberalization in constant-returns-to-scale models.
7. Examples of constant-returns-to-scale models with estimates of welfare gains from trade liberalization of less than 1% of GDP include de Melo and Tarr (1990, 1992, 1993) and Harrison et al. (1997a, b, forthcoming). Imperfect competition and product variety, however, can result in much larger estimated gains (Rutherford and Tarr, 2002).
8. See Jensen and Tarr (2002, appendix) for an explanation of the distortions in energy.
9. There are also some small fees, the most notable of which is the registration fee at the Ministry of Commerce. These fees, however, are collectively still quite small relative to the import duty and the CBT.
10. In addition there are some exemptions from the payment of import taxes, such as duty drawback.
11. Iran intends to disaggregate some of the tariff lines, introducing tariff lines at the eight- or possibly ten-digit level to reflect national needs.
12. Provided licenses are routinely issued within ten working days of application for the import license, licensing is not considered a nontariff barrier under WTO rules.
13. Several sectors in our model are combinations of subsectors. Sometimes, one subsector may receive import subsidies, while another subsector receives no import subsidies, but is pro-

tected by licenses. In these cases, we report the tariff equivalence of the nontariff barrier as the tariff equivalent rate which applies on the protected subsector times its share of the overall sector.

14. Debt repayment (both central government and individual enterprise) also qualifies for foreign exchange at the official exchange rate.

15. We employed Customs Department mimeo data to calculate the share of imports in the farming and food products categories that are comprised of subsidized commodities. For customs valuation purposes, all imports are valued at the official exchange rate. The government intends to value all imports at the rate of exchange from the Tehran Stock Exchange.

16. Of course, the *quantity* of foreign exchange demanded by the government for national defense will have a crowding-out effect on other sectors of the economy, so the decision on how much to spend on national defense is certainly important for foreign exchange and other reasons.

17. We obtained data from the Iranian Ministry of Oil on the domestic consumption price of the four energy products and the world price in 1999/2000.

18. There are no exports of liquid gas, gasoline, kerosene, gas oil, electricity, construction, and postal services in the initial equilibrium. Thus, the requirements for the CET assumption are not satisfied, and we assume that the output of these four sectors cannot be exported.

19. It is an arbitrary choice to group households according to equal numbers as we have done here, or according to an income level. The results should not be affected by the choice.

20. The trade and exchange rate reforms tend to favor the farming, sugar, and weaving and leather products sectors. These sectors should intensively use unskilled labor, the key source of income for the poorest households. This might allow us to predict that the poor would be expected to do no worse than we have estimated from these reforms.

21. This was the process employed in Jordan in the 1990s, where food subsidies were converted initially to a payment to all households, but became targeted to only the poor over several years. Iran has in place an identification card system which could be used as a basis for providing the subsidies.

22. The OPEC quota on oil exports is typically not binding on Iran.

23. Tariffs are a uniform 15% in this scenario except for petroleum products. We assume that the tariffs on petroleum products are part of energy policy that we analyze separately.

24. Even fuel oil exports decline, since the real exchange appreciation of 26% results in a larger decline in the domestic price of exports than in the price of domestic fuel oil products.

25. We have estimated the amount by which the distribution scheme would have to be significantly anti-poor for the poorest household to be no better off than under the status quo. For tariffication with rent dissipation, the share of the fiscal surplus distributed back to the poor would have to be 0.1% (as opposed to an equal share of 3.8%). For exchange rate unification, the share would have to be 0.4% (as opposed to an equal share of 3.8%).

Part IV
Regionalism

THE WORLD BANK ECONOMIC REVIEW, VOL. 16, NO. 1 49–79

Trade Policy Options for Chile: The Importance of Market Access

Glenn W. Harrison, Thomas F. Rutherford, and David G. Tarr

This article uses a multisector, multicountry, computable general equilibrium model to examine Chile's strategy of "additive regionalism"—negotiating bilateral free trade agreements with all of its significant trading partners. Taking Chile's regional arrangements bilaterally, only its agreements with Northern partners provide sufficient market access to overcome trade diversion costs. Due to preferential market access, however, additive regionalism is likely to provide Chile with gains that are many multiples of the static welfare gains from unilateral free trade. At least one partner country loses from each of the regional agreements considered, and excluded countries as a group always lose. Gains to the world from global free trade are estimated to be vastly larger than gains from any of the regional arrangements.

The analysis of regional trade arrangements is typically conducted in the framework of trade creation versus trade diversion, under which preferential tariff reduction is welfare inferior to nonpreferential tariff reduction. However, Wonnacott and Wonnacott (1981) show that regional trade arrangements could produce more gains due to improved market access to trading partners. The logical extension of this argument is that if a country negotiated free trade agreements with all of its trade partners, it would end up with zero effective tariffs on all imports, or free trade, despite the legal existence of positive most-favored-nation (MFN) tariffs. In the process, it would achieve preferential access to its partners' markets. Hence, without transition dynamics, this strategy may produce gains that are considerably larger than unilateral free trade.

We call the process of sequentially negotiating bilateral free trade agreements with all significant trading partners "additive regionalism." There is at least one country, Chile, that is pursuing a clearly articulated strategy of additive regionalism.[1] Does additive regionalism dominate free trade for Chile? If so, by how much?

The government of Chile has successfully concluded a free trade area (FTA) with MERCOSUR and is seeking a free trade agreement with the North American

Glenn W. Harrison is Dewey H. Johnson Professor of Economics at the University of South Carolina and Thomas F. Rutherford is Associate Professor in the Department of Economics at the University of Colorado. David G. Tarr is Lead Economist in the Development Economics Research Group at the World Bank; his e-mail address is dtarr@worldbank.org.

1. Mexico, Singapore, and, to a lesser extent, MERCOSUR may be following the same strategy.

Free Trade Agreement (NAFTA).[2] Moreover, the government of Chile is attempting to add the European Union, the rest of South America, and several other countries to its network of free trade arrangements.[3]

It is well known that most results regarding the welfare effects of regional arrangements are typically ambiguous at the theoretical level and that many questions are quantitative rather than qualitative. Thus, we employ an 11-region global computable general equilibrium (CGE) model to examine quantitatively the network of preferential arrangements that Chile is negotiating as well as unilateral trade policy options in Chile. In addition, we estimate the impact of global free trade as a reference point. Our model includes the Chilean economy as well as the economies of Argentina, Brazil, Mexico, the United States, Canada, Central America, the rest of South America, the European Union, Japan, and an aggregate for the rest of the world. Consequently, we are able to estimate the impact on partner and excluded countries from each of the agreements we evaluate.

Critics of Chile's additive regionalism strategy, such as Donoso and Hachette (1996), argue that agreements with Southern countries are unlikely to be beneficial and that it is not worth delaying the benefits of unilateral and multilateral tariff liberalization to pursue these agreements. They argue that only agreements with the European Union, the United States, or Japan offer sufficient access to be worth pursuing. Advocates for the government's strategy, however, believe that there are gains to be achieved from agreements with smaller Southern countries as well. They also argue, as in Butelmann and Meller (1995), that additive regionalism will progressively reduce trade diversion costs, lower the effective average tariff in Chile, and provide considerably improved market access. Furthermore, they note that Chile can unilaterally lower its external tariff while simultaneously pursuing additive regionalism to further reduce trade diversion costs.

We find that the results for NAFTA, MERCOSUR, and especially additive regionalism all point to the crucial importance of improved market access in preferential trading areas. Considered bilaterally, we find that trade diversion costs do indeed dominate the welfare effects of these agreements unless sufficient market access is obtained in partner countries (or third-country tariffs are lowered).

The results support the view that North–South agreements (for example, Chile with the United States or the European Union) are likely to provide sufficient market access to be beneficial, whereas the results for our South–South agreement (Chile-MERCOSUR) suggest the opposite. Agreements that include a Northern

2. MERCOSUR is a customs union between Argentina, Brazil, Paraguay, and Uruguay. Paraguay and Uruguay are too small to be included as separate countries in the dataset we employ, so our MERCOSUR region excludes them. In a FTA, partner countries eliminate tariffs and export taxes or subsidies against each other but retain separate tariffs against third countries. In a customs union, partner regions adopt a common external tariff. Chile has rejected a customs union with MERCOSUR. Although negotiations for Chile's membership in NAFTA have stalled, many commentators believe that Chile will eventually become the next member of NAFTA.

3. As of early 2001, Chile had reached preferential trade agreements with at least 15 countries.

partner increase the welfare of the members of the group in aggregate; only the Chile-MERCOSUR agreement results in net losses for the members as a group. However, Chile can unilaterally lower the external tariff, reducing trade diversion, so that even its agreement with MERCOSUR is beneficial.[4]

We find that Chile's additive regionalism strategy of combining free trade agreements with four regions—NAFTA, MERCOSUR, the European Union, and rest of South America—produces welfare gains for Chile that are many multiples of the value of unilateral free trade if it were to attain tariff-free access to all these markets. This provides support for the theoretical insight of Wonnacott and Wonnacott (1981). However, if the most highly protected sectors in the European Union and rest of South America are excluded from the agreements, the gains are dramatically reduced.[5]

We estimate that at least one of Chile's potential partners in its additive regionalism strategy will lose in all of the options we evaluate. Adding the rest of South America to its network of agreements would substantially improve Chile's preferential access and welfare but would significantly reduce the real income of the rest of South America, which would suffer large trade diversion losses with very little improved market access. Theory, intuition, and experience indicate that preferential arrangements are unlikely to be implemented if the partner countries do not also expect to gain. Nonetheless, the gains for Chile remain substantial relative to unilateral free trade if it could successfully negotiate these agreements with full market access.

Excluded regions are always estimated to lose from any of the preferential arrangements we consider. Thus, where there are gains to partner countries from preferential arrangements, they come at least partly at the expense of excluded regions.

The gains to the world from global free trade are estimated to be between US$199 billion and $456 billion per year. These gains to the world vastly exceed the gains from any of the regional arrangements. These results emphasize the continuing importance of multilateral liberalization.

Because Chile starts with a relatively efficient uniform tariff of 11 percent, we estimate that it can obtain only small additional gains from improving the efficiency of its resource allocation by further *unilateral* reduction of its tariffs.[6] We show that a country like Chile that starts with a uniform tariff will typically have

4. Chile has enacted legislation that will lower its external tariff from 11 to 6 percent in stages, as suggested by our analysis. Thus our estimates could be viewed as an ex post assessment of the policy of lowering the external tariff. In fact, the vice president of the Chilean Central Bank used estimates from an earlier version of our study in his testimony before the Chilean Parliament in favor of lowering the external tariff.

5. In fact, the experiences of some Mediterranean countries (Morocco, Tunisia, and Turkey) in their preferential trade agreements with the European Union suggest that the highly protected agricultural sectors are likely to be excluded from such an agreement.

6. This conclusion ignores the dynamic gains from trade liberalization, which could lead to much larger gains.

the gains from joining a customs union reduced if it must adopt a nonuniform structure. Conversely, if joining a customs union is a movement toward uniformity, the gains are likely to be augmented.[7] In general, this result indicates that the relative uniformity of the preexisting tariff structure for a country and the proposed common external tariff of any customs union, must be compared on a case-by-case basis to ascertain whether welfare gains will actually be achieved.

We find that the benefits of trade liberalization or regional trade arrangements are considerably reduced if tariff revenue must be replaced by distorting alternative taxes. Similarly, in our optimal tariff calculations, we find that unilateral trade liberalization can proceed to lower tariff levels if efficient replacement taxes are in place.[8]

When there is an optimal tariff, as there is in this model, the amount by which a country can reduce its tariff is limited by the distortions of the replacement tax. Consequently, we have produced an updated estimate of the collected value-added tax (VAT) rates by sector in Chile.[9] We show that Chile could reduce its legal VAT rates to about 50 percent of present levels and improve its welfare by 0.3 percent of gross domestic product (GDP) if it were able to eliminate evasion and collect the VAT uniformly.[10] These gains are significant when compared to unilateral trade liberalization options. We find that the optimal tariff in Chile is almost double with the VAT rate that is currently collected, compared with a VAT that collects taxes at equal rates across sectors.

Section I describes the model and data. Section II explains the policy results for Chile. Section III examines the impact on partner and excluded countries of Chile's agreements as well as the impact of global free trade.

I. A Multiregional Trade Model

General Features

The quantitative model developed to evaluate the trade policy options facing Chile is multi-regional and multi-sectoral. Table 1 lists the 11 regions included explicitly in the model, as well as the 24 sectors included in each region. The general

7. Two other countries with uniform tariffs that may install a nonuniform tariff of a customs union are the Kyrgyz Republic and Estonia. The Kyrgyz Republic has a uniform tariff of 10 percent and has in principle agreed to join in a customs union with Russia, Belarus, and Kazakhstan. The Kyrgyz Republic has not implemented the common external tariff, however, because of fears of the costs of the nonuniformity of the Russian tariff, which is the present common external tariff. See Michalopoulos and Tarr (1997) for details. Estonia also has a uniform tariff of zero and is one of the five transition economies the European Union has designated as candidate countries for accession. Estonian authorities have considerable concerns, however, about the costs of imposing the European Union's common external tariff, especially in the highly protected sectors.

8. However, with low elasticities, there is an adverse terms-of-trade effect that mitigates the welfare gains from reduced costs of trade diversion.

9. See Harrison, Rutherford, and Tarr (1997b).

10. In addition, we eliminate the output tax, which applies primarily to energy, beverages, and tobacco.

TABLE 1. Commodities, Regions, and Factors of Production in the Chile Model

Abbreviation	Meaning
Commodities	
WHT	Wheat
GRO	Other grains
NGC	Nongrain crops
WOL	Wool and other livestock
FRS	Forestry
FSH	Fishing
ENR	Energy products
MIN	Mineral products
MEA	Meat products
MIL	Milk products
FOO	Other food products
B_T	Beverages and tobacco
TEX	Textiles and apparel and leather products
LUM	Lumber and wood
PPP	Pulp and paper
CRP	Chemicals rubber and plastics
I_S	Primary ferrous metals
NFM	Nonferrous metals
FMP	Fabricated metal products
TRN	Transport industries
MAC	Machinery and equipment
T_T	Trade and transport
SER	Services
CGD	Savings good
Regions	
CHL	Chile
ARG	Argentina
BRA	Brazil
RSA	Rest of South America
USA	United States of America
CAN	Canada
MEX	Mexico
CAM	Central America and Caribbean
E_U	European Union 15
JPN	Japan
ROW	Rest of world
Factors	
LND	Land
LAB	Labor
CAP	Capital

specification of this model follows our earlier multiregional model of the effects of the Uruguay Round.[11] The most important differences are the inclusion of data for Chile, updated tariff rates for Argentina and Brazil, and more recent data for all other regions. We adopt a multiregion model rather than a small-open-economy model because we need to consider the possible effects on Chile of a reduction in its import tariffs on other MERCOSUR members. Crucially, we also need to account for the "market access" effects on Chilean exports of a reduction of import tariffs by MERCOSUR, NAFTA, or other regions with which Chile agrees to a free trade agreement either separately or collectively.

Although the general theory of the welfare effects of preferential trading arrangements allows for the impact of changes in partner country tariffs on the home country's terms of trade,[12] some empirical approaches to evaluating preferential trading arrangements ignore them.[13] Our framework allows us to evaluate explicitly the importance to Chile of improved market access to regions such as MERCOSUR and NAFTA as well as losses Chile may suffer as partner countries raise export prices to Chile.

An important feature of the Chilean economy is that its tariff rate is a uniform 11 percent across all traded sectors. The exception to this is the variable levy system for wheat, sugar, and edible oils. Estimates reveal that the variable levy system has resulted in an average level of protection for these three products in excess of 11 percent.[14] We ignore the variable levy system, which will slightly bias downward our estimated gains from unilateral trade liberalization. Harrison, Rutherford, and Tarr (1997b) describe the key data that are important in the analysis.

Argentine tariffs are virtually identical to Brazilian tariffs. In the case of the United States, the tariff estimates include the tariff equivalents of the nontariff barriers, which are quite important in the sectors with high tariffs. If Chile forms an FTA with MERCOSUR or NAFTA, Chilean exporters will not face these tariffs, but outside exporters to these regions will. Thus, these data are crucial in assessing the value of increased access that Chile will obtain from MERCOSUR and NAFTA, respectively.

11. Harrison, Rutherford, and Tarr (1997c). The Web site http://dmsweb.badm.sc.edu/glenn/ur_pub.htm provides access to the model and related publications.

12. See Wooton (1986) and Harrison, Rutherford, and Wooton (1989, 1993).

13. An example is the approach adopted by Bond (1996). He develops a simple general equilibrium specification of the effects on Chile of these preferential trading arrangements with an impressive level of detail with respect to tariff data. However, his results for Chile joining NAFTA differ significantly from ours because his CGE model does not incorporate the impact on Chile of access to NAFTA markets.

14. The variable levy system is applied by examining monthly prices over the previous 2.5 years for wheat and 50 months for sugar. The distribution is truncated at the top and the bottom by an equal percentage (about 15 percent). The range of the resulting truncated distribution determines the upper and lower bounds. A tariff surcharge or reduction of the tariff below the 11 percent rate is applied if the price in the present month is below or above the bounds. Because the system is not based on a domestic support price, its impact varies enormously from year to year. Valdes (1996, p. 55) estimates that between 1985 and 1995 the nominal protection rate for sugar ranged from 6 to 98 percent, and the nominal protection rate for wheat ranged from 45 to −10 percent (see also Quiroz and Valdes 1993).

We also estimate the rates of collected VAT in each industry and the tax on gross output, respectively. These rates are estimated using the procedures explained in Harrison, Rutherford, and Tarr (1997b, appendix A). The different rates of VAT across sectors arise mainly because of evasion of the VAT. The two largest sectors in Chile, trade and transport services and other services, have a combined 61 percent of value added and are the sectors with the lowest rate of collected VAT (about 3 percent as opposed to about 17 percent for most Chilean manufacturing).

Formal Specification

THE MODEL. The general specification of the model follows our earlier work on the Uruguay Round. We concentrate here on what we call our base model, which is static and assumes constant returns to scale. Except for the fact that imports and exports are distinguished by many regions, the structure of the model within any country is very close to the basic model of de Melo and Tarr (1992).

Production entails the use of intermediate inputs and primary factors (labor, capital, and land). Primary factors are mobile across sectors within a region but are internationally immobile. We assume constant elasticity of substitution (CES) production functions for value added and Leontief production functions for intermediates and the value-added composite. Output is differentiated between domestic output and exports, but exports are not differentiated by country of destination.

Each region has a single representative consumer that maximizes utility, as well as a single government agent. In Harrison, Rutherford, and Tarr (1997b, appendix C), we formally characterize the demand structure and elasticities that are critical to the results. Demand is characterized by nested CES utility functions for each agent, which allows multistage budgeting. Demand at the top level, for the composite "Armington" aggregate of each of the 24 goods in table 1, is Cobb-Douglas. Consumers first choose how much of each Armington aggregate good to consume, such as wheat, subject to aggregate incomes and composite prices of the aggregate goods. The Armington aggregate good is in turn a CES composite of domestic production and aggregate imports. Consumers decide how much to spend on aggregate imports and the domestic good subject to the prior decision of how much income will be spent on this sector, and preferences for aggregate imports and domestic goods are represented by a CES utility function. Finally, consumers decide how to allocate expenditures across imports from the 10 other regions based on their CES utility function for imports from different regions and income allocated to consumption on imports from the previous higher-level decision.

DATA AND ELASTICITIES. Except for tariff data and domestic tax data, the data employed to calibrate the model come primarily from the Global Trade Analysis Project (GTAP) database documented in Gehlhar and others (1996). We use the preliminary release of version 3 of this database, current as of May 1996.

The 11-region version of the model retains all regions of the GTAP database that are directly relevant to our policy simulations. The full GTAP database contains 37 sectors.[15]

We generally assume that the lower-level elasticity of substitution between imports from different regions, σ_{MM}, is 30 and that the higher-level elasticity between aggregate imports and domestic production, σ_{DM}, is 15. We refer to these values as our central elasticities. Econometric studies, such as those of Reinert and Roland-Holst (1992) and Shiells and Reinert (1993), suggest lower values. However, Reidel (1988) and Athukorala and Reidel (1994) argue that when the model is properly specified, the demand elasticities are not statistically different from infinity and their point estimates are close to the central elasticity values we have chosen. Moreover, elasticities would be expected to increase over time, and this model presumes an adjustment of about 10 years, a rather long period in the context of these econometric estimates.

To be clear, a value of $\sigma_{MM} = 30$ means that if Chile tried to raise its prices by 1 percent on world markets relative to an average of aggregate imports, Chilean imports would decline relative to aggregate imports by 30 percent. Given that there may be some economists who would prefer lower elasticity estimates, we also perform most of our important policy simulations with $\sigma_{MM} = 8$ and $\sigma_{DM} = 4$. We refer to these as our low elasticities. A high-elasticity scenario for a small open economy such as Chile would be a specification with still less market power for exports, such as would occur in the popular theoretical models of international trade where goods are homogeneous.

The elasticity of transformation between exports and domestic production is assumed to be about four for each sector. Elasticities of substitution between primary factors of production are taken from Harrison and others (1993) and generally reflect econometric estimates for the United States. These estimates are relatively low for primary goods, around unity for manufacturing goods, and elastic for tertiary goods. We assume fixed coefficients between all intermediates and value added.

DISTORTIONS. All distortions are represented as ad valorem price wedges. Border protection estimates combine tariff protection and the tariff equivalents of nontariff barriers. For Brazil and Argentina, these data were estimated by Reincke in Harrison, Rutherford, and Tarr (1997b, appendix B). Otherwise, these data are taken from the GTAP database. They are presented in Harrison, Rutherford, and Tarr (2001, table 9). Other distortions include factor taxes in production, VATs, export subsidies and voluntary export restraints (represented as ad valo-

15. Our aggregation to 24 sectors was undertaken in a manner that ensured that those sectors with significant rates of protection (in the principal trading partners of Chile) are retained as individual sectors. That is, we aggregated sectors that are not important in trade or that have low rates of protection. Aggregation may significantly change the results in applied trade policy analysis, but this type of aggregation results in quite small aggregation bias.

rem export tax equivalents). These are also taken from the GTAP database, except for domestic distortion data in Chile. The latter were estimated for this exercise by Soloaga in Harrison, Rutherford, and Tarr (1997b, appendix A). Lump-sum replacement taxes or subsidies ensure that government revenue in each region stays constant at real benchmark levels. However, for Chile, we capture the marginal efficiency cost of the government having to raise extra revenue through a distortionary domestic tax system. For developing countries, these costs could be quite significant because the revenue losses from trade reform could be sizable.

SOLUTION ALGORITHM. The model is formulated using the GAMS-MPSGE software developed by Rutherford (1999) and solved using the PATH algorithm of Ferris and Munson (2000). Although the model has 11 regions and 24 sectors and is large by historical standards, it is smaller than our Uruguay Round model. Use of demand elasticities as high as those we employ could pose numerical problems in general, but this model solved without difficulty.

II. POLICY RESULTS FOR CHILE

We first discuss how Chile will replace the revenue it will lose from lowering its tariffs and the welfare implications of these options. We then discuss the results regarding the preferential trade area policy options and examine how Chile may use unilateral tariff reduction to optimize its trade policy. Finally, we examine the effects of Chile's strategy of additive regionalism.

The Role of the Replacement Tax

Because Chile is reducing tariffs in most of our scenarios, there is a revenue loss to the government. We impose an equi-revenue requirement in all simulations and stipulate explicitly how the additional tax revenue will be generated. We employ the existing VAT, a uniform VAT, or a lump-sum tax.

WELFARE EFFECTS OF THE REPLACEMENT TAX. Collection of the existing VAT is not uniform in Chile. According to the estimates in Harrison, Rutherford, and Tarr (1997b, table 3), it ranges from 0 percent up to 18 percent across sectors. Hence, raising revenue through the VAT generates distortions: when the VAT is increased, resources move into less highly taxed sectors. This reduces any possible gains from the trade policy change. Results for welfare using the existing VAT are presented in column 1 of table 2.

In fact, we estimate the "marginal cost of public funds" of the existing VAT in Chile to equal 7.6 percent. This implies that consumers and producers will have to be taxed 1,076 pesos for the government to receive 1,000 pesos. The 76 pesos are a welfare loss to the Chilean economy.

We also calculate the marginal cost of public funds of the Chilean tariff, which equals 18.5 percent. Despite the fact that the tariff is uniform across sectors, and

TABLE 2. Welfare and Government Revenue Results for Chile's Trade Policy Options

Policy simulation		With replacement taxes as					Combined effect of uniform VAT and trade policy[b]	
		Existing VAT		Uniform VAT[a]		Lump sum		
		% change in welfare[c]	% change in VAT[d]	% change in welfare[c]	Tariff revenue % of GDP	% change in welfare[c]	% change in welfare[c]	Tariff revenue % of GDP
		(1)	(2)	(3)	(4)	(5)	(6)	(7)
1. FTA with MERCOSUR	(central elasticities)	−0.62	45	−0.40	1.7	−0.43	−0.19	1.8
	(low elasticities)	0.04	17	0.07	2.7	0.08	0.19	2.7
2. Customs union with MERCOSUR	(central elasticities)	−0.95	52	−0.74	1.3	−0.73	−0.62	1.2
	(low elasticities)	−0.20	21	−0.22	2.5	−0.17	−0.14	2.5
3. FTA with NAFTA	(central elasticities)	0.82	48	1.03	0.9	1.04	1.23	0.9
	(low elasticities)	0.30	26	0.31	2.1	0.38	0.43	2.1
4. Zero tariffs on NAFTA imports,	(central elasticities)	−1.11	62	−0.92	0.7	−0.83	−0.64	0.7
no improved access	(low elasticities)	−0.47	30	−0.45	2.0	−0.41	−0.33	2.0
5. FTA with MERCOSUR and	(central elasticities)	0.12	49	0.44	1.7	0.35	0.61	1.7
6% external tariff	(low elasticities	0.06	38	0.11	1.7	0.13	0.21	1.7
6. FTA with NAFTA and	(central elasticities)	1.46	45	1.72	1.1	1.70	1.89	1.1
6% external tariff	(low elasticities)	0.41	41	0.45	1.4	0.49	0.55	1.4
7. Reduce external tariff to 8%	(central elasticities)	0.02	16	0.12	2.9	0.10	0.41	2.9
	(low elasticities)	−0.11	17	−0.08	2.7	−0.06	0.03	2.7
8. Reduce external tariff to 6%	(central elasticities)	0.01	28	0.16	2.3	0.11	0.43	2.3
	(low elasticities)	−0.18	30	−0.14	2.1	−0.14	−0.04	2.1
9. Reduce external tariff to zero	(central elasticities)	−0.26	76	0.02	0	0.09	0.21	0
	(low elasticities)	−0.54	72	−0.45	0	−0.42	−0.37	0

[a]In these scenarios we first create an equilibrium with a uniform VAT, no other domestic taxes, then evaluate the "pure" effects of the trade policy.

[b]These scenarios combine the impacts of the trade policy simulation with going to a uniform VAT and elimination of the domestic output tax, government revenues held constant.

[c]Percentage change in Hicksian equivalent variation as a percentage of GDP.

[d]Required equiproportional increase in the VAT rate across all sectors to keep government revenues unchanged.

therefore imposes no intersectoral distortion costs, the Chilean tariff imposes a higher distortion cost than the VAT because the tariff favors domestic production over imports.

Column 5 of table 2 shows the results of employing a lump-sum tax as the replacement tax. This tax avoids the distortions of a nonuniform VAT because consumer income is taxed in a fixed amount independently of consumer choices. Hence there are no resource allocation effects from the revenue replacement tax instrument. The results show that there is an added welfare cost of using the VAT, as compared with the lump-sum alternative.

Finally, column 3 of table 2 shows the results of using a uniform VAT. In these scenarios, we first counterfactually create an equilibrium in which all other domestic taxes and subsidies are zero and the VAT is uniform. The impact we evaluate is then solely due to the change in trade policy. Because all sectors are taxed and there is no labor-leisure choice, there is no way to take an action that will lower the tax. In other words, there are no resource allocation effects and the uniform VAT is essentially equivalent to a lump-sum or distortionless tax in our model. In addition, any "second-best" interaction effects of distortions between the tariff and the existing VAT will be removed if we start with a uniform VAT and no other distortions (for this reason, the results for the lump-sum tax and the uniform VAT may differ). In these scenarios, we equalize the VAT across sectors and solve for the level of the VAT that is required to compensate for the lost revenue.

REVENUE EFFECTS. Column 2 of table 2 presents the equi-proportional increase in the VAT required to keep government revenue constant. For example, with central elasticities, an FTA with MERCOSUR will require an increase of 45 percent in the VAT rate across sectors. Thus, if the collected VAT rate is 10 percent in a sector, the collected VAT rate will have to increase to 14.5 percent. With central elasticities, there is a strong substitution away from imports that pay tariffs in favor of imports from partner countries that are tariff free. In this case, the revenue requirements for the VAT are quite high to compensate for the lost tariff revenues. With low trade elasticities, the revenue requirement for the VAT is much smaller, ranging from increases between 17 and 26 percent in the three basic preferential trade arrangement scenarios presented in rows 1–3 of table 2.

In columns 4 and 7 of table 2, we show tariff revenues collected in the new equilibrium as a percentage of GDP. In our initial equilibrium, tariff revenues are equal to about 3.6 percent of GDP, but in the preferential trade area scenarios (rows 1–3), they fall to between 0.9 and 2.7 percent of GDP. Thus, in the preferential trade area scenarios, tariff revenues fall to between 25 and 75 percent of the original levels. The loss of tariff revenue is higher with NAFTA (because NAFTA is a larger share of Chilean imports than MERCOSUR) and higher with central elasticities because of the greater trade diversion. The VAT revenues as a percentage of GDP initially constitute about 9 percent of GDP. Depending on the preferential trade area and elasticities, the tariff loss is between 0.9 and 2.7 percent of

GDP. Hence, if the VAT is employed as the replacement tax, it will be necessary for VAT revenues to increase by about 10 to 30 percent.

Some may question whether the implied increase in the VAT is too high. To provide intuition for the model implications for the VAT, consider a particular scenario in which the lost tariff revenue is about 2.5 percent of GDP, as in row 6 of table 2 with central elasticities. Table 2 estimates that the VAT rate will have to increase by 45 percent to a legal rate of about 26 percent. In 1994, the legal VAT rate of 18 percent generated VAT revenues of about 9 percent of GDP, so the legal rate was twice the collected rate. Assuming no change in the rate of VAT evasion, it would appear necessary to raise the VAT by 5 percent to generate 2.5 percent of GDP (that is, from 18 to 23 percent).

The reason that the model predicts a required increase of the legal VAT rate to 26 percent and not 23 percent is that an increase in the tax will induce a shift away from the highly taxed sectors and an erosion of the tax base. Given our model parameters, increases in the VAT continue to generate additions in revenue within the range under consideration. But it is possible that evasion of the VAT could increase. The required legal VAT rate would then increase and the distortion costs of revenue replacement would be still higher than we have estimated. It is possible that the VAT is not a feasible tax for generating considerably more revenue without further reform in collection procedures.[16] Given the uncertainties over rates of evasion of VAT in Chile, these estimates should be taken as indicative of revenue requirements rather than as precise recommendations for the VAT rate. In fact, the next subsection emphasizes the importance of uniformity of collections.

Options for Preferential Trade Areas

RESULTS IN TABLE 2. Table 2 presents the overall welfare results for the trade policy options. Harrison, Rutherford, and Tarr (1997b) give more detailed results on output, imports, and exports for the main scenarios, with central elasticities. Welfare impacts are presented as a percentage of Chile's GDP. They represent changes on a recurring, annual basis, so a 1 percent welfare gain should be interpreted as a 1 percent increase in real income *each year in the future*.

The first row of table 2 presents the results from the scenario where Chile forms an FTA with MERCOSUR. It assumes that each of the MERCOSUR countries represented in the model, Argentina and Brazil, reduces its tariffs, export subsidies, or taxes on its trade with Chile to zero and that Chile does the same for its

16. To quantify these ideas, we simulated Chile's FTA with MERCOSUR and NAFTA, assuming that the services and trade and transportation sectors cannot have their collected VAT rates increased due to evasion. (These are the sectors with low rates of VAT collection and where evasion of the VAT may prevent additional collections; together they produce about 65 percent of Chilean value added.) With central elasticities, the welfare loss in this case from the FTA with MERCOSUR is increased to –0.60 percent of GDP and the gains from the FTA with NAFTA are reduced to 0.12 percent of GDP. As expected, the required rate of VAT increase jumps to about 75 percent.

trade with MERCOSUR. Chile does not adopt the common external tariff of MERCOSUR in this scenario.

The second scenario, shown in row 2 of table 2, represents Chile joining MERCOSUR as part of the customs union. In addition to the requirements of the scenario in row 1, in this case Chile adopts the common external tariff of MERCOSUR. Although Chile has not joined the MERCOSUR customs union, it is a potential policy option, so we evaluate it in this scenario. For simplicity, we assume that the common external tariff that Chile adopts is the import tariff structure that Brazil currently has with the countries that are not in MERCOSUR.[17]

In the third scenario, in row 3 of table 2, Chile forms an FTA with NAFTA. In row 4, primarily to help understand the results, we evaluate the consequences of a free trade agreement between Chile and NAFTA in which Chile does not obtain improved access to the NAFTA market. After discussion of these scenarios, we introduce further simulations to help explain the results and evaluate modified options.

The effects on welfare are dependent on both how Chile chooses to replace the lost tariff revenues and on assumed elasticities. Chile's preferential trade policy options with MERCOSUR lead to a loss of welfare with our preferred central trade elasticities and negligible gains or losses with low trade elasticities. With central trade elasticities, the trade diversion costs of an agreement with MERCOSUR typically dominate the trade creation effects. Moreover, based on the MERCOSUR external tariff, preferential access to the MERCOSUR markets is insufficient to overcome this welfare loss in Chile's markets. Welfare losses are lower with lower assumed elasticities because there is less trade diversion when Chile's consumers are less willing to substitute MERCOSUR's products for those of the rest of the world.[18]

The results indicate that the customs union with MERCOSUR is an inferior outcome for Chile compared with a free trade agreement with MERCOSUR. MERCOSUR's tariff structure is diverse compared with Chile's tariff, which is uniform. Because the welfare costs of trade restrictions tend to increase disproportionately with the height of the tariff, Chile is better off with its own uniform

17. This tariff structure is slightly different than the tariff structure shown for Argentina for two reasons. First, there are exceptions to the common external tariff for Argentina and Brazil, as both countries continue to adapt their tariff schedules over time to the agreed common external tariff. In addition, Argentina and Brazil could well have adopted exactly the same common external tariff at a detailed tariff line level, but have different trade shares across these tariff lines. With the different trade weights, the rates that appear in the GTAP database at the 24-sector level reflect differences in these trade patterns and need not reflect differences in the common external tariff at the detailed tariff line level. For ease of comparison, we also assume in our "Chile customs union with MERCOSUR" scenario that Argentina adopts the tariff of Brazil as its common external tariff. This provides a clean representation of the MERCOSUR customs union for our purposes.

18. These results are consistent with those of Donoso and Hachette (1996) and Muchnik, Errazuriz, and Dominguez (1996). Based on the latter's results, which focus on agriculture, Donoso and Hachette estimate that access to the MERCOSUR market would not offer significant gains to Chile. See also Valdes (1995).

tariff than with the common external tariff of the customs union.[19] That is, part of the costs to Chile of joining a customs union with MERCOSUR derive from the loss of tariff uniformity. Thus, one advantage of a free trade agreement for Chile as opposed to a customs union is that only the customs union requires the adoption of a common external tariff.

In comparing our results in rows 1–3 of table 2 regarding Chile's preferential trade area options, the most important result is that the FTA with NAFTA is beneficial to Chile, whereas the other options are likely to present problems.[20] To ascertain the source of the gain to Chile from a FTA with NAFTA, we performed the simulation in row 4, in which Chile lowers its tariffs against imports from NAFTA countries but does not obtain improved access in NAFTA markets. Although this is not a policy option that Chile would adopt, the results in row 4 show that Chile loses from preferential reduction of its tariffs against NAFTA countries without reciprocal access to NAFTA markets because the trade diversion dominates the trade creation.

To identify even more precisely the source of the access gains from the FTA with NAFTA, we performed a simulation in which access to only one sector was not obtained: nongrain crops. Our estimates of the tariff distortions suggest that the U.S. tariff is likely to be central in this sector: there is a 20 percent tariff on nongrain crops.[21] In other words, Chile applies zero tariffs against NAFTA imports, and NAFTA applies zero tariffs against imports from Chile in all sectors except nongrain crops. Although not shown in table 2, if Chile fails to obtain preferential access in nongrain crops, the welfare gains of 0.82 percent we ob-

19. "Ramsey optimal" tariffs will vary inversely with the elasticity of demand. Typically, however, departures from uniformity do not conform with Ramsey optimal rules, but rather with political economy considerations (see Panagariya and Rodrik 1993).

20. Coeymans and Larrain (1994), Reinert and Roland-Holst (1996), and Hinojosa-Ojeda, Lewis, and Robinson (1995) also find that Chile will gain from a FTA with NAFTA.

21. Although the GTAP database indicates that the U.S. tariff on nongrain crops is 47 percent, we have lowered this to 20 percent in our benchmark equilibrium for two reasons. First, we prefer updated estimates where possible. The most important nongrain crops for Chile are fruits and vegetables, and post–Uruguay Round tariff rates for these products in the U.S. market are the relatively modest figures cited in this note; the higher protection estimates for these products in the GTAP database (averaging 56 percent) were derived from an average of protection estimates in the 1989–94 period. Second, the U.S. protection on these products varies with the season. We have assumed that given production in the opposite hemispheres, when Chilean fruits and vegetables are ready for harvest and export to the United States, they would typically face U.S. tariffs that are in the low range of the seasonal tariffs applied by the United States. Products included in the nongrain crops category of the GTAP database (along with the estimated tariff and tariff equivalent of the nontariff barrier in the United States) are: sugar, 67 percent; oilseeds, including peanuts, 25 percent; coffee, cocoa, and tea, 0 percent; cotton, 31 percent; vegetables (fresh, 0–25 percent; frozen, 17.5–25 percent; dried, 25–35 percent, prepared and preserved, 13.6–14.7 percent); fruits (fresh, 0–20 percent; dehydrated, 0.6–2.2 percent; frozen, 0.7–14 percent; juices, 0–31.3 percent; jams and pastes, 7.0–35 percent; canned, 1.9–20 percent); and other nonfood crops (tobacco and jute), 19 percent. The reduced estimates are closer to the estimates of Butelmann and Meller (1995, p. 376). They report that Chilean fresh, frozen, and canned vegetables face MFN tariff rates in the United States ranging from 9.5 to 17.5 percent (with a few percentage point reductions for the former two categories where GSP treatment applies), and that Chilean fruits face U.S. MFN tariffs from 1 to 10 percent.

tained in the full-access case now drop to a welfare loss of 0.58 percent. Thus, access in nongrain crops is crucial to welfare gains from NAFTA.[22]

These results demonstrate the importance of improved access emphasized by Wonnacott and Wonnacott (1981). Our results show that Chile can gain more from an FTA with NAFTA than it can from global free trade. But Chile can expect to lose from any of the preferential trade agreements we have considered if there is no improvement in access to partner-country markets.

THE IMPORTANCE OF LOW UNIFORM TARIFFS. These results differ from several earlier numerical evaluations of preferential trading areas (Rutherford, Rutström, and Tarr 1997, Harrison, Rutherford, and Tarr 1997a). We speculate that part of the reason that trade diversion dominates trade creation in these estimates is that Chile has a low and uniform tariff. That is, the implementation of a preferential trade agreement in a country that starts with a dispersed tariff structure may result in a reduction in the dispersion of the tariff structure, although this is not true as a general proposition. Potential benefits from a reduction in the dispersion of the tariff, however, are ignored in more aggregated analyses of preferential trade arrangements.[23] To verify this intuition, we have counterfactually created an initial equilibrium in which Chile applies a 22 percent tariff on one-half of its imports and a zero tariff on all others, and then implemented the policy scenarios in rows 1–4 of table 2 (where we have employed existing VAT replacement and central elasticities). The sectors with high tariffs were selected at random, and the experiment was repeated 206 times. The means of the distributions for welfare as a percentage of GDP are as follows: FTA with MERCOSUR, –0.56 percent; customs union with MERCOSUR, –0.44 percent; FTA with NAFTA, 1.47 percent; and FTA with NAFTA but no improved access, –0.52 percent.

The gains of the FTA with NAFTA are significantly larger when based on the hypothetical nonuniform initial tariff structure. Similarly, the losses from the FTA with MERCOSUR are slightly smaller, reflecting a movement toward uniformity. But losses from a preferential reduction in tariffs toward the NAFTA markets remain unless access to the NAFTA market is obtained. These numerical results are consistent with the theoretical results of Hatta (1977), who found that countries will benefit from moving toward uniformity by simultaneously lowering the highest tariff and raising the lowest tariff.

22. Because U.S. protection in milk products is also high, we examined the impact of denial of improved access in NAFTA markets for Chilean products on both nongrain crops and milk products. Chile exports very little milk products, however, so the welfare result was only slightly more adverse for Chile (–0.60 percent of GDP with central elasticities and existing VAT replacement) relative to denial of Chilean access in nongrain crops alone.

23. There is value in further theoretical work into the generality of the impact of preferential arrangements on uniformity. Note also that in our model, elasticities are equal across sectors, so the Ramsey optimal tariff is uniform. A useful exercise would be to evaluate the impact of a preferential trade arrangement where we start from randomly selected elasticities across sectors and see how often Chile gains from preferential trade agreements as we use a large number of distinct sets of elasticities.

In this hypothetical experiment, we find that the ranking of the customs union with MERCOSUR versus the FTA with MERCOSUR is reversed compared with the actual situation represented in table 1. Although Chile still loses from both preferential trade agreements with MERCOSUR, it is intuitive that the customs union produces smaller losses than the FTA because the common external tariff of MERCOSUR is more uniform than the hypothetical Chilean tariff. In the actual situation of table 2, the customs union with MERCOSUR represents *a movement away from uniformity.*

Optimizing Chile's Trade Policy Options

We know from theory that Chile can reduce the trade diversion costs of preferential trade areas if it lowers its external tariff. Thus, a number of economists have recommended that a reduction in Chile's external tariff be combined with its free trade agreements.[24] In rows 5 and 6 of table 2, we evaluate the two FTA options with a simultaneous reduction in the tariff to 6 percent. In rows 7 and 8, we evaluate the impact of lowering the external tariff to 8 and 6 percent, respectively, on a multilateral basis. We evaluate going to global free trade in row 9.

Chile may have a low optimal tariff despite being a small country. If Chilean exports are differentiated from the products of other countries so that Chile in aggregate faces a downward-sloping demand curve for a product, even if individual Chilean producers do not perceive a downward-sloping demand curve, then there will be an optimal export tax to maximize Chilean export profits. The height of the optimal export tax will be inversely related to the elasticity of demand faced by Chile in its export markets, which is in turn determined by how substitutable Chile's products are with those of other countries.[25] In the limit, when Chilean products are perfect substitutes in all its export markets for products from all other countries, Chile has no ability to obtain a higher price by restricting its exports. In this case, the optimal export tax is zero.

Although Chile imposes virtually no export taxes, the Lerner symmetry theorem tells us that in general equilibrium import tariffs are equivalent to export taxes. The import tariff will tax all export sectors roughly uniformly. However, with product differentiation and many sectors, market power on exports differs across sectors and destination markets. Hence the import tariff is not as efficient an instrument as export taxes varying by sector and destination. Nonetheless, if export taxes are ruled out, there is a positive optimal import tariff. However, given the existence of a uniform tariff of 11 percent, we investigate both theoretically and numerically whether the optimal tariff is above or below it.

In our central elasticity scenarios, we have assumed that all countries have an elasticity of substitution between imports from different countries (σ_{MM}) equal

24. Such as Schiff and Sapelli (1996), Corbo (1966), and Leipziger and Winters (1996).

25. Individual competitive firms will price at their marginal costs, but because the country as a whole must accept a lower price to sell more, there is an optimal export tax that equates the marginal revenue received from exports equal to the marginal costs. The more elastic the demand, the lower the optimal export tax.

to 30. We show in Harrison, Rutherford, and Tarr (1997b, appendix C) that the optimal tariff t^* is bounded below by $t^* = \{[\sigma_{MM}/(\sigma_{MM} - 1)] - 1\}$. Thus, even with $\sigma_{MM} = 30$, the optimal tariff is over 3 percent; but in our low elasticity scenarios, with $\sigma_{MM} = 8$, the optimal tariff is over 14 percent.

Considering the preferential trade options in rows 5 and 6 of table 2, there is an expected increase in the estimated welfare gains compared with rows 1 and 3, respectively. With central elasticities, there is a significant improvement in welfare compared with an external tariff of 11 percent. With low elasticities, the adverse terms-of-trade effect of reducing tariffs mitigates the welfare gain from reducing the trade diversion costs. These results show that as long as Chile limits itself to an FTA, it can profit from the increased access it obtains in its partner countries without excessive trade diversion costs, provided it lowers its external tariff sufficiently. In particular, the results in row 5 show that the free trade agreement with MERCOSUR can be expected to yield benefits when the external tariff is lowered to 6 percent. By contrast, comparing rows 5 and 6, we observe that an agreement with NAFTA is worth a lot more than the one with MERCOSUR, largely due to the superior market access of NAFTA.

Rows 7 and 8 of table 2 present estimates of the welfare and replacement tax implications, respectively, to Chile of unilaterally lowering its external tariff. With central elasticities and distortionless domestic taxes (lump sum or uniform VAT), unilateral reduction of the tariff to 6 percent increases welfare, and there are further gains from reducing tariffs from 8 to 6 percent. With the existing VAT as the replacement tax, reducing the tariff to 8 percent increases welfare. However, the distortion costs of the VAT are sufficiently close to the tariff, so that in combination with the small adverse terms-of-trade effects, there are no further gains from tariff reduction below 8 percent. With a distortionless replacement tax, reduction of the external tariff to zero produces positive welfare gains compared with the tariff of 11 percent (row 9). However, because the gains are less than reduction to 6 percent (row 8), the optimal tariff is between 0 and 6 percent.[26]

With existing VAT replacement, there is some limited scope for beneficial reduction of the tariff with central elasticities. Again, with higher elasticities, the optimal tariff is lower and the gains from tariff reduction would increase.

Sectoral Impacts

Tables 6 and 7 in Harrison, Rutherford, and Tarr (1977b) present the impacts under central elasticities on output, exports and imports at the 24-sector level from three of the principal trade policy options: the FTA with MERCOSUR, the FTA with

26. These were the results employed by the vice president of the Central Bank of Chile in his presentation before the lower house committee of the Chilean Parliament when he argued for a reduction of the tariff to 6 percent. In fact, we have separately calculated the optimum tariff with central elasticities at between 3 and 4 percent, and with low elasticities of about 14 percent, assuming lump-sum replacement of tariff revenues in each case.

NAFTA, and unilateral reduction of the tariff to 8 percent.[27] Focusing on the percentage change in output with central elasticities, the sectors that significantly expand under the free trade agreement with MERCOSUR are transportation equipment (dramatically),[28] machinery and equipment, iron and steel, and milk. With the free trade agreement with NAFTA, the sectors that expand more than 10 percent are iron and steel, transportation equipment, milk, nongrain crops, and textiles. With unilateral tariff reduction, the expanding sectors are transportation equipment, iron and steel, and, to a lesser extent, nonferrous metals and mining.

Iron and steel and transportation equipment expand under all three trade policy options, but the other expanding sectors differ. Iron and steel and transportation equipment are both small sectors in Chile; each sector produces less than 1 percent of Chilean value added. However, these are the two sectors that export the most intensively: both export over 90 percent of their output. Preferential or multilateral tariff reduction induces a depreciation in the real exchange rate, which makes exporting more profitable and gives a boost to the sectors that export intensively.

With unilateral tariff reduction, the other sectors that expand (nonferrous metals and mining) are also the ones that export a high percentage of their output. So the real exchange rate impact and export intensity explain the pattern of expanding and contracting sectors with unilateral nondiscriminatory tariff reduction.

With a free trade agreement with NAFTA, textiles, milk, and nongrain crops expand—in addition to the two or three most export-intensive sectors—because these three sectors obtain a substantial improvement in their terms of trade in the U.S. market. We considered earlier how improved access to nongrain crops and milk is crucial to an improvement in Chilean welfare from NAFTA, and these sectoral results are consistent with those welfare results.

With the free trade agreement with MERCOSUR, machinery and equipment and milk expand in addition to transportation and iron and steel. Our data indicate that these sectors are two of the most highly protected in MERCOSUR, so they obtain relatively greater improvement in their terms of trade after implementation of a free trade agreement with MERCOSUR, which induces their expansion.

Additive Regionalism

Butelmann and Meller (1995) articulate the strategy of the government of Chile: to negotiate bilateral free trade agreements with MERCOSUR, NAFTA, and all of its significant and willing trading partners, including the European Union and the rest of South America.[29] They argue that this strategy will progressively lower

27. We also present the sectoral results with low elasticities.

28. Although the expansion is dramatic in percentage terms, it starts from a very small base. Thus, the absolute increase is plausible.

29. The percentage share of Chile's aggregate exports (imports) for its most significant trading partners are: the United States, 14 (25); Brazil, 5 (7); Argentina, 5 (6); the European Union, 32 (23); the rest of South America, 5 (5); and Japan, 17 (10).

the effective average tariff, successively reduce trade diversion costs, and, crucially, will help ensure stability of access to the markets of partner countries. The free trade agreement in late 1996 between Chile and Canada, in which both countries agreed to eschew antidumping actions against each other, is regarded as a notable example of the advantages that the bilateral approach offers. An opposing view within Chile is offered by Donoso and Hachette (1996). They argue that the limited market access of the bilateral agreements with the Southern countries (for example, MERCOSUR) is not worth delaying the benefits of opening up unilaterally, although agreements with the large markets of the United States, the European Union, or Japan would be worthwhile. Moreover, they fear that the MERCOSUR arrangement may restrict broader liberalization.

Table 3 presents estimates of the gains to Chile of progressively adding free trade agreements, using central elasticities and a lump-sum tax as the replacement tax. Columns 1 and 2 reproduce the estimates in table 2. Column 3 shows that although the MERCOSUR agreement independently results in losses to Chile, when combined with an agreement with NAFTA, the impact of an agreement with MERCOSUR is positive rather than negative. The reason is that competition from NAFTA producers greatly reduces the extent and impact of trade diversion.[30] Column 4 of row 1 shows that combining agreements with NAFTA and MERCOSUR with an agreement with the European Union results in a large increase in the gains to more than 5 percent of GDP. Finally, adding a free trade agreement with the rest of South America results in gains of 8.4 percent of GDP. These are enormous estimated gains for a constant-returns-to-scale model. The last column of row 1 excludes the United States from the agreement, but this has only a small negative impact on Chile because it obtains such substantial preferential access in the other markets.

Critics of the government's strategy argue that it is unrealistic to assume that the European Union would grant tariff-free access in its highly protected agricultural products as part of a free trade agreement with Chile. The European Union has steadfastly refused to do so in its Association Agreements with the

30. NAFTA and MERCOSUR combined produce gains of 1.48 percent of GDP, whereas if the results of the NAFTA and MERCOSUR agreements were merely additive (columns 1 and 2) the gains would be only 0.61 percent of GDP. That is, we find that reduced trade diversion from the combined agreements accounts for 0.87 percent of GDP. Because this may appear to be too large a saving due to reduced trade diversion, to verify our explanation we have three additional simulations: (1) Chile unilaterally eliminates tariffs on NAFTA imports without improved access to NAFTA; (2) Chile unilaterally eliminates tariffs on MERCOSUR imports without improved access to MERCOSUR; and (3) Chile unilaterally eliminates tariffs on NAFTA and MERCOSUR without improved access to NAFTA or MERCOSUR markets. If our explanation is correct, simulation 3 should result in reduced trade diversion costs of at least 0.87 percent of GDP, compared with additive losses from the first two simulations. In percentage of GDP, the welfare impacts of these three simulations are: (1) –0.83, (2) –0.82, and (3) –0.77. If the losses of the preferential tariff reduction were additive, the total losses would be –1.65 (= –0.83 – 0.82). Because preferential tariff reduction against the two regions combined results in losses of only –0.77 percent of GDP, trade diversion costs are reduced by 0.88 percent of GDP by combining tariff reductions for the two regions.

TABLE 3. Welfare Results of Additive Free Trade Agreements by Chile
(Chilean gains as a percent of Chilean GDP with central elasticities and lump-sum tax replacement)

	Agreements with					
Product coverage	MERCOSUR	NAFTA	NAFTA & MERCOSUR	NAFTA & MERCOSUR & EU	NAFTA & MERCOSUR & EU & rest of SA[a]	Canada & Mexico MERCOSUR & EU & rest of SA[a]
	(1)	(2)	(3)	(4)	(5)	(6)
1. All products included	−0.43	1.04	1.48	5.24	8.4	8.16
2. Excluded products[b]	−0.43	1.04	1.48	2.02	2.48	0.44
3. Excluded products[b] and 6% external tariff	0.35	1.70	2.01	2.29	2.66	0.87
4. Only EU AG products[c] excluded	−0.43	1.04	1.48	2.02	5.48	3.90
5. Only EU AG products excluded and 6% tariff	0.35	1.70	2.01	2.29	5.71	4.44

[a]Rest of SA is South America except for Chile and the MERCOSUR countries.
[b]Excluded products in the agreement with the EU and their tariffs plus nontariff equivalents in the EU are: wheat (57%), grains (74%), nongrain crops (51%), fishing (14%), meat (63%), and milk (129%). Excluded products in the agreement with the rest of South America (and their tariffs) are: nongrain crops (29%), meat (51%), milk (27%), food (34%), beverages and tobacco (55%), textiles and apparel (46%), chemicals, rubber, and plastics (31%), fabricated metal products (43%), and machinery (52%).
[c]Only the agricultural products from the European Union listed in note b are excluded from any of the FTAS.
Source: Authors' calculations.

Central and Eastern European countries and in its Free Trade and Customs Union Agreements with Mediterranean countries, such as Morocco, Tunisia, and Turkey. Hence, it is unlikely to offer concessions to Chile that it has refused to offer to other countries for which it might be viewed as having more to gain geopolitically. Similarly, although more speculatively, it would be doubtful that tariff-free access in the most highly protected products would be provided by the rest of South America because (following Grossman and Helpman 1995) the political-economy interests that obtained such high protection would resist regional competition as well.

Row 2 of table 3 presents results that more realistically reflect possible outcomes due to excluded products. They exclude agricultural products from the agreement with the European Union, and products with tariffs above 25 percent in the rest of South America from that agreement. The results show, as expected, that without preferential access to these highly protected markets, the gains would be dramatically reduced. The last column shows that the United States is crucial to the whole scenario. If the United States is not included in the additive agreements, the gains drop dramatically to 0.44 percent of GDP. The drop in welfare for Chile exceeds the gains from NAFTA alone, showing that competition from (and in) the United States is important to Chile being able to avoid the trade diversion costs of these agreements. Conversely, if Chile can get a free trade agreement with the United States as part of NAFTA, then free trade agreements with MERCOSUR, the European Union, and the rest of South America each add, impressively, about 0.5 percent to Chilean GDP. These gains accrue even when the European Union and the rest of South America exclude their most highly protected items from the agreements.

Proponents of the government's strategy maintain that the trade diversion costs of the free trade agreements will be diminished because Chile will adopt an external tariff of 6 percent. Moreover, though they concede that access to the European Union in agricultural products is unlikely, they maintain that it is possible that Chile will receive full access to the markets of the rest of South America in view of the sustained trend toward open economies in Latin America. In row 3 of table 3, we evaluate the impact of a 6 percent external tariff with the same products excluded from the agreements with the European Union and the rest of South America as in row 2. There are slightly larger gains to Chile from lowering the external tariff, but the United States remains important for substantial gains. In rows 4 and 5, we evaluate additive regionalism where only European Union agricultural products are excluded, so that full access to the rest of South America is obtained. Columns 5 and 6 show that Chile obtains very substantial gains, with a 6 or 11 percent external tariff, if it can obtain tariff-free access to the highly protected markets of the rest of South America.

Thus, if Chile succeeds in including a wide net of countries in its additive regionalism strategy, the estimates of the welfare gains range from 0.44 to 8.4 percent of Chilean GDP. However, table 2 shows that the gains to Chile from unilateral trade liberalization are only about 0.11 percent of GDP. Hence, the estimated gains to Chile from additive regionalism are 4 to 76 times the gains from unilateral trade liberalization. On balance, it appears that Chile has little to lose by pursuing additive regionalism, especially given that additive regionalism is being combined with lowering the external tariff to about 6 to 8 percent.

III. The Impact of Additive Regionalism

Experience with regional trade arrangements has shown that if the agreement is not mutually beneficial to all parties, then it is unlikely to be effectively implemented or sustained (World Bank 2000). Agreements may exist de facto but are not implemented effectively. Thus, the impact on Chile's partner countries in the trade agreements is relevant to the likely success of the strategy in the long run. Moreover, even if the agreements are beneficial to Chile and its partners, if the benefits are derived from losses to countries that are excluded from the agreements, then clearly the agreements would be unattractive from the perspective of the multilateral trading system. Thus, it is important to estimate the impact on partner and excluded countries from the Chilean strategy of additive regionalism, and to assess the impact on the world in general. As a point of comparison, we also estimate the impact of global free trade on the countries and regions of our model.

Table 4 reports welfare gains as a percentage of own-country GDP, for both our central and low-elasticity cases. For comparisons of gains and losses across countries, table 5 presents the estimated welfare gains in millions of 1995 U.S. dollars. The first five columns in row 1 of table 5 reproduce the results for Chile's additive regionalism strategy, which is presented in the first five columns of table 3. Rows 2–11 present results for the other 10 countries or regions in our model. Column 6 presents results for the global free trade scenario.

Impact on Individual Countries and Regions

From the first five columns of table 4, Chile is too small or its trade pattern is sufficiently different for its regional agreements to have more than a trivial impact on about half of the countries and regions in the model.[31] This group includes Japan and the rest of the world (which are excluded from all the agreements evaluated in table 3) and the United States and the European Union (which are excluded in some of the arrangements in table 3 and included in others). Canada is also essentially unaffected by Chile's trade policy options.

The rest of South America and Central America lose in all the agreements from which they are excluded, although the welfare loss is only about 0.05 percent of their GDP. These regions compete with Chile for the markets in MERCOSUR and NAFTA and compete with producers from MERCOSUR and NAFTA for the Chilean market. In both cases, they lose access to markets because there is a decline

31. When we round welfare to the nearest 0.01 percent of GDP, the impact is either 0 or 0.01 percent.

TABLE 4. The Welfare Impact of Chile's Additive Free Trade Agreements and Global Free Trade[a] (welfare gains as a percent of each country's GDP)

		Agreements with					
Country	Elasticity	MERCOSUR	NAFTA	NAFTA & MERCOSUR	NAFTA & MERCOSUR & EU	NAFTA & MERCOSUR & EU & Rest of SA[b]	Global free trade
		(1)	(2)	(3)	(4)	(5)	(6)
1. Chile	central	–0.40	1.04	1.48	5.24	8.40	1.26
	(low)	(0.00)	(0.37)	(0.60)	(2.55)	(3.31)	(0.68)
2. United States	central	0.00	0.00	0.00	0.00	0.00	0.34
	(low)	(0.00)	(0.01)	(0.00)	(0.00)	(0.00)	(0.18)
3. Canada	central	0.00	0.00	0.00	0.00	0.01	0.42
	(low)	(0.00)	(0.00)	(0.00)	(0.00)	(0.00)	(–0.36)
4. Mexico	central	0.00	–0.02	–0.01	0.00	0.00	–1.38
	(low)	(0.00)	(–0.01)	(–0.01)	(0.00)	(0.00)	(–1.02)
5. Argentina	central	0.06	0.00	0.10	0.12	0.07	0.82
	(low)	(0.00)	(–0.01)	(0.02)	(0.02)	(0.01)	(0.60)
6. Brazil	central	0.02	–0.01	–0.04	–0.04	–0.02	0.94
	(low)	(0.00)	(–0.01)	(0.00)	(0.00)	(–0.01)	(0.24)
7. Central America	central	0.00	–0.06	–0.05	–0.04	–0.06	9.70
	(low)	(0.00)	(–0.03)	(–0.03)	(–0.05)	(–0.06)	(4.42)
8. Rest of SA	central	0.00	–0.03	–0.06	–0.04	–1.19	4.40
	(low)	(0.00)	(–0.02)	(–0.04)	(–0.05)	(–0.22)	(1.25)
9. European Union	central	0.00	0.00	0.00	0.00	0.00	2.74
	(low)	(0.00)	(0.00)	(0.00)	(0.00)	(0.00)	(1.17)
10. Japan	central	0.00	0.00	0.00	0.00	0.00	3.43
	(low)	(0.00)	(0.00)	(0.00)	(0.00)	(0.00)	(1.98)
11. Rest of the world	central	0.00	0.00	0.00	0.00	0.00	1.97
	(low)	(0.00)	(0.00)	(0.00)	(0.01)	(0.01)	(0.54)

[a]All products included in agreements and lump-sum tax replacement.
[b]Rest of SA is South America except for Chile, Argentina, and Brazil.
Source: Authors' calculations.

TABLE 5. The Welfare Impact of Chile's Additive Free Trade Agreements and Global Free Trade[a]
(welfare gains in millions of 1995 US dollars)

Country	Elasticity	Agreements with MERCOSUR	NAFTA	NAFTA & MERCOSUR	NAFTA & MERCOSUR & EU	NAFTA & MERCOSUR & EU & Rest of SA[B]	Global free trade
		(1)	(2)	(3)	(4)	(5)	(6)
1. Chile	central	–291	414	590	2090	3350	504
	(low)	(–67)	(149)	(239)	(1013)	(1318)	(270)
2. United States	central	–7	51	–29	138	60	19,972
	(low)	(–24)	(306)	(231)	(59)	(–11)	(10,833)
3. Canada	central	5	–20	–22	23	49	243
	(low)	(4)	(–15)	(–13)	(14)	(19)	(–2058)
4. Mexico	central	13	–58	–44	–11	15	–4539
	(low)	(1)	(–35)	(–35)	(–3)	(0)	(–3315)
5. Argentina	central	63	–1	222	264	147	1832
	(low)	(44)	(–18)	(54)	(54)	(28)	(1327)
6. Brazil	central	214	–42	–171	–161	–70	3912
	(low)	(108)	(–36)	(15)	(–11)	(–21)	(1004)
7. Central America	central	4	–37	–32	–23	–38	6112
	(low)	(3)	(–21)	(–21)	(–29)	(–36)	(2680)
8. Rest of So. America	central	–34	–56	–95	–73	–2024	7456
	(low)	(–28)	(–39)	(–75)	(–90)	(–376)	(2110)
9. European Union	central	–184	–156	–336	–88	–200	207,413
	(low)	(–28)	(–241)	(–317)	(156)	(86)	(88,720)

10. Japan	central	–58	–19	–30	81	–2	127,664
	(low)	(–30)	(–48)	(–69)	(–76)	(–91)	(73,711)
11. Rest of the world	central	92	–73	–50	–115	6	85,111
	(low)	(29)	(–89)	(–100)	(–229)	(–232)	(23,348)
12. Sum for included[c]	central	–14	387	546	2255	1327	
	(low)	(85)	(405)	(491)	(1282)	(1043)	
13. Sum for excluded[d]	central	–169	–384	–543	–130	–34	
	(low)	(–73)	(–492)	(–582)	(–424)	(–359)	
14. Sum over all countries	central	–183	3	3	2125	1293	455,680
	(low)	(12)	(–87)	(–91)	(858)	(684)	(198,626)

[a]All products included in agreements and lump-sum tax replacement.
[b]Rest of SA is South America except for Chile, Argentina, and Brazil.
[c]Sum of the welfare impact for countries included in the agreement.
[d]Sum of the welfare impact for countries excluded from the agreement.
Source: Authors' calculations.

in the demand for their exports due to preferential access arrangements between Chile and its partners, which adversely affects their terms of trade and welfare.[32]

Perhaps most interesting is that although the rest of South America loses from being excluded by Chile, the biggest loss for this region by far is when the rest of South America *is included* with Chile in a free trade agreement (along with the European Union, NAFTA, and MERCOSUR, as shown in column 5 of table 4). The rest of South America has high protection on the products mentioned in the footnotes for table 3. To the extent that Chilean imports displace imports from other countries in the rest of South America, it loses tariff revenue on imports. Although there is some trade creation from tariff-free access to Chilean imports in the rest of South America, the tariff loss dominates the trade creation due to the high level of the tariffs.[33] Moreover, comparing columns 4 and 5 in table 5, the addition of the rest of South America to the coalition of Chile, MERCOSUR, the European Union, and NAFTA results in an aggregate reduction in welfare for the partner countries (see row 12). The gains to the other partners in this agreement are less than the losses to the rest of South America. So there are insufficient benefits to allow the gainers to compensate the rest of South America for its losses.

For Mexico, competition from Chile for preferred access in the U.S. market results in a very small negative impact of including Chile in NAFTA. However, Chile is too small to make a significant difference to Mexico in the U.S. market. When Chile combines an agreement with NAFTA with an agreement with MERCOSUR, the diversification of Chilean exports results in still less displacement of Mexican exports in the United States, so the negative impact on Mexico of Chile in NAFTA is reduced. When Chile adds the European Union to its group of free trade agreements, the diversification of Chilean exports reduces the small negative impact on Mexico of Chile's preferential access to the United States to virtually zero. By contrast, in the global free trade scenario discussed below, Mexican losses are substantial due to the erosion of preferential access in U.S. markets from the whole world.

Brazil and Argentina both lose from Chile joining NAFTA due to erosion of preference margins in both Chile and NAFTA markets. But Argentina and Brazil both gain small amounts from a MERCOSUR free trade agreement with Chile. The latter fact is partly explained by improved access to the Chilean market for MERCOSUR producers. It is also likely that part of the explanation for this result is that Brazil and Argentina reduce the trade diversion costs of MERCOSUR when they add new partners. That is, Chile will compete with Brazilian producers in Argentine markets. This will reduce the trade diversion costs of Argentina from importing Brazilian products under the MERCOSUR agreement. Of course, Chile could well displace imports from the rest of the world in Argentine markets, which

32. This is consistent with the evidence of Winters and Chang (2000). They find that the price of imports from the United States and Korea in Brazil fell after the formation of MERCOSUR.

33. If the high-tariff products are excluded from the free trade agreement with Chile, the losses are reduced to about one-third of their level (to –0.36 percent).

could increase Argentine trade diversion costs. But as more countries are added to a network of preferential trading arrangements, the trade diversion costs associated with earlier partners are reduced, especially if these are large countries that interject significant competition.[34] Comparing columns 4 and 5 in table 5, Brazil and Argentina both lose from Chile negotiating a free trade agreement with the rest of South America. This is likely due to a terms-of-trade loss in the markets of the rest of South America.

Aggregate Impact of Chile's Additive Regionalism Strategy

Even if Chile gains from an agreement or set of agreements, there is the question of whether Chile gains only because other countries lose. In table 5, we convert the percentage gains and losses of table 4 into gains and losses in millions of 1995 U.S. dollars. This allows us to compare gains and losses across countries and arrive at a total for the world. Row 12 sums the welfare effects for countries that are included in the agreement. For example, Chile-MERCOSUR (column 1) includes Chile, Argentina, and Brazil in our model. Row 13 sums the welfare effect for all countries that are not part of the agreement (for example, all countries other than Chile, Argentina, and Brazil in the case of Chile-MERCOSUR). Row 14 sums over all countries.

From row 12 in table 5, trade diversion dominates the Chile-MERCOSUR agreement to the extent that even the members of the agreement lose in the aggregate. But this agreement is the only one we consider that results in losses for the member countries. Other agreements considered in table 5 are "North–South" agreements (in particular, all include the United States), and we estimate that all of these result in aggregate net benefits for the member countries, although at least one member loses in all of them. The inclusion of the United States means that significant competition is injected into the markets of participating members, and this reduces the likelihood of trade diversion dominating.

From row 13 in table 5, all of the preferential arrangements we consider result in losses for the excluded countries or regions. These results are consistent with the results of Winters and Chang (2000). Employing ex post data, they show that there can be a very significant negative welfare effect (through negative terms-of-trade effects) on countries excluded from regional arrangements. In particular, they estimate that MERCOSUR induced losses for the United States, Germany, Japan, the Republic of Korea, and Chile of about $800 million per year, which was about 9 percent of the value of their exports to MERCOSUR.[35]

For the world as a whole, with central elasticities, the agreement with MERCOSUR results in losses of $183 million, primarily due to the trade diversion costs for Chile and the terms-of-trade loss for the European Union. Independent of elas-

34. It is possible, however, that a new partner could divert imports from an excluded country and add to the trade diversion costs on balance.

35. We estimate a very small negative effect for Central America as a result of Chile forming an FTA with NAFTA.

ticities, the agreements in the first three columns result in essentially a zero impact for the world or for the three excluded regions outside of the Western Hemisphere (rounded to the 0.01 percent of their own GDP). With NAFTA involved, Chile has significant gains, but the terms-of-trade loss for the excluded countries is almost as much as the gains to Chile, so the impact on the world is small.

In columns 4 and 5 of table 5, the gains for the world become significant when the European Union is added or when the European Union and the rest of South America are added to Chile's network of agreements. The main reason for the much larger gains to the world is that the gains to Chile become very large when it obtains preferential access to the markets of the European Union and the rest of South America. As explained, given the high protection on selected products in the rest of South America, the trade diversion costs in this region significantly reduce the gains to the world from including this region in Chile's network of free trade agreements.

Impact of Global Free Trade

The results for global free trade are presented in column 6 of tables 4 and 5. As expected, the gains to the world vastly exceed the gains from any regional arrangement. Even the included countries to any agreement gain more from multilateral global free trade than any individual regional arrangement (although the impact on Chile of an agreement with NAFTA is close). These results emphasize the importance of moving toward lower trade barriers in the multilateral context. Mexico is an exception (as is Canada in the low-elasticity case). Mexico sees losses from global free trade due to the erosion of favored access to the U.S. market.

IV. CONCLUSIONS

Our results for Chile point to some general themes regarding regional trading arrangements. One clear theme is that improved market access in preferential trading areas is important. In the case of Chile, trade diversion costs dominate the welfare effects of bilateral agreements unless sufficient market access is obtained in partner countries (or third-country tariffs are lowered). The North–South agreements generally provide sufficient access to make them beneficial, but the South–South agreement we examined did not (although Chile could lower its external tariff to make the South–South arrangement beneficial). We show that efficient replacement taxes are important with changes in either regional or unilateral trade policy and provide greater scope for trade policy action. Finally, our range of estimates for the gains from additive regionalism indicate that Chile has little to lose by pursuing this strategy and may potentially gain many multiples of the gains from unilateral trade liberalization.

We find that the excluded countries lose from all of the regional arrangements that we examine. In addition, partners to these preferential arrangements sometimes lose.

Chile's additive regional arrangements have an almost imperceptible impact on world welfare. However, we estimate that global free trade generates gains to the world that are enormous in comparison, emphasizing the importance of moving toward lower trade barriers in the multilateral context.

References

Athukorala, Premachandra, and James Reidel. 1994. "Demand and Supply Factors in the Determination of NIE Exports: A Simultaneous Error-Correction Model for Hong Kong: A Comment." *Economic Journal* 104(November):1411–14.

Bond, Eric. 1996. "Using Tariff Indices to Evaluate Preferential Trading Arrangements: An Application to Chile." Unpublished manuscript, Department of Economics, Pennsylvania State University.

Butelmann, Andrea, and Patricio Meller. 1995. "Evaluation of a Chile-U.S. Free Trade Agreement." In Economic Commission for Latin America, *Trade Liberalization in the Western Hemisphere*. Washington, D.C.: Economic Commission for Latin America.

Coeymans, Juan Eduardo, and Felipe B. Larrain. 1994. "Efectos de Un Acuerdo de Libre Comercio Entre Chile Y Estados Unidos: Un Enfoque de Equilibrio General." *Cuadernos de Economia* 31(94):357–99.

Corbo, Vittorio. 1996. "Commentario a 'La integracion de al NAFTA': Temos elegidos." In M. Schiff and C. Sapelli, eds., *Chile en el NAFTA: Acuerdos de Libre Comercio Versus Liberalizacion Unilateral*. Santiago: Centro International Para El Desarrollo Economico.

de Melo, Jaime, and David Tarr. 1992. *General Equilibrium Analysis of U.S. Foreign Trade Policy*. Cambridge, Mass.: MIT Press.

Donoso, B., and Dominique Hachette. 1996. "MERCOSUR y la apertura comercial chilena." Unpublished manuscript, Department of Economics, Catolica University, Santiago, Chile.

Ferris, M. C., and T. S. Munson. 2000. "Complementarity Problems in GAMS and the PATH Solver." *Journal of Economic Dynamics and Control* 24(2):165–88.

Gehlhar, Mark, Denice Gray, Thomas W. Hertel, Karen Huff, Elena Ianchovichina, Bradley J. McDonald, Robert McDougall, Marinos E. Tsigas, and Randall Wigle. 1996. "Overview of the GTAP Data Base." In T. W. Hertel, ed., *Global Trade Analysis: Modeling and Applications*. New York: Cambridge University Press.

Grossman, Gene, and Helpman, Elhanan. 1995. "The Politics of Free Trade Agreements." *American Economic Review* 85(4):667–90.

Harrison, Glenn W., Richard Jones, Larry J. Kimbell, and Randall Wigle. 1993. "How Robust Is Applied General Equilibrium Analysis?" *Journal of Policy Modelling* 15(1):99–115.

Harrison, Glenn W., Thomas F. Rutherford, and David G. Tarr. 1997a. "Economic Implications for Turkey of a Customs Union with the European Union." *European Economic Review* 41(3–5):861–70.

———. 1997b. "Trade Policy Options for Chile: A Quantitative Evaluation." Policy Research Working Paper 1783, World Bank. Updated version entitled "Chile's Regional Arrangements and the Free Trade Agreement of the Americas: The Importance of Market Access." Policy Research Working Paper 2634, World Bank, 2001. Both papers available online at: www.worldbank.org/research/trade/archive.html.

———. 1997c. "Quantifying the Uruguay Round." *Economic Journal* 107(444):1405–30.

———. 2001. "Chile's Regional Arrangements and the Free Trade Agreement of the Americas: The Importance of Market Access." Policy Research Working Paper 2634, World Bank. Available online at: www.worldbank.org/research/trade/archive.html.

Harrison, Glenn W., Thomas F. Rutherford, and Ian Wooton. 1989. "The Economic Impact of the European Community." *American Economic Review (Papers & Proceedings)* 79(2):288–94.

———. 1993. "An Alternative Welfare Decomposition for Customs Unions." *Canadian Journal of Economics* 26(4):961–68.

Hatta, Tatsu. 1977. "A Theory of Piecemeal Policy Recommendations." *Review of Economic Studies* 44(1):1–21.

Hinojosa-Ojeda, Raul, Jeffrey Lewis, and Sherman Robinson. 1995. "Convergence and Divergence Between NAFTA, Chile and MERCOSUR: Overcoming Dilemmas of North and South American Economic Integration." Unpublished manuscript, Department of Economics, UCLA.

Leipziger, Danny, and L. Alan Winters. 1996. "Chile y el NAFTA: lecciones y orientaciones futuras." In M. Schiff and C. Sapelli, eds., *Chile en el NAFTA: Acuerdos de Libre Comercio versus Liberalizacion Unilateral.* Santiago: Centro Internacional Para El Desarrollo Economico.

Michalopoulos, Constantine, and David Tarr. 1997. "The Economics of Customs Unions in the Commonwealth of Independent States." *Post-Soviet Geography and Economics* 38(3):125–43.

Muchnik, Eugenia, L. F. Errazuriz, and J. I. Dominguez. 1996. "Efectos de la asociation de Chile al Mercosur en el sector agricola y agroindustrial." *Estudios Publicos* 63:113–64.

Panagariya, Arvind, and Dani Rodrik. 1993. "Political Economy Arguments for a Uniform Tariff." *International Economic Review* 34(3):685–703.

Quiroz, Jorge, and Alberto Valdes. 1993. "Price Bands for Agricultural Stabilization: The Chilean Experience." Unpublished manuscript, World Bank, Washington, D.C.

Reidel, James. 1988. "The Demand for LDC Exports of Manufactures: Estimates from Hong Kong." *Economic Journal* 98(March):138–48.

Reinert, Kenneth A., and David W. Roland-Holst. 1992. "Armington Elasticities for United States Manufacturing Sectors." *Journal of Policy Modelling* 14(5):631–39.

———. 1996. "Chilean Accession to the NAFTA: General Equilibrium Estimates." In K. Fatemi, ed., *Western Hemispheric Economies in the 21st Century.* Laredo, Tex.: Graduate School of Business, Texas A&M University.

Rutherford, Thomas F. 1999. "Applied General Equilibrium Modeling with MPSGE as a GAMS Subsystem: An Overview of the Modeling Framework and Syntax." *Computational Economics* 14(1/2):1–46.

Rutherford, Thomas F., E. E. Rutström, and David G. Tarr. 1997. "Morocco's Free Trade Agreement with the European Community." *Economic Modelling* 14(2):237–69.

Schiff, Maurice, and Claudio Sapelli, eds. 1996. *Chile en el NAFTA: Acuerdos de Libre Comercio Versus Liberalizacion Unilatera.* Santiago: Centro Internacional Para El Desarrollo Economico.

Shiells, C. R., and K. A. Reinert. 1993. "Armington Models and Terms-of-Trade Effects: Some Econometric Evidence for North America." *Canadian Journal of Economics* 26(2):299–316.

Valdes, Alberto. 1995. "Joining an Existing Regional Trading Agreement from the Perspective of a Small Open Economy: Chile's Accession to NAFTA and MERCOSUR." *American Journal of Agricultural Economics* 77:1292–97.

———. 1996. "Surveillance of Agricultural Price and Trade Policy in Latin America during Major Policy Reforms." World Bank Discussion Paper No. 349, Washington D.C.

Winters, L. Alan, and Won Chang. 2000. "Regional Integration and Import Prices: An Empirical Investigation." *Journal of International Economics* 51(2):363–77.

Wonnacott, Paul, and Ronald Wonnacott. 1981. "Is Unilateral Tariff Reduction Preferable to a Customs Union? The Curious Case of the Missing Foreign Tariffs." *American Economic Review* 71(4):704–14.

Wooton, Ian. 1986. "Preferential Trading Agreements: An Investigation." *Journal of International Economics* 21:81–97.

World Bank. 2000. *Trade Blocs*. Oxford and New York: Oxford University Press.

Journal of Economic Integration
11(3), September 1996; 332–365

Increased Competition and Completion of the Market in the European Union: Static and Steady State Effects

Glenn W. Harrison
University of South Carolina

Thomas F. Rutherford
University of Colorado

David G. Tarr
The World Bank

Abstract

We model the effects of completion of the internal market in the European Union on trade, production and market structure. The impetus for change comes from the removal of border costs, as well as increased competition from the greater ability of EU buyers to substitute among the products of different EU producers. In turn, this increased competition arises from the single market program on standards, government procurement, and dynamic learning

* Correspondence Address: Dewey H. Johnson Professor of Economics, Department of Economics, College of Business Administration, University of South Carolina, Columbia, SC 29208, U.S.A.; Assistant Professor, Department of Economics, University of Colorado; and Lead Economist, The World Bank. This study is part of the World Bank's research on "The Impact of EC 1992 and Trade Integration in Selected Mediterranean Countries," supported under grant RPO #67564. The authors would like to thank two anonymous referees of this journal and seminar participants at the EU Commission, the U.S. International Trade Commission, the World Bank and Georgetown University for their helpful comments. The views expressed are those of the authors alone and should not be interpreted as the opinion of the World Bank.

effects. Removing the border costs results in relatively small welfare gains. Increased competition more than doubles the estimated benefits, and the steady state growth effect more than quadruples the welfare gains.

I. Introduction

Completion of the market in the European Union has generated enormous interest among policy-makers and academic modellers. Estimates of the gains from the single market program are based in part on the removal of barriers on trade between member states. More importantly, the single market program involves "deep" integration. The largest estimates of gains come from models with imperfect competition which assume that completion of the market will induce a single integrated market in which international price discrimination is impossible. That is, in these analyses a uniform EU-wide price is imposed in imperfectly competitive markets.[1]

Strikingly, virtually all key authors have expressed dissatisfaction with how increased competition under the single market program has been modelled.[2] In large part this stems from the fact that no clear rationale has been articulated for how the integration process will induce a common price. That is, if arbitrage fails to eliminate price differences (net of transportation, border and standards costs) prior to 1993,[3] it is not clear why it

1. Gasiorek, Smith and Venables [1992], Haaland and Norman [1992] and Mercenier [1992] estimate the gains at between 0.5 and 1.35 percent of GDP. The official forecasts, from Cecchini et al. [1988; p.83] and Emerson et al. [1988; Table 10.1.1, p.203], were that the welfare gains would be between 4.3% and 6.4% of 1988 GDP. Since these estimates were based on extrapolations of partial equilibrium calculations for a handful of industries from the work of Smith and Venables [1988], Winters [1992; p.105] has appropriately characterized these extrapolations as "heroic".
2. For example, see Karp [1992; p.63], Smith and Venables [1988; p.1523], Mercenier [1992; p.1] and Winters [1992; p.20].
3. We use the date "1993" to refer to the nominal year in which completion of the market is to begin. The delays in national legislative efforts to implement necessary statutes, as well as other delays in application of those laws, makes this date a matter of pedagogic convenience rather than a prediction about when the EU will in face have completed the single-market program. We also refer throughout to the "European Union," despite it historically being the "European Community" at the time of some of the policy changes or data we discuss.

would eliminate price differences (net of transportation costs) after 1993.[4] We review the theory of monopolistically competitive markets and empirical work on the relatively integrated markets in the United States. Both indicate the implausibility of the modelling exercises that assume that no price discrimination is possible after the implementation of the EU92. In addition, we note that the imposition of uniform pricing results (due to the elimination of reciprocal dumping implied by uniform pricing) in the counterintuitive result that intra-EU trade *declines* subsequent to the EU92 program.[5] Thus, we model market integration within the EU92 program with an approach that captures the idea that EU92 will increase competition and rationalization in imperfectly competitive markets without imposing *complete* elimination of firm level price discrimination across the EU. We provide a rationale for the reduction of price discrimination occasioned by the EU92 program in which the extent of remaining price discrimination is endogenously determined.

The impetus for change in our framework comes from two interrelated effects. One effect is the, now standard, 2.5 percent reduction of border and supply side standards costs. In addition, we maintain that increased competition will come from an increase in the willingness of EU buyers to substitute among the products of producers in different countries. This increased willingness is due to the single market program on standards, rules on government procurement, and an increase in intra-EU trade (from border costs reductions) which is likely to lead to consumers trying new varieties they

4. Karp [1992; p.63] makes the same point: "If it were possible to price discriminate before 1992, then lowering transportation costs (broadly defined) might either increase or decrease the incentive for price discriminate before 1992, then lowering transportation costs (broadly defined) might either increase or decrease the incentive for price discrimination." Smith and Venables [1988; p.1523] note that "... it is not obvious that there exist feasible changes in EU trade policy and competition policy that could impose such a change. In practice policy may be expected to be some combination of our two experiments."

5. See, for example, Smith and Venables [1988; pp. 1520-1523]. Tarr [1994] notes that the segmented markets approach of Gasoriek, Smith and Venables assumes that there are no taste differences across countries or firms. That is, all price differences in the benchmark are calibrated as due to non-tariff barriers and all these are eliminated in the integrated markets counterfactual.

sometimes like.[6]

These effects are best modelled as a change in the elasticity of substitution of consumers in EU countries for the varieties of output of other EU firms. We simulate this change along a continuum from an initial situation, characterized by firm level product differentiation where consumers regard the output of other EU firms are equally substitutable with other ***non-EU imports***, to an endpoint where consumers regard the varieties of all other EU firms as equally substitutable with ***home varieties***.[7]

We develop a monopolistic competition model in which each firm's post-1992 markup is endogenously determined as a function of the substitutability of the outputs of different EU firms in the preference structure of national consumers. We show, however, that even in the extreme case of no national preferences, pricing differences and market segmentation are not eliminated. As long as arbitrage is imperfect, price differences (net of transportation costs) may persist. Firms then determine their optimal markups in each national market based on perceived elasticities that vary, among other things, with the firm's market share in each national market.[8]

---

6. This assumption is supported by the views of businessmen surveyed in the "Costs of non-Europe" project who believed that they would have greater access to new regional markets and there would be increased price and non-price competitiveness as a result of the single market (Nerb [1988; p.27]).
7. Since we may calibrate the initial equilibrium as an optimum for any elasticity of substitution, we recalibrate the initial equilibrium to the new elasticities, while preserving the assumed optimality of the initial data point. This allows us to meaningfully calculate the Hicksian equivalent variation in counterfactual simulations. Our approach was independently adopted by Burniaux and Waelbroeck [1992] in a prototype model of EU92.
8. Haaland and Wooton [1992] have shown that, if trade barriers or national preferences continue to exist in the post-1992 environment, uniform EU-wide pricing that results from complete elimination of segmentatin can, contrary to the conventional wisdom, reduce welfare. The reason is that if firms are forced to charge a uniform price across the EU, but national preferences are retained, they will raise prices on their intra-EU exports and this may dominate the effects of lower markups on their domestic sales. In other words, EU92 could reduce welfare due to the loss of the beneficial aspects of a type of reciprocal dumping described by Brander and Krugman [1983]. A similar result is shown analytically by Malueg and Schwartz [forthcoming]. The Haaland-Wooton model does not, however, explain why EU92 would force uniform pricing in markets which were previously characterized by price dis

Our estimates are that the reduction of border and standards costs associated with the EU92 program will result in welfare gains of about 0.5% of EU welfare. Allowing for the additional effects of standardization on consumer substitution elasticities (our version of integration), however, more than doubles the estimated welfare gains.

We also estimate the steady state growth effects of EU92. Building on the single sector approach of Baldwin [1989; pp.266, 269], we integrate our multisector approach and the steady state effects into a single model. We estimate that the benefits in the steady state more than *quadruple* the estimate of the welfare benefits (about 2.4% of EU GDP) compared to the segmented markets comparative statics estimate, explaining some of the anticipatory euphoria.

Our general equilibrium model is described in section II, and the policy simulations are discussed in section III. In section III we develop partial equilibrium analyses to facilitate the intuitive understanding of the numerical general equilibrium results. Compared with earlier studies, we estimate dramatically greater disparity in the expected benefits from EU92 across EU countries. We show that this is explained primarily by differences in intra-EU trade intensities which we are able to uncover due to our greater regional disaggregation.

II. A Multi-Regional Trade Model

A. General Model Features[9]

The model separately identifies nine regions of the EU. Along with their intra-EU trade intensities, they are: Belgium (35.6), Denmark (14.9), France (11.1), Germany (11.9), Italy (10.1), the Netherlands (29.1), Portugal (12.0), Spain (08.8), and the United Kingdom (11.9). The model also identifies

crimination. The problems that they identify, however, have led Winters [1992; p.20] to call for further research to distinguish trade barriers and consumer preferences as a rationale for home market bias.

9. See Harrison, Rutherford and Tarr [1994, Appendix A] for a detailed algebraic formulation of the model; for the decomposition algorithm employed for solution see Rutherford [1992a] [1992b].

Morocco, Turkey, and a residual Rest of World (ROW), making twelve regions in all.

There are twenty-six sectors per region, twelve of which are characterized by increasing returns to scale (IRTS). In IRTS sectors we assume firms are Cournot oligopolists, with free entry and exit assuring zero profits. The Cost Disadvantage Ratio (CDR), which is defined as the ratio of fixed to total costs, provides a measure of the importance of scale economies in IRTS sectors.[10] All other sectors exhibit constant returns to scale (CRTS) and have a competitive market structure. The sectors are as follows: Agriculture (3), Food (3, 11), Beverage and Tobacco (2), Energy (4), Utilities (2), Iron and Steel (1, 5), Non-Metallic Mineral Products (1, 6), Chemicals (2, 6), Metal Products (2, 5), Industrial Machinery (2, 6), Office Machinery (1, 4), Electrical Goods (3, 5), Motor Vehicles (2, 11), Other Transport Equipment (1, 14), Textiles and Clothing (2), Wood (1), Paper and Printing (2, 11), Rubber and Plastics (1, 4), Construction and Repair (8), Trade (12), Financial Services (15), Transport and Communication (6), Health Services (4), Education Services (4), Other Market Services (6), General Public Services (10). The first number in parentheses is the value added of the sector as a percent of total EU value added; the second number in parentheses is the CDR for those sectors subject to IRTS.

By received standards in the literature this makes for a "big model". We adopt this relatively detailed level of sectoral and regional disaggregation since disaggregation has, as we show below, an important impact on the estimated effects of EU92. Gasiorek, Smith and Venables [1992] note that regional aggregation entails a nontrivial assumption in these exercises, since it is primarily through the reduction in border and standards costs of exporting between regions that the EU92 program will have its impact. Regional aggregation in effect converts exports, on which a cost reduction would be achieved, into domestic production. We show below that greater regional disaggregation is fundamental in revealing the considerable differences in the welfare benefits that will accrue to the EU countries with different intra-EU trade intensities.

10. The methodology for estimation of the CDR is discussed in Harrison, Rutherford and Tarr [1994, Appendix B].

Regarding sectoral aggregation, our 26-sector model allows us to keep separate virtually all of the sectors which have significant IRTS as estimated at the 44-sector level. It also allows us to maintain some disaggregation of CRTS sectors, along the lines that might be expected to influence results (viz., traded versus non-traded, labor-intensive versus capital-intensive).

The rest of our static model is relatively standard. We have multiple price-wedge distortions, such as factor taxes in production, value-added taxes, import tariffs, export subsidies, voluntary export restraints (represented as ad valorem equivalents) and non-tariff barriers (also represented as *ad valorem* equivalents). Production entails the use of intermediate inputs and primary factors. Primary factors are mobile across sectors within a region, but are internationally immobile. Each region has a single representative consumer, as well as a single government agent.

B. Modelling the Reduction in Border and Standards Costs of Intra-EU Trade

The two types of real trade costs which constitute the "sand in the gears" in our model are border costs and standardization costs on the supply side. *Border costs* represent the costs of undertaking trade, such as administrative costs of transacting and transporting over international boundaries. These are modelled as additional purchases of the domestic "transportation" good in each region. This good represents the activity of shipping, handling and warehousing for customs purposes. *Standardization costs* on the supply side are due to differences in technical specifications and regulations across national boundaries, and are associated with the production costs of fulfilling technical regulations in foreign EU markets. These costs are more likely to be reflected in extra costs of producing the specific good itself, rather than the purchase of inputs of any specific good. Thus we model supply side standardization costs as additional value-added in each sector in which trade takes place. They do not fall on domestic sales, and hence should be interpreted as the *differential* costs of transacting with other EU countries.

Following previous studies, we assume that the sum of real trade costs from border costs and supply side standardization costs equals 2.5% for each region. From Cawley and Davenport [1988; Tables B2, A3] we have estimates of border costs for the regions in our model. The weighted averages are as follows: Belgium, Denmark, France and Spain (1.7%), Germany (1.8%), United Kingdom (1.9%), Italy and the Netherlands (1.6%), and Portugal (1.5%). The region-specific standardization costs are derived residually from 2.5%. These estimated supply side standardization costs are then assumed to apply to all traded goods within the indicated region.

C. Theory and Evidence Against Uniform Pricing

Previous studies have modelled completion of the market in two stages, with the first stage being the same as ours. In the second stage, previous studies have attempted to capture the presumption that EU integration will have its strongest impact by increasing competition in IRTS sectors. Their second stage involves a shift in the pricing behavior of national firms as the result of completion. Pricing is originally undertaken with "segmented markets", and with monopolistic competition in IRTS sectors this results in lower prices in foreign markets than at home.[11] With completion of the market these segmented markets are replaced with an integrated market in which price discrimination between home and foreign markets is assumed to be impossible.

We claim that it is inappropriate either on *theoretical or empirical grounds* to model EU integration as a process that imposes complete pricing uniformity. First consider the theory. Although the possibility of price discrimination by a monopolist selling in segmented markets has long been accepted in economic theory, recent theoretical work has shown the existence of price discrimination equilibria in a variety of multi-firm settings, even with free entry (*e.g.*, Katz [1984], Borenstein [1985] and Holmes [1989]).[12] These analyses suggest that price discrimination may arise even when market power over price arises only from monopolistically competitive product differentiation.

---

11. This result assumes, plausibly enough, that foreign market shares for a given firm are smaller than domestic market shares. Hence the perceived demand elasticity is different in the two markets, resulting in differences in mark-ups.
12. See Varian [1989] for a review of the theory of price discrimination under non-monopoly conditions.

On empirical grounds, consider the United States market, which is considerably more integrated than the EU is likely to become in the immediate future. Although there are generally alternative theoretical explanations for the observed pricing practices,[13] there are a wide variety of observed pricing practices in the United States that are consistent with price discrimination. These include: (1) two-part tariffs, in which a lump sum fee is charged and a usage charge per unit applies;[14] (2) discount coupons, which allow those consumers with lower opportunity cost of time to obtain a lower price; (3) selling the same product under different brand names and charging a premium for the label as occurs in supermarkets;[15] (4) discounts on products that face stiff competition, for example in the shoe machinery (Kaysen [1956]) and computer markets (Fisher, McGowan and Greenwood [1983]); and (5) geographic price discrimination under single or multiple basing points, with some absorption of transportation charges by the producer.[16]

---

13. See Carlton and Perloff [1990] for alternate explanations. The welfare economics of these practices is a separate matter which we do not address.
14. Tie-in sales, where the purchaser of the product is required to purchase related products, is one type of two part tariff. For example, IBM, in requiring purchasers of its computers to buy its tabulating cards was able to obtain a higher price for the machine from the more intensive users. Xerox, is charging a per unit rental fee for copies that exceeded the marginal maintenance costs, price discriminated against intensive users. See Scherer and Ross [1990].
15. See Wolinsky [1987].
16. Some form of basing point system has been adopted by many U.S. industries including the steel, cement, lead and wood pulp industries. See Scherer and Ross [1990] for further discussion. In addition, recent studies have found evidence of price discrimination in monopolistically competitive markets. Using data from retail gasoline markets, Borenstein [1991] developed a model of spatial competition in which differences in the willingness of buyers to switch stations results in price discrimination between leaded and unleaded gasoline. As gasoline stations which offered leaded gasoline diminished, the relative price of leaded to unleaded gasoline rose. Shepard [1991] found the price difference between full service and self-service gasoline in stations that offered both services was considerably greater than the price difference across different stations that only offered one type of service. Based on a similar model, Borenstein and Rose [1991] found price discrimination in the U.S. airline industry. Pashigian and Bowen [1991] have found that the greater use of sales in the pricing of apparel in retail stores is consistent with a price discrimination theory of

A further highly counterintuitive result of the uniform pricing assumption is that intra-EU trade declines as a result of EU integration. This is because firms charge higher markups on their domestic sales than on export sales prior to integration. Uniform pricing in the EU causes firms to raise export markups and lower domestic markups, which reduces intra-EU trade.

D. Modelling the Price Effects of Integration

Impact of Standards, Government Procurement and Dynamic Learning Effects on Substitution: The single market program should increase the ability and willingness of EU buyers to substitute among the products of EU suppliers due to the impact of standards, government procurement and dynamic learning effects on substitution. Regarding standards, the EU92 program involves ***interchangeability*** standards which are designed for the express purpose of allowing buyers greater substitution possibilities among different suppliers. Interchangeability standards have had a powerful impact on competition in the United States. Well known interchangeability standards are those in the auto industry which were imposed on parts suppliers by the Society of Automotive Engineers (SAE) on behalf of auto assemblers; these standards were designed so that assemblers would be able to substitute among different suppliers of parts such as wheel rims, spark plugs and screws and bolts.[17]

Standards are sometimes imposed by suppliers for anticompetitive purposes.[18] For example, fearing anticompetitive standards, the U.S. Federal Communications Commission mandated standardized interconnection for terminal equipment and open network architecture (ONA), which means that the components of the telephone system are made available on an

---

pricing (as well as greater uncertainty), in which consumers who are more interested in being in fashion have less elastic demand and pay higher prices early in the season.

17. It is also possible that ***quality standards*** will arise. Products that are graded for quality typically have little product differentiation advantages. This includes milk, eggs, meat, lumber, soybeans, diamonds and mushrooms. See Hemenway [1975] for a detailed discussion of the impact of standards on competition.

18. Another prominent reason for suppliers to desire standards is to gain economies of scale. This was discussed above and included in the model.

unbundled basis so that competing supplier services can be combined in any manner desired. These standards have been highly successful, at least judged by the wide variety of independent supplier equipment and services that have developed.[19]

As part of its single market program, EU policy is attempting to implement similar reforms in standards. The EU green paper on telecommunications policy indicates that through the promotion of Europe-wide standards it shall provide equal access to all market participants (EC [1987; p.5]). Moreover, ONA has been mandated by the Maastricht treaty partly to insure the uniform interpretation of essential requirements across the EU in order to limit the possibilities for the imposition of restrictive licensing conditions.[20]

Probably the best known example of supplier-based anticompetitive standards is national standards that have the force of law for the purpose of protection, which the EU refers to as technical regulations. For example, EU courts interpreted German beer purity laws as protectionist and required that beer manufactured in any member state could be imported into Germany. This is an application of the mutual recognition principle in which products produced in one member state may be sold throughout the EU. In the absence of specific EU legislation however, EU states may still block intra-EU imports if certain national interests are involved. So the EU has attempted to achieve harmonization of technical regulations in which EU directives indicate mandatory requirements for national regulations.[21] In either event, the European consumer will be able to consume products from other EU states that previously were illegal to import.

Regarding ***government procurement***, broadly speaking the single market program is designed to require governments to accept the goods and ser-

19. See Besen and Saloner [1987] for further details.
20. See XIII, September 1993, p.12 (the magazine of DG XIII of the EU) and Emerson et al. [1988; p.86].
21. A manufacturer may meet the technical requirements either by producing a product that meets the defined essential requirements (which allows manufacturer variety subject to the constraint of meeting the essential requirements of the product) or by producing a product in conformity with European standardization bodies (Emerson et al. [1988; p.40]).

vices of non-national EU producers as closer substitutes to products of their national producers. Finally, based on the surveys of the "Costs of non-Europe" project, some observers concluded that "there is a dynamic of demand associated with the *learning process* of consumers and enterprises which is released or accelerated when barriers are removed" (Nerb [1988; p.26]). Thus, due to standards, government procurement rules and dynamic learning effects, the EU92 program should substantially increase the ability of buyers to substitute among the products of EU suppliers, justifying our modelling focus.

Modelling the Impact of Increased Substitution: Consumers may have preferences for the products of firms depending on region of origin. Prior to the EU92 program consumers are assumed to possess weakly separable utility functions that allow multiple stage budgeting of their choice decisions. First, based on a Cobb-Douglas utility function at the top level, they choose between the 26 different composite goods which were listed earlier, such as "motor vehicles" and "textiles and clothing". Having chosen how much to spend on each aggregate commodity, they then choose between domestic and imported composites of this commodity: between "domestic autos" or "imported autos", for example. This decision is based on a CES sub-utility function. Having decided how much to allocate to imported autos, consumers then decide how much to allocate to imports from different regions in the model. This decision is also based on a Constant Elasticity of Substitution (CES) sub-utility function. Finally, given the decision on how much to spend on autos from each country, consumers allocate expenditures on the different varieties from each country based on the lowest level CES sub-utility function.[22] Figure 1 displays the typical structure of preferences, after the initial Cobb-Douglas choice of how much to spend on the aggregate commodity, taking French consumers of autos as an example.

---

22. Given that the elasticities of substitution for these last two levels of choice with respect to foreign country and foreign firm variety (within a country) are the same, the structure is equivalent to firm level competition among all imports. A special case of this structure, with all elasticities of substitution equal, yields firm level competition among all firms that is independent of the country of origin.

Figure 1
Structure of Preferences before the EU92 Program

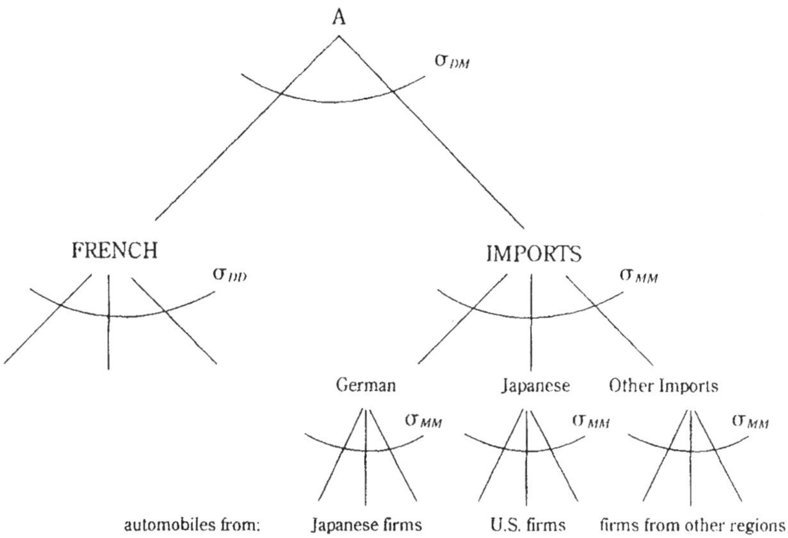

Due to EU92 programs regarding standards, government procurement, and due to dynamic learning effects, EU-produced goods become better substitutes, and this is perceived by EU consumers. This reflects a demand change by EU consumers, which we simulate along a continuum where in the limit consumers regard the products of all EU firms as equally substitutable. The latter preference structure is shown in Figure 2, again taking French consumers of autos as an example.

Specifically, in the fully integrated scenario the preference structure of consumers is directly analogous to the segmented scenario prior to EU92. Having decided how much to spend on any aggregate commodity, such as autos, consumers allocate that income among imported and domestic varieties of the commodity. However, now the notion of a "domestic variety" includes all other EU-produced varieties, even if they are not produced in the EU country in which the consumer lives. That is, we shift from treating other EU products as being "foreign varieties" and treat them as if they were "domestic varieties". The preference structure is modelled as a weighted average of the two extreme preference structures, where

Figure 2
Structure of Preferences after the EU92 Program

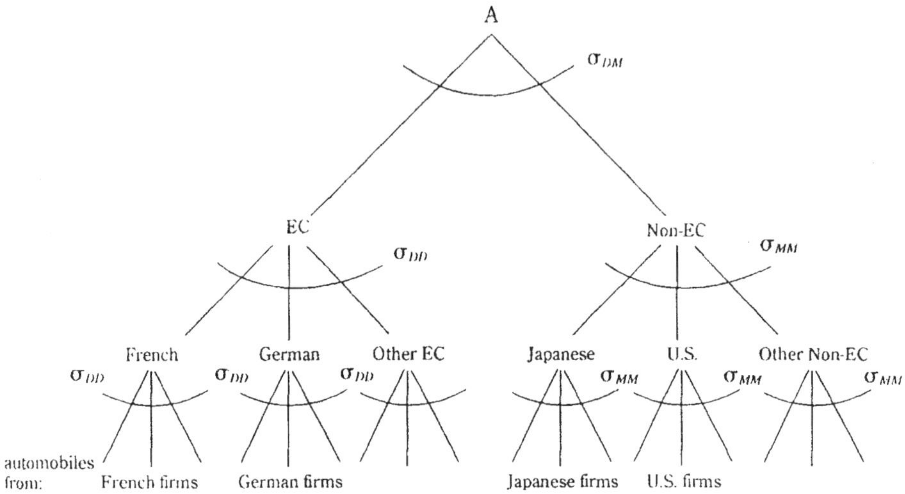

"percent integration" represents the weight of the fully integrated structure.[23]

Our measure of Hicksian equivalent variation is well defined because when we employ the post-EU92 preference structure (elasticities), we recalibrate the initial equilibrium with the same preference structure (elasticities). This is possible because given prices, incomes and quantity choices, the initial data point can be calibrated as an optimum for any elasticity of substitution.[24] That is, nothing is changed in the benchmark equilibrium by

23. We assume that this fraction is constant across all countries, reflecting the overall progress towards completion of the EU92 program. It would be a simple matter to let it vary across EU countries, perhaps reflecting the differential speed with which EU countries are accepting EU-wide standards and are removing border costs on EU imports. There is some anecdotal evidence of such differentials, at least as measured by the speed of enacting national legislation to implement the EU92 program (*e.g.*, *The Economist*, July 3-9, 1993, Survey on the European Community).

24. For example, in two dimensions suppose that prices, income and the consumer's budget constraint are given along with the observed quantity choice. Then given an initial elasticity of substitution from the utility function, the observed point is calibrated as an optimum by choosing other parameters of the utility function such that the indifference curve is tangent to the budget line at the observed quantity choice, i.e.,

the recalibration, but the different elasticity structure impacts the results in the counterfactual.

The key elasticities of substitution are denoted σ_{DM}, σ_{DD} and σ_{MM}, and reflect the substitutability between domestic (D) and imported (M) goods, alternative domestic varieties, and alternative foreign countries (and varieties), respectively. Our priors are that products produced in the same country will be more substitutable among themselves than products from different countries. This gives us the relationship that $\sigma_{MM} < \sigma_{DD}$; this inequality plays a crucial role in the analysis.[25] Although it does not play an important role in the analysis, we also posit that domestic consumers are less willing to substitute foreign varieties for domestic varieties than they are among different varieties from foreign sources. In the absence of data-based estimates of these elasticities we initially specify $\sigma_{DM} = 5$, $\sigma_{MM} = 10$, and $\sigma_{DD} = 15$. These three key elasticities of substitution remain the same when applied to the pre or post EU92 preference structure.

A formal derivation is provided in Harrison, Rutherford and Tarr [1994, Appendix A], but intuition into how market integration affects markups and intra-EU trade can be obtained through examination of the markup equations. Define the markup for firms from one EU country (r) selling into another EU country (r') in the segmented market situation as $m_{rr'}$, and in the fully integrated equilibrium as $m^{*}_{rr'}$. The markup under segmented markets is:

$$m^{*}_{rr'} = \frac{1}{\sigma_{MM}} + \left[\frac{1}{\sigma_{DM}} - \frac{1}{\sigma_{MM}}\right]\frac{\theta_{rr'}}{N_r \theta^{M}_{r'}} + \left[1 - \frac{1}{\sigma_{DM}}\right]\frac{\theta_{rr'}}{N_r} \tag{1}$$

and the markup under fully integrated markups is:

$$m^{*}_{rr'} = \frac{1}{\sigma_{DD}} + \left[\frac{1}{\sigma_{DM}} - \frac{1}{\sigma_{DD}}\right]\frac{\theta_{rr'}}{N_r \theta^{EC}_{r'}} + \left[1 - \frac{1}{\sigma_{DM}}\right]\frac{\theta_{rr'}}{N_r} \tag{2}$$

where

it is optimal. Changing the curvature of the utility function will not change the point of tangency in the initial equilibrium. The curvature of the utility function is important in the counterfactual because the slope of the budget constraint changes or because of imperfect competition, but it is irrelevant in determining the initial equilibrium.

25. It also implies, along with later assumptions, that $\sigma_{DM} < \sigma_{DD}$.

$$\theta_{r'}^{M} = \sum_{r \neq r'} \theta_{rr'} \qquad \theta_{r'}^{EC} = \sum_{r \in EC} \theta_{rr'}$$

$\theta_{rr'}$ denotes the market share of region r firms in region r', and N_r is the number of firms in region r. The change in markup, defined as the fully integrated minus the segmented markup, simplifies to:

$$m^{*}_{rr'} - m_{rr'} = \left[\frac{1}{\sigma_{DD}} - \frac{1}{\sigma_{MM}}\right] + \frac{\theta_{rr'}}{N_r}\left[\frac{1}{\theta_{r'}^{EC}}\left[\frac{1}{\sigma_{DM}} - \frac{1}{\sigma_{DD}}\right] - \frac{1}{\theta_{r'}^{M}}\left[\frac{1}{\sigma_{DM}} - \frac{1}{\sigma_{MM}}\right]\right] \quad (3)$$

When this expression is negative, markups on intra-EU trade will fall and trade will tend, *ceteris paribus*, to increase. We assumed that $\sigma_{DM} = 5$, $\sigma_{MM} = 10$, and $\sigma_{DD} = 15$. The first term in this simplified expression is negative when $\sigma_{DD} > \sigma_{MM}$, and for our specific values equals –0.033; however, there is some ambiguity with respect to the second term. Given the ranking of the elasticities of substitution, the second term will be positive the smaller is $\theta_{r'}^{EC}$ in relation to $\theta_{r'}^{M}$, *i.e.*, the smaller the share domestic firms have of the domestic market relative to non-EU imports in the domestic market.[26] Given our specific values, the change in the markup equals:

$$-0.033 + \frac{\theta_{rr'}}{N_r}\left[\frac{(.133)}{\theta_{r'}^{EC}} - \frac{(.1)}{\theta_{r'}^{M}}\right].$$

Numerically, we find that the sign of the second term is positive in most cases, but considerably smaller than the first term because it is multiplied by the ratio of a share ($\theta_{rr'}$) divided by the number of firms. For example, for Belgium's markup in Germany we have the share of Belgian exports in the German market divided by the number of Belgian firms. Thus, we find that the change in the markup is uniformly negative, and in most cases the decline in the markup is between 2 and 3.3 percent.

III. The Effects of Completion of the Market

A. Static Welfare Effects

Table 1 displays the results of completion of the market on aggregate EU welfare. In effect, this measure of the welfare effects adopts a utilitarian

26. Specifically, the second term will be positive if and only if $4\sum_{r \notin EC} \theta_{rr'} + \sum_{\substack{r \notin EC \\ r \neq r'}} \theta_{rr'} > 3\theta_{r'r'}$.

Table 1
Welfare Effects of EU92 on the EU [a]

Percent Integration		Percent Removal of Border and Standards Costs									
		0%		25%		50%		75%		100%	
		Static (1)	Steady state (2)	Static (3)	Steady state (4)	Static (5)	Steady state (6)	Static (7)	Steady state (8)	Static (9)	Steady state (10)
0%	IRTS	0.00	0.00	0.12	0.38	0.25	0.85	0.38	1.33	0.52	1.79
	CRTS	0.00	0.00	0.11	0.34	0.22	0.74	0.34	1.15	0.46	1.56
25%	IRTS	0.11	0.30	0.24	0.72	0.37	1.14	0.51	1.57	0.66	2.03
	CRTS	0.00	0.00	0.11	0.33	0.23	0.70	0.35	1.08	0.47	1.48
50%	IRTS	0.23	0.59	0.36	0.98	0.50	1.38	0.65	1.80	0.81	2.25
	CRTS	0.00	0.00	0.11	0.30	0.23	0.64	0.35	0.99	0.49	1.37
75%	IRTS	0.36	0.83	0.50	1.20	0.65	1.59	0.81	2.00	0.98	2.44
	CRTS	0.00	0.00	0.11	0.27	0.23	0.57	0.36	0.90	0.50	1.24
100%	IRTS	0.50	1.04	0.65	1.38	0.82	1.76	0.99	2.16	1.18	2.60
	CRTS	0.00	0.00	0.11	0.23	0.23	0.49	0.36	0.79	0.50	1.10

Note: a. Welfare effects are in each case the aggregate equivalent variation as a percent of aggregate EU GDP.
Source: Model estimates.

social welfare function for the EU, such that we simply add up the welfare effects for individual EU countries. In Table 1 we display a matrix of results where we simulate partial and full removal of border and supply side standards costs and well as partial and complete change in the elasticities of substitution (referred to in the table as percent of integration).

First, consider the static welfare effects with IRTS in Table 1. These estimates imply that ***removal of internal trade barriers and market integration are complementary*** to each other, which is consistent with the received wisdom from previous studies. Full integration with complete removal of internal trade barriers results in an aggregate welfare gain of 1.13% of GDP per annum.

Table 2

Country Composition of the Welfare Effects of EU92[a]: 100% Integration and Removal of Border and Standards Costs

Region	Percent change in: Welfare[b]		Welfare in dollars[c]		Real wages		Real price[d] of capital	Real consumer prices	
	Static	Steady state	Static	Steady state	Static	Steady state		Static	Steady state
Belgium (BE)	3.37 (1.53)	6.39	3.32 (1.51)	6.31	5.2 (2.6)	6.7	3.3 (1.3)	1.4 (0.7)	1.0
Germany (DE)	1.10 (0.44)	2.03	7.27 (2.90)	13.39	1.0 (0.4)	1.6	0.9 (0.3)	0.1 (0.1)	0.1
Denmark (DK)	1.82 (0.81)	3.78	1.21 (0.54)	2.51	2.4 (1.2)	3.0	1.7 (0.8)	0.7 (0.4)	0.4
Spain (ES)	0.80 (0.36)	1.96	2.19 (0.98)	5.36	0.8 (0.4)	1.4	1.2 (0.5)	0.4 (0.2)	0.0
France (FR)	1.13 (0.50)	2.47	7.07 (3.14)	15.44	1.1 (0.5)	1.8	1.4 (0.7)	0.3 (0.2)	0.1
Italy (IT)	1.05 (0.46)	2.03	4.62 (2.03)	8.88	1.0 (0.4)	1.5	0.8 (0.3)	0.0 0	–0.1
The Netherlands (NL)	2.48 (1.20)	7.73	3.41 (1.65)	10.63	3.0 (1.3)	4.9	4.0 (2.5)	1.2 (0.7)	1.1
Portugal (PT)	1.04 (0.42)	1.72	0.53 (0.21)	0.87	0.5 (0.3)	0.6	1.3 (0.8)	–0.2 0	–0.6
United Kingdom (UK)	0.80 (0.29)	1.49	4.31 (1.57)	7.97	0.1 (–0.2)	0.4	1.0 (0.4)	–0.3 (–0.3)	–0.3
Rest of World (ROW)	–0.00 (–0.005)	0.05	–0.35 (–0.42)	4.06	–0.00 (–0.1)	0.0	0.3 (0.1)	0 0	0.0

Notes: a. Numbers without parentheses are for IRTS in fully integrated scenario with all border and standards.

b. Equivalent variation s a percent of GDP.

c. Equivalent variation in billions of 1985 U.S. dollars.

d. Real price of capital is fixed in the steady state scenario.

The ***relative contribution of market integration and removal of trade barriers appears to be roughly additive and, as it turns out, somewhat symmetric.*** That is, x% integration and y% removal of sand achieves about the same welfare increase as y% integration and x% removal of sand, provided neither x nor y are zero.

CRTS Results and Comparison with IRTS: To build intuition, it is helpful to consider the results in the case in which all sectors are subject to CRTS. We implement this by setting the CDR equal to zero for all sectors. Given that there are no rationalization gains to be realized from improved scale efficiency in a CRTS model, we would expect that the welfare effects of EU92 would be much smaller, and indeed they are. In Table 1 the effect of assuming IRTS and monopolistically competitive pricing in our model is seen to increase the welfare gains by almost nothing (if we assume zero price integration) or by as much as 100% (if we assume full price integration).

In Table 2 we present results showing the distributional effects across countries. We find considerable disparity in the welfare effects across EU countries, even though all gain. Table 2 shows the effect on welfare in percentage and in absolute terms (equivalent variation as a percent of GDP and in billions of 1985 U.S. dollars, respectively), the percentage change in the real wage and the real price of capital, and finally the percentage change in the real cost of living. The numbers without parentheses are for the IRTS fully integrated scenario in which all border and standards costs "sand" are removed. The CRTS results are in parentheses.

Examining Table 2 for the distribution of welfare gains across the countries of the EU in the CRTS case, one sees that Belgium and the Netherlands are the countries which experience the largest increase in welfare as a percent of GDP. The key to understanding this is to recognize that we have modelled the impact of the EU92 program on standards and borders costs as costs which will be reduced on intra-EU exports only. That is, there are no cost reductions on production for the domestic market. Border costs require resources of the domestic transportation sector in our model, and supply side standards costs are a component of value-added to the extent that the good is exported. Since the single market program is assumed to

Figure 3
Distribution of EU92 Benefits under CRTS:
Case of Belgian Steel in Germany

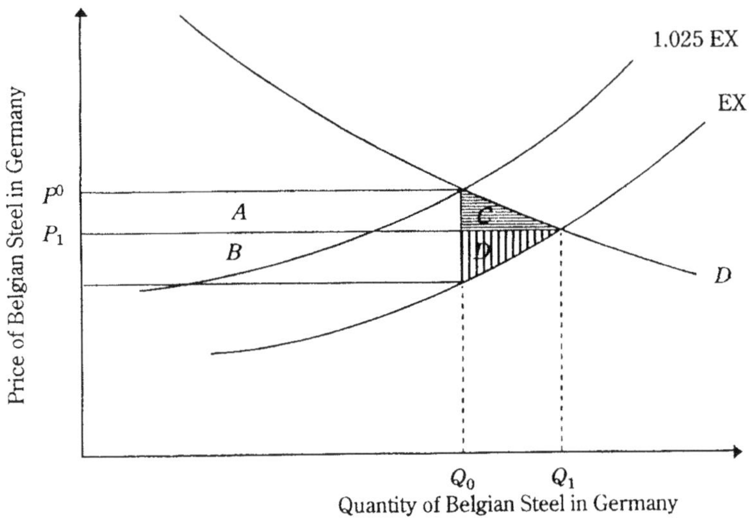

Note: The initial equilibrium for Belgian steel in Germany is at (P_0, Q_0), determined by the intersection of the export supply curve of Belgian steel producers to Germany (1.025 EX), and the demand by German consumers for Belgian steel (D). Following the changes of EC92, the export supply curve shifts down by 2.5 percent to EX, resulting in a new equilibrium (abstracting from general equilibrium effects) at (P_1, Q_1). There are rectangles of benefits **A** (to Germany) plus **B** (to Belgium), the sum of which is 2.5 percent of the initial exports; plus triangles of benefits from reduced distortion costs equal to **C** (to Germany) and **D** (to Belgium).

reduce the border and standards costs of intra-EU exporting by 2.5 percent, the first order effect on welfare (as a percent of GDP) will be approximately equal to the share of intra-EU trade in GDP times 2.5 percent. But there will be additional gains from removing distortion costs.

In Figure 3 we depict the partial equilibrium welfare economics of a 2.5% reduction in the costs of intra-EU exporting under CRTS. We take the example of Belgian exports of steel to Germany. There is a rectangle of benefits from the reduction of the costs of exporting Belgian steel to Germany, equal to 2.5% of the initial costs of exporting. Provided neither German demand for steel, nor Belgian supply of steel, are limiting elasticity cases, the initial rectangle of benefits will be shared between the exporting and importing country (*A* to German consumers and B to Belgian producers in the figure).

In addition, the border and standards costs are analogous to distortions to trade. Their removal allows a reallocation of resources with an increase in intra-EU trade. That is, there are "triangles" of benefits that augment the "rectangles" of benefits from the reduced costs of exporting. In Figure 3 triangle *C* is a benefit to German consumers and triangle *D* is a gain to Belgian exporters. These reallocation benefits will be increased or decreased to the extent that the country is responsive to changes in relative prices of imports and exports. Figure 3 also reveals that the more elastic is a country's demand or supply curves in relation to the other countries of the EU, the smaller will be its share of the benefits of EU92.

The intra-EU trade intensities of the EU countries in our model were noted earlier. The three countries that trade most intensely within the EU are Belgium, Netherlands and Denmark, and these are the three countries that gain the most from the EU92 program in the CRTS case. For the remaining countries there is little difference in their intra-EU trade intensities (ranging from 12% to 8.8%), and there is also relatively little difference in their welfare gain as a percent of GDP (ranging from 0.5% to 0.29%).

The benefits for all countries under CRTS exceed the first order effect of the lowering of the cost of production. In particular, 2.5% times the trade intensity ratio yields the following first order welfare effect in percent of GDP: Belgium 0.89, Netherlands 0.37, Denmark 0.37, Germany 0.30, Portugal 0.30, U.K. 0.30, France 0.28, Italy 0.25, and Spain 0.22. Other than for the U.K. and Denmark, the welfare benefits are between 1.4 and 2.2 times this "first order" effect, suggesting that the triangles in Figure 3 are quite large.[27] By the standards of CRTS models, we have assumed rather large trade elasticities in our benchmark equilibrium, so the triangles in Figure 3 are almost as large as the rectangles.[28] Examining Figure 3 reveals that the

27. For the U.K. the benefits are close to the first order effect, indicating that the U.K. is obtaining a relatively small share of the benefits of integration. As discussed above, this suggests that U.K. import demand or export supply is more elastic than that of the other EU countries.

benefits would be closer to the rectangles the more inelastic are the demand elasticities.[29] When we counterfactually reduce all three import demand elasticities for all countries in our model to one-fourth their original values, the benefits for most EU countries are reduced to between 1.17 and 1.28 of the simple rectangle effect.[30]

Thus, the intensiveness with which a country engages in trade is of first order importance in explaining the benefits that are likely to be achieved from CRTS sectors. More aggregated models have aggregated small countries such as Belgium with larger countries. In so doing they have produced a region which is closer to average with respect to trade intensities, which will mask important distributional effects across the EU countries.[31]

In column 9 of Table 1 the CRTS welfare gain to the aggregate EU from complete removal of border and standards costs barriers to intra-EU trade varies from 0.46% to 0.5%, depending on the degree of market integration. Market integration, which in our model is greater substitutability among EU products, has only a very small effect on welfare in a CRTS model (by inducing slightly more resource movement) because it does not affect markups or entry and exit.

The Impact of IRTS: Examination of Tables 1 and 2 reveals that the wel-

28. Similar to the approach of Gasiorek, Smith and Venables [1992], we choose to calibrate with elasticities to be consistent with price-cost margins given by estimates of the CDR subject to a zero profit model assumption. Nonetheless, the trade elasticities are small in relation to those used in their models.

29. We show below, however, that the higher elasticities reduce the additional welfare gain from rationalization and consumption efficiency gains in IRTS sectors. Thus, the high elasticities have offsetting effects regarding their welfare impact.

30. Exceptions are Denmark, which remains an outlier and obtains benefits equal to 1.78 times the rectangle effect, and Germany and the U.K. which obtain less than the rectangle effect. The large demand elasticities that we have employed, however, result in somewhat higher estimates of the welfare effects and of the adjustment across industries in both the CRTS and IRTS cases.

31. Our interpretation of border costs follows Smith and Venables [1988] and others, who have modelled EU92. An alternate view is that border costs are highest where trade is lowest. Thus, when border costs are removed, the countries with the lowest trade intensities will gain more for the same shares of trade. Although trade intensities would still matter, the results across countries could change significantly.

fare benefits of the complete removal of border and standards costs roughly double, both for the aggregate EU as well as for individual EU regions, when the impact of IRTS with full market integration is incorporated. The key to explaining the impact of IRTS is the role of market integration on elasticities, markups and entry and exit. To clarify this point first compare the CRTS and IRTS results with 0% integration (row 1 of Table 1). Then the static effects of removing border or standards costs are virtually identical between IRTS and CRTS. That is, without additional effects from market integration, the beneficial effects of removing border and standards costs can be attributed to "traditional" efficiency gains found in a standard CRTS framework.

The key to understanding the impact of IRTS in our model is that integration increases the elasticity of demand on intra-EU exports, thereby inducing markup declines. The equation for the markup was discussed earlier. A decline in the equilibrium markup can only be achieved through an improvement in the realization of scale efficiency.

Despite the fact that we employ equivalent variation in a general equilibrium, a partial equilibrium analysis is useful to isolate the crucial variables in IRTS sectors. In Figure 4 we present a consumer surplus interpretation of a symmetric monopolistically competitive industry with a given level of fixed costs per firm and constant marginal costs (MC). An additional simplification in Figure 4 is that it presumes a homogeneous output, so the elasticity increase is represented simply as a rotation of the market demand curve.[32] Originally there are n_0 firms charging price P_0 and producing q_0. We assume zero profits, so rectangles $A+C$ equal fixed costs per firm. As a result of an increase in the market elasticity of demand, the perceived marginal revenue of the firm will equal marginal costs at a larger output level. In the absence of general equilibrium effects which change factor costs, the marginal and average cost curves for the representative firm remain unchanged. Then, due to the zero profit constraint, exit must occur such that the new perceived demand curve of the representative firm, d_1, is tangent to the average

32. The analysis of Figure 4 extends naturally to our firm level product differentiation case by defining the market output as the CES aggregate of the output of the individual firms, and the market price as the price dual to the CES quantity aggregate.

Glenn W. Harrison, Thomas F. Rutherford and David G. Tarr

Figure 4
Rationalization and Consumption Efficiency Gains from Increased Elasticities

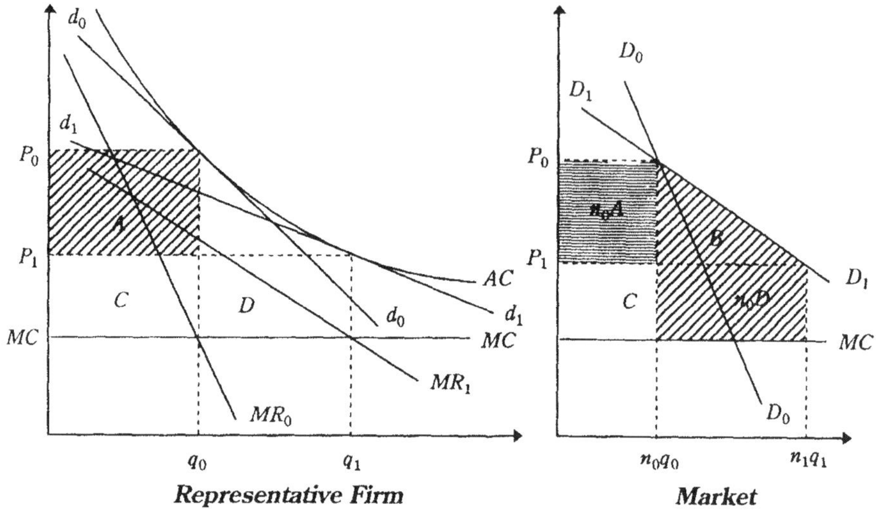

Note: Increased market demand elasticity induces representative firms to lower price and some to exit industry in the new zero profit equilibrium. The welfare gain equals the area under the market demand curve above MC, *i.e.*, the consumption efficiency gain B plus the rationalization gain n_0D, where $n_0D = n_0A$.

cost curve at the new lower markup. It follows that $P_1 < P_0$ and industry output increases.

Welfare effects are shown in the panel of Figure 4 labeled Market, where D_0 and D_1 are the initial and new market demand curves. Since price exceeds marginal costs in the initial equilibrium, the expansion of output increases welfare. This welfare gain can be decomposed into two parts. First there is the typical consumption efficiency triangle B, as might occur with removal of a tax.[33] Unlike a tax, however, there is an additional gain of consumers' surplus equal to the rectangle n_0A that has no offsetting cost or lost tax revenue. The additional consumers' surplus gain derives from the rationalization gain of spreading fixed costs. That is, the expansion of output

33. Following the procedure of Burns [1973], the efficiency triangle is obtained by connecting the pre and post equilibria by a straight line.

costs society resources at the rate of MC per unit but is valued as the area under the demand curve.[34] These consumption efficiency and rationalization gains from increased elasticities in IRTS sectors are gains from the EU92 program over and above the gains from the reduction of the costs of exporting that were characterized in Figure 3.[35]

A similar interpretation will apply even when general equilibrium effects are incorporated that will induce shifts in the market demand curves. For IRTS industries that experience an output decline or only a small output increase, exit occurs. For those that experience output increases, entry can occur with a markup decline only with a significant output expansion. All of these scenarios result in rationalization in the use of fixed costs and, since price-marginal costs markups decline, a decrease in consumption deadweight loss. These are benefits above those that would occur in a CRTS sector.

In Table 3 we present some of the key data for the IRTS sectors in three representative countries: Belgium, France and Spain. We focus on these countries because Belgium is the country that gains the most from the EU92 program, France is a representative large country, and Spain is a country with relatively small trade shares in Germany. We present results for the scenario of 100 percent integration and 100 percent removal of border and standards costs.

In the first three columns we present the percent decline in the "Lerner" markup: price minus marginal costs, all divided by price. The equation for the change in the Lerner markup was presented as equation 3. Note that markups on export sales in Germany change between −1.0 and −3.3 percent for industries in all three countries. For some products there are no exports

34. Since fixed costs per firm are unchanged $A + C = C + D$, *i.e.*, $A = D$ and $n_0A = n_0D$. Then the welfare increase equals the area under the demand curve between n_0q_0 and n_1q_1 that lies above industry marginal costs.

35. The greater the absolute value of the decline in the markup, the larger will be the welfare benefits from rationalization and consumption efficiency. A proportional reduction in the elasticities of substitution in the model, however, will increase the absolute value of the decline in the markup. That is, given benchmark elasticities, $\sigma_{DD} = 15$, $\sigma_{MM} = 10$, the dominant first term in equation 3 is $(1/15) - (1/10) = -1/30$. If the elasticities of substitution were scaled down, for example by 1/5, then the first term in equation 3 would equal $(1/3)-(1/2) = -5/30$. This would result in a larger drop in the new equilibrium price in Figure 4 and greater welfare gains.

Table 3
Changes in IRTS Sectors in Belgium, France and Spain: 100% Integration and Removal of Border and Standards Costs

	Percent Change in:											
	Mark Up in Germany			Number of firms			Output per firm			Production[a]		
	BE (1)	FR (2)	SP (3)	BE (4)	FR (5)	SP (6)	BE (7)	FR (8)	SP (9)	BE (10)	FR (11)	SP (12)
Food	-3.3	NA[b]	-3.3	-19.6	-7.7	-1.0	30	11	6	4.7 (-5.2)	2.9 (1.8)	5.1 (1.6)
Steel	-1.6	-2.9	-3.3	4.5	0	-6.2	54	12	4	60.9 (32.1)	12.3 (6.0)	-2.7 (-7.3)
Nonmetallic Minerals	NA	NA	NA	-33.1	-11.0	2.4	17	5	9	-21.6 (11.3)	-6.6 (1.1)	11.1 (0.5)
Chemicals	-2.8	-3.1	NA	-4.1	-4.6	-8.6	28	7	-1	22.8 (4.3)	1.8 (1.0)	-9.8 (-4.5)
Metal Products	NA	-3.3	-3.2	-27.2	1.4	1.4	5	3	5	-23.9 (-11.8)	4.9 (1.7)	6.9 (-1.5)
Industrial Machinery	-2.8	-3.1	-3.3	-10.9	-5.3	-11.2	33	-1	0	18.5 (11.3)	-5.9 (-4.4)	-11.1 (-12.4)
Office Machinery	NA	-2.6	-3.1	-29.6	-8.8	-0.1	13	15	1	-20.7 (-12.1)	5.3 (2.6)	0.6 (0.0)
Electrical Goods	-1.0	-3.2	-3.3	-22.9	-8.3	-12.5	44	1	2	11.1 (9.7)	-7.4 (-3.0)	-10.7 (-0.4)
Motor Vehicles	-3.1	-3.2	-3.3	49.5	-16.3	-12.1	60	27	20	139.4 (45.5)	6.7 (2.7)	5.4 (-6.1)
Other Transport Equipment	NA	-3.0	NA	-29.1	-6.7	-12.6	20	12	8	-14.8 (-12.3)	4.8 (0.4)	-5.3 (0.0)
Paper	-3.3	-3.3	-3.3	-17.0	-11.2	-7.8	51	8	11	25.2 (-0.5)	-4.5 (-2.0)	2.8 (3.8)
Rubber and Plastics	NA	-3.3	-3.3	-10.2	-2.7	-2.8	46	0	0	30.8 (25.0)	-2.8 (-2.7)	-2.3 (-8.7)

Notes: a. Value in parentheses is percent change in production under CRTS.

b. NA = Not applicable since there are no exports to Germany from this country of this product in the benchmark.

to Germany in the benchmark data, hence the markup equation is not applicable. Since the Spanish share of the German market is small, when the markup equation applies the decline in the markup is close to –3.3 percent, which is the value of the first term on the right hand side of equation 3.

In columns 4-6 we present the percent change in entry and exit, and in columns 7-9 we present the percent change in output per firm. The key differences appear in the output per firm columns. We see that rationalization is much greater in Belgium than in the other two countries. Again the reason is that the intra-EU trade intensity of Belgium is much greater than the other two countries considered here. Since export sales constitute a much larger percentage of output for Belgium, the same percentage decline in markup on exports to the various EU markets induces a much larger reallocation of resources in Belgium's IRTS sectors.

Columns 10-12 show the percent change in output in the IRTS sectors, and the numbers in parentheses show the percent change in production when these sectors are presumed to operate under CRTS. One can see that different IRTS scenarios expand and contract in the different countries (a full presentation of the output changes by industry and region is presented in Harrison, Rutherford and Tarr [1994, Appendix]). The interesting pattern is that the sign of the output change in the IRTS scenario is generally the same as the sign of the output change in the CRTS scenario. The magnitude of the change in absolute value, however, is generally larger with IRTS. Thus, traditional determinants of resource allocation, factor intensities and remaining tax wedges, play a key role in influencing industrial structure. Shifts in relative costs that occur in a CRTS world provide an impetus for output decline or expansion. If relative costs decline and output expands due to a change in factor intensities, in an IRTS world the output expansion induces a further decline in average costs and price, which magnifies the output increase.

Returning to Table 2, note that despite the fact that markups decline and real incomes[36] increase with integration, real prices also increase. For a sharp example, Belgian real incomes increase while real prices also increase by 1.4% despite some significant declines in specific IRTS sectors.[37] The key

36. Our numeraire is a basket of final consumption in the Rest of the World.

is that the relative price of labor increases by 5.2%, and the relative price of capital by 3.3%, so factor earnings increase at a faster pace than commodity prices.[38] Factor earnings increase so much in Belgium because resources are being allocated more efficiently, hence the value of the marginal product of each factor is greater than with the previous allocation of resources. In addition to the benefits that occur under CRTS, as discussed above, there are significant gains from rationalization and markup declines. All of these gains are dependent on the intra-EU trade intensity of the country.

Intra-EU Trade: In Harrison, Rutherford and Tarr [1994, Tables A2, A3] we present the percentage change in exports and imports to EU countries and non-EU countries, respectively. We have argued that a counterintuitive feature of modelling EU integration as uniform pricing is that intra-EU trade declines as a consequence. With our approach to integration, however, there is a strong increase in trade among the EU countries, and a modest decline in trade between EU countries and the rest of the world. We also note that domestic sales of EU firms typically decline. Although domestic markups increase for EU firms, the largest declines in domestic sales are not explained by differences in markup changes. Rather, the largest declines in domestic sales occur in those countries that have the highest intra-EU trade intensities.

Thus, overall we have a picture of EU countries trading much more with each other and relying less on their domestic markets for sales. Moreover, since their economies become more trade intensive, there is only a slight decline in trade with countries outside of the EU.

Regarding the decline in EU trade with the rest of the world, we have

37. For example, the following IRTS sectors experience price declines: Food by 3.3%, Iron & Steel by 4.7%, Chemicals by 3.2%, Industrial and Office Machinery by about 4.5%, and Vehicles by 5.5%. Most CRTS sectors in Belgium experience an increase in relative prices (*e.g.*, Beverages & Tobacco by 2.4%, Utilities by 2.6%, and virtually all service sectors by about 3%). In the CRTS version of the model the Belgian increase in the price level is only about 0.7% . The structural pattern of price increases and decreases is approximately the same as in the IRTS version, even though no sector has IRTS in this case.

38. The same qualitative effect occurs in the CRTS model, with the relative price of labor increasing by 2.6% and the relative price of capital by 1.3%.

modelled EU92 as a shift in relative costs for EU countries toward trading with EU countries rather than non-EU countries. That is, the 2.5% cost decrease on exports to EU countries accrues only to firms in EU countries. It is possible that some, if not all, of the border and standards costs reductions that accrue to EU firms will also benefit non-EU firms.[39] To the extent that this occurs then there would be an increase in non-EU exports and imports to and from the EU for ROW relative to what we have reported. This would also allow a welfare increase for the rest of the world in the static model since then a picture similar to Figure 3 would also apply to the rest of the world exports to EU countries.[40]

B. Modelling the Steady State Welfare Effects

In our steady state model we assume that in the initial (pre-single market) equilibrium the capital stock in each country is optimal given the rate of return on capital in the initial equilibrium. That is, increases in the rate of return on capital would induce an increase in investment until the marginal productivity of capital is driven down to the initial rate of return. The single market will produce a new equilibrium, where for almost all countries the rate of return on capital increases (relative to a price index of consumption) due to a more efficient allocation of resources. This implies that in a dynamic sense the new capital stock can no longer be optimal: investment must be forthcoming until the marginal productivity of capital is reduced to the long run equilibrium rate of return on capital.[41] Analogous to the medium-term growth bonus of Baldwin [1989], this expansion of the capital stock then

---

39. For example, a Moroccan truck delivering vegetables to Belgium should have reduced border costs as it passes between Spain and France and between France and Belgium.
40. In Harrison, Rutherford and Tarr [1994] we compare the welfare results of our model with those of the other principal models of EU92: Gasiorek, Smith and Venables [1992], Haaland and Norman [1992] and Mercenier [1992]. We show that the greater sectoral disaggregation of the CRTS sectors in our model results in substantial differences in the results for some EU countries, although there is little impact on the aggregate welfare results.
41. See Hansen and Koopmans [1972] and Dantzig and Manne [1974] for early multisectoral applications of this approach.

works like an "endowment effect", generating larger welfare gains since there are more resources available. In addition, as the income of the world increases, demand for goods and the derived demand for factors increases. In this model the quantity of capital will increase in response, producing a further endowment effect.[42]

We emphasize that this calculation measures an *upper bound* on potential welfare gains in the long run without endogenous growth. The capital stock can only be produced through investment, and that requires reduced consumption along the transition path. For sufficiently high discount rates, the cost of the foregone consumption could easily outweigh the longer-run benefits of the capital accumulation it allows.[43]

Table 1 shows that the steady-state welfare gains are slightly more than double those from the comparable static model. Completion of the program results in an aggregate steady-state welfare gain of 2.38% of GDP for the EU. The distribution of these welfare gains, and related economic effects, is shown in Table 2.

References

Baldwin, Richard [1989], "The growth effects of 1992," *Economic Policy*, October; pp. 248-270.

Baldwin, Richard E., Forslid, Rikard and Haaland, Jan, "Investment Creation and Investment Diversion: Simulation Analysis of the Single Market Programme," in R. Baldwin and J. Francois (eds.), *Dynamic Issues in Applied Commercial Policy Analysis*, A Centre for Economic Policy Analysis conference volume, forthcoming.

Besen, Stanley and Garth Saloner [1987], "The Economics of Telecommunications Standards," in R. Crandall and K. Flamm (eds.), *Changing the*

42. Baldwin, Forslid and Haaland [forthcoming] have recently applied our steady state approach to an evaluation of the single market program. Harrison, Rutherford and Tarr [forthcoming] and Francois, McDonald and Nordstrom [forthcoming] apply an analogous approach to an analysis of the Uruguay Round.

43. Of course, our estimates would fail to capture endogenous growth effects. Rutherford and Tarr [forthcoming] offer a fully dynamic endogenous growth model that has a true welfare measure.

Rules: Technological Change, International Competition and Regulation in Communications (Washington, D.C.: The Brookings Institution).

Borenstein, Severin [1985], "Price Discrimination in Free-Entry Markets," *Rand Journal of Economics*, 16, Autumn; pp. 380-397.

Borenstein, Severin and Rose, N.L. [1991], "Competition and Price Dispersion in the U.S. Airline Industry," *Working Paper #3785*, National Bureau of Economic Research, July.

Brander, James A., and Krugman, Paul R [1983], "A Reciprocal Dumping Model of International Trade," *Journal of International Economics*, 15; pp. 313-321.

Brooke, Anthony; Kendrick, David, and Meeraus, Alexander, *GAMS* [1988], *A User's Guide* (Redwood City, CA: The Scientific Press).

Burniaux, Jean-Marc and Waelbroeck, Jean [1992], "Preliminary Results of Two Experimental Models of General Equilibrium with Imperfect Competition," *Journal of Policy Modelling*, 14; pp. 65-92.

Burns, Michael [1973], "A Note on the Concept and Measure of Consumers' Surplus," *American Economic Review*, 63(3); pp. 335-344.

Carlton, Dennis and Perlof, Jeffrey [1990], *Modern Industrial Organization* (New York: Harper Collins).

Cawley, Richard, and Davenport, Michael [1988], "Partial Equilibrium Calculations of the Impact of Internal Market Barriers in the European Community," *Economic Paper No. 73*, European Commission, Brussels.

Cecchini, Paolo; Catinat, Michel; and Jacquemin, Alexis [1988], *The European Challenge:* 1992 (Aldershot, UK: Wildwood House).

Dantzig, George, and Manne, Alan S. [1974], "A Complementarity Algorithm for an Optimal Capital Path with Invariant Proportions," *Journal of Economic Theory*, 9; pp. 312-323.

Emerson, Michael; Aujean, Michel; Catinat, Michel; Goybet, Philippe; and Jacquemin, Alexis [1988], *The Economics of 1992: The E.C. Commission's Assessment of the Economic Affects of Completing the Internal Market* (Oxford: Oxford University Press).

European Community [1987], *Towards a Dynamic European Economy: Green Paper on the Development of the Common Market for Telecommunications Equipment* (Brussels: EC Commission).

Fisher, Franklin; McGowan. John; and Greenwood, Joel [1983], *Folded, Spindled and Mutilated: Economic Analysis and U.S. v. IBM* (Cambridge, MA: MIT Press).

Francois, Joseph; McDonald, Brad, and Nordstrom, Håkan, "Trade Liberalization, Investment and the Capital Stock," in R. Baldwin and J. Francois (eds.), *Dynamic Issues in Applied Commercial Policy Analysis*, A Centre for Economic Policy Analysis conference volume, forthcoming.

Gasiorek, Michael; Smith, Alasdair; and Venables, Anthony J. [1992], "1992: Trade and Welfare; A General Equilibrium Model," in Winters, L.A. (ed.), *Trade Flows and Trade Policy After '1992'* (New York: Cambridge University Press).

Haaland, Jan I, and Wooton, Ian [1992], "Market Integration, Competition and Welfare," in Winters, L.A. (ed.), *Trade Flows and Trade Policy After '1992'* (New York: Cambridge University Press).

Haaland, Jan I. and Norman, Victor [1992], "Global Production Effects of European Integration," in Winters, L.A. (ed.), *Trade Flows and Trade Policy After '1992'* (New York: Cambridge University Press).

Hansen, Terje, and Koopmans, Tjalling [1972], "On the Definition and Computation of a Capital Stock Invariant Under Optimization," *Journal of Economic Theory*, 5; pp. 487-523.

Harrison, Glenn W.; Rutherford, Thomas F., and Tarr, David G. [1994], "Product Standards, Imperfect Competition, and Completion of the Market in the European Union," *Policy Research Working Paper No. 1293*, The World Bank, April.

Harrison, Glenn W.; Rutherford, Thomas F., and Tarr, David G., "Quantifying the Uruguay Round," in W. Martin and L. Alan Winters (eds.) *The Uruguay Round and the Developing Countries*, Cambridge University Press, forthcoming.

Hemenway, David [1975], *Industrywide Voluntary Product Standards* (Cambridge, MA.: Ballinger).

Holmes, T. J. [1989], "The Effects of Third Degree Price Discrimination in Oligopoly," *American Economic Review*, 79, March; pp. 244-250.

Katz, Michael [1984], "Price Discrimination and Monopolistic Competition," *Econometrica*, 52, November; pp. 1453-1471.

Kaysen, Carl [1956], *United States versus United States Shoe Machinery Cor-*

poration (Cambridge, UK: Cambridge University Press).

Karp, Larry [1992], "Discussion of Gasiorek, Smith and Venables," in Winters, L.A. (ed.), *Trade Flows and Trade Policy After '1992'* (New York: Cambridge University Press).

Malueg, David, and Schwartz, Marius, "Parallel Imports, Demand Dispersion and International Price Discrimination," *Journal of International Economics*, forthcoming.

Melo, Jaime de, and Tarr, David [1992], *General Equilibrium Analysis of U.S. Foreign Trade Policy* (Cambridge, MA: MIT Press).

Mercenier, Jean [1992], "Completing the European Internal Market: A General Equilibrium Evaluation Under Alternative Market Structure Assumptions," *Working Paper 0892*, Department of Economics, University of Montreal, March.

Nerb, G. [1988], "The Completion of the European Market: A Survey of European Industry's Perception of the Likely Effects," *The Costs of Non-Europe* (Luxembourg: Office for Official Publications of the European Communities, Volume 3).

Norman, Victor [1989], "EFTA and the Internal European Market," *Economic Policy*, October; pp. 423-465.

Pashigian, Peter and Bowen, Brian [1991], "Why Products are Sold on Sale?: Explanations of Pricing Regularities," *Quarterly Journal of Economics*, 106, November; pp. 1015-1038.

Rutherford, Thomas F. [1992a], "Extensions of GAMS for Complementarity and Variational Problems Arising in Applied Economics," *Economics Working Paper 92-9*, Department of Economics, University of Colorado at Boulder.

Rutherford, Thomas F [1992b]., "Sequential Joint Maximization," *Economics Working Paper 92-8*, Department of Economics, University of Colorado at Boulder.

Rutherford, Thomas and Tarr, David, "Blueprints, Spillovers and the Dynamic Gains from Trade Liberalization in a Small Open Economy," in R. Baldwin and J. Francois (eds.), *Dynamic Issues in Applied Commercial Policy Analysis,* A Centre for Economic Policy Analysis conference volume, forthcoming.

Scherer, F.M., and Ross, David [1990], *Industrial Market Structure and Eco-*

nomic Performance (Boston: Houghton Mifflin).

Shepard, Andrea [1991], "Price Discrimination in Retail Configuration," *Journal of Political Economy*, 99, February; pp. 30-53.

Smith, Alasdair, and Venables, Anthony J. [1988], "Completing the Internal Market in the European Community: Some Industry Simulations," *European Economic Review*, 32; pp. 1501-1525.

Tarr, David [1994], "Comments on Trade Policy Under Imperfect Competition," in P. Krugman and A. Smith (eds.), *Empirical Studies of Strategic Trade Policy* (Chicago: University of Chicago Press).

Varian, Hal R. [1989], "Price Discrimination," in R. Schmalansee and R. Willig (eds.), *Handbook of Industrial Organization* (Amsterdam: North Holland).

Winters, L. Alan [1992], "The Welfare and Policy Implications of the International Trade Consequences of '1992'," *American Economic Review (Papers & Proceedings)*, 82, May; pp. 104-108.

Winters, L. Alan (ed.1992), *Trade Flows and Trade Policy After '1992'* (New York: Cambridge University Press).

Wolinsky, Asher [1987], "Brand Names and Price Discrimination," *Journal of Industrial Economics*, 35, March; pp. 255-268.

ELSEVIER European Economic Review 41 (1997) 861–870

EUROPEAN ECONOMIC REVIEW

Turkey's Customs Union with the EU

Economic implications for Turkey of a Customs Union with the European Union

Glenn W. Harrison [a], Thomas F. Rutherford [b], David G. Tarr [c,*]

[a] *University of South Carolina, Columbia, SC 29208, USA*
[b] *University of Colorado, Boulder, CO 80309, USA*
[c] *The World Bank, Room N-5-037, 1818 H. St. N.W., Washington D.C. 20433, USA*

Abstract

With a CGE model, we quantify the impact of the Customs Union between Turkey and the European Union (EU). Since the average tariff on non-agricultural imports will be less than 2 percent, the trade diversion costs of the Customs Union are quite small. Improved access to third country markets (through reciprocal preferential access agreements of the EU) results in the largest gains from the Customs Union, estimated overall to be about 1–1.5 percent of Turkish GDP. Applying the VAT uniformly (rather than raising it to compensate for the tariff revenue loss) will increase the welfare gain from joining the EU. © 1997 Elsevier Science B.V.

JEL classification: F15; F14; C68

Keywords: Customs Union; Computable general equilibrium model; Regional agreements; European Union; Turkey

1. Introduction and summary

Turkey has joined in a Customs Union with the European Union. We employ a computable general equilibrium model to quantify the impact of the Customs

* Corresponding author. E-mail: dtarr@worldbank.org, Fax: +1 202 522-1159, Tel.: +1 202 473-7677.

PII S0014-2921(97)00043-3

Union (CU) on Turkish welfare, employment and value-added by sector, revenue implications for the government, real exchange rate effects, and other relevant variables. Although not typically quantified in small open economy applied general equilibrium models, we quantify the impact of the most important 'deep integration' elements of the agreement between Turkey and the European Union (EU), in addition to the traditional tariff changes. The model forms the basis for our policy conclusions which we believe will allow the government to optimize its entry into the CU with the EU. We begin by summarizing the principal elements that we quantify, presented in Table 1.

1.1. Low average tariffs

It is well known that the CU with the EU will imply that Turkey will eliminate its tariffs and levies on imports of manufacturing products originating from the EU. In addition, Turkey will apply the Common External Tariff (CET) of the EU on imports from third countries. It may be less understood that application of the CET for most products will also involve a substantial reduction of tariffs against imports from third countries. In part this is true because the 'most favored nation' (MFN) tariff of the EU is only about 7 percent on average. But equally important, application of the EU's CET implies that Turkey will be obligated to provide preferential access to its markets for all countries to whom the EU grants preferential access. [1] By the year 2001, it is expected that Turkey will negotiate preferential trade agreements with all countries with whom the EU has a preferential agreement. Based on Turkey's present import shares, this means that the average tariff on non-agricultural imports will be less than 2 percent (zero for imports from the EU and slightly over 3 percent on average for third countries). Since Turkey is complementing its tariff elimination on EU imports with tariff reductions on imports from third countries, Turkey will become a relatively open economy in non-agricultural sectors. This complementary tariff reduction to third countries should be regarded optimistically since it reduces the trade diversion costs of the CU and results in additional gains from trade.

1.2. Improved access to third markets and to the EU

Since the preferential access agreements with third countries will typically be negotiated reciprocally, Turkish exporters can anticipate improved access to the markets of the third countries to whom it grants preferential access. According to

[1] This includes the Eastern European countries with whom the EU has 'Association agreements', Mediterranean countries subject to the EU's Mediterranean policy, the African, Caribbean and Pacific countries that are part of the Lome convention, as well as GSP treatment for eligible countries.

our estimates, improved access to third country markets results in gains to Turkey that are quantitatively the most important element in the CU arrangements. This indicates that the government should expedite its negotiations with all countries with whom it will negotiate preferential agreements, analogous to the steps it has already taken with Hungary. In addition, Turkey will obtain improved access to EU markets in selected 'sensitive' products.

1.3. Deep integration (product standards and reduced costs of trading)

As explained below, this includes improved terms-of-trade on sales in the EU for Turkey due to the program on product standards (0.1% of GDP), and reduced costs of trading with the EU for reasons analogous to the reduction in border costs in the single market program (0.1% of GDP).

1.4. Overall gains

Our estimates are that the gains to Turkey of the CU with the EU are between 1% and 1.5% of its GDP per year depending on the complementary policies adopted by Turkey. These gains recur annually, and incorporate the welfare costs of imposing higher taxes to compensate for the revenue loss of the tariff. Of course, the results are dependent on the model structure. In particular, the long run dynamic impact on the growth rate of the Turkish economy is not estimated in our model, so the gains from the CU are likely to be larger than we have estimated. [2]

In Section 2 we discuss the principal quantitative results of the model. In Section 3 we quantitatively evaluate complementary policies Turkey may adopt to optimize its entry into the CU, including an analysis of the revenue replacement challenge. Finally, we note similarities in the experience of Spain and Greece compared with the starting point of Turkey. The Greek experience shows that simply adopting the common external tariff of the EU does not guarantee a high growth rate. Crucially, we argue, Turkey will have to reduce the role of the state in production.

2. Quantitative results for the CU

The principal results from our model are presented in Table 1. More detailed results, such as the impact on the value added of specific sectors, returns of factors

[2] See Baldwin (1989) and Rutherford and Tarr (forthcoming) for estimates of the dynamic gains from trade liberalization. On the other hand, the estimates may be high to the extent that they ignore the costs of adjustment. Estimates of the costs of adjustment, however, are typically small in relation to the gains from trade liberalization (see Morkre and Tarr, 1980). Moreover, the EU has allocated funds to assist Turkey in its adjustment to the CU.

Table 1
Welfare and revenue implications for Turkey of the Customs Union with the European Union

		Access	Standards	Tariff reduction	Reciprocal access	Export subsidy reduction (EU)	Trading costs reduction	Full Customs Union	Full + export subsidy reduction	Second best	First best
1.	Welfare (billions of Turkish lira)	904.3	272.9	286.4	1203.0	−75.4	182.0	2861.3	3246.6	3639.7	4027.7
2.	Welfare (% of GDP)	0.3	0.1	0.1	0.5	–	0.1	1.1	1.2	1.4	1.5
3.	VAT rate (% of benchmark rate)	98.7	99.4	124.6	97.7	97.6	99.8	116.2	109.1	174.9	12.8 [a]

[a] Uniform rate of VAT applied in the new equilibrium.

Access: Improved access to EU markets in steel, textiles and apparel and some agricultural products.

Standards: Improved product quality standards in Turkey leading to 1% export price increase in the EU.

Tariff reduction: Zero tariffs on manufactured goods from the EU; application of the common external tariff of the EU.

Reciprocal access: Improved access to markets where the EU has preferential access.

Export subsidy reduction (EU): Removal of export subsidies to the EU.

Trading costs reduction: Reduction in the costs of importing from and exporting to the EU by 0.3%.

Full Customs Union: All of the above.

Full + export subsidy reduction: Full CU plus removal of export subsidies to all destinations.

Second best: Full CU plus elimination of all taxes and subsidies and use of a VAT as the revenue replacement tax.

First best: Full CU plus elimination of all taxes and subsidies and use of a uniform VAT as the revenue replacement tax.

of production, our systematic sensitivity analysis, as well as detailed documentation of the model, data and elasticity choices may be found in Harrison et al. (1996a).

We report results for aggregate welfare, where we aggregate the 40 households of the full model into a single representative consumer, both in terms of billions of 1990 Turkish lira and as a percent of GDP. In all experiments, we impose a constraint that the fiscal deficit of the government of Turkey cannot increase. We implement this constraint by allowing the VAT rate to adjust in all sectors. The variable 'VAT rate' in Table 1 shows the amount that the VAT must change. For example, a value of 124.6 for VAT in the '*Tariff Reduction*' column means the VAT rate must increase to 124.6% of its original level in all sectors, i.e., a 24.6% increase. This implies that the distortion costs of replacing tariff revenue with a non-uniform VAT are incorporated in our estimates.

In the column of Table 1 labelled '*Access*' we estimate the impact of improved access to EU markets. Turkey already has tariff free access to EU markets in manufactured products, and agriculture is for the most part excluded from the CU agreement However, Turkish exporters should obtain improved access in textiles and apparel, steel and to a small extent in agriculture. Restrictions on exports of Turkish exports to the EU derive from voluntary export restraints, and not from the MFA; both the EU and Turkey expect the VERs to be promptly removed. In steel, Turkish exports will not be subject to the 6% import tax, and there is some hope of a reduction in other non-tariff barriers that the EU applies against Turkish exports. Finally, although agriculture is essentially out of the agreement, it is expected that some limited improved access to the EU markets will be obtained. Thus, in '*Access*' we assume the price received by Turkish exporters to the EU will increase by: 5% in textiles, 15% in apparel, 10% in steel, and 1% in agricultural products, resulting in an increase in Turkish welfare by 0.3% of GDP.

In the scenario '*Standards*' we simulate the impact of improved access to EU markets due to harmonization of product quality standards and improvement in testing laboratories in Turkey. It is recognized that additional testing laboratories are necessary for Turkey, and the pressure of increased EU competition in import markets is likely to improve Turkish product quality and the price of Turkish products in EU markets. [3] In '*Standards*' we assume that the price of Turkish exports will increase by 1% in EU markets. This results in an increase in welfare of 0.1% of GDP.

In the scenario '*Tariff Reduction*' we simulate the impact of Turkey lowering its non-agricultural tariffs against the manufactured products of the EU and implementing the CET of the EU, including the preferential access agreements.

[3] In Harrison et al. (1996b) we show how product standards improvement may magnify the gains from trade liberalization in imperfectly competitive markets.

We take as our initial equilibrium the situation that prevailed in 1993 (based on actual collections of tariffs, as opposed to MFN rates). By 1993, Turkey has already implemented a large portion of the tariff changes by phasing in the tariff changes over a 12 year or 22 year period, depending on the product. We take as our counterfactual scenario the tariffs that will prevail in 2001, after preferential agreements have been negotiated with those countries that the EU has preferential agreements. [4] This scenario results in an improvement of welfare equal to 0.1% of GDP. The benefits from this aspect of the CU are perhaps smaller than some would anticipate, but these estimates follow for a number of reasons: [5] First, in our base year data, the total value of all EU imports was only about 9% of GDP, and the tariff reductions induce 'triangles' of consumption efficiency gains that are only a fraction of the value of the imports. Second, because tariff changes required by the CU were phased in over time and already significantly implemented in our benchmark year of 1993, there already was a low level of tariffs in Turkey in 1993. In fact, the average tariff reduction induced by the CU is only about 7%, and welfare gains from tariff reductions increase more than proportionally with the height of the initial tariff. Third, the tariffs on agricultural products are not reduced, so there are some non-uniform distortions introduced as the new tariff structure strongly favors agriculture. Finally, there are some trade diversion costs in any CU. The latter costs should not be high in Turkey's case since third country tariffs will not be high.

The EU has negotiated preferential trade arrangements with a number of countries, such as the central European countries and a number of Mediterranean countries. Turkey is obligated to negotiate similar preferential trade agreements with these countries. The impact of Turkey reducing its tariffs against these countries is already incorporated in the scenario '*Tariff Reduction*'. But Turkey should obtain improved access to the markets of these countries, since the tariffs of these countries will be reduced against Turkish exports. The impact on Turkey of its improved access to these third countries is estimated in the scenario '*Reciprocal Access*'. We assume that the improved access for Turkish exports in third markets will equal the improved access that Turkey will offer third country imports. This implies that improved access will increase the price Turkish exporters can obtain on exports to third countries by 4.2%. [6] Improved access to

[4] Tariffs in the initial equilibrium are based on actually collected rates, and are taken from Arslan (1995). Tariffs in the counterfactual are taken from data provided by Professor Subidey Togan.

[5] These estimates are consistent with partial equilibrium calculations, see Harrison et al. (1996a, ftn. 9).

[6] The difference between the EU's most favored nation CET and Turkey's third country tariff, taking into account preferences and weighted by Turkey's trade weights is 4.2%. This may be an underestimate of the improved access Turkey will receive in third markets since Turkish external tariffs under the CET of the EU are lower on average than the MFN rates of developing countries receiving preferential access to the EU.

these markets results in a gain in Turkish welfare of 0.5%, which is the largest gain of all the components. [7]

In the scenario labelled '*Export Subsidy Reduction*' we simulate elimination of the remaining export incentives program for exports of non-agricultural products destined to the EU only. Compared with non-discriminatory reduction of export subsidies, which appears to be the more likely policy choice, this does not affect Turkish welfare significantly (there is a negligible reduction in welfare). The reason is that with removal of export subsidies only to the EU, exporters have the incentive to switch export markets away from the EU so they continue to receive export subsidies. Thus, the distortion costs of the export subsidy program are not reduced, unless they are reduced to all export markets. [8]

In the scenario labelled '*Trading Costs Reduction*' we simulate the impact of reduction in the costs of trading between the EU and Turkey. As a result of the CU, closer relations with the EU will likely bring with it a possible reduction in costs of clearing goods at the frontier. This is an effect similar to that of the single market program of the EU. The 'Costs of Non-Europe' studies estimated that in the EU, border costs added 1.5% to 2% to the costs of exports. The impact should be quantitatively less important for Turkey so we assume that there will be a 0.3% reduction in the costs of goods imported from the EU and the costs of exporting to the EU will also decline by 0.3%. This results in an improvement in Turkish welfare of 0.1%.

In the scenario '*Full CU*' we combine all of the above elements. The overall annual gain in Turkish welfare is equal to 1.1% of GDP. We estimate that the real exchange rate will have to depreciate by about 0.5% to maintain external balance (see Harrison et al., 1996a, for further details on the real exchange rate).

3. Conclusions and policy challenges

What complementary policies can Turkey adopt to optimize its entry into the CU? Given the crucial importance in Turkey of reducing the fiscal deficit and creating a stable macroeconomic regime, Turkey must adopt policies to confront the revenue replacement challenge. [9] We estimate that Turkey will lose tariff revenue equal to 1.4% of GDP. [10] If the VAT is used to replace lost revenue, in the '*Full CU*' we estimate that VAT rates will have to increase by 16.2% in each

[7] Improved access, by improving the prices received by Turkish exporters, results in 'rectangles' of gains on all previous sales in these export markets plus triangles of gains on new sales.

[8] See Morkre and Tarr (1995) for a similar result.

[9] For example, many hope the CU will encourage foreign direct investment. But the Mexico crisis demonstrates that financial flows can flow out of Turkey if the macroeconomic situation deteriorates.

[10] See Krueger et al. (1995, p. 64) for a similar result.

sector to compensate for the revenue loss from implementing the full CU (for example from 10% to 11.6%). However, some tax experts in the government of Turkey believe that a VAT rate increase will generate little revenue due to tax evasion problems driving more of the economy into the informal sector. This argues for subsidy reductions, which would serve the dual purpose of increasing efficiency directly by reducing distortions as well as reducing the revenue needs of the state and the indirect distortions imposed by additional taxes.

The CU imposes no restraints on export subsidies to third countries or in agricultural products to any destination. In the column labelled '*Full with Export Subsidy Reduction*' we estimate the impact of eliminating export subsidies to all destinations in addition to the elements of the CU. [11] There is an additional 0.1% of GDP gain in welfare. (See Harrison et al., 1996a, for estimates of the gains from reducing agricultural tariffs.) In addition, we estimate that the VAT would have to increase by only 9.1% (rather than 16.2%) if export subsidy reduction to the rest of the world complemented implementation of the CU.

In order to assess the relative importance of other trade and tax distortions in Turkey, we also implement a scenario, called '*Second Best*' in Table 1, in which, all tariffs, subsidies, and taxes other than the VAT are removed in addition to the elements in '*Full*', and the VAT is used as the replacement tax. Since the welfare gain is 1.4% of GDP, removal of these other distortions results in a gain of 0.3% over implementation of the full CU; but the existing VAT must increase by 74%. Finally, in the scenario called '*First Best*' we impose a uniform VAT along with the other changes in '*Second Best*'. Since there are no untaxed sectors and no labor–leisure choice, the uniform VAT is equivalent to a lump sum tax with no distortions. Welfare increases another 0.1% relative to Second Best, but the uniform rate of VAT need only be 12.8% because all the exempted sectors are now included.

Probably the most important challenge from the CU is that it will result in Turkish industries being exposed to international competition to a greater extent than has been the case to date. The increasingly competitive industrial structure brought on by the CU will further expose inefficient State Owned Enterprises (SOEs). The loss-making SOEs will likely lose even more, making it increasingly costly to maintain inefficient SOEs. The drain on the state budget and the rest of the economy would then become even more of a constraint on growth of the Turkish economy.

In summary, the reduction of state subsidies of various types and the reduction of the role of the state in production will significantly contribute to the solution of

[11] Any actions on export subsidy reduction in Turkey will almost certainly be taken in a non-discriminatory manner, in part because there are many in Turkey who believe that the Framework Agreement for the CU between the EU and Turkey imposes comparable restraints as GATT/WTO rules regarding the subsidies and export incentives code.

all challenging problems identified. With participation with the EU in a CU, Turkey now stands at historical crossroads. One road it can take at this time is the successful road taken by Spain after it decided to accede to the EU. Spain complemented its accession (and anticipated accession) to the EU with a significant reduction in the role of the state in the domestic economy.

On the other hand, despite rapid growth in the 1960s, Greece has made much less progress after its accession to the EU. Although both Greece and Spain adopted the external trade policies of the EU, Greece continued to support its SOEs to a much greater degree. Its consolidated fiscal deficit and public sector borrowing requirements rose to a large share of GDP in the 1980s, and this crowded out private investment and contributed to stagnant growth. Moreover, even the private sector is highly regulated. As a result, between 1980 and 1992 Spain grew at over twice the rate of Greece such that by 1992 Spanish per capita income (at $14,000) was about twice the level of Greece. [12]

Although Turkey in 1995 is a more open economy than either Greece or Spain at the start of their accession to the EU, and the precise form of state intervention in the domestic economies differed, all three economies experienced the problem of excessive state involvement in their domestic economies. In Turkey's case, SOEs are its analogous achilles heel. The example of Greece demonstrates that simply adopting the external trade policy of the EU will not be sufficient to propel the economy forward to much higher growth rates. Bold and dramatic action to reduce the role of the state with respect to subsidies and ownership of production are crucial for a fully effective integration with the EU that will be capable of significantly boosting the growth of the Turkish economy.

Acknowledgements

The authors would like to thank: Ismail Arslan for his extensive comments and background paper; Roberto De Santis and Gazi Ozhan for preparation of the Social Accounting Matrix; Subidey Togan for his background paper and tariff calculations; Jacob Kolster and Costas Michalopoulos of the World Bank, Olivier Bodin and Bertin Martins of DGII and B. Hanbuckers of DGI in the Commission of the European Union; numerous individuals in both the private sector and government of Turkey for their helpful discussions and comments; and Minerva Pateña for logistical support. The views expressed are those of the authors and do not necessarily reflect those of the World Bank, the government of Turkey, the European Union or those acknowledged.

[12] See Harrison et al. (1996a) for sources and additional details regarding the Greek-Spanish experience.

References

Arslan, I., 1995, Turkey: The CU and beyond, Background paper for the Country Economic Memoranda, The World Bank, Ankara, mimeo.

Baldwin, R., 1989, The growth effects of 1992, Economic Policy 9, 247–281.

Harrison, G.W., T.F. Rutherford and D.G. Tarr, 1996a, Economic implications for Turkey of a CU with the European Union, Policy and research working paper no. 1599, The World Bank, Washington, DC.

Harrison, G.W., T.F. Rutherford and D.G. Tarr, 1996b, Increased competition and completion of the market in the European Union: Static and steady-state effects, Journal of Economic Integration, 11, 332–365.

Krueger, A.O., O. Aktan, P. Dohlman, C. Ozden and J. Whalley, 1995, Industrial and fiscal impact on Turkey of Customs Union with the European Union, Ankara, Treasury, mimeo.

Morkre, M.E. and D.G. Tarr, 1980, Effects of restrictions on United States imports: Five case studies and theory (United States Government Printing Office, Washington, DC).

Morkre, M.E. and D.G. Tarr, 1995, Reforming Hungarian agricultural trade policy, Weltwirtschaftliches Archiv 131, 106–131.

Rutherford, T.F. and D.G. Tarr, forthcoming, Blueprints, spillovers and the dynamic gains from trade liberalization in a small open economy, in: R. Baldwin and J. Francois, Eds., Dynamic issues in applied commercial policy analysis (Cambridge University Press, Cambridge).

ELSEVIER

Economic Modelling 14 (1997) 237–269

Economic Modelling

Morocco's free trade agreement with the EU: A quantitative assessment

Thomas F. Rutherford[a], E. Elisabet Rutström[b], David Tarr[c,*]

[a]University of Colorado, Economics Department, Boulder, CO 80309-0256, USA
[b]University of South Carolina, Dept. of Economics, BA College, Columbia, SC 29 208, USA
[c]The World Bank, 1818 H. St., N.W., Washington D.C. 20433, USA

Abstract

Using an applied general equilibrium model, we find that the EU–Morocco free trade area (FTA) will increase Moroccan welfare by about 1.5% of its GDP, showing that trade diversion is not dominant. The gains increase to about 2.5% of GDP if Morocco adds trade liberalization with the rest of the world while adjustment costs are only slightly higher, partly reflecting the absence of trade diversion with global liberalization. We show what are the key modeling assumptions and parameter choices that affect the estimates in models of this type, employing systematic sensitivity analysis as well as graphical exposition.

JEL classification: F14, F15, F021

Keywords: Free trade areas; General equilibrium modeling; Systematic sensitivity analysis; Welfare analysis

1. Introduction[1]

With the completion of the North American Free Trade Agreement (NAFTA) and a number of Association agreements on trade and economic assistance

* Corresponding author. E-mail: dtarr@worldbank.org.

[1]An earlier French language version of this paper, that emphasized the effects on the Moroccan economy, appeared as Rutherford et al. (1994). The present paper examines the consequences of modeling assumptions in greater detail, presents the equations of the model in detail which are not otherwise available, and develops new graphical interpretations of the results.

PII S0264-9993(96)01032-2

between the European Union (EU) and most of the countries of Central and Eastern Europe (the 'Europe Agreements'), and the development of the Mediterranean policy of the European Union,[2] there has been a great surge of interest in regional trade integration among developing countries. These agreements differ from the old (and in many cases failed) regionalism among developing countries in that the partner country or region is a major industrialized country that is also the most significant trading partner of the developing country.[3] Concern about the welfare and sectoral implications of the NAFTA in particular has led to the development of over thirty applied general equilibrium models designed to estimate these effects. The results, however, are quite varied and reasons for the differences sufficiently opaque that the United States International Trade Commission (USITC) convened a conference for the purpose of determining why the NAFTA models produced different results (see USITC, 1992).

Given that there is widespread interest among policy-makers of results from applied general equilibrium models, and that the quantitative importance of a number of assumptions is now well known, as well as the fact that correspondence between the theory of regional integration and its implementation in the applied models is not always straightforward, we believe it is important to identify the key assumptions and parameters that affect the results.

The purpose of this paper is twofold. First, we provide a careful applied general equilibrium modeling exercise of the economic effects of an EU–Morocco free trade area (FTA), as well as some of the other principal trade policy options open to Morocco. Second, we use our Moroccan model as a vehicle to demonstrate the key modeling assumptions and parameter choices that affect the estimates in models of this type, by sequentially altering a number of modeling assumptions and parameter values and comparing the results to our central case.

Concrete discussions for an FTA between the EU and Morocco began in March 1992. To some the Moroccan interest in a reciprocal FTA may be surprising, since Morocco already enjoys privileged relations with the EU. It has free access to markets in industrial products (there are some minor exceptions such as trousers), and is not obligated to provide reciprocal access to its market to producers in the EU. However, EU agricultural protection impedes Moroccan exports (notably in the areas of vegetables and citrus fruits), so that improved access to EU markets is an important issue. Moreover, the reciprocal obligations of a free trade agreement (FTA) with the EU will require that Morocco lower its moderately high tariffs against its most important trade partner. These tariff reductions against the EU may provide additional trade liberalization benefits to Morocco, provided the trade diversion costs of preferential tariff reduction do not dominate. For the task of

[2]The countries covered by the EU's Mediterranean policy are Morocco, Algeria, Tunisia, Libya, Malta, Cyprus, Egypt, Israel, Jordan, Lebanon, Syria and Turkey. The EU Commission believes that if events proceed as planned, Europe and the Mediterranean could complete creation of a new free trade area, the biggest in the world, by the year 2010. See Commission of the European Communities (1994) for an elaboration of the objectives of the European Union.

[3]See de Melo and Panagariya (1992) for an elaboration of the issues in the 'new regionalism'.

evaluating the FTA, we develop our central model which we assess is the most accurate model to characterize the Moroccan economy, and base our best estimates on this central model.

In our central case we find that the welfare benefits to Morocco from the free trade agreement are about 1.5% of GDP, and are about 2.5% of GDP if Morocco adds trade liberalization with the rest of the world to the free trade agreement. These welfare gains are quite substantial in the context of other model estimates with constant returns to scale such as ours, and partly reflect benefits from eliminating dispersion in the tariff regime, since dispersion is eliminated in the process of liberalization.

The larger welfare gains found from Morocco's adding elimination of protection against the rest of the world to a free trade agreement with the EU can be obtained with only slightly higher adjustment costs. This reflects the trade diversion costs associated with discriminatory trade liberalization, and can be seen as an important argument in favor of the efforts towards lowering tariffs against non-EU sources subsequent to achieving an FTA. On the other hand, the significant benefits that accrue from discriminatory liberalization against either EU or rest of the world imports indicate that trade diversion is not dominant.

In this paper we devote considerable effort to investigating what are the key parameters driving the results. This is investigated numerically and to aid the exposition graphically. We show that trade creation and welfare increase with the elasticity of substitution between domestic varieties and import substitutes on the one hand; but that trade diversion and welfare losses increase with the elasticity of substitution between imports from different regions. We perform many thousands of simulations to systematically investigate the impact of the elasticities and find that our basic results are quite robust.

In Section 2 we provide a brief overview of the structure of the Moroccan economy, its trade regime and our model.[4] In Section 3 we present the results in our central model case. In Section 4, we investigate the impact of key elasticities of demand. In Section 5 we perform systematic sensitivity analysis with respect to the elasticities; this allows us to provide estimates within a range (with probability assessments over the range).

2. A small open economy model

2.1. Trade protection in Morocco and free trade agreement shocks

2.1.1. Structure of protection

Since 1993 Morocco has dramatically liberalized its foreign trade regime. By 1993, the maximum rate for customs duties had been lowered to 45% and, most

[4] Further details are available in Rutherford et al. (1993), available to the reader upon request. Please send an e-mail message to: mpatena@worldbank.org.

[5] See Mateus et al. (1988) and UNDP–World Bank (1992) for details on these liberalizations.

impressively, no imports required a license (other than for health and safety reasons). On the export side only minor restraints remain.[5] We therefore take as our point of departure a trade regime that is free of non-tariff barriers.

Tariff rates as of 1991 by sector are presented in column 10 of Table 1. The *structure* of the rates is taken from legal applicable rates at the tariff line level that are aggregated, based on an unweighted average, to the 39 sectors of our model. The rates that appear in Table 1 have been proportionately adjusted for all sectors, such that the total tariff collections in the economy, based on 1991 imports, equal actual aggregate tariff collections from budget data for 1991.[6] The average import tariff based on collections is 19%, which includes tariff surcharge (fiscal import duty).[7] The most important sectors regarding import revenues are industrial machinery, and coal and crude oil, which together account for over 30% of revenues from trade taxes.

Among the most important non-tariff barriers scheduled to be removed in early 1993 are those in several agriculture sectors: sugar, cereals, meat, dairy and edible oils. These non-tariff barriers are believed to be quite binding, and Morocco intends to increase tariffs in the meat and dairy industries, and impose variable levies in the others to cushion the adjustment costs. We therefore assume in our benchmark that the tariff levels in the meat and dairy, sugar and cereals sectors are 45%.

2.1.2. *Shocks of the free trade agreement*

As a result of the decade-long liberalization of trade, some diversification in exports has been achieved, mainly in textiles and phosphate derivatives, but the development of export markets in agriculture has been inhibited by protectionist policies in the EU. Given the generally free access to EU markets by Moroccan producers, EU restrictions of importance on imports from Morocco only remain in fruit and vegetables, trousers, and canned sardines. At the level of aggregation of our model, increased access to the EU markets for Moroccan products will primarily influence the export price of the fruit and vegetable sectors.[8]

---

[6]Appendix B of Rutherford et al. (1993) discusses this adjustment.

[7]As members of the Maghreb preferential trading area, imports from Algeria and Tunisia are exempted from the fiscal import duty.

[8]Morocco's exports in fruit and vegetables are dominated by oranges and other citrus fruit, which are both the major components of our citrus fruits, and by tomatoes, potatoes, and preserved vegetables, which are the major components of our vegetables sector.

[9]There is some question of whether a free trade agreement which excludes agriculture formally, but which negotiates agriculture separately would be the outcome. This was how agriculture was handled in the Europe Agreements and in the customs union between the EU and Turkey (see Intermedia, 1995). GATT rules require that preferential trade agreements include substantially all trade. With the conclusion of the Uruguay Round, with its strengthened restraints on the interpretation of substantially all trade within a preferential trade agreement, some experts in the European Commission now believe that agriculture cannot be excluded from the agreements. Even if agriculture is excluded from the agreements, its separate negotiation will lead to some improved preferential access for both parties to the agreement.

Table 1
Morocco: basic data for the social accounting matrix

Sector (abbrev.)		Sector share of total (1) Output	(2) Labor	(3) Capital	(4) Imports	(5) Percentage from EC	(6) Exports	(7) Percentage to EC	Trade by sector, (%) (8) Imports (consumption)	(9) Exports (output)	Tariff rate, (%) (10)
Agriculture											
1. Cereals (CER)	R[a]	5.44	3.04	10.32	7.16	53.8	0.85	54.2	13.20	1.50	45[b]
2. Sugar (SUG)	R	0.26	0.12	0.41	0.00	0.0	0.00	0.0	0.00	0.00	45[b]
3. Citrus fruits (CIT)	R	2.18	1.50	2.84	0.03	64.8	9.26	69.8	0.40	40.20	31.56
4. Vegetables (VEG)	R	1.84	1.14	2.15	0.26	100.0	2.75	89.6	2.40	14.00	11.35
5. Meat and dairy (MAD)	R	4.90	1.62	9.88	0.23	50.2	0.02	100.0	0.70	0.00	45[b]
6. Fishing (FSH)	R	0.38	0.08	0.25	0.00	64.8	0.66	53.6	0.00	16.30	
7. Forestry and other agriculture (FOR)		1.02	0.51	1.74	2.44	59.4	0.77	86.6	32.80	7.00	29.54
Mining and related											
8. Phosphates (PHS)		2.52	2.85	4.04	0.00	0.0	22.45	51.1	0.00	89.20	
9. Other non-metallic mining (NMM)	R	0.40	0.46	0.30	1.99	7.7	0.73	41.2	41.10	15.40	16.48
10. Metals mining (MIN)	R	0.59	0.58	0.91	0.14	86.4	4.57	80.6	18.30	81.40	14.74
11. Coal and crude oil (CAO)	R	0.16	0.47	0.08	18.82	1.6	0.14	84.2	96.20	22.90	11.35
12. Refined oil (OIL)		4.14	0.31	0.20	1.89	51.6	2.19	73.9	19.50	7.50	23.80
13. Electricity and water (ELE)		1.80	1.54	1.77	0.00	0.0	0.00	0.0	0.00	0.00	
Manufacturing											
14. Food products (FOO)		4.10	5.38	0.96	3.38	53.6	0.44	95.7	10.90	1.00	35.23
15. Other food products (OFF)		5.40	4.24	2.16	3.98	47.7	7.40	65.3	12.90	13.30	27.91
16. Beverages and tobacco (BEV)		1.01	1.84	0.61	0.34	76.8	1.53	94.2	5.30	15.00	30.02
17. Textiles (TXT)		4.10	6.07	2.28	5.30	71.0	6.25	61.0	21.10	14.40	25.30
18. Clothing (CLO)		2.31	2.27	1.81	0.02	86.7	4.02	94.1	0.20	15.50	34.13

Table 1 (*continued*)

Sector (abbrev.)	Sector share of total (1) Output	(2) Labor	(3) Capital	(4) Imports	(5) Percentage from EC	(6) Exports	(7) Percentage to EC	Trade by sector, (%) (8) Imports (consumption)	(9) Exports (output)	Tariff rate, (%) (10)
19. Leather and shoes (LEA)	1.24	1.88	0.68	0.15	89.5	4.78	71.5	2.40	38.50	24.01
20. Wooden products (WDN)	1.95	2.93	0.64	2.36	31.4	0.26	83.7	17.60	3.00	19.98
21. Paper and printing (PAP)	1.11	1.92	0.29	2.27	47.1	0.92	69.4	28.20	8.20	27.65
22. Cement (CEM)	1.66	3.58	0.41	0.95	38.1	0.11	68.2	11.00	0.70	21.86
23. Iron and steel (IAS)	0.46	0.44	0.12	6.57	63.3	1.87	79.2	75.60	31.90	16.84
24. Electro-mechanical industry (EMI)	1.79	3.93	1.12	2.29	88.9	0.11	87.3	22.60	0.60	21.45
25. Industrial machinery (IND)	0.98	0.74	0.62	17.83	45.3	0.06	68.2	74.10	0.60	20.44
26. Transport equipment (TEQ)	1.14	1.53	0.46	4.96	62.4	0.25	66.1	46.90	2.10	15.04
27. Electrical equipment (EEQ)	0.78	1.40	0.17	3.84	57.4	0.13	99.4	49.80	1.60	26.43
28. Office machinery (MAC)	0.07	0.04	0.02	1.06	73.9	0.02	98.2	73.70	1.90	30.54
29. Chemicals (CHM)	3.41	3.80	2.45	8.15	67.1	7.41	29.4	34.90	21.20	19.40
30. Rubber and plastics (RBR)	0.75	1.22	0.24	1.10	74.5	0.15	20.5	21.50	0.80	23.16
31. Other industries (OTH)	0.33	0.44	0.18	0.19	77.2	0.05	44.7	11.00	1.50	26.26
Services										
32. Construction (CON)	9.51	3.83	6.44	0.00	0.0	0.00	0.0	0.00	0.00	
33. Trade (TRD)	12.57	2.99	21.61	0.00	0.0	0.00	0.0	0.00	0.00	
34. Transport (TRN)	5.49	3.87	4.19	1.41	100.0	9.39	57.2	4.80	20.90	10.00
35. Communications (COM)	0.50	0.46	0.70	0.01	100.0	0.02	57.2	0.40	0.60	10.00
36. Banking (BNK)	1.63	1.73	2.10	0.00	100.0	0.02	57.2	0.00	9.30	
37. Insurance (INS)	0.34	0.38	0.00	0.00	100.0	1.24	57.2	3.20	10.70	10.00
38. Other services (SRV)	11.82	6.99	14.87	0.86	100.0	7.70	57.2	1.20	7.60	10.00
39. Administration (ADM)	12.86	21.85	0.00	0.00	0.0	0.00	0.0	0.00	0.00	

[a] Sectors marked R (for resource) have sector specific capital.

[b] Non-tariff barrier estimated at 45% legal tariff rates after adjustments for collections are 10%, 16% and 28% in cereals, sugar and meat and dairy respectively.

The free trade agreement would involve a lowering and eventual elimination of all remaining trade barriers on all imports from the EU (i.e. lowering of the tariff), with correspondingly increased market access for Moroccan products to the EU, most notably in agriculture.[9]

We estimate the price distortion in agriculture due to border barriers in the EU to be about 8%, following the EU model developed by Harrison et al. (1989). An 'upperbound' scenario would assume that the EU demand schedule for Moroccan fruits and vegetables is infinitely elastic, so that a removal of tariffs and other barriers will be entirely passed on to Moroccan producers as an increase in the export price. If the EU demand schedule were less than infinitely elastic, the price increase passed on to Moroccan exporters would be less than 8%. Moreover, if Moroccan exporters are currently capturing some of the rents from the EU trade barriers, then the export price increase would result in less than the full 8% of benefits to Moroccan exporters. Since Moroccan production is small relative to EU demand (suggesting highly elastic demand in the EU), and since the variable levy is assumed to capture rents in the EU, we take as our base case scenario the full 8% increase in the price of fruits and vegetables from improved access to the EU market.

Domestic taxes consist of value-added tax (VAT), employment and corporation taxes, and production taxes and subsidies. Since we do not have good updated data

[10] In Rutherford et al. (1993) we provide a detailed documentation of the tax rates applied in our model. Briefly, however, total Moroccan value added in 1991 was 189.4 billion dirhams, while total imports were 59.7 billion dirhams. Value-added tax on domestic sales (imports) was 5359 (7853) million dirhams, which represents 3% of value-added and 11% of imports. We applied these rates to the structure of value-added and imports in our social accounting matrix (see below), which yields an amount of value-added government revenue equal to 32% of total government revenue.

Import taxes (including the fiscal import duty P.F.I.) equal 11,465 million dirhams in 1991, or 19% of the value of imports. We scale all actual tariff rates in 1991 so that the weighted average rate equals this 19%. This yields that 30% of government revenue in our model is from tariff collections.

Actual value-added and tariff collections in 1991 were 24 and 21% of government revenue, respectively, but there are many taxes employed in Morocco that are not present in our model (such as a personal income tax, excise taxes, licensing fees and a corporate tax). With our mapping we have assured that the structure of VAT and import tax from 1991 is implemented in our model. Moreover, regarding what is important for the revenue implications of the model, the relative importance of VAT to import taxes as a percentage of total government revenue is preserved approximately (32/30 versus 24/21).

[11] Given that VAT is applied on all production and in our model it is not rebated on exports, the entire VAT applied on imports is a discriminatory tax on imports. There are two methods of value-added taxation that do not discriminate against imports: (1) apply VAT on all domestic production, including that destined for exports, but do not apply VAT on imports (the origin principle); or (2) apply VAT on imports and domestic production for the domestic market only (the destination principle). If all domestic production is subject to VAT and imports are also taxed, the VAT on imports is a discriminatory tariff.

In Morocco, an effort is made to rebate VAT on exports. Then, in principle, Morocco implements the VAT according to the destination principle, and provided the rebate of VAT on exports is complete, the VAT is not discriminatory against imports.

on collections by sector, all of these rates have been set uniformly. The most important tax in our model is VAT, and import taxation is the next most important. The legal VAT rate is 19%, applied to both imports and domestic production. As with important taxation, however, there are exemptions to VAT. In order to be consistent with aggregate VAT revenues collected on domestic production and imports, the domestic VAT rate has been set to 3% and the rate applied to imports to 11%.[10] VAT taxation on imports introduces further distortion in the trade regime.[11] The other tax rates are calibrated based on aggregate tax collections as recorded in the social accounting matrix (SAM). They are: a 1% production tax (net of subsidies), an 8% labor tax (net of subsidies), and a 5% corporation tax (net of subsidies).

2.2. General model structure

Our small open economy (SOE) model is designed for trade policy analysis with a large number of sectors. The model is a 'generic' general equilibrium model of a single economy along the lines of de Melo and Tarr (1992) and Harrison et al. (1993). The model is formulated as a system of nonlinear equations corresponding to the three classes of equilibrium conditions associated with an Arrow–Debreu general equilibrium: price–cost equality for producers, supply–demand balance for commodity and factor markets (including balance of payments), and income–expenditure balance for domestic consumers and government.

Goods are produced using primary factors and intermediate inputs, according to a linearly homogeneous nested Leontief–CES (Constant Elasticity of Substitution) production function:

$$Y_i = \min\left[\frac{X_{1i}}{a_{1i}}, \frac{X_{2i}}{a_{2i}}, \ldots, \frac{X_{ni}}{a_{ni}}, \frac{V_i(f_i) + \sum_k f_{ki}^{\mathrm{F}}}{a_{VA}}\right], \tag{1}$$

where

$$V_i(f_i) = \left(\sum_k \delta_{ki} f_{ki}^{(\sigma-1)/\sigma}\right)^{\sigma/\sigma-1}.$$

In this equation x_{ki} represents intermediate inputs of good k in sector i, f_{ki} is the variable input of primary factor k in sector i, $V_i()$ represents the value-added function for variable factors, f_i represents primary factor inputs to variable cost in sector i, and f_{ki}^{F} represents the input of factor k to the formation of fixed costs in sector i, due to the possibility of sector-specific capital. Appendix A gives a complete listing of all variables and parameters of the model.

Primary factors include labor and capital. Land is not included explicitly, but we nonetheless have a sector specific factor by varying the share of capital that is sector specific in 'resource' sectors (the nine resource sectors are denoted by an R following their names in Table 1). Labor is assumed to be fully mobile across sectors.

Production exhibits constant returns to scale, and producers behave competitively, selecting output levels such that marginal cost at those output levels equals the given market price gross of subsidy, providing the following zero profit condition:

$$(1 + s_i^{\mathrm{P}})(p_i D_i + p_i^{\mathrm{X}} X_i) + p_i^{\mathrm{X}} X_i s_i^{\mathrm{X}} = c_i Y_i. \tag{2}$$

In this equation the first term represents the value of output gross of production subsidy, and the second term captures the effect of the export subsidy.

In export sectors, output is differentiated between goods destined for the domestic, EU and all other export markets. This relationship is characterized by the following two-level constant elasticity of transformation frontier:

$$Y_i = \phi_i(D_i, X_i) = \left(\alpha_{DX_i} D_i^{(\epsilon_i - 1)/\epsilon_i} + \alpha_{X_i} X_i^{(\epsilon_i - 1)/\epsilon_i}\right)^{\epsilon_i/(\epsilon_i - 1)}. \tag{3}$$

Composite output is an aggregate of domestic output (D_i) and composite exports (X_i) for two or more destinations r (EU and non-EU markets):

$$X_i = \left(\sum_r \beta_{X_{ir}} x_{ir}^{(e_i - 1)/e_i}\right)^{e_i/(e_i - 1)}. \tag{4}$$

Our model has one representative consumer. Final demand by private households arises from nested constant elasticity of substitution utility functions. This allows consumer decision-making to occur in multi-stage budgeting. At the top level, goods from different sectors compete subject to the budget constraint of the consumer, where all income elasticities are unity. In the second stage, the consumer decides how much to spend on domestic versus aggregate imports, subject to income allocated to spending in the sector from the first stage, with possibly different elasticities of substitution by commodity. Finally, having decided how much to spend on imports, the consumer allocates this expenditure on EU versus non-EU imports. The aggregation of domestic and imported varieties is characterized by a nested constant-elasticity function of domestic and imported goods:

$$S_i = \psi_i(D_i, M_i) = \left(\alpha_{DM_i}^{1/\sigma_i} D_i^{(\sigma_i - 1)/\sigma_i} + \alpha_{M_i}^{1/\sigma_i} M_i^{(\sigma_i - 1)/\sigma_i}\right)^{\sigma_i/(\sigma_i - 1)}. \tag{5}$$

where M_i represents a composite import from two or more regions r:

$$M_i = \left(\sum_r \beta_{M_{ir}} m_{ir}^{(s_i - 1)/s_i}\right)^{s_i/(s_i - 1)}.$$

[12] By an Armington sector we mean a sector where imported goods and domestic goods are differentiated products based on country of origin. In these sectors we also assume that exported goods and domestic goods are differentiated by country of destination. See de Melo and Tarr (1992, chapter 2) for a fuller explanation of the impact of the Armington assumption.

For simplicity (and due to limitations of data) we assume that the import composition and import–domestic substitution possibilities in investment, intermediate and final demand are identical.

In two sectors, meat and dairy, and sugar, we depart from the 'Armington'[12] assumption and assume that imports and domestic production are perfect substitutes. This is because there are no (or negligible) imports in the initial equilibrium due to the non-tariff barriers discussed above; the Armington assumption, without very high elasticities of substitution, will imply (contrary to expectations) that trade liberalization yields very little increase in imports. In principle, the appropriate model is the one that is benchmarked to an econometrically estimated elasticity of supply in the sugar and meat and dairy industries. Absent explicit estimates, we use the model that is closest to our assessment of the supply elasticity. We show below, however, that the homogeneous versus Armington assumption has very important implications and that the homogeneous model is not easily approximated in the Armington framework by choosing a high Armington elasticity.

The market clearance condition for domestic supply balances output from the Armington aggregation function with intermediate, investment and final demand. This condition is:

$$S_i = \sum_j a_{ij} Y_j + G_i + I_i + C_i, \tag{6}$$

in which Y_j is the activity level of sector j, a_{ij} is the input requirements of good i in sector j, and G_i, I_i and C_i are components of final demand associated with government, investment and final consumption. Factor markets always clear with flexible prices:

$$\sum_i f_{ki} + f_{ki}^{F} = E_k. \tag{7}$$

As discussed above, the only Moroccan trade distortions currently included in the model are ad valorem tariffs (or subsidies) on imports and a value-added tax that is applied at different rates on imports and domestic products. The model allows tariff rates on imports to differ depending on whether the import is from the EU or the rest of the world (ROW); and we allow exports to have different prices depending on whether they are sold in the EU or ROW. These distinctions allow us to study policies such as accession to a free trade area. The free trade agreement with the EU also involves changes in Morocco's access to EU markets. The main effect of increased access would be an increase in the Moroccan export prices, and these are therefore included as policy instruments that can be varied in counterfactual simulations.

Government expenditures and investment demand are exogenous. Funding of government expenditures is provided by net tax revenues. There are three other components of government income in addition to import tariffs. These are (i) value-added taxes on factor inputs to production and on imports, (ii) employment and corporation taxes on factor employment, and (iii) ad valorem production subsidies net of excise taxes on production output.

Given the importance of the tariff as an instrument of revenue generation in Morocco, we exploit the ability of a 'simulation laboratory' to control for this effect by adopting value-added tax (VAT) as an explicit replacement tax such that government revenue remains constant. The VAT induces distortion costs (marginal excess burden). We indicate the extent that VAT would have to be changed in order to avoid a reduction in government revenue. The marginal excess burden of raising government revenue from VAT is incorporated in the analysis.

Since private consumption equals the income from primary factors plus net transfers to the consumer by the government (from domestic and foreign trade taxes), Walras law is satisfied. The budget constraint for the private consumer is written:

$$\sum_i \pi_i C_i = \sum_k w_k E_k + B - \tau_T T. \tag{8}$$

In this equation w_k represents the market price of primary factor k, B represents the foreign exchange balance and $\tau_T T$ represents the level of lump sum transfer.

Public consumption is balanced with the value of public endowments and tax revenue. The government budget is:

$$\begin{aligned}\sum_i \pi_i G_i = {} & \tau_T T + \tau_f \sum_{ik} w_k t_{ik} f_{ik} + \tau_v \sum_{ik} v_i w_k f_{ki} + \sum_{ir} p_{ir}^{\mathrm{M}} t_{ir} m_{ir} \\ & - \sum_i s_i^{\mathrm{P}} (p_i D_i + p_i^{\mathrm{X}} X_i) - \sum_i s_i^X p_i^X X_i.\end{aligned} \tag{9}$$

World market import and export prices are fixed, so there are no endogenous changes in the terms of trade. In other words, import supplies and export demands are infinitely elastic. The current account balances the value of exports and imports taking into account exogenously fixed capital inflows:

$$\sum_i p_i^{\mathrm{X}} X_i + B = \sum_{ir} p_{ir}^{\mathrm{M}} m_{ir}, \tag{10}$$

where p^{X} and p^{M} are the exogenously given international prices and B is the exogenous capital flow. This guarantees no 'free lunch' either taken from or given to foreigners.

2.3. Empirical implementation of the Morocco model

We employ a social accounting matrix (SAM) for Morocco, based on a SAM constructed by Mateus et al. (1988), which distinguishes 39 production sectors, but which also incorporates updated data where deemed crucial. This level of disaggregation captures most of the important sectors of the Moroccan economy that would be affected by the free trade agreement. In particular, citrus fruits, vegetables, cereals, sugar, meat and dairy products, textiles, apparel, fishing and phosphates are included as separate sectors.

The SAM incorporates an internally consistent set of relationships. Among the most important identities in the SAM are zero profits for each production activity, market clearance for all commodities and factors, budget balance for households and the government, and the value of imports equals the value of exports, net of capital flows. In fact, an Arrow–Debreu type applied general equilibrium model, such as ours, must be based on a SAM; otherwise the data would be inconsistent with the underlying behavior assumptions of the model (which are based on optimizing behavior of all agents subject to budget constraints and adding up conditions).

A basic component of a SAM is an input–output table. Based on the work of Mateus et al., we employed the most recent input–output table available from survey work, which is a 1890 table. We have also shown (Rutherford et al., 1993) that, at the nine-sector level of aggregation, value-added shares did not significantly change between 1980 and 1991. Over 40% of value added originates in services sectors, about 30% in manufacturing (food, and textiles and apparel comprise about half the manufacturing sector) and the remaining 30% is in agriculture and mining. Thus, utilizing data from 1980 for production and value-added should not present a great problem.

On the other hand, tariff rates have changed significantly since 1980, and we know that results in models that examine changes in trade policy are highly dependent on the tariff rates employed in the SAM. Thus, we updated the protection data to 1991 rates, as discussed above, but kept the import value at domestic prices constant, to maintain consistency. In addition, we have disaggregated imports and exports by trading partners according to source and destination shares of 1991, so that we have captured any significant changes in the mix of imports from the EU and the rest of the world. Introducing this data on tariffs and shares does not affect the balancing of the SAM in any way, and therefore does not affect the consistency of our data.

A final choice we made was to preserve the sectoral pattern of trade. Although the trade liberalizations since 1983 have changed the sectoral pattern of trade, updating the model to reflect this new pattern would necessitate (due to consistency requirements) altering the sectoral composition of value-added or final demand or altering the input–output table such that they would not have reflected the actual structure of either 1980 or 1991. Thus, we preferred to stay with the production structure of the 1980 SAM, since that is based on an empirical survey.

Table 1 summarizes some of the most important industry data employed in our model, and displays the names of each of our sectors along with a three-letter acronym for later reference. Columns 1–3 show the share of Moroccan output, employment and capital by sector, derived from the 1980 SAM.

Columns 4 and 6 display the sectoral decomposition of imports and exports, where the share accounted for by EU imports and exports is displayed in columns 5 and 7. These shares are updated 1991 data, aggregated from tariff line data provided by the government of Morocco. Phosphates are the most important export sector, and they encounter no trade barriers in the EU. Fruit and vegetables exports together make up 14% of all exports to the EU.

Columns 8 and 9 show the importance of trade for each sector. Clearly the mining sectors are very dependent on exports, as is the citrus fruit sector to a lesser degree. We therefore expect some benefits to this latter sector from increased access to EU markets.

Estimates of elasticities must be assembled for primary factor substitution, import demand, import source, domestic demand, and the transformation of domestic supply into domestic and exported products.[13] Despite our literature search, there are many elasticities about which there is considerable uncertainty. We assess the consequences of varying the elasticities with 'systematic sensitivity analysis' in Section 5.

The SOE model is generated with the GAMS software developed by Brooke et al. (1988) and solved with the MPS/GE software developed by Rutherford (1989, 1992). The systematic sensitivity analyses are undertaken with the MPSS software developed by Harrison (1990) and using the procedures developed by Harrison and Vinod (1992).

3. Results

Given the questions of improved market access of Moroccan fruits and vegetables and of trade diversion and trade creation (which arises in any preferential trade area), we evaluate the following six policy scenarios: (a) improved access for Moroccan fruits and vegetables in the EU (*ACCESS*); (b) unilateral tariff reductions in Morocco against the EU alone (*EULIB*), against imports from the rest of the world alone (*LIBROW*), and against all trading partners (*LIBALL*), without improved access to EU agricultural markets; (c) cooperative tariff reductions with the EU, where on the EU side this implies extended market access for Moroccan fruit and vegetables (*FTA*); and (d) full free trade agreement with the EU augmented by unilateral liberalization of tariffs against rest of the world imports (*FTAALL*). The aggregate results on welfare and taxes are summarized in Table 2. The impact on employment by sector is presented in Table 3.

The first three columns of Table 2 show the welfare gain measured as the equivalent variation as a percentage of benchmark GDP. Columns 7–9 show the percentage labor adjustment measured by the necessary reallocation of labor across sectors as a percentage of total labor supply. Columns 10–12 likewise measure the necessary reallocation of capital across sectors as a percentage of total capital supply.

Before discussing the results in detail, we first present a partial equilibrium consumer surplus analysis in Fig. 1. Although our model is general equilibrium and employs Hicksian equivalent variation as the welfare measure, the figure should be

[13] In detail, these elasticities refer to the elasticity of substitution between primary factors of production in each sector; the elasticity of substitution between domestic production and an imports composite in each sector; the elasticity of substitution between imports distinguished by source, also by sector; the elasticity of substitution between domestic consumption of each good (the components of which are, in turn, composites of domestic and imported production); and the elasticity of transformation of domestic production into domestic uses and export. The benchmark values of all elasticities in the model are reported in appendix A of Rutherford et al. (1993).

Table 2
Free trade agreement with the EU and related trade liberalization: welfare, tax and factor adjustment effects on Morocco[a]

	change in welfare (%)			change in VAT rate (%)			Percentage of labor that changes jobs			Percentage of capital that adjusts		
	(1) H	(2) M	(3) L	(4) H	(5) M	(6) L	(7) H	(8) M	(9) L	(10) M	(11) M	(12) H
FTA[b]	2.28	1.52	1.20	54.0	58.3	60.3	3.2	2.5	2.2	5.1	3.3	2.7
EULIB[c]	2.05	1.29	0.97	54.6	58.9	60.9	3.3	2.6	2.3	5.4	3.6	3.0
ACCESS[d]	0.31	0.27	0.25	−1.8	−1.2	−1.0	0.4	0.3	0.3	0.6	0.4	0.3
LIBROW[e]	1.86	1.10	0.78	55.7	60.1	62.0	3.2	2.5	2.2	5.3	3.5	2.9
LIBALL[f]	3.12	2.37	2.06	80.7	85.5	87.7	3.7	3.0	2.8	6.0	4.3	3.6
FTAALL[g]	3.36	2.60	2.29	80.0	84.9	87.1	3.6	3.0	2.7	5.6	3.9	3.3

[a]All simulations use value-added tax as replacement tax. Results are for high (H), medium (M), and (L) elasticity of supply in resource sectors.
[b]Full free trade agreement with the EU. Increased export prices for citrus fruits and vegetables for EU destinations by 8% and elimination of import protection from EU sources.
[c]Unilateral elimination of import protection against EU imports.
[d]Increased export prices for citrus fruits and vegetables to EU destinations by 8%.
[e]Elimination of import protection against non-EU imports.
[f]Elimination of import protection against all imports, EU and non-EU.
[g]Full free trade agreement with the EU, augmented by elimination of import protection from non-EU sources as well.

helpful in illustrating some of the key elements of the welfare economics. The demand curves of Moroccan consumers for imports from the EU and from the ROW are drawn to show that they depend on their own tariff inclusive price, the tariff inclusive price of the other import substitute good, and the income allocated to all imports.[14]

Preferential tariff reduction against EU imports will reduce the tariff inclusive price of EU imports (a movement along the demand curve for EU imports). The reduction in the price of EU imports will induce shifts in the demand curves for imports of both varieties and for the domestic substitute. First consider the demand curve for imports from the EU. The decline in the price of EU imports implies that composite imports have declined in price; thus, there will be a shift away from domestic goods and toward imports.[15] That is, the income allocated to

[14]That is, we have assumed that imports substitute for each other in a CES nest, and composite imports substitute with the domestic good, also within a CES framework. It follows from the theorems on weak separability that the price of the domestic good in the sector will affect the demand for any import variety only through the impact of the income allocated to composite imports. Although not fundamental to our analysis, and easily changed, we have also assumed that demand for the composite output of the various sectors substitute for each other in a Cobb–Douglas model of final consumption choices. Consequently, the expenditures on the output of any sector are independent of relative prices.
[15]As discussed in Section 2.2, our structure of demand allows multistage budgeting.

Table 3
Percentage employment change by sector and scenario

Sector (abbrev.)		FTA H	FTA M	FTA L	ECLIB H	ECLIB M	ECLIB L	ACCESS H	ACCESS M	ACCESS L	LIBROW H	LIBROW M	LIBROW L	LIBALL H	LIBALL M	LIBALL L	FTALL H	FTALL M	FTALL L
Agriculture																			
1. Cereals (CER)	R[b]	−11.3	−9.4	−8.6	−11.5	−9.5	−8.7	0.0	0.1	0.1	−11.1	−9.1	−8.3	−13.4	−11.6	−10.9	−13.3	−11.5	−10.8
2. Sugar (SUG)	R	−82.5	−68.4	−61.5	−82.3	−68.1	−61.2	−2.4	−1.3	−1.0	−82.6	−68.5	−61.6	−78.5	−63.7	−56.6	−78.7	−78.7	−56.9
3. Citrus fruits (CIT)	R	22.4	17.6	15.9	2.3	1.7	1.6	17.6	14.6	13.3	2.2	1.5	1.4	2.9	2.2	2.1	23.1	18.2	16.4
4. Vegetables (VEG)	R	9.1	8.4	8.1	−1.1	−1.4	−1.6	8.9	8.7	8.7	−1.6	−2.0	−2.2	−1.4	−1.7	−1.9	8.6	8.0	7.7
5. Meat and dairy (MAD)	R	−67.3	−52.0	−45.3	−67.1	−51.7	−45.1	−1.8	−0.3	−0.8	−67.7	−52.4	−45.7	63.6	−48.2	−41.6	−63.8	−48.5	−41.9
6. Fishing (FSH)	R	−2.0	−2.0	−3.8	−2.2	−3.3	−4.2	0.1	0.2	0.2	0.7	0.2	−0.8	1.7	1.0	0.4	1.9	1.3	0.8
7. Forestry and other agriculture (FOR)		−4.7	−4.9	−5.0	−4.5	−4.7	−4.8	−0.4	−0.3	−0.3	−3.1	−3.3	−3.5	−6.9	−7.1	−7.2	−7.1	−7.3	−7.3
Mining and related																			
8. Phosphates (PHS)		92.6	68.5	58.1	108.7	79.9	67.3	−8.6	−7.1	−6.2	102.2	73.3	60.7	120.3	91.5	79.1	104.1	80.0	69.7
9. Other non-metallic mining (NMM)	R	6.4	5.7	5.4	6.8	6.1	5.8	−1.0	−0.7	−0.6	−2.7	−2.5	−2.4	−1.3	−1.1	−1.0	−1.7	−1.4	−1.3
10. Metals mining (MIN)	R	3.8	2.7	2.4	4.0	2.9	2.6	−0.7	−0.4	−0.3	2.9	2.1	1.9	4.2	3.0	2.7	3.9	2.8	2.5
11. Coal and crude oil (CAO)	R	9.3	8.5	8.1	9.7	9.0	8.6	−0.9	−0.7	−0.7	−0.7	−0.3	−0.1	2.4	2.6	2.7	2.0	2.1	2.2
12. Refined oil (OIL)		−2.0	−3.4	−4.0	−1.8	−3.3	−3.9	0.1	0.1	0.0	6.6	5.0	4.2	4.4	2.8	2.1	4.2	2.7	2.0
13. Electricity and water (ELE)		−1.1	−0.4	−0.1	−1.0	−0.2	0.1	−0.1	−0.1	−0.1	−1.0	−0.2	0.1	−1.0	0.1	0.4	−1.0	−0.1	0.2

Table 3 (*Continued*)

Sector (abbrev.)	*FTA*			*ECLIB*			*ACCESS*			*LIBROW*			*LIBALL*			*FTALL*		
	H	M	L	H	M	L	H	M	L	H	M	L	H	M	L	H	M	L
Manufacturing																		
14. Food products (FOO)	−6.0	−5.2	−4.9	−6.1	−5.3	−5.0	0.1	0.1	0.1	−6.0	−5.2	−5.0	−8.0	−6.8	−6.5	−7.4	−6.7	−6.4
15. Other food products (OFP)	−3.9	−3.1	−2.8	−4.0	−3.1	−2.8	−0.3	−0.6	−0.1	−4.9	−4.1	−3.8	−5.8	−5.0	−4.7	−5.7	−4.9	−4.6
16. Beverages and tobacco (BEV)	−2.2	−2.3	−2.3	−2.3	−2.3	−2.4	−0.2	−0.2	−0.1	−1.8	−1.9	−1.9	−3.0	−3.1	−3.1	−3.0	−3.0	−3.1
17. Textiles (TXT)	−4.0	−3.7	−3.8	−4.0	−3.9	−3.9	−0.3	−0.2	−0.1	−2.8	−2.7	−2.7	−5.5	−5.3	−5.3	−5.4	−5.3	−5.2
18. Clothing (CLO)	−1.0	−1.1	−1.1	−1.0	−1.1	−1.2	−0.2	−0.2	−0.1	−1.7	−1.8	−1.9	−1.8	−1.8	−1.9	−1.7	−1.8	−1.9
19. Leather and shoes (LEA)	13.2	10.9	9.7	14.1	11.6	10.3	−1.6	−1.3	−1.1	8.0	5.7	4.5	12.7	10.5	9.4	12.0	9.9	8.9
20. Wooden products (WDN)	0.5	0.5	0.5	0.4	0.4	0.5	−0.1	−0.0	0.0	−2.7	−2.7	−2.7	−2.0	−2.0	−2.0	−2.0	−1.9	−1.9
21. Paper and printing (PAP)	−2.8	−2.7	−2.7	−2.8	−2.7	−2.6	−0.3	−0.2	−0.2	−3.3	−3.2	−3.2	−5.0	−4.8	−4.8	−5.0	−4.8	−4.8
22. Cement (CEM)	−1.3	−1.1	−1.0	−1.3	−1.1	−0.9	−0.1	−0.1	−0.1	−1.6	−1.3	−1.2	−2.2	−2.0	−1.8	−2.2	−2.0	−1.9
23. Iron and steel (IAS)	2.5	1.8	1.5	3.0	2.3	2.0	−1.3	−1.0	−0.9	3.2	2.7	2.4	1.0	0.4	0.1	1.0	−0.1	−0.3
24. Electro-mechanical industry (EMI)	−4.2	−3.7	−3.4	−4.3	−3.8	−3.5	0.1	0.00	0.00	0.00	0.6	0.9	3.8	−3.2	−2.9	−0.7	−3.1	−2.8
25. Industrial machinery (IND)	−3.7	−2.8	−2.5	−3.6	−2.6	−2.2	−0.4	−0.4	−0.4	−7.0	−6.1	−5.7	−11.2	−10.3	−9.9	−11.3	−10.5	−10.1
26. Transport equipment (TEQ)	−1.8	−1.3	−1.1	−1.7	−1.2	−0.9	−0.3	−0.3	−0.3	0.2	0.7	1.0	−2.6	−2.0	−1.7	−2.6	−2.1	−1.9
27. Electrical equipment (EEQ)	−6.3	−6.1	−6.0	−6.1	−6.0	−5.9	−0.4	−0.3	−0.3	−4.7	−4.5	−4.4	−10.0	−9.3	−9.2	−10.0	−9.4	−9.3

Table 3 (*Continued*)

Sector (abbrev.)	*FTA*			*ECLIB*			*ACCESS*			*LIBROW*			*LIBALL*			*FTALL*		
	H	M	L	H	M	L	H	M	L	H	M	L	H	M	L	H	M	L
28. Office machinery (MAC)	−17.2	−17.0	−16.8	−16.9	−16.6	−16.5	−0.8	−0.7	−0.6	−3.2	−2.9	−2.8	−20.0	−19.2	−19.1	−19.9	−19.5	−19.4
29. Chemicals (CHM)	1.2	0.3	−0.1	1.6	0.7	0.3	−0.9	−0.7	−0.7	5.7	4.8	4.4	3.0	2.2	1.9	2.5	1.8	1.5
30. Rubber and plastics (RBR)	−0.7	−1.5	−1.8	−0.4	−1.2	−1.6	−0.3	−0.2	−0.2	2.4	1.5	1.1	−0.1	−0.9	−1.3	−0.4	−1.2	−1.5
31. Other industries (OTH)	−1.8	−1.8	−1.8	−1.8	−1.9	−1.9	0.1	0.1	0.1	−1.4	−1.5	−1.5	−1.2	−1.3	−1.3	−1.2	−1.2	−1.3
Services																		
32. Construction (CON)	−1.5	0.1	0.8	−1.5	0.2	1.0	0.0	−0.1	−0.2	−1.6	0.2	1.0	−1.4	0.3	1.1	−1.4	0.2	0.9
33. Trade (TRD)	−4.0	−1.9	−0.9	−5.7	−2.8	−1.5	1.2	0.7	0.4	−5.3	−2.5	−1.1	−6.1	−3.3	−2.0	−4.5	−2.4	−1.4
34. Transport (TRN)	2.3	2.2	2.1	2.8	2.7	2.6	−0.5	−0.5	−0.5	5.3	5.2	5.1	5.5	5.4	5.4	5.0	4.9	4.9
35. Communications (COM)	−1.0	−0.1	0.3	−1.0	0.0	0.5	−0.1	−0.1	−0.2	−0.6	0.5	0.9	−0.5	0.5	0.9	−0.5	0.4	0.7
36. Banking (BNK)	0.4	1.0	1.2	0.7	1.3	1.6	−0.3	−0.3	−0.4	0.8	1.4	1.7	0.7	1.3	1.6	0.5	1.0	1.2
37. Insurance (INS)	0.4	0.9	1.1	0.4	1.0	1.2	−0.4	−0.3	−0.3	1.7	2.2	2.4	1.2	1.8	2.0	1.2	1.7	1.9
38. Other services (SRV)	−0.3	0.5	0.9	−0.3	0.7	1.1	0.1	−0.2	−0.2	−0.3	0.6	1.1	0.1	1.0	1.4	0.1	0.9	1.2
39. Administration (ADM)	−0.1	−0.2	−0.2	−0.2	−0.2	−0.2	0.00	0.00	0.00	−0.1	−0.2	−0.2	−0.1	−0.1	−0.1	−0.1	−0.1	−0.1

[a] H, M, L refer to high, medium and low industry-wide elasticity of supply in the resource (R) sectors.
[b] Sectors denoted with R (resource) have sector specific capital.
Source: model estimates.

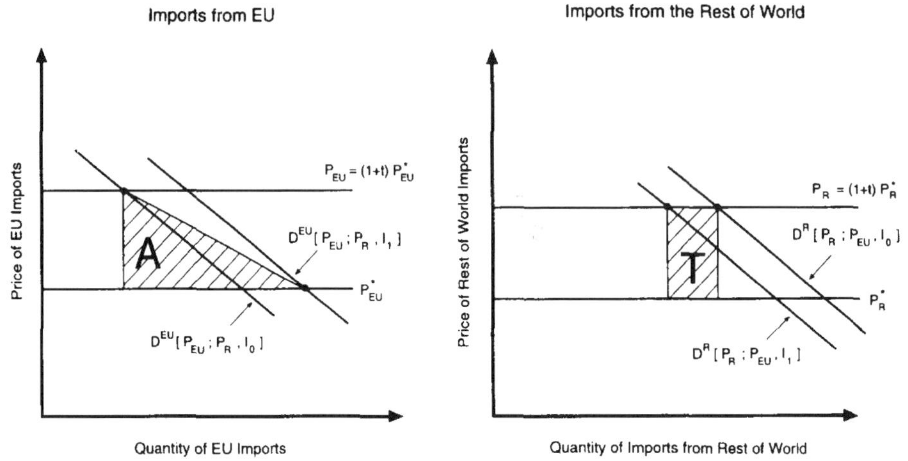

Fig. 1. Welfare effects of trade integration: tradeoff of trade creation and trade diversion. If tariffs are eliminated preferentially against the EU, the welfare change is equal to the trade creation triangle A minus the trade diversion rectangle T.

imports will increase (from I_0 to I_1 in the figure) as a share of total sectoral expenditures. That increase in income allocated to imports will induce an increase in the demand for imports from the EU, as shown in the figure as an outward shift of the demand for EU imports.[16] Also, the demand for the domestic variety of the good, which is not pictured, will decrease.

Now consider the demand curve for imports from the rest of the world. The decline in the price of EU imports means that there will be a substitution away from ROW imports toward the EU, i.e. an inward shift in the demand for imports from the ROW. On the other hand, the reduction in the price of composite imports, which induces an increase in the demand for EU imports, also induces an increase in the demand for imports from the ROW, i.e. this is an offsetting effect, analogous to an income effect, that mitigates the reduction in demand from the substitution effect. We have drawn the figure under the presumption that the substitution effect is dominant and that therefore the demand for imports from the ROW declines.

Regarding the welfare analysis, there is a triangle A of gains (trade creation) in the market for EU imports. Following the principles derived by Burns (1973), one side of triangle A is obtained by connecting the before and after equilibria points. Following from the principles developed by Harberger (1971), there is a rectangle

[16] The decline in the price of EU imports is partly illusory since it involves a loss of government revenue from tariffs for which the government will have to obtain compensatory sources. If the government applies taxation evenly across production from all sources, such as through VAT, then there will nonetheless be a decline in the relative price of imports which will shift the demand curve for EU imports in the direction indicated in the figure.

of trade diversion losses in the market for imports from the ROW, equal to the rectangle T; but we ignore the domestic market in the welfare analysis since there is no difference between price and marginal costs which we model.[17]

The net effect is equal to A − T. The figure takes into consideration that the reduction in price of EU imports reduces the demand for the domestic good and therefore shifts to the right the demand for imports from both sources (a partial equilibrium effect). This demand increase for imports increases the triangle A and reduces the rectangle T.

Now turn to the results. They depend importantly on the industry-wide elasticity of supply assumed in the resource sectors. The greater the elasticity of supply, the more resource movement across sectors (more labor has to change jobs), but the more welfare gain as well. For example, under *ACCESS*, the citrus fruits and vegetables sectors obtain higher EU prices. With larger elasticity of supply, they expand output more. This results in greater welfare gain to the economy, but also more movement of capital and labor between sectors. Conversely, the meat and dairy, sugar, and cereal producers will suffer a decline in demand as a result of lowering tariffs under all scenarios except *ACCESS*. The greater the elasticity of supply, the more output, labor and capital reduction there will be in these sectors, but the larger the welfare gain as a result of shifting these resources into more efficient sectors.[18] All the results of columns 1–3, 7–9 and 10–12 follow this pattern.

First consider the policy scenario *ACCESS*. Improved access to the EU for citrus fruits and vegetables will improve Moroccan welfare by slightly more than one-fourth of a percentage point of GDP, due to improved resource allocation and better terms of trade in citrus fruits and vegetables. Since columns 7 through 12 show that factor movement is small under *ACCESS*, it is primarily the terms of trade improvement that is providing the benefits from improved access.

Removing tariffs against EU imports (*EULIB*) results in an improvement in Moroccan welfare of between 1 and 2%, which is about four to seven times the

[17]The justification for the welfare analysis of Fig. 1 is equation (8) (or its special case, equation (5‴) in Harberger (1971). Harberger considers the case where there is a change in the tax on good 1 (in our case lowering the tariff against EU imports) in the presence of taxes on other goods in the economy, say good $2, \dots, n$. In our case, the most notable other tax is the tariff on competing imports from the rest of the world in the same sector. Then, the change in welfare is the change in surplus on good 1, plus the change in surplus on goods $2, \dots, n$, where the latter is equal to the tax in the other sectors times the change in quantity in those sectors, summed over all such sectors. To simplify Fig. 1, and because the cross-substitution effect in demand will be smaller and of either sign in other sectors, we have ignored sectors outside the directly competing import sector. Our quantitative analysis, however, which is based on Hicksian equivalent variation, incorporates the welfare changes from all goods.

[18]The different elasticities of supply are implemented through varying the share of sector specific capital. Given sector specific capital, in response to a change in demand, the rent on capital in the sector will change, which implies there will be less movement of resources in or out of the sector. For example, specific capital owners in citrus fruits and vegetables earn greater rents under *ACCESS*, but the increase in their rents increases their prices and diminishes the expansion of output. Conversely, in contracting sectors, sector specific capital results in a reduction of rents, costs and prices, and a diminished reduction in output.

benefits of improved access alone. The free trade agreement (*FTA*), which combines the policies of *ACCESS* and *EULIB*, results in gains in Moroccan welfare that are roughly additive in the separate policies. Removing tariffs against the non-EU rest of the world (*LIBROW*) results in gains of about 80% of those from liberalizing trade with the EU alone, reflecting the fact that the EU is the larger trade partner.

If tariffs are lowered against all imports (*LIBALL*) another substantial increase in Moroccan welfare (of about 1% of GDP) is obtained (compared with *EULIB*), interestingly, without significant additional shifting of labor and capital among sectors. The reason that the additional welfare is obtained with little additional resource movement is that lowering tariffs against only the EU induces resource movement, but that resource movement is not necessarily toward the most efficient sectors by world standards, i.e. *there is trade diversion from the Morocco–EU free trade agreement.*[19] Resource movement that is induced by trade diversion will not occur when tariffs are lowered to all supplying countries. The significant benefits that accrue from discriminatory liberalization against either EU or rest of the world imports indicate, however, that trade diversion is not dominant.

Liberalizing tariffs to the rest of the world in combination with a free trade agreement (*FTAALL*) with the EU results in benefits that are roughly additive in the separate policies that make up *FTAALL*, i.e. *LIBALL* plus *ACCESS*.

All simulations are performed assuming that the rate of VAT would be altered so that revenue to the government is unchanged. For scenarios involving reduced tariffs against the EU, columns 4–6 of Table 2 show that VAT would have to be increased by about 55–60%. This means that the VAT collection rate on imports would rise to about 16–17% (from the collected 11%) and on domestic products to about 4–5% (from the collected 3%). For scenarios involving full tariff liberalization against all imports, the VAT rate would have to rise by about 80–90%.

To sum up the aggregate effects, there are significant trade diversion costs when only partially liberalizing import protection, implying that a complete elimination of the protective system would result in higher welfare gains than a free trade agreement with the EU. Moreover, there is a clear correlation between the welfare effects and the necessary factor adjustments. The higher the welfare gain, the higher is generally the adjustment needed. One interesting conclusion is that broader trade liberalization yields greater welfare gain than the *FTA*, but with only slightly higher adjustment costs. This can be seen as an important argument in favor of the efforts towards lowering tariffs against non-EU sources subsequent to achieving an FTA. Finally, welfare benefits of 1.5 to 2.5% of GDP, from the free

[19]Trade diversion would occur in a Moroccan free trade agreement with the EU when a supplier outside the EU supplied the product to Morocco at a cheaper price than the EU supplier, but the *tariff inclusive* price of the EU supplier is cheaper. Trade diversion costs are more likely to be high relative to trade creation benefits: (1) the higher the tariff rate against and (2) the larger the share of trade with the countries that are excluded from the integration agreement. We also show in Section 4.1 that (3) the lower the elasticity of substitution of composite imports and (4) the higher the elasticity of substitution for imports from different countries of origin, the greater the relative costs of trade diversion.

trade agreement or broader liberalization, are quite substantial for models with constant returns to scale. We have shown, however, that a considerable portion of the benefits derives from eliminating dispersion in the tariff regime, since dispersion is eliminated in the process of liberalization.[20]

4. Impact of key modelling parameters

Sensitivity analysis over the parameters of our model has revealed the parameters that are most important regarding the welfare, revenue and factor adjustment estimates. One which we discussed above in detail is the industry-wide elasticity of supply. We have also found that the results are sensitive to the elasticity between imports and domestic consumption (the Armington elasticity), and to a lesser extent the elasticity of substitution in consumption between imports from the EU and the ROW. In this section we discuss the impact of these parameters as well as the Armington assumption in sectors with small initial shares of imports.

4.1. Industry-wide elasticity of supply and sector specific capital

As interpreted below, one parameter that stands out in importance regarding some of the results is the industry-wide elasticity of supply assumed in the resource sectors. Consequently, in this section, we present results for the cases of low, medium and high industry-wide elasticities of supply. We implement a change in the elasticity of supply by assuming three different shares of sector specific capital in the resource (R) sectors: 50, 75 and 90%. Ceteris paribus, the larger the share of capital that is sector specific, the lower the industry-wide elasticity of supply. Appendix C of Rutherford et al. (1993) numerically elaborates the relationship between the assumed share of sector specific capital in the citrus and vegetable sectors, and the supply elasticity of the composite output for domestic firms in these sectors. In the case of citrus fruits, the industry-wide elasticity of supply varies from about unity with 90% sector specific capital to 3.5 with 50% sector specific capital, but takes slightly lower values in the vegetable sector.

The relationship between the share of sector specific capital (and therefore the industry-wide elasticity of supply) and the transformation elasticity is crucial in determining whether domestic and export production are gross substitutes or complements. Although this relationship is important for sectors such as citrus fruits and vegetables, which are expected to experience export price increases, it is typically not transparent in models of this type for the following reason.

[20] In fact, when we first harmonized tariffs for all sectors to their weighted average level in the benchmark (21.5%) and subsequently simulated the various policies shown in Table 2 (in the medium elasticity scenarios) we obtained considerably smaller benefits. In particular, the welfare benefits as a percentage of GDP are as follows: *FTA*, 0.549; *EULIB*, 0.325; *ACCESS*, 0.243; *LIBROW*, 0.290; *LIBALL*, 1.233; *FTAALL*, 1.456. This shows that about two-thirds of the benefits in many of the scenarios derive from harmonization of the tariff regime.

Let φ_i denote the supply elasticity of the composite output in a sector and ϵ_i denote the elasticity of transformation between domestic and exported output in a sector. Abstracting from general equilibrium effects from other markets, de Melo and Tarr (1992) show that if and only if $\varphi_i > \epsilon_i$, an increase in the export price will increase output of the domestic variety and raise the domestic price, i.e. the export and domestic varieties are gross complements in production.[21] Although a similar condition exists in consumption, all elasticities in consumption are entered parametrically, and it is straightforward to examine whether the import and domestic varieties are gross substitutes.[22] Although φ is entered parametrically, ϵ (the industry-wide elasticity of supply) is only defined implicitly and, in a model with constant returns to scale such as ours, could potentially assume extremely large values, especially for small sectors where output expansion will not significantly alter the relative costs of its inputs.

Given that the elasticity of transformation (φ) is 5 in our benchmark, and that with the shares of sector specific capital the maximum industry-wide elasticity of supply is 3.5, exports and domestic output in these sectors are gross substitutes in our model. However, if we were to choose shares of sector specific capital less than 35%, the industry-wide elasticity of supply would exceed 5, and domestic output and exports would be gross complements.[23]

4.2. Elasticity between domestic consumption and composite imports

In the results reported in Table 2, the Armington elasticity is equal to 2 for all sectors other than sugar and meat and dairy (imports and domestic production are assumed to be perfect substitutes in these latter two sectors). Increasing the Armington elasticity (σ_i) for all Armington sectors increases the welfare benefits, as shown in Table 4. At a value of 10 for the Armington elasticity, the welfare benefits of the integration–liberalization strategies increase more than three times in all scenarios except *ACCESS* (where trade diversion is not an issue). At a value of 1 for the Armington elasticity the welfare benefits are reduced.

[21] The intuition for this result is as follows. When the export price increases, firm revenues will increase if output levels are held constant. Firms will therefore purchase more inputs in order to produce more. Disregarding the relative price change between domestic and export markets for a moment, this would result in an increase in composite production, i.e. of goods destined for both the domestic and export market. This increase in composite output we label the output effect. The extent of this effect depends on ϵ. It is equivalent to the income effect in consumer theory. There is also a transformation effect, however, from producing domestic goods in favor of export production, due to the change in the relative price of exports to domestic varieties. The extent of this transformation effect depends on φ, the transformation elasticity, and it is equivalent to the substitution effect in consumer theory. When $\epsilon > \varphi$, the output effect dominates the transformation effect, and the goods are gross complements.

[22] de Melo and Tarr (1992) show that a necessary and sufficient condition for the price of the domestic import competing good in a sector to be a gross substitute with the import good is that the price elasticity of demand for the composite Armington good is less than the Armington substitution elasticity. This condition ensures that the substitution effect will dominate the income effect in demand. A similar result is discussed in Rutström (1992).

[23] The industry-wide elasticity of supply in small sectors rises rapidly and reaches 10 with a sector specific capital of 20% in citrus fruits and vegetables.

Table 4
Welfare effects of variations in elasticities of substitution in demand[a]

	FTA	ECLIB	LIBALL	ACCESS	LIBROW	FTAALL
σ_i = 1[b]	1.184	0.962	1.814	0.243	0.882	2.035
σ_i = 2	1.518	1.288	2.369	0.265	1.099	2.598
σ_i = 3	1.859	1.622	2.939	0.285	1.317	3.176
σ_i = 4	2.213	1.970	3.535	0.306	1.541	3.777
σ_i = 5	2.587	2.338	4.164	0.326	1.775	4.412
σ_i = 6	2.986	2.732	4.837	0.347	2.024	5.089
σ_i = 7	3.419	3.160	5.557	0.368	2.292	5.814
σ_i = 8	3.890	3.676	6.323	0.389	2.584	6.584
σ_i = 9	4.406	4.137	7.127	0.411	2.905	7.393
σ_i = 10	4.969	4.695	7.956	0.433	3.260	8.225
σ_i = 1[c]	2.005	1.774	2.369	0.265	1.652	2.598
σ_i = 2	1.857	1.626	2.369	0.265	1.499	2.598
σ_i = 3	1.723	1.493	2.369	0.265	1.351	2.598
σ_i = 4	1.610	1.380	2.369	0.265	1.216	2.598
σ_i = 5	1.518	1.288	2.369	0.265	1.099	2.598
σ_i = 6	1.448	1.219	2.369	0.265	1.002	2.598
σ_i = 7	1.398	1.169	2.369	0.265	0.927	2.598
σ_i = 8	1.365	1.136	2.369	0.265	0.871	2.598
σ_i = 9	1.346	1.117	2.369	0.265	0.832	2.598
σ_i = 10	1.339	1.110	2.369	0.265	0.809	2.598

[a]Table values represent the change in welfare (equivalent variation) as a percentage of GDP. See Table 2 for an explanation of the policies.
[b]σ_i = the Armington elasticity of substitution between domestic output and composite imports.
[c]σ_i = the elasticity of substitution between imports from different sources.
Source: model estimates.

In Fig. 2 we provide an interpretation of the welfare economics of why an increase in the Armington elasticity increases the welfare benefits of trade integration. To simplify, and to isolate the impact of the Armington elasticity, we assume that imports from EU and ROW sources are homogeneous in the preferences of consumers. The case of trade diversion in a given sector is depicted. Tariffs are lowered preferentially against imports from the EU, but imports from the ROW are the cheapest. The cost advantage of ROW suppliers is not large enough to overcome the tariff preference toward the EU, so that Moroccan importers shift from all ROW imports to all EU imports. Initially equilibrium is at E^0 and shifts to either E^1 or E^E depending on the elasticity of demand for composite imports. Ceteris paribus, the larger the Armington elasticity, the larger the elasticity of demand for composite imports. Consumer surplus analysis (our general equilibrium model uses Hicksian equivalent variation) implies that the net change in welfare is equal to A − T in the inelastic case, or A + B − T in the elastic demand case, i.e. the triangle B represents the net difference in the welfare between the elastic and inelastic demand cases. In the case of trade creation, there is no rectangle T to subtract and the triangles A and B extend down to the delivered price of the low

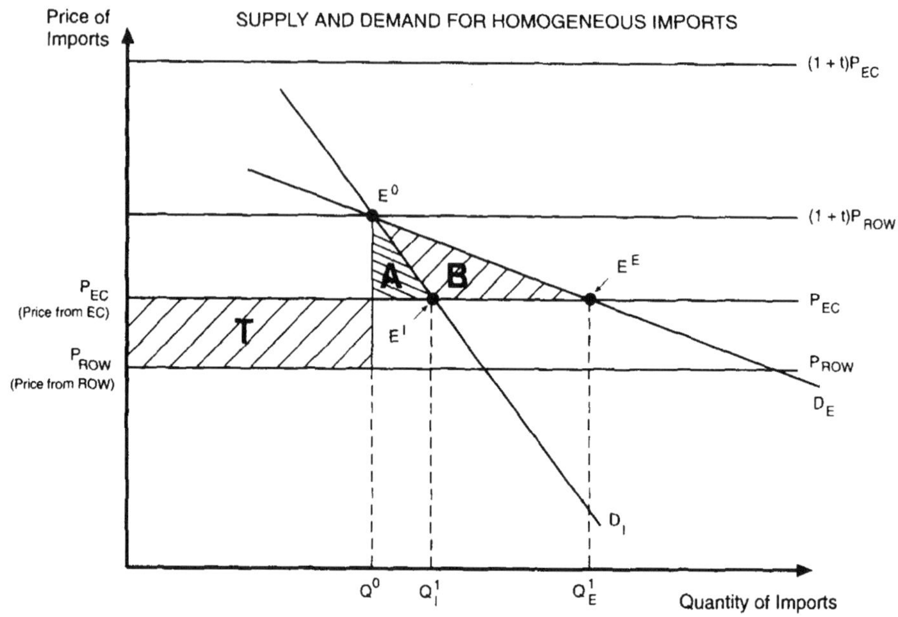

Fig. 2. Welfare benefits of trade integration increase with the elasticity of demand for composite imports. The trade diversion case, where consumers regard imports from different sources as homogeneous, is pictured. If tariffs are eliminated preferentially against the EC, the welfare change is equal to A − T with D_I (inelastic demand for imports), or A + B − T with D_E (elastic demand for imports). In the trade creation case there is no area T to subtract, and the triangles A and B extend down to the price of the low cost supplier.

cost supplier; but an enlarged triangle B remains the net difference in welfare between the elastic and inelastic demand cases.

4.3. Elasticity of substitution between imports from different sources

Our benchmark value of the elasticity of demand between imports from the EU and imports from the ROW is 5. In Table 4, we show that increasing this value reduces the welfare benefits of preferential tariff reduction, either against the EU or against the ROW. This parameter has no effect on the welfare effects when the tariff changes are not preferential.

Fig. 3 depicts how an increase in the elasticity of substitution among imports impacts on the estimates of the change in welfare. The demand curves of Moroccan consumers for imports from the EU and from the ROW are drawn analogously to Fig. 1. The difference between Figs. 1 and 3 is that we depict alternate new shifts in demand and new equilibria depending on the elasticity of substitution between EU and ROW imports. The inward shift in the demand curve for imports from the ROW will be larger the larger the elasticity of substitution among imports from

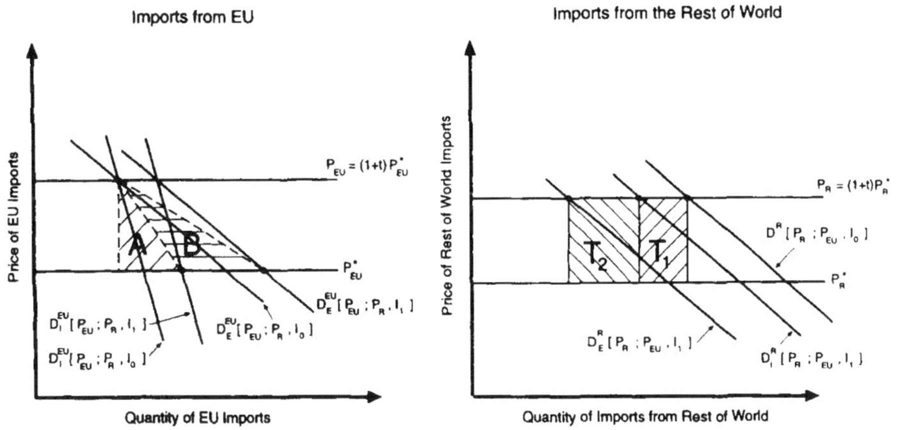

Fig. 3. Welfare benefits of trade integration decrease with greater substitutability among imports. If tariffs are eliminated preferentially against the EU, the welfare change is equal to A − T, with respectively inelastic demands D_I, and equal to A + B − T_1 − T_2 with relatively elastic demands D_E.

different sources. In the market for EU imports, triangle A is the gain in consumer surplus that is not offset by lost tariff revenue in the low elasticity case. With higher elasticities of substitution the demand for EU imports would be flatter so that the larger triangle A + B is the gain in consumer surplus in the market for EU imports.

In the market for ROW imports, there is a loss of tariff revenue equal to T_1 in the low cross-elasticity case or equal to $T_1 + T_2$ in the high cross-elasticity case, that is not offset by a consumer surplus change. Thus, the net change in welfare is equal to $A - T_1$ in the low elasticity case or $A + B - T_1 - T_2$ in the high elasticity case. In our simulations the rectangle T_2 exceeds the area B, so that trade diversion costs are higher with increases in the elasticity of substitution among imports.

4.4. Homogeneous or Armington sectors

Since both the sugar and the meat and dairy sectors have few or no imports, we have assumed that they are homogeneous sectors in our model. An alternative modeling procedure would be to assign a very small amount of imports to a sector that has no imports and treat the sector as an Armington sector. In view of the above discussion on the impact of the Armington elasticity, it should be apparent that treating the sector as a homogeneous sector (equivalent to an infinite Armington elasticity) will increase the welfare benefits of our trade integration

[24] See de Melo and Tarr (1992, chapter 2) for an elaboration.

scenarios, i.e. the Armington assumption mutes resource movement and reduces the welfare impact.[24] What may be less apparent is that under the Armington assumption, in response to a change in trade policy in a given sector, resource movement and the welfare impact will be quite small in sectors with a small import share compared with sectors with a large share of imports. For example, with our point estimate Armington elasticity (elasticity of substitution) of 2, a 50% decline in the relative price of imports will induce a 100% increase in the ratio of imports to domestic sales in consumption. But if imports were less than 0.5% of consumption, they will remain under 1% after their relative price reduction, i.e. the absolute increase in the import share of consumption is less than 0.5%. With the same elasticity of substitution, if a sector has a significant initial share, the same relative price reduction will result in a much larger absolute increase in imports as a percentage of total consumption in the sector. That is, ceteris paribus, there is dramatically less resource movement (and consequently welfare impact) in the case of a small initial import share.

In the case of sugar and meat and dairy, it appears appropriate to model these sectors as homogeneous products such that after quantitative restraints are removed there will be a substantial increase in the import share. These sectors have been protected by quantitative restraints because of the fear that they would contract precipitously. On the other hand, the homogeneous product assumption will tend to result in excessive resource movement without the presence of specific factors of production. Thus, as discussed in Section 3, we have employed specific factors in the homogeneous sectors to approximate the appropriate supply response.

5. Sensitivity analysis

Estimates of elasticities for primary factor substitution, import demand, import source, domestic demand, and the elasticity of transformation from domestic into exported output must be assembled. Despite our literature search for elasticity values, there are many elasticities in our model about which there is uncertainty. Our 'remedy' for this uncertainty, which is endemic to any large-scale model of this kind, is to undertake systematic sensitivity analyses of our major results with respect to plausible bounds on these elasticities. Even if we are unable to specify a point estimate with any precision, our priors over the likely bounds that these elasticities could take are quite strong. To the extent that our major conclusions are robust to perturbations over these bounds, we do not see our uncertainty over specific values of these elasticities as a weakness of the model.[25] We report the

[25] These remarks should not be interpreted as denying the value of any new empirical work on generating such elasticities. On the contrary, any effort that could generate better bounds on these point estimates is useful in generating policy conclusions that carry greater credibility, even if those conclusions will still be probabilistic in nature.

results of these sensitivity analyses in this section, which involve a minimum of 1000 simulations for each counter-factual policy. They will allow us to conclude whether or not our main results are robust, at least with respect to plausible uncertainty over elasticities.[26]

Our sensitivity analysis employs the procedures developed by Harrison and Vinod (1992). Essentially these procedures amount to a Monte Carlo simulation exercise in which a wide range of elasticities are independently and simultaneously perturbed from their benchmark values. These perturbations follow prescribed distributions, such as a t distribution with a specified standard deviation and degrees of freedom, or a uniform distribution over a specified range. The point estimates employed in the simulations underlying Table 2 are the means of these distributions, with one exception. The exception is that the point estimate for the elasticity of substitution between intermediates and value added is zero, i.e. Leontief; whereas in the systematic sensitivity analysis we allow for a CES production structure.[27] For each Monte Carlo run we solve the counter-factual policy with the selected set of elasticities. This process is repeated until we arrive at the desired sample size, in our case 1000. The results are then tabulated as a distribution, with equal weight being given (by construction) to each Monte Carlo run. The upshot is a probability distribution defined over the endogenous variables of interest. In our case we focus solely on the welfare impacts of each policy.

The results of the sensitivity analysis are reported in Table 5. In the interests of reporting all of the pertinent data in a compact manner, some of the column and row headings are necessarily somewhat cryptic at first glance. The acronyms for each simulation (column heading) are defined in Table 2. The 'sample size' row refers to the number of Monte Carlo runs that were actually completed. In each case we have at least 1000 runs, which should be enough to obtain a reliable picture of the distribution of results. The 'point estimate' (PE) row shows the effect of the policy when all elasticities are set equal to their benchmark, or point estimate, values. These are the results reported and discussed earlier. As before, we report the change in welfare due to the policy as a percentage of GDP, the revenue as the change in the VAT rate required, and the labor adjustment as the percentage of the labor force that is reallocated.

The remaining rows report the results of the sensitivity analysis proper. We list the median, the mean, and the standard deviation, so as to provide simple indicators of the location and dispersion of the distribution of results. We do not report here the skewness and kurtosis statistics that are necessary to gain a more complete impression of the distribution. In all cases we find that both the skewness and kurtosis are insignificant.

---

[26] We appreciate that there are many other assumptions that remain fixed as we vary just elasticities, but regard those extensions as beyond the scope of the present study.

[27] The exact distributional assumptions used are documented in appendix A of Rutherford et al. (1993). For the purposes of this paper suffice it to notice here that we employ uniform distributions for the Armington elasticities (values = {1, 2, 3}), the elasticity of substitution between EU and non-EU sources (values = {3, 5, 7}).

Table 5
Results from sensitivity analysis

	FTA	*ACCESS*	*EULIB*	*LIBROW*	*LIBALL*	*FTAALL*
Sample size	1005	2284	1096	1002	1002	1078
Welfare	1.52	0.27	1.29	1.10	2.37	2.60
PE[a]						
Median	1.72	0.29	1.51	1.39	2.73	2.96
Mean	1.74	0.29	1.51	1.39	2.72	2.96
St.d.[b]	0.39	0.02	0.31	0.32	0.35	0.35
Prob. ≥ 0	1.0	1.0	1.0	1.0	1.0	1.0
Prob. ≥ PE	0.705	0.789	0.721	0.870	0.809	0.826
50% LB[c]	1.49	0.28	1.27	1.11	2.43	2.69
50% UB[d]	2.00	0.31	1.77	1.64	2.96	3.23
75% LB	1.38	0.27	1.14	1.00	2.26	2.52
75% UB	2.14	0.32	1.90	1.79	3.12	3.40
VAT rate	58.3	−1.20	58.90	60.10	85.50	84.90
PE						
Median	56.33	−1.55	57.08	57.11	81.69	80.99
Mean	56.39	−1.58	57.11	57.25	81.75	81.01
St.d.	2.95	0.03	3.07	3.24	3.13	3.07
Prob. ≥ 0	1.0	0.0	1.0	1.0	1.0	1.0
Prob. ≥ PE	0.262	0.086	0.297	0.197	0.133	0.129
50% LB	54.42	−1.81	54.96	55.06	79.52	78.75
50% UB	58.49	−1.39	59.35	59.63	84.19	84.34
75% LB	53.02	−1.99	53.53	53.72	78.11	77.32
75% UB	59.90	−1.29	60.60	61.55	85.70	85.00
Labor adj. PE	2.4	0.3	2.5	2.5	3.0	2.9
Median	2.65	0.32	2.75	2.77	3.48	3.38
Mean	2.67	0.32	2.78	2.80	3.49	3.39
St.d.	0.36	0.04	0.38	0.39	0.48	0.45

[a] PE = point estimate.
[b] St.d. = standard deviation.
[c] LB = lower bound.
[d] UB = upper bound.

In order to obtain an indication of the *qualitative* policy results we report the 'prob. ≥ 0' row for the welfare and the VAT rate results, which shows the probability from the empirical distribution that welfare increased in the counterfactual policy. This gives us a measure of the confidence that we have the *sign* right when we look at the point estimate effect or the mean or median. Similarly, we report a row showing the probability that an effect greater than or equal to the PE effect was obtained. If the PE result is perfectly representative of the location of the distribution of results we should see this value around one-half; this would be the case if the PE result exactly equalled the reported median result. A value lower

[28] With the exception of the intermediate input substitution, where the point estimate is zero.

(higher) than one-half indicates that the distribution generally lies below (above) the PE result.[28]

Finally, to gain a better sense of the confidence to be attached to the PE or mean welfare and VAT rate result, we report lower and upper bounds from 50% and 75% symmetric confidence intervals around the median result. These confidence intervals simply show the smallest and largest values that lie within 50% or 75% of the distribution centered on the median. Thus a 50% confidence interval between 1.1 and 2.3 can be interpreted as saying that 50% of the Monte Carlo runs resulted in welfare results between these values.

What, then, do we learn from these sensitivity analyses regarding our policy conclusions? Most notably, since the standard deviation of the estimate is 0.39, a 95% confidence interval for the welfare impact of the FTA gives a range of welfare improvement from 1.06 to 2.42% of GDP. Thus, even at the low end of the confidence interval of the estimates, there is a welfare improvement, establishing robustness of the basic policy message with respect to the elasticity parameters.

Most mean and median welfare effects are above the point estimates reported earlier due to the fact, as mentioned above, that the point estimate between intermediates and value-added is Leontief, whereas greater substitution possibilities are allowed in the systematic sensitivity analysis. These higher welfare effects are also coupled with higher adjustment costs. We can confirm our conclusion above that *FTA* is a preferred policy package to *EULIB* in the sense of providing higher median welfare gains at lower median adjustment costs. Note, however, that the mean welfare effect for *EULIB* lies within one standard deviation of the mean for *FTA*. There is therefore considerable overlap between the two distributions, so the conclusion regarding which policy package is preferred might still not be robust. We find, however, that the welfare effect in *FTA* is greater than the median welfare effect in *EULIB* with a probability of 0.711. The reverse case that the welfare effect in *EULIB* is larger than the median welfare effect in *FTA* only occurs with a probability of 0.282, however.

Similarly, we find the second-best argument in favor of eliminating all import protection and not just protection from EU competition to be robust to variations in the value of key parameters. The welfare effect in *LIBALL* is much larger than the welfare effect of *EULIB*, but with not much additional labor adjustment.

Interestingly we find that the median revenue effects are smaller than the point estimates. In no case would the VAT rate have to increase to more than about 5.5 and 20% from a benchmark value of 3 and 11% for domestically produced and imported goods, respectively.

In summary, we find that our general conclusions are quite robust with respect to any uncertainty in key parameters. Welfare and labor adjustments tend to be higher, due to the inclusion of higher Armington elasticities, but the revenue effect is smaller.

6. Conclusions

The purpose of this paper has been to illustrate the importance of several key parameters in a general equilibrium model for a small open economy. This is done within the framework of a model exercise of the economic effects of an EU–Morocco free trade area. The model is a 'generic' general equilibrium model with a large number of production sectors, each employing intermediate and primary factors in constant returns to scale production processes, and a representative consumer that derives income from these factors and maximizes utility subject to that income constraint. A number of innovative features are introduced to allow better control of the properties of the model. For example, to allow for differential degrees of substitution in consumption, products are differentiated into domestic and imported, as well as EU and non-EU varieties. For some commodities, however, a homogeneous good assumption is employed in order to better capture expected supply responses. For the same reason the model also allows both mobile and sector specific capital to be employed across sectors, with the proportion of mobile to sector specific capital being variable. On the export side we also adopt a differentiation across output varieties, both according to whether products are destined for domestic and foreign markets, and according to whether the foreign markets are EU or non-EU.

Our general results for the EU–Moroccan free trade agreement show that fairly large welfare gains are to be expected for Morocco. More gains are expected to arise out of the import liberalizations in Morocco than out of the improved access to EU markets. Expanding the import liberalizations to incorporate all trading partners will give substantial added benefits with very little additional adjustment cost. We conclude that there is some trade diversion in the EU–Moroccan FTA, but that it is dominated by trade creation effects such that the net effects are positive.

The key parameters responsible for whether a regional trade agreement leads to net positive or negative results are, in addition to import shares and tariff levels, the substitution elasticities in consumption. We generally find that regional agreements are more likely to be detrimental to welfare when domestic varieties are not close substitutes to imported varieties, i.e. when the Armington elasticity is low. With a higher Armington elasticity the own elasticity of demand for partner imports is larger, which allows more trade creation. Moreover, the decline in the composite price of imports results in a substitution away from domestic goods in favor of imports of all varieties, i.e. a shift in demand for imports; with a larger Armington elasticity, this leads to greater trade creation effects in the market for partner country imports and a reduction in the trade diversion costs of lost tariff revenue in the market for imports from the rest of the world.

The elasticity of substitution between import sources has a more ambiguous influence on the welfare effects. On the one hand a higher elasticity will lead to a larger shift away from the non-partner imports, causing larger losses in tariff revenues. On the other hand, it will also yield larger consumer gains on the market for partner imports. In the Morocco model, where the Armington elasticity is set at 2.0 and the cross-elasticity is set at 5.0, we find net positive welfare effects from a regional agreement. Due to uncertainties in the estimates of many elasticities, we have performed systematic sensitivity analysis and have found that our results are quite robust with respect to the elasticities.

Acknowledgements

The authors would like to acknowledge the help and comments of Ali Khadr, Martin Rama and Eric Abalahin of the World Bank; Hasan Bernoussi, Jamal Kilito, Fat Allah Sujilmassi and Zahra Maafiri of the Moroccan Ministry of External Commerce; Glenn Harrison and Jean Luc Grosso of the University of South Carolina; and an anonymous referee of this journal. This research was partially supported by the World Bank under RPO 675–64, The Impact of EC92 and Trade Integration on Selected Mediterranean Countries'. The views expressed are those of the authors and do not necessarily reflect those of the World Bank, the Government of Morocco or those acknowledged.

Appendix

Variables

X_i Exports of good i
X_{ir} Exports of good i to region r
D_i Domestic sales of good i
M_i Composite imports of good i
m_{ir} Imports of good i from region r
S_i Armington aggregate of domestic goods and imports
V_i Value-added function for variable factors
C_i Private consumer demand for good i
W Welfare index for the representative domestic consumer
L_i Labor inputs used in sector i
K_i Capital inputs used in sector i
x_{ki} Intermediate inputs of good k in sector i
f_{ki} Variable input use of primary factor k in sector i
f_{ki}^{F} Fixed input use of primary factor k in sector i
Y_i Domestic production of good i
p_i Price of domestically produced good i
π_i Price of domestic–import good i composite
w_k Price of factor k
τ_T Replacement tax multiplier on lump-sum transfers
τ_v Replacement tax multiplier for value-added taxes
τ_f Replacement tax multiplier for factor taxes
p_i^{X} Export price of good i (exogenous)
p_{ir}^{M} Import price of good i from region r (exogenous)

Parameters

G_i Government demand for good i

I_i	Final demand for output of sector i for investment purposes
t_{ir}	Import tariff rate on commodity i from region r
t_{ik}	Factor taxes on factor k in sector i
s_i^{P}	Rate of production subsidy for good i
s_i^{X}	Export subsidy rate for good i
ν_i	Tax rate on factor inputs in sector i
T	Lump-sum tax on consumers
B	Current account balance (equal to net capital inflows)
E_k	Endowment of factor k
a_{ij}	Intermediate input requirements; amount of good i required to produce one unit of good j
$'' \alpha_{DX_i}$	Distributive parameter for domestic composite good i in export transformation function, Y_i
α_{X_i}	Distributive parameter for export composite good i in export transformation function, Y_i
α_{M_i}	Distributive parameter for import composite good i in import aggregation function, M_i
α_{DM_i}	Distributive parameter for domestic composite good i in import aggregation function, M_i
$\beta_{X_{ir}}$	Distributive parameter for exports of good i to region r in regional export transformation function, X_i
$\beta_{M_{ir}}$	Distributive parameter for imports of good i from region r in regional import transformation function, M_i
F_k	Primary factor supplies
δ_{ki}	Distributive parameter for primary input k in value added for good i
σ	Elasticity of substitution between primary factor inputs in value added
ϵ_i	Elasticity of transformation between domestic production and exports in sector i
e_i	Elasticity of transformation between exports to different regions
σ_i	Elasticity of substitution between domestic goods and aggregate imports in sector i
s_i	Elasticity of substitution in consumption in sector i between imports and from different regions.

References

Brooke, A., D. Kendrick and A. Meeraus, 1988, GAMS: A user's guide (Scientific Press, Redwood City, CA).

Burns, M., 1973, A note on the concept and measure of consumers' surplus, American Economic Review 63, 335–344.

Commission of the European Communities, 1994, Strengthening the Mediterranean policy of the European Union: Establishing a Euro-Mediterranean partnership (European Commission, Brussels).

Harberger, A., 1971, Three basic postulates for applied welfare economics: An interpretive essay, Journal of Economic Literature 9, 785–797.

Harrison, G.W., 1990, The sensitivity analysis of applied general equilibrium models with MPSS: User's guide, Unpublished manuscript (Department of Economics, University of South Carolina).

Harrison, G.W., T.F. Rutherford and I. Wooton, 1989, The economic impact of the European Community, American Economic Review (Papers & Proceedings) 79, 288–294.

Harrison, G.W., T.F. Rutherford and D. Tarr, 1993, Piecemeal trade reform in partially liberalized economies, World Bank Economic Review 7.

Harrison, G.W. and H.D. Vinod, 1992, The sensitivity analysis of applied general equilibrium models: Completely randomized factorial sampling designs, Review of Economics and Statistics 74.

Intermedia, 1995, Customs Union with the EU (Istanbul).

Mateus, et al., 1988, A multisector framework for analysis of stabilization and structural adjustment policies: The case of Morocco, Discussion Paper 29 (World Bank, Washington D.C.).

Melo, J. de and A. Panagariya, 1992, The new regionalism in trade policy (World Bank, Washington D.C.).

Melo, J. de and D. Tarr, 1992, General equilibrium analysis of U.S. foreign trade policy (MIT Press, Cambridge Mass).

Rutherford, T.F., 1989, General equilibrium modelling with MPS/GE, Unpublished monograph (Department of Economics, University of Western Ontario).

Rutherford, T.F., 1992, Extensions of GAMS for complementarity and variational problems arising in applied economics, Economics Working Paper 92–9 (Department of Economics, University of Colorado at Boulder).

Rutherford, T.F., E.E. Rutström and D. Tarr, 1993, Morocco's free trade agreement with the European Community: A quantitative assessment, Working Paper 1173 (Policy Research Department, World Bank, Washington D.C.).

Rutherford, T.F., E.E. Rutström and D. Tarr, 1994, L'Accord de libre-échange entre le Moroc et la CE: Une evaluation quantitative, Revue d'Economie du Developpement, Vol. 2, 97–133.

Rutström, E.E., 1992, Friends, enemies and rentseeking: Who protects whom in Indonesia?, Working Paper B-92-04 (College of Business Administration, University of South Carolina).

UNDP–World Bank, 1992, Morocco 2000: An open and competitive economy, Country Report 7 (UNDP–World Bank Trade Expansion Program).

USITC, 1992, Economy-wide modeling of the economic implications of an FTA with Mexico and a NAFTA with Canada and Mexico, (Publication 2508 USITC Washington D.C.).

Introduction and Key Tables from: Services Liberalization in Preferential Trade Arrangements: The Case of Kenya*

Edward J. Balistreri and David G. Tarr

Despite the fact that many modern preferential trade agreements include commitments to foreign investors in services, the literature does not contain a modeling framework to analyze these commitments. In this paper we fill that void by developing a computable general equilibrium model of Kenya with monopolistic competition, foreign direct investment in services and Dixit-Stiglitz endogenous productivity effects. We use this model to assess preferential commitments by Kenya to foreign services providers. We show that there is an imperfect competition analogy to trade diversion in goods, whereby preferential commitments in services could be immizerising. Sensitivity analysis shows that losses are more likely the more technologically advanced are the excluded regions relative to the partner region, and, very importantly, the greater the rent capture on initial barriers in services. So an agreement with the technologically rich European Union is both worth more to Kenya and is more likely to be welfare increasing than an agreement with its less technologically rich African partners. From our systematic sensitivity analysis, in which the model is executed 30,000 times, and results are reported as confidence intervals of the sample distributions, we find that there is only a two percent chance that a services agreement with the Africa region would be immizerising for Kenya, but an agreement with the EU should produce gains with probability one.

1. Introduction

Both economic theory and the empirical literature have shown that foreign direct investment and the wide availability of business services results in total factor productivity gains to the manufacturing sector and the economy broadly. International commitments to national treatment and market access for foreign investors in key business services sectors may help developing countries obtain better access to these services that contribute to the productivity gains. Some developing countries, however, are hesitant to make substantial multilateral commitments, but may be more inclined to proceed in regional arrangements with other neighboring developing

*The full World Bank Policy and Research Working Paper is available at the following link: http://econ.worldbank.org/external/default/main?pagePK=64165259&theSitePK=469372&piPK=64165421&menuPK=64166093&entityID=000158349_20110131090808

countries, rather than with a major developed country partner. But refusing to open up to FDI from the more technologically advanced countries could mean that developing countries do not obtain the most significant productivity advances, or possibly even regress if developed country technology is diverted.

Since the early 1990s, regional trade agreements have surged; 283 have been notified to the WTO and were in force as of February 2010.[1] Commitments to foreign investors in services are key aspects of modern FTA agreements negotiated with the EU, the US and in some other agreements. Policy-makers have expressed demand for analysis of the implications of these agreements, and applied general equilibrium modelers have responded with a substantial number of studies that examine regional agreements in goods, but which exclude analysis in services. These studies include Harris (1984), Levy and van Wijnbergen (1995), Smith and Venables (1988) and Harrison *et al.* (1996, 1997, 2002, 2003, 2004).There have also been several papers in recent years that examine FDI in services, without a regional dimension, including Markusen, Rutherford and Tarr (2005), Konan and Maskus (2006), Rutherford and Tarr (2008), Brown and Stern (2001), Dee *et al.* (2003), Jensen *et al.* (2007, 2010), and Balistreri *et al.* (2009). Given that commitments to foreign investors in services are key aspects of modern FTA agreements, and the evidence on the productivity gains of FDI in services, economists need to have a framework to be able to assess the impact of preferential commitments to foreign investors in services. This paper fills that void.

Kenya, like many developing countries, is faced with multiple preferential trade and FDI options as well as multilateral decisions. In 2011 it is involved in negotiations of commitments in services in various regional arrangements, including the Economic Partnership Agreements with the European Union, the Common Market for Eastern and Southern Africa (COMESA), the East African Customs Union and the South African Development Community (SADC) as well.[2] In the context of its international negotiations under the Doha Development Agenda, Kenya may be called upon to make further commitments in the business services area. Kenya is making commitments in services within the East African Customs Union, including a mutual recognition agreement in professional services, but its policy-makers seek an assessment of the impact of these agreements for Kenya as well as for its partners.

In this paper, we develop an innovative 55 sector small open economy computable general equilibrium model of Kenya to assess the impact of Kenya's preferential agreements that include commitments to foreign investors in services. We build on

[1]See http://www.wto.org/english/tratop_e/region_e/region_e.htm. This does not include a significant number of regional agreements that are in force (among developing countries) that have not been notified to the WTO.

[2]See Balistreri and Tarr (2011, Table 1) for a list of COMESA and East African Customs Union countries. While Kenya is not presently a member of the SADC, COMESA and SADC are negotiating a free trade agreement.

Table 18.1. Benchmark Distortions.

	Tariff	Sales tax	Regulatory barriers	
			All firms	Foreign firms
Business Services				
Communication			6.0	4.0
Insurance		0.6	13.0	26.0
Banking and other financial services		0.6	17.0	
Professional business services			3.7	11.9
Road services			15.0	30.0
Railway transport			25.0	
Maritime transport			57.0	40.0
Pipeline transport				
Airline transport			2.0	2.0
Dixit-Stiglitz Goods				
Beverages & tobacco	30.4	44.0		
Grain milling	25.8	9.4		
Sugar & bakery & confectionary	23.5	19.5		
Petroleum	10.4	22.4		
Chemicals	8.8	4.8		
Metals and machines	9.5	5.2		
Non metallic products	19.3	0.7		
Agriculture				
Maize	29.6			
Wheat	11.0			
Rice	27.6			
Barley	9.9			
Cotton	12.5	12.5		
Other cereals	9.9			
Sugarcane	64.2	19.4		
Coffee	19.7			
Tea	19.7	5.1		
Roots & tubers				
Pulses & oil seeds	6.7	0.0		
Fruits	19.5			
Vegetables	19.7	0.1		
Cut flowers	19.7			
Others crops	2.7	3.4		
Beef	19.7			
Dairy	28.9			
Poultry	19.7			
Sheep goat and lamb for slaughter				
Other livestock	19.7			
Other CRTS				
Fishing	19.7			
Mining	1.2	4.1		
Meat & dairy	27.6	15.5		
Other manufactured food	15.8	5.5		
Printing and publishing		12.1		
Textile & clothing	14.4	8.5		

(*Continued*)

Table 18.1. (*Continued*)

	Tariff	Sales tax	Regulatory barriers: All firms	Regulatory barriers: Foreign firms
Leather & footwear	13.8	14.5		
Wood & paper	9.2	5.9		
Other manufactures	17.2	3.0		
Trade		1.9		
Hotels		13.9		

Note: The following are also CRTS sectors of the model, but with zero benchmark distortions: forestry, water, electricity, construction, real estate, administration, health, education.
Source: Authors' estimates. See Balistreri, Rutherford, and Tarr (2009) for details.

Table 18.2. Market Shares in Kenyan Services Sectors with FDI (%) and Estimates of Elasticity of Firms' Supply with Respect to Price for Kenya (by Sector and by Kenyan Trading Partner Region).

	Market Shares in Services Sectors with FDI				Elasticity of supply with respect to price by Kenyan trading partner region			R&D expenditures divided by sales (times 1000) for the US*
Business Services	Kenya	EU	Africa	ROW	Africa	EU	ROW	
Communication	26	49	0	25	2.5	13.4	20	52-high
Insurance	85	4	0	11	3.3	3.3	10	4-low
Banking	62	29	0	9	3.3	3.3	10	4-low
Professional services	94	2	2	2	2.5	13.4	20	116-high
Road services	80	2	14	4	3.3	3.3	10	low
Railway transport**	0	0	0	100	1.9	10	15	medium
Maritime transport**	45	25	15	15	1.9	10	15	medium
Pipeline transport**	70	0	13	18	1.9	10	15	medium
Airline transport**	30	30	10	30	1.9	10	15	medium
Manufacturing								
beverages and tabacco					3.3	3.3	10	14-low
grain milling***					3.3	3.3	10	7-low
sugar & bakery & confectioners***					3.3	3.3	10	7-low
petroleum					3.3	3.3	10	2-low
chemicals					1.9	10	15	34-medium
metals and machines***					1.9	10	15	33-medium
non-metallic products***					3.3	3.3	10	0-17-low

*Based on average R&D expenditures for the years 2004 and 2005. The average for all US industries was 36.
**We evaluate transportation as a medium R&D sector since three sectors dominate R&D expenditures of US multinationals operating abroad. These are transportation, chemicals and computers and electronics. Moreover, about two-thirds of all R&D expenditures of foreign multinationals operating in the US was performed in the same three sectors. See "U.S. and International Research and Development: Funds and Technology Linkages," at http://www.nsf.gov/statistics/seind04/c4/c4s5.htm
***Food is the proxy for grain milling and sugar, bakery and confectioners; machinery is used for metals and machines; for non-metallic products, we used plastics, rubber, mineral and wood products.
Source: Authors' estimates. For details, see Balistreri and Tarr (2011).

Table 18.3. Summary of Results (Results are Percentage Change from Initial Equilibrium, Unless Otherwise Indicated) No Initial Rent Capture Case Except Numbers in Parentheses. Values in Parentheses are for the Initial Rent Capture Case.

Scenario definition	Bench-mark	**EU FTA**	EU Discrimi-natory Services	EU Tariffs	**Africa FTA**	**EU-Africa FTA**	**Unilateral**	Unilateral Discrimi-natory Services	Unilateral Tariffs	**Unilateral & Domestic**
50% reduction of discriminatory barriers on EU services firms	No	**Yes**	Yes	No	**No**	**Yes**	**Yes**	Yes	No	**Yes**
50% reduction of discriminatory barriers on African services firm	No	**No**	No	No	**Yes**	**Yes**	**Yes**	Yes	No	**Yes**
50% reduction of discriminatory barriers on ROW services firms	No	**No**	No	No	**No**	**No**	**Yes**	Yes	No	**Yes**
50% reduction of regulatory barriers for all services firms	No	**No**	No	No	**No**	**No**	**No**	No	No	**Yes**
Removal of tariffs on EU sourced goods	No	**Yes**	No	Yes	**No**	**Yes**	**Yes**	No	Yes	**Yes**
Removal of tariffs on ROW sourced goods	No	**No**	No	No	**No**	**No**	**Yes**	No	Yes	**Yes**

(*Continued*)

Table 18.3. (*Continued*)

Scenario definition	Bench-mark	**EU FTA**	EU Discrimi-natory Services	EU Tariffs	**Africa FTA**	**EU-Africa FTA**	**Unilateral**	Unilateral Discrimi-natory Services	Unilateral Tariffs	**Unilateral & Domestic**
Aggregate welfare										
Welfare (EV as % of consumption)		**0.7** (0.5)	0.5 (0.3)	0.2 (0.2)	**0.3** (0.1)	**1.0** (0.5)	**3.6** (2.9)	1.5 (0.9)	2.0 (2.0)	**10.3** (7.0)
Welfare (EV as % of GDP)		**0.6** (0.4)	0.4 (0.3)	0.1 (0.1)	**0.2** (0.0)	**0.8** (0.5)	**3.0** (2.5)	1.3 (0.7)	1.7 (1.7)	**8.6** (5.9)
Government budget										
Tariff revenue (% of GDP)	3.6	**2.1**	2.9	2.1	**2.9**	**2.1**		2.9		
Tariff revenue		**−29.0**	−0.1	−28.9	**−0.1**	**−29.1**	**−100.0**	−0.3	−100.0	**−100.0**
Aggregate trade										
Real exchange rate		**0.9**	0.3	0.6	**0.2**	**1.2**	**4.0**	0.9	3.1	**5.8**
Aggregate exports		**3.2**	0.1	3.1	**0.3**	**3.5**	**12.6**	0.5	11.9	**15.4**
Factor Earnings										
Skilled labor		**2.2**	0.7	1.5	**0.5**	**2.7**	**9.0**	2.2	6.5	**15.3**
Semi-skilled labor		**1.1**	0.5	0.6	**0.3**	**1.4**	**5.6**	1.5	4.1	**10.3**
Unskilled labor		**1.5**	0.6	0.9	**0.3**	**1.9**	**7.4**	1.9	5.3	**14.3**
Capital		**1.5**	0.5	0.9	**0.3**	**1.8**	**7.0**	1.7	5.1	**12.4**
Land		**2.6**	0.4	2.2	**0.5**	**3.0**	**7.7**	1.4	6.1	**10.0**
Factor adjustments										
Skilled labor		**0.5**	0.3	0.3	**0.2**	**0.7**	**2.1**	0.9	1.3	**4.2**
Semi-skilled labor		**0.7**	0.2	0.7	**0.1**	**0.8**	**2.5**	0.6	1.9	**4.5**
Unskilled labor		**0.2**	0.1	0.1	**0.0**	**0.2**	**0.7**	0.2	0.5	**1.3**
Capital		**0.3**	0.1	0.3	**0.0**	**0.3**	**1.3**	0.3	1.2	**2.2**
Land		**1.0**	0.5	0.7	**0.4**	**1.4**	**3.7**	1.4	2.2	**7.2**

Source: Authors' estimates.

Table 18.4. Piecemeal Sensitivity Analysis of Kenya-EU and Kenya-Africa FTAs.

in Equivalent Variation (EV) as a percentage of consumption

	Parameter Value			**EV of EU-Kenya FTA**			**EV of Africa-Kenya FTA**		
Parameter	Lower	Central	Upper	Lower	Central	Upper	Lower	Central	Upper
$\sigma(q_i, q_j)$ – services sectors	2	3	4	1.19	0.67	0.54	0.62	0.29	0.19
$\sigma(q_i, q_j)$ – goods sectors		see below		1.06	0.67	0.59	0.32	0.29	0.28
σ(va, bs)	0.625	1.25	1.875	0.55	0.67	0.82	0.25	0.29	0.33
σ(D, M)	2	4	6	0.65	0.67	0.69	0.28	0.29	0.29
σ(L, K)	0.5	1	1.5	0.64	0.67	0.70	0.28	0.29	0.29
$\sigma(A_1, \ldots A_n)$	0	0	0.25	0.67	0.67	0.67	0.29	0.29	0.29
σ(D, E)	2	4	6	0.65	0.67	0.69	0.28	0.29	0.29
ε_{TZA}	Central values of all 4 sets of eta			0.61	0.67	0.72	0.31	0.29	0.27
ε_{EU}	parameters are listed in table 2.			0.25	0.67	0.96	0.29	0.29	0.29
ε_{AFR}	Lower values are 0.5 all central values and			0.68	0.67	0.67	0.14	0.29	0.43
ε_{ROW}	upper values are 1.5 times all central			0.90	0.67	0.55	0.29	0.29	0.29
ε_{AFR} & θr =1	values for the selected ε.			0.49	0.49	0.48	-0.09	0.05	0.20
θ_r	NA	0	1	NA	0.67	0.49	NA	0.29	0.05
θ_r - CRTS model	NA	0	1	NA	0.09	-0.06	NA	0.14	-0.06
IRTS by sector	goods only	services only	goods & services	0.21	0.51	0.67	0.14	0.27	0.29
AVE	Lower (upper) values of the ad valorem			0.39	0.67	1.05	0.14	0.29	0.45
AVE & θr =1	equivalents are 0.5 (1.5) times all the AVEs			0.29	0.49	0.77	0.02	0.05	0.11
AVE, θr =1 & ε_{AFR}= low.	listed in table 1.			0.30	0.49	0.77	-0.04	-0.09	-0.15
export demand	NA	Central	perf. elastic in all	NA	0.67	0.78	NA	0.29	0.30
θ_m	0.025	0.05	0.075	0.67	0.67	0.67	0.29	0.29	0.29
$\sigma(q_i, q_j)$ – goods sectors									
sugar and bakery	2.12	2.93	3.74						
beverages and tabacco	1.52	2.33	3.14						
chemicals	2.01	2.82	3.63						
metals and machines	8.35	16.69	25.04						
grain milling	2.43	3.24	4.05						
nonmetallic products	2.805	5.61	8.415						
petroleum	2.75	3.56	4.37						

Key:
$\sigma(q_i, q_j)$: Elasticity of substitution between firm varieties in imperfectly competitive sectors.
$\sigma(v_a, b_s)$: Elasticity of substitution between value-added and business services.
σ(D, M): Elasticity of substitution between domestic and imported varieties.
σ(L, K): Elasticity of substitution between primary factors of production in value added.
$\sigma(A_1, \ldots A_n)$: Elasticity of substitution in intermediate production between composite Armington aggregate goods.
σ(D, E): Elasticity of transformation (domestic output versus exports).
ε_{TZA}: Elasticity of national service firm supply with respect to price of output.
ε_{EU}: Elasticity of EU service firm supply with respect to price of output.
ε_{AFR}: Elasticity of AFR service firm supply with respect to price of output.
ε_{ROW}: Elasticity of Rest of World service firm supply with respect to price of output.
θ_r: Share of rents in services sectors captured by domestic agents.
IRTS by sector: in goods (services) only, business services (Dixit-Stiglitz goods) in Table 1 are CRTS.
AVE: *ad valorem* equivalents of regulatory barriers in services; ε_{AFR} = low means ε_{AFR} = 0.5 central values.
export demand: in the upper case, perfectly elastic export demand is assumed for all model sectors.
θ_m: Shares of value added in multinational firms due to specialized primary factor imports.
Source: Authors' estimates.

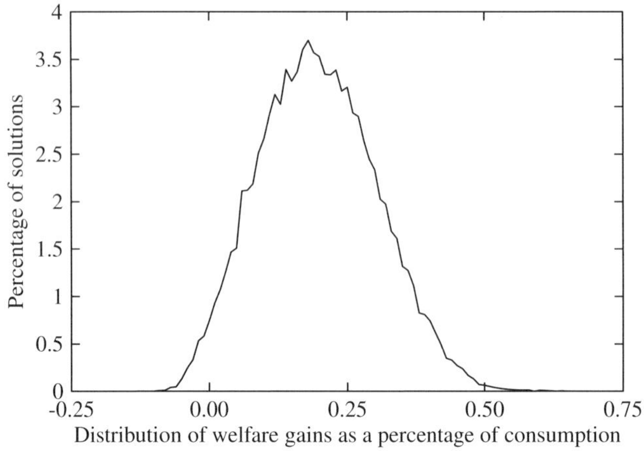

Figure 18.1. Sample Frequency Distribution of the Welfare Results of Kenyan Preferential Reduction of Services Barriers against African Partners — 30,000 Simulations.

the model of Balistreri, Rutherford and Tarr (2009), but decompose the rest of the world into the European Union, our Africa region and the Rest of the World. This allows us to assess regional trade issues. The model contains foreign direct investment in services from each foreign region in the model with Dixit-Stiglitz endogenous productivity gains from additional varieties of services. In each imperfectly competitive sector, firm types differ by sector and region. Based on the now extensive econometric literature begun by Coe and Helpman (1995), we allow the endogenous productivity effects to vary by the level of development of the partner region, and by sector.

To assess the robustness of the results to parameter uncertainty, we conduct systematic sensitivity analysis, where we execute the model 30,000 times. Each simulation is based on a random draw of all the parameter values, including the share of initial rents captured by Kenyan agents. We then present the key results as sample distributions and sample confidence intervals. We estimate that Kenya would realize gains from an agreement with the European Union with a probability of one, but there is a 1.9 percent chance that Kenya would lose from a preferential arrangement with the Africa region.

Preferential liberalization of services barriers results in an increase in varieties (with productivity gains) from regional partners, but losses of varieties (and lost productivity) from excluded countries. The possible losses for Kenya in a services agreement with our Africa region show that, with some plausible parameter values,

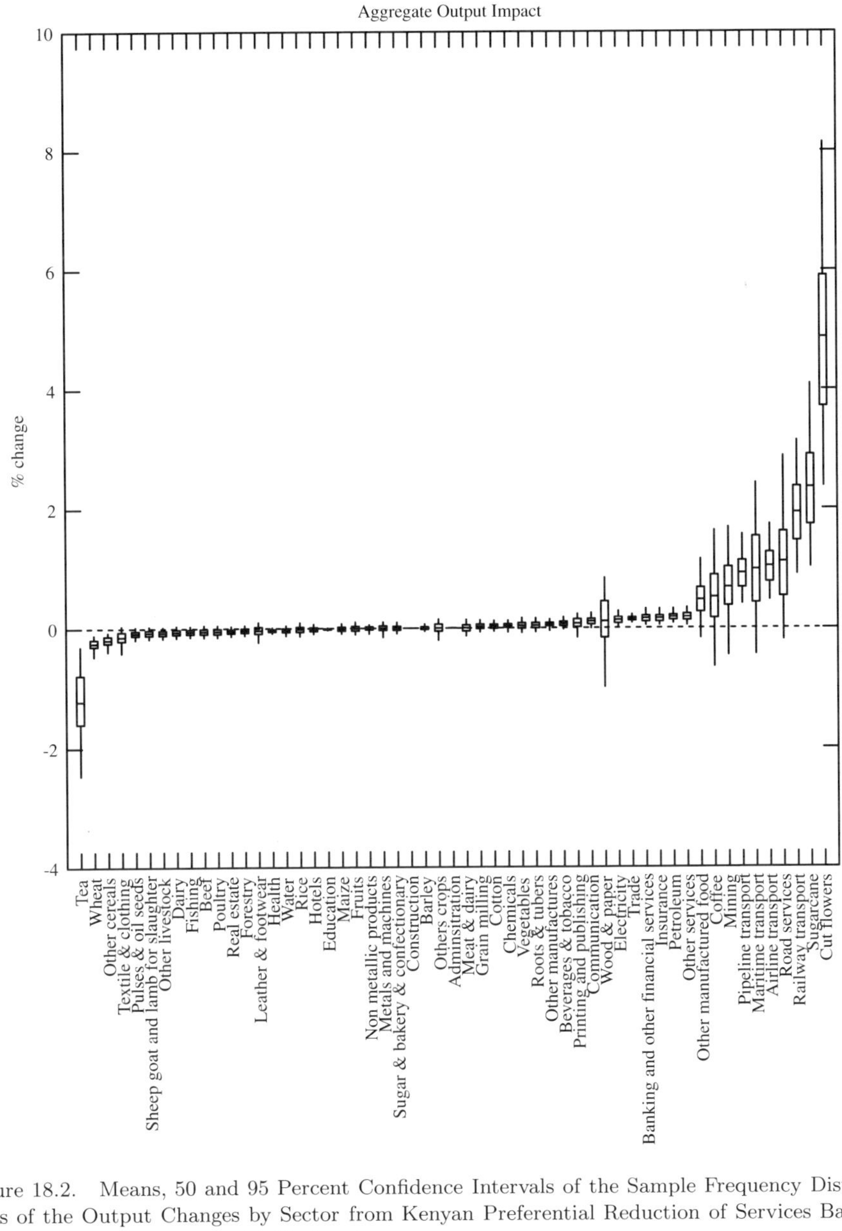

Figure 18.2. Means, 50 and 95 Percent Confidence Intervals of the Sample Frequency Distributions of the Output Changes by Sector from Kenyan Preferential Reduction of Services Barriers Against African Partners — 30,000 Simulations.

Note: The boxes are limited vertically by the 25% and 75% quartiles. The bars in the box are the means. The vertical lines extend to the 2.5% and 97.5% percentiles.

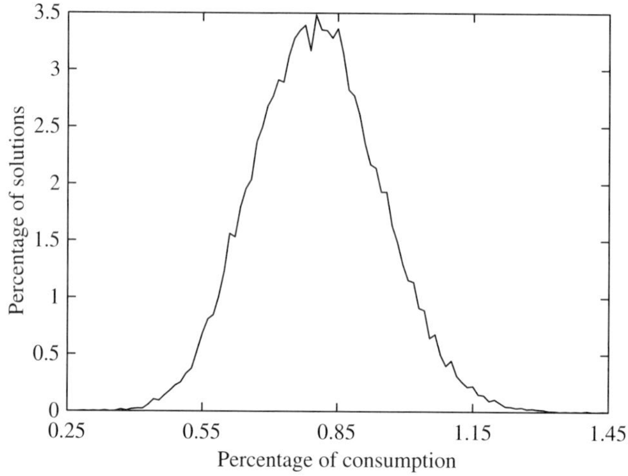

Figure 18.3. Sample Frequency Distribution of the Welfare Results of Kenyan Preferential Reduction of Services Barriers Against EU Partners — 30,000 Simulations.

there is an imperfect competition analogy to trade diversion in goods whereby preferential commitments in services could be immizerising due to a loss of varieties of services from excluded countries combined with lost domestic rents.

Piecemeal sensitivity analysis shows that the two most important parameters in the model are the share of rents captured by domestic agents and the parameter that captures the capacity of a region to transfer technology to Kenya. Detailed sensitivity analysis with these parameters shows that the gains are both larger and more likely to be positive the more technologically advanced is the partner region relative to the excluded regions, and the less the rent capture on initial barriers in services.

It is well known that preferential liberalization of goods can lead to welfare losses, due to the loss of tariff revenue on diverted trade from excluded partners. While there are no tariffs on FDI in services, if the home country captures rents from regulatory barriers, they play an analogous role as tariffs in service liberalization. If Kenyans are assumed to capture the rents from barriers in services, then, even in a constant returns to scale version of our model, the mean estimate is that Kenya would lose.

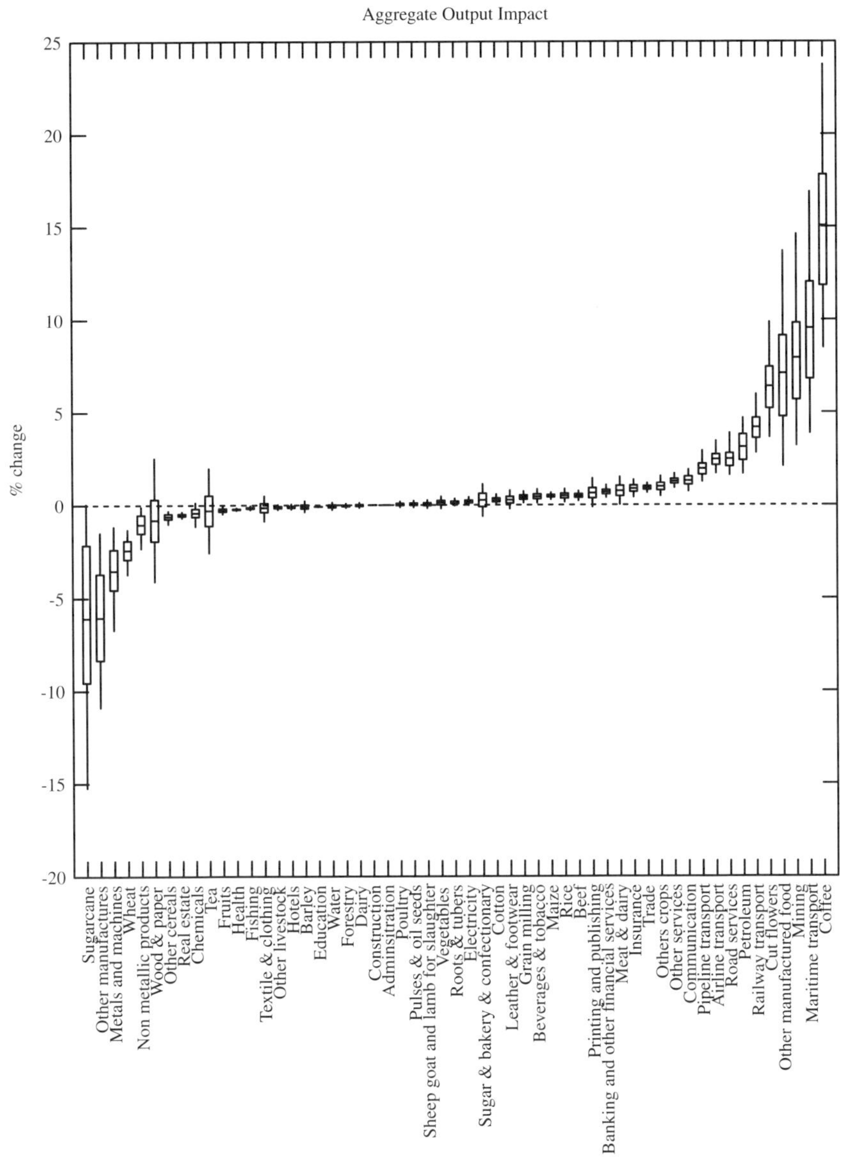

Figure 18.4. Means, 50 and 95 Percent Confidence Intervals of the Sample Distributions of the Output Changes by Sector from Kenyan Preferential Reduction of Services Barriers Against EU Partners — 30,000 Simulations.

Note: The boxes are limited vertically by the 25% and 75% quartiles. The bars in the box are the means. The vertical lines extend to the 2.5% and 97.5% percentiles.

References

Balistreri, Edward J., Thomas F. Rutherford and David G. Tarr (2009). "Modeling Services Liberalization: The Case of Kenya," *Economic Modeling*, **26**(3), 668–679.

Balistreri, Edward J. and David G. Tarr (2011). "Services Liberalization in Preferential Trade Arrangements: The Case of Kenya," World Bank Policy and Research Working Paper number 5552, January.

Brown, Drusilla and Robert Stern (2001). "Measurement and Modeling of the Economic Effects of Trade and Investment Barriers in Services," *Review of International Economics*, **9**(2), 262–286.

Coe, David T. and Elhanen Helpman (1995). "International R&D Spillovers", *European Economic Review*, **39**(5), 859–887.

Dee, Philippa, Kevin Hanslow and Tien Phamduc (2003). "Measuring the Costs of Barriers to Trade in Services," in Takatoshi Ito and Anne Krueger (eds.), *Trade in Services in the Asia-Pacific Region*, Chicago: University of Chicago Press, pp. 11–46.

Harris, Richard (1984). "Applied General Equilibrium Analysis of Small Open Economies with Scale Economies and Imperfect Comp," *The American Economic Review,* **74**(5), 1016–1032.

Harrison, Glenn W., Thomas F. Rutherford, David G. Tarr and Angelo Gurgel (2004). "Trade Policy and Poverty Reduction in Brazil," *The World Bank Economic Review*, **18**, 289–317.

Harrison, Glenn W., Thomas F. Rutherford and David G. Tarr (2003). "Trade Liberalization, Poverty and Efficient Equity," *Journal of Development Economics*, **71**(1), 97–128.

Harrison, Glenn W., Thomas F. Rutherford and David G. Tarr (2002). "Trade Policy Options for Chile: The Importance of Market Access," *World Bank Economic Review*, **16**(1), 49–79.

Harrison, Glenn H., Thomas F. Rutherford and David G. Tarr (1997). "Economic Implications for Turkey of a Customs Union with the European Union," *European Economic Review*, **41**(3–5), 861–870.

Harrison, Glenn H., Thomas F. Rutherford and David G. Tarr. (1996). "Increased Competition and Completion of the Market in the European Community: Static and Steady-State Effects," *Journal of Economic Integration*, **11**(3), 332–365.

Jensen, Jesper, Thomas F. Rutherford and David G. Tarr (2007). "The Impact of Liberalizing Barriers to Foreign Direct Investment in Services: The Case of Russian Accession to the World Trade Organization," *Review of Development Economics,* **11**(3), 482–506.

Jensen, Jesper, Thomas F. Rutherford and David G. Tarr (2010). "Modeling Services Liberalization: The Case of Tanzania," *Journal of Economic Integration*, **25**(4), 644–675. http://dx.doi.org/10.11130/jei.2010.25.4.644

Konan, Denise E. and Keith E. Maskus (2006). "Quantifying the Impact of Services Liberalization in a Developing Country," *Journal of Development Economics*, **81**, 142–162.

Levy, Santiago and van Wijnbergen, Sweder (1995). "Transition Problems in Economic Reform: Agriculture in the North American Free Trade Agreement," *American Economic Review*, **85**(4), 738–54.

Markusen, James R., Thomas Rutherford and David G. Tarr (2005). "Trade and Direct Investment in Producer Services and the Domestic Market for Expertise," *Canadian Journal of Economics*, **38**(3), 758–777.

Rutherford, Thomas F. and David G. Tarr (2008). "Poverty Effects of Russian WTO Accession: Modeling "Real" Households with Endogenous Productivity Effects," *Journal of International Economics,* **75**(1), 131–150.

Smith, Alasdair and Anthony J. Venables (1988). "Completing the Internal Market in the European Community: Some Industry Simulations", *European Economic Review*, **32**, 1501–1525.

Economics
The Open-Access, Open-Assessment E-Journal

Vol. 6, 2012-1 | January, 2012 | http://dx.doi.org/10.5018/economics-ejournal.ja.2012-1

Deep Trade Policy Options for Armenia: The Importance of Trade Facilitation, Services and Standards Liberalization

Jesper Jensen
Teca Training, Denmark
David Tarr
The World Bank

Abstract In this paper the authors develop an innovative 21 sector computable general equilibrium model of Armenia to assess the impact on Armenia of a Deep and Comprehensive Free Trade Agreement (DCFTA) with the EU, as well as further regional or multilateral trade policy commitments. They find that a DCFTA with the EU will likely result in substantial gains to Armenia, but they show that the gains derive from the deep aspects of the agreement. In order of importance, the sources of the gains are: (i) trade facilitation and reduction in border costs; (ii) services liberalization; and (iii) standards harmonization. A shallow agreement with the EU that focuses only on preferential tariff liberalization in goods will likely lead to small losses to Armenia primarily due to a loss of productivity from lost varieties of technologies from the Rest of the World region in manufactured products. Additional gains can be expected in the long run from an improvement in the investment climate. The authors estimate only small gains from a services agreement with the CIS countries, but significant gains from expanding services liberalization multilaterally.

Special Issue
Trade Facilitation, Transport Costs and Logistics: A New Challenge for European Competitiveness

JEL F12, F13, F14, F15, F17, C68, L16
Keywords Trade facilitation; services liberalization; standards harmonization; preferential liberalization; multinationals; monopolistic competition; foreign direct investment; endogenous productivity effects

Correspondence David G. Tarr, The World Bank, MSN MC3-303, 1818 H Street, NW, Washington, D.C. 20433, USA; email: dtarr@Worldbank.org

Citation Jesper Jensen and David Tarr (2011). Deep Trade Policy Options for Armenia: The Importance of Trade Facilitation, Services and Standards Liberalization. *Economics: The Open-Access, Open-Assessment E-Journal*, Vol. 6, 2012-1. http://dx.doi.org/10.5018/economics-ejournal.ja.2012-1

Economics: The Open-Access, Open-Assessment E-Journal

1 Introduction

Armenia, along with Ukraine, Georgia and Moldova, is one of four countries to the east of the European Union (EU) that has been targeted by the EU for negotiation of a "Deep and Comprehensive Free Trade Agreement" (DCFTA). Based on the EU-Ukraine ongoing negotiation, we know that a DCFTA between Armenia and the EU will contain numerous chapters and go well beyond tariff liberalization on goods. Notably, a DCFTA would include negotiation of liberalization of business services sectors, and the EU has traditionally placed considerable emphasis on harmonization of standards with the EU, as well improved trade facilitation and lower border costs. Evaluation of these deeper aspects of free trade agreements presents challenges for modelers.

Since the early 1990s, regional trade agreements have surged; 283 are in force and have been notified to the WTO as of February 2010. [1] Given the inclusion of services in modern FTAs negotiated with the EU, the US and in some other agreements, economists need to be able to assess the impact of services commitments as part of their advice to governments regarding preferential trade agreements. Since both economic theory and empirical literature have shown that wide availability of business services results in productivity gains to the manufacturing sector and contributes to its international competitiveness.[2] Services commitments in regional agreements could lead to substantial productivity improvements. But is there an analogy to trade diversion in goods whereby preferential commitments in services could be immizerising? Moreover, regional agreements with the EU and the US are "deep" involving elements of standards harmonization and trade facilitation, among other chapters. Are developing countries likely to obtain substantially larger welfare gains from a deep agreement with a developed country, rather than a free trade agreement with a

1 http://www.wto.org/english/tratop_e/region_e/region_e.htm. This does not include a significant number that are in force but which have not been notified to the WTO.

2 See Francois and Hoekman (2010) for a summary of the evidence.

developing country? How do the welfare gains of preferential versus global liberalization compare?

Armenia is an example of a country facing regional trade policy choices with both developed and developing countries, as well as multilateral trade policy choices. In addition to being a candidate for a Deep and Comprehensive Free Trade Agreement (DCFTA) with the European Union, it has existing free trade agreements with the countries of the Commonwealth of Independent States (CIS). Moreover, in the context of its international negotiations under the Doha Development Agenda, Armenia may be called upon to make further commitments in the business services area.

Policy-makers have expressed considerable demand for analysis of their actual or potential regional agreements. Applied modelers have responded with applied general equilibrium models that focus on goods. Among the better known papers are Levy and Van Wignbergen (1995), Harris (1984), Smith and Venables (1988) and Harrison, Rutheford and Tarr (1993; 1996; 1997a; 2002; 2004). So the literature now contains a substantial number of good studies that examine regional agreements in goods. But except of Jensen and Tarr (2010), the literature does not contain any numerical studies of regional arrangements that involve commitments to multinational firms who will undertake foreign direct investment in services. We attempt to fill that gap in this paper. Crucial to the analysis, we incorporate the Dixit-Stiglitz-Ethier mechanism of endogenous productivity gains from additional varieties of imperfectly produced goods and services. Moreover, as a component of the DCFTA, we evaluate the impact on Armenia of establishing a national quality infrastructure that would facilitate Armenian firms that wish to export to the EU to comply with EU voluntary standards, technical regulations in goods and meet EU sanitary and phyto-sanitary requirements. (We refer to this simply as standards harmonization in this paper, although this subject is broader than standards on manufactured goods.) As we explain below, however, we do not recommend that Armenia adopt all EU sanitary and phyto-sanitary (SPS) requirements as requirements for producing for the Armenia or CIS markets; rather a case by case approach would be advisable based on an evaluation of the costs versus benefits.

In this paper we develop a 21 sector small open economy comparative static computable general equilibrium model of Armenia that we believe is appropriate to evaluate the impact of an EU-Armenian DCFTA along with other trade policy options of Armenia. We build on the model of Jensen, Rutherford and Tarr (2007) and Jensen and Tarr (2010), but we decompose the rest of the world into three regions: the European Union; our CIS region; and the Rest of the World. All foreign regions are sources of foreign direct investment in some of the business services sectors. In addition, and crucially for the results, we evaluate the impact of lowering standards and border costs as a result of the DCFTA with the EU.

We find that a DCFTA with the EU will likely result in substantial gains to Armenia, but we show that the gains derive from the deep aspects of the agreement. We estimate that a shallow free trade agreement with the EU that focuses only on preferential tariff liberalization in goods will likely lead to small losses to Armenia due to traditional trade diversion (tariff losses on displaced imports from the Rest of the World region) and, more importantly, due to a loss of productivity from lost varieties of technologies form the Rest of the World region in manufactured products. We estimate that the gains to Armenia from a DCFTA with the EU derive from further liberalization of barriers in services (by 50 percent of the ad valorem equivalents), harmonization of standards[3] and most importantly, from a trade facilitation which includes a reduction in border costs. Additional gains can be expected in the long run from an improvement in the investment climate. But we calculate slightly smaller gains if Armenians presently capture the rents from the barriers against foreign service-providers.

Preferential liberalization of barriers against CIS services providers could add additional gains, but these gains would be very small. The gains from further integration with the CIS are small for two reasons: first, institutional development through standards harmonization and trade facilitation are not considered part of the scenario, since it is not considered a likely outcome. Although we do consider deeper service commitments on a preferential basis in the CIS, technology diffusion obtained through trade and FDI with transition and developing countries has been estimated to be much smaller than the technology diffusion obtained through trade and FDI with developed countries.

[3] As we discuss in Section 3 below, this does not imply that we recommend that Armenia adopt all technical regulations and sanitary and phyto-sanitary requirements of the European Union.

Economics: The Open-Access, Open-Assessment E-Journal

We find that unilateral liberalization of services and trade barriers on a non-discriminatory basis would yield gains that are about three times the gains from preferential liberalization of goods and services with the EU alone. This policy would assure that Armenia receives goods and services from the least cost supplier and would eliminate any trade diversion costs. Liberal rules of origin in any preferential agreement would help move Armenia toward achieving the gains from unilateral liberalization. Finally, we estimate that a reduction in non-discriminatory regulatory barriers (that is, barriers that raise the costs of Armenians as well as foreign services providers in Armenia) would provide significant additional benefits in Armenia.

We devote considerable attention to the sensitivity of our results to uncertainty in the parameters. First, to understand the model better, we conduct piecemeal sensitivity of the results, where we isolate the impact of each of the parameters to ascertain which parameters most strongly impact the results. Second, to assess the robustness of the results to parameter uncertainty, we conduct systematic sensitivity analysis, where we execute the model 30,000 times. Each simulation is based on a random draw of all the parameter values; we then present sample distributions and sample confidence intervals of the key variables. Finally, we conduct sensitivity on a range of values of key parameters that determine the productivity impacts in imperfect competition.

An earlier estimate of the gains to Armenia from the DCFTA is Dyker et al. (2008), known as the CASE study. The CASE study estimates gains to Armenia from the DCFTA that are about 2.5 times larger than the gains estimated in the present study. We explain in Appendix I that the larger estimated gains of the CASE study are due to due to a combination of two effects: (i) larger assumed distortions in the CASE study; and (ii) different modeling assumptions. Regarding the distortions, the larger the distortions are, the more gains there are from their removal. As we explain in Jensen and Tarr (2011, Appendix I), the larger distortions in the CASE study partly reflect the fact that our study was based on estimates of distortions in 2010, while the CASE study uses estimates of distortions from 2006 or 2007. Since Armenia has implemented substantial reforms in the interim, the initial distortions in the CASE study are significantly higher. This is the case with border costs. But it is also due, in some cases, to the fact that we had greater data available to us that allowed a more accurate estimate, for example in the services survey and estimates that we conducted.

Finally, we mention that we conducted surveys in Armenia to assess the regulatory environment in the services sectors and calculated the shares of ownership by foreign region in the services sectors. We employed the former survey to estimate the ad valorem equivalents of the barriers to investment in the services sectors. We also constructed an input-output table for Armenia. This work is an example of our experience that shows that data limitations is a small developing economies can be overcome so that modern models can be applied in these countries.

The paper is organized as follows. In Section 2, we provide an overview of the estimation of the ad valorem equivalents of barriers in Armenian services sectors. We provide an overview of the model in Section 3 and a discussion of the data in Section 4. The central results are presented in Section 5 and sensitivity results are presented in Section 6. Conclusions are presented in Section 7. Further documentation is available in the appendixes of Jensen and Tarr (2011). This includes a discussion of the trade and tariff data; our calculation of ownership shares by sector and region; how we obtained estimates of the Dixit-Stiglitz elasticities in goods; our estimation of the reduction in trade or border costs as a result of a DCFTA; our estimate of the reduction in standards costs; and our construction of a balanced input-output table for Armenia. The estimates and methodology of the ad valorem equivalents of barriers in services is explained in Modebadze and Eroyants (2010).

2 Estimation of the Ad Valorem Equivalents of the Border and Trade Cost Barriers, the Regulatory Barriers in Services and the Standards Costs

In Table 1, we present the sectors and regions of our model and the factors of production. In Table 2 and 3, we show the value added by sector and the trade flows by sector for Armenia. We need to estimate key distortions in the traded goods sectors and the services sectors with foreign direct investment.

Economics: The Open-Access, Open-Assessment E-Journal

Table 1: List of Sectors, Factors and Regions in the Armenia Model

Business Services	**Other goods and services**
Telecommunication	Agriculture, hunting, forestry and fishing
Insurance	Electricity, gas and water supply
Banking	Construction
Air transport	Wholesale, retail trade and repair
Transport via pipelines	Hotels and restaurants
Railway transport	Road transport
	Auxiliary transport activities
Dixit-Stiglitz Goods	Post and courier activities
Mining and quarrying	Real estate and professional services
Manufacturing	Public administration and defence
	Education
Regions	Health and social work
Armenia	Other social and personal services
EU: The 27 members of the European Union	
CIS+Georgia: Azerbaijan, Belarus, Georgia, Kazakhstan, Kyrgyzstan, Moldova, Russia, Tajikistan, Turkmenistan, Ukraine, Uzbekistan	**Factors of Production**
Rest of the World: All other countries	Labor, capital

Services Barrier Estimates

Estimates of the ad valorem equivalents of the regulatory barriers in services are crucial to the results. In order to make these estimates, we first need to assess the regulatory environment in the services sectors in our model. We commissioned a 112 page survey of the regulatory regimes in key Armenian business services sectors, namely, insurance, banking, fixed line and mobile telecommunications services and air transportation services. We supplemented that information with research by regional experts into the relevant sector.[4] This questionnaire and research provided us with data and descriptions and assessments of the regulatory environment in these sectors.

[4] We thank Karine Eroyants and Grigol Modebadze for this research.

Table 2: Sectoral value-added (%, unless otherwise indicated)

	Capital (%)	Labor (%)	GDP bnDram	GDP % of total
Business Services				
Transport via railways	46.0	54.0	12.0	0.4
Transport via pipelines	46.0	54.0	7.3	0.2
Air transport	46.0	54.0	42.0	1.4
Telecommunications	46.0	54.0	90.1	2.9
Insurance	66.3	33.7	0.9	0.0
Banking	66.3	33.7	70.9	2.4
Dixit-Stiglitz Goods				
Mining and quarrying	47.9	52.1	51.6	1.7
Manufacturing	46.9	53.1	332.8	10.9
Other goods and services				
Agriculture, hunting, forestry and fishing	75.6	24.4	575.2	19.2
Electricity, gas and water supply	38.5	61.5	122.7	4.1
Construction	56.0	44.0	865.5	29.0
Wholesale and retail trade and repair	61.6	38.4	363.0	12.0
Hotels and restaurants	25.2	74.8	10.6	0.3
Other land transport	46.0	54.0	36.1	1.2
Auxiliary transport activities	46.0	54.0	14.2	0.5
Post and courier activities	46.0	54.0	1.0	0.0
Real estate and professional services	85.7	14.3	107.2	3.5
Public administration and defence	7.6	92.4	90.7	3.0
Education	23.1	76.9	98.5	3.3
Health and social work	56.0	44.0	89.6	3.0
Other social and personal services	43.1	56.9	34.3	1.0

Modebadze (2010) then estimated the ad valorem equivalents of barriers to foreign direct investment in fixed line and mobile telecommunications, banking, insurance and maritime transportation services. The process involved converting the answers and data of the questionnaires into an index of restrictiveness in each industry. Modebadze followed the methodology of Kimura, Ando and Fujii(2004a, 2004b, 2004c) to generate these estimates. The methodology involves classifi-

Economics: The Open-Access, Open-Assessment E-Journal

Table 3: Trade Flows

	Imports			Exports		
	bnDram	% of total	% of supply	bnDram	% of total	% of output
Business Services						
Transport via railways	5.9	0.5	27.4	3.1	0.7	16.5
Transport via pipelines	3.6	0.3	27.4	1.9	0.4	16.5
Air transport	20.9	1.9	27.4	11.0	2.5	16.5
Telecommunications	44.7	4.1	27.4	23.5	5.4	16.5
Insurance	0.1	0.0	12.7	0.1	0.0	9.5
Banking	11.2	1.0	12.7	8.0	1.9	9.5
Dixit-Stiglitz Goods						
Mining and quarrying	70.4	6.4	63.5	50.5	11.7	57.3
Manufacturing	823.0	74.6	54.6	254.6	58.8	39.0
Other goods and services						
Agriculture, hunting, forestry and fishing	42.7	3.9	5.0	6.2	1.4	0.8
Electricity, gas and water supply	4.3	0.4	2.5	7.4	1.7	4.3
Construction	1.4	0.1	0.1	4.0	0.9	0.3
Wholesale and retail trade and repair						
Hotels and restaurants	16.2	1.5	42.6	7.8	1.8	26.3
Other land transport	17.9	1.6	27.4	9.4	2.2	16.5
Auxiliary transport activities	7.1	0.6	27.4	3.7	0.9	16.5
Post and courier activities	0.5	0.0	27.4	0.3	0.1	16.5
Real estate and professional services	8.7	0.8	6.3	20.1	4.6	13.5
Public administration and defence	6.8	0.6	4.2	3.9	0.9	2.5
Education	10.7	1.0	9.0	9.8	2.3	8.3
Health and social work	2.7	0.2	2.1	5.0	1.2	3.8
Other social and personal services	3.6	0.3	5.7	2.4	0.6	4.6

cation of the possible restrictions into separate categories with unique weights summing to one, where the weights are determined based on the significance of each category. Next, Modebadze assigned a score to each potential restriction, where the score reflects the level of restriction imposed by the economy. Modebadze estimated two indices: an index of "regulatory barriers" (RB index) where the regulatory barriers impose costs on both domestic and multinational firms in a non-discriminatory manner; and an index of discriminatory barriers against multinational service providers, which we call the foreign discriminatory index (FDR index).[5]

[5] In order to obtain the estimated score for each restriction, the assigned score is multiplied by the corresponding weight. Finally, the estimated scores for all categories are summed to obtain the restrictiveness indices.

Economics: The Open-Access, Open-Assessment E-Journal

This methodology further involves building on the estimates and methodology explained in the volume by C. Findlay and T. Warren (2000), notably papers by Warren (2000), McGuire and Schulele (2000) and Kang (2000). For each of these service sectors, the authors evaluated the regulatory environment across many countries. The price of services is then regressed against the regulatory barriers to determine the impact of any of the regulatory barriers on the price of services. Modebadze then assumed that the international regression applies to Armenia in the case that the above mentioned restrictiveness indexes are used. Applying that regression and their assessments of the regulatory environment in Armenia from the questionnaires and other information sources, he estimated the ad valorem impact of a reduction in barriers[6] both for discriminatory and non-discriminatory barriers. Modebadze then weighted his fixed line and mobile telecommunications estimates by their market shares to obtain her estimate for communications. The results of the estimates of the ad valorem equivalents of the barriers are listed in Table 4. Details are provided in Modebadze and Eroyants (2010). While we believe our approach uses the best available methodology and is based on a survey we conducted, we acknowledge that, as with the estimation of the ad valorem equivalents of non-tariff barriers in goods, the estimation is subject to a margin of error.

Trade Facilitation and Border Costs

According to the World Bank Logistics Performance Index of 2010, Armenia ranks 111th in the world out of 155 countries.[7] This is an improvement from 131st in the world in 2007,[8] but still leaves considerable room for improvement. Given the focus of the EU on institutional development for trade facilitation, a deep and comprehensive free trade agreement with the EU is likely to reduce these costs for

6 Warren estimated quantity impacts and then using elasticity estimates was able to obtain price impacts. The estimates by Modebadze that we employ are for "discriminatory" barriers against foreign direct investment.

7 See: http://info.worldbank.org/etools/tradesurvey/mode1b.asp.

8 See http://siteresources.worldbank.org/INTTLF/Resources/lpireport.pdf.

Table 4: Benchmark Distortions (%)

			Border costs		Standards	Regulatory barriers	
	Output tax	Tariff	Imports	Exports	for EU exports	All firms	Foreign firms
Business Services							
Transport via railways	2.5					20.0	
Transport via pipelines	2.5					40.0	
Air transport	2.5						106.8
Telecommunications	2.5					1.7	0.3
Insurance	0.7					9.6	15.8
Banking	0.7					1.5	5.6
Dixit-Stiglitz Goods							
Mining and quarrying	2.4		9.1	8.9			
Manufacturing	1.5	4.3	9.1	8.9	21.6		
Other goods and services							
Agriculture, hunting, forestry and fishing	0.7	10.1	9.1	8.9	15.8		
Electricity, gas and water supply	0.8						
Construction	0.3						
Wholesale and retail trade and repair	1.2						
Hotels and restaurants	4.5						
Other land transport	2.1						
Auxiliary transport activities	2.1						
Post and courier activities	2.1						
Real estate and professional services	1.9						
Public administration and defence	0.5						
Education	0.1						
Health and social work	0.3						
Other social and personal services	6.3						

exports to the EU. We therefore assume that the costs of exporting to the EU from Armenia will fall and the costs of importing into Armenia from the EU will also fall. Moreover, improved institutional development for trade facilitation is likely to reduce trade facilitation costs for imports from and exports to all regions. If customs is more efficient in processing imports from the EU, these procedures will generally facilitate trade with all regions. For example, if trucks with imports from the EU can pass through Armenian borders more quickly, trucks with imports from other countries are also likely to see reduced delays. Given that the EU will monitor trade with the EU much more carefully, it is possible that not all institutional reforms in trade facilitation will transmit to trade with non-EU countries. So we shall assume that the border costs of exporting to or importing from non-EU countries will fall by a smaller percentage.

To obtain quantitative estimates, we rely on a survey of Armenian firms undertaken for the study by Dyker et al., (2008) and data from the Cost of Doing Business study of the World Bank. We estimate that the costs of importing from and exporting to the EU will fall by 2.5 percent of production costs, while the costs of importing into Armenia from non-EU countries will fall by 2.3 percent of production costs and the cost of exporting to non-EU countries from Armenia will fall by 2.2 percent of production costs. Details of the estimation are available in Jensen and Tarr (2011, Appendix D).

Standards Costs

The EU devoted considerable resources to assisting its new member states with standards and, similarly it is allocating resources to this problem for the countries with which it may potentially have a DCFTA. Consequently, we assume these costs will fall as a result of a Deep and Comprehensive Free Trade Agreement. That is, for firms who will sell in the EU, after adaption by the firms and Armenian development of the National Quality Infrastructure, we assume the production costs of selling in the EU by Armenian firms will decline. We rely on a survey by Jakubiak et al., (2006) and adapt it for Armenia. We estimate that the costs of compliance with EU standards as a percentage of production costs will fall for Armenian exports to the EU of agricultural (manufacturing) products from 15.8 (21.6) percent of production to 11.8 (16.2) percent of production. But there are costs of facilities to meet EU standards and in development of the National Quality

Infrastructure that we estimate will diminish the cost reduction by about 2 percent. Since the CIS market is predominantly regulated by "GOST" regulations, we do not assume that production costs for Armenian exporters would fall on exports to any market other than the EU. Details are in Jensen and Tarr (2011, Appendix E).[9]

9 An important policy caveat to the above paragraph is that we do not recommend that Armenia adopt all EU technical regulations and sanitary and phyto-sanitary (SPS) measures. On the one hand, facilitating but not compelling voluntary harmonization to standards in goods should be beneficial and is the core of what we estimate. Armenian firms could continue to produce according to Gosstandard (GOST) standards for the CIS market or at home if they choose to do so. On the other hand, requiring Armenian firms to adopt EU technical regulations in goods and especially all SPS requirements will likely impose very high costs. It does not appear that the benefits of these mandatory requirements are justified in all cases without actual membership in the EU. Experience of the new Eastern Expansion EU members during accession shows that, despite vast accession support from the EU, large parts of their food industry were forced out of business, since the upgrades needed to meet the EC requirements were not commercially feasible. As a result, a more gradual adaptation to EU SPS requirements through choosing to adopt EU SPS requirements on a case by case basis where the benefits exceed the costs seems appropriate.

A similar view was expressed in the report of the World Bank (2007, p. 65). It states: Several of the CIS countries have expressed the desire to harmonize their standards with the EU. ...For the CIS countries, even those intending to join the EU, complete harmonization with EU food safety and agricultural health legislations is neither necessary nor, at present, realistic, considering the high costs involved. The new EU members received large-scale financial and technical support from the EU for their accession process. The new EU member states received, over a seven-year period, accumulated SAPARD support for agro-processing and marketing of about 18 percent of their agricultural GDP in 2000, or €357 per person employed in agriculture in 2003, of which the EU paid more than one-third. Under PHARE they also received sizable EC support for their public sector for SPS-related expenses, with accumulated amounts in the range of one-third of the EC support under SAPARD. For non-EU accession countries, implementing the required changes without such support would outstrip public and private capacities. Realistic options are selective convergence or obtaining third-country status to EU accession, each of which has different strategic and resource implications. Selective convergence can mean that selected parts of the relevant legislation and regulations are used as specimens for modernization or for harmonization for purposes of trade in particular products. Third country status—used for livestock and fisheries products—means that a country's regulations, inspection methods, and capabilities are considered equivalent to those of the EC. EU accession, on the other hand, requires full adoption of the Acquis Communautaire for domestic production, processing, and marketing. Experience of the new EU members during accession shows that, despite vast accession support from the EU, large parts of their food industry were forced out of business, since the upgrades needed to meet the EC requirements were not commercially feasible. Given the tremendous costs involved, it is therefore not realistic for CIS countries to pursue full adoption of EU standards.

Economics: The Open-Access, Open-Assessment E-Journal

3 Overview of the Model

This paper builds on the algebraic structure of the models of Jensen, Rutherford and Tarr (2007; 2010) and especially Balistreri and Tarr (2011, Appendix F) where a full algebraic description of the model is available (except for the trade facilitation and standards costs extensions). Here we provide a general description of the structure described there and provide more details where we depart from that structure. There are 21 sectors in the model shown in Table 1. These include six imperfectly competitive business services sectors, two imperfectly competitive goods sectors and thirteen competitive goods and services sectors. Labor and capital are the two primary factors of production. In each imperfectly competitive sector there is sector-specific capital that is unique to production from each region in the model; and there are primary inputs imported by multinational service providers, reflecting specialized management expertise or technology of the firm. The existence of sector specific capital in the imperfectly competitive sectors implies that there are decreasing returns to scale in the use of the mobile factors and supply curves in these sectors slope up. In our central model, we assume that 50 percent of the capital in each of the imperfectly competitive sectors is sector specific. We conduct sensitivity analysis with respect to this share by allowing 25 percent and 75 percent of the capital in each sector to be sector specific.

There are three categories of firms in the model: (1) perfectly competitive goods and services sectors: (2) imperfectly competitive goods sectors; and (3) imperfectly competitive services sectors with foreign direct investment. The cost, production and pricing structures in the three categories differ widely. As in Jensen, Rutherford and Tarr (2010), we disaggregate the rest of the world region into three regions. In this case the three regions are: (1) the European Union; (2) the CIS plus Georgia[10]; and (3) the Rest of the World. In the imperfectly competitive sectors, this requires introducing different firm types with distinct cost structures for each region. We retain the small open economy model framework, so only Armenia is modeled fully.

[10] Georgia is not a member of the CIS, but Armenia and Georgia have a bilateral free trade agreement and provide equivalent preferential treatment to each other.

Economics: The Open-Access, Open-Assessment E-Journal

Perfectly Competitive Goods and Services Sectors

Regardless of sector, all firms minimize the cost of production. In the 13 competitive goods and services sectors, goods or services are produced under constant returns to scale and where price equals marginal costs with zero profits. In these sectors, products are differentiated by country of origin, i.e., we employ the Armington assumption. All goods producing firms (including imperfectly competitive firms) can sell on the domestic market or export. Firms optimize their output decision between exports and domestic sales based on relative prices and their constant elasticity of transformation production function. Having chosen how much to allocate between exports and domestic sales, firms also optimize their output decision between exports to the three possible export regions, based on relative prices the three regions and their constant elasticity of transformation production function for shifting output between the regions.

Goods Produced Subject to Increasing Returns to Scale

We have two goods in this category in the model: mining and an aggregate manufacturing sector. These goods are differentiated at the firm level. We assume that these goods may be produced domestically or imported for firms in any region in the model. Firms in these industries set prices such that marginal cost (which is constant) equals marginal revenue; and there is free entry, which drives profits to zero. For domestic firms, costs are defined by observed primary factor and intermediate inputs to that sector in the base year data. Foreigners produce the goods abroad at constant marginal cost but incur a fixed cost of operating in Armenia. In each of these two sectors, we have four firm types: one firm type for each region. Firms in each region have the same cost structure. We assume that each firm type requires sector specific capital unique to its firm type. The cif import price of foreign goods is simply defined by the import price, and, by the zero profits assumption, in equilibrium the import price must cover fixed and marginal costs of foreign firms.

All imperfectly competitive goods enter the production function of firms and consumption function of the representative consumer as Dixit-Stiglitz aggregates. That is, if Z is an imperfectly competitive good, we assume (suppressing sector subscripts) that:

$$(1) \quad Z = \left[\sum_{i=1}^{m} Z_i^{\rho}\right]^{1/\rho} \text{ and } Z_i = \left[\sum_{j=1}^{n_i} z_{ij}^{\rho}\right]^{1/\rho} \quad i=1,\ldots.m,$$

where m is the number of regions, Z_i is the Dixit-Stiglitz aggregate of firm output in the sector from region i and z_{ij} is the output of firm j in region i. We assume that $1 > \rho > 0$, which implies that the elasticity of substitution $\sigma = 1/(1-\rho) > 1$. Given that the elasticity of substitution is equal at all levels, this is equivalent to pure firm level product differentiation. Given identical costs for firms within a region i, firms in the same region i in equilibrium will charge the same price p_{zi} (although prices will differ between regions). Then dual to the Dixit-Stiglitz quantity aggregates Z_i are the Dixit-Stiglitz unit cost functions C_i. These represent the quality adjusted minimum cost of purchasing the inputs z_{ij}. We have:

$$(2) \qquad C_i = \frac{p_{zi}}{n_i^{1/(\sigma_i-1)}}$$

Since $\sigma_i > 1$, C_i declines in the number of varieties available from region i. This is the Dixit-Stiglitz externality.

Domestic firms set prices using the Chamberlinian large group monopolistic competition assumption within a Dixit-Stiglitz framework, which results in constant markups over marginal cost for both foreign firms and domestic firms.

Unlike Jensen, Rutherford and Tarr (2007), but following Jensen, Rutherford and Tarr (2010) all imperfectly competitive domestic firms (both goods and services producers) face a downward sloping demand curve in each of their three export markets. Consistent with firm level product differentiation, we assume that the elasticity of demand in each of the export markets is the Dixit-Stiglitz elasticity of demand. Firms then set marginal revenue equal to marginal costs in each of the three export markets; then the export markets contribute to the quasi-rents of the firm and affect the entry and exit decisions of firms. Without this modeling extension, firms would have to sell at marginal costs on exports, and fixed costs would have to be covered by domestic sales alone. It has been established empirically that there are significant fixed costs of exporting and the heterogeneous firms literature has built on that idea, showing that only the most efficient firms export. Although we do not have heterogeneous firms, our new

Economics: The Open-Access, Open-Assessment E-Journal

modeling extension allows us to be consistent with the heterogeneous firms models by allowing markups on fixed costs of exports.

Introducing downward sloping demand curves into the model means that there are possible terms of trade effects to consider in this model that were not present in the Jensen, Rutherford and Tarr (2007) model. Balistreri and Markusen (2009) have shown, however, that there should be virtually no role for optimal tariffs to exploit terms of trade effects. The reason is that, unlike perfectly competitive firms, imperfectly competitive firms are pricing such that marginal revenue equals marginal costs on export markets, which is the objective of optimal tariffs.

For simplicity we assume that the composition of fixed and marginal cost is identical in all firms producing under increasing returns to scale (in both goods and services). This assumption in a Dixit-Stiglitz based Chamberlinian large-group model assures that output per firm for all firm types remains constant, i.e., the model does not produce rationalization gains or losses.

The number of varieties affects the productivity of the use of imperfectly competitive goods based on the standard Dixit-Stiglitz formulation. The effective cost function for users of goods produced subject to increasing returns to scale declines in the total number of firms in the industry.

Service Sectors That Are Produced under Increasing Returns to Scale and Imperfect Competition

These sectors are telecommunications, banking services, insurance services, air transportation services, railroad transportation services and pipeline transportation services. In these services sectors, we observe that some services are provided by foreign service-providers on a cross border basis analogous to goods providers from abroad. But a large share of business services are provided by service providers with a domestic presence, both multinational and Armenian.[11] Our model allows for both types of foreign provision of services in these sectors. There are cross border services allowed in this sector and they are provided from abroad

[11] One estimate puts the world-wide cross-border share of trade in services at 41% and the share of trade in services provided by multinational affiliates at 38%. Travel expenditures 20% and compensation to employees working abroad 1% make up the difference. See Brown and Stern (2001, Table 1).

at constant costs—this is analogous to competitive provision of goods from abroad. Cross border services, however, are not good substitutes for service providers who have a domestic presence.[12]

Crucial to the results, we allow multinational service firm providers that choose to establish a presence in Armenia in order to compete with Armenian firms directly. As in the goods sectors, services that are produced subject to increasing returns to scale are differentiated at the firm level. There are four firms types in each of these sectors: one firm type for each region. The cost structures of firms within a region are identical, and each firm type requires its own sector specific capital. Firms in these industries set prices such that marginal cost (which is constant) equals marginal revenue; and there is free entry, which drives profits to zero. We assume firm level product differentiation and employ the Chamberlinian large group monopolistic competition assumption within a Dixit-Stiglitz framework. Given our assumption on the composition of fixed and variable costs, we have constant markups over marginal cost for both foreign firms and domestic firms, i.e., no rationalization impacts.

For domestic firms, costs are defined by observed primary factors and intermediate inputs to that sector in the base year data. When multinationals service providers decide to establish a domestic presence in Armenia, they will import some of their technology or management expertise. That is, foreign direct investment generally entails importing specialized foreign inputs. Thus, the cost structure of multinationals differs from national only service providers. Multinationals incur costs related to both imported primary inputs and Armenian primary factors, in addition to intermediate factor inputs. Foreign provision of services differs from foreign provision of goods, since the service providers use Armenian primary inputs. Domestic service providers do not import the specialized primary factors available to the multinationals. Hence, domestic service firms incur primary factor costs related to Armenian labor and capital only. These services are characterized by firm-level product differentiation. For multinational firms, the barriers to foreign direct investment affect their profitability and entry. Reduction in the constraints on foreign direct investment

12 Daniels (1985) found that service providers charge higher prices when the service is provided at a distance.

will induce foreign entry that will typically lead to productivity gains because when more varieties of service providers are available, buyers can obtain varieties that more closely fit their demands and needs (the Dixit-Stiglitz variety effect).

Closure Rules

Total labor and capital is fixed. Labor is mobile across sectors, so receives the same real wage in all sectors. Total capital is constant. A share of capital is mobile and receives the same real rental rate across all sectors; a share is sector and firm type specific in each of the imperfectly competitive sectors. We assume that the real exchange rate adjusts so that the balance of trade is constant. We also assume that government revenues are unchanged, so that any loss of revenue due to tax or tariff decreases must be made up in alternate taxes. The latter two assumptions allows us to conduct welfare analysis based on equivalent variation of the representative consumer.

Comparative Steady State Formulation.

In this version of our model, we allow the capital stock to adjust to its steady state equilibrium along with all of the model features we employ in our WTO reference case, i.e., we allow for tariff and FDI liberalization with endogenous productivity effects as above. We call this our comparative steady state model. In the comparative static model, we assume that the capital stock is fixed and the rental rate on capital is endogenously determined. In the comparative steady state model, the logic is reversed. We assume that the capital stock is in its initial steady state equilibrium in the benchmark dataset, but that the capital stock will adjust to a new steady state equilibrium based on a fixed rate of return demanded by investors. That is, if the trade policy shock happens to induce and increase in the rate of return on capital so that it exceeds the initial rate of return, investors will invest and expand the capital stock. Expansion of the capital stock drives down the marginal product of capital, i.e., it drives down the rental rate on capital, until the rate of return on capital falls back to the initial level.[13] To analyze trade policy, this comparative steady state approach has been employed by many authors,

[13] The rate of return on investment in our model is the rental rate on capital divided by the cost of a unit of the capital good.

including Harrison, Rutherford and Tarr (1996, 1997), Baldwin et al. (1999) and Francois et al. (1996). The approach, however, dates back to the 1970s, when both Hansen and Koopmans (1972) and Dantzig and Manne (1974) used it. The approach ignores the foregone consumption necessary to achieve the higher level of investment and thus, is an upper bound estimate on the long run gains within the framework of the model assumptions.

4 Data of the Model and Evidence for Key Elasticities

Input-Output Matrix

The core of the model data consists of an input-output table. No official recent input-output table for Armenia exists, so we produced the table based on data provided by the National Statistical Office of the Republic of Armenia. Our data sources include an unbalanced supply-use table with 16 sectors for the year 2006 and detailed data on GDP for 2007 by types of income, expenditure, and production. The supply-use table contains all the elements we need for the input-output table, but supply deviates significantly from use in most of the sectors. We therefore develop a balancing procedure to arrive at a balanced input-output table.[14] The procedure involves an optimization problem in which the elements of the table are adjusted such that the sum of the squared deviations from the initial values are minimized and subject to a number of side constraints, including supply-use balance. As part of the procedure, we also use detailed GDP data to update the dataset to the year 2007. Finally, we disaggregate two services sectors to get more details on transport, communication and financials sectors. The final table contains 21 sectors. Details of the construction are explained in Jensen and Tarr (2011, Appendix G).

Trade Data by Regional Partner and Sector

To obtain the shares of imports and exports from the different regions of our model, we used trade data published by the National Statistical Service of the

[14] We thank Miles Light for his contribution to this work.

Republic of Armenia.[15] The data is for the year 2007 and shows exports and imports by country and commodity.

The regions of our model are Armenia, the European Union, the CIS, and the Rest of the World. For the European Union, we took the 27 member countries as of 2007. For the CIS, we include Azerbaijan, Belarus, Kazakhstan, Kyrgyzstan, Republic of Moldova, Russian Federation, Tajikistan, Turkmenistan, Ukraine, and Uzbekistan. Rest of the World is the residual.

The data is reported according to the Harmonized System (HS) classification at the two digit level. We mapped the HS-commodities into the sectors of our model. The exact mapping and results for both exports and imports are reported in Jensen and Tarr (2011, Appendix A). The results are shown in Table 5.

Tariff Data—Collected Rates at the Tariff Line Level

We received data on collected import duties (tariffs) and import values at the four digit tariff line level (again using the Harmonized System classification) from the Armenian Customs Authority. The collected tariff rates for the sectors in our model are obtained by first aggregating the four digit tariff line level tariff collections and import values to the sectors of our model. The ratio of tariff collections to import values for each sector of our model is then calculated to give estimates of the collected tariff rates, which in turn are incorporated into our dataset. The tariff rates are shown in Table 4 of Jensen and Tarr (2011, Appendix A). Applying these tariff rates across all sectors implies that tariff revenue in the revised database is about 1% of GDP, which is consistent with collected revenues in Armenia.[16]

Given that Armenia participates in preferential trade areas with the other CIS member states, it was necessary to make further adjustments. That is, since in principle, tariff rates should be zero within these preferential trade areas, we set tariff collections on imports from CIS countries at zero. We then increased the

15 http://www.armstat.am/file/article/ft_2nish_07_14.pdf

16 For the year 2008, aggregate data from Armenia show that tariff collections are 1% of GDP.

Table 5: Trade Flows by Trading Partner (%)

	Imports			Exports		
	European Union	CIS	Rest of the World	European Union	CIS	Rest of the World
Business Services						
Transport via railways	0	100	0	0	100	0
Transport via pipelines	0	100	0	0	100	0
Air transport	30	30	41	30	30	41
Telecommunications	6	39	55	6	39	55
Insurance	30	57	14	30	57	14
Banking	21	49	30	21	49	30
Dixit-Stiglitz Goods						
Mining and quarrying	28	62	9	42	23	35
Manufacturing	30	25	45	33	31	36
Other goods and services						
Agriculture, hunting, forestry and fishing	6	49	45	13	83	4
Electricity, gas and water supply	0	0	100	0	0	100
Construction	0	0	100	0	0	100
Wholesale and retail trade and repair	0	0	100	0	0	100
Hotels and restaurants	0	0	100	0	0	100
Other land transport	0	0	100	0	0	100
Auxiliary transport activities	0	0	100	0	0	100
Post and courier activities	0	0	100	0	0	100
Real estate and professional services	0	0	100	0	0	100
Public administration and defence	0	0	100	0	0	100
Education	0	0	100	0	0	100
Health and social work	0	0	100	0	0	100
Other social and personal services	0	0	100	0	0	100

Source: Authors' estimates.

tariff rates for the other regions in our model so that the overall weighted average collected tariff rate is unchanged at the tariff line level. We used the trade flow data, disaggregated by regions and sectors of our model to weight the tariff rates. This adjustment has the impact of raising the collected tariff rates for the regions in our model where positive tariff rates apply. The resulting adjusted tariff rates are also reported in Table 4.

We also note that we have only three sectors where tariff rates apply in our model. It is well known that the distortion costs of a diverse tariff structure decline with aggregation. Thus, the limited number of sectors in our model is likely to lead to an underestimate of the welfare gains from tariff reduction.

Share of Market Captured by Multinational Service Providers

It was necessary to calculate the market share of multinational firms in the services sectors by region of the model. Take the banking sector as an example. We need to know the share of the market captured by Armenian, EU, CIS and Rest of the World firms, where the countries in the regions are defined in Table 1. This entailed acquiring a list of all banks operating in Armenia along with their market share, and, when the bank is owned by multiple parties, allocating the ownership across the regions of our model. The database www.armbanks.am was sufficient for this task in most cases, but websites of the banks had to be consulted to allocate ownership shares in several cases. The results, by region and sector, are presented in Table 6A and explained in more detail in Jensen and Tarr (2011, Appendix B).

Table 6A: Market Shares in Sectors with FDI (%)

	Armenia	European Union	CIS	Rest of the World
Business Services				
Transport via railways	0	0	100	0
Transport via pipelines	0	0	100	0
Air transport	70	9	9	12
Telecommunications	0	6	39	55
Insurance	31	20	39	10
Banking	26	16	36	22

Source: See Appendix

Share of Expatriate Labor Employed by Multinational Service Providers

The impact of liberalization of barriers to foreign direct investment in business services sectors on the demand for labor in these sectors will depend on the share of expatriate labor used by multinational firms. Despite the fact that multinationals use Armenian labor less intensively than their Armenian competitors, if multinationals use mostly Armenian labor, their expansion is likely to increase the demand for Armenian labor in these sectors.[17] As estimates of the share of expatriate labor or specialized technology not available to Armenian firms that is used by multinational service providers in Armenia, we used estimates from other studies in these sectors.[18] We have found that multinational service providers use mostly local primary factor inputs and only small amounts of expatriate labor or specialized technology.

Estimates of the Dixit-Stiglitz Elasticities of Substitution for Goods

It was necessary for us to obtain estimates of the Dixit-Stiglitz product variety elasticities of substitution for the imperfectly competitive sectors in our model. Christian Broda, Joshua Greenfield and David Weinstein (2006) estimated Dixit-Stiglitz product variety elasticities of substitution at the 3 digit level in 73 countries. Among the 73 countries, there were no CIS countries, but Lithuania is in their sample. As a former Soviet Union economy with a population about the size of Armenia, we choose Lithuania as our proxy. We explain in Jensen and Tarr (2011, Appendix C), how we mapped the 3 digit elasticities for 130 goods sectors estimated by Broda et al. into the sectors of our model. The mapping and resulting elasticities by relevant sector in our model are shown in Jensen and Tarr (2011, Table C1). For the manufacturing sector, we get a trade weighted elasticity of 8.

---

[17] See Markusen, Rutherford and Tarr (2005) for a detailed explanation on why FDI may be a partial equilibrium substitute for domestic labor but a general equilibrium complement.

[18] Based on Jensen, Rutherford and Tarr (2007) for Russia and Jensen and Tarr (2008) for Kazakhstan, we employed the following shares: railway transportation, 3%; pipeline transportation, 3%; air transportation, 12.5%; telecommunications, 10%; insurance, 10%; banking, 10%.

Economics: The Open-Access, Open-Assessment E-Journal

Elasticities of Varieties with Respect to Price—Evidence on the Role of Trade and FDI in Increasing Total Factor Productivity through Technology Transfer as a Function of Research and Development Intensity of the Trading Partner

Grossman and Helpman (1991) have developed models of economic growth that have highlighted the role of trade in providing a greater variety of intermediate goods as a vehicle for technological spillovers that allow less developed countries to close the technological gap with industrialized countries. Similarly, Romer (1994) has argued that product variety is a crucial and often overlooked source of gains to the economy from trade liberalization.

Some of the key articles regarding product variety are the following. Broda and Weinstein (2004) find that increased product variety contributes to a fall of 1.2 percent per year in the "true" import price index. Hummels and Klenow (2005) and Schott (2004) have shown that product variety and quality are important in explaining trade between nations. Feenstra et al. (1999) show that increased variety of exports in a sector increases total factor productivity in most manufacturing sectors in Taiwan (China) and Korea, and they have some evidence that increased input variety also increases total factor productivity. In business services, because of the high cost of using distant suppliers, the close availability of a diverse set of business services may be even more important for growth than in goods. Winters et al. (2004) summarize the empirical literature by concluding that "the recent empirical evidence seems to suggest that openness and trade liberalization have a strong influence on productivity and its rate of change."

As discussed above, we employ the Dixit-Stiglitz-Ethier[19] mechanism, whereby additional varieties of business services increase the productivity of the firms that use the services. This is the key mechanism used in the Grossman Helpman models, endogenous growth theory as well as the economic geography literature. It provides a micro-foundation for the link between a change in policy and productivity growth.

[19] Ethier (1982) made the key extension of the Dixit-Stiglitz framework for our purposes; he showed how liberalization of international trade could lead to productivity increases when imports are used as intermediate inputs. We use the phrases Dixit-Stiglitz framework and Dixit-Stiglitz-Ethier framework synonymously in the paper.

Beginning with the path-breaking work of Coe and Helpman (1995), a rich literature now exists that has empirically investigated the transmission of knowledge through the purchase of imported intermediate goods and through foreign direct investment. We summarize this literature in Jensen and Tarr (2011, Appendix H). In summary, this literature shows that the purchase of intermediate inputs and FDI from industrialized countries is an important mechanism for the transmission of R&D and productivity growth in developing countries. For small developing countries, trading with large technologically advanced countries is crucial for TFP growth. But for products in which developing countries have a comparative advantage, developing country trade may be important for spillovers.

In our model, the parameter that reflects the ability of a region to increase total factor productivity through the transmission of new technologies is the elasticity of varieties with respect to the price. Schiff et al., (2002, Table 1) have shown that for R&D intensive sectors, trade with industrialized countries contributes significantly to total factor productivity in developing countries, but trade with developing countries does not. Averaging over the industries in Schiff et al.,(2002, Table 3) yields that trade with industrialized countries in R&D intensive products is about eight times more valuable for developing country TFP increases. On the other hand, for sectors that are low in R&D intensity, their results suggest that for technology diffusion trade with developing countries can be as important as trade with industrialized countries.

Based on these considerations, we first classify the increasing returns to scale sectors of our model into low, medium and high technology sectors. Due to lack of data for Armenia, the classification is defined by the share of R&D expenditures in total sales, based on U.S. data. For low R&D intensive sectors, we assume that the elasticity of firms with respect to price is the same for the CIS region as for the EU, but the elasticity is only one-third of Rest of the World elasticity (trade with the CIS or EU regions misses out on trade with China or the U.S.). For medium and high R&D intensive sectors, we assume that trade and FDI with the CIS region is only one-eighth as valuable as trade with the Rest of the World (as discussed above), while trade with the EU is two-thirds as valuable as trade with the Rest of the World. Finally, we allow the elasticity of the Rest of the World to vary depending on the R&D intensity of the sector, where we allow for more

Economics: The Open-Access, Open-Assessment E-Journal

technology diffusion in more R&D intensive sectors. The results of these assumptions are in Table 6b.[20]

Table 6B: Estimates of supply elasticity of firms with respect to price

	Armenia	European Union	CIS	Rest of the World
Business Services				
Transport via railways	2	10	2	15
Transport via pipelines	2	10	2	15
Air transport	2	10	2	15
Telecommunications	3	13	3	20
Insurance	3	3	3	10
Banking	3	3	3	10
Dixit-Stiglitz Goods				
Mining and quarrying	3	3	3	10
Manufacturing	2	10	2	15

Source: See Appendix

5 Results for Deep Liberalization: Central Elasticity Case

We execute several scenarios to assess the impacts of Armenia's broad trade policy options. First, we consider the impact of Armenia entering into a Deep and Comprehensive Free Trade Agreement (DCFTA) with the European Union. Second, we evaluate the impact of deepening the CIS free trade agreement by adding preferential liberalization of services in the CIS; third, we evaluate combining a DCFTA with the EU with preferential liberalization of services with the CIS; fourth, in the scenario we call "unilateral," we combine the impact of a DCFTA with the EU, preferential liberalization of services with the CIS, and unilateral liberalization of tariffs and services with the rest of the world; finally, we add the impact of reducing geographically non-discriminatory services barriers

[20] On the other hand, Table 6a shows that the CIS has a larger share of the market than the EU in most services sectors. This will have the effect of yielding larger gains for liberalization with respect to the CIS.

Economics: The Open-Access, Open-Assessment E-Journal

in Armenia to the unilateral scenario. We discuss the results for each of these broad policy options in turn.

Unless otherwise stated, all results in this section are reported in Table 7. In Table 7 we present results with no rent capture of the barriers against foreign direct investment by Armenians. We have also executed all the scenarios under the assumption that Armenians capture the rents from the barriers against FDI. The results with rent capture lower the gains from regional integration, but do not change the sign of the results (although there is almost a sign reversal in one case discussed below). So we discuss the key results with rent capture in the text and refer the reader to Jensen and Tarr (2011) for detailed results.

Impact of the DCFTA with the EU

Aggregate effects (Table 7, EU-FTA column). A DCFTA with the EU is a complex agreement that will contain numerous chapters. Overall, we assess that the agreement will result in gains to Armenia of 1.4 percent of consumption in the medium term, and 1.8 percent of consumption in the long run (see the EU-FTA steady state column). We estimate that in this scenario, there will be a substantial increase in EU firms operating in Armenia in the air transportation services sector (329 percent increase) and insurance sector (21 percent increase), and a substantial increase in varieties of EU goods available in the manufacturing sector (31 percent increase). Although varieties decline from other regions in this scenario, there is a net increase in varieties, and this leads to a reduction in the quality adjusted price of these goods and services. For details, and comparison with the CIS preferential agreement, see Jensen and Tarr (2011, Tables 18, 21). We focus on five of the most important impacts that impact on trade and real incomes and assess their impacts separately to determine the source of these gains. These are: (i) preferential reduction in the of barriers in services with the EU that reduced the ad valorem equivalents of the barriers by 50 percent; (ii) a reduction in border costs; which will reduce border costs for trade with the EU most strongly, but will also reduce border costs with third countries, including the CIS; (iii) a reduction in standards costs of trading with the EU; (iv) elimination of tariff barriers against the EU; and (v) the impact on the investment climate from the four above mentioned impacts. We analyze each of these components in turn.

Economics: The Open-Access, Open-Assessment E-Journal

Table 7: Summary of Results—no initial capture of rents in services by Armenians (results are percentage change from initial equilibrium, unless otherwise indicated)

Scenario definition	Benchmark	EU FTA	EU Discriminatory Services	EU Tariffs	Border Costs	EU Standards	EU FTA Steady-state	CIS FTA	EU-CIS FTA
Reduction of discriminatory barriers on EU services firms	No	**Yes**	Yes	No	No	No	Yes	**No**	**Yes**
Reduction of discriminatory barriers on CIS services firms	No	**No**	No	No	No	No	No	**Yes**	**Yes**
Reduction of discriminatory barriers on ROW services firms	No	**No**	No	No	No	No	No	**No**	**No**
Reduction of regulatory barriers for all services firms	No	**No**	No	No	No	No	No	**No**	**No**
Removal of tariffs on EU sourced goods	No	**Yes**	No	Yes	No	No	Yes	**No**	**Yes**
Removal of tariffs on ROW sourced goods	No	**No**	No	No	No	No	No	**No**	**No**
Reduction in border costs	No	**Yes**	No	No	Yes	No	Yes	**No**	**Yes**
Reduction in standards for EU exports	No	**Yes**	No	No	No	Yes	Yes	**No**	**Yes**
Steady-state capital stock	No	**No**	No	No	No	No	Yes	**No**	**No**
Aggregate welfare									
Welfare (EV as % of consumption)		**1.4**	0.4	-0.1	1.0	0.1	1.8	**0.1**	**1.5**
Welfare (EV as % of GDP)		**1.0**	0.3	-0.1	0.7	0.1	1.2	**0.1**	**1.1**
Government budget									
Tariff revenue (% of GDP)	1.0	**0.6**	1.0	0.5	1.0	1.0	0.6	**1.0**	**0.6**
Tariff revenue		**-40.9**	0.3	-44.2	5.0	0.7	-40.4	**0.1**	**-40.8**
Aggregate trade									
Real exchange rate		**0.6**	0.2	0.5	0.2	-0.3	0.9	**0.1**	**0.6**
Aggregate exports		**13.9**	-0.1	2.5	9.3	1.8	15.1	**0.2**	**14.2**
Factor Earnings									
Capital		**2.0**	0.4	0.5	0.8	0.2	1.0	**0.1**	**2.0**
Labor		**2.0**	0.5	0.4	0.9	0.1	2.9	**0.1**	**2.0**
Factor adjustments									
Capital		**0.4**	0.1	0.2	0.1	0.2		**0.0**	**0.4**
Labor		**0.4**	0.2	0.2	0.1	0.1	0.6	**0.0**	**0.4**
Capital stock and investment							1.9		

Source: Authors' estimates.

Economics: The Open-Access, Open-Assessment E-Journal

Table 7: Summary of Results—no initial capture of rents in services by Armenians—continued
(results are percentage change from initial equilibrium, unless otherwise indicated)

Scenario definition	**Unilateral**	Unilateral Discriminatory Services	Unilateral Tariffs	Unilateral Steady-state	**Unilateral & Domestic**	Unilateral & Domestic Steady-state
Reduction of discriminatory barriers on EU services firms	**Yes**	Yes	No	Yes	**Yes**	Yes
Reduction of discriminatory barriers on CIS services firms	**Yes**	Yes	No	Yes	**Yes**	Yes
Reduction of discriminatory barriers on ROW services firms	**Yes**	Yes	No	Yes	**Yes**	Yes
Reduction of regulatory barriers for all services firms	**No**	No	No	No	**Yes**	Yes
Removal of tariffs on EU sourced goods	**Yes**	No	Yes	Yes	**Yes**	Yes
Removal of tariffs on ROW sourced goods	**Yes**	No	Yes	Yes	**Yes**	Yes
Reduction in border costs	**No**	No	No	No	**No**	No
Reduction in standards for EU exports	**No**	No	No	No	**No**	No
Steady-state capital stock	**No**	No	No	Yes	**No**	Yes
Aggregate welfare						
Welfare (EV as % of consumption)	**1.1**	0.9	0.1	1.4	**1.4**	1.8
Welfare (EV as % of GDP)	**0.8**	0.7	0.1	1.0	**1.0**	1.3
Government budget						
Tariff revenue (% of GDP)		1.0				
Tariff revenue	**-100.0**	0.8	-100.0	-100.0	**-100.0**	-100.0
Aggregate trade						
Real exchange rate	**2.0**	0.5	1.4	2.3	**2.2**	2.5
Aggregate exports	**7.0**	0.1	6.9	8.2	**7.6**	8.9
Factor Earnings						
Capital	**2.3**	1.0	1.3	1.3	**2.6**	1.6
Labor	**2.3**	1.0	1.3	3.3	**2.6**	3.7
Factor adjustments						
Capital	**0.8**	0.2	0.6	0.2	**0.8**	0.2
Labor	**0.8**	0.3	0.5	0.9	**0.8**	0.9
Capital stock and investment				1.9		2.1

Source: Authors' estimates.

Services liberalization (Table 7, EU Discriminatory Services column). In view of the evidence on the importance of services for productivity growth (see Francois and Hoekman, 2010), it is crucial to estimate these impacts. We estimate that the impact of preferential liberalization of services with EU will result in a welfare gain to Armenia of 0.4 percent of Armenian consumption (measured by Hicks an equivalent variation). In this scenario we assume that Armenian discriminatory barriers against EU multinational service providers are reduced by fifty percent in all sectors except airline services. In airline services, we assume that barriers are reduced by 25 percent due to the fact that several barriers in airlines will not be affected by a DCFTA.[21] The gains from preferential services liberalization are smaller than we have observed in other applications, such as in Russia (Jensen, Rutherford and Tarr, 2007), Kazakhstan (Jensen and Tarr, 2008), Tanzania (Jensen, Rutherford and Tarr, 2010) and Kenya (Balistreri, Rutherford and Tarr, 2009). There are two reasons for this. First, the estimated discriminatory ad valorem equivalents of the barriers against multinational providers of services in Armenia are a lot lower than we have observed in these other applications. As we show in Table 4, only insurance and air transportation services have significant discriminatory barriers against foreign direct investment. Second, the liberalization is preferential, so there are lost services varieties from all regions other than the EU. The loss in varieties from other regions results in a loss of productivity and ultimately welfare. There could be further losses from preferential services liberalization if there are rents captured by Armenians on the barriers to FDI.[22]

EU tariff liberalization (Table 7, EU Tariffs column). We assess the impacts of preferentially removing tariffs on imports of goods imported from the EU, with no other policy changes. We find this will lead to a loss of welfare for Armenia equal to –0.08 percent of consumption. Although the welfare loss is not large, it deserves explanation. There are two primary explanations—loss of tariff revenue

[21] For example, airline services can only be provided within the framework of an international agreement. This is not likely be changed by a DCFTA.

[22] We note that tariff liberalization results in lost fiscal revenue that the government must replace, but services liberalization does not involve a loss of revenue to the government. The lost tariff revenue on third country imports is a welfare loss.

of displaced imports from the Rest of the World and loss of manufactured good varieties from the Rest of the World.

The EU has a minority share in manufactured and agricultural goods imports in Armenia. For manufactured goods, 45 percent of imports come from the Rest of the World region, while only 30 percent is from the EU. In agriculture, only six percent of imports originate in the EU, while 45 percent originate in the Rest of the World. Preferential tariff liberalization with respect to the EU results in a displacement of Rest of the World imports and a loss of tariff revenue on those imports.

To isolate the tariff loss impact from the productivity impact, we executed the preferential tariff liberalization scenario in model with perfect competition and constant returns to scale model in all goods sectors. In this scenario, there are no productivity impacts from additional varieties of goods. We find that there is a very small welfare loss for preferential reduction of barriers against EU imports equal to –0.001 percent of consumption. Thus, the tariff loss on rest of world imports is enough to offset any welfare gains from additional imports from the EU region, but the tariff loss is not sufficient to give significantly negative welfare impacts.

The difference between the welfare loss of –0.001 in the perfectly competitive case and the welfare loss of –0.08 in the full model must be due to loss of varieties from regions other than the EU. That is, preferential liberalization of tariffs against the EU induces additional varieties from the EU, but loss of varieties from the Rest of the World, CIS and Armenia. Given the large share of the Rest of the World in manufacturing imports of Armenia, the number of varieties lost from this region is relatively large.

Improved trade facilitation, including reduced border costs (Table 7, Border Costs column). We evaluate the impact of improved trade facilitation in Armenia as a result of the DCFTA with the EU. We assume that the costs of importing from or exporting to the EU declines by 2.5 percent of total production costs and the costs of non-EU trade fall by 2.3 or 2.2 percent of total production costs. (See Jensen and Tarr (2011, Appendix D) for an elaboration of the methodology.) We evaluate the welfare gain from improved trade facilitation at 1.0 percent of consumption. That is, this scenario suggests that the largest source of gains from

Economics: The Open-Access, Open-Assessment E-Journal

the DCFTA with the EU is due to its impact on lowering the costs of trade transport on both imports and exports on both EU and non-EU trade.

Harmonization with EU standards (Table 7, EU standards column). We evaluate the impact of harmonization with EU standards as part of the DCFTA. As we explain in Jensen and Tarr (2011, Appendix E), we assess that the costs of meeting EU standards for Armenian exporters will fall by 25 percent for agricultural and manufacturing exports to the EU (from 15.8 of production costs to 11.8 percent of production costs in agriculture and from 21.6 percent of production costs to 16.2 percent of production costs in the case of manufacturing. On the other hand, there are adjustment costs of adapting to the new standards that we assess raise the costs of production by two percentage points. This cost reduction applies only to Armenian firms exporting to the EU and only on the agriculture and manufacturing sectors.

We assess that Armenia will gain 0.1 percent of consumption as a result of the harmonization of standards. The gains in standards are considerably less than from trade facilitation. This is due to the fact that the standards costs reduction is limited to exports to the EU on a subset of all exports, whereas trade facilitation cost reduction is assumed to apply to all products, on both imports and exports and there is some cost reduction for all trade partners.

EU DCFTA steady-state (Table 7, EU-FTA Steady-state column). As discussed above, we assess the potentially positive impact of the DCFTA on the investment climate by executing a "steady-state" scenario. We assume the capital stock adjusts to its long run equilibrium in response to an increase in the real return on capital. We estimate that the welfare gain will increase to 1.8 percent of consumption in this scenario. This is a modest increase over the comparative static result, but not striking. It reflects that the real return on capital increases only modestly in the comparative static scenario.

Similarly, in the scenario "unilateral steady state" and the scenario "unilateral and domestic steady state" we estimate approximately a 30 and 70 percent increase, respectively, in the welfare gain in the steady state scenario relative to the comparative static scenario. Again, this reflects a modest increase in the rate of return on capital in the comparative static scenario.

Small gains from preferential liberalization of services with the CIS region (Table 7, "CIS FTA" column). In the case of preferential liberalization of services barriers with the CIS region (to reduce the ad valorem equivalent by 50 percent), the gains are smaller—0.10 percent of consumption. In the case of rent capture by Armenians of the barriers against FDI, the gains are almost zero (see Jensen and Tarr, 2011). The agreement with the EU includes tariff reduction, while tariff free access in the CIS region is considered part of the status quo; so the appropriate scenario for comparison of the relative gains for Armenia is the scenario labeled EU Discriminatory Services. The gains for Armenia of an agreement with the EU are four times greater than the gains from an agreement with the CIS region.

Why are the gains larger for the agreement with the EU? As we discussed above, trade and FDI from large technologically advanced regions can be expected to lead to technology diffusion that increases total factor productivity. Although trade and FDI from small developing countries can contribute to technology diffusion, it has been estimated to do so to a significantly lesser extent, at least for research and development intensive sectors. The elasticity of the number of varieties (firms) with respect to price is the parameter in our model that captures that effect, and the values we have chosen are in Table 6B.[23] We estimate that the number of varieties from the EU substantially increases in air transportation, banking and insurance as a result of preferential liberalization with the EU, while the estimated expansion of varieties from the CIS region is much more modest in response to preferential liberalization with respect to the CIS region. In air transportation services, we estimate a 41 percent increase in the number of CIS firms and a 17 percent increase in insurance. For details, see Jensen and Tarr (2011, tables 18, 21). This is a more modest increase than in the DCFTA with the EU. We show in the sensitivity analysis below that this elasticity of supply parameter is very important for the results: preferential agreements in services are more likely to be beneficial the higher the supply elasticities of the partner

[23] The elasticity of supply corresponds to the share of the sector's costs that are due to a specific factor of production. In all of the imperfectly competitive sectors, we assume there are four specific factors: one for each region in the model. Then, as industry output expands, the price of the specific factor necessary for production of that variety increases, thereby increasing the cost of production of firms. Since the cost of production of firms increases as the industry supply increases, the supply curve of each region will slope up in each of these sectors. And higher cost shares of the specific factor will lead to less elastic supply curves in that sector.

country's services suppliers and the lower the supply elasticities of the excluded countries services suppliers.

Combining the CIS FTA with a DCFTA with Europe—More substantial gains (Tables 7, "EU-CIS FTA" column). We show our estimates for the impacts of agreeing to a FTA with both the EU and the CIS region. The estimated gains are approximately the sum of the separate agreements. This shows that Armenia can augment the gains it may realize from an agreement with the EU, by adding a preferential services agreement with its CIS partners.

Harrison, Rutherford and Tarr (2002) found that, for Chile, the gains from combining free trade agreements would be more than additive. Harrison, Rutherford, Tarr and Gurgel (2004) found similar results for Brazil. That is, the gains of the two agreements combined exceeded the gains of the two separate agreements. The reason is that if Chile, for example, agreed to a free trade agreement with the U.S., then competition from the U.S. would greatly reduce the trade diversion associated with an agreement with neighboring developing countries. But there are the possibilities of trade diversion with the rest of the world region, so the gains from combined agreements are not necessarily greater than the gains from the separate agreements.

Non-discriminatory liberalization of services and tariff barriers would result in about a three-fold increase in the gains compared with preferential liberalization of goods and services with the EU alone (Table 7, "Unilateral" column). Preferential services liberalization can result in losses or reduced gains due to a loss in rents, if Armenians are capturing rents from the barriers to FDI in services. In addition, it will result in losses or reduced gains due to the exit of firms from excluded countries and the loss of varieties that entails. With non-discriminatory liberalization, Armenians would be able to access goods and services from the least cost supplier in the world. This would eliminate all trade diversion losses from preferential services liberalization and result in the maximum number of new foreign varieties for productivity improvement from trade and FDI liberalization. Consequently, the gains, which are equal to 1.1 percent of consumption, are much larger in this case than in the comparable case of preferential liberalization with the EU (between 0.4 and 0.3 percent of consumption for service and goods liberalization alone) or the CIS alone. Over 85 percent of the gains from unilateral liberalization come from liberalization of services and less than 15 percent comes from tariff liberalization.

Additional gains would be derived from reduction in the barriers that domestic as well as foreign firms face (Table 7, "Unilateral and Domestic" column)**.** If inefficient regulatory barriers that do not discriminate against foreign firms were also reduced by 50 percent, additional gains of 0.4 percent of consumption would be realized. This is a relatively low additional gain in comparison with some earlier work (Balestreri, Rutherford and Tarr, 2009; Jensen, Rutherford and Tarr, 2010). It reflects a relatively efficient legal framework for domestic services in Armenia.

Sector impacts (Table 8). In Table 8, we present results for the percentage change in output by sector for four scenarios: an FTA with the EU; and FTA with the CIS region; and FTA with the EU and the CIS region combined; and unilateral liberalization. Details of what is included in these scenarios are provided in Table 7.

Business services. In general we see an expansion of the output of the business services sectors, as the removal of discriminatory barriers induces more foreign direct investment. We define the output of multinational firms in the business services sectors who locate in Armenia as part of Armenian industry output (as is the case under a GDP calculation). Preferential reduction of barriers against one region generally reduces the number of firms from the other three regions in the model, but on balance the number of firms operating in Armenia and the output of the sector expands. Since multinational firms operating in Armenia use primarily Armenian labor, employment in these sectors also expands. To see what happens to EU firms, versus Armenian and other firms, it is necessary to view the tables that report the change in the number of firms by scenario.

Manufacturing, agriculture and other services. Given that we assume that total employment and the capital stock are fixed in the medium term, if labor expands in some sectors, it must contract in other sectors. Given the expansion in several sectors, we must have declines in others in the medium term. Sector output will tend to increase relative to other sectors based primarily on the following three considerations: (i) the more intensively the sector exports (due to a depreciation of the real exchange rate from trade liberalization); (ii) the lower the tariff was

Economics: The Open-Access, Open-Assessment E-Journal

Table 8: Output and Employment Impacts from Liberalization
(% change from benchmark)

	Unilateral Liberalization		EU-CIS FTA		CIS FTA		EU FTA	
	Output	Labor income	Output	Labor income	Output	Labor income	Output	Labor income
Business Services								
Transport via railways	1.8	2.2	0.6	1.5	0.2	0.1	0.5	1.4
Transport via pipelines	1.8	2.2	0.6	1.5	0.2	0.1	0.5	1.4
Air transport	14.2	14.7	7.1	8.1	-0.7	-0.7	7.9	9.0
Telecommunications	2.7	3.2	1.0	2.0	0.3	0.2	0.8	1.8
Insurance	4.5	5.7	1.4	2.8	0.9	0.6	0.5	2.2
Banking	4.1	5.4	1.2	2.6	0.7	0.4	0.5	2.2
Dixit-Stiglitz Goods								
Mining and quarrying	1.0	3.1	3.2	5.2	0.1	0.1	3.1	5.1
Manufacturing	-1.8	-0.1	-0.5	1.2	0.1	0.1	-0.6	1.1
Other goods and services								
Agriculture, hunting, forestry and fishing	-1.7	0.3	-0.6	1.2	0.1	0.1	-0.7	1.2
Electricity, gas and water supply	-0.2	1.4	-0.2	1.4	0.1	0.1	-0.3	1.4
Construction	0.0	2.1	0.0	1.9	0.0	0.0	0.0	1.9
Wholesale, retail trade and repair	4.2	6.1	2.7	4.5	0.1	0.1	2.6	4.4
Hotels and restaurants	7.2	7.4	-0.2	0.6	1.3	0.8	-1.4	-0.2
Other land transport	2.8	3.6	-0.3	0.8	0.2	0.2	-0.5	0.6
Auxiliary transport activities	2.8	3.6	-0.3	0.8	0.2	0.2	-0.5	0.6
Post and courier activities	2.8	3.6	-0.3	0.8	0.2	0.2	-0.5	0.6
Real estate and professional services	1.5	3.5	-0.4	1.4	0.1	0.1	-0.5	1.3
Public administration and defence	0.3	1.5	-0.1	1.3	0.0	0.0	-0.1	1.3
Education	-0.5	1.6	-0.9	1.0	0.0	0.1	-1.0	0.9
Health and social work	-0.2	1.9	0.1	2.0	0.0	0.1	0.0	1.9
Other social and personal services	0.1	1.9	-0.4	1.4	0.1	0.1	-0.4	1.3

Source: Authors' estimates.

relative to other sectors prior to liberalization; and (iii) the more intensively the sector uses services that are liberalized. What is striking about the output results is how small the output declines are in the unilateral liberalization scenario. In other applications, we have observed small output declines in the declining sectors in preferential liberalization scenarios, but significant output declines in some sectors in the unilateral liberalization scenario. The greater sector impacts in the unilateral scenario are because we assume zero tariffs in our unilateral reform scenario. The mild output declines reflect the low level of tariff protection in Armenia in the benchmark equilibrium. In our unilateral liberalization scenario, we do observe output declines in agriculture and manufacturing of 1.7 and 1.8 percent, respectively, as these are the only sectors that are protected by tariffs in the initial data.

Outside of business services, the sectors that expand depend on the scenario. In our unilateral liberalization scenario, we estimate that the hotel and restaurant sector, other transport services and wholesale and retail trade, and post and courier services are the sectors that will expand the greatest. These sectors are relatively intensive users of business services, such as transportation and banking services. Regulatory reforms will decrease the price and allow for quality improvements in these business services, which permits the using sectors to operate more cheaply and offer better quality services.

With the EC DCFTA, we estimate that wholesale and retail trade and mining and quarrying would be the main sectors that expand outside of business services. ince the liberalization is preferential, not multilateral, the expansion of business services is less strong than in unilateral liberalization. Then the intensive users of business services, like hotels and restaurants, gain less.

6 Sensitivity Analysis

In this section we assess the impact of parameter values and key modeling assumptions on the results. Through our "piecemeal sensitivity analysis" we will determine the most important parameters for the results, and we will assess how important for the results are rent capture or additional varieties from reform in services sectors under increasing returns to scale. In the piecemeal sensitivity analysis, we change the value of a single parameter while holding the values of all other parameters unchanged at our central elasticity values. We present piecemeal sensitivity analysis of the two most relevant policy scenarios. In Table 9, we examine the prospective free trade agreement with the EU and in Table 10 we examine the agreement with the CIS region.

Given uncertainty of parameter values and the rent capture assumption, point estimates of the results may be viewed with skepticism. In our "systematic sensitivity analysis," we execute 30,000 simulations. In each simulation, we allow the computer to randomly select the values of all parameters, subject to the specified probability distributions of the parameters. Through the systematic sensitivity analysis we will be able to assess how robust the results are and obtain confidence intervals of the results.

Rent Capture Assumption

In the row labeled θr we retain the increasing returns to scale assumption in the services sectors and selected goods sectors, but allow initial rent capture in the services sectors to be either zero (central value) or 100 percent (upper value). The welfare gain with no rent capture is 1.44 percent of consumption but falls to 1.37 percent of consumption with initial rent capture. The fall is modest in relation to the overall gains, due to the fact that border costs, not service sector gains dominate the welfare results.

In the case of an agreement with the CIS region, the gains fall even more dramatically in percentage terms, from a welfare gain of 0.10 percent of consumption to 0.01 percent of consumption in our central elasticity case.

Impact of Constant Returns to Scale—Possible Negative Welfare Effects

In the row labeled "θr –CRTS model," we assume constant returns to scale in all sectors; this eliminates the Dixit-Stiglitz externality from additional varieties. We allow initial rent capture in the services sectors to be either zero (central value) or 100 percent (upper value). We see that without the Dixit-Stiglitz variety externality, the gains from an agreement with the EU fall dramatically and are estimated to be negative with the CIS region (–0.03 percent of consumption) in the case of initial rent capture. With no initial rent capture, the gains for the EU agreement would be approximately 0.73 percent of consumption and would fall to

0.67 with initial rent capture. In the case of an agreement with the CIS region, the gains are 0.06 with no initial rent capture and are –0.03 with initial rent capture.

Table 9: Piecemeal Sensitivity of impact on Armenia of a DCFTA with the EU
Results are estimated changes in welfare (Hicksian EV) as a percent of consumption

Parameter	Parameter value Lower	Central	Upper	Results for EV Piecemeal sensitivity analysis Lower	Central	Upper
$\sigma(q_i, q_j)$ – services sectors	2	3	4	1.39	1.44	1.51
$\sigma(q_i, q_j)$ – goods sectors		See below		1.76	1.44	1.30
$\sigma(va, bs)$	0.625	1.25	1.875	1.39	1.44	1.52
$\sigma(D, M)$	2	4	6	1.42	1.44	1.46
$\sigma(M, M)$	4	8	12	1.44	1.44	1.44
$\sigma(L, K)$	0.5	1	1.5	1.44	1.44	1.44
$\sigma(A_1,\ldots A_n)$	NA	0	0.25	NA	1.44	1.45
$\sigma(D, E)$	2	4	6	1.44	1.44	1.44
ε_{ARM}	Central values of all 4 sets of ε parameters are listed in table 6B. Lower and upper values are 0.5 and 1.5 times central values.			1.46	1.44	1.43
ε_{EU}				0.96	1.44	1.77
ε_{CIS}				1.44	1.44	1.45
ε_{ROW}				1.53	1.44	1.39
θ_r	NA	0	1	NA	1.44	1.37
θ_r - CRTS model	NA	0	1	NA	0.73	0.67
θ_m	0.025	0.05	0.075	1.44	1.44	1.45
$\sigma(q_i, q_j)$ – goods sectors						
Mining & quarrying	8.5	17.00	25.5			
Manufacturing	4	8.00	12			

Key:
$\sigma(q_i, q_j)$: Elasticity of substitution between firm varieties in imperfectly competitive sectors
$\sigma(va, bs)$: Elasticity of substitution between value-added and business services
$\sigma(D, M)$: Elasticity of substitution between domestic production and imports
$\sigma(M, M)$: Elasticity of substitution between imported varieties
$\sigma(L, K)$: Elasticity of substitution between primary factors of production in value added
$\sigma(A_1,\ldots A_n)$: Elasticity of substitution in intermediate production between composite Armington aggregate goods
$\sigma(D, E)$: Elasticity of transformation (domestic output versus exports)
ε_{ARM}: Elasticity of national service firm supply with respect to price of output
ε_{EU}: Elasticity of EU service firm supply with respect to price of output
ε_{CIS}: Elasticity of CIS service firm supply with respect to price of output
ε_{ROW}: Elasticity of Rest of World service firm supply with respect to price of output
θ_r: Share of rents in services sectors captured by domestic agents
θ_m: Shares of value added in multinational firms due to specialized primary factor imports

Source: Authors' estimates.

Table 10: Piecemeal Sensitivity of impact on Armenia preferential services liberalization with the CIS region

Results are estimated changes in welfare (Hicksian EV) as a percent of consumption

Parameter	Parameter value Lower	Central	Upper	Results for EV Piecemeal sensitivity analysis Lower	Central	Upper
$\sigma(q_i, q_j)$ – services sectors	2	3	4	0.22	0.10	0.07
$\sigma(q_i, q_j)$ – goods sectors		See below		0.11	0.10	0.10
$\sigma(va, bs)$	0.625	1.25	1.875	0.09	0.10	0.12
$\sigma(D, M)$	2	4	6	0.10	0.10	0.10
$\sigma(M, M)$	4	8	12	0.10	0.10	0.10
$\sigma(L, K)$	0.5	1	1.5	0.10	0.10	0.10
$\sigma(A_1,\ldots A_n)$	NA	0	0.25	NA	0.10	0.10
$\sigma(D, E)$	2	4	6	0.10	0.10	0.10
ε_{ARM}	Central values of all 4 sets of ε			0.11	0.10	0.10
ε_{EU}	parameters are listed in table 6B.			0.11	0.10	0.10
ε_{CIS}	Lower and upper values are 0.5			0.05	0.10	0.15
ε_{ROW}	and 1.5 times central values.			0.11	0.10	0.10
θ_r	NA	0	1	NA	0.10	0.01
θ_r - CRTS model	NA	0	1	NA	0.06	-0.03
θ_m	0.025	0.05	0.075	0.10	0.10	0.10
$\sigma(q_i, q_j)$ – goods sectors						
Mining & quarrying	8.5	17.00	25.5			
Manufacturing	4	8.00	12			

Key:

$\sigma(q_i, q_j)$: Elasticity of substitution between firm varieties in imperfectly competitive sectors
$\sigma(va, bs)$: Elasticity of substitution between value-added and business services
$\sigma(D, M)$: Elasticity of substitution between domestic production and imports
$\sigma(M, M)$: Elasticity of substitution between imported varieties
$\sigma(L, K)$: Elasticity of substitution between primary factors of production in value added
$\sigma(A_1,\ldots A_n)$: Elasticity of substitution in intermediate production between composite Armington aggregate goods
$\sigma(D, E)$: Elasticity of transformation (domestic output versus exports)
ε_{ARM}: Elasticity of national service firm supply with respect to price of output
ε_{EU}: Elasticity of EU service firm supply with respect to price of output
ε_{CIS}: Elasticity of CIS service firm supply with respect to price of output
ε_{ROW}: Elasticity of Rest of World service firm supply with respect to price of output
θ_r: Share of rents in services sectors captured by domestic agents
θ_m: Shares of value added in multinational firms due to specialized primary factor imports

Source: Authors' estimates.

Piecemeal Sensitivity Analysis

Three parameters stand out as having a strong impact on the results. The elasticity of substitution between firm varieties in imperfectly competitive goods and

Economics: The Open-Access, Open-Assessment E-Journal

services sectors, $\sigma(q_i, q_j)$ has a very strong impact. Following from the Le Chatelier principle, larger elasticities typically lead to larger welfare gains in response to welfare improving reforms, as the economy can adapt more readily. This holds for the elasticities in the EU DCFTA scenario. Unlike other elasticities, however, a lower value of $\sigma(q_i,q_j)$ can increase the welfare gains. This holds for the lower value of this elasticity in goods and services and the upper value in goods. This is because lower values of this elasticity imply that varieties are less close to each other, so additional varieties are worth more. In the case of goods in the EU DCFTA and in the case of the CIS piecemeal sensitivity, lower values of this parameter increase the estimated welfare gains. The elasticity of substitution between value-added and business services, $\sigma(va, bs)$, also has a strong impact. The better firms are able to substitute business services for labor and capital, the more the economy will gain from the reforms that reduce the quality adjusted price of business services. Finally, for the agreement with the EU, a strong impact comes from changes in the value of ε_{EU}, the elasticity of EU multinational service firm supply with respect to the price of EU services in Armenia. Larger values of this parameter mean that tariff preferences that open opportunities for EU service firms to provide new varieties, will not be so quickly choked by the increased cost of the specific factor required for EU firm expansion. Similarly, for the agreement with the CIS region, ε_{AFR}, the elasticity of CIS multinational service firm supply with respect to the price of CIS services in Armenia has a strong impact. We conduct more detailed sensitivity analysis on this parameter below.

Systematic Sensitivity Analysis

In the systematic sensitivity analysis, we execute the model 30,000 times and harvest the results for desired variables. In each individual simulation, we allow the computer to select values of all the parameters in the model (the parameters in Table 10), based on the specified probability density functions (pdfs) of the parameters. We assume uniform probability density functions, with upper and lower values of the pdfs given by the upper and lower values in the piecemeal sensitivity analysis table. We include initial rent capture in the systematic sensitivity analysis, with the rent capture parameter allowed to take values between zero and one with a uniform pdf.

The welfare results for a deep and comprehensive free trade agreement with the EU are depicted in Figure 1. A 95 percent confidence interval for the gain in equivalent variation as a percent of consumption is: 1.01 percent to 1.84 percent. There are no simulations with negative estimated welfare changes.

In Figures 2 and 3, we show "box and whisper" diagrams for the sample distribution of the percentage change in output by sector. Sectors are on the horizontal axis and the percentage change in output is shown on the vertical axis. The bars in the box are the means of the distributions. Fifty percent confidence intervals are depicted by the boxes, while the vertical lines show 95 percent confidence intervals.

Figure 1: Sample Distribution of the Welfare Results of Armenian-EU DCFTA 30,000 simulations.

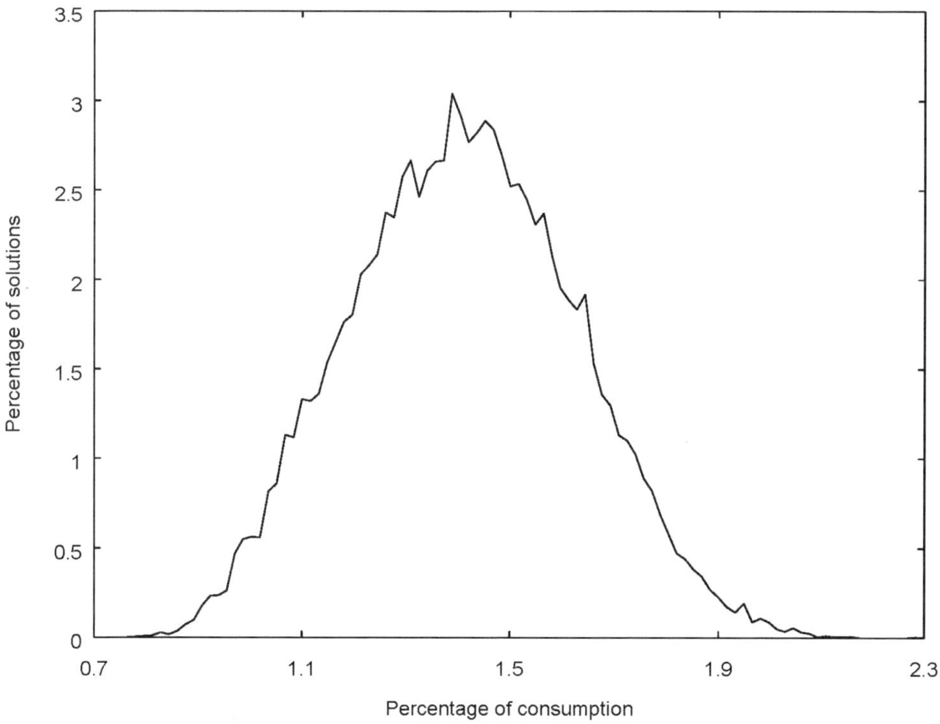

Economics: The Open-Access, Open-Assessment E-Journal

Figure 2: Means, 50 and 95 Percent Confidence Intervals of the Sample Distributions of the Output Changes by Sector from Armenian-EU DCFTA—30,000 simulations.

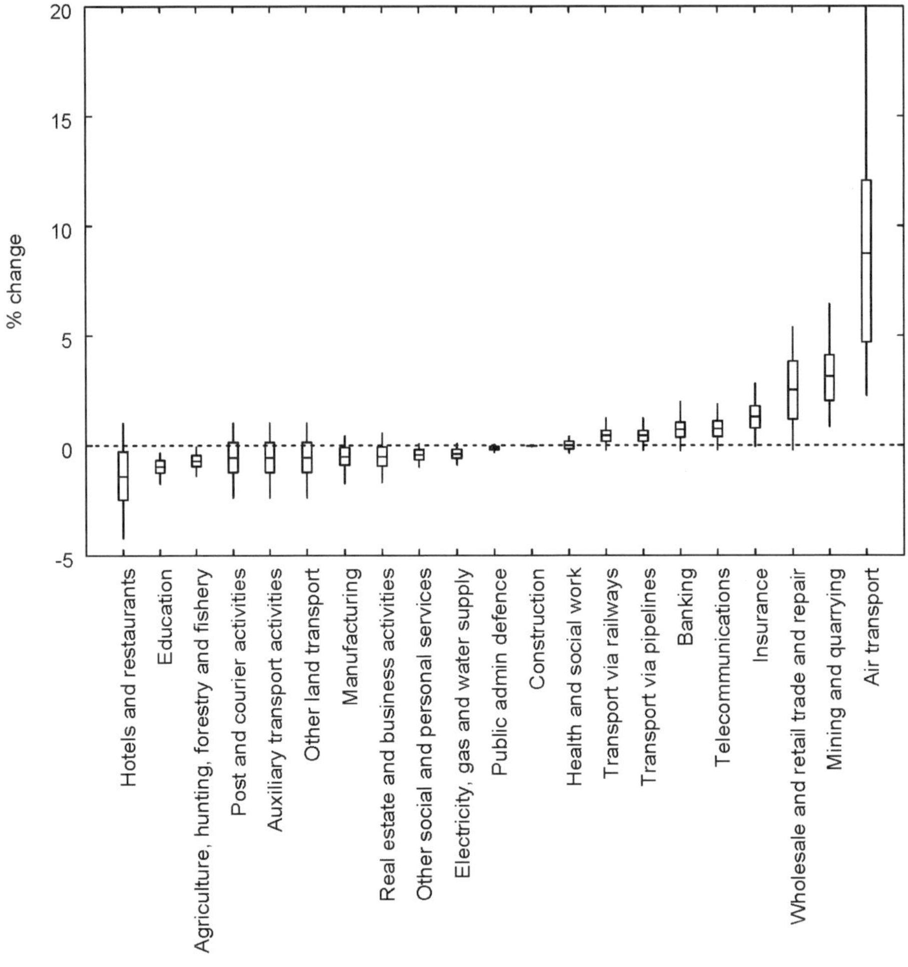

Note: The boxes are limited vertically by the 25% and 75% quartiles. The bars in the box are the means. The vertical lines extend to the 2.5% and 97.5% percentiles.

The means of the systematic sensitivity results show a similar pattern to the point estimates regarding the expansion of the services sectors. The business services sectors, mining and quarrying and wholesale and retail trade sectors are the sectors that we estimate will expand. While the confidence intervals are rather tight for most sectors (95 percent confidence intervals for the significantly expanding sectors are virtually all positive), they reveal a large range of uncertainty for hotels and restaurants.

Figure 3: Means 50 and 95 Percent Confidence Intervals of the Sample Distributions of the Labor Payment Changes by Sector from Armenian-EUFTA—30,000 simulations

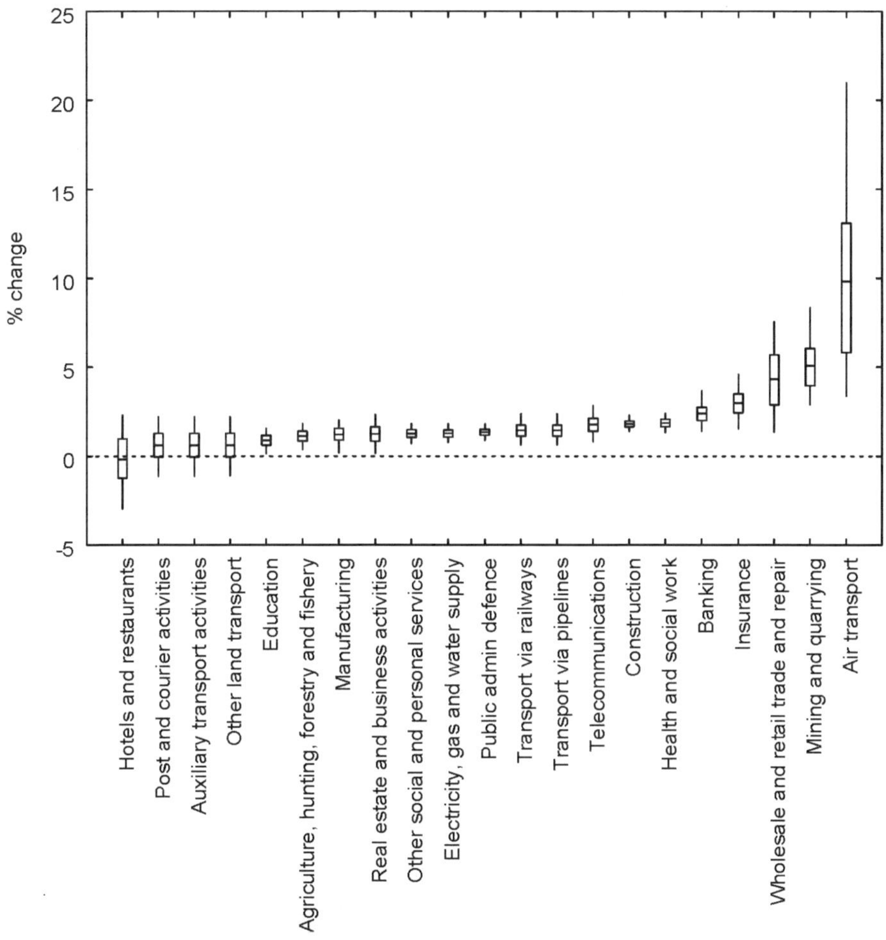

The results for preferential reduction of barriers with CIS partners on welfare, output and labor are shown in Figures 4–6. The welfare results for preferential reduction of barriers in services with the CIS region, depicted in Figure 6, are impacted significantly by the fact that we allow the rent capture parameter to vary between 0 and 1. The median result is between the two extreme values in the piecemeal sensitivity table for rent capture. Losses can occur when the share of rent capture in services by Armenian nationals is high. A 95 percent confidence interval for equivalent variation as a percent of consumption is: 0.003 to 0.147. There is a negative value for equivalent variation in 576 simulations.

Regarding output impacts of a services agreement with the CIS, results appear rather robust within a 95 percent confidence interval with the exception of air

Figure 4: Sample Distribution of the Welfare Results of Armenian-CIS FTA 30,000 simulations.

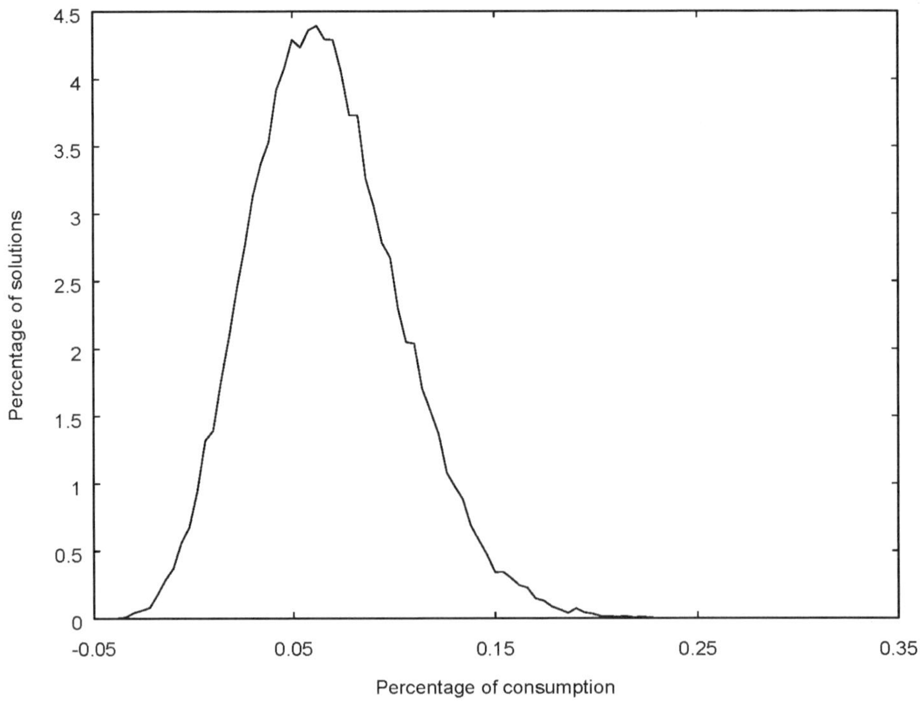

transport and telecommunications. The sensitivity analysis reveals that we cannot have a great deal of confidence in the sign of the impacts for air transportation.

Figure 5: Means 50 and 95 Percent Confidence Intervals of the Sample Distributions of the Output Changes by Sector from Armenian-CISFTA—30,000 simulations.

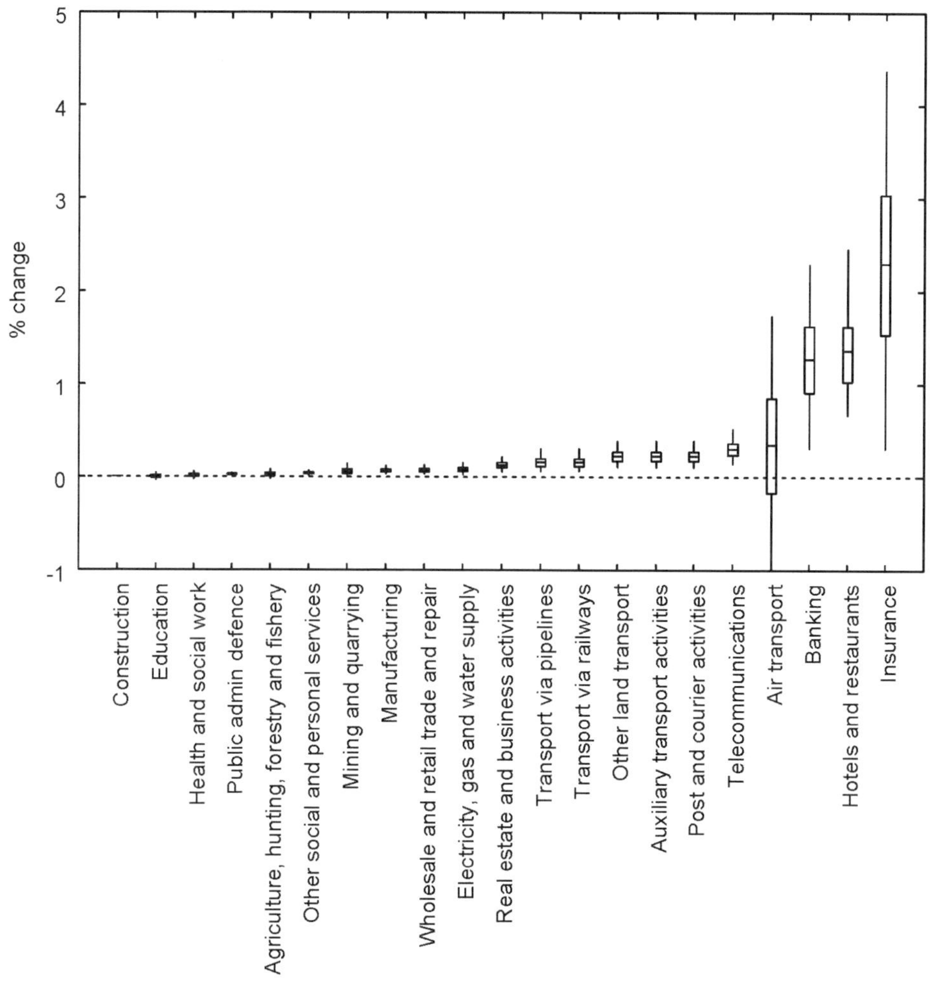

Note: The boxes are limited vertically by the 25% and 75% quartiles. The bars in the box are the means. The vertical lines extend to the 2.5% and 97.5% percentiles.

Economics: The Open-Access, Open-Assessment E-Journal

Figure 6: Means 50 and 95 Percent Confidence Intervals of the Sample Distributions of the Labor Payment Changes by Sector from Armenian-CIS FTA—30,000 simulations.

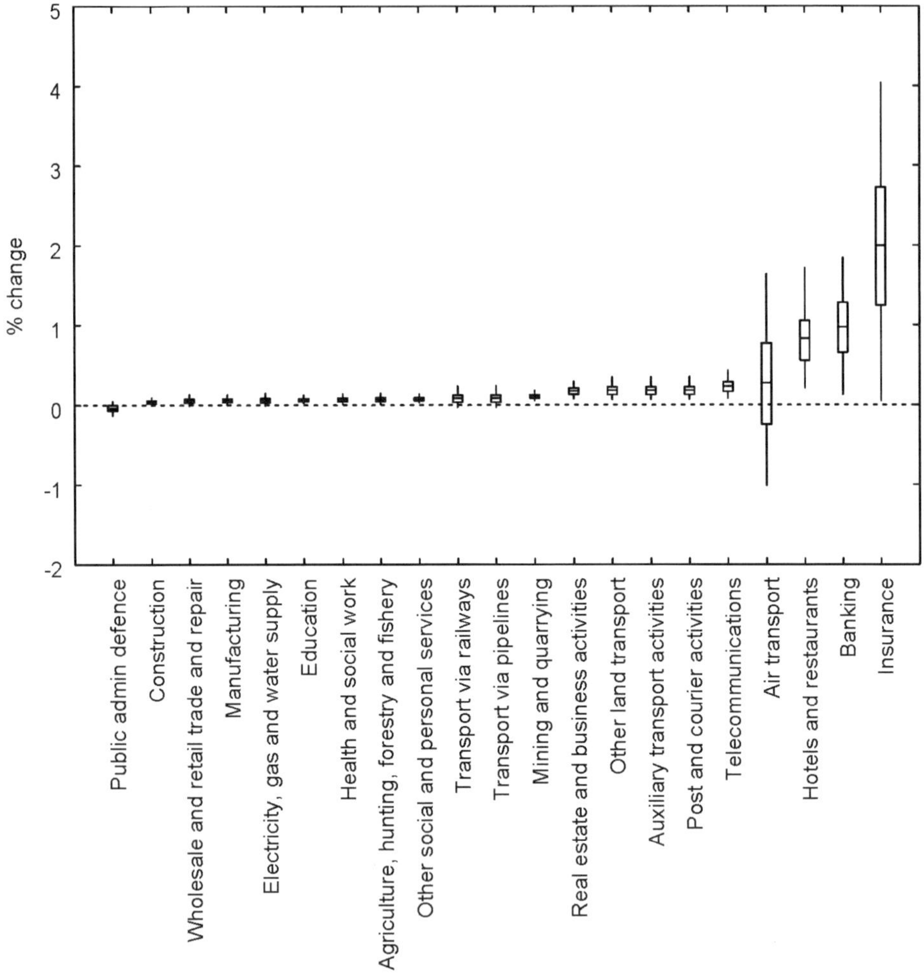

Note: The boxes are limited vertically by the 25% and 75% quartiles. The bars in the box are the means. The vertical lines extend to the 2.5% and 97.5% percentiles.

7 Conclusions and Possible Extensions for Future Work

Conclusions. In this paper we have developed an innovative small open economy computable general equilibrium model of the Armenian economy that is capable of assessing the impact of a deep and comprehensive free trade agreement with the European Union. In addition to preferential tariff liberalization, we have examined preferential liberalization of barriers against multinational service providers, harmonization of Armenian standards with EU standards and reduction of trade and border costs. We have also assessed the impact of preferential liberalization of services with the CIS region and compared all results with wider non-discriminatory liberalization. We find that Armenia would lose from a shallow free trade agreement with the EU, that is, a free trade agreement that preferentially liberalizes good alone. This is due primarily to a loss of productivity from excluded varieties of manufactured products from the non-EU regions. But Armenia would gain substantially from a DCFTA with the EU, due to inclusion of services liberalization, reduction of trade and border costs and harmonization of standards.

Armenia would obtain only small gains from a preferential reduction of barriers in services with the CIS region in our central elasticity case. Gains from liberalization with the EU region are considerably larger because of the larger amount of technology diffusion associated with trade and FDI with large industrialized countries, captured in our model as a relatively large increase in the number of varieties. Non-discriminatory liberalization of goods and services, however, will produce gains about three times larger than preferential liberalization of goods and services with the EU alone.

Possible Extensions. Future work could usefully examine the distributional and poverty consequences of the DCFTA, by introducing multiple households. Rutherford and Tarr (2008) have applied this style of model with an aggregate rest of world to examine the case of Russian WTO accession. But, we have not seen a regional model with FDI and monopolistic competition that has examined poverty and distributional impacts. An important extension would be to extend the model to a heterogeneous firms model, to better assess the consequences for industry structure. Balistreri, Hillberry and Rutherford (2010, 2011) have developed a heterogeneous firms CGE model, but it does not include FDI in services. Further, although we have captured the impacts of market shares of multinationals and their differences in the use of imported inputs, there are other dimensions in the way multinationals might differ from domestic firms. The paper by Latorre and Gomez-Plana (2011) is an interesting effort to capture some of these aspects.

References

Baldwin, R.E., R. Forslid, and J. Haaland (1999). Investment Creation and Investment Diversion: Simulation Analysis of the Single Market Programme. In R. Baldwin and J. Francois (eds.), *Dynamic Issues in Applied Commercial Policy Analysis*. Cambridge: Cambridge University Press.

Balistreri, E.J., R.H. Hillberry, and T.F. Rutherford (2010). Trade and Welfare: Does Industrial Organization Matter? *Economic Letters* 109: 85–87. http://ideas.repec.org/a/eee/ecolet/v109y2010i2p85-87.html

Balistreri, E.J., R.H. Hillberry, and T.F. Rutherford (2011). Structural Estimation and Solution of International Trade Models with Heterogeneous Firms. *Journal of International Economics* 83: 95–108. http://ideas.repec.org/a/eee/inecon/v83y2011i2p95-108.html

Balistreri, E.J. and J. Markusen (2009). Sub-national Differentiation and the Role of the Firm in Optimal International Pricing. *Economic Modeling* 26(1): 47–62. http://ideas.repec.org/a/eee/ecmode/v26y2009i1p47-62.html

Balistreri, E.J., T.F. Rutherford, and D.G. Tarr (2009). Modeling Services Liberalization: The Case of Kenya. *Economic Modeling* 26(3), May, 668–679. http://ideas.repec.org/a/eee/ecmode/v26y2009i3p668-679.html

Balistreri, E.J. and D.G. Tarr (2011). Services Liberalization in Preferential Trade Arrangements: The Case of Kenya. World Bank Policy and Research Working Paper No. 5552. https://www.gtap.agecon.purdue.edu/resources/download/5457.pdf

Broda, C. and D. Weinstein (2004). Variety, Growth and World Welfare. *American Economic Review* 94(2): 139–144. http://ideas.repec.org/a/aea/aecrev/v94y2004i2p139-144.html

Broda, C., J. Greenfield, and D. Weinstein (2006). From Groundnuts to Globalization: A Structural Estimate of Trade and Growth. National Bureau of Economic Research, NBER Working Paper No. 12512. http://ideas.repec.org/p/nbr/nberwo/12512.html.

Coe, D.T., and E. Helpman (1995). International R&D Spillovers. *European Economic Review* 39(5): 859–887. http://ideas.repec.org/a/eee/eecrev/v39y1995i5p859-887.html

Daniels, P.W. (1985). *Service Industries: A Geographical Appraisal.* New York: Methuen & Co.

Dantzig, G. and A. Manne (1974). A Complementarity Algorithm for an Optimal Capital Path with Invariant Proportions. *Journal of Economic Theory* 9(3): 312–323. http://ideas.repec.org/a/eee/jetheo/v9y1974i3p312-323.html

Dixit, A. and J. Stiglitz (1977). Monopolistic Competition and Optimum Product Diversity. *American Economic Review* 67(3): 297–308. http://ideas.repec.org/a/aea/aecrev/v67y1977i3p297-308.html

Dyker, D., M. Emerson, M. Gasiorek, P. Holmes, M. Jakubiak, A. Jungmittag, V. Korchagin, A. Kudina, E. Polyakov, A. Roudoi, and G. Torosyan (2008). Economic Feasibility, General Economic Impact and Implications of a Free Trade Agreement Between the European Union and Armenia. CASE Network Report No. 80. Warsaw: CASE. http://ideas.repec.org/p/sec/cnrepo/0080.html

Ethier, W.J. (1982). National and International Returns to Scale in the Modern Theory of International Trade. *American Economic Review* 72(2): 389–405. http://ideas.repec.org/a/aea/aecrev/v72y1982i3p389-405.html

Francois, J. and B. Hoekman (2010). Services Trade and Policy. *Journal of Economic Literature* 48: 642–692. http://ideas.repec.org/a/aea/jeclit/v48y2010i3p642-92.html

Grossman, G. and E. Helpman (1991). *Innovation and Growth in the World Economy.* Cambridge, MA: MIT Press.

Hansen, T. and T. Koopmans (1972). On the Definition and the Computation of a Capital Stock Invariant Under Optimization. *Journal of Economic Theory* 5(3): 487–523 http://ideas.repec.org/a/eee/jetheo/v5y1972i3p487-523.html

Harris, R. (1984). Applied General Equilibrium Analysis of Small Open Economies with Scale Economies and Imperfect Competition. *The American Economic Review* 74(5): 1016–1032.
http://ideas.repec.org/a/aea/aecrev/v74y1984i5p1016-32.html

Harrison, G.H., T.F. Rutherford, and D.G. Tarr (1993). Trade Reform in the Partially Liberalized Economy of Turkey. *The World Bank Economic Review* 7(2): 191–217. http://www.jstor.org/stable/3989864

Harrison, G.H., T.F. Rutherford, and D.G. Tarr. (1996). Increased Competition and Completion of the Market in the European Community: Static and Steady-State Effects. *Journal of Economic Integration* 11(3): 332–365.

Harrison, G.H., T.F. Rutherford, and D.G. Tarr (1997). Quantifying the Uruguay Round. *Economic Journal* 107(444): 1405–1430.
http://ideas.repec.org/a/ecj/econjl/v107y1997i444p1405-30.html

Harrison, G.H., T.F. Rutherford, and D.G. Tarr (1997a). Economic Implications for Turkey of a Customs Union with the European Union. *European Economic Review* 41(3–5): 861–870.
http://ideas.repec.org/a/eee/eecrev/v41y1997i3-5p861-870.html

Harrison, G.H., T.F. Rutherford, and D.G. Tarr (2002). Trade Policy Options for Chile: The Importance of Market Access. *World Bank Economic Review* 16(1): 49–79. http://ideas.repec.org/a/oup/wbecrv/v16y2002i1p49-79.html

Harrison, G.H., T.F. Rutherford, D.G. Tarr, and A. Gurgel (2004). Trade Policy and Poverty Reduction in Brazil. *The World Bank Economic Review* 18(3): 289–317. http://ideas.repec.org/a/oup/wbecrv/v18y2004i3p289-317.html

Hummels, D. and P. Klenow (2005). The Variety and Quality of a Nation's Trade. *American Economic Review* 95: 704–723.
http://ideas.repec.org/a/aea/aecrev/v95y2005i3p704-723.html

Jensen, J., T.F. Rutherford, and D.G. Tarr (2010). Modeling Services Liberalization: The Case of Tanzania. *Journal of Economic Integration* 25(4): 644–675. Also available as World Bank Policy and Research Working Paper No. 4801. http://ideas.repec.org/p/wbk/wbrwps/4801.html

Jensen, J., T.F. Rutherford, and D.G. Tarr (2007). The Impact of Liberalizing Barriers to Foreign Direct Investment in Services: The Case of Russian Accession to the World Trade Organization. *Review of Development Economics* 11(3): 482–506.
http://ideas.repec.org/a/bla/rdevec/v11y2007i3p482-506.html

Jensen, J. and D.G. Tarr (2008). Impact of Local Content Restrictions and Barriers against Foreign Direct Investment in Services: The Case of Kazakhstan Accession to the WTO. *Eastern European Economics* 46(5): 5–26. http://ideas.repec.org/a/mes/eaeuec/v46y2008i5p5-26.html

Jensen, J. and D.G. Tarr (2011). Deep Trade Policy Options for Armenia: The Importance of Services, Trade Facilitation and Standards Liberalization. World Bank, World Bank Policy and Research Working Paper number 5662. http://econ.worldbank.org/external/default/main?pagePK=64165259&theSitePK=469372&piPK=64165421&menuPK=64166093&entityID=000158349_20110518082525

Kang, J.-S. (2000). Price Impact of Restrictiveness on Maritime Transportation Services. In C. Findlay and T. Warren (eds.), *Impediments to Trade in Services: Measurement and Policy Implications*. London: Routledge.

Kimura, F., M. Ando, and T. Fujii (2004a). Estimating the Ad Valorem Equivalent of Barriers to Foreign Direct Investment in the Telecommunications Services Sectors in Armenia. Available at http://www.worldbank.org/trade/russia-wto.

Latorre, M.C. and A. Gomez Gomez-Plana (2011). On the Differential Behaviour of National and Multinational Firms: A Within and Across Sectors Approach. Paper presented at the 14th Annual GTAP Conference, Venice, Italy. https://www.gtap.agecon.purdue.edu/resources/res_display.asp?RecordID=3495

Levy, S. and van Wijnbergen, S. (1995). Transition Problems in Economic Reform: Agriculture in the North American Free Trade Agreement. *American Economic Review* 85(4): 738–754. http://ideas.repec.org/a/aea/aecrev/v85y1995i4p738-54.html

Markusen, J.R, T.F. Rutherford, and D.G. Tarr (2005). Trade and Direct Investment in Producer Services and the Domestic Market for Expertise. *Canadian Journal of Economics* 38(3): 758–777. http://ideas.repec.org/a/cje/issued/v38y2005i3p758-777.html

McGuire, G. and M. Schuele (2000). Restrictiveness of International Trade in Banking Services. In C. Findlay and T. Warren (eds.), *Impediments to Trade in Services: Measurement and Policy Implications*. London: Routledge.

McKee, D.L. (1988), *Growth, Development, and the Service Economy in the Third World*. New York: Praeger Publishers.

Modebadze, G. and K. Eroyants (2010). Ad Valorem Equivalence to FDI Restrictiveness in Armenia. Mimeo. https://docs.google.com/leaf?id=0B0V-t-Bs4-hXYjA3MTQ5MDctNTAxYy00M2I4LWI3NDAtZGRiNDI3NmYwOGU2&hl=en

National Bureau of Statistics of Armenia. Gross Domestic Product at Current Prices by Selected Economic Activities for the Years 2001–2006. Unpublished data.

Navaretti, G. and D.G. Tarr (2000). International Knowledge Flows and Economic Performance: A Review of the Evidence. *World Bank Economic Review* 14(1): 1–15. http://ideas.repec.org/a/oup/wbecrv/v14y2000i1p1-15.html

Rutherford, T.F. and D.G. Tarr (2008). Poverty Effects of Russian WTO Accession: Modeling "real" Households with Endogenous Productivity Effects. *Journal of International Economics* 75(1): 131–150. http://ideas.repec.org/a/eee/inecon/v75y2008i1p131-150.html

Rutherford, T.F. and D.G. Tarr (2003). Regional Trading Arrangements for Chile: Do the Results Differ with a Dynamic Model? *Economie Internationale* 2003(2Q-3Q):261–281. http://ideas.repec.org/a/cii/cepiei/2003-2q-3qk.html

Rutherford, T.F. and D.G. Tarr (2002). Trade Liberalization, Product Variety and Growth in a Small Open Economy: A Quantitative Assessment. *Journal of International Economics* 56(2): 247–272.

Rutherford, T.F., E.E. Rutstrom, and D.G. Tarr (1997). Morocco's Free Trade Agreement with the European Community: A Quantitative Assessment. *Economic Modeling* 14(9): 237–269. http://ideas.repec.org/a/eee/ecmode/v14y1997i2p237-269.html

Rutherford, T.F., E.E. Rutstrom, and D.G. Tarr (1995). The Free Trade Agreement between Tunisia and the European Union. World Bank: Washington, D.C. Mimeo. Reprinted as Rutherford, T.F.; E.E. Rutstrom, and D.G. Tarr. (2000). A Free Trade Agreement Between the European Agreement and a Representative Arab Mediterranean Country: A Quantitative Assessment. In B. Hoekman and J. Zarrouk (eds.), *Catching Up with the Competition: Trade Opportunities and Challenges for Arab Countries.* Ann Arbor, MI: University of Michigan Press.

Schiff, M. and Y. Wang (2006). North-South and South-South Trade Related Technology Diffusion: An Industry Level Analysis of Direct and Indirect Effects. *Canadian Journal of Economics* 39(3): 831–844. http://papers.ssrn.com/sol3/papers.cfm?abstract_id=944945

Schiff, M., Y. Wang, and M. Olarreaga (2002). Trade Related Technology Diffusion and the Dynamics of North-South and South-South Integration. World Bank, World Bank Policy and Research Working Paper 2861. http://ideas.repec.org/p/wbk/wbrwps/2861.html

Schott, P. (2004). Across-Product versus Within-Product Specialization in International Trade. *Quarterly Journal of Economics* 119(2): 647–678. http://ideas.repec.org/a/tpr/qjecon/v119y2004i2p646-677.html

Smith, A. and A.J. Venables (1988). Completing the Internal Market in the European Community: Some Industry Simulations. *European Economic Review* 32(7): 1501–1525. http://ideas.repec.org/a/eee/eecrev/v32y1988i7p1501-1525.html

Tarr, D.G. (2002). On the Design of Tariff Policy: Arguments for and Against Uniform Tariffs. In B. Hoekman, A. Mattoo and P. English (eds.), *Development, Trade and the WTO: A Handbook.* Washington: World Bank.

Warren, T. (2000). The Impact on Output of Impediments to Trade and Investment in Telecommunications Services. In C. Findlay and T. Warren (eds.), *Impediments to Trade in Services: Measurement and Policy Implications.* London: Routledge.

World Bank (2007). *Food Safety and Agricultural Health Management in CIS Countries: Completing the Transition.* Agriculture and Rural Development Department, Washington D.C.: The World Bank. http://siteresources.worldbank.org/INTARD/825826-1111134598204/21422839/FoodSafetyCIS.pdf

Economics
The Open-Access, Open-Assessment E-Journal

Please note:

You are most sincerely encouraged to participate in the open assessment of this article. You can do so by either recommending the article or by posting your comments.

Please go to:

http://dx.doi.org/10.5018/economics-ejournal.ja.2012-1

The Editor

The Eurasian Customs Union among Russia, Belarus and Kazakhstan: Can It Succeed Where Its Predecessor Failed?

David G. Tarr

In 2010, Russia, Belarus and Kazakhstan formed the Eurasian Customs Union and imposed the Russian tariff as the common external tariff of the Customs Union. This resulted in almost doubling the external average tariff of the more liberal Kazakhstan. Russia has benefited from additional exports to Kazakhstan under the protection of the higher tariffs in Kazakhstan. But estimates reveal that the tariff changes resulted in substantial transfers from Kazakhstan to Russia as importers in Kazakhstan now purchase lower quality or higher priced Russian imports that are protected under the tariff umbrella of the common external tariff. Transfers from the Central Asian countries to Russia were the reason the Eurasian Economic Community (known as EurAsEC) failed, so this bodes badly for the ultimate success of the Eurasian Customs Union. What is different, however, is that the Eurasian Customs Union and its associated Common Economic Space aim to reduce non-tariff barriers and improve trade facilitation, and also to allow the free movement of capital and labor, liberalize services, and harmonize some regulations. Estimates by my colleagues and I show that if substantial progress could be made in trade facilitation and reducing non-tariff barriers, this could make the Customs Union positive for Kazakhstan and other potential Central Asian members. Unfortunately, so far the Customs Union has made these matters worse. But Russia's accession to the World Trade Organization will eventually substantially reduce the transfers from Kazakhstan to Russia. Progress with non-tariff barriers and trade facilitation, however, will take a strong political commitment from Russia which we have not yet seen. But if that Russian political leadership is forthcoming, the Eurasian Customs Union could succeed where its predecessor failed.

Keywords: Eurasian customs union, Russia, Kazakhstan, Belarus, trade diversion, trade facilitation, non-tariff barriers, WTO accession.

JEL classification: F13, F15, F55, F63.

1. The Eurasian Customs Union: Can It Succeed Where Its Predecessor Failed?

In January 2010, Russia, Belarus and Kazakhstan formed the Eurasian Customs Union. In January 2012, the three countries agreed to even closer economic ties, by signing the agreement to form a "common economic space." Their earlier effort at a Customs Union failed due to high transfers from Kazakhstan and the other Central Asian member countries to Russia; unfortunately, the current Customs Union imposes a tariff structure that repeats that mistake. But Russian WTO accession will substantially reduce those transfers, and the present Customs Union is charged with reducing non-tariff barriers among the member countries and hopes to improve trade facilitation. So far, the Customs Union has moved backwards on non-tariff barriers and trade facilitation. It will take strong political will and leadership from Russia to make the required progress in non-tariff barriers and trade facilitation to avoid a repeat of the failure of its predecessor customs union.

2. What is the Eurasian Customs Union

Regarding tariffs, the key change was that the three countries agreed to apply the tariff schedule of the Customs Union as their common external tariff for third countries. With few exceptions, the initial common external tariff schedule was the Russian tariff schedule. Kazakhstan negotiated exceptions from the common external tariffs for slightly more than 400 tariff lines, but was scheduled to phase out the exceptions over a period of five years (Shepotylo, 2011).[1] In addition, the members agreed to have the Customs Union determine the rules regarding sanitary and phyto-sanitary standards (SPS) and standards on good. Fearing transshipment of goods from China through Kazakhstan and from the European Union through Belarus, Russia negotiated and achieved agreement on stricter controls on the origin of imports from countries outside of the Customs Union. The common economic space (CES) stipulates that, in principle, there will be free movement of labor and capital among the countries, there will be liberalization of services on the CES and coordination of some regulatory policies such as competition policy. In February 2012, the Eurasian Economic Commission began functioning. It is intended to act as the regulatory authority for the Customs Union in a manner similar to the European Commission for the European Union.

3. Economics of the Tariff Changes — Gains for Russia and Losses for Kazakhstan

Some proponents of the Eurasian Customs Union argue that as a result of the Customs Union, firms in the three countries will have improved market access through having tariff free access to the markets in all three countries. But prior to 2010, along with other countries in the Commonwealth of Independent States (CIS), the three countries had agreements in place that stipulated free trade in goods among them.Thus, the Customs Union could not provide improved market access due to reducing tariffs on goods circulating among the three countries.

Since the common external tariff was essentially the Russian tariff, there was little change in incentives regarding tariffs in Russia. The big change occurred in

[1]Shepotylo followed the Methodology of Shepotylo and Tarr (2008). See Tochitskaya (2010) for a discussion of tariff changes in Belarus.

Kazakhstan, who had a much lower tariff structure than Russia prior to implementing the Customs Union tariff. Despite the exemptions allowed Kazakhstan on a transition basis, Kazakhstan almost doubled its tariffs in the first year of the Customs Union by imposing the common external tariff (see Jandosov and Sabyrova, 2011; and World Bank, 2012). The increase in tariffs on many items not produced in Kazakhstan, but produced in Russia, led to a substantial increase in imports from Russia and displacement of imports from Europe. From Russia's perspective, the Customs Union does represent an expansion of the market. Many of its manufacturing firms that were not competitive in Kazakhstan with the low tariffs of Kazakhstan prior to the Customs Union; but they were able to expand sales to the Kazakhstani market under the tariff umbrella. This represents gains for Russian industry. Given the deeper manufacturing base in Russia compared with most countries of the CIS, and the resulting uneven benefits of the common external tariff in favor of Russia, acceptance of the common external tariff has been a fundamental negotiating position of Russia regarding acceptance of members in the Customs Union.

Some cite the expanded Russian exports in Kazakhstan as evidence of success of the Customs Union. But the displacement of European imports in Kazakhstan, under the tariff umbrella of the common external tariff, by higher priced or lower quality imports (including lower tech goods that reduce access to modern Western technologies) from Russia represents a substantial transfer of income from Kazakhstan to Russia, and is an example of what economists call "trade diversion." It is the reason that the World Bank (2012) has evaluated the tariff changes of the Customs Union as a loss of real income for Kazakhstan.

Further, the three countries together (and even a broader collection of CIS countries) constitute too small a market to erect tariff walls against external competition. They would lose the benefits of importing technology from advanced countries, and would rely on high priced production from within the Customs Union.

4. Political Consequences of the Customs Union — Large Transfers Lead to Tensions and Conflict

Some would argue that there are political benefits of trade to be taken into account. The European Union has shown that despite a long history of wars, the increased interdependence of France and Germany due to increased trade now makes it appear inconceivable that they would engage in hostilities. But when a customs union is inefficient and the benefits and the costs of the customs union are very unequal, the customs union can inflame conflicts. Schiff and Winters (2003, pp. 194–195) have effectively argued that a clear example of how integration can inflame conflict is the civil war of the United States. The United States constituted a customs union among the states. In the 1800s, the North produced manufactures that were sold to the South and the South produced cotton that was exported to Europe. In 1828, Congress passed the "Tariff of Abominations" that resulted in a massive transfer of income from the South to the North. South Carolina threatened to secede and Federal troops were sent to South Carolina; but Congress reduced the tariffs before fighting ensued. In 1860, however, tariffs were raised again and this time Congress did not back down. Adams (1993) concludes that the high tariffs were as important as slavery in driving the South to secede from the Union and initiate the civil war. Another example is the East African Customs Union. Kenya was seen as the country with the relatively advanced base in manufactures that resulted in transfers from Tanzania and Uganda to Kenya. The customs union collapsed in 1978 with the closing of borders among the countries. This led to tensions and contributed to the conflict between Tanzania and Uganda in 1979. On the other hand, the success of the European Union in promoting peace in the region is partly explained by a strategy of avoiding policies that create transfers large enough to trigger conflicts.

5. Non-Tariff Barriers — Extremely Costly Methods of Regulating Standards Worsened by the Customs Union

Non-tariff barriers are a significant problem in the Customs Union. International evidence shows that command and control barriers, such as quotas and licenses, have become much less important as instruments of protection in world trade. They have been replaced by sanitary and phyto-sanitary (SPS) conditions on food and agricultural products and technical barriers to trade (TBTs) on goods. In the case of the Eurasian Customs Union and the CIS, SPS conditions and TBTs are even more important than in other regions of the world. There are standards based trade disputes between Belarus and Russia on several products, including milk, meat, buses, pipes and beer (see Petrovskaya, 2012). Anecdotal evidence indicates that Kazakhstani exporters complain bitterly regarding the use by the Russian authorities of SPS and TBTs measures, either to extract payments from them or for protection.

If the Customs Union could make substantial progress on reducing these barriers, it would be a significant accomplishment. My colleagues and I estimated that progress on the non-tariff barriers and trade facilitation could outweigh the negative impact of the tariff changes for Kazakhstan (see World Bank, 2012). Unfortunately, so far the Customs Union has taken a step backward on both non-tariff barriers and trade facilitation.

A big problem in reducing standards as a non-tariff barrier is that standards regulation, in all three countries, is still based on the Soviet system of standards regulation. There are reportedly about 20,000 standards that apply in the Customs Union. Standards in the three countries remain dominated by Soviet style standards, known as GOST: 62 percent of the standards are GOST standards; 23 percent are Russian; and 14.5 percent are Belorussian.[2] Lacking a market to control quality, GOST standards controlled the quality of a product, even when there was no health

[2]See Shymulo-Tapiola (2012) and www.minpromtorg.ru/industry/metrology/59.

or safety issue. That is, mandatory technical regulations were employed where market economies allow voluntary standards to apply. Even the process under which the product was produced was controlled in many cases. This regulatory system makes innovation and adaption to the needs of the market very costly as firms must negotiate with regulators when they want to change a product or how it is produced. This overly mandatory regulatory system is a bigger problem than a trade problem as it impacts virtually all producers, regardless of the destination of the product. Legislation in both Russia and Kazakhstan calls for conversion to a system of voluntary standards, and there is a desire to move to a system of voluntary standards where no health and safety problem exists; but this is happening too slowly in all three countries. The problem is that the Customs Union has worsened the situation. Technical regulations are now decided at the level of the Customs Union; so firms that previously negotiated with their national standards authority, have had to get agreement from the Customs Union, and this has reportedly caused further delays, impeding innovation and the ability of firms to meet the demands of the market.

A second problem with efforts to reduce the non-tariff barriers is that the Customs Union is trying to harmonize standards of the three countries by producing mandatory technical regulations. The alternative is to use Mutual Recognition Agreements (MRAs). Experience has shown that no customs union has been able to broadly harmonize standards based on mandatory technical regulations, with the exception of the European Union. And even in the European Union, they had to use MRAs and only harmonized technical regulations after decades of work. While each member of the Customs Union is expected to create a system of mutual recognition of certificates of conformity, these certificates are not presently recognized in the other countries of the Customs Union. There is little hope for a significant reduction in standards of non-tariff barriers unless the system of mutual recognition is more widely recognized and adopted.

Finally, although Mutual Recognition Agreements are required for significant progress, the "National Quality Infrastructure" will need to be developed in all three countries. That is, facilities such as laboratories, testing and metrology facilities will need to be developed and mutually recognized to allow the implementation of MRAs. This is a non-trivial investment.

6. Trade Facilitation — Participation in International Production Chains Made More Difficult by the Customs Union

Customs posts between the member countries have been removed, and this has reduced trade costs for exporters and importers operating in the three countries. But Russia's concerns regarding transshipment have led to an opposite impact on trade with third countries, i.e., the costs of trading with countries outside of the Customs Union have increased. Participation in international production chains has become a key feature of modern international production and trade. If goods can't move easily in and out of the country, multinational firms will look to other countries to make their foreign direct investment and for international production sharing. Addressing this significant problem will take a change of emphasis on the part of Russia.

7. Russian WTO Accession — Liberalization that Will Significantly Reduce Transfers to Russia

It has apparently been agreed by the Customs Union members that the common external tariff of the Customs Union will change to accommodate Russia's WTO commitments. As a result, the applied un-weighted average tariff will fall in stages from 10.9 percent in 2012 to 7.9 percent by the year 2020 (see Shepotylo and Tarr, forthcoming).[3] This will have the effect of lowering the trade diversion costs of Kazakhstan. In addition, the Customs Union will be expected to adapt its rules on standards to conform with commitments Russia made as part of its WTO accession commitments. In the case of Belarus, it remains to be seen if it will implement the changes, as this will increase competition for its industries.

8. Customs Union Implications for the entry of Kazakhstan into the WTO — Surmountable Complications

Prior to joining the Customs Union, Kazakhstan had signed bilateral market access agreements with many of the WTO members on its Working Party on WTO accession,[4] and had committed to lower tariffs than the tariffs of the Customs Union on many tariff lines. Thus, to join the Customs Union, Kazakhstan would have to exceed its bound tariff level on many tariff lines. This may require "compensation" from the Customs Union in the form of lowering the common external tariff to provide offsetting market access. Shepotylo and I (forthcoming) have estimated, however, that there are about 1,500 tariff lines where the applied tariff rate of Russia is below its final bound rate. Consequently, Russia should be able to agree to lower the bound tariffs of the Customs Union to pay "compensation" to the WTO members for Kazakhstan applying higher tariffs than its commitments, without actually having to lower any applied tariffs in Russia.

[3]The final "bound rate" of Russia is higher at 8.6 percent on an un-weighted average basis; but there are about 1,500 tariff lines where the applied rate of Russia is below the bound rate. The applied weighted average tariff will fall from 9.3 percent in 2012 to 5.8 percent in 2020.
[4]As of October 2012, it had reportedly signed bilateral market access agreements with all members of its Working Party except one.

9. Conclusion — The Need to Russia to Exercise Political Leadership for Standards and Trade Facilitation Reform for Success of the Customs Union

In 1996, the same three countries formed a customs union; they were joined by Kyrgyzstan in 1996, later by Tajikistan and still later by Uzbekistan in 2005. As Michalopoulos and I (1997) anticipated, the earlier Customs Union failed because it imposed large costs on the Central Asian countries, who had to buy either lower quality (including lower tech goods) or higher priced Russian manufactured goods under the tariff umbrella. The present Customs Union also started with the Russian tariff, which protects Russian industry and suffers from the same problem that led to the failure of the earlier Customs Union. Nonetheless, the present Customs Union could succeed. Crucially, due to Russia's accession to the WTO, the tariff of the Customs Union will fall by about 40 to 50 percent.[5] This will make the Customs Union a more open Customs Union, significantly reduce the transfers from Kazakhstan to Russia, and thereby reduce the pressures from producers and consumers in Kazakhstan on their government to depart from enforcement of the tariffs of the Customs Union. Further, the present Customs Union aims to reduce non-tariff barriers and improve trade facilitation and includes "deep integration" on its agenda, i.e., services liberalization, the free movement of labor and capital and some regulatory harmonization. Although,to date, the Customs Union has moved backwards on non-tariff barriers and trade facilitation, one could optimistically hope for substantial progress. In the important area of non-tariff barriers, given the common history of Soviet mandatory standards, Russia will have to take the lead in moving the Customs Union toward a system of voluntary standards where no health and safety issue is involved, and toward a system of mutual recognition agreements and away from commonly negotiated technical regulations. On trade facilitation, Russia will have to reverse its pressure and find a way to allow the freer movement of goods with third countries while addressing its transshipment concerns.

References

Adams, Charles, (1993), *For Good and Evil: The Impact of Taxes on the Course of Civilization*, Lanham, Md.: Madison Books.

Jandosov, Oraz, and Lyaziza Sabyrova (2011), "Indicative tariff protection level in Kazakhstan: before and after the customs union (part I)," Rakurs Discussion Paper 5.3. March.

Michalopoulos, Constantine and David G. Tarr (1997), "The Economics of Customs Unions in the Commonwealth of Independent States," *Post-Soviet Geography and Economics*, **38**(3), 125–143.

[5]Russian tariffs fall more on an un-weighted average basis than they do on a weighted average basis. See Shepotylo and Tarr (forthcoming).

Petrovskaya, Galina (2012), "Belarus, Rossia, Ukraina. Obrechennye na torgovye konflikty" (Belarus, Russia, Ukraine. Doomed for trade conflicts), Deutsche Welle, June 14. www.dw.de/dw/article/0,,16023176,00.html.

Schiff, Maurice and L. Alan Winters (2003), *Regional Integration and Development*, Washington DC: World Bank and Oxford University Press.

Shepotylo, Oleksandr (2011), "Calculation of the tariff rates of Kazakhstan before and after the imposition of the customs union common external tariff in 2010." Available as part of World Bank (2012).

Shepotylo, Oleksandr, and David G. Tarr (2008), "Specific tariffs, tariff simplification and the structure of import tariffs in Russia: 2001–2005," *Eastern European Economics*, **46**(5), 49–58.

Shepotylo, Oleksandr, and David G. Tarr (forthcoming), "Impact of WTO Accession on the Bound and Applied Tariff Rates of Russia," *Eastern European Economics*.

Shymulo-Tapiola, Olga (2012), "The Eurasian Customs Union: Friend or Foe of the EU?" The Carnegie Papers, Carnegie Endowment for International Peace, October. Available at: www.CarnegieEurope.eu,

Irina Tochitskaya (2010), "The Customs Union between Belarus, Kazakhstan and Russia: An Overview of Economic Implications for Belarus," paper no 405/2010, Case-Network. Available at: www.caseresearch.eu/sites/default/files/publications/32701553_CNSA_405_0.pdf.

World Bank (2012), Assessment of Costs and Benefits of the Customs Union for Kazakhstan, Report Number 65977-KZ, Washington DC, January 3, 2012. Available at: http://documents.worldbank.org/curated/en/2012/01/15647043/assessment-costs-benefits-customs-union-kazakhstan

Author Index

Subject Index